William Hazlitt
The First Modern Man

William Hazlitt self portrait
(Maidstone Museum and Art Gallery/The Bridgeman Art Library)

William Hazlitt

The First Modern Man

*Yet he alone is truly great who is so without the
aid of circumstances and in spite of fortune,
who is as little lifted up by the tide of opinion,
as he is depressed by neglect or obscurity, and
who borrows dignity only from himself.*

Hazlitt, *Characteristics* xc

DUNCAN WU

*For Carol
with lots of love
Duncan
x x x*

May '09

OXFORD
UNIVERSITY PRESS

OXFORD
UNIVERSITY PRESS

Great Clarendon Street, Oxford OX2 6DP

Oxford University Press is a department of the University of Oxford.
It furthers the University's objective of excellence in research, scholarship,
and education by publishing worldwide in

Oxford New York

Auckland Cape Town Dar es Salaam Hong Kong Karachi
Kuala Lumpur Madrid Melbourne Mexico City Nairobi
New Delhi Shanghai Taipei Toronto

With offices in

Argentina Austria Brazil Chile Czech Republic France Greece
Guatemala Hungary Italy Japan Poland Portugal Singapore
South Korea Switzerland Thailand Turkey Ukraine Vietnam

Oxford is a registered trade mark of Oxford University Press
in the UK and in certain other countries

Published in the United States
by Oxford University Press Inc., New York

© Duncan Wu 2008

British Library Cataloguing in Publication Data

Data available

Library of Congress Cataloging in Publication Data

Wu, Duncan.
William Hazlitt : the first modern man / Duncan Wu.
p. cm.
Includes bibliographical references and index.
ISBN 978-0-19-954958-0 (acid-free paper)
1. Hazlitt, William, 1778-1830. 2. Authors, English-19th century-Biography.
3. Critics-Great Britain-Biography. 4. Romanticism-Great Britain I. Title.
PR4773.W8 2008 824'.7-dc22
[B] 2008031678

Typeset by SPI Publisher Services, Pondicherry, India
Printed in Great Britain
on acid-free paper by
CPI Antony Rowe

ISBN 0-19-954958-3 978-0-19-954958-0

1 3 5 7 9 10 8 6 4 2

To my parents

ACKNOWLEDGEMENTS

WORK on this biography grew naturally out of my editorial work on Hazlitt, and I pay tribute here to the scholars without whose achievements Hazlittians would be the poorer: William Hazlitt Jr, W. C. Hazlitt, A. R. Waller, Arnold Glover, Jules Douady, P. P. Howe, Geoffrey Keynes, Ernest J. Moyne, Herschel Moreland Sikes, Stanley Jones, Charles E. Robinson, and Eleanor Gates. Barbara Rosenbaum's account of Hazlitt in her *Index to English Literary Manuscripts* has been a constant companion throughout my work. I have learnt much from previous biographers: Jules Douady, P. P. Howe, Catherine Macdonald Maclean, Herschel Baker, Ralph Wardle, Stanley Jones, A. C. Grayling, and Jon Cook. In particular, I single out Jules Douady, often neglected in accounts of Hazlitt scholarship. His *Liste Chronologique*, though dated, remains an invaluable guide to Hazlitt's career, as does his excellent *Vie de William Hazlitt, l'Essayiste*—as readable now as when it first appeared in 1907.

During the years I have worked on this book, I have incurred debts and obligations which are a pleasure to acknowledge here. Firstly I thank the many librarians, archivists, and experts who welcomed me during research trips, and smoothed my path in ways too numerous to mention: Virginia Murray at the John Murray Archive in London; Nick Savage, Liz King, and Mark Pomeroy at the Library of the Royal Academy of Arts; Janet Birkett, Assistant Curator of the Theatre Museum; Rob Cox, Roy Goodman, and Valerie-Ann Lutz at the American Philosophical Society; Frances O'Donnell, Curator of Archives and Manuscripts at the Andover-Harvard Theological Library; the staff of the Pusey Library, Harvard; Ted Hutchinson, Kim Nusco, Brenda Lawson, Anne E. Bentley, Peter Drummey, Rakashi Khetarpal, and the staff of the Massachusetts Historical Society; Lee Arnold, Director of the Library of the Historical Society of Pennsylvania; Jim Green of the Library Company of Philadelphia; Hal Worthley of the Congregational Library of Boston; Stephen Z. Nonack of the Boston Athenaeum; Bridget Clancey, Beth Bensman, and the staff of the Presbyterian Historical Society, Philadelphia; Glenys A. Waldman, Librarian at the Masonic

Acknowledgements

Library and Museum of Pennsylvania; Earl K. Holt III, Betsy Draper, and Lucy Sewall, King's Chapel Archive, Unitarian Universalist Association, Boston; Michelle LeBlanc, Old South Meeting House, Boston; Charles Carter of the Pforzheimer Library, New York Public Library; Isaac Gewirtz and Stephen Crook of the Berg Library, New York Public Library; Jennifer B. Lee and Tara C. Craig at the Columbia University Rare Book and Manuscript Library; Alex Rankin at the Howard Gotlieb Archival Research Center, Boston University; Roberta E. Zonghi and her colleagues at the Boston Public Library; Sidney F. Huttner at the University of Iowa Library; Polly Armstrong and the staff of Stanford University Library; Chatham Ewing, Curator of Modern Manuscripts, Washington University Library; Stephanie Philbrick of the Maine Historical Society; Flossie Dere, Corresponding Secretary of the Maine Genealogical Society; Bruce Kirkham of the Kennebec Historical Society; Amey Hutchins, University Archives, University of Pennsylvania; Mary B. Dunhouse of the Boston Public Library; Sumner A. Webber, City Historian, Hallowell; Earl K. Holt III, Minister of King's Chapel, Boston; James Gerencser, Archivist and Librarian, Dickinson College; Leslie A. Morris and the staff of the Houghton Library, Harvard University; Kathryn James and the staff of the Beineke Library, Yale University; Martha Smalley, Yale Divinity School Library; Heidi Hass and the staff of the Morgan Library, New York; Barbara Austen, Manuscript Archivist at Connecticut Historical Society Museum, Hartford, Connecticut; the staff of the National Archives and the Library of Congress, Washington, DC; Nicole Murray and the staff of the Folger Shakespeare Library; Eric L. Pumroy, Director of Library Collections, Bryn Mawr College; Ellen Healy, Gomez Mill House, New York; John Hurley, Director of Information and Public Witness, Unitarian Universalist Association; Susan Palmer, Archivist at Sir John Soane's House and Museum; Nigel Roche, Curator of St Bride Printing Library; Vanessa Bell and Eamon Dyas at the News International Archive, Wapping; Elizabeth James, Sally Brown, and the staff of the British Library, London; Lucinda Jones and the staff of the Wiltshire Record Office; Tom Mayberry and the staff of the Somersetshire Record Office; the staff of the Central Reference Library, Birmingham; Jo Hutchings, Archivist at Lincoln's Inn Library; Gina Douglas, Librarian of the Linnean Society; Deborah McVea and Catherine Fuller at the Bentham Project; Mike Bott at Reading University Library; Aidan Flood at the Camden Public Library; the staff of the Westminster Record Office; the staff of the Local Studies and Archives Centre, Holborn Library; the staff of the National Archives, Kew; David Mullin, Director of the

Acknowledgements

Edward Jenner Museum, Berkeley; Nicholas Robinson of the Department of Manuscripts and Printed Books, Fitzwilliam Museum, Cambridge; Janet Graham and staff of the Liverpool Central Library; Mrs. S. M. Laithwaite, Archivist at the Devon Record Office; Rowan Watson, Head of Documentary Materials, National Art Library, V&A; Dan Mitchell, Special Collections, University College Library Library, London; John R. Hodgson, Keeper of Manuscripts and Archives, John Rylands University Library of Manchester; Malcolm C. Davis, Manuscript Archivist at Leeds University Library; Irene Ferguson, Assistant to the University Archivist, University of Edinburgh; the staff of the National Library of Scotland; Sue Killoran, Librarian of Harris Manchester College, Oxford; Christina Mackwell, Assistant Librarian at Lambeth Palace Library; Tina Gee and Roberta Lewis of Keats House, Hampstead; the staff of Reading Central Library; the staff of Manchester Central Library; Jeff Cowton and the staff of the Wordsworth Library, Grasmere; Katrina Jowett, Senior Assistant Librarian, Library and Museum of Freemasonry, Freemasons' Hall, London; the staff of the Department of Special Collections, Glasgow University Library; the staff of the London School of Economics Library; the staff of Senate House Library, University of London; the staff of the Guildhall Library and the Guildhall Record Office, City of London; Alan Crookham, Archivist at the National Gallery, London; Catherine Payling, Josephine Greywoode, and the staff of the Keats–Shelley Memorial House, Rome; and Gerard Hayes, State Library of Victoria, Australia. There are a number of librarians to whom I owe particular thanks. Firstly, I thank Sally Collins and Ludmila Gromova, librarians of St Catherine's College, Oxford, for making readily available to me the runs of the *London Magazine* and the *Edinburgh Review* acquired years ago by my late colleague Michael Gearin-Tosh, and for other good turns besides. I am grateful also to Clive Hurst, Head of Rare Books and Printed Ephemera, and Bruce Barker-Benfield, Senior Assistant Librarian, Department of Special Collections and Western Manuscripts, at the Bodleian Library, Oxford, as well as their helpful colleagues at the Map Room, Duke Humfrey's library, Room 132, and the Upper Reading Room, particularly Vera Ryhajlo and Helen Rogers, who so often traced 'missing' or 'out of place' materials. I also acknowledge the assistance of Michael Basinski, Curator of the Poetry Collection, State University of New York at Buffalo, and his predecessor Robert Bertholf, both of whom helped me navigate the intricacies of the Goodyear Hazlitt collection. Mr Basinski's assistants, Margaret Konkol and Karlen Chase, kindly secured copies of items in the collection on my behalf. Dr David Wykes, Director of Dr Williams' Library, assisted my survey of the Henry Crabb Robinson papers, and gave advice on aspects of Unitarianism.

Fellow academics and researchers have been generous with their expertise, often sending information or unpublished research; some have assisted with funding applications. I am grateful to them all: Susan Wolfson, Daniel W. Howe, Peter Tufts Richardson, Helen Braithwaite, Derek Jewell, N. J. Thorne, Lynda Pratt, W. A. Speck, William St Clair, Pamela Clemit, Donald John, Robert Ryan, Doucet Fischer, Tom Mayberry, Gary Dyer, G. M. Ditchfield, Peter Thompson, Jules Prown, David Bjelajac, Richard Carwardine, Jack Stillinger, Peter Cochran, Cecilia and Nicholas Powell, David Stam, Eric Walker, Ann Wroe, Joseph Riehl, Crystal B. Lake, Roger Pearson, Caroline Warman, Charles Rzepka, Kyle Grimes, Geoffrey Bindman, Rob Morrison, John Strachan, Joshua Getzler, Charles Mahoney, Leo Lemay, D. D. Raphael, David Sutton, Melanie Wright, Clara Kidwell, Karen Racine, Theda Purdue, Alvise Zorzi, Timothy Webb, the Reverend Dr Alicia McNary Forsey, the Venerable Clive Cohen (Archdeacon of Bodmin), Emily Lorraine de Montluzin, James Harris, David Sutton, Stephen Burley, Quentin Bailey, Paul F. Betz, Grant Scott, David Bromwich, Uttara Natarajan, Matthew Scott, Stephen Gill, David Wickham, Jane Stabler, Grevel Lindop, and Berta Joncus. I owe a particular debt to Nicholas Roe and Tom Paulin who have encouraged my research throughout, and read the typescript at various stages.

Thanks to the Internet I was fortunate in making contact with family and local historians who generously shared with me their hard-won knowledge, most of whom are descendants of those who either knew, or worked with, Hazlitt: Jacob Dicus 8th, Peter Ostle, Clive Gudsell, Pauline Harkness, and Jenny Marley. Fergal Crossan, Assistant Manager of Hazlitt's Hotel in Frith Street, helpfully provided me with information about the building both before and after its restoration in 1986. I thank fellow Trustees of the Charles Lamb Society, the Keats–Shelley Memorial Association, and the Hazlitt Society for their encouragement and assistance. Conversations with members of the Hazlitt Day-School, held annually at St Catherine's College, Oxford, since 2001, have often cast light of one kind or another on aspects of my work.

I am grateful to the Master and Fellows of St Catherine's College, Oxford, for help of various kinds, and owe a particular debt to my English colleagues, Bart Van Es and Jeremy Dimmick, for holding the fort when I went on research leave, 2004–6. I am no less grateful to colleagues at Georgetown University for granting me the freedom to conclude work on this work in early 2008, especially Dean Jane D. McAuliffe and my new head of department, Penn Szittya. My agent, Charlie Viney, proposed the subtitle and theme of this book, and has been a true friend throughout work on it, assisting me through numerous tribulations. In Philadelphia, Professor Charles E. Robinson and his wife, Nanette, of the University of Delaware were welcoming hosts, and I thank them for their hospitality. It has been a privilege once more to work with Andrew McNeillie, Jacqueline Baker, Charles Lauder, Jr, and other colleagues at Oxford University Press. The writing of this book has coincided with Hazlittian traumas in my own life, through which I have been assisted by the kindness of friends: I thank Sue Lewis, Constance Parrish, Brad Peterson, Richard S. Tomlinson, Roby Harrington, Libby Purves, and Paul Heiney.

My greatest debt is to the Leverhulme Trust for the award of a Major Research Fellowship, which released me from teaching and administrative duties for two years for the purpose of completing archival work on this volume. I would not have been able to do so otherwise. I am no less grateful to the American Philosophical Society and its Research Administrator, Linda Musumeci, for its award of a Franklin Research Grant, which provided me with the means to visit American libraries holding Hazlitt-related materials— an appropriate connection given that Hazlitt's father almost certainly attended meetings of the Society in its early years, and was a friend and admirer of the man after whom its grants are named. Financial assistance from the Faculty of English Language and Literature, University of Oxford, was instrumental in completing research on this book. I am hugely grateful to these institutions for their support.

William Hazlitt: The First Modern Man is in many respects a tribute to the late Stanley Jones, who introduced me to Hazlitt's world and shared his scholarship with me when I began work on this volume. His magisterial biography, *Hazlitt: A Life*, continues to set the standard for work in the field, and remains an indispensable resource for anyone with a serious interest in its subject. At his death, Stanley's widow, Dorothea, gave me his research notes, which have been invaluable reference sources; now at the Bodleian Library in Oxford, they may be consulted on application to the superintendent at Room 132. Stanley once thanked Michael Foot 'for his boundless generosity and unflagging

Acknowledgements

encouragement', sentiments I can only reiterate. Mr Foot has been a great friend to Hazlittians, not least as the guardian of manuscripts and rare volumes which he has made available to researchers over the years. He has given me access to numerous items without which I could not have completed this volume, and urged me on to the finishing line. I thank him and all those who have assisted me.

Georgetown University, February 2008

CONTENTS

Contents

Part IV: The Plain Speaker

Part V: The New Pygmalion

Part VI: Mr Hazlitt's Grand Tour

Part VII: London Solitude

LIST OF FIGURES

FRONTISPIECE William Hazlitt self portrait
(Maidstone Museum and Art Gallery/The Bridgeman Art Library)

List of Figures

LIST OF PLATES

1. Hazlitt's death mask.
2. John Hazlitt, Self-portrait, painted during the 1790s.
   (Maidstone Museum and Art Gallery/The Bridgeman Art Library)
3. Mary Peirce Hazlitt, wife of John Hazlitt.
   (Maidstone Museum and Art Gallery/The Bridgeman Art Library)
4. Hazlitt's letter requesting a copy of Baron Fain's memoirs, an essential
   source for his *Life of Napoleon*.
   (Maidstone Museum and Art Gallery/The Bridgeman Art Library)
5. Hazlitt's letter to his father from Hackney New College, October 1793.
   (Maidstone Museum and Art Gallery/The Bridgeman Art Library)
6. Hazlitt as a boy, painted in America by John Hazlitt.
   (Maidstone Museum and Art Gallery/The Bridgeman Art Library)
7. Margaret Hazlitt, by John Hazlitt.
   (Maidstone Museum and Art Gallery/The Bridgeman Art Library)
8. William Hazlitt, by John Hazlitt.
   (Maidstone Museum and Art Gallery/The Bridgeman Art Library)
9. Charles Lamb, by William Hazlitt.
   (Private collection/The Bridgeman Art Library)

LIST OF ABBREVIATIONS

Baker	Herschel Baker, *William Hazlitt* (Cambridge, MA, 1962)
Bennett	*The Letters of Mary Wollstonecraft Shelley*, ed. Betty T. Bennett (3 vols., Baltimore and London, 1980–8)
Bewick	Thomas Landseer, *Life and Letters of William Bewick (Artist)* (2 vols., London, 1871)
BL	British Library, London
Bonner	*The Journals of Sarah and William Hazlitt*, ed. Willard Hallam Bonner, in *The University of Buffalo Studies* 24 (February 1959), 171–281
Bromwich	David Bromwich, *Hazlitt: The Mind of a Critic* (New Haven, 1999)
Champneys	Basil Champneys, *Memoirs and Correspondence of Coventry Patmore* (2 vols., London, 1900)
Chorley	*Letters of Mary Russell Mitford*, ed. Henry Chorley (2 vols., London, 1872)
Clare	*John Clare By Himself*, ed. Eric Robinson and David Powell (Ashington and Manchester, 1996)
Clarke	Charles and Mary Cowden Clarke, *Recollections of Writers* (London, 1878)
Coleridge Notebooks	S. T. Coleridge, *Notebooks*, ed. Kathleen Coburn and Anthony John Harding (5 vols., Princeton, NJ, 1957–2002)
Curry	*New Letters of Robert Southey*, ed. Kenneth Curry (2 vols., New York, 1965)
De Quincey	*The Works of Thomas De Quincey*, ed. Grevel Lindop et al. (21 vols., London, 2000–3)
Douady	Jules Douady, *Liste Chronologique des Oeuvres de William Hazlitt* (Paris, 1906)
Farington	*The Diary of Joseph Farington*, ed. Kenneth Garlick, Angus Macintyre and Kathryn Cave (17 vols., New Haven and London, 1978–98)
Fenner	Theodore Fenner, *Opera in London: Views of the Press 1785–1830* (Carbondale, IL, 1994)

List of Abbreviations

Foakes	S. T. Coleridge, *Lectures 1808–19 On Literature*, ed. R. A. Foakes (2 vols., Princeton, NJ, 1987)
Four Generations	W. C. Hazlitt, *Four Generations of a Literary Family* (2 vols., London and New York, 1897)
Gates	*Leigh Hunt: A Life in Letters*, ed. Eleanor M. Gates (Essex, CT, 1998)
Gordon	Mary Gordon, *'Christopher North': A Memoir of John Wilson* (2 vols., Edinburgh, 1862)
Grayling	A. C. Grayling, *The Quarrel of the Age: The Life and Times of William Hazlitt* (London, 2000)
Griggs	*Collected Letters of Samuel Taylor Coleridge*, ed. Earl Leslie Griggs (6 vols., Oxford, 1956–71)
Haydon, *Life*	*Life of Benjamin Robert Haydon*, ed. Tom Taylor (3 vols., London, 1853)
Haydon Table Talk	*Benjamin Robert Haydon: Correspondence and Table-Talk*, ed. Frederic Wordsworth Haydon (2 vols., London, 1876)
Hazlitt Papers	'The Hazlitt Papers', *The Christian Reformer* 5–6 (August 1838 to January 1839), 505–12, 697–705, 756–64, 15–24
Hazlitts	W. C. Hazlitt, *The Hazlitts* (Edinburgh, 1911)
Howe	*The Works of William Hazlitt*, ed. P. P. Howe (21 vols., London, 1930–4)
Howe, *Life*	P. P. Howe, *The Life of William Hazlitt* (3rd edn, London, 1947)
Hunt Correspondence	*The Correspondence of Leigh Hunt*, ed. Thornton Leigh Hunt (2 vols., London, 1862)
Jones	Stanley Jones, *Hazlitt: A Life* (Oxford, 1989)
Jones (1966)	Stanley Jones, 'Nine New Hazlitt Letters and Some Others', *Etudes Anglaises* 19 (1966), 263–77
Jones (1977)	Stanley Jones, 'Some New Hazlitt Letters', *Notes and Queries* 24 (1977), 336–42
Keats Circle	*The Keats Circle: Letters and Papers 1816–1878*, ed. Hyder Edward Rollins (2 vols., Cambridge, MA, 1948)
Keynes	Sir Geoffrey Keynes, *Bibliography of William Hazlitt* (2nd edn, Godalming, 1981)
Lamb and Hazlitt	W. C. Hazlitt, *Lamb and Hazlitt* (New York, 1899)
Le Gallienne	*Liber Amoris or the New Pygmalion by William Hazlitt with Additional Matter now Printed for the first time from the Original Manuscripts*, ed. Richard Le Gallienne (privately printed, London, 1894)

List of Abbreviations

Letters	*The Letters of William Hazlitt*, ed. Herschel Moreland Sikes, assisted by Willard Hallam Bonner and Gerald Lahey (New York, 1978)
Lucas	*The Letters of Charles and Mary Lamb*, ed. E. V. Lucas (3 vols., London, 1935)
McGann	*The Complete Poetical Works of Lord Byron*, ed. Jerome J. McGann and Barry Weller (7 vols., Oxford, 1980–93)
Maclean	Catherine Macdonald Maclean, *Born under Saturn: A Biography of William Hazlitt* (London, 1943)
Marchand	*Byron's Letters and Journals*, ed. Leslie A. Marchand (12 vols., London, 1973–82)
Marrs	*The Letters of Charles and Mary Anne Lamb*, ed. Edwin W. Marrs, Jr (3 vols., Ithaca, NY, 1975–8)
Medwin (1839)	Thomas Medwin, 'Hazlitt in Switzerland: A Conversation', *Fraser's Magazine* 19 (March 1839), 278–83
Memoirs	W. Carew Hazlitt, *Memoirs of William Hazlitt* (2 vols., London, 1867)
Mitford Letters	Mitford MSS correspondence, 6 volumes (B/TU/MIT), Reading Central Library
Morley	*Henry Crabb Robinson on Books and Their Writers*, ed. Edith J. Morley (3 vols., London, 1938)
Morpurgo	Leigh Hunt, *Autobiography*, ed. J. E. Morpurgo (London, 1949)
Moyne	*The Journal of Margaret Hazlitt*, ed. Ernest J. Moyne (Lawrence, KS, 1967)
Murray papers	Papers of John Murray, now retained at the National Library of Scotland, Edinburgh
New Letters	*William Hazlitt to his Publishers, Friends, and Creditors: Twenty-Seven New Holograph Letters*, ed. Charles E. Robinson (Heslington, York, 1987)
O'Leary	Patrick O'Leary, *Regency Editor: Life of John Scott* (Aberdeen, 1983)
Patmore	P. G. Patmore, *My Friends and Acquaintance* (3 vols., London, 1854)
Pope	*The Diaries of Benjamin Robert Haydon*, ed. Willard B. Pope (5 vols., Cambridge, MA, 1960–3)
Procter (1830)	B. W. Procter, 'My Recollections of the Late William Hazlitt', *New Monthly Magazine* 29 (November 1830), 469–82
Procter (1877)	B. W. Procter, *An Autobiographical Fragment and Biographical Notes* (London, 1877)
Remains	*Literary Remains of the Late William Hazlitt*, ed. William Hazlitt Jr (2 vols., London, 1836)

List of Abbreviations

Robinson diary	Henry Crabb Robinson, MS diary in Dr Williams's Library, London
Rollins	*The Letters of John Keats 1814–21*, ed. Hyder E. Rollins (2 vols., Cambridge, MA, 1958)
Shaver	*The Letters of William and Dorothy Wordsworth: The Early Years 1787–1805*, ed. Ernest de Selincourt, rev. Chester L. Shaver (Oxford, 1967)
Shelley Circle	*Shelley and His Circle*, ed. K. N. Cameron, Donald Reiman, Doucet Devin Fischer, et al. (10 vols. ongoing, Cambridge, MA, 1961–)
Stillinger	*The Letters of Charles Armitage Brown*, ed. Jack Stillinger (Cambridge, MA, 1966)
Storey	*The Letters of John Clare*, ed. Mark Storey (Oxford, 1985)
Super	R. H. Super, *Walter Savage Landor: A Biography* (London, 1957)
Wardle	Ralph M. Wardle, *Hazlitt* (Lincoln, NE, 1971)
WH	William Hazlitt
Wilcox	Stewart C. Wilcox, *Hazlitt in the Workshop: The Manuscript of* The Fight (Baltimore, 1943)
Wu	*The Selected Writings of William Hazlitt*, ed. Duncan Wu (9 vols., London, 1998)
Wu *Library*	Duncan Wu, 'Hazlitt's Unpublished *History of English Philosophy*: The Larger Context', *The Library* 7 (March 2006), 25–64
Wu (2007)	*New Writings of William Hazlitt*, ed. Duncan Wu (2 vols., Oxford, 2007)

PREFACE

ROMANTICISM is where the modern age begins, and Hazlitt was its most articulate spokesman. No one else had the ability to see it whole; no one else
knew so many of its politicians, poets, and philosophers. By interpreting it for
his contemporaries, he speaks to us of ourselves—of the culture and world we
now inhabit. Perhaps the most important development of his time, the creation
of a mass media, is one that now dominates our lives. Hazlitt's livelihood was
dependent on it. As this biography argues, he took political sketch-writing to
a new level, invented sports commentary as we know it, and created the essay-
form as practised by Clive James, Gore Vidal, and Michael Foot.

His writings were read by a contemporary readership larger than had been
previously available, thanks to technological advances. When in 1814 John
Walter II introduced the steam-press to the printing-house of *The Times*, it
became possible to produce newspapers in thousands rather than hundreds
of copies, and new forms of transport enabled them to reach all parts of the
country within a day. The new mass media created a mass consciousness, giving
rise to such phenomena as the hysteria that gripped the nation at the death of
Lord Byron. It had political repercussions too, for it is no accident that this was
the moment at which working people began to campaign for their rights. The
Romantic period was the gateway to a new world, and needed a writer who
could analyse it. It found that writer in Hazlitt.

Of those who fed this new industry, he was the most gifted, the most wide-
ranging in his talents, the most percipient, and by far the best prose stylist.
What he wrote was a revelation, for none of his predecessors had spoken to the
reader as he did. An emotional man, he was unafraid of declaring his feelings
and prejudices, of revealing the flaws in his emotional and psychological constitution. Here was a writer who articulated more eloquently than any other what
it felt to be human in the age of industry and revolution. As one of his closest
friends said—'I do enjoy the conversation and sincerity of Hazlitt, perhaps
more than any one else; he is natural,—unaffected,—expresses himself with a
frankness, impetuosity, and passion, that arrest one's attention and secure one's

confidence.'[1] It is because his writing enshrines these qualities that it retains its appeal today.

He stood at the centre of his world, his sensibilities forged at the heart of the new culture that came into being as he came of age. He was nineteen when he spent three weeks with Wordsworth and Coleridge in Somerset in 1798—'the figures that compose that date are to me like the "dreaded name of Demogorgon" ', he wrote[2]—and was one of the first to hear the *Lyrical Ballads* before publication, as well as some of the verse composed for Wordsworth's monumental, never-to-be-completed epic, 'The Recluse'. Here was a glimpse of the future, of the world to come—a society in which all men were equal, and the tyranny of property and power no more. He would never forget it.

Hazlitt was an idealist, and as such became first a philosopher, then a painter, journalist, and lecturer. He came to know the major figures of his time, including John Horne Tooke, William Godwin, J. M. W. Turner, Sir John Soane, Charles Kemble, and Edmund Kean. Among writers his judgement was second to none. He was the intimate of Coleridge, Shelley, Keats, Lamb, and Leigh Hunt, and the friend of Landor, Stendhal, and Thomas Moore, among others. He understood the culture at first hand, and was to be its greatest interpreter.

He hailed the coming of a new age when the French deposed their monarch, and wept when Napoleon abdicated. He foresaw a time when people would claim the right to speak on their own account, and determine the composition of their own government. He deplored the abandonment of such hopes in his contemporaries, but never forsook the belief that reform would one day change the world. 'I deny that liberty and slavery are convertible terms,' he wrote, 'that right and wrong, truth and falsehood, plenty and famine, the comforts or wretchedness of a people, are matters of perfect indifference.'[3] It was a remarkably modern statement, addressing issues with which we are still grappling.

From an early age he was a citizen of the world. 'Give me the clear blue sky over my head, and the green turf beneath my feet, a winding road before me, and a three hours' march to dinner...I laugh, I run, I leap, I sing for joy.'[4] As an infant he spent nearly two years in the new republic of America, the child of a singularly enlightened father who denied the arbitrary power of kings and bishops; he travelled the Continent as an adult—to Paris in 1802, and then to France and Italy after the Napoleonic Wars. He was most like us in regarding boundaries as a human concept with little bearing on the republic of ideas, eagerly devouring the work of Madame de Staël, Cervantes, Molière, and Goethe.

Preface

Not only did Hazlitt shape the understanding his own age had of itself, but in doing so shaped our own. We are the inheritors of the Romantic sensibility: its values and aspirations remain compelling, like some dream remembered from childhood. We recall the acting of Kean through Hazlitt's eyes, and through his analyses comprehend the writings of Wordsworth, Coleridge, Byron, and Scott. His commentaries on government spies, the hereditary monarchy, and the Church remain relevant nearly two centuries after their first publication. And like all great writers Hazlitt had an intuitive understanding of human psychology that, despite the passage of time, gives his writings a resonance and urgency lacking from those of his contemporaries. In that sense the most memorable of his subjects was himself, dissected with extraordinary candour in *Liber Amoris*, the chronicle of his obsession with his landlady's nineteen-year-old daughter, Sarah Walker: 'I intend these Essays as studies of human nature; and as, in the prosecution of this design, I do not spare others, I see no reason why I should spare myself.'[5] No contemporary wrote so coolly of the insanity of love, so dispassionately of their own failings and flaws—nor would they have wanted to. For it led him to confess to urges and impulses which were almost taboo. The result was outrage. The problem was (and remains) cultural. In France such a book would have raised barely an eyebrow, but in England it created a scandal exploited so successfully by his political enemies as to blight his reputation for the rest of the nineteenth century.

When I began working on this book, my aim was largely academic: it seemed to me that the full story of Hazlitt's life had yet to be told. And the years that have passed have only confirmed that belief, as I have discovered many facts which my predecessors have overlooked. But as I approach the conclusion to my labours, a more pressing reason spurs me on. It is true that Hazlitt consorted with prostitutes, had affairs with actresses, and frequented low-life dives. The available evidence indicates also that he acted honourably and kindly to those around him, often to a fault. He was impeccably honest, direct, and straightforward; lent money to anyone who needed it; and took care of family members without regard to his own welfare—which explains why he was so often in debt. Nor did the quality of his writing ever flag: called upon for the smallest contribution to a newspaper column, he would give generously of his talents to produce something unique, amusing, and thought-provoking. Yet this was a man who was attacked mercilessly throughout his life; indeed, Hazlitt-baiting became a recognized subgenre of literary journalism at which everyone was expected to excel. Between 1817 and 1830 there was not a single

Preface

Tory journal that did not carry at least one article condemning him as an infidel, a Jacobin, and a whoremonger (as if Tories did not have anything so disgusting as a sexual appetite and never frequented the stews); many journals of more Whiggish tastes followed suit. This was nothing other than government-sponsored persecution, and must count as one of the most successful smear campaigns in literary history. Sales of any book bearing his name collapsed, and his reputation remained flat until the end of the nineteenth century. Even then, the literary establishment was slow to accept him, and he continues to bear the slings and arrows of less well-informed critics today. Were there any doubting this, one need only take a look at recent comment on *Liber Amoris*, which unwittingly adopts the same morally superior posture as government stooges of his own time. The fact is that Hazlitt's achievement surpasses that of Lamb and De Quincey, and judgements on his private life (right or wrong) should not be permitted to detract from it. This biography is an attempt to reveal Hazlitt as he was, with all his faults and virtues, stripping away the propaganda that continues to obscure our view of him. It is designed to reveal both his contribution to the genre of essay-writing, and his qualities as a man.

This is the first fully researched biography to comprehend Hazlitt as he was in his own time, at the epicentre of his cultural milieu, the commentator par excellence on its achievements and failures. It draws on over a decade of archival research in libraries across Britain and North America, to reveal for the first time such matters as why Godwin broke with Hazlitt; how Hazlitt came to know Sir John Soane and J. M. W. Turner; the true nature of Hazlitt's dealings with Thomas Medwin; and what the likes of Joseph Farington and Sir Thomas Lawrence thought of him. In addition, I have drawn for the first time on manuscript sources to shed new light on his dealings with such figures as Francis Jeffrey, Robert Stodart, John M'Creery, Henry Crabb Robinson, Joseph Parkes, John Cam Hobhouse, and Stendhal. I have also uncovered much new material relating to Hazlitt's father, the Reverend William Hazlitt Sr, and his American sojourn; in particular, this volume benefits from new discoveries relating to his journalistic career in Philadelphia and Boston, and his relations with the Boston Association of Ministers. Work on this biography has proceeded concurrently with that on a related project, *New Writings of William Hazlitt*, published in two volumes by Oxford University Press in autumn 2007. Many of the 205 newly attributed works make their appearance here, illuminating hitherto obscure passages of Hazlitt's life.

Preface

In truth, his influence has never waned, nor will it do so. For we are inheritors of the culture he helped forge. His restless, inexhaustible passion is echoed in the endless editorials, columns, and feature pages of our newspapers and magazines. The age that configured itself round the related concepts of freedom, imagination, and infinite possibilities retains its chief interpreter, who continues to speak to us. To hear that voice clearly is to understand ourselves the better. Besides reminding us of his continuing power to surprise and entertain, this biography aims to confirm Hazlitt's stature as philosopher, journalist, and artist, while recognizing the relation he bears to us as the first modern man.

No man ever treasured his youth more joyously than Hazlitt did; no man ever honoured his father better; no man ever discharged with such good faith the debts of honour he owed to the favourite authors of his youth—Burke, Rousseau, Cervantes, Montaigne and a legion more. No critic (except perhaps a few fellow poets, and not many of them) ever heard the strange language of a new school of poetry with such an alert sympathy, and certainly no critic ever welcomed the innovation with greater daring and, despite all subsequent political feuds, with more persistence and warmth.

Michael Foot, *Debts of Honour* (London, 1980)

. . . no one was more certain that happiness is not separable from sadness, that pain is to be lived no less than joy, and that there is bound to be fear as well as hope.

Stanley Jones, *Hazlitt: A Life* (Oxford, 1989)

To be remembered after we are dead is but a poor recompense for being treated with contempt while we are living.

William Hazlitt, *Characteristics* ccccxxix

You know I am a fervent Hazlittite; I mean, regarding him as the English writer who has had the scantiest justice.

Robert Louis Stevenson, *c*.9 December 1881

Il y a des impressions que ni le temps ni les circonstances peuvent effacer.

Jean-Jacques Rousseau, *La Nouvelle Héloïse*

John Lamb: This is the strangest tale that e'er I heard.
Charles Lamb: It is the strangest fellow, brother John.

Manuscript in Hazlitt's hand, now at the Wordsworth Library, Grasmere; concluding lines of 'Self-Love and Benevolence'

PROLOGUE

To be young is to be as one of the Immortal Gods.

Hazlitt, 'On the Feeling of Immortality in Youth'[1]

THE Worcester stagecoach clattered along the Shrewsbury road. It was a cold January night in 1798 and the occupants of the vehicle would normally have been shivering as well as uncomfortable. But on this occasion they were warmed by the non-stop conversation of the young, dark-haired man before them. It was the 26-year-old Samuel Taylor Coleridge, already a noted figure in the intellectual world, renowned for his political and religious lectures as well as his poetry. He was to take up the position of Unitarian minister at Shrewsbury in succession to John Rowe, recently appointed to a new position in Bristol.

At 8pm the carriage ascended the hill to Shrewsbury High Street where a small cluster of friends and relatives stood in the cold, including Rowe, who was to accommodate Coleridge at his home. He had heard a great deal about the young man, said to be a prodigy who had outstripped his elders and looked set to achieve great things. The coach drew to a halt, its door swung open, and the travel-worn passengers climbed down—among them, a round-faced fellow in a short black coat like a shooting-jacket. He was deep in conversation with another passenger, who was laughing, and clearly not the sober, scholarly individual for whom he was waiting. In the end, none of the passengers answered to his expectations and Rowe returned home disappointed. As he entered the front door, his wife stepped into the hallway. 'No sign of the man,' he said to her. 'Perhaps he has been delayed.' They went together into the sitting-room where a fire blazed merrily away, only to hear a loud knock at the door. Rowe opened it and found the man wearing a shooting-jacket; smiling, he stood with cap in hand.

'Samuel Taylor Coleridge, sir,' he said. 'How do you do?' And without waiting for an answer, he stepped into the drawing-room and began to talk. He did not cease all evening, nor did he stop all the while he was there.

Prologue

Fig. 1. The Unitarian Chapel in Shrewsbury High Street, as it appeared to Hazlitt on the day he attended Coleridge's sermon in January 1798.

Early next morning the nineteen-year-old William Hazlitt awoke while it was dark, put on his clothes, and stepped into the freezing air. A ten-mile slog lay ahead of him. The road was muddy and wet,[2] and it was hard-going underfoot—'cold, raw, comfortless'.[3] But he had heard of Coleridge and was determined to see him preach.

When he arrived at the dark-panelled chapel, the organist was playing Psalm 100 which commands 'Make a joyful noise unto the Lord, all ye lands.' Hazlitt took his place in one of the box-pews, packed with other Salopians eager to see their new minister. When the organist was done, there was silence. Then a rustling and a shuffling, and Mr Coleridge stepped up to the large central pulpit.

'And he went up into the mountain to pray, HIMSELF, ALONE!', he intoned. The effect was stunning, as Hazlitt later recalled.

As he gave out this text, his voice 'rose like a steam of rich distilled perfumes,' and when he came to the two last words which he pronounced loud, deep, and distinct, it seemed to me who was then young, as if the sounds had echoed from the bottom of the human heart, and as if that prayer might have floated in solemn silence through the universe. The idea of St John came into mind, 'of one crying in the wilderness, who had his loins girt about, and whose food was locusts and wild honey.' The preacher then launched into his subject, like an eagle dallying with the wind.[4]

He spoke on the subject of 'peace and war; upon church and state—not their alliance, but their separation—on the spirit of the world and the spirit of Christianity, not as the same, but as opposed to one another.'[5] Hazlitt was enraptured.

Coleridge was at the height of his powers having in recent months composed two of his greatest poems, 'Kubla Khan' and 'The Ancient Mariner'; in need of money, he had applied for the post at Shrewsbury. A few weeks earlier, he had been the recipient of £100 from the Wedgwoods, pottery magnates with Unitarian sympathies, but returned it because the Shrewsbury job carried a salary of £120 and a house worth £30 in rent. So he was pleased to find himself a hit with the congregation, who had never seen anything like it. To them, he appeared possessed by divine afflatus: he horrified them with talk of war, enraged them with his account of government-sponsored injustice, and filled them with 'holy dread' on return to his biblical text. They were spellbound. Hazlitt's walk home was different from that earlier; high in the sky, the sun now seemed 'an emblem of the *good cause*' whose chief representative on earth was Samuel Taylor Coleridge.

Coleridge arranged to visit Hazlitt's father, Unitarian priests being accustomed to the hospitality of colleagues in neighbouring towns, and turned up for dinner the following Tuesday. He rambled the ten miles to Wem along the same route Hazlitt had taken, whistling all the way. Having found the Hazlitts' little house on Noble Street, he knocked at the door and was shown in. By the time William came down, Coleridge was talking animatedly to Hazlitt's father and the rest of the family. Up close, he looked different; in church, he appeared pock-marked and swarthy, but William now saw he was clear-complexioned with a broad high forehead, large projecting eyebrows, and enormous eyes 'rolling beneath them like a sea with darkened lustre'.[6] The mouth, he later recalled, was 'gross, voluptuous, open, eloquent', the chin round and good-humoured, but the nose—'the rudder of the face, the index of the will'[7]—small and feeble.

Hazlitt's father was swept away by this effusive man. It was as if all the conversation for which he yearned since returning from America over a decade earlier had been given him at once. He had probably heard the tale of how at one party Coleridge held forth on Berkeley's philosophy, persuading his listeners

[3]

the entire cosmos was 'a transparency of fine words'; or how, another time, he smoked his pipe and fell asleep, only to amaze the company when he sprang up five minutes later and launched into an hour-long description of 'the third heaven'. If so, neither the Reverend Hazlitt nor his family were disappointed, for the man was even better than the legend. Over dinner—leg of Welsh mutton with turnips—they got onto the topic of Revolutionary pamphleteers including James Mackintosh, who defended the French Revolution, and Edmund Burke, who condemned it.

'Mackintosh', said Coleridge, 'is a clever scholastic man, a ready warehouse-man of letters who knows exactly where to lay his hand on what he wants, though the goods were not his own. But he is no match for Burke in style or matter. Burke is a metaphysician, Mackintosh a mere logician. Burke is an orator (almost a poet) with an eye for nature; Mackintosh has an eye only to commonplaces.'

Young William intervened: 'I too have always held Burke in high esteem. Speaking of him with contempt might be made the test of a *vulgar* democratical mind.'

'A just and striking observation, sir!', replied Coleridge.[8] Nothing could have pleased Hazlitt more. The point was that both sided with Mackintosh (and the Revolution) but prided themselves on recognizing Burke's superior talents.

Coleridge told them about Wordsworth, who was composing the great poem of the age. He was, Coleridge observed, 'a Republican and at least a semi-atheist'[9]—which made the obscure poet seem not only glamorous but rather dangerous. He also recounted how one day, when Mackintosh made a slighting comment about Wordsworth, Coleridge replied: 'He strides on so far before you that he dwindles into the distance!'[10]

Coleridge discoursed with Hazlitt and his father late into the night.

'Have you ever seen Mary Wollstonecraft?' he asked Hazlitt.

'Only once, for a few minutes.'

'I have seen her with Mr Godwin, turning off his objections to one of her arguments with quite a playful, easy air. This was but one instance of the ascendancy which people of imagination exercise over those of mere intellect.' Hearing someone talk in this unexpected way about two of the foremost radical figures of the time was rather shocking.

'But Mr Godwin is a clever man, is he not?' asked Hazlitt.

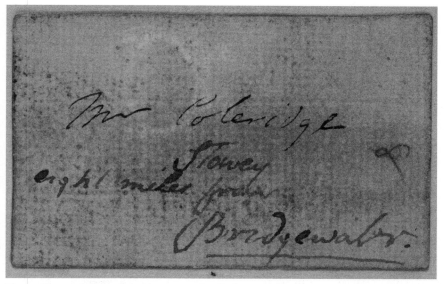

Fig. 2. The card which Coleridge gave to Hazlitt in 1798 when inviting him to Nether Stowey later that year. I am grateful to Tom Mayberry for this illustration.

'I do not rate him very high. Mrs Wollstonecraft, however, is a woman possessed of rare powers of conversation, though of little talent as a writer.'[11]

Coleridge's ideas on politics and religion depended partly on those of Joseph Priestley, and there can be little doubt Priestley was among the subjects discussed that evening. Two years earlier, Coleridge had told a friend Priestley's belief that 'God not only *does*, but *is*, every thing' led to that in an 'eating, drinking, lustful *God*—'with no *unity* of *Consciousness*'.[12] This was the kind of rant into which he could easily have slipped with Hazlitt's father, though he would have taken care to be more respectful with the older man, if no less combative.

The next morning a letter arrived for Coleridge. It was from Thomas Wedgwood, increasing the annuity he would offer to £150; Coleridge seemed to 'make up his mind to close with this proposal in the act of tying on one of his shoes'.[13] The course of his life changed in an instant. He decided to withdraw from the Shrewsbury post and instead to return to Stowey and devote himself to poetry and philosophy. Though pleased for him, the Hazlitts were understandably disappointed at the thought of losing such an interesting neighbour.[14] Coleridge cheered William up by asking for a pen and paper and scribbling

[5]

something on a card, which he placed in his hand. Hazlitt looked at it: 'Mr Coleridge', it said, 'Stowey eight miles from Bridgewater'.[15]

'I would be glad to see you in a few weeks' time', Coleridge said. 'What do you say to that, sir?'

Hazlitt stammered out his acceptance of the invitation, stumbling over his words. Then he had a thought. 'May I accompany you on your way?' he asked. Of course he could. For six miles he walked with Coleridge along the Shrewsbury road, a one-man audience to his digressions and dilations. 'He talked far above singing.'[16] They covered a multitude of subjects including Hazlitt's own 'philosophical discovery', which he attempted to explain, though without making much sense. In turn, Coleridge rattled off a litany of thinkers—Dr Johnson, Bishop Berkeley, William Paley—criticizing their sentiments and style.

'How do you like Hume?' asked Hazlitt, as they rambled along the Shrewsbury road.

'Hume? He stole his essay on miracles from South's sermons!'[17] replied Coleridge. 'He can't even write! He's unreadable.'[18] The younger man, who in his spare time was slaving over Hume's *Treatise on Human Nature*, 'that completest of all metaphysical *choke-pears*',[19] was astonished. Even then, for all his scepticism, Hume was regarded as one of the greatest philosophers of the century—and Coleridge regarded him as a charlatan.

The intensity with which Hazlitt experienced this was as much the product of youth as of the turmoil against which it was played out. A world war was in progress. Over the past five years, France had steadily subjugated the nations ranged against it with the sole exception of Britain, now under threat of invasion. Hazlitt and his family were in a difficult position as their sympathies rested with the French, who had exchanged a hereditary monarchy for a more democratic form of government. Coleridge agreed with them in siding with the Revolutionaries—but towards the end of his stay in Shrewsbury news arrived of Napoleon's invasion of Switzerland (a neutral country), which made it harder to support them, and inspired one of Coleridge's most anguished political poems, 'France: An Ode'.

There was another development of which Hazlitt and his family were aware. For several months the government had been attempting to suppress the United Irishmen—an underground organization devoted to the overturning of British rule in Ireland. Hazlitt's father was connected with it[20] and may have been related to one of its founders, Henry Haslett. He was certainly associated with William Drennan, the first of the Irishmen to be tried for sedition in 1794,[21] so that when, in the spring of 1798, the Irishmen attempted a revolution against the British, he and his family listened avidly for news. Were the Irish and French to be victorious, it would mean an end to Britain and its constitution—something the Hazlitts had long wished for. To them (and to many of like mind), the hereditary monarchy by which they were governed was little other than a form of institutionalized tyranny.

In April, Hazlitt walked thirty miles north-west to the Vale of Llangollen and celebrated his twentieth birthday at an inn with his favourite novel, Rousseau's *La Nouvelle Héloïse*, feasting on a bottle of sherry and a plate of cold chicken. Among other things he re-read St Preux's description of his return to Switzerland, which described

> the Alpine air so wholesome and so pure; the gentle breeze of the country, more fragrant than the perfumes of the orient; that rich and fertile land, that matchless countryside, the most beautiful ever beheld by human eyes; that charming place to which I had found nothing equal in my tour of the world; the aspect of a happy and free people; the mildness of the season, the serenity of the weather; a thousand delightful memories which aroused again all the sentiments I had enjoyed—all threw me into ecstasies which I cannot describe and seemed to infuse me with all the joy of my whole life at once.[22]

William experienced similar feelings as he walked through the Vale: 'The valley at this time "glittered green with sunny showers," and a budding ash-tree dipped its tender branches in the chiding stream.'[23] As he strode along the high road the thought of the liberties enjoyed by the French made the lush fields seem 'a heavenly vision on which were written, in letters large as Hope could make them, these four words, LIBERTY, GENIUS, LOVE, VIRTUE'.[24] Political developments in Ireland and Europe gave him the sense that a truly egalitarian world was in sight, and that awareness infused his perception of the world around him. On his way home, he stopped at an inn and gazed at drawings by the artist Richard Westall, including one of a female figure which made him think longingly of 'a girl who had ferried me across the Severn, standing up in the boat between me and the twilight'.[25]

On return to Wem he found a letter from Coleridge who was keen to see him but requested a week's grace as his wife was about to deliver a baby. Hazlitt was so thrilled at the expectation of seeing him again that his father had to restrain him from leaving there and then. Over the next few days he occupied himself with various tasks, including another vain attempt to write up his 'philosophical discovery', but impatience finally got the better of him and he set out regardless.

Prologue

The walk was nearly two hundred miles and, if he was to satisfy Coleridge's request, it would have to last nearly two weeks. He decided to follow the River Severn through Shropshire, then went across country to Worcester via Kidderminster. One bright day he heard singing; he turned to see a man declaiming from a score he held in his hand—it was an actor, his pockets stuffed with playbills. 'Bonjour!' cried the man before passing on, singing 'to the echo of the babbling stream, brisk as a bird, gay as a mote, swift as an arrow from a twanging bow, heart-whole, and with shining face that shot back the sun's broad rays!'[26] The man's carefree mood echoed his own. The excitement William felt at journeying south to see Coleridge and the awareness of the momentous events taking place in the world gave everything the same vivid, intense appearance.

> Bliss was it in that dawn to be alive,
> But to be young was very heaven![27]

The following day he tried to befriend some local girls but found them 'coarse and hard'.[28]

He travelled about 25 miles each day, and six days after setting out undertook the penultimate leg of his journey from Lulsgate Bottom (now a suburb of Bristol) to Bridgwater. It rained solidly, he got drenched, and he concluded his journey by running into an inn where he sat up all night, drying off, reading Jacques de St Pierre's novel, *Paul and Virginia*.[29] 'Sweet were the showers in early youth that drenched my body, and sweet the drops of pity that fell upon the books I read!'[30]

He was within a day's walk of Stowey and much earlier than expected, so decided to cool his heels for a while in Bridgwater. Despite amusing himself there a day or so, the town's novelty soon wore thin, and he became eager to press on to Stowey, a mere seven-and-a-half miles away. He walked into the village on the morning of 20 May 1798, found Mr Coleridge's cottage, and knocked on the door.

His host was in buoyant mood, having just become father to a son named after an Irish Bishop whose philosophical works he revered—Berkeley. ('You remember, I am a *Berkleian*!', he told Robert Southey the previous year.[31]) The elder of his boys was just over eighteen months old and named after another philosopher, Hartley.

What did Coleridge's wife Sara make of their guest? For most of her marriage she had little choice but to put up with her husband's hare-brained friends, most of whom she couldn't stand. The previous year, before Coleridge went

Fig. 3. Coleridge's cottage in Nether Stowey as it appears today. This was where Hazlitt arrived on the morning of 20 May 1798 after a week-long trek from Wem.

out for a long walk with Charles Lamb, she 'accidentally' poured a skillet of boiling milk over his foot. As for the idea of putting anyone up, their cottage had only three rooms downstairs and two upstairs—close quarters for two adults, let alone two squealing infants and a guest. Yet her own daughter would testify that Sara always liked Hazlitt: 'uncouth & morbid & melancholy as he was—She found him civil'.[32] High praise from a woman who failed to get on with most of her husband's friends.

Coleridge's close collaboration with Wordsworth had produced some of the greatest poetry in the language. Since meeting Hazlitt, Coleridge had composed the third indisputably great poem of his career, 'Christabel' Part I, as well as others including 'The Nightingale', which would appear in *Lyrical Ballads*, a volume he and Wordsworth would publish as a means of funding a trip to Germany in the autumn. At that time, Germany was the intellectual hub of the Western world, boasting Goethe, Schiller, Kant, and the Schlegel brothers.

These were the architects of the new Romantic sensibility that was about to change the world.

In Germany, Wordsworth hoped to complete 'The Recluse'. Though appalled by the bloody aftermath of the French Revolution, he remained loyal to its aims and wanted to find a non-violent means of achieving them. The answer was a philosophical poem by which humanity would be re-educated to understand how love of nature led irresistibly to love of mankind. It would create a new kind of society in which there was no need for money, property or social class, and universal love would reign supreme. By his own count, Wordsworth already had over 1,500 lines of the new work: 'The Giant Wordsworth—God love him!', Coleridge declared.[33]

Although Wordsworth was in Bristol, not to return till the following day, Hazlitt could at least meet his sister, Dorothy. The walk to Holford was a mere two-and-a-half miles and as they strode down the shady Somerset lanes, Coleridge revealed that the Wordsworths had moved from Dorset because they wanted to be close to him. These three young people were living through the most important year of their artistic lives, and each brought something different to the collaboration: Wordsworth's vision of nature as a redemptive force was new to Coleridge, who, having grown up in London, had little instinctive feeling for it; conversely, Coleridge's philosophical expertise provided Wordsworth with something hitherto lacking from his work. Dorothy possessed a refined version of Wordsworth's sensitive observation of the natural world, which she documented in a diary kept at her brother's request.

As they emerged from the trees that overhung the driveway, Hazlitt and Coleridge found themselves gazing at an elegant foursquare Queen Anne mansion nestling in a dell at the foot of the Quantock hills. Though Dorothy was not expecting visitors, Coleridge was sure she would be pleased to see them. 'She is a woman indeed!—in mind, I mean, & heart', Coleridge had written.[34] The feeling was mutual: Dorothy loved him with the affection of a sister. It didn't matter that she wasn't pretty in the conventional sense, with her gipsy-brown skin, sparkling wild eyes, and slight stoop, which 'gave an ungraceful, and even an unsexual character to her appearance when out of doors';[35] she had 'simple, ardent, impressive'[36] manners, a powerful mind, 'and her taste [was] a perfect electrometer—it bends, protrudes, and draws in, at subtlest beauties & most recondite faults'.[37]

She welcomed them into Alfoxden House and set before them a 'frugal repast'.[38] After they had eaten, she showed them manuscripts of her brother's poems, and Hazlitt became one of the first to read 'The Thorn', 'Goody Blake and Harry Gill', and 'The Mad Mother', written weeks earlier. 'I dipped into these with great satisfaction, and with the faith of a novice,' he recalled.[39] They talked into the small hours and when he could stay awake no longer, was shown upstairs to an old room with blue hangings, covered with old family portraits dating from the age of George I, and fell asleep. He was awakened next morning by stags bellowing from the fringes of the wood.

After breakfast, they strolled round the estate, sat at the foot of an ancient oak, and listened to Coleridge reading Wordsworth's poem 'The Idiot Boy'. It was like nothing Hazlitt had previously heard. At a time when poets were expected to address abstract entities such as Hope and Fear or paraphrase passages from the Bible, here was 'a new style and a new spirit'[40] that spoke of working people, articulating their hopes, fears, and sufferings. Not only did these poems address the deplorable state of the real world, but their declared agenda was one of political change. As Wordsworth later told the leader of His Majesty's opposition, Charles James Fox, his poems were 'written with a view to shew that men who do not wear fine cloaths can feel deeply'.[41]

That evening, as they returned to Stowey, Coleridge lamented Wordsworth's refusal to believe in fairies. 'There is a something corporeal, a matter-of-factness, a clinging to the palpable, or often to the petty, in his poetry,' he remarked. This was true. Wordsworth did have a whimsical side to him—as 'The Idiot Boy' proved—but lacked the qualities by which Coleridge created the nightmarish fairytales of 'Christabel' and 'The Ancient Mariner'. However, added Coleridge, 'That objection does not apply to Wordsworth's philosophic poetry, which has a grand and comprehensive spirit in it, so that his soul seems to inhabit the universe like a palace, and to discover truth by intuition rather than by deduction.'

Wordsworth arrived at Coleridge's cottage the following day. Hazlitt was struck by his 'gaunt and Don Quixote-like' appearance. He was 'quaintly dressed' in a brown fustian jacket and striped pantaloons, and took his seat next to half a cheddar cheese, which he proceeded to demolish.[42] His face was equine, Hazlitt observed—a high forehead, long Roman nose, furrowed cheeks, and 'a convulsive inclination to laughter about the mouth, a good deal at variance with the solemn, stately expression of the rest of his face'.[43] As Wordsworth spoke, Hazlitt was conscious of his Cumbrian accent—'a strong tincture of the northern *burr*, like the crust on wine'.[44] Wordsworth had seen a play in Bristol the previous evening, Matthew Lewis's *The Castle Spectre*, the latest hit to reach the provinces. 'It fitted the taste of the audience like a glove,' Wordsworth remarked.[45] Which just about said it all: high-class hokum, but hokum nonetheless.

Wordsworth arrived with a publisher friend, Joseph Cottle, who had driven him down from Bristol in a gig. Cottle had known Coleridge since he planned to emigrate to America with Southey and set up a 'pantisocratic' commune in 1794. So taken was he with Coleridge that he published his journal *The Watchman*, enlisted subscribers for it, and lent him money. They remained in touch about various publishing ventures, and now he wanted to discuss *Lyrical Ballads*.[46]

When justice was done to the cheese, Wordsworth went to the window. 'How beautifully the sun sets on that yellow bank!', he said. This was the kind of observation by which he would change the culture. 'With what eyes these poets see nature,' thought Hazlitt.[47] The natural world was not yet understood to be a living thing; that insight was bequeathed us by the Romantics.

The next day Hazlitt accompanied Coleridge to Alfoxden; they sat under the oak and listened to Wordsworth reciting 'Peter Bell'. While chanting his tale of crime and punishment, 'his face was as a book where men might read strange matters.' Afterwards, they walked to Stowey and along the way Hazlitt and Wordsworth got into 'a metaphysical argument' in which 'neither of us succeeded in making ourselves perfectly clear and intelligible.'[48]

The argument concerned the Wordsworthian concept of 'wise passiveness'—the belief that the mind, when relaxed, was 'content to feel | As nature feels, and to receive her shapes | As she has made them'.[49] The process by which the perceiving sensibility was shaped by the beneficent influence of the natural world was fundamental to Wordsworth's 'Recluse', whereby love of nature led inexorably to love of mankind. It was essential to his philosophy that the process was necessitarian—that is, the individual was unable to resist it. Like many left-leaning intellectuals, Wordsworth had something of the totalitarian about him, and was quite at home with that aspect of his theory; as an instinctive libertarian, Hazlitt detested it. It amounted to enforced re-education of the masses. Unfortunately for Wordsworth, Hazlitt was expert at metaphysical discourse: his father studied under Adam Smith at Glasgow and had tutored him in the finer points of theology, philosophy, economics, and political theory. He read David Hume in his spare time. Like most educated people Wordsworth had ploughed his way through Locke and had read his share of philosophy at university. But he had a down-to-earth sensibility with little real interest in the sort of intellectual gymnastics Hazlitt took in his stride. Most of the ideas incorporated into 'The Recluse' were imbibed from Coleridge.[50]

The argument went off the rails when Hazlitt opposed Wordsworth's half-baked notions with his theory of disinterestedness—the philosophical 'discovery' he had failed to describe to Coleridge in February. On this occasion, the need to demolish Wordsworth's house of cards lent him an eloquence he had not previously enjoyed. It was uncomfortably obvious to everyone, long before he was done, that he had bested his opponent, and afterwards there was an uncomfortable silence. The moon shone through the boughs of the trees above their heads, and he could hear the tread of his companions' shoes. Too late, Hazlitt realized what he had done. Wordsworth regarded himself as the great poet of the age, an opinion shared by Coleridge. He was not to be defied by a young upstart from Shropshire! Coleridge, more than either of the Wordsworths, realized the significance of Hazlitt's theory. It was more subtle and penetrating than anything he could have devised, and placed its emphasis on the freedom of the individual will. If it was right, he realized, 'The Recluse' was unworkable.

'You wish merely to argue me out of my own existence, sir!' retaliated Wordsworth. 'The mind is not so easily anatomized.'

'Indeed', chimed Coleridge. 'You want to take in pieces, by metaphysical aid, the inner self; to expose the brain as a fine illusion. It is no such thing!'[51] There was a moment's silence and then Wordsworth turned to Hazlitt.

'This argument of yours—is this your grand theory of human disinterestedness?' he asked. 'The one you mentioned to Coleridge?'

'Yes sir.'

Wordsworth smiled, his equine face turning back along the road they had been walking, as he prepared to return to Alfoxden. Then he looked straight into Hazlitt's face. 'There is doubtless *something* in it,' said he. 'Yet it is what every shoemaker must have thought of.'[52] With that, he disappeared into the gloom, followed closely by his sister.

Wordsworth knew his comment was unfair, inspired by awareness of the younger man's superior expertise. The argument continued to rankle, and as soon as he arrived at Alfoxden Wordsworth composed two poems re-enacting it in fictionalized form, 'Expostulation and Reply' and 'The Tables Turned', which would be published in *Lyrical Ballads*. In one of his most famous stanzas Wordsworth condemned Hazlitt's metaphysical insights as inadequate to the 'lore' vouchsafed by the natural world:

> Sweet is the lore which nature brings;
> Our meddling intellect
> Misshapes the beauteous forms of things;
> —We murder to dissect.[53]

Wordsworth was rattled because he recognized that, were he to expound the philosophy of 'The Recluse', he had to train himself to the point at which he could engage with the likes of Hazlitt on their own terms. Hazlitt, after all, had no antipathy towards the project; he was merely questioning the detail. That was why Wordsworth sailed to Germany later that year—to study at its universities—and it is why traces of the 'philosophical dispute' are to be found in the first version of his poem *The Prelude*, which was composed there.[54]

Hazlitt remembered the exchange for the rest of his life, and was deeply hurt by it. He had intended no disrespect to either Wordsworth or Coleridge and was taken aback by their hostility to his ideas. Coleridge must have felt sorry for him, and was probably as surprised by the harshness of Wordsworth's parting shot as Hazlitt. He had occasionally noted Wordsworth's brittleness when under threat—which would in due course generate tensions in their own friendship.[55] He cheered his young friend up during sunny afternoons in the lime-tree bower of his next-door neighbour, the tanner Thomas Poole. Poole had trained the branches of a lime tree to form a large circle, embracing anyone who sat within them, providing shelter from the winds that blew off the Bristol Channel. A year earlier, Coleridge made it the subject of one of his greatest poems, 'This Lime-Tree Bower My Prison', which he recited to Hazlitt. The two men would retire to the bower with large tankards of flip (a mixture of hot beer and spirits sweetened with sugar, enlivened by a fresh egg) and engage for hours in conversation. They had much to discuss. Although they enjoyed each other's company, their opinions were sharply divergent. Hazlitt was all his life an unswerving republican but Coleridge stopped short of that, preferring to describe himself as 'a Democrat & a Seditionist'.[56] What was more, Coleridge despised those who 'assumed to themselves the exclusive title of Philosophers & Friends of Freedom', claiming his own opinions to be 'utterly untainted with

French Metaphysics, French Politics, French Ethics, & French Theology'.[57]
If he said as much to Hazlitt—which he is likely to have done—they would
have been in the bower until late at night. The same thing would have happened when they ventured onto the subject of religion—Coleridge being a
devout Unitarian, Hazlitt an 'Infidel'. Yet for all their differences, Hazlitt was
seduced by the older man, as were most of those who encountered him at this
period. Coleridge was voluble, emotional, charming, and amusing, even when
describing the suspicion he and the Wordsworths aroused among the locals.
At a time when the French were widely expected to invade Britain, fears of a
'fifth column' of republican sympathizers only intensified political paranoia at
an already frenzied moment. It was not unlike the feverish speculation about
communist sympathizers in America during the 1950s. The British government
was sufficiently concerned to dispatch a spy to Somerset, one James Walsh, to
find out what Wordsworth and Coleridge were up to. At first Walsh thought
they were French émigrés, then jumped to the equally outlandish conclusion
that they were 'a sett of Violent Democrats' likely to foment revolution in
the event of an invasion.[58] This was a factor in their decision to leave the
country, as Coleridge pointed out: 'Wordsworth has been caballed against *so
long and so loudly*, that he has found it impossible to prevail on the tenant of the Allfoxden estate to let him the house after their first agreement is
expired.'[59]

It was probably on one such afternoon in the bower that Coleridge drew
from his pocket a small leather-bound notebook in which he had, he said, a
'curiosity'. A curiosity? thought Hazlitt. What can he mean? There was a glint
in Coleridge's eye—yet he seemed almost apologetic. He opened the book,
settled on a page, and looked Hazlitt in the eye, before intoning, in a sort of
chant:

> In Xannadù did Cubla Khan
> A stately pleasure-dome decree,
> Where Alph, the sacred river, ran
> Through caverns measureless to man
> Down to a sunless sea.

It was the earliest version of 'Kubla Khan'—a poem now so integral to our
literary heritage that it is impossible to recreate the shock-value it would have
had for its first readers in 1798. It was totally unlike anything Hazlitt—or anyone
else—had ever encountered. Was poetry supposed to do this? Should it be

allowed to do this? Yet he could not help but set aside all such questions as he surrendered to its hypnotic cadences and rhythms.

> But oh, that deep romantic chasm that slanted
> Down a green hill athwart a cedarn cover!
> A savage place, as holy and enchanted
> As e'er beneath a waning moon was haunted
> By woman wailing for her demon-lover!
> For from this chasm, with hideous turmoil seething,
> As if this earth in fast thick pants were breathing,
> A mighty fountain momently was forced
> Amid whose swift half-intermitted burst
> Huge fragments vaulted like rebounding hail,
> Or chaffy grain beneath the thresher's flail!
> And mid these dancing rocks at once and ever,
> It flung up momently the sacred river.
> Five miles meandering with a mazy motion
> Through wood and dale the sacred river ran,
> Then reached the caverns measureless to man
> And sank in tumult to a lifeless ocean.
> And mid this tumult Cubla heard from far
> Ancestral voices prophesying war!

Women wailing for the demon lovers! Orgasmic fountains! Weird landscapes! What can Hazlitt have made of it? He probably questioned Coleridge, but the author himself was puzzled. 'I composed it in a sort of reverie brought on by two grains of opium taken to check a dysentery,' he admitted. Yet even he had no idea what it was about. Hazlitt stared at his friend, thunderstruck, certain he was in the presence of genius. 'Let me hear it again,' he demanded.[60]

Late into the night, they would sit and discuss books in the front parlour of the cottage while infant Berkeley squalled in the upstairs bedroom. One evening the racket got so much on Hazlitt's nerves that, against his usual inclinations, he suggested it was evidence of innate wickedness.

'Why, the infant is merely straining its lungs a little!'[61] Coleridge replied.

'If the child had been in pain or fear, I should have said nothing', Hazlitt said. 'But it cried only to vent its passion and alarm the house, and in its frantic screams and gestures I see that great baby, the world, tumbling about in its swaddling clothes, and tormenting itself and others for the last six thousand years!' Hazlitt would always hold to the view that love of mischief for its own sake was the original sin of human nature. In the case of the infant, he thought, its love of power was allied to evil. This led them to discuss childhood reading, and Coleridge declared his early love of fairy tales and the Arabian Nights, which had habituated his mind 'to the Vast'.[62]

'I don't like the Arabian Nights', said Hazlitt.

'If you do not like them', replied Coleridge, 'it is because you do not dream!'[63]

That night Hazlitt heard Coleridge recite 'The Ancient Mariner', soon to be published in *Lyrical Ballads*. He recognized its power immediately, and always insisted it was the one work 'we could with confidence put into any person's hands, on whom we wished to impress a favourable idea of [Coleridge's] extraordinary powers.'[64] So pleased was Coleridge with Hazlitt's reaction that he promised to show him the weird landscape by which it was inspired. The previous November, Coleridge and the Wordsworths had gone for an eight-day hike along the Somerset coastline, during which 'The Ancient Mariner' was conceived as a means of paying their expenses.

Coleridge and Hazlitt would follow the same route but in three days rather than eight, Coleridge having other things to get on with. They set out on 5 June with John Chester, a farmer's son who Hazlitt regarded as an ass. A slightly comic figure in brown coat, boots, and corduroy breeches, Chester kept up a 'sort of trot' at Coleridge's side, like a footman beside a state coach, listening avidly to whatever fell from the great man's lips. 'If you want my private opinion, sir,' Chester whispered to Hazlitt, 'Mr Coleridge is a wonderful man!'

They headed west along the coastal path, passing Dunster, before rambling on to Minehead, Porlock and Culbone (where Coleridge had written 'Kubla Khan'). He showed them Culbone church, a Lilliputian structure 33 feet in length and 12 in breadth, its quaint cemetery dotted with rustic gravestones set in a small clearing in a dense wood. Hazlitt would not forget the wild, heathy landscape of the moors, with the Welsh hills visible on the far side of the Bristol Channel, and the undulations of the coastline, which ushered them into countless small valleys. Towards evening he pointed out to Coleridge the masts of a sailing vessel on the edge of the horizon, within the crimson disc of the setting sun, like the spectre-ship in 'The Ancient Mariner'.

By the time they reached the small village of Lynton it was nearly midnight. They had covered 35 miles. At that hour most inns were shut, but they found one they thought was open and banged loudly on the door. The innkeeper proved obliging, perhaps remembering Coleridge from his earlier visit. He fried them some bacon and eggs before they went to bed.

The next morning they were getting ready to leave when they heard the deafening roar of thunder; Coleridge ran outside, bareheaded, to enjoy 'the commotion of the elements', but the clouds declined to cooperate, letting fall no more than a few drops of rain. They laughed and walked on a mile or so to the Valley of the Rocks, a craggy wall of stone overlooking the sea, topped with huge boulders. Even today, it is like something out of a horror film; a contemporary guidebook describes it as 'a line of ragged rock fantastical and grotesque in the extreme'.[65] Hazlitt began to understand how this strange landscape shaped the fearful vision of 'The Ancient Mariner'.[66]

They headed back to Stowey, stopping at an inn for breakfast. In an old wood-panelled room they feasted on tea, toast, eggs, and honey within sight of the hives from which it had been taken, and the wildflowers and thyme which had produced it. Coleridge discoursed on Virgil's *Georgics*, but Hazlitt thought he had little feeling for classical literature. While he was talking, Hazlitt noticed a copy of James Thomson's poem *The Seasons* on a window-seat and pointed it out.

'*That* is true fame!' Coleridge exclaimed, meaning that its presence in a public tavern was better than the good opinion of countless critics. 'Yet Thomson is a good poet rather than a great one, his style as meretricious as his thoughts are natural.'[67]

'Who *is* the best modern poet?' asked Hazlitt.

'Cowper.'[68] Though little-read today, the reflective blank verse of William Cowper's *The Task* was a powerful influence on Wordsworth and Coleridge.

As they continued, Coleridge argued the merits of other writers: he didn't like Junius or Dr Johnson but thought Burke a better orator and politician than either Fox or Pitt. When they reached Porlock Weir they met a fisherman who told them how the previous day he had tried unsuccessfully to save the life of a drowned boy. 'I do not know how we ventured, but, Sir, we have a *nature* towards one other,' the man said.[69] This stuck in Coleridge's head, and as they proceeded on their way he suggested it was a perfect illustration of Hazlitt's theory of disinterestedness. Not only had Hazlitt managed to explain his philosophical theory—but perhaps there was something to it.

The day after their return, Coleridge set out for Bristol early in the morning while Hazlitt dozed. By the time he woke up, Coleridge was long gone. Hazlitt pulled on his clothes and scribbled a brief note to his father, letting him know he was on his way home.[70] Hazlitt Sr was relieved to hear it. These were uncertain times. On the other side of the Irish Sea, the United Irishmen had begun their rebellion on 23 May and the bloodshed would continue until the third week of June. In a matter of weeks over 30,000 people were slaughtered, peasants charging British cannon armed only with pitchforks and staves. That such a multitude thought that sacrifice worthwhile testifies to the severity of British rule. It was a tragedy—and one reason why Hazlitt said that the figures composing the year 1798 'are to me like the "dreaded name of Demogorgon" '.[71]

But there was another reason too. This was the defining experience of his life. Coleridge, in particular, was 'the only person from whom I ever learnt any thing in conversation', 'the only person I ever knew who answered to my idea of a man of genius'.[72] From the moment he met them it was clear that Wordsworth and Coleridge were the last hope of a revolution derailed by Robespierre and the Terror, for their millenarian aspirations were faithful to the convictions of Condorcet, Voltaire, and Rousseau—its intellectual godfathers. A cause which by 1798 seemed in danger of being lost in the confusion of war was once more within the grasp of humanity, thanks to a philosophical poem devised by two contemporaries. Were they to succeed, poetry would no longer be an ornament in the drawing-room but the vehicle for political change. As he walked past the hedgerows on the Bridgwater road, Hazlitt knew he would never be the same. He had been vouchsafed a glimpse of the future.

PART I

The Road to Nether Stowey

CHAPTER 1

Say nothing about my father, he was a good man. His son is
a devil, and let him remain so.

Hazlitt, probably after 1823[1]

I am by education and conviction inclined to republicanism
and puritanism.

Hazlitt, 'Trifles Light as Air'[2]

HAZLITT's father was an extraordinary man. An Irishman born at Shronell, County Tipperary, Hazlitt Sr was educated at Glasgow University from 1756 to 1761. A bastion of free thought in the midst of sectarianism, the University boasted some of the finest minds in the United Kingdom including James Watt (who Hazlitt Sr assisted on experiments leading ultimately to the discovery of latent heat[3]) and Adam Smith (whose lectures he attended[4]). Despite opposition from the local synod, the professors at Glasgow encouraged students to think for themselves rather than accept the assumptions handed down by church elders. That unshakeable belief in liberty of thought and worship had a profound effect on the personality of Hazlitt Sr, and in turn on his son.[5]

The result was that many of those graduating from the 'Old College' on the High Street turned out dissenters; that is, they rejected the Thirty-Nine Articles, preferring to worship outside the confines of the Anglican church. This was the case with Hazlitt Sr, who, when he graduated, did so a Socinian—one who rejects Trinitarian Christianity as a human invention, preferring a Unitarian God (without deified Christ or Holy Spirit). This went against the creed of his father, who never overcame 'disappointment at his son's going over to the Unitarian side of the question'.[6] Disappointing one's father would become a family tradition among the Hazlitts.

After graduation, Hazlitt Sr preached for various ministers in London and in his spare time visited the theatres. He passed his love of drama on to his son who evoked this period in 'On Actors and Acting':

What a rich treat to the town, what a feast for the critics, to go and see Betterton, and Booth, and Wilks, and Sandford, and Nokes, and Leigh, and Penkethman, and Bullock, and Estcourt, and Dogget, and Mrs. Barry, and Mrs. Montfort, and Mrs. Oldfield, and Mrs. Bracegirdle, and Mrs. Cibber, and Cibber himself, the prince of coxcombs, and Macklin, and Quin, and Rich, and Mrs. Clive, and Mrs. Pritchard, and Mrs. Abington, and Weston, and Shuter, and Garrick, and all the rest of those who 'gladdened life, and whose deaths eclipsed the gaiety of nations'! We should certainly be there. We should buy a ticket for the season.[7]

After gaining a 'testimonial of approbation' recommending him to serve as a dissenting minister, Hazlitt Sr was introduced to a number of congregations including that at Wisbeach, Isle of Ely, where he fell in love with Grace Loftus, daughter of an ironmonger, 'a very beautiful young girl, elegant in her person and manners, and beloved by all who knew her'.[8] They were married on 10 January 1766 at Peterborough and settled in Marshfield, Gloucestershire, where Hazlitt was appointed minister of the Presbyterian meeting.

Marshfield was, and remains, a small isolated village on the ridge of an exposed valley. Their first children, John and Loftus, were born here. And it was here Hazlitt Sr wrote his first book, *A Sermon on Human Mortality*, co-published by Joseph Johnson and Benjamin Davenport in 1766.[9] Finding Marshfield remote, he was relieved at being appointed four years later to the Earl Street congregation in Maidstone, 'a large and respectable society'[10] within striking distance of London. Here he became part of a growing network of Unitarians in and around the capital. There were several focuses for this activity, one being his publisher. Johnson issued a journal called the *Theological Repository* edited by another Socinian, Joseph Priestley,[11] to which Hazlitt Sr was soon contributing.[12]

Shortly after arrival in Maidstone, Hazlitt Sr encountered Benjamin Franklin, then in the midst of his second English agency. They shared a fascination with the latest scientific developments; Hazlitt told him of Watt's experiments at Glasgow while Franklin revealed his own interest in electricity, which extended to kiteflying in the midst of Lake District thunderstorms. They had much in common politically, for Hazlitt was sympathetic to the cause of the American colonists. And despite the fact that Franklin was thought to be 'an unbeliever in Christianity',[13] they apparently found agreement on religious matters: when Hazlitt Sr published *An Essay on the Justice of God* in

1773 he gave a copy to Franklin, now preserved at the Library Company of Philadelphia.[14]

Hazlitt Sr became a minister at a time when dissenters were gaining ground politically. In 1772 Priestley was appointed 'literary companion' to William Fitzmaurice-Petty, second earl of Shelburne. A cabinet minister who served in Pitt's second ministry, Shelburne spearheaded a bill in 1771 to release dissenting clergy from having to sign the Thirty-Nine Articles. He 'professed a warm regard to the Dissenters, as friends of liberty, &c., and promised, if ever he came into power, to exert himself in supporting their rights, and placing them on the same footing with other Protestant subjects'.[15] Even though his bill was defeated, Shelburne would prove a valuable ally.[16]

William Hazlitt was born on 10 April 1778, probably in the family's small Maidstone house in Rose Yard, a narrow passage between the High Street and Earl Street.[17] Baptized by his father on 21 June,[18] William was his parents' fourth child; there was also a seven-year-old sister, Margaret (also called Peggy, born 1770), and an eleven-year-old brother, John. As a baby he was exceptionally good-looking and called 'the evening star' on that account. The death of his infant brother Loftus, aged two-and-a-half, shortly after the family moved to Maidstone, made his mother doubly protective of him, and he was spoilt from the outset.

He was not two years old when in March 1780 the family moved to Ireland. A dispute over money matters divided the Maidstone congregation,[19] and rather than become embroiled in it, Hazlitt Sr accepted an invitation to move to Bandon, County Cork. By now the American War of Independence was in full swing and at nearby Kinsale prison British soldiers were torturing American prisoners of war. As a 'hearty well-wisher to the Americans',[20] Hazlitt Sr wrote a newspaper article exposing the abuses and brought a private action against those concerned.[21] He was soon the recipient of death threats, which led him to appeal to Lord Shelburne, now Prime Minister. Shelburne ordered the regiment to a different part of Ireland, confirming there was 'nothing in [Hazlitt's] conduct with respect to them that was blameable'.[22] It was typical of Hazlitt Sr to stand up for the rights of the oppressed without regard to himself. His fidelity to his principles was absolute, and his son would be the same.

By now, the American War was nearing its end: a treaty was signed in Paris in November, and Britain declared an end to hostilities in February 1783. Hazlitt Sr was eager to leave Britain: it was a den of injustice, America a haven of freedom.

By the time Congress declared an end to the war on 11 April, Hazlitt and his family were at sea.

The six-week sea voyage cannot have been pleasant, especially for Grace, now six months' pregnant and nursing baby Harriet, nearly eighteen months old. But the weather was kind, and young William, who had his fifth birthday in mid-Atlantic, was spared seasickness. The only thing that marred their journey was the disapproval of the ship's captain when he realized they 'were the friends of liberty, which he cordially hated'.[23]

Their hearts lifted when they saw the woods of New Jersey and the highlands of Neversunk, and as they entered American waters they fished for fresh mackerel, dangling home-made lines over the side of the ship. They were relieved finally to dock in New York on 26 May 1783. Theirs was the first ship to arrive after the peace, bringing news of it to the British officers who controlled the port. Young William witnessed 'how they raved and swore, cursing both the Congress and those at home who had thus put a stop to their ravaging with fire and sword their brothers' land'.[24] This was an early glimpse of John Bull—who, Hazlitt later wrote, 'beats his wife, quarrels with his neighbours, damns his servants, and gets drunk to kill the time and keep up his spirits, and firmly believes himself the only exceptionable, accomplished, moral and religious character in Christendom'.[25]

New York at this time was a small township in Lower Manhattan, the rest of the island being largely agricultural. Jeremy Belknap noted that its streets were crooked except for Broadway, 'a noble wide street & strait'. Its buildings were residential, substantial houses of stone or brick, constructed in the Dutch manner with high, stepped gables: 'on these are large Irons in ye shape of figures denoting ye year in wh ye house was built & serving also as braces to strengthen ye brickwork'.[26] A few such buildings, reconstructed, are to be seen in South William Street today (see Fig. 4).

Two days later they set out for Philadelphia, of which Hazlitt Sr probably heard much from Benjamin Franklin. This was where independence had been declared in 1776. It now boasted a state-run University, the leading medical school and hospital in the country, the American Philosophical Society, and a zoo. With about 350,000 citizens it was larger than either New York or Boston.

They found lodgings in Strawberry Alley, then took a house in Union Street. Hazlitt's father believed he could offer the land of liberty his compassionate, Unitarian version of the Christian religion, and convert others merely by

Fig. 4. South William Street, NYC, today. Though a reconstruction, this building gives some idea of what much of New York looked like when the Hazlitts first visited in April 1783.

reasoning with them. He contacted all the ministers in town to ask whether they would allow him to address their congregations but had not counted on the ingrained anti-Britishness of the Irish and Scotch Presbyterians by whom the city was dominated. To them, he appeared arrogant, offensive—and, what was worse, a heretic.[27] The only minister to welcome him was John Ewing, pastor of the First Presbyterian church, known as the buttonwood church because of the trees surrounding it. The fifty-year-old Ewing became one of Hazlitt's closest friends, inviting him frequently to preach. 'I always heard him with high satisfaction', he remembered, 'and I never heard him drop a sentiment [to] which the most orthodox divine among us could not subscribe.'[28]

Tragedy hit the Hazlitts weeks after their arrival when on 25 June baby Harriet, then eighteen months old, died of the croup. Grace was well advanced in another pregnancy, giving birth to another girl, Esther, barely a month later. But on 12 September a nurse 'let the baby fall' and that child died as well.[29] Not yet recovered from the death of Harriet, her parents were inconsolable. Ewing, who had ten children of his own, recalled that Hazlitt Sr's 'distressed condition affected every person that knew him'.[30] These losses left their mark on the five-year-old William, who would be as protective of his own son as his parents were of him.

Others who helped the Hazlitts through their difficult first months included the Gomez family, near neighbours on Union Street. Moses Daniel Gomez was nearly ten years older than Hazlitt Sr—in his mid-fifties—and before the war had been a successful merchant based in New York. Rather than submit to British occupation, Moses moved to Philadelphia with his father, wife, and mother-in-law. There were two boys and two girls in the house—Esther, Deborah, Isaac, and Benjamin, his late brother-in-law's orphaned children. Free of the prejudices found among many at this time, Hazlitt Sr made friends with them. For his part, Gomez could not understand 'why the orthodox were so bitter against him, and he thought the Unitarian doctrine the most reasonable scheme of Christianity he had ever heard.'[31] While they talked these matters over, young William played with the Gomez children in the yard—contact that influenced him at a fundamental level, for he grew up to be a lifelong opponent of anti-semitism, one of his last essays arguing for Jewish emancipation.[32] The Hazlitts were deprived all too soon of their friendship when Moses moved his family back to New York in the summer of 1783.

It was soon clear that Hazlitt Sr would not find a post in Philadelphia, compelling him to leave the family for long periods while he sought postings elsewhere. This had disastrous results. In the autumn of 1783 he was invited to Centreville, Maryland, and lodged at the house of a vestryman, Richard Tilghman Earle, then in his mid-fifties. On the first Sunday of his stay he delivered, as always, a service reflecting his distinctive beliefs, using his own prayers (free of references to the Trinity) and a sermon articulating his rational interpretation of the New Testament. The congregation reacted positively and asked him back the following week. If all went well, he would be appointed. Unfortunately, he contracted a form of swamp fever common in that part of America, and by the next Sunday was in a state of delirium. He managed to get himself to the church but fainted in the pulpit. It was thanks only to Earle and Earle's son-in-law, Solomon Clayton (a doctor), that he survived. In the end, the church voted 'unanimously' against appointing him[33] because of 'some difficulties ... concerning an Unitarian liturgy'.[34] His intention was probably to substitute for the Trinitarian liturgy that used by Theophilus Lindsey at the Essex Street chapel in London, and the congregation could not agree on its acceptability.

Chapter 1

Hazlitt Sr said that fever 'rendered me useless, whilst I was groaning under a great expence, almost six months',[35] indicating he did not recover until March 1784. When he was well enough to travel, his son John came to fetch him, and they returned to Philadelphia together. He spent much of the winter recuperating, so the children saw more of him than in preceding months. The principal beneficiary was young William, whom he prepared for the education he would give him in later years. Already acquainted with such tales as Jack the Giant Killer, the Seven Champions of Christendom, and Guy of Warwick, the boy was now venturing upon *Robinson Crusoe* by that famous dissenter, Daniel Defoe.

'Heaven lies about us in our infancy'; and it cannot be denied, that the first perusal of that work makes a part of the illusion:—the roar of the waters is in our ears,—we start at the print of the foot in the sand, and hear the parrot repeat the well-known sounds of 'Poor Robinson Crusoe! Who are you? Where do you come from; and where are you going?'—till the tears gush, and in recollection and feeling we become children again![36]

In the spring of 1784 Hazlitt Sr began to receive invitations from other congregations. During March he was asked to preach in Charleston, South Carolina, but turned down the offer because of the heat—so intense in summer that churches were obliged to close. And in April two farmers visited from Pittsburgh, nearly 300 miles to the west.[37] Then in the wilderness, Pittsburgh remained the target of attacks by Iroquois indians, but Hazlitt Sr thought he owed it to the farmers at least to discuss the prospect. Thirteen-year-old Peggy was in favour, and perhaps her young brother was too, sharing her desire to see the 'wild and beautiful forests' of Pennsylvania.[38] But Hazlitt Sr had already sustained enough loss in this young, dangerous country, and declined.

Within weeks, another offer came his way. At the end of 1783, Samuel Cooper, pastor of the Brattle Street church in Boston, had died. Not only had he been a Unitarian, but Priestley was his 'idol'.[39] Hazlitt Sr travelled to Boston, preached, and found the congregation amenable to his beliefs; even Jeremy Belknap (no supporter) conceded he had 'preached in one of ye politest vacant assemblies, & been much admired'.[40] Hazlitt came away with the impression that the post was his, took lodgings in State Street, and wrote to Grace, saying he finally had a job; she and the children would have to make the 266-mile passage to Boston on their own.

The stagecoach moved swiftly past ash and oak woods, wild trees bearing peaches, hickory, and other nuts. Peggy later recalled its progress along the

Delaware through Burlington and the small towns of Bristol and Bath, 'shining in the morning sun, whose very names brought back to my mother many sad and pleasing recollections of former days'.[41] (Grace had been a frequent visitor to both British towns during their time at Marshfield, and felt homesick.) They crossed into New Jersey and arrived at a point of land at the mouth of the Raritan River—Perth Amboy.

The name was a reminder of its turbulent history: the Earl of Perth was one of its earliest 'proprietors', or governors, in the seventeenth century; Amboy derived from Ompoge, the name given by its earliest inhabitants, the Algonquin indians. It was known for the Proprietary House, built in 1762 for William Franklin, Benjamin Franklin's son.[42] Though damaged during the war, the house had been refurbished and rooms were now rented out to passing travellers: Peggy remembered it as 'a very large inn said to contain an hundred beds. . . . It stands alone, and its green lawn in front gently slopes down to the river. From the rising ground, on which the house stands, there is a beautiful and extensive view, and more than one river is seen from thence.'[43] To this day, it stands only a few blocks from the water, looking out over Raritan Bay and the Arthur Kill.

That humid August night in 1784, Peggy, Grace, and young William shared a room with a little girl of William's age called Maria, and her mother. In the middle of the night, Peggy had an adventure: 'I awoke and heard a snoring under the bed. I crept softly out to feel and, hoping it was only a dog, I made up my mind not to speak, but to watch till daylight, when seeing a large Newfoundland dog who was come to guard us stretched at his full length under the bed, I went quietly to sleep.'[44] Peggy's alertness may reflect the anxieties that lurked in her mind as the family made yet another move.

Next morning they joined a large party on the lawn in front of the house for 'tea, coffee, cakes, pastry, eggs, ham, etc.'[45]—the scale of an American breakfast still a wondrous thing for the Hazlitts. Peggy's attention was seized by 'a puritanical old gentleman of the name of Shakespeare' who she imagined to have 'inherited the talents of his immortal namesake'. He closely resembled 'all the prints I had seen of the great poet . . . and took his coffee with the air of a prince in disguise'. Perhaps she told young William. Some thought he was a Jesuit 'and others made many different conjectures!'[46]

Later that morning they boarded a boat for New York which drifted off course when the captain left it in the care of 'an ignorant black boy',[47] running aground on a sandbank where it stayed for the next five hours. Fortunately this was one of the finest days of the summer, so at least they did not need to fret about the weather. All the same, on hearing some passengers express fears they might drown, young William burst into tears. Eventually the incoming tide freed the ship and it continued on its way, arriving in New York as the sun set.

This was their second visit to New York—not the city we know, but taking shape. Where once the masts of British warships dominated the harbour, it was now filled with those of trading vessels and ships carrying migrants from faraway Europe. The city was returning to life after the privations of war: recently designated state capital, colonial records were being returned to it; the Bank of New York had opened for the first time in June at the Walton House in St George's Square; James Duane was voted City Mayor in February (to hold office for the next six years).[48] The British left traces of their occupation everywhere, including numbers on the houses, an innovation Americans decided to retain. The numbers were useful when the Hazlitts visited the Gomez family, now settled at 203 Water Street.[49] It was the last time they were to see 'these good and friendly Israelites'.[50]

Two days after their arrival, on a Sunday, they boarded the Rhode Island packetboat with many other passengers including 'a little solitary Frenchman who, by keeping aloof from the rest, made himself the jest of the party'.[51] The vessel passed safely through the whirlpool of Hell's Gate, the narrow channel between Wards Island and Astoria, and the rushing waters of Hog's Back, where the Harlem and East Rivers converge: 'It was a very fine evening and pleasant sailing between the mainland and Long Island. The views of each side were very beautiful, and we remained on deck until a late hour, enjoying the moonlight and the fresh air.'[52]

At noon the next day they came ashore at Newport, Rhode Island. Once a bustling trading post, it had been devastated by British occupation during the war. The blockade of the harbour forced the soldiers to fell trees for fuel, and Peggy observed that 'many of the floors bore the marks of the axes where they cut up the mahogany furniture of the houses for firing.'[53] It was a wasteland, not to regain its status as a resort until the middle of the next century.

There they sampled the black sea bass, still found in local waters, and John Hazlitt (now seventeen) joined a party of ladies and gentlemen exploring the island on horseback. The following day they travelled north by road to Providence, which had escaped occupation. Grace, Peggy, and a Mrs Enderwick lodged in a boarding house, while John accompanied the men to another lodging. At first it looked as if William would be separated from his mother, for the landlady objected to his remaining with her, but Grace refused to part with him, declaring that if he was billeted elsewhere, she would go too. 'At last an ungracious consent was given, and the child was admitted within the sacred walls,' Peggy recalled. 'This affair afforded no small amusement the next day.'[54]

Boston was a mere thirty miles off. They started out at six in the morning, passing through woods thronged with birds 'whose matin and vesper hymns rose sweetly on the ear.'[55] Hazlitt Sr was waiting for them on arrival, and took them to his lodgings in the heart of the city, kept by Catherine Gray and her two sisters; their journey had taken the best part of a week.

Boston was situated on a 487-acre spit of land extending into the Harbour, defined by three hills—Trimont, Copps Hill, and Fort Hill. Like other places they had seen, the town was picking itself up after the war: a second bank had opened the previous year, and a theatre was built in Market Place (which Hazlitt Sr is bound to have visited). This was a more liberal town than Philadelphia, thanks partly to Harvard College in nearby Cambridge, which having freed itself from puritanism nurtured a brand of Protestantism that gave way to full-blown Unitarianism later in the century. In that development Hazlitt Sr was to be a catalyst.

On the day he arrived in Boston, 15 May 1784, Hazlitt's father was introduced to the Boston Association of Ministers, some of whom were more liberal in their views than him. Almost all had been educated at Harvard and were members of a social and cultural elite[56] with the power to appoint ministers to the two hundred-odd churches in and around Boston.[57] Their unofficial chairman was Charles Chauncey, who immediately 'entered into a familiar conversation' with Hazlitt Sr and 'shewed him every possible respect'.[58] Now in his eightieth year, Chauncey entered Harvard at the age of 12, went on to become pastor of Boston's First Church in 1727 when 22, and had been in post ever since. He had tutored most of those present, and his kindly welcome signalled Hazlitt's admission to the Association as honorary member. They were in the midst of a debate about ordination when someone asked: 'Who do *you* think should have the power to ordain?'

Without hesitation, Hazlitt Sr replied: 'The people. The congregation are the proper ordainers of any minister.' It was the best answer he could have given. That, after all, was what Independence was about; the rule of Bishops was tyranny writ small.

Fig. 5. King's Chapel (formerly the stone chapel) in Boston—the first church in America to declare itself Unitarian, thanks in part to the efforts of Hazlitt's father.

As soon as he said this, another voice piped up. 'I wish you could prove that, Sir.'

'Few things could admit of an easier proof,' replied Hazlitt Sr, with a friendly smile.[59]

This was a turning-point in the fortunes of Boston Unitarianism. The man who had replied to Hazlitt was the 25-year-old James Freeman, who officiated as a lay reader at the King's Chapel.[60] (Founded in 1686, King's Chapel moved into a handsome stone building in the centre of Boston in the early 1750s, which still stands.) The appointment was thought of as temporary until he could be ordained, but that would not come easily. Freeman was an Arian and believed Christ neither divine nor immortal, a view incompatible with Trinitarianism. The Bishops demanded he subscribe to the Thirty-Nine Articles, but that would have meant renouncing his convictions.

Which explains why, on hearing the Reverend William Hazlitt say that 'the people, or the congregation, who chose any man to be their minister, were his proper ordainers', Freeman was galvanized. Was this possible? If so, it was a licence to exchange the arbitrary dictat of the Episcopalian Bishops for the authority of his own congregation. The prospect was exciting because nothing was more in the spirit of the American Revolution. The Association debated it for the rest of the afternoon, and Freeman afterwards planned with Hazlitt the first steps towards his ordination.[61]

Young William was told of these events as they unfolded, which shaped him no less than the country to which they had come. His father's distrust of human authority in matters of church government was to enter his own bloodstream as a suspicion of institutions. There was something of the anarchist in both Hazlitts. They saw human organizations as inherently corrupt. The essayist would be a member of no one's club; he flattered no one in the hope of patronage; and even though he was to travel across Europe more than once, never applied for a passport. His father's defiance of Bishops is echoed in his own contempt for courtiers, politicians, placemen, and poets laureate. That's why, years later, he honoured dissenting ministers as those who 'incur a certain portion of obloquy and ill-will, for the sake of what they believe to be the truth: they are not time-servers on the face of the evidence, and that is sufficient to expose them to the instinctive hatred and ready ribaldry of those who think venality the first of virtues, and prostitution of principle the best sacrifice a man can make to the Graces or his Country.'[62]

Faithful to his principles, Hazlitt's father was denied the job at Brattle Street Church, the Presbyterians in Philadelphia having spread the story that he was a heretic,[63] and before long was in more financial difficulty than before.[64]

In order to save money, the family moved to Lower Dorchester, five miles south of Boston. It was now September 1784 and for the remainder of his time in America, Hazlitt Sr journeyed round the countryside delivering sermons at the invitation of the Boston Association of Ministers. At the same time he wrote for the *Boston Magazine* and the *American Herald* as part of a campaign to soften up public opinion for developments at King's Chapel. In one of the most audacious, he denounced each of the Thirty-Nine Articles in turn; his commentary on the doctrine of predestination is typical of his style and manner:

> The seventeenth article asserts fully the Calvinistic doctrine of predestination, and then teaches that this doctrine is full of sweet, pleasant, and unspeakable comfort to *godly* persons. I should rather have said *inhuman, malicious* persons. For, if the doctrine of predestination, as it is here described, were true, and if the elect persons themselves, contrary to the article, which says that the affair is *secret*

to us, and only existing *in the decree of God's counsel*, could have any assurance of their own election, it must fill them with bitter, tormenting, and unspeakable sorrow, unless they possess the spirit of infernals incarnate, to reflect that a vast multitude of their fellow creatures, as innocent in fact as they are, and without any fault of their own, should be remedilessly devoted to eternal misery.[65]

This was no shrinking violet and no timeserver. He concluded this essay with an exhortation to the people of America to set themselves free from 'the dominion of unreforming Bishops' and reject 'doctrinal corruptions'— referring to the Thirty-Nine Articles as a whole. Such declarations could only spell career suicide. But Hazlitt Sr nurtured a compassionate view of the Christian religion based on a patient, close analysis of the New Testament, and had no intention of compromising for the sake of advancement—the option taken by many like-minded colleagues. His articles struck a chord within the hearts and minds of many of the Bostonians who read them and, despite making many enemies among the Bishops, he won an enthusiastic following among the liberal churchgoers of Boston and the surrounding area. They included such luminaries as Benjamin Lincoln, recently retired as Secretary for War in Washington's government, whom Hazlitt Sr later described as 'noble minded',[66] and John Hancock, signatory to the Declaration of Independence, former President of the Continental Congress and, since 1780, Governor of Massachusetts.[67]

Ebenezer Withington, to whose farm the Hazlitts had moved, was a widower in his mid-fifties who Peggy Hazlitt remembered as a 'good man'.[68] Young William was less interested in him than in a native American who worked on the farm. 'He had a good voice and sung some songs about Washington,' Peggy recalled, 'He had a little girl who might have passed for one of our handsome brunettes. It is said that those Indians that come to live among the white people are generally such as have been turned out of their own tribe, and so it proved in this instance.'[69] William had seen other instances of Indian subjugation while in America. He was probably with his sister when in Philadelphia she saw 'six Cherokee chiefs...dressed in their robes of state with feathers bound round their heads like a coronet. These were come to conclude a treaty with the Pensilvanians.'[70] Their talks with Henry Knox, Secretary of War, eventually produced compensation for the loss of many thousands of acres of land they had occupied for centuries before the arrival of Europeans. The money was woefully inadequate, and loss of their habitat brought about disintegration of their tribe. As he grew up, young William became increasingly sensitive to the injustice and, in his earliest surviving letter, written when he was eight, he said of America 'that it would have been a great deal better if the white people had not found it out. Let the [Indians have] it to themselves for it was made for them.'[71]

Hazlitt's father heard about 'a good and cheap house at Weymouth',[72] five miles down the road. It belonged to Mary Cranch, wife of Richard Cranch, Justice of the Court of Common Pleas. Mary's sister was Abigail Adams, wife of John Adams, who would become Vice-President under Washington and second President of the United States (1797–1801). The entire family was friendly to Unitarianism.

Their journey to Weymouth took two days because they were invited to stay with the Cranches en route; their landlady wanted to meet them. 'We here found a very pleasant family', recalled Peggy Hazlitt, 'and spent an agreeable evening, and they always treated us with the greatest kindness.'[73] The plain-speaking Mary Cranch told Hazlitt Sr how she sympathized with his liberal views but counselled him to be 'more prudent' about how he expressed himself.

'What do you mean?' he asked.

'Exercise more caution, sir. Or you will never get a parish. You have built up a good reputation among those to whom you have preached. The people at Weymouth wish to hear you. But however they might like you as a preacher, I fear your outspokenness will prevent your ever settling here, be your heart and head ever so good.'[74] This sort of advice was impossible for him to accept; on the contrary, when he encountered a new congregation, Hazlitt's father confronted them with his ideas so they would know exactly what they were getting. His son would aspire to such unstinting honesty, with a similar disregard for the consequences.

The next morning, Peggy walked to Weymouth with Mrs Cranch's maid, ahead of the family, to get the house 'in some order before the arrival of my father and mother, who came with William in the one horse chaise so common there at that time.'[75] Mary Cranch had given Peggy a wild duck she would cook as a welcoming feast. On arrival, she found a beautiful south-facing house in the middle of the countryside, a mile or so from the Atlantic coastline, 'a most romantic spot surrounded on three sides by very steep hills that sloped down just in sight of the windows, covered with locust trees'.[76] A peach-tree grew in the garden, the blossoms of which were 'visited by the humming bird, the most beautiful and irascible of the feathered race'.[77] William was bewitched by hummingbirds, all of them small, about an inch and a half in length, not including the needle-like bills with which they sucked nectar from the flowers. The plot in front of the house had a large pear tree 'beyond the shade of which in the hot days William was not allowed to go until four o'clock, when the sun was in some sort shaded by the neighbouring hills'[78]—further evidence of Grace's protectiveness. There was a fence enclosing the sloping green on which 'woodpeckers were wont to sit and make a noise with their bills like a saw'.[79] Beyond the garden was a large meadow which attracted fireflies in the evenings.

One of the first things Peggy noticed inside the house was a painting of Esau and Jacob embracing by the American artist John Singleton Copley. 'On this picture I used to gaze with delight, and wondered at the skill of the artist who had made so natural and lively a representation of the scene!'[80]

This was home for the next eighteen months, during which young William thrived. The rural township of Weymouth was full of spaces where he could play, populated by a profusion of local fauna: wild turkey, teal, woodpigeon, parrots, moose, snakes, monkeys, wolves, lynx, and bears. Fowl peculiar to America included bluebirds, the red linnet, the oriole, the mockingbird, and the bobolink (or Bob Lincoln). On one occasion William saw a catamount, a tree-climbing wildcat; local hunters sent eighteen dogs after it, but it killed six of them and ran away.

His earliest memories dated from this time. In 'Why Distant Objects Please', he recalled: 'The taste of barberries, which have hung out in the snow during the severity of a North American winter, I have in my mouth still, after an interval of thirty years, for I have met with no other taste, in all that time, at all like it. It remains by itself almost like the impression of a sixth sense.'[81]

Hazlitt Sr preached at the local church on 5 and 12 December 1784, and on both occasions Cotton Tufts and his family were among the congregation.[82] Besides being a physician, Tufts served on the state senate and shared Hazlitt's fascination with the sciences. Tufts and his wife were related to Abigail Adams; they had one son and looked after Tufts's niece, Lucy Jones. Now sixteen years old, Lucy became a 'constant companion' of Peggy. 'I fancy I see her now', Peggy remembered years later, 'in her polonaise dress, which set off her fine figure to advantage. I think Sophia Western must have looked like her.'[83] Her glamorous looks attracted someone else—John Hazlitt, who fell passionately in love with her. He was now eighteen, and she was the first love of his life. He tried to paint her portrait, but his hands shook so much he was unable to complete it.

He tried to talk to her, but the tremor in his voice gave him away. In desperation he poured his emotion into letters but she treated them with such contempt as to drive him mad.

Mary Cranch, who witnessed the entire thing, told her sister of John's sufferings: 'In the silent watches of the night, when the Moon in full orb'd Majisty had reach'd her nocturnal height, He left his Bed and upon the cold ground told her his tale of woe, in accents loud and wild as wind.'[84] A far from compassionate recipient of this attention, Lucy reacted coquettishly. During the hot summer of July 1785, while John raked hay in the fields, she dressed in her fanciest white dress and paraded under a nearby oak, singing with the birds. When she had his attention, she fled back to the house 'as if she had been pursu'd by a snake'.[85] None of which escaped the notice of John Quincy Adams, son of Abigail Adams and future President of the United States, recently returned from negotiating the Treaty of Paris. He described John as 'violently' smitten: 'he did not sit like patience, on a marble monument smiling at grief. But called the Earth; the Sun, moon, Stars, and every other planet, to witness, that she was the fairest, noblest, sweetest, most beauteous damsel, that was ever beheld by mortal eyes. In short he was nearly raving. And it has been thought necessary to keep him out of her sight, that he might not have a relapse.'[86] It was a foreshadowing of the fate that awaited young William when, decades hence, he encountered a woman by the name of Sarah Walker. William certainly witnessed his brother's torments close up, for John distracted himself by painting a delicate miniature of his brother as a beautiful, otherworldly, long-haired creature gazing confidently and unselfconsciously at the viewer.[87]

The one person unaware of these developments was their father, who was in Boston visiting James Freeman. The summer of 1785 was punctuated by a major development at King's Chapel. On 19 June the congregation voted to adopt a Unitarian liturgy, 600 copies of which were soon printed.[88] Hazlitt Sr presided over its drafting and ensured that copies were sent to the Bishops who had refused Freeman ordination.[89]

Over the following year he continued to search for a post, preaching at churches as far afield as Dorchester, Jamaica Plain, and Providence. Fearing long absences would make him a stranger to young William, he took him along and, when delivering sermons, had him stand in the pulpit, hoping it would inspire him to follow in his footsteps. One of the places they visited was Cape Cod, then populated by fisherman. Despite the season, it was bleak and forbidding—rocks, sand, and boundless ocean.

'Do any robins or Bob Lincolns come here?' William asked his father.

'I suppose they do not like such an ugly place,' he replied.[90]

Towards the end of summer 1786 Hazlitt Sr realized he would never find a job: the land of liberty had yet to catch up with his brand of rational dissent. It was still something of a shock for congregations versed in Anglican orthodoxies to hear a visiting clergyman disavow the Trinity, and his readiness to do so made him enemies. A visit to Salem marked his last tour of duty in an American pulpit.[91] It was sickening to accept he had no option but to return to Britain.

There was one consolation. The event he predicted on his first day in Boston was within sight. The congregation of King's Chapel had decided to ordain James Freeman as minister, without reference to the Bishops. During Hazlitt's last months in Boston he assisted in preparations for this important event and made friends among the congregation, in particular Kirk Boott, originally from Derby, who set up a general store in early 1784 and acquired a partner, William Pratt, another Englishman. Both were as fervent in support of the plan to ordain Freeman as they were of Hazlitt Sr himself. Boott was the first person outside the family to realize there was something special about young Billy Hazlitt. The boy used to play with his daughter Frances, and he would watch them. 'He has uncommon powers of mind,' he told Hazlitt's father, '&, if nothing happens to prevent his receiving a liberal education, he must make a great man.'[92] When he visited England several years later, Boott offered to train him as a merchant, but the Reverend Hazlitt had other plans.

On 18 November 1787 James Freeman was ordained by the Senior Warden of King's Chapel, Thomas Bulfinch, using a form of words still used today—'to be the Rector, Minister, Priest, Pastor, Public Teacher, and Teaching Elder'. At that moment King's Chapel terminated the affiliation with the Episcopal Church which had endured since its founding and became America's first Unitarian institution. Two days after ordination, Freeman told Hazlitt it was a 'blow at the root of superstition and priestly usurpation. It will tend, I hope, to render alterations in the Episcopal church easy; for the Bishops will now be shewn, when they refuse to ordain a man on account of supposed heresy, that the people can proceed without them.'[93]

He was right. Other Episcopalian churches invited Freeman to preach, using the Unitarian liturgy he had devised with Hazlitt Sr. Freeman sent copies to William Oxnard in Portland and William Bentley in Salem, both of whom adopted it.[94] Though Hazlitt Sr left America believing himself to have failed, he had sparked a revolution that would make Boston the centre of Unitarian worship in America. 'I bless the day when that honest man first landed in this country,' Freeman told one correspondent.[95] In 1789 he went further: 'Before Mr Hazlitt came to Boston, the Trinitarian doxology was almost universally used. That honest good man prevailed upon several respectable ministers to omit it. Since his departure, the number of those who repeat only scriptural doxologies has greatly increased, so that there are now many churches in which the worship is strictly Unitarian.'[96] In after-years, the essayist never ceased to feel pride at his father's achievements and his facing-down of the bigotry of the orthodox. Fidelity to one's principles, whatever the price, would become a family heirloom. As late as 1829, Hazlitt boasted to a friend that the liturgy used by William Ellery Channing, the foremost American Unitarian clergyman of the nineteenth century, 'was drawn up by my father forty years ago & upwards, who went to America to plant Unitarianism there.'[97]

CHAPTER 2

When I was a boy, I lived within sight of a range of lofty
hills, whose blue tops blending with the setting sun had often
tempted my longing eyes and wandering feet. At last I put
my project into execution, and on a nearer approach,
instead of glimmering air woven into fantastic shapes,
found them huge lumpish heaps of discoloured earth.

Hazlitt, 'Why Distant Objects Please'[1]

L ONDON was endlessly stimulating. Young William fell in love with its restlessness, often wandering out of the front door and rambling about on
his own. His parents were terrified he would get lost but he seemed always to
find his way home. Hazlitt Sr occasionally walked him to the Montpelier Tea
Gardens in Walworth, planted with trees, shrubs, and exotic flowers.[2] These
were the first green things the boy had seen after the long sea voyage back to
England and he was fascinated by them—their names, colours, and odours.
Years later, he summoned them up in his mind's eye:

> A new sense comes upon me, as in a dream; a richer perfume, brighter colours
> start out; my eyes dazzle; my heart heaves with its new load of bliss, and I am a
> child again. My sensations are all glossy, spruce, voluptuous, and fine: they wear
> a candied coat, and are in holiday trim. I see the beds of larkspur with purple
> eyes; tall holly-oaks, red and yellow; the broad sun-flowers, caked in gold, with
> bees buzzing round them; wilderness of pinks, and hot-glowing pionies; poppies
> run to seed; the sugared lily, and faint mignonette, all ranged in order, and as thick
> as they can grow; the box-tree borders; the gravel walks, the painted alcove, the
> confectionary, the clotted cream:—I think I see them now with sparkling looks; or
> have they vanished while I have been writing this description of them? No matter;
> they will return again when I least think of them.[3]

After several months, Hazlitt Sr was appointed to a meeting house in Wem,
Shropshire, 170 miles to the north. 'It was our evil destiny to pass the best

Fig. 6. The house in Noble Street, Wem, where the Hazlitts lived after their return from America. Although the family found it 'old and ugly', Hazlitt himself loved it.

of our days in a little, disagreeable market town, where we could not see the green fields and scarcely the blue vault of heaven,' Peggy reflected, years later.[4] Even the house to which they moved was 'old and ugly'.[5] The Hazlitts had seen a land in which the people had liberated themselves from the fetters of a hereditary monarch and his corrupt, unrepresentative government. Having tasted that brave new world, it was a crushing humiliation to return to the routine oppressions of the old country. Those feelings were aggravated by the recollection of the distinguished revolutionaries they had known in America— John Quincy Adams, Benjamin Lincoln, John Hancock; in Wem they were surrounded by the 'dullness, petty jealousies, and cabals of a little country town',[6] which made their lives unbearable.

Except for William. These were days in which 'my path ran down with butter and honey',[7] and he came to love the Shropshire landscape as much as Wordsworth did the fells of Cumberland. The strong winds that swept across the countryside were good for kites, he recalled:

Chapter 2

I feel the twinge at my elbow, the flutter and palpitation, with which I used to let go the string of my own, as it rose in the air and towered among the clouds. My little cargo of hopes and fears ascended with it; and as it made a part of my own consciousness then, it does so still, and appears 'like some gay creature of the element,' my playmate when life was young, and twin-born with my earliest recollections.[8]

On summer evenings he watered the cabbage-plants and rows of beans in the garden; years later, he reflected: 'If I see a row of cabbage-plants or of peas or beans coming up, I immediately think of those which I used so carefully to water of an evening at Wem, when my day's tasks were done, and of the pain with which I saw them droop and hang down their leaves in the morning's sun.'[9]

Though unvarying and flat, the countryside contained many places where he could play. One witness remembered how 'at night he would ramble forth no one knew where: & in the moon-light might be used to scamper about the fields like . . . any wild thing'.[10] Another acquaintance, a female farming labourer, was horrified when he jumped out of the hedge without warning; 'Almost frighted me to death!' she later recalled.[11]

Advancing in his career as portraitist, William's brother John remained in London and studied with Sir Joshua Reynolds, then in his mid-sixties. Reynolds encouraged John to exhibit, which he did every year at the Royal Academy from 1788 to 1819. Deprived of John's company, Hazlitt Sr focused on William, ten years old in April 1788, of whose gifts he was increasingly aware. If the boy lived up to his promise, what an addition he would make to the faith. Shortly after moving to Wem, Hazlitt Sr took over the small school run by his predecessor and turned it into a model crammer for the dissenting rationalist. William was his star-pupil. Himself the product of a sterling education, Hazlitt Sr wanted his son to transcend the heights he had scaled, 'a task which the docility and vivid comprehension of the pupil rendered not merely easy, but delightful'.[12] Soon William was reading at mealtimes and staying indoors, hunched over his books; in March 1788 William told John that besides reading Ovid and Eutropius he was drawing the faces of busts: 'I shall not I suppose paint the worse for knowing every thing else.'[13]

He excelled, beating other boys at school with the occasional exception of his friend Joseph Swanwick. It is good he had one friend, because his intellectual prowess alienated him from everyone else. By the age of ten he had learned to despise his contemporaries: 'they cannot learn & are fit only for fighting like stupid dogs & cats.'[14] In later years he cautioned his own son against such overweening confidence:

> It was my misfortune (perhaps) to be bred up among Dissenters, who look with too jaundiced an eye at others, and set too high a value on their own peculiar pretensions. From being proscribed themselves, they learn to proscribe others; and come in the end to reduce all integrity of principle and soundness of opinion within the pale of their own little communion. Those who were out of it and did not belong to the class of *Rational Dissenters*, I was led erroneously to look upon as hardly deserving the name of rational beings.[15]

The family returned briefly to London when, in May 1789, John Hazlitt married Mary Peirce at St Anne's church, Soho, for they surely attended the wedding. John's bride hailed from Portsmouth, and he probably met her while seeking work there. She was descended from clergyman James Peirce, who rejected Trinitarianism in 1719 only to be dismissed from his post. To the Reverend Hazlitt that would have been an impeccable pedigree, and he welcomed his daughter-in-law into the family. She was an able and intelligent woman who would struggle to give her children the best possible start in life. Something of a bluestocking, she would later win the respect of Lamb and Coleridge.

In July 1789, the month in which events in France became full-blown Revolution, eleven-year-old William suffered intense illness brought on by overwork.[16] His father was driving him too hard. Where the intellect was concerned, Hazlitt Sr knew no moderation—a zealot, he inculcated equal zealotry in his son. The extent of this is revealed by William's remark, almost an aside, in a letter to his brother—'We cannot be happy without being employed.'[17] According to Peggy, William 'set himself to work in earnest and with such intense application as had nearly cost him his life!'[18] In later years he was mindful of this when advising his own son: 'I applied too close to my studies, soon after I was of your age, and hurt myself irreparably by it. Whatever may be the value of learning, health and good spirits are of more.'[19] The likelihood is that unremitting application brought on stomach trouble—probably an ulcer—that would dog him for the rest of his life. His indisposition lasted weeks, though by the end of August Theophilus Lindsey told his father: 'I hope your son is well, and that he has changed his condition agreeably and with good prospects.'[20]

Henceforth William's natural posture was that of the scholar—'slow, cautious, circuitous, instead of being prompt, heedless, straightforward'.[21] He was happier dealing with 'historic personages and abstract propositions'[22] than with men and things. And in adulthood he suffered a 'depression of spirits' that 'leads a man, from a distrust of himself, to seek for low company, or to forget it by matching below himself.'[23] Thus he was led to consort with lowlife characters—badger-baiters, publicans, and prostitutes. But the most immediate consequence was the seed of doubt it planted in his mind about his father. William never stopped loving him but now began to question his father's judgement—and this, ultimately, would bear unwelcome fruit.[24]

After his first bout of stomach trouble, Hazlitt was always delicate. He tried valiantly to join other boys in their sports, but to his chagrin found himself less robust than they. One summer when playing in the River Roden he was 'seized with cramp'[25] and would have drowned had he not been saved by an older lad. This near-disaster made his parents more protective of him than ever.

One of his father's parishioners, a widow called Mrs Tracey, moved out of Wem with her two daughters in early 1790 to settle in Liverpool. She had been a frequent visitor to the Hazlitts', often bringing her daughters with her, who for a time learnt French with young William. She wrote to ask whether he might like to spend the summer with them in Liverpool, also inviting William's friend George Dicken. William was thrilled. He got on well with Mrs Tracey's daughters and was keen to see the city. Despite some initial hesitation, his father was reassured by the thought of the well-established network of Unitarians there who would tutor William, and finally agreed he could go.

Liverpool was a booming commercial hub, prospering from its eminence as the pre-eminent English slaving port of the late eighteenth century. It was also a hive of dissenting activity, of which Mrs Tracey was part. As soon as they arrived, the two thirteen-year-old boys were drawn into her social and cultural network—taking tea with Mrs Hudson and Mr Clegg (who taught geography), and dinner with Mr Fisher ('a very rich man'[26]), Mrs Corbett, Mrs Chilton, and Mrs Sydebotham—all Unitarian. There were extensive lessons with private tutors such as John Yates, a minister with whom William read Horace. And he studied conversational French with John de Lemprière, author of the *Bibliotheca Classica* (1788), which throughout the next century provided many (including Keats) with a key to the classics. Lemprière had graduated at Oxford a couple of months earlier, and was teaching privately while seeking permanent employment. 'I have every thing ready for Mr. Dolounghpryée, who comes this evening,' William told his father (indicating that Lemprière took the pronunciation—if not the spelling—of his name seriously).[27] As if that were not

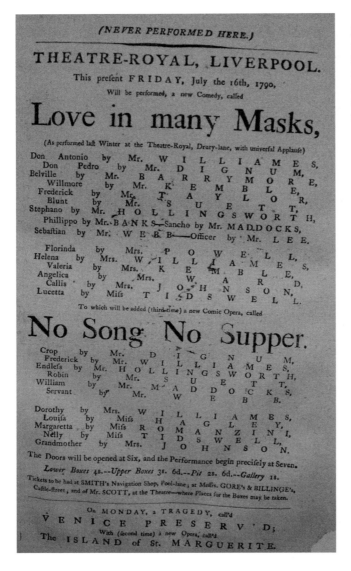

Fig. 7. Playbill for the Theatre Royal, Liverpool, 16 July 1790, the night of Hazlitt's first visit to the theatre when he was twelve.

enough, William was learning the harpsichord, on which (to his father's dismay, one imagines) he could play 'God save the King'.[28]

On Friday 16 July, Mr Corbett took him and Dicken to the theatre for the first time. They saw the double-bill at the Theatre Royal, consisting of *Love in Many*

Masks (John Philip Kemble's adaptation of Aphra Behn's *The Rover*[29]) and Stephen Storace's comic opera, *No Song, No Supper*.[30] Both productions had succeeded in London the previous spring, and went down well in Liverpool, as William told his father: 'It was very entertaining, and was performed by some of the best players in London.'[31] John Philip Kemble had been a star since coming out as Hamlet in 1783, and had managed Drury Lane since 1788. His first acting engagement having been in Liverpool, he returned each summer, bringing the company to perform the previous season's repertoire. This tall, distinguished, dark-haired man became identified with an acting style by which he articulated his lines with deliberation, honouring every pause and syllable. It was a style with which Hazlitt fell in love, and was what he meant when declaring years later that the 'Kemble religion [was] ... the religion in which we were brought up'.[32] He followed the career of this great actor until Kemble's retirement, reviewing his farewell appearance con amore.[33]

Hazlitt's first exposure to theatre was an experience he stored in his imagination for the rest of his life—a 'bright vision of my childhood [that] has played round my fancy with unabated, vivid delight'.[34] None of his subsequent Liverpool correspondence mentions another such outing but Mr Corbett cannot have detained him from the splendours to come: on 2 August Kemble appeared as Macbeth and on 6 August Prospero. It may have been in order to throw his parents off the scent that instead of mentioning any more theatre visits, William filled his letters home with sanctimonious declamations on politics and religion. Thrilled, his father wrote that his 'piety ... was a great refreshment to me; continue to cherish those thoughts, which then occupied your mind, continue to be virtuous, & you will finally be that happy being whom you describe.'[35] William was on the road to becoming a clergyman.

But the trip to Liverpool had other, less desirable results. Though fond of him, Mrs Tracey did not lavish upon William the fuss he received from his parents; in fact, she was in the habit of sending him on errands or leaving him alone in the house. William's response was characteristic: he became diffident, brooding, introspective. His almost pathological shyness, which may be connected with the onset of adolescence, probably dates from this moment. It is possible that, as one memoirist claims, by the time he returned to Wem he was so inward-looking that he declined ever again to accompany his family to church, preferring to worship at home[36]—something his parents may have been prepared to indulge.

The early 1790s were a traumatic period in which to grow up. George III and his government watched events in France with mounting anxiety, terrified the Revolution would jump the Channel. There were repercussions throughout the land: in Liverpool William had seen press gangs at work—groups of roughnecks armed with clubs and cutlasses dredging the alehouses for new recruits. 'The world is not quite perfect yet', he told his mother, 'nor will it ever be so whilst such practices are reckoned lawful.'[37] Pitt was returned with an increased majority in the election of November 1790, making it certain the Government would be robust in its reaction to events in France. Anxiety mounted the following year as the French National Assembly grappled with the question of how best to dispose of their monarch. Paine then published *The Rights of Man* in London, effectively a republican manifesto, igniting a furious debate about democracy—in which many of his allies happened to be Unitarian. Months later came an event that horrified dissenters across Britain.

Hazlitt Sr's colleague and friend Joseph Priestley was now well known—not so much as an eminent scientist and theologian but as a sympathizer with the French. He set up a Constitutional Society in Birmingham where he now lived, its first act being to hold a 'Gallic Commemoration Dinner' on 14 July 1791 to honour the second anniversary of the storming of the Bastille. Pro-Government newspapers condemned it. Such was the intensity of their attacks that Priestley withdrew from the event, but that did not discourage an angry Church-and-King mob organized by local magistrates from setting fire to his house, laboratory, and library. They then went on a spree: four meeting houses and twenty-seven domestic residences were destroyed; eight rioters and one special constable were killed and many others injured. The official response was to endorse the rioters' actions and publish propaganda claiming (falsely) that treasonous toasts had been made at the dinner.[38]

If this was a catastrophe for Priestley, it was worse for the dissenting community as a whole, not least the Hazlitts. A mere 40 miles to the east, Birmingham was the largest neighboring city, and they realized that, had they been a little closer, they would almost certainly have been among the mob's targets. (They were mindful that the old meeting house in Wem was burnt down by rioters in 1715.[39]) One of Hazlitt Sr's friends, John Ralph, wrote to deplore what had happened: 'What a regular, systematic scene of High-church villainy! What deliberate malignancy in those who planned, what execrable flagitiousness in those who executed it!' He went on to request news of the family's welfare:

Chapter 2

'What is your eldest son doing? and what have you done with your *scholar*?'[40]
Good question.

In the circumstances, it was impossible for young William not to become politicized, as everyone of his generation was. When the *Shrewsbury Chronicle*[41] attacked Priestley's 'impious and erroneous doctrines', the thirteen-year-old leapt to his defence:

> Religious persecution is the bane of all religion; and the friends of persecution are the worst enemies religion has; and of all persecutions, that of calumny is the most intolerable. Any other kind of persecution can affect our outward circumstances only, our properties, our lives; but this may affect our characters for ever. And this great man has not only had his goods spoiled, his habitation burned, and his life endangered, but is also calumniated, aspersed with the most malicious reflections, and charged with every thing bad, for which a misrepresentation of the truth and prejudice can give the least pretence.[42]

Given the character of his mature writing, it is not surprising that Hazlitt's first publication was a denunciation of political and religious oppression; what is surprising is its eloquence—a tribute to William's father, thanks to whose tuition this (barely) teenage boy was writing with the fluency of someone twice his age. Hazlitt Sr had revealed similar qualities when dealing with the British soldiers at Kinsale, the bigots of Philadelphia, and the episcopalians of Boston. How proud he was, boasting to his old friend Thomas Milner, who replied: 'Your account of your youngest son gives me great pleasure.'[43]

Six months later, in May 1792, William overheard his father arguing with an old lady, one of his congregation, about the repeal of the Corporation and Test Act,[44] which since 1673 had debarred Dissenters from military, political, and public office. Many Dissenters welcomed the French Revolution, believing it to herald repeal of the Test Acts. Now fourteen, William began to meditate a 'system of political rights and general jurisprudence',[45] a project he pursued for several years.

During the summer he read for the first time the great novels of the century. An enterprising publisher, Charles Cooke, had just begun to issue *Tom Jones* in pocket-sized instalments, equivalent to our 'modern classics'. They sold in huge quantities. One of those who subscribed was Hazlitt's father. William's first reading of Fielding's masterpiece 'broke the spell' of more rarefied intellectual pursuits:

It smacked of the world I lived in, and in which I was to live—and shewed me groups, 'gay creatures' not 'of the element', but of the earth; not 'living in the clouds', but travelling the same road that I did;—some that had passed on before me, and others that might soon overtake me. My heart had palpitated at the thoughts of a boarding-school ball, or gala-day at Midsummer or Christmas: but the world I had found out in Cooke's edition of the British Novelists was to me a dance through life, a perpetual gala-day. The six-penny numbers of this work regularly contrived to leave off just in the middle of a sentence, and in the nick of a story, where Tom Jones discovers Square behind the blanket; or where Parson Adams, in the inextricable confusion of events, very undesignedly gets to bed to Mrs Slip-slop.[46]

Cooke also published *Amelia* (1793), *Tristram Shandy* (1793), *Peregrine Pickle* (1794), *Gil Blas* (1797–8), and Smollett's translation of *Don Quixote* (1799),[47] each of which Hazlitt read as they were issued, luxuriating in the imaginative realm to which they gave access:

Ah! never again shall I feel the enthusiastic delight with which I gazed at the figures, and anticipated the story and adventures of Major Bath and Commodore Trunnion, of Trim and my Uncle Toby, or Don Quixote and Sancho and Dapple, or Gil Blas and Dame Lorenza Sephora, or Laura and the fair Lucretia, whose lips open and shut like buds of roses. To what nameless ideas did they give rise,—with what airy delights I filled up the outlines, as I hung in silence over the page!—Let me still recal them, that they may breathe fresh life into me, and that I may live that birthday of thought and romantic pleasure over again! Talk of the *ideal*! This is the only true ideal—the heavenly tints of Fancy reflected in the bubbles that float upon the spring-tide of human life.

> Oh! Memory! shield me from the world's poor strife,
> And give those scenes thine everlasting life![48]

William was fifteen in April 1793 and had developed more rapidly than anyone could have predicted. It was time for him to go where he could receive specialized tuition—but where? After the riots at Birmingham, that 'great man' Priestley had accepted the post of lecturer at the Unitarian College in Hackney, East London—and his defender was eager to follow. The principal difficulty was money, but William applied to the Presbyterian Fund in London for an exhibition, and was awarded the munificent sum of £12 a year.[49]

Shortly before leaving Wem, he had an attack of 'the nervous disorders, to which, you well know, I was so much subject'.[50] This may have been related to the indisposition which struck when he was eleven, or perhaps his father was pushing him hard in the weeks before his departure for London. At any rate, his sister thought it bad enough to be regarded as a 'fit'; 'And although he had no return of it, it was long before he recovered.'[51]

When first he arrived in London, William stayed with his brother John at 139 Long Acre, to the immediate north of Covent Garden. Long Acre runs north-west from St Martin's Lane for about three-quarters of a mile before it intersects Drury Lane and during much of the eighteenth century was home to furniture-makers and cabinet-designers. Hazlitt fell in love with this part of London and his heart never left it; he would be buried in a church less than a mile away. Its charms are best evoked by Charles Lamb: 'The Lighted shops of the Strand and Fleet Street, the innumerable trades, tradesmen and customers, coaches, wag-gons, play houses, all the bustle and wickedness round about Covent Garden, the very women of the Town, the Watchmen, drunken scenes, rattles;—life awake, if you awake, at all hours of the night, the impossibility of being dull in Fleet Street, the crowds, the very dirt & mud, the Sun shining upon houses and pavements, the print shops, the old book stalls, parsons cheap'ning books, coffee houses, steams of soups from kitchens, the pantomimes, London itself a pantomime and a masquerade.'[52] Now building up a reputation as a miniaturist and portrait-painter, John Hazlitt had begun to make a precarious living. The house he shared with his wife was not extensive, but he gave his younger brother shelter until he was lodged in Hackney. Thereafter, William returned once a fortnight.

The Hackney College occupied a 'large and noble building' in an eighteen-acre plot enclosed by a brick wall. Its grounds contained walks, an extensive garden, offices, and teaching rooms. As its report remarked in 1787, 'The sit-uation is in a healthful and gravelly soil, well-watered, and affording agreeable and extensive prospects'[53]—among them, a tendency to radical politics. After the Birmingham riots, the students sent Priestley an address of condolence commending him for 'those generous sentiments which you and the other enlighteners of Europe have excited', declaring their intention of 'pursuing, with however unequal steps, the course which you have pointed out'.[54] Before a warrant was issued for the arrest of Paine in May 1792, they invited him to dinner and found him 'as agreeable and striking in conversation as he is in his writings'.[55] All this at a period when Government-sponsored propagandists demonized such men as bloodthirsty, king-killing republicans, attacks which intensified after the execution of Louis XVI in Paris on 21 January 1793, an event that altered the political landscape by precipitating war between Britain and France. Because both countries had international trading interests, the conflict quickly spread to all parts of the known world. Despite claims that it would last a matter of months, the war dragged on for more than two decades—more than half Hazlitt's adult life.

When he arrived in London, radicals were still considering how to respond to the upsurge in patriotic fervour that accompanied the war, a trend aggravated by the orgy of bloodletting in Paris following Marat's murder by Charlotte Corday on 13 July—the Reign of Terror. Against that background, William embarked in September 1793 on his studies. On Monday and Wednesday he was tutored for two hours by Abraham Rees in mathematics and algebra; at 2pm he attended shorthand classes[56] and at 8pm classes in Hebrew. Tuesdays and Thursdays were devoted to the Classics—Latin and Greek, as well as lectures on Greek antiquities. Years later, he reflected on the benefit of language studies, lamenting that 'our divines no longer introduce texts of the original Scriptures into their sermons. The very sound of the original Greek or Hebrew would impress the hearer with a more lively faith in the sacred writers than any translation.'[57]

By the end of his first month, he thought himself 'liked, very well, by the students, in general'.[58] He was liked by tutors too, though they found him intractable to begin with. During his first weeks he was given an essay topic by classics professor John Corrie. Judging it was 'not a subject suited to my genius',[59] he did not attempt it. The deadline was Saturday morning, when William had to confess his dereliction.

'You should have a very good reason, indeed, sir, for neglecting it,' said Corrie.

'Why, really, I couldn't write it,' Hazlitt replied.

'Did you never write *anything*?'

'Yes, sir. I have written some things.'

'Very well, then, go and write your theme immediately.'

He made as little headway as before and began to cry. By the time Corrie summoned him an hour later his eyes were swollen, 'and I assumed as sullen a countenance as I could, intimating that he had not treated me well.' Corrie liked this intelligent, sensitive boy who wouldn't write to order; perhaps he saw similarities with his son Richard, six months William's junior.

'Have you written *anything*, sir?' Corrie enquired. 'Anything at all?' Hazlitt produced the beginning of the essay he had begun after hearing his father and an old lady arguing about the Test Acts the previous year. Corrie read it and was astonished. 'Well, sir, I wish you'd write more such things.'

'Why, sir', William answered, 'I intended to write several things which I have planned, but that I could not write any of them in a week, or two or three weeks.'

'*What* do you intend to write?' Corrie asked. Hazlitt said he would enlarge and improve the essay he had just given him. 'Aye, sir, I wish you would,' said Corrie.

'Well I will do it then, sir,' said Hazlitt.

'Do so. Take your own time, now; I shall not ask for it. Only write it as soon as you can; for I shall often be thinking of it, and very desirous of it. Very desirous indeed.'[60]

This exchange illustrates both William's sensitivity and the unease with which he approached any institution; throughout his life he was chary of them, refusing to conform to their rules and regulations.[61] At the end of October he finished an introduction to his essay and showed it to Corrie. 'He seemed very pleased with it,' Hazlitt told his father.[62]

Thanks partly to Corrie's encouragement he began to work like a demon, leading his parents to fear for his health. During November the Reverend Hazlitt wrote to approve the plan of his essay while begging him to slow down. William replied, assuring him that 'I can finish in a manner equal to the introduction' despite 'many imperfections'.[63] More concerned than ever, his father wrote again, ordering him to stop altogether. 'I was sorry to hear from your two last letters that you wish me to discontinue my essay', William replied, 'as I am very desirous of finishing it.'[64] He told his father that, 'so far is my studying this subject from making me gloomy, or low-spirited, that I am never so perfectly easy, as when I am, or have been, studying it.'[65] He retained the capacity for hard work throughout his life but, as his father sensed, was capable of exhausting himself.

William was eager to attend Priestley's history lectures in November, thinking him 'the Voltaire of the Unitarians'.[66] He later recalled the lecturer's person better than what he said: Priestley's 'frame was light, fragile, neither strong nor elegant; and in going to any place, he walked on before his wife (who was a tall, powerful woman) with a primitive simplicity, or as if a certain restlessness and hurry impelled him on with a projectile force before others.'[67]

His personal appearance was altogether singular and characteristic. It belonged to the class which may be called *scholastic*. His feet seemed to have been entangled in a gown, his features to have been set in a wig or taken out of a mould. There was nothing to induce you to say with the poet, that 'his body thought'; it was merely the envelope of his mind. In his face there was a strange mixture of acuteness and obtuseness; the nose was sharp and turned up, yet rounded at the end, a keen glance, a quivering lip, yet the aspect placid and indifferent, without any of that expression which arises either from the close workings of the passions or an intercourse with the world. . . . He stammered, spoke thick, and huddled his words ungracefully together.[68]

'History' may have been a convenient cover under which to discuss current affairs; it would explain why Hazlitt later commended him as 'an able controversialist'.[69] Priestley did not long remain in the country. The Birmingham riots led to his being shunned by the establishment and his sons were unable to find employment. After a final course of lectures, on 'Experimental Philosophy, particularly including Chemistry', he sailed for America, never to return.

Priestley's persecution was symptomatic: thought to be subversive, dissenters were now receiving 'special attention' from the Government. During the autumn of 1793 a Unitarian minister, Thomas Fysshe Palmer, who opposed the Anglo-French war, was tried for sedition and after a rigged trial transported to Botany Bay with Thomas Muir and William Skirving, vice president and secretary of the Friends of the People in Edinburgh. They became known as the 'Scottish martyrs' and their conviction regarded as a human rights outrage. Sheridan and Fox lobbied to have the sentences overturned, but to no avail. The young William Wordsworth followed events closely. Then twenty-three, the Cumbrian poet was as fired up with revolutionary ardour as Hazlitt. He lived in France during 1791–2, acquired a French girlfriend whom he got pregnant, and returned to London to publish some of his poems. But before he could return to France, war broke out and he found himself stranded in London in a state of emotional anguish. His friends were so concerned that they sat up all night playing cards with him 'as the best mode of beguiling his sense of distress'.[70] He vented his frustrations in a pamphlet, 'A Letter to the Bishop of Llandaff. By a Republican',[71] which laid into the mob that 'set fire to the house of the philosophic Priestley'.[72] Fortunately for him, no publisher would touch it, or he would have been transported along with the Scottish martyrs.[73] Unfortunately, Hazlitt did not meet him at this moment. The poet was a more likeable man now than he would become—more vulnerable, and as 'hot' in the republican cause as Hazlitt (if not hotter). They might have discovered much common ground and forged an alliance that could have survived what fate had in store for them.

By the end of 1793 both were aware of the most effective radical response to the war: William Godwin's *Political Justice*. An atheist who believed in free love, Godwin proposed that human beings were innately reasonable, and that rationality would cause institutions to wither away—the money system, property, marriage, and government. This paved the way for anarchist and socialist thinkers of the nineteenth century, not least Marx and Engels, who Godwin influenced. Radicals were suddenly galvanized: 'I am studying such a book!' the nineteen-year-old Robert Southey exclaimed with delight.[74] Wordsworth became a disciple too, visiting Godwin's house for animated breakfast conversations about the future of mankind. John Hazlitt met Godwin at the house of the playwright and radical Thomas Holcroft in February 1794, and became friendly with both.

When on Wednesday 17 September 1794 William attended a party thrown by his brother, Godwin was present. In May Godwin had published *Caleb Williams*, forerunner of the modern detective novel. It was an immediate success, and by the time he met its author, the sixteen-year-old Hazlitt was probably an admirer. 'We conceive no one ever began Caleb Williams that did not read it through', he later recalled, 'no one that ever read it could possibly forget it, or speak of it after any length of time but with an impression as if the events and feelings had been personal to himself.'[75] Besides wanting to talk about that, young Hazlitt would have been intrigued by Godwin's views on the Government's latest attempt to suppress radical opinion: the arrest of twelve activists who would be prosecuted on the trumped-up charge of treason, the penalty for which was capital punishment (by being hung, drawn, and quartered). Arrestees included such high-profile figures as John Thelwall, John Horne Tooke, and Thomas Holcroft. Godwin knew most of them personally.[76]

Even the slightest acquaintance with Godwin must have been intoxicating. At around this moment Hazlitt heard a man 'of remarkable candour and ingenuity' (probably Godwin) launch into a violent attack on the established church, saying 'all prayer was a mode of dictating to the Almighty, and an arrogant assumption of superiority.'[77] This was daring, for the Church of England was still a potent political force. Someone else pointed out there was at least one prayer that did not come under that heading. 'And what is that, sir?' asked Godwin. 'The Samaritan's—"Lord, be merciful to me a sinner!!"' Godwin was unconvinced. 'I'm afraid we have shocked that gentleman's prejudices!' he remarked loudly. William was more than a little dismayed—'This did not appear to me at that time quite the thing,' he later remarked,[78] yet he was too thoughtful not to be unsettled by it. What if Godwin was right?

Godwin's finest hour was fast approaching. In October 1794, just as the Treason Trials were to begin, he wrote for the *Morning Chronicle* a devastating attack on the Government, arguing: 'If men can be convicted of High Treason, upon such constructions and implications as are contained in this charge, we may look with conscious superiority upon the republican speculations of France, but we shall certainly have reason to envy the milder tyrannies of Turkey and Ispahan.'[79] He made mincemeat of the prosecution case and showed the defence how to fight its corner. The article, reprinted as a pamphlet, had immediate results: the first defendant, Thomas Hardy, founder and secretary of the London Corresponding Society, was acquitted following a nine-day trial on 5 November: 'in his fate seemed involved the fate of the nation, and the verdict of Not Guilty appeared to burst its bonds, and to have released it from inconceivable miseries, and ages of impending slavery.'[80] The next trial, of John Horne Tooke and his colleagues from the Society for Constitutional Information, ran from 17 to 22 November. Tooke was a star-turn in his own defence: 'he baffled the Judge, dumb-founded the Counsel, and outwitted the Jury'.[81] He was acquitted after eight minutes' deliberation. Next in the dock was John Thelwall, also found not guilty. He went home and threw a party at which Godwin was an honoured guest. John and Mary Hazlitt were also invited. Realizing the game was up, the Government abandoned the remaining prosecutions. This threw London into a frenzy. It was as much a victory for the forces of liberalism as for Godwin, who became an overnight 'star' (his own word). Tooke regarded him as his personal saviour and at a dinner-party led him to the head of the table and ceremonially kissed his hand.[82]

William's acquaintance with this impressive man made the affairs of the world more pressing than ever, fuelling the desire to join him as a pamphleteer. Be this as it may, he pursued his studies at Hackney to 'the satisfaction of the Board',[83] as Andrew Kippis reported to the Presbyterian Fund on 5 December 1794.

CHAPTER 3

*The doctrine of self-love, as an infallible metaphysical
principle of action, is nonsense.*

Hazlitt, *Aphorisms on Man*[1]

'**D**o you like Sterne?' asked William.
  'Yes, to be sure. I should be hanged if I didn't!' He was talking to
Joseph Fawcett, 'almost the first literary acquaintance I ever made'. Twelve years
his senior, Fawcett was an energetic, excitable Unitarian preacher. A decade
before, he started to give his Sunday evening lectures at the Old Jewry Meeting
House in London, and became the most popular dissenting clergyman of the
day. Crowds flocked to hear him, including Sarah Siddons, the Kembles, and
Wordsworth. But Hazlitt did not meet him until introduced by Godwin in early
1795, shortly before Fawcett resigned to become a farmer at Edge Grove, near
Aldenham in Hertfordshire.[2] As Hazlitt recalled, 'the conversations I had with
him on subjects of taste and philosophy (for his taste was as refined as his
powers of reasoning were profound and subtle) gave me a delight such as I can
never feel again.'[3]

One day Fawcett entertained him by reciting Milton's *Comus*, intoning the
verse with his deep, fruity tenor:

> I have oft heard
> My mother Circe with the Sirens three,
> Amidst the flowery-kirtled Naiades
> Culling their potent herbs, and baleful drugs,
> Who as they sung, would take the prisoned soul,
> And lap it in Elysium[4]

He then delivered an appreciation of the entire work, which Hazlitt found 'a
feast to the ear and to the soul'. Fawcett read the poetry of Milton with the same
spirit of devotion others lavished on their own. 'What I want', he would say,
'is something that will make me *think*.' This was an exemplary man of letters:

'A heartier friend or honester critic I never coped withal.'[5] By the time Hazlitt knew him, it may be (as Wordsworth claims) that Fawcett had 'fallen into habits of intemperance',[6] for Hazlitt recalled that 'the disappointment of the hopes he had cherished of the freedom and happiness of mankind, preyed upon his mind and hastened his death.'[7]

During 1795 John Hazlitt and his wife met regularly with Godwin and his circle, often taking William with them. Among others, he met Thomas Holcroft, former stocking-weaver, cobbler, actor, and now a dramatist. He was part of the informal think tank that worked out the ideas in Godwin's *Political Justice* and a member of the Society for Constitutional Information—which led the Government to prosecute him in 1794. When years later Hazlitt commended him as a man whose principles 'were of such a kind, that they could not but strike and win upon the admiration of young and ingenuous minds, of those whose hearts are warm, and their imaginations strong and active, and whose generous and aspiring impulses seem almost to demonstrate the efficacy of disinterested and enlightened motives over the human mind',[8] he was recalling his own feelings at the time of their meeting.

Everyone went to the theatre. In those days Drury Lane could hold up to 3,000 people at a time (three times the capacity of the Olivier at London's National Theatre). People of all classes were welcome, admission being available for as little as sixpence—the price of two pints of ale. Among other things, Hazlitt 'wept outright' when on 11 October 1794 he saw Mrs Siddons playing Isabella in Southerne's tragedy.[9] Then in her fortieth year, Sarah Siddons had been the foremost actress of her day for the best part of two decades, renowned for her intense portrayal of tragic heroines. In later years, Hazlitt remembered how 'she not only hushed the tumultuous shouts of the pit in breathless expectation, and quenched the blaze of surrounding beauty in silent tears, but to the retired and lonely student, through long years of solitude, her face has shone as if an eye had appeared from heaven; her name has been as if a voice had opened the chambers of the human heart, or as if a trumpet had awakened the sleeping and the dead':

> The enthusiasm she excited had something idolatrous about it; she was regarded less with admiration than with wonder, as if a being of a superior order had dropped from another sphere to awe the world with the majesty of her appearance. She raised Tragedy to the skies, or brought it down from thence. It was something above nature. We can conceive of nothing grander. She embodied to

our imagination the fables of mythology, of the heroic and deified mortals of elder time. She was not less than a goddess, or than a prophetess inspired by the gods. Power was seated on her brow, passion emanated from her breast as from a shrine. She was Tragedy personified.[10]

The 'retired and lonely student' did not go just to tragedies; Hazlitt also loved *The School for Scandal*, 'one of our great theatrical treats in our early play-going days. What would we not give to see it once more, as it was then acted, and with the same feelings with which we saw it then?'[11] Nor can he have missed the prostitutes in the galleries, many of whom were soon known to him.[12]

It was probably from around this time that Hazlitt saw prostitutes regularly, assuming he was not already doing so. He never made a secret of it and, in a late essay, analysed the motives that impelled him to consort with streetwalkers, locating the principal explanation in anxiety:

> The scholar is not only apprehensive of not meeting with a return of fondness where it might be most advantageous to him, but he is afraid of subjecting his self-love to the mortification of a repulse, and to the reproach of aiming at a prize far beyond his deserts. Besides, living (as he does) in an *ideal* world, he has it in his option to clothe his Goddess (be she who or what she may) with all the perfections his heart doats on; and he works up a dowdy of this ambiguous description *à son gré*, as an artist works up a piece of dull clay, or the poet the sketch of some unrivalled heroine. The contrast is also the greater (and not the less gratifying as being his own discovery) between his favourite figure and the back-ground of her original circumstances; and he likes her the better, inasmuch as, like himself, she owes all to her own merit—and *his* notice![13]

It is easy, from our perspective, to condemn Hazlitt on moral grounds, but his conduct is mitigated in part by the fact that his involvement could be as emotional as this passage suggests. He was quite capable of falling in love with prostitutes, unlike James Boswell, whose various encounters speak of a more calloused sensibility. Moreover, Regency London took a different view of the sex industry, which was more widespread than it is now. In 1817 there were 360 brothels in just three parishes in the City of London, containing over 2,000 prostitutes. Brothels operated throughout most of the eighteenth and nineteenth centuries without fear of legal constraint, their employees engaged in a trade not prohibited by law (a situation that prevails to this day). In fact, they went about their business with the benefit of some legal protection. Social historians agree that the benign attitude of the authorities towards prostitution in eighteenth-century London indicates it was regarded as 'a fact of life',[14] so that Hazlitt's visits to the stews of the West End would have been unexceptionable to those who knew of them. They included Coleridge, who also visited prostitutes, as did Wordsworth, Shelley, and Keats.[15] No one talks about Lamb's sex-life, but it would be naive to suppose he never had one. What did it consist of? 'These are thy Pleasures O London with-the-many-sins— O City abounding in whores,' he once told Manning, which suggests more than a passing acquaintance with them.[16] Shortly after, he referred to 'London, whose dirtiest drab-frequented alley, and her lowest bowing Tradesman, I would not exchange for Skiddaw, Helvellyin, James, Walter, and the Parson in the bargain.'[17] And when writing to Wordsworth, Lamb rubbed his nose in the metropolitan glories he preferred to the morally improving ones of Cumbria— 'all the bustle and wickedness about Covent Garden, the very women of the Town'.[18] If Hazlitt was unusual, it was only in the candour with which he acknowledged his sex drive, described in his first book as 'a perpetual clog and dead-weight upon the reason'[19]—though, given his fear of highwaymen, footpads, and the like, it is likely that he kept away from alleyways, instead visiting the knocking-shops or inviting female guests to his rooms.

All the same, Hazlitt's sexual proclivities contravened codes the Unitarians held sacred, and can only have led him to question his religious convictions. Ironically, his studies at Hackney lent support to this, for his tutors encouraged his reading of Hume, as well as of Godwin's *Political Justice*, with its godless heaven on earth.[20] In short, it was thanks partly to the College's openness to atheistic philosophies that Hazlitt lost his faith. Even tutors accepted the course had backfired, creating disbelievers out of the devout. 'It may be very true, that at Hackney they learnt, too many of them, Infidelity,' Coleridge later observed, 'the Tutors, the *whole* plan of Education, the place itself, were all wrong.'[21] If so, blame lay at the door of Thomas Belsham, professor of divinity, who was compelled to admit 'there is an unaccountable tendency in the young men, in this part of the world, to infidelity, and the studious and virtuous part of our family have very generally given up Christianity.'[22] He was later to note that the high dropout rate 'raised a great outcry against Unitarianism, and against me in particular, as being either an unbeliever, or at least indifferent to the Christian religion'.[23]

By June 1795, shortly after his seventeenth birthday, William knew he no longer believed in God and left Hackney 'an avowed infidel'.[24] This was the most catastrophic event of his life and would have an effect on everything that followed. From his earliest years his father had been training him up to be a Unitarian minister. Every sinew strained, every breath taken under his father's roof had that end in view. Now he would deliver to his loving parents the mother of all disappointments: not only was he to withdraw from his studies, but he rejected their religion. He knew what pain this would cause them. Ever since returning from America, the Reverend Hazlitt's sole consolation for the apparent failure of his own ambitions was the expectation that William would become a Unitarian minister. It was all the old man had ever wanted from him—and he would be denied it. The resulting guilt was a burden Hazlitt was to carry for the rest of his life. It shaped him. He spent his entire career knowing how inadequately even the most inspired of his essays repaid his father for the pains he had taken over his education and the grief caused by his apostasy. *His* apostasy. For it was he, William Hazlitt, who started out as the biggest turncoat of all. It made him determined not to fail his political aspirations, and that in turn made him a zealous monitor of other peoples'.

When his father heard the news, he was grief-stricken. The career he envisaged for his son was swept aside in a single blow. It broke the old man, and years passed before he came to terms with it; yet it was typical of him that, when William returned home, he welcomed him with loving kindness and not a word of reproach.

Hazlitt's studies had been funded by the Presbyterian Fund thanks to the advocacy of his father's colleague, Andrew Kippis. When Hazlitt's father wrote to apologize, Kippis returned a letter of condolence: 'I can only say that I sincerely sympathize with you in your affliction. I deeply feel for your distress and disappointment, and wish that I could impart to you any sufficient thoughts or words of consolation.'[25] Hazlitt's defection was to have consequences no one could have foreseen, for it was the start of a trend: in May 1796 Kippis had the doleful job of reporting to the Presbyterian Fund that two other students it financed had 'left the Academy & declined the Ministry'.[26] There must have been raised voices on the committee, as there were within the Unitarian community at large. Recently retired, Theophilus Lindsey told John Rowe that in 'Hazlitt's conduct there seems to be not only a ground of infinite self-conceit, but something that bespeaks an unsound state of mind, not guided by any rational principles.'[27] To some, it was impossible to regard young William as other than insane.

This was the beginning of the end for the Hackney College which was already in financial trouble, Priestley's appointment having deterred many backers. It soon shut down and in June 1796 the buildings were auctioned off.

His father loved him, whatever decision he made about his future, but it was impossible for William to remain long in Wem, where his father's grief at what had happened was a constant reproach. After a while he went to stay with his brother in London. One day, he picked up a copy of the *St James's Chronicle* for 1 March 1796, which lay in the hallway, and read extracts from Edmund Burke's recently published *Letter to a Noble Lord*.[28] He was struck immediately by Burke's 'familiar, inimitable, powerful prose-style'.[29] 'This is true eloquence,' he thought, 'this is a man pouring out his mind on paper.'[30] At the time, he was a devotee of Junius who between 1769 and 1772 defended the liberties of the British people;[31] next to Burke, however, his prose 'shrunk up into little antithetic points and well-trimmed sentences. But Burke's style was forked and playful as the lightning, crested like the serpent. He delivered plain things on a plain ground; but when he rose, there was no end of his flights and circumgyrations.'[32] Though Hazlitt did not always care for Burke's sentiments, he loved his style.[33]

It was also at this time he discovered 'French romances and philosophy, and devoured them tooth-and-nail'.[34] In particular, he admired *La Nouvelle Héloïse*, Rousseau's account of the passionate love of St-Preux for a fallen woman, Julie. It was unlike anything in the English language for its handling of emotion, and Hazlitt responded to it immediately: 'the description of the kiss; the excursion on the water; the letter of St Preux, recalling the time of their first loves; and the account of Julia's death; these I read over and over again with unspeakable delight and wonder.'[35] He relished Rousseau's novel for the rest of his life, and would one day compose a variation on it—*Liber Amoris*.

In summer 1796, at his brother's house, he saw Godwin deep in conversation with a woman he did not recognize. It was Mary Wollstonecraft, author of what is now regarded as the founding text of modern feminism, *A Vindication of the Rights of Woman*. Then aged thirty-seven, she was devastatingly attractive, with a line in waggish conversation. A number of suitors had proposed to her in recent years, including (so it was believed) Holcroft. By this time, she and Godwin were in love. Hazlitt was always to remember how 'she seemed to turn off Godwin's objections to something she advanced with quite a playful, easy air.'[36]

Hazlitt was miserably aware of the havoc he caused by leaving the Hackney College, and in October apologized to his father for the deed which had 'served to overcast & to throw into deep obscurity some of the best years of my life'.[37] All the same, his education had produced an important dividend: a 'philosophical discovery' he wanted to enshrine in writing. Half a dozen pages were in shorthand, he told his father: 'I have proceeded some way in a delineation of the system, which founds the propriety of virtue on its coincidence with the pursuit of private interest.'[38] He knew his father would approve, as it was a justification for his lifelong opposition to the Calvinist view that man was inherently evil.

Hazlitt theorized, quite simply, that humans could be motivated by objects in the future—which, like all such objects, were imaginary. And that was the point: other people exist, in their future state, on the same imaginative level as ourselves. If that was so, he reasoned, the ability to conceive of our future selves implies an equal capacity to imagine others'. He thus confronted the belief that mankind was self-seeking with the theory that disinterestedness was built into the human psyche. It was one thing to have worked this out, quite another to justify it. He would turn from Rousseau, Fielding, or Burke to find that, far from sharing their eloquence, he was woefully inarticulate. Time and again he took the few disjointed sentences he had written, crumpled them into a ball, and hurled them into the fireplace.

Having disappointed his father once, he was not about to compound the blow by announcing his intention to become a philosopher. It was reasonable at this stage to suppose writing would be merely a hobby. Instead he continued to paint, and by the end of 1796 was working in Liverpool, where he met William Roscoe, the wealthy Unitarian lawyer fascinated by Italian art who fostered young painters through the Society for the Encouragement of the Arts, Painting, and Design which he founded in 1773. Hazlitt went regularly to Roscoe's soirées at his family home at Mount Pleasant, where he met Roscoe's wife, Jane, and son, William, who was four years Hazlitt's junior. Roscoe shared Hazlitt's distrust of institutions—after only a term at Gray's Inn he abandoned attempts to become a barrister—and they enjoyed each other's conversation. Hazlitt made friends within the Roscoe circle including the Reverend William Shepherd, Unitarian minister at Gateacre, Liverpool, as radical in politics as he was in religion. Roscoe encouraged Shepherd's interest in Italian literature, and would assist publication of his *Life of Poggio Bracciolini* in 1803. Its printer was John

M'Creery, an Irishman who, in autumn 1793, had begun printing Roscoe's *Life of Lorenzo de Medici*, a labour which absorbed him for the next two and a half years. Its successful publication established M'Creery as house printer to the Roscoe circle. Ten years later M'Creery moved to London where he and the awkward young painter would meet again, under different auspices.

William soon returned to London to visit John and Mary Hazlitt, now at 6 Suffolk Street, which backed onto Middlesex Hospital. It may have been through his brother that he was asked to paint the children of lexicographer James Knowles. Hazlitt depicted Knowles's daughter Charlotte in white muslin, weeping over a dead bird in her lap—a pose recalling early Reynolds. Knowles's son, James Sheridan, was then around twelve, and Hazlitt found him difficult to pose. 'Hang your fat cheeks—frown, James!', he ordered. Outside the studio, artist and sitter got on famously: when Hazlitt could do no more, he set up a tightrope in the drawing room and danced upon it while James applauded.[39] (Hazlitt was a great admirer of Jack Richer, the legendary artiste who danced a hornpipe on the rope at Sadler's Wells.[40])

He became friend and mentor to the boy at an important moment in his life. Three years hence, after the death of James's mother, his father remarried, which led to a falling-out between father and son. James left home and was looked after by a succession of friends, including Hazlitt. In the midst of that, James managed to write poetry and plays; Hazlitt 'cheered me on', Knowles later testified, and 'read to me examples of good composition from good Poets'.[41] Moreover, Hazlitt 'had an endearing tenderness of heart towards those whom he loved, and this was just the quality, and the only quality, which could gain complete mastery over the young poet'.[42] Knowles never ceased to feel grateful for Hazlitt's generosity: 'He was honest, and, when he met with a friend, intensely affectionate.'[43]

By 1797 William was known to Godwin, Holcroft, and Thelwall, the kind of metropolitan company in which he was to flourish, made all the more attractive by having 'rendered themselves obnoxious to Government'.[44] These excitable, opinionated men, all older than him, provided the stimulus to his hard-nosed republicanism. He looked up to them, Holcroft in particular: 'He was a man of too honest, and of too independent a turn of mind to be a time-server, to lend himself as a tool to the violence of any party; his habits and studies rendered him equally averse to political intrigues or popular tumults; and he had no other desire than to speak the truth, such as he saw it, with a conviction that its effects must be beneficial to society.'[45] The self-educated son of a cobbler, a jockey, and actor who had found success as a playwright, Holcroft was as intense, passionate, and energetic in debate as Hazlitt himself. Hazlitt once asked Coleridge whether he was not struck with Holcroft, to which Coleridge responded that he was 'in more danger of being struck *by* him'.[46] Abrupt and outspoken, Holcroft was impressed by young Hazlitt, and found the only way of arguing with him was to make him define his terms. 'What do you mean by a *sensation*, sir?' he would demand. 'What do you mean by an *idea*?'[47]

Thelwall had much in common with Hazlitt, not least that he was once a painter. He had also been a tailor, actor, and lawyer's clerk. In recent years he had become famous for journalism and poetry, including a book of verse written while imprisoned in the Tower. He was exactly the kind of loose talker Hazlitt loved. Once, drinking beer at a political rally, he skimmed the froth from the head with a penknife, declaring to those around him (including government spies): 'Thus should all tyrants be served!'

In conversation with Hazlitt, Thelwall revealed how after the Treason Trials he retreated to Wales and one morning found himself at an inn at Llangollen. Having ordered his breakfast, he sat expectantly at the table and gazed absently out of the window at passers-by. When his breakfast arrived he found to his surprise that his appetite had deserted him, 'the day had lost its freshness in his eye, he was uneasy and spiritless; and without any cause that he could discover, a total change had taken place in his feelings.'[48] What was wrong? While he pondered this, he glanced out of the window, and noted a face that had passed several times before: that of Taylor, a government spy.

> To the flitting, shadowy, half-distinguished profile that had glided by his window was linked unconsciously and mysteriously, but inseparably, the impression of the trains that had been laid for him by this person;—in this brief moment, in this dim, illegible short-hand of the mind he had just escaped the speeches of the Attorney and Solicitor-General over again; the gaunt figure of Mr Pitt glared by him; the walls of a prison enclosed him; and he felt the hands of the executioner near him, without knowing it till the tremor and disorder of his nerves gave information to his reasoning faculties that all was not well within.[49]

Hazlitt admired Thelwall as an orator, and went often to see him speak: 'he was like a volcano vomiting out *lava*. . . . He was the model of a flashy, powerful demagogue—a madman blest with a fit audience. He was possessed, infuriated with the patriotic mania; he seemed to read and tear the rotten carcase of corruption with the remorseless, indecent rage of a wild beast: he mourned over the bleeding body of his country, like another Antony over the dead body of Caesar, as if he would "move the very stones of Rome to rise and mutiny": he pointed to the "Persian abodes, the glittering temples" of oppression and luxury, with prophetic exultation; and, like another Helen, had almost fired another Troy!'[50]

Another of the Treason Trial defendants, John Horne Tooke, had by now withdrawn to a villa in Wimbledon, an excellent home for the financially stretched bohemian. Here he held weekly Sunday dinners to which he invited a throng of luminaries from the world of politics and letters, including Sir Francis Burdett, Godwin, Thelwall, Holcroft, and Hazlitt. Hazlitt always retained a high regard for Tooke who, 'besides being the inventor of the theory of grammar, was a politician, a wit, a master of conversation'.[51] In an earlier time, Tooke had been friend and supporter of John Wilkes, defender of liberty and father of the British free press.[52] As Tooke reminisced about his first meeting with Wilkes in the mid-1760s, it seemed to young Hazlitt that the conversation mellowed 'like the wine with the smack of age'.[53] One afternoon, Holcroft got into an argument with Tooke about politics. Tooke, a more agile and cool-headed thinker and speaker, spun a paradox around Holcroft's assertions that enraged him so much that his opponent jumped up and declared,

'Mr Tooke, you are a scoundrel!'

Without missing a beat, Tooke gazed calmly at him and replied: 'Mr Holcroft, when is it that I am to dine with you? Shall it be next Thursday?'

Holcroft looked about himself, blinked, and answered, 'If you please, Mr Tooke!', and sat down again.

Hazlitt had mixed in intellectual circles before, but must have felt somewhat overawed by the remarkable men he met at Tooke's gatherings. He adopted the watchful, thoughtful attitude he would maintain in society for the rest of his life, restraining his impulsive nature so as not to make a fool of himself, pre-ferring instead to listen politely, contributing occasionally with an observation or insight that would take his interlocutors to the heart of the subject under discussion. Sometimes, when sure of his ground, he would enter into the sort of conversation he described as 'thinking aloud': 'I like very well to speak my mind on any subject (or to hear another do so) and to go into the question according to the degree of interest it naturally inspires, but not to have to get up a thesis upon every topic.'[54]

It is no accident that his contact with these radical voices increased after his departure from Hackney; as disbelievers, their strongly held views lent support to his own atheism. They also encouraged him to test the political assumptions with which he had grown up. When we call them 'radical' (a label often attached to Hazlitt), what do we mean? The word covers a range of views over which they themselves were perpetually arguing. Moreover, the same person might change their mind from year to year or month to month. Religious affiliations ranged across the spectrum from Anglicanism to dissenting forms of religion (Unitarianism was popular) to outright atheism. Some wished merely to restrict the power of the monarch while others wanted to make Britain a republic. But all had one thing in common: the aspiration to a fairer world. This was to provide the impulse for an equally powerful revolution—the movement we now call Romanticism. Hazlitt's introduction to it would take place that 'raw, comfortless' morning in January 1798 when he went to see the new preacher at Shrewsbury—Mr Coleridge, whose sermon was a religious explication of Hazlitt's most deeply held convictions. It was a revelation, and was to change him forever:

> I could not have been more delighted if I had heard the music of the spheres. Poetry and Philosophy met together, Truth and Genius had embraced, under the eye and with the sanction of Religion. This was even beyond my hopes. I returned home well satisfied. The sun that was still labouring pale and wan through the sky, obscured by thick mists, seemed an emblem of the good cause: and the cold dank drops of dew that hung half melted on the beard of the thistle, had something genial and refreshing in them; for there was a spirit of hope and youth in all nature, that turned every thing into good.[55]

PART II

Beyond Xanadu

CHAPTER 4

*A mist passed away from my sight: the scales fell off.
A new sense came upon me, a new heaven and a
new earth stood before me.*

Hazlitt, 'On the Pleasure of Painting'[1]

ORLEANS ITALIAN PICTURES.

This superb assemblage of Italian Pictures is now exhibiting for sale by private
contract at Mr. Bryan's Gallery, No. 88 Pall-mall, and at the Lyceum, from 11 till
4——Admittance, 2s.6d. each.

Advertisement in *The Times*, 1 January 1799, p. 1 col. 1

THE collection of Italian masters formerly in the possession of the Regent
Orleans was on display at a gallery in Pall Mall, and Hazlitt visited it
many times, never to forget what he saw.[2] He gazed at Ludovico Carracci's
'Susannah and the Elders' 'till our heart thrilled with its beauty, and our eyes
filled with tears. How often had we thought of it since, how often spoken of it!'[3]
Sebastiano del Piombo's 'The Raising of Lazarus' moved him for its portrayal
of the revived man: 'The flesh is well-baked, dingy, and ready to crumble
from the touch, when it is liberated from its dread confinement to have life
and motion impressed on it again.'[4] He adored Annibale Carracci's 'Danaë',
with its 'fine, up-turned, expectant'[5] face. Most of all, two paintings by Titian
burned themselves into his memory. In 'Venus Rising from the Sea', the central
figure was in shade—'a kind of veil through which the delicate skin shows more
transparent and aerial'[6]—while 'The Death of Actaeon' worked beautifully as
a landscape: 'The winds seemed to sing through the rustling branches of the
trees, and already you might hear the twanging of bows resound through the
tangled mazes of the wood.'[7] For the rest of his life Hazlitt would return to them
in his imagination. 'From that time I lived in a world of pictures. Battles, sieges,

speeches in parliament seemed mere idle noise and fury, "signifying nothing," compared with those mighty works and dreaded names that spoke to me in the eternal silence of thought.'[8]

After his encounter with Wordsworth and Coleridge in Somerset, the twenty-year-old Hazlitt was more convinced than ever that his future lay in the visual arts, and in the New Year of 1799 he moved in with his brother, now resident at Rathbone Place in the heart of the artists' quarter to the north of Oxford Street. This part of the capital was to be Hazlitt's residence for the rest of his life, relished partly for its literary associations. It was, Leigh Hunt commented, 'classic ground: from Fleet-street, where Johnson and Goldsmith lived, to Gerrard-street, Soho, which contains the residence of Dryden. It includes the chief places of resort, during the three periods in which poetry and wit were allied with familiar life;—Dryden's period, with Etherege, Wycherley, Rochester, and others;—the time of Steele and Addison, Garth, Vanbrugh, Congreve, &c. and that of the two authors above mentioned, who left us just before the French Revolution.'[9]

A principal attraction of Oxford Street was its book- and printsellers' shops, in which he spent many hours. One day, when a shower came on, he rushed into a picture dealer's. He found himself looking at the engraving of a painting by Thomas Gainsborough—*The Shepherd-Boy*. He would never forget it. 'What truth and beauty was there!', he later recalled. 'He stands with his hands clasped, looking up with a mixture of timidity and resignation, eying a magpie chattering above his head, while the wind is rustling in the branches. It was like a vision breathed on the canvas. I have been fond of Gainsborough ever since.'[10]

This was a period when he 'was treated as a cipher',[11] yet Hazlitt was now acquiring the friends whose regard would follow him into the 1810s. He began to visit Godwin on 12 February 1799, a habit he continued for the next 27 years, and through him came contact with John Stoddart. The son of a navy lieutenant on half-pay (and, latterly, master of a press gang in Poole), Stoddart passed through Christ Church, Oxford, before making his way to Grub Street in 1796, full of Godwinian self-righteousness, where he became acquainted with Wordsworth and Coleridge. A puritan by nature, he affected the cropped haircut of the sans-culottes while voicing the belief that Napoleon's invasion of Britain would be 'of more advantage than victory'.[12] Such humourless fervency possessed little charm for Lamb, who saw him as 'a cold-hearted, well-bred, conceited disciple of Godwin'.[13] Stoddart's steeliness owed much to his determination to elevate himself from the poverty in which he had grown up. He had ambition and, in

Fig. 8. Thomas Gainsborough, *The Shepherd-Boy*. 'What truth and beauty was there! He stands with his hands clasped, looking up with a mixture of timidity and resignation, eying a magpie chattering above his head, while the wind is rustling in the branches. It was like a vision breathed on the canvas.'

1797–8, probably under the influence of his friend Basil Montagu, kept terms at Gray's Inn.

Hazlitt came to know Montagu as well. He was the natural son of the fourth Earl of Sandwich and his mistress Martha Ray, shot dead on the steps of Drury Lane theatre by a rejected suitor, James Hackman, in 1779.[14] Montagu had class on his side, but little else. While a law student in London, he married against his father's wishes only for his wife to die giving birth to a son, Basil Caroline Montagu. By then he had relinquished his studies under Godwin's influence, whose disciple he had become. In 1795 his father deprived him of his inheritance, leaving him in such straitened circumstances that Wordsworth and his sister offered to take care of Basil Caroline for him, which they did for several years. (He became 'Edward' in Wordsworth's 'Anecdote for Fathers' and 'To my Sister'.) Montagu resumed his study of the law 'from a desire to save the lives of the culprits' (as Holcroft wryly noted[15]) and was called to the bar in May 1798. Though on the Norfolk circuit, Montagu was based at Paper Buildings, Inner Temple, where he entertained Stoddart and Hazlitt.

Together the three young men talked politics and metaphysics late into the night. Stoddart seemed loud and conceited even then (Holcroft found him 'pertinacious and verbose'[16]), and Hazlitt thought his exhibition of radical disdain contrived. Montagu was more congenial company; Hazlitt liked his determination to work hard and distinguish himself. They remained friends, on and off, till the end of Hazlitt's life.

One day in February 1799, Stoddart (now at Lincoln's Inn) invited Hazlitt to a momentous series of lectures. James Mackintosh's 'On the Law of Nature and Nations' was delivered at Lincoln's Inn Hall between February and June 1799. A man of impeccable liberal credentials, Mackintosh was the associate of Godwin, Horne Tooke, Sheridan, and Charles James Fox, his *Vindiciae Gallicae* (1791) ranking alongside *The Rights of Man* as a statement of pro-Revolutionary ardour. Now, he shocked his audience by abandoning that cause, arguing instead that the British constitution was 'the most truly & properly democratick C[onstitution] ever known'.[17] The Revolution, he declared, was a mistake 'which has rooted up every Principle of Democracy in the Country & banished the People from all concern in the Government'.[18] As Hazlitt recalled, 'The volcano of the French Revolution was seen expiring in its own flames, like a bon-fire made of straw: the principles of Reform were scattered in all directions, like chaff before the keen northern blast. He laid about him like one inspired; nothing could withstand his envenomed tooth.'[19] In a swipe, 'visionary sceptics and Utopian philosophers' (Paine and Godwin) were confounded. Fascinated by the spectacle of a former Revolutionary shredding 'the good cause', Hazlitt attended 'day after day', and was 'at last at some loss to know *whether two and two made four*, till we had heard the lecturer's opinion on that head.'[20] It was typical of Hazlitt to listen disinterestedly to Mackintosh even though he could not agree with him.

The Tories were jubilant. Pitt congratulated Mackintosh on lectures that seemed 'to promise more useful Instruction and just Reasoning on the Principles of Government than I have ever met with in any Treatise on that subject'.[21] Godwin, on the other hand, experienced 'mingled emotions of pleasure & pain' (principally the latter) and asked Mackintosh 'who are the speculators whom you designate by the following epithets—superficial & most mischievous sciolists—mooters of fatal controversies—men who, in pursuit of a transient popularity, have exerted their art to disguise the most miserable common-places in the shape of paradox—promulgators of absurd & monstrous systems—of abominable & pestilential paradoxes—shallow metaphysicians— sophists swelled with insolent conceit—savage desolators?' The answer was, of course, himself. 'It seems that our personal intercourse is likely to be much diminished,' he concluded.[22]

Godwin's star was waning. Mackintosh's desertion induced in him a period of self-doubt[23] during which it was comforting to find young admirers like Hazlitt. That was not to say Hazlitt was ever a Godwinian. Unlike Stoddart and Montagu, he never espoused Godwin's philosophy but revered him as a hero of 1790s Britain, never tiring of his company. It was particularly irritating to Hazlitt that Mackintosh denied the existence of benevolence in the human psyche, as he thought exactly the opposite. This led Hazlitt to explain to Godwin his own theories which revealed how Mackintosh could be rebutted. Godwin listened with interest. The youth's arguments were, on the face of it, sound. Perhaps some use might be made of them. But there were bigger beasts in the jungle than Mackintosh. The previous year an obscure clergyman with a penchant for political economy had written a response to Godwin entitled *An Essay on the Principle of Population*. The Reverend Thomas Robert Malthus accused him of having overlooked the tendency of people to reproduce more rapidly than the food supply would permit; so far as Malthus was concerned, wars, famines, plagues, delayed marriages, prostitution, and contraception were useful checks on overpopulation. He thought poor relief should be abolished and death from starvation encouraged as 'natural'. This was the flowering of Utilitarianism in its most pernicious form, and Hazlitt would worry away at it for years to come.

Godwin was drawn to Hazlitt not just by his politics, but the fact that he saw something of himself in the young man. Both were shy and tended to come off badly in society. For his part, Hazlitt admired Godwin not just for his writings, but his courage in bringing up the baby daughter who had taken her mother's name. Throughout her girlhood the future Mary Shelley saw the young philosopher arriving at her father's house and considered him, for all his social awkwardness, a friend.

A young solicitor's clerk called Henry Crabb Robinson was also among the audience at Mackintosh's lectures. Three years Hazlitt's senior, he was an avowed Unitarian and dedicated supporter of Revolutionary principles, and so regarded Mackintosh as 'an apostate from liberty'.[24] He was struck by Hazlitt's 'bashfulness, want of words, slovenliness in dress &c', which 'made him an object of ridicule'.[25] For all that, he saw (as did Godwin) that there was something special about him, and they soon became friends, meeting over talkative, sociable breakfasts. Robinson was no 'live wire' but had an acute and piercing intelligence, and enjoyed the same bantering debates as Hazlitt. When that autumn Robinson made his first visit to Shropshire, he asked for the address of Hazlitt's parents and called on them along the way. He thought Hazlitt's father 'a very worthy old Presbyterian minister—not worse than an Arian'; on the other hand he had to contend with 'John the miniature painter & his vixenish wife whom I did not like'.[26]

Another young lawyer Hazlitt met at this moment was Robert Southey, who in May 1799 was keeping terms at Gray's Inn where he had begun legal training two years earlier.[27] Stoddart, a friend of Southey's from Oxford days, may have introduced them.[28] Hazlitt already knew Southey through his political poetry, which made him a whipping-boy for the Tory satirists.[29] He knew also that Southey had been Coleridge's collaborator in the failed scheme by which they planned to sail to America and set up a commune. There had been disagreements on the details—Coleridge wanted free love, Southey disagreed and insisted they marry before setting sail. In 1799, Southey was as committed to revolution as ever, but was more pragmatic than Coleridge: why else was he studying the law? He and Hazlitt would meet again.

Southey was gone by the time Coleridge descended on London at the end of November. His sojourn in Germany had been productive but he needed to pursue a profession and now intended to become a journalist. He settled at Buckingham Street, close to the newspaper offices in the Strand, where his family soon joined him; his work was appearing in the *Morning Post* by 7 December. By 3 January 1800, when Godwin found Hazlitt conversing with Coleridge in his rooms, Hazlitt was a regular visitor. Later that month Mackintosh delivered a repeat performance of his lectures, the first of which Coleridge attended courtesy of the lecturer, who sent him a ticket. It did not improve their acquaintance, Coleridge referring a few months later to the 'Animalcula who live on the dung of the great Dung-fly Mackintosh'.[30]

In the face of Mackintosh's attacks, Godwin busied himself with books: his second novel, *St Leon*, was published on 2 December 1799. He gave a copy to Hazlitt who when he began it decided 'I do not at present admire [it] very much.'[31] But by the time he finished it he had fallen in love with the 'gorgeous and flowing eloquence, and . . . crown of preternatural imagery, that waves over it like a palm-tree!'[32] Still believing his destiny to lie in the visual arts, Hazlitt was making visits to Manchester and Liverpool in search of work, with some success: 'I shall be glad to hear that your son's prospects improve at Manchester', Joshua Toulmin, a colleague, told the Reverend Hazlitt.[33]

On one such trip he was commissioned to paint the head of a countrywoman. 'I certainly laboured it with great perseverance,' he later recalled.

> It took me numberless sittings to do it. I have it by me still, and sometimes look at it with surprise, to think how much pains were thrown away to little purpose,— yet not altogether in vain if it taught me to see good in every thing, and to know that there is nothing vulgar in nature seen with the eye of science or of true art.[34]

In manner and style he imitated Rembrandt, whose portraits he had seen at Burleigh House. He was so successful that when the artist Benjamin Robert Haydon saw it years later, he asked: 'Hallo! where did you get that Rembrandt? It looks like an early performance.'[35]

On another occasion Hazlitt was asked to copy the half-length portrait of a Manchester industrialist 'who had died worth a plum',[36] for a fee of five guineas. While working on it, he lived solely on coffee and rushed his work towards the end because he was so hungry. The moment he had money in his pocket, he went to the nearest tavern and gorged himself on sausages and mash: 'Neither Monsieur de Very, nor Louis XVIII, over an oyster-pâté, nor Apicius himself, ever understood the meaning of the word *luxury* better than I did at that moment!'[37]

On his way back to Wem he called on Daniel Stringer, a Royal Academician at Knutsford who had 'the finest hand and the clearest eye of any artist of the time, and produced heads and drawings that would not have disgraced a brighter period in the art.'[38] At his house William saw 'some spirited comic sketches in an unfinished state, and a capital female figure by Cignani'.[39] But Stringer was no longer the inspired genius he had once been. He had sacrificed himself to the company of country squires, downing endless jars of Cheshire ale. Yet no one who saw his work doubted his talent: a friend of this moment, Tom Kershaw, told William that 'he would rather have been Dan Stringer than Sir Joshua Reynolds at twenty years of age.'[40] Stringer's fate was a dire warning of what awaited young artists.

His parents' home was a good base for someone whose work often took them north, and William was there at the end of 1801, hoping to retrieve something of the intimacy he had enjoyed with his father in earlier years. In later life he wrote about 'schisms, coldness, and incurable heart-burnings in families', reflecting on an instance in which the son

> is brought up to the church, and nothing can exceed the pride and pleasure the father takes in him while all goes well in this favourite direction. His notions change, and he imbibes a taste for the Fine Arts. From this moment there is an end of any thing like the same unreserved communication between them. The young man may talk with enthusiasm of his 'Rembrandts, Correggios, and stuff': it is all *Hebrew* to the elder; and whatever satisfaction he may feel in hearing of his son's progress, or good wishes for his success, he is never reconciled to the new pursuit, he still hankers after the first object that he had set his mind upon.[41]

As part of the attempt to reclaim their former closeness he embarked during the winter of 1802 on his father's portrait. 'I drew it with a broad light crossing the face, looking down, with spectacles on, reading. The book was Shaftesbury's Characteristics, in a fine old binding, with Gribelin's etchings.'[42] The choice of text was not accidental. Shaftesbury had expounded the theory of disinterestedness—the very quality in which Hazlitt and his father vested the virtuous potential of humanity.[43] The portrait was painted con amore, and for both artist and sitter the period of its execution was one of the happiest of their lives.

He sent the portrait to the Royal Academy where it was exhibited during the summer of 1802. It hung alongside Masquerier's picture of fop and playwright Sir Lumley Skeffington; seeing them together Hazlitt reflected 'that they were the portraits of two very good-natured men.'[44] In London he renewed old friendships, being given supper at Godwin's house, where he stayed on 12 May. The following week he was at Drury Lane to see *The Winter's Tale* with Sarah Siddons as Hermione and John Philip Kemble as Leontes—a performance he would remember for the rest of his life. 'Nothing could go off with more *eclat*, with more spirit, and grandeur of effect. ... We shall never see these parts so acted again; or if we did, it would be in vain.'[45]

Weeks before, it had become possible for the British to visit Paris, peace having been negotiated with the French. No one knew how long it would hold, so everyone made the most of it; fortunately the Treaty was signed on 25 March 1802, in time for the summer vacation. There were illuminations across London and the English flocked across the Channel, eager to sample the delights of the Continent, of which they had been deprived for over a decade. Hazlitt had no plans to join them until commissioned by a Mr Railton, one of his Liverpool patrons, to copy ten paintings in the Louvre.[46] The fee would be £105. Nothing could have held him back: he was going to the greatest art gallery in Europe!

Hazlitt had taken to visiting James Northcote, the academician who in former years had studied with Reynolds and befriended Johnson, Goldsmith, and Boswell. Now 56 years old, Northcote enjoyed Hazlitt's company and entertained his visits for the rest of his life. Hazlitt was fascinated by the Johnson circle, and enjoyed Northcote's anecdotes—how Reynolds saw Alexander Pope at an auction shortly after first arriving in London; how Johnson was once taken for a tramp, so slovenly was his dress; Reynolds's belief that childrens' gestures were natural, and that distortions in physique came with the dancing master. These stories brought their protagonists to life, and Hazlitt may have been instrumental in encouraging Northcote to publish them in 1813.[47]

One day when Hazlitt arrived, Northcote had a print of Titian's portrait of Cardinal Ippolito de Medici in Hungarian dress laid out on the floor. 'This is one of the finest pictures in the world!' he told him. Hazlitt would soon be able to see it for himself, for it was in the Louvre, and he told him about the Railton commission.

'If you would give me leave, sir, I will make a copy of it for you.'

'You would delight me, Hazlitt, if you would!' replied Northcote.[48]

* * *

Calais was peopled with novelty and delight. The confused, busy murmur of the place was like oil and wine poured into my ears; nor did the mariners' hymn, which was sung from the top of an old crazy vessel in the harbour, as the sun went down, send an alien sound into my soul. I only breathed the air of general humanity. I walked over 'the vinecovered hills and gay regions of France' erect and satisfied; for the image of man was not cast down and chained to the foot of arbitrary thrones: I was at no loss for language, for that of all the great schools of painting was open to me.

Hazlitt, 'On Going a Journey'[49]

Part II: Beyond Xanadu

On 14 July 1790, the young William Wordsworth had landed at Calais to join the Revolutionaries in the midst of their exaltations: 'All hearts were open, every tongue was loud | With amity and glee.'[50] In October 1802, Hazlitt was no less aware of the achievements of preceding years. The French had toppled their monarch and were to some extent self-determining. His aim was partly to bear witness to the only country in Europe that had taken a step towards democracy as we know it.

He moved into the Hotel Coq Heron, less than ten minutes from the Louvre, on 15 October 1802. The countryside round Paris was 'barren and miserable', full of beggars, and the city 'dirty and disagreeable, except along the river side'[51]—France was suffering the effects of nearly a decade of war. The following morning he got up and went to the gallery, heading straight for the Italian masters, only to be denied access by 'the old Republican door-keepers, with their rough voices and affectation of equality',[52] though he could glimpse the paintings within when the doors opened—'(vile hindrance!) like looking out of purgatory into paradise!'[53] Realizing he was expected to slip the porters a sweetener, he put some coins in their hands, entered, and was stunned by what he saw.

> It was *un beau jour* to me. I marched delighted through a quarter of a mile of the proudest efforts of the mind of man, a whole creation of genius, a universe of art! ... Reader, 'if thou hast not seen the Louvre, thou art damned!'[54]

He walked about in a dream-like state, surrounded by works he knew only from engravings. And he never forgot his first encounter with Titian's *Ippolito de Medici*. It stood on an easel, with its back to him; he walked past, turned, and recognized it immediately, having seen the image most recently on Northcote's floor. But this was a different thing entirely, far superior to the copy he had seen in London. The Cardinal glared at him. He thought he saw the man draw breath, and the boar-spear in his hand seemed to quiver. Titian's painting 'seemed "a thing of life"', with supernatural force and grandeur'.[55]

Before he could copy anything, he had to obtain a permit, and was assisted in this by J. F. L. Merimée (father of the author Prosper Merimée, born the following year), to whom Holcroft had given him a letter of introduction. From that day onwards, Hazlitt displayed the same discipline he had shown when studying Latin and Greek in earlier years. He went to the Louvre at about 9.30 in the morning and worked continuously until 4pm, when the gallery closed. Early

Fig. 9. Titian's
Ippolito de Medici,
one of Hazlitt's
favourite paintings,
which he saw for the
first time at the
Louvre in 1802.

one morning Merimée visited his hotel and saw two of Hazlitt's paintings—the head of the countrywoman and another of a black man—'which he liked very much, though they are contrary to the French style', as Hazlitt told his father.[56] There was a world of difference between French and British notions of taste. One day at the Louvre, Merimée asked what he thought of one of the French landscapes.

'It is too clear', Hazlitt observed, without hesitation.

'Mais, c'est impossible!', Merimée replied.

'What I meant', Hazlitt continued, 'is that the various parts of the several objects are painted with too much distinctness across the picture; the leaves of the trees in shadow are as distinct as those in the light; the branches of the trees at a distance are as plain as those nearby. Perspective arises in this picture only from the diminution of objects, and there is no interposition of air.' He noticed Merimée's look of incredulity. 'Look, there: one cannot see the leaves of a tree a mile off!' Merimée shook his head, despairing of his young friend.[57]

A day or two later Hazlitt saw Bonaparte, as he led his entourage through the palace. The First Consul of the French Republic was in the habit of taking the air without ceremony, affirming his credentials as a man of the people. Hazlitt would remember the sighting for the rest of his life: 'What a fine iron binding Buonaparte had round his face, as if it had been cased in steel! What sensibility around the mouth! What watchful penetration in the eye! What a smooth unruffled forehead!'[58]

Hazlitt was now working on a copy of Titian's man in black—a painting he loved. He had nearly completed it when, on 28 October,[59] he overheard a large man immediately behind him, talking rapidly about some paintings at the other end of the gallery: 'All those blues and greens and reds are the Guercinos; you may know them by the colours.'[60] He turned to see Charles James Fox, former leader of the Whig opposition in the Commons. Sidelined by George III who, at Pitt's resignation, appointed his doctor's son, Henry Addington, as Prime Minister, Fox was now taking advantage of the Treaty of Amiens to visit a country he loved. Hazlitt gazed admiringly at a 'great man',[61] aware that his grey hair, pale face and furrowed brow indicated not only age but fragility. When a day or so later Fox passed through the gallery again, Hazlitt was bold enough to compliment him on his achievements; he responded warmly, and Hazlitt always remembered his 'frank, simple, unaffected manners' at 'the affection and esteem of strangers'.[62]

One day an Englishman came up to Hazlitt and admired his work: 'Upon my word, Sir', he said, 'you get on with great spirit and boldness; you do us great credit, I am sure.'[63] Another wanted to know whether he taught oil painting, at which he said he was 'more in need of instruction myself; that that sort of rapid sketching was what I did better than anything else; and that, after the first hour or two, I generally made my pictures worse and worse, the more pains I took with them.'[64]

There was quite an artists' colony in the Louvre—many of them British. A few weeks before, Joseph Farington toured it with Fuseli, Opie, and Flaxman.[65] One whom Hazlitt came to know was the miniaturist Richard Cosway, now in his sixtieth year. The two men got on from the moment they met on the morning of 29 November 1802; Cosway, Hazlitt recalled, 'was Fancy's child':

> he believed whatever was incredible. Fancy bore away in him; and so vivid were his impressions, that they included the substances of things in them. The agreeable and the true with him were one. He believed in Swedenborgianism— he believed in animal magnetism—he had conversed with more than one person of the Trinity—he could talk with his lady at Mantua through some fine vehicle of sense, as we speak to a servant down-stairs through a conduit-pipe. Richard Cosway was not the man to flinch from an *ideal* proposition.[66]

Cosway's marriage to Maria Hadfield, a talented artist and musician, had broken down years earlier, partly as a result of their daughter's death, and she now lived independently in Paris. But they remained on good terms, and invited the young artist for tea the following evening. Hazlitt was as charmed by Mrs Cosway as he was by her husband, regarding her as 'the most lady-like of Englishwomen'.

'And pray, madame, what is your husband really like?' he asked, while Cosway looked on.

She laughed and, smiling at Cosway, remarked, 'Toujours riant, toujours gai!'[67]

The following evening Hazlitt was strolling through the Paris streets when he heard a peal of female laughter. He turned to see Maria Cosway arm in arm with a dashing young man in a 'light drab-coloured great-coat':[68] Lucien Bonaparte, younger brother to the Emperor, member of the legislative Tribunat, and senator of the First French Empire. Years later, when Bonaparte published a poem, *Charlemagne*, Hazlitt went out of his way to read it, judging it 'as clever a poem as can be written by a man who is not a poet'.[69]

On 1 February 1803 Hazlitt was granted a certificate confirming he had copied ten pictures in the Louvre (including works by Titian, Raphael, Tintoretto, and Poussin), endorsed by the director-general of the museum, Baron Vivant-Denon.[70] A few days later he was in the *diligence* to Calais on his way home where he fell into conversation with an Englishman and a Frenchman. When it was mentioned that a man had married his wife after thirteen years' courtship, the Englishman observed: 'At least he would then have been acquainted with her character.'

'Mais non, Monsieur', interrupted the Frenchman, 'for the very next day she might turn out the very reverse of the character that she had appeared in during

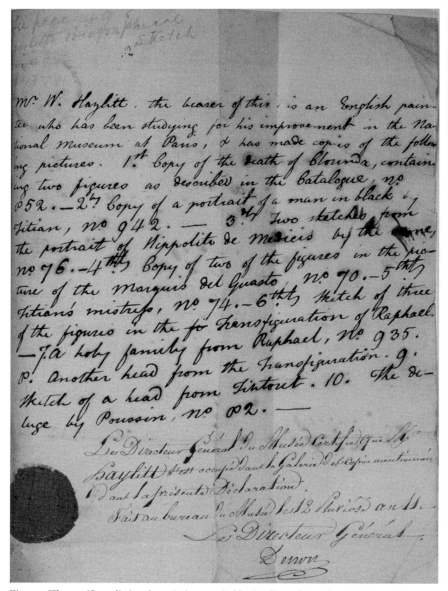

Fig. 10. The certificate listing the paintings copied by Hazlitt on his visit to the Louvre in 1802–3, signed by Baron Vivant-Denon. Most of the writing on the sheet is Hazlitt's; only the hand at the bottom is Denon's. I am grateful to Tom Mayberry for this illustration.

all the preceding time!' Hazlitt could not help admiring these words of wisdom, which would resound in his head for years to come, though they would not save him from disaster.[71]

He was fortunate to have left when he did. The Peace of Amiens was under strain, and broke down completely when on 22 May 1803 Napoleon decreed all British men between 18 and 60 were to be imprisoned. Safely in London, Hazlitt sent Mr Railton his copies and gave Northcote that of Titian's Ippolito. His old friend crowed over the image for weeks.

CHAPTER 5

*All country-people hate each other. . . . There
is nothing good to be had in the country, or, if
there is, they will not let you have it.*

Hazlitt, review of Wordsworth, *The Excursion*[1]

COLERIDGE eventually finished speaking and gazed expectantly round the table. Godwin, whose house it was, turned to his guests. The man in the frock coat, Charles Lamb, leant forward: his former schoolfriend had just discoursed on 'man as he was, or man as he is to be'—one of the catchphrases of the moment, often in the mouths of those inclined to radical causes.

Reddening slightly, Lamb exclaimed: 'Give me . . . give me man as he is *not* to be!'[2] There was a moment's silence, and the company fell about, helpless with laughter. Lamb brought them back to earth with wit and grace, and Godwin's guests could now enjoy themselves without any obligation to respond to Coleridge's oration.

It was the beginning of a beautiful friendship. Three years Hazlitt's senior, Lamb had a strange history. He had not gone to University partly due to bouts of mental instability severe enough to require incarceration. Instead he took a clerical job with the East India Company, one of the biggest trading concerns in London, where he remained until retirement. Yet his existence was anything but humdrum: returning home on the afternoon of Thursday 22 September 1796, he found his mother stretched out on the floor in a pool of blood, lifeless; his father stumbling around the dining room with a serving fork protruding from his forehead; and his sister Mary whimpering quietly to herself. Her shaking hand gripped a knife and was covered in blood. She had gone crazy, murdering their mother and severely injuring their father. Lamb would never forget the 'day of horrors'.

He kept a cool head. Aware he could save his sister from life in a mental institution, he promised the authorities he would nurse her at home for the rest of his life, placing her under professional supervision if further episodes threatened. He remained true to his word for the rest of his life. It was a sacrifice born of love.

Though Lamb and Hazlitt did not meet before the dinner-party of Tuesday 22 March 1803,[3] they must have heard of each other through Coleridge and Godwin, who had known both for years.[4] Indeed, Lamb visited Coleridge at Nether Stowey in 1797 and was the addressee of 'This Lime-Tree Bower My Prison', which Hazlitt had read. If the character in the poem seemed earnest, Hazlitt was happy to be disabused. Not only was Lamb willing to prod one of the lions of literary London but, as Hazlitt soon found, his sense of humour respected no one's *amour propre*. This was the sort of companion to whom he warmed and, despite occasional hiatuses, they remained close to the end, meeting regularly to smoke, drink, and talk into the small hours. Lamb once described himself thus: 'I want individuals. I am made up of queer points and I want so many answering needles.'[5] Hazlitt was the ideal needle to Lamb's 'queer point'.[6]

A few days later Coleridge decided to take Hazlitt in hand and manage his career, though his motives were not entirely pure. It was clear that Hazlitt was a man of greater substance than Coleridge first realized: what better way of keeping him in his place than to administer his job applications? In June, Coleridge wrote to Godwin, asking whether he could find a publisher for an abridgement of Abraham Tucker's obscure philosophical epic, *The Light of Nature Pursued*, which Hazlitt would distil from seven volumes to a few hundred pages—a feat of mind-numbing tedium. It would serve as a platform for Coleridge, who would write an introduction; the abridger, Coleridge puffed, was 'a young man of profound Genius and original mind, who wishes to get his *Sabine* Subsistence by some Employment from the Booksellers, while he is employing the remainder of his Time in nursing up his Genius for the destiny which he believes appurtenant to it.'[7] This pompous endorsement led nowhere, at least for the moment, and it is not clear whether Godwin even knew to whom it referred. But it suggests Hazlitt had resumed work on his metaphysical manuscript, which Tucker influenced.[8] Hazlitt found his writing skills had improved, and the draft on which he was working began to grow into *An Essay on the Principles of Human Action*.

During the spring of 1803, Coleridge met Sir George Beaumont, art patron and landscape painter, who at first detested him. But they met again in June, this time at Keswick, where Coleridge was now resident. Beaumont began by thinking 'how He should shun Him',[9] but was slowly won round by the excitable speaker, who despite increasing drug addiction had lost none of his charm. By the end of their second encounter, Beaumont was so taken by him that he had agreed to commission Hazlitt to paint Coleridge's portrait.[10]

Years hence, Hazlitt said that 'The Lakes in the North of England are not picturesque, though certainly the most interesting sight in this country'[11]—such was the equivocation he felt towards Cumbria and its denizens. But at the time of his first visit, he fell in love with it. As long before as 1769 Thomas Gray described 'the repose of this little unsuspected paradise';[12] more recently, Coleridge and Wordsworth had become tourist attractions in their own right. The author of a guide in 1802 enthused over 'The animated, enthusiastic, and accomplished Coleridge whose residence at Keswick gives additional charms and interest to its impressive scenery' and 'a kindred intellect, his friend and neighbour at Grasmere, Wordsworth'.[13]

The summons to paint Coleridge was prestigious not merely because of the man paying for it, but for the sitter's renown. As part of his duties, Hazlitt was expected to entertain Sir George and his wife when they dined with the Coleridges. What can the Beaumonts have made of the shy dropout who was to immortalize one of the finest intellects of the day? Not only was Hazlitt constitutionally incapable of flattery, but he would have declined to attempt it had a gun been placed at his temples. While his friends were fighting for their lives at the Treason Trials, Beaumont had been a Tory MP with zero tolerance for republicanism and regicides.

Coleridge, however, was adept at playing to an audience and, in order to impress his guests, launched into a vicious harangue against Junius. Hazlitt heard him do this during their walking-tour of 1798,[14] so it was not a complete shock. But on this occasion Coleridge was more declamatory than usual, aware that his past required some energetic whitewashing.

'Junius? He cannot manage a long sentence; whenever he tries it, his style degenerates into inelegance and cumbrousness!' The Beaumonts nodded sagely over their claret. 'His antitheses are false. At worst, he combines sneer and irony with such gross violation of good sense as to be perfectly nauseous!'[15] More nodding.

Hazlitt listened in silence as Coleridge condemned a writer whose cadences he regarded as sacred. When he shut his eyes he imagined Coleridge's triumphant glance about the table. He could envisage Lady Beaumont applauding him with her dainty, lace-covered hands. He could hear Sir George barking

'Hear, hear!' It was too much. He exploded, catching Coleridge in mid-sentence and defending Junius's 'felicities of style, turns of expression, and refinements of thought and feeling'.[16] He had walked straight into it. The evening did not last much longer. There were cleared throats, an embarrassed silence, and a shuffling of feet. The Beaumonts bade their farewells and left. Hazlitt had committed an unforgivable offence against his host in the presence of honoured guests—guests who, moreover, were his patrons. Beaumont would not seek out Mr Hazlitt's services a second time, nor (so far as we know) did he ever speak to him again.

Hazlitt was still in bed when, next morning, there came a knock at the door. It was Coleridge. 'Good morning!' he cried, throwing a book onto the counterpane. 'I am come to show you how foolish it is for persons who respect each other to dispute warmly—for, after all, they will probably think the same!'[17] Hazlitt sleepily opened his eyes. He picked the book up and examined the title page: it was Coleridge's copy of *Junius's Letters*, its pages 'full of expressions of admiration, from which it appeared that Coleridge himself really agreed with Hazlitt.'[18] Knowing from their conversations in Somerset that Hazlitt would not tolerate his attacks, Coleridge staged the previous night's drama as a means of displaying to a Tory benefactor the extent to which he had renounced his radical past. He thus enhanced his eligibility as Beaumont's pensioner at Hazlitt's expense.

This was a harbinger of what would eventually tear them apart. Coleridge was prepared to say almost anything to win the favour of those whose opinions he despised. Hoping to secure Beaumont's long-term assistance, he sent him lengthy screeds claiming to have 'detested Revolutions in my calmer moments'.[19] Hazlitt by contrast was ready to go to the scaffold for his principles, and remained true to them till the day he died. Nor would he stand idly by while others laid them waste. If he failed his religious ideals, he always remained loyal to his political ones.

In the studio, Hazlitt placed Coleridge against a dark background like one of Titian's Italian statesmen. The likeness, he explained, was secondary: he wanted to create 'a fine Picture'.[20] Suddenly, the job but half-finished, he declared his intention of painting Wordsworth's picture, packed, and left for Grasmere. Why? In all likelihood, his humiliation before the Beaumonts rankled, and a break from Coleridge was the only way of containing himself. 'You would be as much astonished by Hazlitt's coming, as I at his going', Coleridge told Wordsworth.[21]

Part II: Beyond Xanadu

Hazlitt had not seen Wordsworth since 1798, and they may not have spoken since the philosophical argument which ended when Wordsworth told him his 'metaphysical discovery' was 'what every shoemaker must have thought of'. Here was a chance for them to re-establish their friendship. By now, Hazlitt was an enthusiastic admirer of *Lyrical Ballads* which in 1801 was republished as a two-volume work, incorporating poems written in Germany and the Lake District, along with a lengthy Preface that spelt out its egalitarian aims: 'Low and rustic life was generally chosen because in that condition the essential passions of the heart find a better soil in which they can attain their maturity, are less under restraint, and speak a plainer and more emphatic language.'[22] Hazlitt would have recognized this as the agenda of 'The Recluse', a new kind of poetry designed not only to discuss the lives of working people but to speak directly to them. Hazlitt did not care that Wordsworth had spoken slightingly of his own ideas; he was convinced of his greatness as a poet and was certain he would yet change the world for the better. Perhaps Wordsworth felt awkward about their last encounter, and wanted to make up for it—or perhaps Dorothy persuaded him to do so. At all events, he agreed to sit for Hazlitt, and the artist journeyed twelve miles south to the vale of Grasmere.[23]

Wordsworth and Dorothy had been at Dove Cottage since returning from Germany in 1799, and the poet had just become a family man: his first son, Johnny, was born on 18 June, and Hazlitt met the child and its mother in an upstairs room. As the baby slumbered in Mary Wordsworth's arms, not yet baptized, her husband told Hazlitt it was impossible not to take pleasure in the sight, to admire it even.

'Admire? That's a strange word. Why admire?' asked Hazlitt.

'There is a grandeur in it', replied Wordsworth. 'The child knows nothing of the ills of life, and that unconsciousness is the germ that implies future good to the world—an untouched, untold treasure.' Here in a nutshell was the urge behind Wordsworth's poetry—to return the world to the childlike state from which evil had been purged.[24]

In the five years since last they met, Wordsworth had written some of his greatest verse including *The Two-Part Prelude*, part of which he agreed to recite. He was famously protective of this poem during his lifetime. *The Prelude* went unpublished until after his death, and the two-part version, now considered by many the best, did not appear in print until 1979. Hazlitt was one of a few contemporaries who saw 'the Poem on my own life'.[25]

[90]

> Ah! not in vain ye Beings of the hills!
> And ye that walk the woods and open heaths
> By moon or star-light, thus from my first dawn
> Of childhood did ye love to intertwine
> The passions that build up our human soul[26]

Hazlitt was swept away by Wordsworth's flowing lines, and remembered snatches of them for the rest of his life. He would refer to the 'building up of the human mind' in his *Essay on the Principles of Human Action*.[27] Wordsworth read also from his abandoned drama, *The Borderers*, which contained the speech:

> Action is transitory, a step, a blow—
> The motion of a muscle—this way or that—
> 'Tis done—and in the after vacancy
> We wonder at ourselves like men betray'd.
> Suffering is permanent, obscure and dark,
> And has the nature of infinity.[28]

The play was a curate's egg, but these lines made up for its shortcomings: Hazlitt was always to remember them as proof of Wordsworth's genius.[29] From both quotations it is clear he admired Wordsworth's understanding of the mind—not surprisingly, for Hazlitt's own philosophy was psychological in substance.

It was July, the sun beamed down on Wordsworth's cottage, lambs bleated in the fields, birds twittered, and Grasmere looked like the Paradise it had been to Gray. But in his makeshift studio, Hazlitt posed Wordsworth as if he were an undertaker. It was oppressive work, and one hot afternoon Hazlitt proposed a boating expedition on Grasmere Lake. Wordsworth had probably told him of William Gell, the artist whose boat he borrowed for occasional fishing expeditions.[30] The two men stepped on board and rowed out.

Politically they had something in common: both were republicans and had visited France during the Treaty of Amiens.[31] But there they parted company. Hazlitt revered Napoleon as a bulwark against the tyranny of kings; Wordsworth despised him as he did all despots.

> Happy is he who, caring not for Pope,
> Consul, or King, can sound himself to know
> The destiny of Man, and live in hope.[32]

So had Wordsworth declared in a sonnet published a few months before. And in October he would enlist in the Grasmere Volunteers when invasion threatened—something Hazlitt would never have done. Wordsworth detested *all* politicians.

'I would hang the entire House of Commons,' he declared. 'You remember Tierney, who fought Pitt in a duel? I wish he had shot out Pitt's tongue and put an end to his eloquence.'

Shocked, Hazlitt said that he was an admirer of Lords Chatham (Pitt's father) and Mansfield for the beauty of their speeches, though he agreed with neither.

'I see nothing to admire in their speeches,' Wordsworth snapped. 'And what did it all end in, but their being made Lords?'

Hazlitt had no more respect for lords than Wordsworth, but thought genius should be honoured wherever it was found. Knowing Wordsworth to be a Cambridge man, he praised Newton for his 'vast power of comprehension'. That a man should see an apple fall, and deduce 'the law that holds the universe together'[33]—was not that genius?

'He was a man of little mind, if we can believe the stories Coleridge has to tell about him.' Oh dear. Hazlitt moved onto what he hoped was safer ground. What of Shakespeare? There was a genius indeed!

'Shakespeare? There is something in the man I cannot make up my mind to, for I detest those interlocutions between Lucius and Caius.' Lucius and Caius? Wordsworth meant the conspirators in *Julius Caesar*. If he couldn't confess to an admiration for Shakespeare, what of Milton, on whose *Paradise Lost* he modelled his *Prelude*?

'Milton? The only merit of the *Paradise Lost* is in the conception or in getting rid of the horns and tail of the Devil—for, as to the execution, I could do as well or better myself.'[34] This was unbelievably arrogant, and for once Hazlitt found himself at a loss. Wordsworth came to his rescue. 'Chaucer—now there's a poet. I have rendered some of his *Canterbury Tales* for the modern reader. Do you know his *Troilus*?'[35] Hazlitt loved the *Tales*, and had read Dryden's translations of them; Wordsworth scoffed, condemning Dryden's Odes. As evidence he cited Bacchus in *Alexander's Feast*—'Flush'd with a purple Grace | He shews his honest Face'[36]—pointing out Dryden's error: 'Instead of presenting the god returning from his conquest of India, crowned with vine-leaves, drawn by panthers, and followed by troops of satyrs, wild men and animals he had tamed, he shows him as if he were merely a good-looking youth!'[37] Hazlitt had to laugh. 'Ingenious poets', Wordsworth continued, 'were of small and delicate frames, like Dryden and Pope; but the very greatest of them, such as Shakespeare and Milton, were healthy fellows, cast in a larger and handsomer mould.'

'So, I would wager, were Titian, Raphael, and Michelangelo,' countered Hazlitt.[38]

Now his mood had softened slightly, Wordsworth seemed less reluctant to enumerate those works he admired—Walton's *Compleat Angler*, Paley's *Moral Philosophy*, books of voyages and travels, and Daniel's 'To the Lady Margaret, Countess of Cumberland'.[39] What they had in common, it seemed to Hazlitt, was that they were 'of an inoffensive modesty of pretension',[40] posing Wordsworth no threat.

Hazlitt realized Wordsworth probably wanted to talk about his own poetry rather than others'. The second volume of *Lyrical Ballads*, published in early 1801, contained 'Poems on the Naming of Places', centred on parts of the Lake District with personal associations. 'Did you take that idea from *Paul and Virginia*?' he asked. It was an innocuous question. *Paul and Virginia* was a sentimental novel by Jacques de St Pierre which enjoyed success when translated in 1796; Wordsworth kept a copy at Dove Cottage.[41]

Wordsworth took this very badly indeed, denying the influence and claiming that his poems differed from *Paul and Virginia* in several respects, which he enumerated. As Hazlitt later observed, 'Any the slightest variation would be sufficient for this purpose in his mind; for whatever *he* added or omitted would inevitably be worth all that anyone else had done, and contain the marrow of the sentiment.'[42] With that outburst, Wordsworth turned back to shore, and their boating trip came to an abrupt end.

Where did this tension come from? It was not that Wordsworth nursed a particular dislike of Hazlitt—at least, not at this stage; De Quincey found the poet similarly unapproachable when he came to Grasmere five years later. The fact is, there was a patrician streak in Wordsworth who was in any case prickly in the company of other men. Brought up in the finest house in the prosperous market town of Cockermouth, Wordsworth regarded himself as Hazlitt's social superior and never acknowledged Hazlitt's intellectual achievement. Years later, he could not accept Hazlitt's right to review *The Excursion*, and despite not having read his books, stated that he 'had little imagination, and no wholesome or well regulated feeling. But for what he learned from Coleridge and Lamb, he never would have been listened to as a critic.'[43]

Hazlitt took refuge from his sitter in the comparatively welcoming company of Dorothy Wordsworth. He loved his own sister and was quite prepared to enjoy someone else's. But this was more than a repetition of the sibling relationship he enjoyed with Peggy, for it always had a slight frisson to it. Dorothy had liked Hazlitt ever since finding him at the door of Alfoxden House five years earlier, and now lost no time in showing him the fells of Grasmere, which she knew intimately. Perhaps, in her manner, there was a touch of flirtatiousness; even if there wasn't, Hazlitt's imagination was capable on its own of turning Dorothy into the seductress of his dreams. Having persuaded himself that her interest in him was more than that of a friend, he fell in love with her. It was not surprising. Although she was not a conventional beauty, Dorothy's kindly manner, acute intelligence, and sensitivity to others made her tremendously appealing to those who knew her. Out of sheer impulsiveness, he offered her his hand in marriage. 'No', she said. 'It is impossible. I am married to poetry.' It was true. She was devoted to her brother and his literary ambitions, and would never desert him. Hazlitt took rejection hard. Humiliated, he left for Manchester, promising to return in a few weeks' time. His passion for Dorothy left him frustrated, and he probably disappeared into the city's stews.[44]

During Hazlitt's absence, Coleridge was asked by Tom Wedgwood whether he could recommend the artist as a travelling companion. This was an opportunity to do both men a good turn as they would probably have liked each other, instead of which Coleridge warned Wedgwood against Hazlitt's 'singularly repulsive' manners—'brow-hanging, shoe-contemplative, *strange*'. On the other hand, he went on, Hazlitt liked children (probably an indication of how well he got on with Hartley), 'but he is jealous, gloomy, & of an irritable Pride— & addicted to women as objects of sexual Indulgence.' Having demolished any chance of the two men meeting, let alone travelling in each other's company, Coleridge made a show of listing Hazlitt's virtues, saying he was

> strangely confused & dark in his conversation & delivers himself of almost all his conceptions with a Forceps, yet he says more than any man I ever knew, yourself only excepted, that is his own in a way of his own—& oftentimes when he has warmed his mind, & the synovial juice has come out & spread over his joints, he will gallop for half an hour together with real Eloquence. He sends well-headed & well-feathered Thoughts straight forwards to the mark with a Twang of the Bow-string.

After all this, he had the gall to 'recommend him as a Portrait-painter'.[45] These remarks are taken at face value only by those unaware of their context.[46]

Chapter 5

They were written the day after Coleridge's return from a tour of Scotland with the Wordsworths whom he abandoned halfway through in order to go cold turkey—complete opium withdrawal. But the cure failed and Coleridge was left to contemplate 'The self-created Hell within', which he described as consisting of

> Deeds to be hid that were not hid,
> Which, all confus'd I might not know,
> Whether I suffer'd or I did:
> For all was Horror, Guilt & Woe,
> My own or others, still the same,
> Life-stifling Fear, Soul-stifling Shame![47]

By the time he returned to Keswick, Coleridge knew his life was a mess—his health irredeemably shattered; his talents unfulfilled; his love-life confused (besotted as he was with Wordsworth's sister-in-law, Sara Hutchinson).[48] In those circumstances the temptation to undermine Hazlitt was irresistible—out of spite and an anxiety to keep pretenders in their place.

On 23 July 1803 the United Irishmen attempted another Revolution, funded and organized by Robert Emmet, a Protestant from County Tipperary, from where Hazlitt's father also hailed. In fact, connections between the Hazlitt and Emmet families went back many years.[49] They were so close that when Emmet's invalid niece needed somewhere to live, Hazlitt's father took care of her for the rest of her life—no small gesture for a man on an irregular pension from the Presbyterian Fund.[50] So that when news of the rebellion broke, Hazlitt followed its progress.

Despite Emmet's careful preparation, it was a fiasco. He made a number of crucial mistakes, most obviously failing to raise popular support, and in the end was compelled to abandon his assault on Dublin Castle and go into hiding. Nonetheless, he and his colleagues managed to kill the Lord Chief Justice and several British soldiers, and the authorities resolved to track him down. They caught him in August and on 19 September he was sentenced to death in a show trial and executed next day. This had a powerful effect on radicals, not least because (like many of them) he was a well-connected, middle-class intellectual. It prompted Coleridge to write a hysterical letter to the Beaumonts, assuring them he was 'disgusted beyond measure by the manners & morals of the Democrats'.[51] Southey reacted less self-interestedly. He thought Emmet 'an admirable young man, of ardent genius, pure morals, &

martyr-like intrepidity'[52] and contributed an elegy to the Norwich newspaper, *The Iris.*[53]

These events weighed heavily on Hazlitt's mind when he returned to Cumbria in October—after all, he was Emmet's exact contemporary—and perhaps he hoped to talk them over with Coleridge. However, Coleridge was in no state to talk about anything except himself. Less than a week before Hazlitt's arrival, he celebrated his thirty-first birthday by scrawling in his notebook: 'O me! my very heart dies!—This *year* has been one painful Dream | I have done nothing!'[54] He had begun to realize he would never shake off the addiction that was shutting him down; he must take steps. The first concerned his old friend Robert Southey who (though he did not realize it) was about to take over the family Coleridge was preparing to abandon. When Hazlitt arrived, Southey and his wife had been resident at Greta Hall for several weeks, unaware they were to remain there for the rest of their lives. The next step was to secure a patron. Coleridge's addiction rendered him unfit for any profession, especially one in which regular deadlines had to be observed, and required an alternative income stream: the Beaumonts.

None of this was evident to Hazlitt when he arrived at Greta Hall on 23 October. So far as he was concerned, the Southeys were houseguests and Coleridge was publishing articles in the *Morning Post* as usual.[55] Doubtless he was surprised to find Southey there, but they always got on, and Coleridge proposed a ramble. The next day the three men walked along the western side of Derwentwater into Borrowdale, over Grange Fell to Watendlath, and then back up the eastern side of the lake to a 'late dinner'.[56] In the evening Southey entertained them by singing ballads, accompanying himself on the lute,[57] and they talked politics into the small hours. Southey felt as strongly as Hazlitt about Emmet, and revealed that 'I knew much of him from many conversations with his most intimate friend at Dublin. He was an admirable man. God Almighty seldom mixes up so much virtue & so much genius in the intellect as ennobled him.'[58] This would have led Hazlitt to reveal his own family connections with the Emmet family. Their conversations were congenial and enjoyable, and Southey concluded Hazlitt to be 'a man of real genius' and his portrait of Coleridge 'very fine'.[59]

The ostensible reason for Hazlitt's return was to finish the portraits—he could paint his subjects only when they were before him—and that was probably why Wordsworth visited Greta Hall on Wednesday 26 October. When Wordsworth's last sitting was over that evening, they sat down with Coleridge and debated the existence of God. Normally this would have been a reasonable pastime but in Coleridge's present condition it was ill-advised, to say the least. But there was little choice: Coleridge had been meditating the argument for several days. Shortly after arriving at Keswick, Hazlitt seems to have made a slighting reference to the Deity, provoking Coleridge's notebook description of Watendlath with the comment: 'O what is there on Earth that can better deserve the name of Divine?'[60] The three-cornered discussion with Wordsworth soon degenerated into what Coleridge later described as 'A most unpleasant Dispute'.[61] Wordsworth and Hazlitt, neither of whom subscribed to the creed espoused by Coleridge, spoke 'so irreverently so malignantly of the Divine Wisdom, that it overset me', he confided to his notebook.[62] Of his two antagonists, the most vociferous was Hazlitt who, recognizing Coleridge's references to 'the Divine Wisdom' as an insult, threw them back in his face. Coleridge consoled himself with pieties: 'Hazlitt how easily roused to Rage & Hatred, self-projected/but who shall find the Force that can drag him up out of the Depth into one expression of Kindness, into the shewing of one Gleam of the Light of Love on his Countenance.—Peace be with *him!*'[63] He was no less self-righteous when casting Wordsworth as Hazlitt's conspirator: 'Dear William, pardon Pedantry in others & avoid it in yourself, instead of scoffing & reviling at Pedantry in good men in a good cause, & *becoming* a Pedant yourself in a bad cause—even by that very act becoming one!'[64]

Coleridge was a hopelessly deluded man. At this time, most of his notebook jottings were made in the middle of the night during periods of wakefulness brought on by brandy and opium. Notes toward his great philosophical work had long been displaced by howls of self-loathing. As he moved into a phase of permanent illness he cast a younger, more promising talent (Hazlitt) as his tormentor in a drug-fuelled psychodrama, giving rise to fantasies of martyrdom: 'Hazlitt to feelings of Anger & Hatred Phosphorous—it is but to open the Cork, & it flames—but to Love & serviceable Friendship, let them, like Nebuchadnezzer, heat the Furnace with a 7 fold Heat, this Triune Shadrach, Meshach, Abednego, will shiver in the midst of it.'[65]

Hours after writing those words, Coleridge sat for his portrait on the morning of Thursday 27 October. Hazlitt assumed the previous day's argument was over but in Coleridge's frenzied imagination it continued, fixated as he was on Hazlitt's godless philosophy.[66] If his notebooks are anything to go by, it would appear that during the sitting Coleridge burst into a rant, whether out loud or in his head, concerning 'the whole business of the Origin of Evil'.[67] Nor did his disturbed state resolve itself, for having retired to bed after tea he woke up screaming in the middle of the night, continuing even after his wife tried to calm him. The entire household awoke in terror, including the children. The next day Coleridge was unable to drop his obsessive thoughts about 'the Question of Evil',[68] which produced a self-justifying note that asked (apparently with reference to Hazlitt): 'Is this the metaphysics that bad Spirits in Hell delight in?'[69]

His true anxiety was the knowledge that Hazlitt would surpass him. Five years earlier, Coleridge had the potential to be a great poet, political pamphleteer, philosopher, and preacher. Opium addiction and his own natural indolence had since thwarted that promise, and it was as much as he could do to stifle competitors. Hazlitt was the one who threatened him most. Coleridge knew Hazlitt was close to finishing his *Essay* and publication could not be far off. What had *he* achieved?

These tensions were broken by an event no one could have foreseen. Hazlitt had taken to visiting the local tavern, eager to escape Greta Hall, and one evening found himself in close quarters with a girl who teased him with promises of sex. When he responded in what he thought the appropriate manner, she slapped him down with the taunt: 'You're a black-faced rascal, sir!' The entire tavern burst into laughter, ribald remarks shot across the room, and Hazlitt was made 'the laughing-stock of the village'.[70] His reaction was characteristic. He threw her over his knee, lifted her petticoats, and spanked her on the bottom.[71]

The peasantry of the Lakes, then as now, was tight-knit: they were unlikely to tolerate any such action by an outsider. Hazlitt was lucky to get out of the building, and probably subjected to physical violence in the process. He ran the half mile to Greta Hall, where he explained what had happened to Coleridge and Southey.[72] To him it was hardly worth bothering about, but Coleridge took a different view: a gang had already formed to give Hazlitt a ducking, soon to arrive at their door.[73] He would arrange to get him out of harm's way. There was no time to pack, and Hazlitt left his possessions, including his painting materials and the portraits. Coleridge later claimed to have given him 'all the money I had in the world, and the very Shoes off my feet, to enable him to escape over the mountains'.[74]

They smuggled him out of Keswick, probably with the aid of a servant, and Hazlitt reached Dove Cottage around midnight, leaving his pursuers no clue as to his whereabouts. Wordsworth worried about harbouring a fugitive from a ducking-party, but the man at his door was filthy, exhausted, and in no shape to continue. He let him in and found him a dry, warm place in which to sleep. Early next morning, while still dark, he gave him clothes and money,[75] and set him on the Ambleside road. Hazlitt would never return.

At the time this incident was not seriously regarded by anyone who knew of it.[76] Their attitude was akin to that of Lamb who referred to 'The "scapes" of the great god Pan...and his narrow chance of being submerged by the swains'.[77] But that did not stop it being used as ammunition by enemies, who unfortunately came to number Wordsworth and Coleridge. This was hypocrisy. Throughout his life Wordsworth kept secret the illegitimate daughter he abandoned in France, while Coleridge remained tight-lipped about his dealings with prostitutes at Cambridge. They never admitted to 'beastly appetites', though they were no less subject to them than Hazlitt. Critics in our own time have followed suit, invoking the affair of the 'Keswick rapist' as if Hazlitt were a uniquely depraved example of human sexuality. In some respects this is a function of class: why else could it be that for Lord Byron, Lady Caroline Lamb, and Georgiana, Duchess of Devonshire, their love-lives remain elemental to their appeal? The fact is that Hazlitt was remarkable less for his sexual appetite than for the honesty with which he wrote about it. It is a sad reflection on us that we continue to use his candour to repudiate him. Sexual need is, after all, a trait we share. Hazlitt's crime was to bring to light things his contemporaries preferred to deny—a tribute to both his courage and modernity.

In time, Hazlitt was made uneasy by the episode. Had there really been reason for him to leave Greta Hall at dead of night? He had only Coleridge's word for it. As the months passed, and he waited vainly for a show of friendship from Coleridge, it began to dawn on him that he had been humiliated unnecessarily. Feelings of hurt hardened into suspicions of malice, which in turn gave rise to doubts as to whether Coleridge was anything other than a self-esteeming windbag.

As for the portraits of that summer, neither have come down to us, and their true qualities remain unknown. One thing is for sure: they were not appreciated. Of his portrait, Coleridge noted that 'Every single person without one exception cries out!—What a likeness!—but the face is too long! you have a round face!'[78] Some thought it made him look twenty years older than he really was.[79] Wordsworth thought it a respectable likeness, albeit 'dolorous and funereal',[80] a judgement that may have had something to do with the manner adopted by Hazlitt, who remembered Coleridge's face to have had 'a purple tinge as we see it in the pale and thoughtful complexions of the Spanish portrait-painters, Murillo and Velasquez'.[81] Wordsworth later revised his opinion, referring to the portrait as 'not producible for fear of fatal consequence to married Ladies, but [it] is kept in a private room, as a special treat to those who may wish to sup upon horrors.'[82] Southey taunted the sitter by saying he looked as if he were on trial 'and certainly had stolen the horse; but then you did it cleverly,—and it had been a deep, well-laid scheme, and it was no fault of yours that you had been detected.'[83] Last sighted in 1938, its present whereabouts is unknown.[84]

The portrait of Wordsworth attracted mixed opinions. Hartley Coleridge saw the likeness immediately but thought the poet 'far handsomer', while Mary Stamper, the Coleridges' maid, said, 'It is very *leek*; but it is not canny enough— though Mr Wordsworth is not a canny man, to be sure.'[85] It was the brooding, Titianesque pose that flummoxed most viewers. One person thought its subject looked as if he were 'at the gallows—deeply affected by his deserved fate—yet determined to die like a man'.[86] Walking into the room in which it was hung, Wordsworth's pious brother Richard shrieked 'God zounds!'—for 'never, till that moment, had he conceived that so much of the diabolical lurked under the innocent features of his quondam playmate'.[87] Wordsworth paid Hazlitt three guineas and took ownership of it. Supposing its 'diabolical' aspects to be the artist's invention, he had by 1816 consigned it to the flames.[88] Years later, in a letter to Hazlitt's son, he declared airily that 'I sat to him, but as he did not satisfy himself or my friends, the unfinished work was destroyed.'[89]

CHAPTER 6

*There are but few authors who should marry: they are
already wedded to their studies and speculations.*

Hazlitt, *Aphorisms on Man*[1]

T HE year 1804 brought sad news of old friends. Halfway through February
the Hazlitts heard of Joseph Fawcett's death at the age of 46, probably
from alcoholism. The star turn of the Old Jewry had subsided into despair
when the Revolution failed. Perhaps Hazlitt saw the obituary in the *Gentleman's
Magazine*, which described him as 'an eccentric character'.[2] Wordsworth did,
and wrote saying so: 'I was sorry to see from the Papers that your Friend poor
Fawcett was dead; not so much that he was dead but to think of the manner
in which he had sent himself off before his time.'[3] It was later proposed that
Hazlitt write his biography—a Fawcettiad, as Lamb put it—but that was not to
be.[4] Instead Wordsworth portrayed him in *The Excursion* as the Solitary, whose
life was blighted by disillusionment.[5] That was not how his friends remembered
him, and Hazlitt put the record straight when describing him as 'one of the most
enthusiastic admirers of the French Revolution'.[6]

A month later came more bad tidings: the death of Joseph Priestley in
America, an exile since leaving Britain in 1794.[7] This was the greater loss, at
least to Hazlitt's father and his generation. Their leading light throughout years
of bigotry was extinguished. Had all their hard work come to nothing? So it
must have seemed.

In the midst of these reminders of mortality, Hazlitt felt a peculiar exal-
tation, for he had completed his first book. Years before, he cried with the
humiliation of not being able to articulate himself. But he had worked unceas-
ingly and now had a manuscript with which he was satisfied. No literary
task would ever be so challenging. The finished text, which elucidated his
secular hopes for humanity, was a kind of apologia to his father for his failure to become a minister, and the Reverend Hazlitt was the first to read it.

Thrilled on his son's behalf, he urged that he travel to London and find a publisher.

When summer arrived, Hazlitt visited his brother and wife at their new house in Great Russell Street at the heart of Bloomsbury, where they were bringing up their young daughter, Harriet. He lodged in a corner of the studio and knocked on the doors of publishers, none of whom were interested in something called *An Essay on the Principles of Human Action*. Eventually John suggested he speak to Godwin—still at the Polygon in Somers Town, barely twenty minutes' walk away[8]—who was better connected in the publishing world than anyone else he knew. From this period onwards, Hazlitt was a frequent visitor to Godwin's home, where he became familiar with the entire family which at this time included the six-year-old Mary Shelley. Unlike Coleridge, Godwin seems to have ruled his children with a rod of iron, for they would sit in the drawing room in a state of 'cadaverous Silence'[9] while the adults talked. At all events, Godwin was the ideal person to consult, for Hazlitt had in his sights one of his oldest friends, the publisher Joseph Johnson.

When Godwin heard Hazlitt's request, he sighed a long and dolorous sigh, being enough of a businessman to realize this was the last thing Johnson needed. Now in his sixty-sixth year (a year younger than Hazlitt's father), Johnson was in precarious health, no longer the young Turk he had been when he opened his shop nearly five decades earlier. Nothing could be less appealing than a book of philosophical musings by a complete unknown. However, Hazlitt told Godwin, he had one advantage: Johnson *did* know who he was, having retailed his father's writings since 1766.

On 31 July 1804 Godwin visited Johnson's shop in St Paul's Churchyard to offer him Hazlitt's *Essay*. At first Johnson kept him waiting, finally summoning him upstairs to the L-shaped room where once he had thrown weekly dinners for his writers. The cream of dissenting culture had passed through its portals, including Godwin's late wife Mary Wollstonecraft, the eccentric engraver and poet William Blake, and the equally strange visionary artist Henry Fuseli.

'What can I do for you, Godwin?' From the look on his face Johnson knew the answer: he wanted a favour. Godwin knew better than to argue that the world was waiting for a new philosophical opus from a first-time author and began by reminding him of the Hazlitt name.

'What of it?' asked Johnson.

'There is a son, a philosopher', explained Godwin.

[102]

Fig. 11. William Godwin, painted by his friend James Northcote in 1802. Godwin acted as Hazlitt's literary agent at the outset of his career, urging Joseph Johnson to publish his first book.

Johnson remembered Hazlitt Sr with respect, and probably recalled that his son was the first of the Hackney dropouts. Whether or not he made that connection, he continued to listen. The *Essay* was written, so there would be no wait for copy, and it could be published in a small edition that would minimize the risk. Johnson could afford to take risks: four years hence he would die worth £60,000, an enormous sum for the time. Godwin had high regard for the publisher, describing him not long after as 'the only bookseller upon whose unalterable integrity I have reason to place the most perfect reliance.'[10] Perhaps, as he argued Hazlitt's case, he flattered Johnson a little, but it is equally likely he did not need to do so. Johnson had come into the publishing business with a sincere desire to help dissenters expound ideas which the establishment found offensive. As he listened to Godwin, he realized that there were principled reasons for publishing this obscure volume by the neophyte Hazlitt. He agreed to take the *Essay*, providing its author agreed that publishing expenses be met before sharing out of profits. In effect, Hazlitt was asked to waive income from the book, as sales were unlikely to cover costs: he did not hesitate, aware he was lucky to get into print at all.

But Johnson was slow to put it into production and, for the time being, Hazlitt set aside thoughts of authorial fame and cast around for more sitters. He soon found one in Charles Lamb, who came regularly to John Hazlitt's studio after work. This brought him into contact with the Hazlitt family, especially young Harriet Hazlitt, with whom he got on well. She became so fond of him as to approach complete strangers with the words, 'Mr Lamb is coming to see me!'[11] Charles brought his sister with him, and together they laughed and joked with her. This helps explain the series of childrens' books the Lambs produced during this period, including their *Tales from Shakespeare* (1806), which has never been out of print.[12] These were Hazlitt's first meetings with Mary Lamb, whom he reckoned the 'one reasonable woman' he ever knew.[13]

For the portrait, Lamb dressed as a Venetian senator against a dark background—intended by the artist to be a brooding, Titianesque pose.[14] Each time he arrived, Lamb donned a black cloak with red silk lining and did his utmost to submit to the command that he 'Adopt a magisterial manner!' A whimsical, self-deprecating man, Lamb was utterly unsuited to this, and the expression Hazlitt gave him speaks not of the dark eminence of the Medici but of Lamb's good humour—as if the model were indulging the artist's pretensions.[15]

The portrait was completed as a new career beckoned: *An Essay on the Principles of Human Action* was published by Johnson on 19 July 1805. It established its author as a force to be reckoned with, at least for anyone who bothered to read it. There were not many. Johnson printed 250 copies, most of which remained in his warehouse.[16] Hazlitt made nothing from it,[17] but would always cherish it as containing 'an important metaphysical discovery, supported by a continuous and severe train of reasoning nearly as subtle and original as anything in Hume or Berkeley.'[18] It led him to construct a theory of psychology and aesthetics that informed everything that followed. Copies were sent to friends, including Coleridge, who was now in the Mediterranean attempting a last-ditch cure for his addiction. Readers included Wordsworth (who said it was the only book of Hazlitt's he ever read[19]), James Mackintosh, and James Scarlett.[20] Scarlett, who would eventually rise to become Attorney General and first Lord Abinger, wrote to the author, complimenting him. Anyone in Hazlitt's shoes would have sniffed the prospect of a patron but his father intervened, warning that 'his new correspondent had sinister designs upon his liberty of action'.[21] Scarlett may claim to be a Whig, argued the Reverend Hazlitt, but his instincts were Tory.[22] This may seem overscrupulous, even priggish, but it was true to the hard line taken by both Hazlitts on matters of patronage. They believed it was impossible to accept the assistance of a political enemy without compromising one's hard-won principles.

Hazlitt was beginning to see himself as a writer, and enjoyed working with printers and publishers. For his part, Johnson took a shine to the awkward young man in whom he saw echoes of Hazlitt Sr's dogged determination. With a favourable word from him, Hazlitt began another volume—the abridgement of Tucker's *Light of Nature Pursued* proposed by Coleridge two years earlier. At that time, Coleridge probably hoped Hazlitt would not emerge from a task that combined editorial drudgery with intellectual exertion on a Herculean scale, but the manuscript flowed from Hazlitt's pen and was done 'quicker, and with less trouble, than I expected'.[23]

It was completed at Wem, where he returned for the new year of 1806, which began with news of Napoleon's greatest triumph. Victory at Austerlitz on 2 December 1805 brought the third coalition to an end with the simultaneous defeat of the Russian and Austrian armies. *The Times* reported it on 30 December, and its dispatch was reprinted in regional newspapers on New Year's Eve. Hazlitt was thrilled. He hoped Napoleon's victory would herald future French success, compelling Britain to sue for peace. He would never forget the day he heard the news: 'I walked out in the afternoon and, as I returned, saw the evening star set over a poor man's cottage with other thoughts and feelings than I shall ever have again. Oh for the revolution of the great Platonic year, that those times might come over again!'[24] Hazlitt was not alone in supporting Napoleon. Although other republicans such as Wordsworth had decided that in crowning him Emperor the French were like 'the dog | Returning to his vomit',[25] others (including Thelwall and Godwin) regarded Napoleon as the Revolution's last hope.

Hazlitt's exultant mood may have been influenced by the first review of his *Essay* which appeared at that moment in the *Annual Review*, praising 'the acuteness, discrimination, and *analytical* talent, which are stamped upon every page of his work'.[26] Unfortunately that was the exception to the rule; other reviewers thought it an 'innocent absurd little essay', 'wearisomely protracted'.[27] With that, Hazlitt's first book disappeared—not quite 'still-born from the press', as he later claimed,[28] but near enough. It was a shame: philosophers have since noted that 'had Hazlitt's views on personal identity received the attention they deserved, the *philosophical* discussion of personal identity may well have leaped ahead 150 years and the *psychological* discussion have been significantly advanced'.[29]

He sent the manuscript of the *Abridgement* to Godwin on 5 January 1806, asking him to extract a decision, one way or the other, from Johnson.[30] The old publisher proved less than forthcoming. When Godwin visited his shop he 'would not come down, or give any answer, but has promised to open the manuscript & to give you an answer in one month'.[31] This turned out to be optimistic. Returning four weeks later, Godwin discovered there had been a fire at the publishers' which delayed a decision further. Hazlitt remained in Wem, where Lamb sent regular news of goings-on in town, including the preparations made for Nelson's funeral and a racy new travel-book—James Bruce's *Travels to the Source of the Nile*: 'he's a fine dashing fellow & intrigues with Empresses & gets into Harams of Black Women, & was himself descended from the Kings of Scotland'.[32] As the weeks passed, Hazlitt's continuing residence in Wem was becoming less explicable, for he was missing the paintings that passed through the salerooms, an interest he shared with Lamb. 'What do you in Shropshire', Lamb asked on 15 March, 'when so many fine pictures are a going a going every day in London?'[33]

The answer was that he was writing, now in the midst of his first sustained political pamphlet, addressed to the Ministry of All the Talents formed after Pitt's death the previous month. Entitled *Free Thoughts on Public Affairs*, it attacked Pitt's administration of the war and pleaded with Fox, now Foreign Secretary, to make peace with Napoleon. Hazlitt felt strongly about this: as he saw it, Napoleon had safeguarded the advances of the Revolution. The rest of Europe was run by a network of robber barons and gangsters, but Napoleon was a man of the people, the product of egalitarian ideals. Were Fox to settle with him, France would have the potential to become the first European democracy of modern times. (Alas, Fox would die in September having done little more than propose the bill for the abolition of the slave trade.)

When his manuscript was ready, Hazlitt hastened to London to find a publisher. Godwin had by now set up his own bookshop in Hanway Street, the narrow lane that still runs between Oxford Street and Tottenham Court Road, from where he published a range of titles, and sold stationery, paper, ink, paints, cards, maps, puzzles, and toys. In the third week of May 1806 Hazlitt visited Godwin and offered him the pamphlet for publication. Godwin ushered him quickly into the back room and told him he wanted nothing to do with it. Cowed by poverty, intimidated by the abuse of political opponents,[34] the philosopher was terrified of getting into further trouble with the Government. He and his second wife, Mary Jane, had a growing family. All he wanted was to raise them as quietly as he could. He even employed a stooge, one Thomas Hodgkins, to manage the shop on his behalf, lest his involvement goad the Government into closing it down. 'Therefore I cannot help you,' said Godwin to his young friend. Seeing the look of disappointment on Hazlitt's face, he offered him a suggestion: 'If you have the money to pay for its printing yourself, you don't need a publisher. All you need is a printer and a willing bookseller.'[35] He then offered his young friend a piece of information that would prove an enormous help—the name and address of Richard Taylor.

Taylor had for years been printer of choice to the dissenting community in London, working from his premises in Shoe Lane, on the north side of Fleet Street.[36] Hazlitt would work closely with him on a series of publications, spending long hours in the printing house with Taylor's compositors. Taylor ran off 250 copies of *Free Thoughts on Public Affairs*,[37] on sale by 2 July when it was advertised in the *Morning Chronicle*. There were fewer takers than for the *Essay* and it attracted no reviews.[38]

If Hazlitt's second book earned its author neither money nor fame, it did bring an unexpected dividend in the form of association with its proof-reader-in-chief, Charles Lamb, of whom Hazlitt saw more than ever. Together they toured the taverns and brothels of the West End, staying out late into the night.[39] Mary believed her brother liked Hazlitt better than anyone (except their old friend Thomas Manning, who was in China).[40] Charles and William had a good deal in common. They were about the same age (Lamb being just three years Hazlitt's senior) and unlike most of their acquaintances had missed out on university, both being of a dissenting background. Most important of all, they were temperamentally well suited to one another, sufficiently relaxed to argue, rant, shout, and get drunk without either taking offence.

It was at this moment that the Lambs introduced Hazlitt to a new acquaintance. Sarah Stoddart was sister to one of Hazlitt's old acquaintances from Gray's Inn, John Stoddart, who had shed his former Jacobinism to become King's Advocate in Malta. Sarah had lived there with her brother for several years but had recently returned to find a husband in London. Aged thirty-one (three and a half years Hazlitt's senior), she knew time was running out if she was to have children. She already knew Hazlitt's brother, John, and had heard many good things from the Lambs about his shy younger sibling.[41]

She had a lot going for her. A fluent French-speaker, she admired Rousseau (whom she read in the original) and among the possessions she brought back from Malta was a commonplace book containing the poetry of Campbell, Susanna Blamire, Scott, Lamb, and Coleridge (whose 'Christabel' she knew by heart).[42] She was 'a remarkable and learned woman, and one whose society was sought'.[43] Her character could not have been further removed from that of her disciplined, ambitious, worldly brother, for besides having a good sense of humour, she was plain-spoken and direct,[44] fun-loving and slightly eccentric— which endeared her to the Lambs. 'She is one of the few people who are not in the way when they are with you,' Charles told William.[45] Her habits included that of 'pouring her tea into her saucer, which scandalized more strait-laced folks'.[46] That would have been quite acceptable to the Lambs, who probably followed suit. And Charles would have been pleased to find a woman who shared his enjoyment of alcohol. An old family story describes how as children the Stoddarts were offered grog by their father.[47] 'John, will you have some?', asked Stoddart Sr. 'No thank you, father,' responded the future King's Advocate of Malta. 'What about you, Sarah, will you?' 'Yes please, father!', she answered.[48] Even her grandson saw the implication, commenting: 'Not that she ever indulged to excess, but she was *that sort of woman*'[49]—by which I think he meant, quite simply, that she enjoyed a convivial drink with friends, again something that can only have endeared her to the Lambs. This sort of thing would have shocked her brother, who in later years felt impelled to lecture her against 'Extravagance, Dissipation & Taudriness ... coarseness, Rusticity & vulgarity',[50] and would recount with horror her gin binges late into the night with Hazlitt.[51]

Mary Lamb wrote to Sarah to reveal that Hazlitt 'is in town, I believe you have heard us say we like him.'[52] This was far from innocent—she knew Sarah was on the prowl—but they did not take to each other immediately. For one thing, she was unimpressed by tales of Hazlitt's bachelor escapades. She certainly heard about the debauch following the acceptance of Lamb's farce, *Mr. H——*, by the management of Drury Lane. When Lamb and Hazlitt returned late from the fleshpots of Sadler's Wells that night, Mary 'gave them both a good scolding—*quite a setting to rights*', as she boasted to Sarah.[53] (Comically, Mary seems to have thought that a telling-off from her was all that was required to reform their morals.) And perhaps Charles told Sarah about the summer evening when he and Hazlitt went to 'see a very pretty girl'. In fact, they were met by two pretty girls who 'neither laughed nor sneered nor giggled nor whispered'. Hazlitt's response was to frown 'blacker & blacker indignant that there should be such a thing as Youth & Beauty, till he tore me away before supper in perfect misery & owned he could not bear young girls. They drove him mad.'[54]

During the summer Hazlitt renewed his friendship with Henry Crabb Robinson, the young lawyer he had known in the late 1790s who had just returned from the University of Jena, where he had befriended Goethe, Schiller, the Schlegels, and Madame de Staël. Robinson and Hazlitt lunched together on 10 June and spent the evening at the house of Thomas Clarkson with the Lambs.[55] Though defeated in 1791, the bill to abolish the slave trade was about to be presented once more to Parliament, and Clarkson was travelling far and wide in an effort to lobby ministers. Those at his house that evening supported him. And they had something else in common: all of them knew Coleridge, from whom nothing had been heard for weeks. What condition was he in?[56] As they speculated, Lamb and Hazlitt amused the company with their witticisms; it was a pleasant evening. 'Mrs. Clarkson pretty well', Lamb later reported to Wordsworth. 'Mr. C. somewhat fidgety, but a good man.'[57]

There was another cause for celebration: Joseph Johnson suddenly decided to pay Hazlitt an advance of £80 for his *Abridgement*.[58] Why? Johnson had only just got round to reading Hazlitt's 'Introduction' to the volume and was struck immediately by its command. He saw that the informed book-buyer would acquire the *Abridgement* for that alone. This has not previously been reported, and it reveals that Johnson was the first London publisher to comprehend Hazlitt's potential as an author, to the extent of investing seriously in him. Even Hazlitt was amazed, and took encouragement from it. Eighty pounds was a larger sum than he had yet earned for his writing, and made it hard seriously to contemplate a painterly career. He burned to pursue another book project, and soon had the idea for one, which he took to Johnson. Collections of parliamentary speeches were at that moment doing good business. Wordsworth's sardonic remark that the entire House of Commons should be hanged gave Hazlitt the idea of compiling an anthology of 'greatest hits' (Burke, Sheridan, Pitt), interspersed with appreciative headnotes on their authors—one in the eye for the scoffer of Grasmere.

But who would publish? Not, on this occasion, Johnson, who may have thought the craze for political speeches was on the wane. Instead, Hazlitt consulted Henry Crabb Robinson, who introduced him to Anthony Robinson (no relation), a wealthy sugar refiner who had grown up in Cockermouth, the same town as Wordsworth. When Hazlitt realized this, he told Robinson about his less-than-satisfactory encounters with the poet, which drew from Robinson a series of indecent anecdotes which fuelled Hazlitt's scepticism of Wordsworth's ability to fulfil the promise he had shown in 1798.[59] Formerly a Baptist preacher, Robinson retained contacts in the dissenting community including the printer Thomas Ostell (a Quaker), who expressed interest in Hazlitt's idea.[60] Robinson put them in touch and, by 21 July 1806, Ostell had agreed to issue Hazlitt's *Eloquence of the British Senate*,[61] production of which was probably financed by Robinson.[62]

Coleridge returned to Britain on 17 August after a 55-day voyage spent in a state of permanent constipation, not eased by the application of no less than twelve enemas.[63] He did not tell his old friends he had arrived, instead wandering the streets of London listening to passers-by talk of blockades, food shortages, conscription, and unrest in the provinces. During his two-and-a-half-year absence the country had changed beyond recognition. He wandered down the Strand into Fleet Street before stopping at the Mitre Court doorway of his old friend Charles Lamb. He knocked on the door, which was opened to him. The man who entered was altered utterly from the one who sailed south nearly three years previously—and not for the better. Fat and inert, he displayed a deadness in the eyes, which had become lost in the pasty flesh, and his voice declaimed in a strange 'puppet' voice. He was sicker than ever, his body-chemistry permanently enslaved to opium.[64] It was as much as he could do to sit in the Lambs' parlour, slumped on an easy-chair, puffing mechanically on one of a large supply of cigars acquired on his travels.[65] Hazlitt heard as much from Lamb, but did not seek out his former mentor.

In November the Lambs instituted their 'Wednesdays'[66]—social evenings to which they invited a select few: besides Hazlitt, the musician William Ayrton, James White (Lamb's schoolfriend and author of the spoof volume *Falstaff's Letters*), Captain James Burney (brother of the novelist Fanny Burney and naval explorer), Burney's son Martin, John Rickman (who in 1801 conducted the first census), Edward Phillips (Rickman's clerk), and Elizabeth Reynolds, Lamb's old schoolteacher. On these evenings 'cribbage & pipes'[67] (card-games and tobacco) were the order of the day.

'Who would you wish to have seen?' Lamb began. Smoke hung in the air, glasses clinked, and everyone looked questioningly at everyone else. 'Who in history, I mean?'

Chapter 6

Ayrton started: 'I suppose the two first persons you would choose would be the two greatest names in English literature, Sir Isaac Newton and Mr Locke.' He gave a smug grin, at which everyone looked at Lamb.

'Yes', said Lamb, 'they are the greatest names, but not persons—not persons!'

'Not persons?' queried Ayrton, who feared his moment of triumph was about to pass.

'That is', continued Lamb, 'not *characters*, you know. By Mr Locke and Sir Isaac Newton, you mean the *Essay on the Human Understanding* and the *Principia*, which we have to this day. But beyond their contents there is nothing personally interesting in either of them. What we want to see anyone bodily for, is when there is something peculiar, striking in the individuals, more than we can learn from their writings, and yet are curious to know.'[68] This was Lamb's attitude to humanity in a nutshell. He was interested in people's oddities, not their intellectual prowess.

'I suppose', said Ayrton, downcast, '*you* would like Shakespeare or Milton?'

'No!' said Lamb. 'Neither! I've seen so much of Shakespeare on the stage and on bookstalls, in frontispieces and on mantelpieces, that I'm tired of the everlasting repetition. As to Milton's face, it is too starched and puritanical.'

'I shall guess no more,' said Ayrton, who was beginning to feel a bit of a fool. 'Who is it, then, you would like to see "in his habit as he lived", if you had your choice of the whole of English Literature?'

'Sir Thomas Browne and Fulke Greville', Lamb replied. 'I should like to encounter them in my apartment in their nightgown and slippers, and exchange friendly greeting with them!' This was a typically nutty Lambian comment— as if the appearance in nightgown and slippers of two equally eccentric literary personalities, long dead, were something to be sought after. Ayrton laughed, but he was the only one. 'The reason why I pitch upon these two', continued Lamb, 'is that their writings are riddles, and they themselves the most mysterious of personages. They resemble the soothsayers of old, who dealt in dark hints and doubtful oracles. And I should like to ask them the meaning of what no mortal but themselves can fathom.'

'What of Dr Johnson and Mr Boswell?' asked someone from the back of the room. 'Would not they be worthy dining companions?'

'No!' said Lamb, who was getting excited. 'I have no curiosity about the good doctor, no uncertainty about him, for he and Boswell have pretty well let me into the secret of what passed through their minds. He and other writers like him are sufficiently explicit.' This too was typical of Lamb and Hazlitt; for neither did Johnson and Boswell, despite their brilliance as writers, hold much interest. 'Browne and Greville, whose repose I should be tempted to disturb (were it in my power), are implicit, inextricable, inscrutable!' And then, to underline his point, Lamb quoted a couplet from Milton: 'And call up him who left half-told | The story of Cambuscan bold.' One of Lamb's favourite literary works was Browne's *Hydriotaphia. Urn-Burial; or, A Discourse of the Sepulchral Urns Lately Found in Norfolk* (1658), a bizarre volume if ever there was one, which used the discovery of bronze age tombs as the inspiration for a meditation on death and earthly fame. 'When I read that obscure but gorgeous prose composition the *Urn-Burial*', he declared, 'I seem to look into a deep abyss, at the bottom of which are hid pearls and rich treasure; or it is like a stately labyrinth of doubt and withering speculation, and I would invoke the spirit of the author to lead me through it. Besides, who would not be curious to see the face of a man who, having himself been married, wished that mankind were propagated like trees? As to Fulke Greville, he is like nothing but one of his own "Prologues spoken by the ghost of an old king of Ormus", a truly formidable and inviting personage. His style is apocalyptical, cabalistical, a knot worthy of such an apparition to untie; and for the unravelling a passage or two, I would stand the brunt of an encounter with so portentous a commentator!'

Hazlitt, who was sitting next to Ayrton, noticed the look of horror that had passed over his face. 'I'm afraid', said Ayrton, 'that if the mystery were cleared up, the merit of the writing might be lost.' He then turned to Hazlitt, and whispered: 'As long as dear Charles continues to admire these crabbed old authors, he will himself never become popular.' It was true that literary fame had so far eluded Lamb, for all his efforts to attain it. But the joke would be on Ayrton.

Others now began to make suggestions—Hazlitt proposed Chaucer, Donne, and Dante; Mary nominated Alexander Pope. The conversation began to take off, and they moved onto history, philosophy, painters, Frenchmen, and a host of other topics, as they would continue to do for years to come.

On 10 December, just over a week later, the chance to test Ayrton's comment about Lamb's literary ambitions arrived. His comedy, *Mr. H——*, was staged at Drury Lane. If it had a good run, Lamb could make £200 in royalties and £100 from the copyright; if it failed, he would get nothing.[69] The sun beamed brightly that morning upon the playbills, and the streets thronged with people asking each other whether they were to go. Lamb sent complimentary tickets to friends including Hazlitt, who sat several rows behind him in the pit. Hazlitt was thrilled when laughter greeted the Prologue—he could hear Lamb in the front row roaring 'with laughter at his own wit'. Cheers and applause followed. 'Encore! Encore!', the audience shouted. What better promise of success?

The play's premise was as silly as anything in *Monty Python*—that Mr H——, who did all he could to conceal his name, was actually called 'Hogsflesh'. As soon as that was revealed, the steam went out of the drama and the audience lost interest. In fact, they positively detested it. 'Off, off, off!' someone cried.[70] People began booing and hissing, and finally the entire pit heckled so loudly that no one could hear the actors, who were forced to mime their way to the end, by which time Lamb too was on his feet, 'the loudest hisser in the house'.[71]

In the green room, Lamb was surrounded by the friends and well-wishers who had failed to drown out the rest of the audience. He accepted their commiserations as if they were congratulations, puffing on his pipe. Though he detested tobacco smoke, Henry Crabb Robinson made a point of staying to console him.[72] Over the ensuing weeks Robinson was 'truly kind & friendly about the farce',[73] instrumental in helping the Lambs get over its failure. Hazlitt too was sad for his friend, and dreamt of revivals at provincial theatres.[74] As this was Hazlitt's first Christmas and New Year away from home for some time, he decided to spend it with the Lambs. His parents sent a basket from Wem containing pigs' cheeks (a delicacy), two fowl, some pickled pork, and a tongue.[75] He took it along and, when it was empty, they set about a bottle of port and some fine Virginia tobacco. It was a Christmas to remember.

One of Hazlitt's first deeds in 1807 was to move to 34 Southampton Buildings. This L-shaped road, running south from Holborn, parallel to Chancery Lane, was a warren of one- or two-room apartments let to bachelors—legal clerks and trainee lawyers, in the main—well placed for the courts around the corner. It put Hazlitt less than ten minutes from the Lambs and about the same distance from his brother. Close at hand were the major booksellers, theatres, and brothels. (Indeed, one of the attractions of the place was that his landlady had no objection to prostitutes calling at his rooms.[76]) Hazlitt was in the habit of waking at noon and ordering two platefuls of buttered toast and tea before staring at the fire for a few hours, doing nothing until snapping out of his torpor late in the afternoon and working frantically into the evening. This was an odd way of proceeding, especially for someone so productive, but it was a method he followed for most of his life, related to a trait inherited from his father—'a constitutional tendency to meditate and brood over questions, and to prefer to think about a subject than to write about it.'[77]

There is no doubt he was working hard. Anthony Robinson was impressed: 'Hazlitt blotts much paper', he told Henry Crabb Robinson. Besides everything else, Hazlitt was writing a 'Quarto Gazetteer' (which would not come to fruition). 'If this be not meddling with many coloured Life, what is?', Robinson asked. 'Well—God speed his Plough!'[78] Hazlitt had also to proof-read the *Abridgement* of Tucker, which Joseph Johnson published in February. It sank without a trace.[79] Now ill with the respiratory ailment that would kill him two years hence, Johnson had lost interest in it, despite the handsome advance he had paid its editor.[80]

Hazlitt soon finished his anthology of parliamentary speeches, *The Eloquence of the British Senate*, an editorial job the magnitude of which dwarfed the *Abridgement*, as it required rummaging through endless volumes of turgid debates. Its introductory sketches showed how far he had travelled as a writer; the best were on Chatham, Burke, Fox, and Pitt, reprinted in his *Political Essays* (1819). *Eloquence* was published by Thomas Ostell on 4 July[81] but attracted only hostile reviews and few sales.[82]

Hazlitt was now in the thick of London's publishing world. There were a host of opportunities for jobbing writers, many of whom kept afloat on exactly the kind of work he was now doing. He looked for more openings and soon came into contact with William Cobbett, who became his first editor.[83] Cobbett had enlisted in the army as a young man and been stationed in New Brunswick. There he became a writer of pro-government propaganda attacking such figures as Paine and Priestley. Yet Cobbett is a rare example of a Tory propagandist who changed sides. Returning to Britain, he established his *Political Register*, which published weekly from January 1802 until his death in 1835. After Robert Emmet's execution in 1803, he criticized the Government's treatment of Ireland, attracting a charge of seditious libel. This made him regard the Government differently, and he took to criticizing its financial and political policies as well— all the more so when, with the collapse of the Ministry of All the Talents, he saw how little difference there was between the Whigs and Tories. By 1807 he was publicly supporting Burdett and Cartwright, parliamentary reformers.

Though resident in Hampshire, Cobbett was a frequent visitor to the capital, and encountered Hazlitt in early 1807—for the first and only time—at a coffeehouse.[84] Cobbett was 44 and coming into his own as a journalist. He had a tall, portly figure with a 'good sensible face—rather full, with little grey eyes, a hard, square forehead, a ruddy complexion, with hair grey or powdered', and wore a scarlet waistcoat with the flaps of the pockets hanging down, as was the custom for gentleman-farmers in the eighteenth century. This was somewhat eccentric, and made Hazlitt like him all the more. He found Cobbett 'a very pleasant man—easy of access, affable, clear-headed, simple and mild in his manner, deliberate and unruffled in his speech, though some of his expressions were not very qualified.'[85] What Hazlitt meant was that Cobbett used such words as 'rogue' and 'scoundrel'—and stronger epithets too; he 'went on just the same in a room as on paper',[86] an important lesson in good journalism.

'So, Mr Hazlitt, what think you of the damned Poor Law?', demanded Cobbett, combatively.[87] He wanted to find out where Hazlitt stood. Recent legislation had put in place a system whereby parishes supplemented the income of the poor to subsistence level, depending on the price of bread and the number of children in each family. Cobbett thought this robbed them of self-respect and made them the target of middle-class contempt; Hazlitt could see that, but worried about what might replace it. Neither agreed with Malthus, who argued that the law encouraged the poor to marry and produce children— both undesirable results, in his view. Hazlitt spoke so eloquently that Cobbett suggested he write some articles on the subject, which began to appear in the *Political Register* on 14 March 1807. These were Hazlitt's most accomplished compositions thus far—less formal in tone than earlier ones and full of the brio that makes his voice so compelling. For instance, the opening paragraph of the first letter condemns Malthus for having attacked the poor:

> His name hangs suspended over their heads, *in terrorem*, like some baleful meteor. It is the shield behind which the archers may take up their stand, and gall them at their leisure. He has set them up as a defenceless mark, on which both friends and foes may exercise their malice or their wantonness, as they think proper. He has fairly hunted them down, he has driven them into his toils, he has thrown his net over them, and they remain as a prey to the first invader, either to be sacrificed without mercy at the shrine of cold, unfeeling avarice, or to linger out a miserable existence under the hands of ingenious and scientific tormentors.—There is a vulgar saying, 'Give a dog a bad name, and hang him.' The poor seem to me to be pretty much in this situation at present. The poor, Sir, labour under a natural stigma; they are *naturally* despised.[88]

This is vintage, rabble-rousing Hazlitt, his indignation articulated in these cascading clauses with their gradually accelerating rhythms. What's more, he was right to attack Malthus, whose ideas were the culmination of a philosophical tradition that saw humanity as selfish, evil, and grasping—the same bogey condemned by Hazlitt's father when doing battle with Calvinism. Cobbett applauded his new contributor, telling readers that 'the check-population philosopher, Mr. Malthus, has met with a formidable opponent who will, I confidently hope, continue on till he has completely put down the hard-hearted doctrine of this misanthropic economist.'[89] Sadly, it was not to be. Hazlitt joked that Malthus was like 'the clown in Shakespear' and should lay 'aside his harlequin's coat and sword',[90] but fate was on his opponent's side. Malthus's appointment as Professor of History and Political Economy at Haileybury gave him the means to inculcate his views among those who would propagate them across the Empire. His became the dominant ideology of the new century and provided justification for all manner of inhumanity in the schoolroom, workplace, and home—as Dickens's novels illustrate.

Hazlitt published three letters with Cobbett, wrote two more, and collected them as a pamphlet, *A Reply to the Essay on Population*, issued on 6 August by Longman. This well-established London publisher had noticed Hazlitt's talents, and his admiration was not misplaced: all but 48 of the 500 copies sold.[91]

Hazlitt sent a copy to Godwin, only to receive a hurt letter in response because of a footnote in which he said Godwin 'does not regard a new-born infant with any particular complacency'.[92] Godwin couldn't abide accusations of hard-heartedness because they were based on an essential truth: his philosophy denied the importance of the emotions. Godwin declared himself 'astonished at your feeling willing to hold up a man with whom you hold in habits of kindness, to the aversion of your readers'.[93] Hazlitt answered that 'I looked upon it as a joke, & thought you would do the same', concluding:

> No one has ever been more ready than I have to take part with my friends on all occasions. I have committed four or five riots in my zeal for the reputation of Coleridge & Wordsworth: & all the thanks I ever got for this my zeal in their favour was some of the last indignities that can be put upon any person. In my list of friends it has always been my good luck to come in like the tale of an etc. & to subsist only upon sufferance.[94]

This can only be a reference to the humiliation of being bundled out of the Lake District in the belief that he was pursued by a ducking party. Perhaps he had got wind of the fact that no such thing had existed, or perhaps he simply resented the indignity of it. But it is clear, too, that Wordsworth and Coleridge never treated him as anything other than a hanger-on, a miscellaneous junior rather than an equal. And that hurt more than anything else, for he was to prove loyal to the last—insisting, even to their enemies, on their essential genius, even when they condemned him. Hazlitt was not an embittered or grudgeful man, but the treatment he suffered at the hands of Wordsworth and Coleridge was to rankle for the rest of his life. His friendship with Godwin would endure, however; if anything, this exchange bonded them more closely. Godwin wrote the next day, apologizing: 'I am gratified, though with some mixture of pain, that this occurrence has furnished the first occasion for us to talk the language of friendship.'[95]

By now, Hazlitt was speaking the language of friendship with someone else: Sarah Stoddart. They were thrown together by chance when both gave moral support to Charles Lamb during Mary's temporary confinement in a madhouse. One afternoon Hazlitt confided to Sarah that he was recovering from a love affair.[96] She was a good listener, and one thing she was always able to do was draw him out, engaging him in conversation about the most intimate matters, even his peccadilloes. She soon realized that, despite his affected slovenliness, Hazlitt was a disciplined man who worked hard and cared passionately about his principles—a trait that boded well for other aspects of his character: in short, she saw he was good husband material camouflaged as its opposite. To him, she held a number of attractions, not least 'her unaffected good sense'.[97] Their courtship proceeded at breakneck speed: within weeks he was showering her with love letters and began 'to spout amorous verses, & sing licentious ditties & burthens of old songs'.[98]

All the same, it was always a troubled relationship. By November they were accusing each other of infidelity when Mary Lamb, now released to her brother's care, wrote to Sarah confessing her wish to know 'how your comical love affair would turn out.'[99] This suggests that the Lambs thought this was a mere fling for both parties, rather than what we would call a 'committed relationship'. How wrong they were. Charles and Mary joked about the ill-assorted couple for months, failing to appreciate Sarah's seriousness about having babies—for she was determined not to let this one get away. Hazlitt *had* been unfaithful, but Sarah was confident of her ability to tug him back, as indeed she did. She seemed to know instinctively how to handle him—a skill that would serve her well.

There was only one possible obstacle: her brother, now practising law at Doctors' Commons. Get him on your side, she advised William, who promptly invited his prospective brother-in-law for dinner. By the end of November

John Stoddart was 'on very friendly visiting terms with Hazlitt'[100] and dined again *chez* Hazlitt on 8 December, with the Lambs, Godwin, and Joseph Hume (Lamb's chum from the Victualling Office).

It is a tribute to Hazlitt's powers of persuasion that by the third week of December the couple were engaged. John Hazlitt declared himself 'mightily pleased with the match', though he had ominous advice for Sarah: if they did not start out debt-free they would 'always be behindhand'.[101] John knew his brother's spendthrift ways and was concerned about his ability to keep his prospective family in the black. Perhaps he hoped Sarah had sufficient means to ensure it would not matter.

Belatedly, this began to occur to John Stoddart as well. The thought of surrendering his sister to a hired gun from Grub Street who spent money as soon as it was earned began to seem less than prudent.[102] After all, Sarah had an income of £80 and two properties to her name (one in Salisbury, the other in Winterslow).[103] Though modest, that was a fortune compared with what Hazlitt could bring to a marriage. Stoddart put these anxieties to his sister but found her impervious: she was determined to marry. There had been other suitors in the past, and she would not lose this one. Stoddart mulled the situation over and realized what he had to do.

The day before the wedding, his lawyers drew up a settlement designed to safeguard Sarah's private income while ensuring the couple had sufficient to raise a family, were they to have one. He set up a trust into which he would pay £100 a year, rising to £150 after five years, for the duration of their married lives, the money to be spent as they pleased.[104] It was, on the surface, extraordinarily generous. But Hazlitt would not have perceived it as such: this was the regular income which he, by implication, was incapable of providing. Sarah, on the other hand, saw the sense in it. It guaranteed financial security up to a minimum level which, given the irregularity of Hazlitt's earnings, was something they needed. She declared she would not marry unless he signed: reluctantly, he did.

On the eve of his wedding, Hazlitt became the pensioner of his brother-in-law, something that filled him with disgust for years to come. It poisoned their friendship and was one of several corrosive forces that ate away at the marriage—which may have been what Stoddart intended.

CHAPTER 7

For indeed I never love you so well as when I think of
sitting down with you to dinner on a boiled scrag-end of
mutton, & hot potatoes. You please my fancy more then than
when I think of you in . . . No, you would never forgive me if I
were to finish the sentence. Now I think of it, what do you
mean to be dressed in when we are married?

William Hazlitt to Sarah Stoddart, January 1808[1]

THEIR engagement lasted longer than expected, John Stoddart's prevari-
cations dragging on into the new year of 1808. Lamb's reaction was to
invent the story that Hazlitt's fretfulness had caused him to commit suicide by
slitting his throat with a palette knife.[2] That someone whose life was marred
by tragedy could mount such a hoax seems astonishing until one considers
that it was only by such gestures that Lamb maintained his own sanity.[3] It
prompted a robust response from the alleged suicidee, who penned a series
of proofs demonstrating he was still extant, concluding he could see 'no reason
why [Lamb] should not be considered as much a dead man as himself, and the
undertaker spoken to accordingly'.[4]

Being thought dead cannot have been much good for Hazlitt, whose moods
went up and down like a yo-yo. He wanted to marry Sarah as soon as he
could and hated celibacy (having renounced the stews on her behalf); yet for
decency's sake, they were compelled to remain apart, Sarah remaining in the
Wiltshire cottage inherited from her father. 'If Hazlitt were to go down to Salisbury', Mary Lamb warned her, 'you know it would never do'[5]—and Charles
must have given the same advice to William. For her part, Sarah was untroubled
by the delay. But Hazlitt lived on his emotions, increasingly wound up by
frustration. 'What is become of you?', he wrote to her in January 1808, 'are you
gone into a nunnery? Or are you fallen in love with some of the amourous heroes
in Boccacio?'[6] Sarah thought it a good thing for him to be kept in suspense,

not realizing what a creature of impulse he could be: on 6 February he left for Winterslow without informing the Lambs, his brother, or indeed Sarah herself. What a surprise when he arrived at her door! She cannot have been wholly displeased, for he remained there over the next fortnight.

This was Hazlitt's first visit to the small village four miles to the east of Salisbury which he was to make his second home. The main road to Andover was two miles to the north where, at the local inn, coaches dropped mail, and on his first visit he disembarked there. In later years he preferred to walk in and out of the village using the ancient path (now the Clarendon Way) that led all the way to Salisbury Cathedral.

He took to the place immediately—after all, he had grown up in the countryside—and explored the area with Sarah. To the south were Tytherley woods around stately Norman Court, seat of Charles Baring Wall MP (with whom Hazlitt would become friendly[7]); to the southwest, Clarendon Wood, famous 'for the Constitutions signed in the palace which once rose proudly amongst its stately trees';[8] to the northwest, Thorny Down, site of a Bronze Age settlement, 'a wood of the oldest looking trees that seemed as if they had stood there for centuries, so entangled were their branches';[9] and, beyond that, Stonehenge, nexus of a series of earthworks and stone circles scattered round the region. Hazlitt walked across the Plain to bear witness to 'that "huge, dumb heap" that stands on the blasted heath, and looks like a group of giants, bewildered, not knowing what to do, encumbering the earth, and turned to stone, while in the act of warring on Heaven.'[10] There were art galleries too. Longford Castle, owned by Lord Radnor, contained landscapes by Teniers, while to the west of Salisbury he would visit Wilton House to stare in wonder at Van Dyck's portrait of the Pembroke family.[11] He arrived 'a willing exile', he later recalled, 'and as I trod the lengthened greensward by the low wood-side, repeated the old line, "My mind to me a kingdom is!" '[12]

On this first visit Hazlitt probably encountered the Armsteads, the elderly couple living close by, who were already good friends of Sarah's. In later years, Mrs Armstead would supply the Hazlitts with puddings; indeed, hers were the only ones Hazlitt would eat. She even 'contrived to persuade him that she had the art of making egg puddings *without egg*'.[13]

This brief foretaste of married life came to an untimely end when the Lambs forwarded Hazlitt's mail to Wem, assuming he was there. Hazlitt's father wrote an alarmed letter back, wondering where on earth his son could be if he wasn't in London. Alarmed in their turn, the Lambs spoke to Hazlitt's landlady, who revealed the awful truth. Soon everyone knew what the unmarried couple were up to, and Hazlitt was compelled to return to London, for form's sake if nothing else.

In the weeks before the wedding they met regularly at the Lambs', drinking and making merry. One evening in mid-March[14] there came a knock on the door and in walked William Wordsworth. He was in town partly on Coleridge's account: claiming to be opium-free, Coleridge had attempted to deliver some lectures at the Royal Institution and promptly fallen ill. Believing this the result of addiction, Wordsworth had come to return his friend to Cumberland. During the years since 1803, Wordsworth's stature in the literary world had grown thanks to the slow-burning success of *Lyrical Ballads*, and his valu- ation of himself as the Milton of his day was firmly established, in his own mind at least. He carried himself accordingly, with a gravitas that would have inspired contempt in the firebrand who in 1793 had written a pamphlet arguing for the execution of Louis XVI. Though no longer republican, Wordsworth still considered himself a 'democrat'—code for one who espoused egalitarian principles.

In the years that had passed since the Keswick incident, Hazlitt had been hurt by Wordsworth's silence, aware it could only signify disapprobation. Yet he was too generous-hearted to lose hope in Wordsworth's essential genius, believing the poet could still achieve the ambition of which he had spoken in 1798—of writing the epic poem that would wipe out inequalities of wealth and class. For his part, Wordsworth had been wary enough of Hazlitt in earlier years, but rumours of his debauches in London knocking shops brought out all the priggishness he could muster. Wordsworth was a frightful prude. Then in his late thirties, he was unhesitatingly censorious, especially when confronted with the follies and foibles of his fellow man. This put the two writers on a collision course.

As he walked into the Lambs' front parlour, Wordsworth's heart sank. Not only had it seemed to him that Lamb, who met him at the door, was at his most skittish—an aspect of his character he could barely tolerate—but as he walked along the hallway he thought he could hear giggling. His heart sank even further when he set eyes on its source. 'There unluckily I found Hazlitt and his Beloved', Wordsworth later told Coleridge, as if their betrothal had been rubbed unpleasantly in his face. Perhaps Sarah was sitting on Hazlitt's lap when he entered and jumped up in embarrassment. Wordsworth must have wanted to turn round immediately and walk back into the street, but it was too late for that. Lamb was a different person in Hazlitt's company—more unbuttoned, prone to vulgarity, gossip, bawdy talk—which made him a less desirable companion, at least as far as Wordsworth was concerned. Worse still, the parlour was full of tobacco smoke, for Hazlitt and Lamb were indulging their favourite (or, in Hazlitt's case, second-favourite) vice. Though a connoisseur of wine, Wordsworth despised the carousing in which Lamb and Hazlitt indulged, which smacked of the tavern; he hadn't inebriated himself since undergraduate days (or so he said).[15]

On the way in, Wordsworth made the mistake of mentioning to Lamb that, besides his desire to assist Coleridge, he had come to London to find a publisher for a new poem, *The White Doe of Rylstone*, the manuscript of which was in his coat-pocket. There were instant calls for a recital. He had no intention of reading it to this disorderly company and declined.

> But as they were very earnest in entreating me, I at last consented to read one Book, and when it was done I simply said that there was a passage which probably must have struck Hazlitt as a *Painter* 'Now doth a delicate shadow fall' etc, and mentioned that Sir G. Beaumont had been greatly pleased with it. We then had a short talk about that part and nothing more took place.

Wordsworth should have known better than to present Beaumont as a critical authority; for Hazlitt it could only have revived memories of the dinner party at which Coleridge had, not for the last time, humiliated him. It was also a reminder of Wordsworth's acceptance of Beaumont's patronage—which Hazlitt thought a mistake, believing you could not take the Tory coin without turning Tory yourself. When Hazlitt needed assistance, he had been careful only to seek out that of dissenters and radicals—Thomas Clarkson, Joseph Johnson, Anthony Robinson, William Roscoe. He would never have accepted money from the supporter of a party he despised. Hazlitt did not now venture into such deep waters, merely declining either to criticize or compliment *The White Doe*, which disappointed him. That was insulting enough, but Wordsworth was horrified by what Lamb had to say about the poem.

'I fear it will not be popular,' said Lamb, who echoed the feeling among his guests.

'Popular?', said Wordsworth. 'I do not suppose it could *ever* be popular, first because there is nothing in it to excite curiosity, and next because the main catastrophe is not a material but a spiritual one!'[16] He did not stop there, discoursing on the poem's content and context, halting only when he noticed a vaguely unpleasant smile on Lamb's face, at which he excused himself and left. This was a horrible way for Wordsworth's evening to end, and left a bitter taste in his mouth for years afterwards. 'Let Lamb learn to be ashamed of himself,' he told Coleridge, in the hope his remarks would be passed on. 'Lamb has not a reasoning mind, therefore cannot have a comprehensive mind, and, least of all, has he an imaginative one.'[17] For Wordsworth, criticism was the bitterest of pills.[18] In retrospect, he blamed Hazlitt for Lamb's unreceptiveness. That was why he ensured this was their last encounter; henceforth he demanded that his London hosts exclude Hazlitt from whatever gathering he deigned to attend.

William Hazlitt and Sarah Stoddart were married at the church of St Andrew, Holborn, by special licence on the morning of Sunday 1 May 1808. Despite the solemnity of the occasion, Charles Lamb laughed so much he 'had like to have been turned out several times during the ceremony'.[19] There was nothing comic about the occasion; Lamb's laughter was a nervous response to solemnity— hardly surprising in someone whose life was shaped by tragedy and bloodshed. But perhaps his laughter was also the product of nerves, as the wedding would have been more tense than expected. For the strain between Hazlitt and his brother-in-law, John Stoddart, soon to erupt into outright hatred, began to manifest itself in differences over the preparations. First, Hazlitt wanted the marriage to take place in Winterslow but Stoddart overruled that plan, probably because he would not be able to oversee it at that distance.[20] Well, thought Hazlitt, if it had to take place in London, Sarah could at least stay with the Lambs, which would enable the lovers to see each other beforehand. Realizing what was afoot, Stoddart ordered that Sarah reside under his roof instead, otherwise 'it would have a very strange appearance'.[21] As consolation, the Lambs offered to throw a 'wedding-breakfast' at their home, but Stoddart insisted on his right to host that too. In the end, Stoddart even took responsibility for obtaining the wedding license.[22] The entire thing was his doing, arranged without reference either to his sister's wishes or those of the groom. Hazlitt must have been infuriated, but the Lambs advised him not to make a fuss. They reminded him that, if Stoddart wanted, he could still deny the couple the right to marry and, until that was done, it was best to humour him; as Mary Lamb told Sarah: 'it is better to take him along with us, in our plans, if he will good-naturedly go along with us, than not.'[23] This uneasy peace would not hold for long.

Part II: Beyond Xanadu

After the celebrations were over, bride and groom repaired to a cottage on a farm at Camberwell Green to the south of London, where Sarah was to conceive her first child. In those days Camberwell was a village famous for its unspoilt pastures, flowers, and fruit trees, although the property developers were starting to build the terraces that survive there today. The Hazlitts may have come here because William remembered the Montpelier tea gardens less than a mile away, where his father brought him after their return from America.

The marriage was tempestuous from the outset, and would remain so because of Hazlitt's lack of funds and seeming inability to generate them. Temperamentally, he was quite happy to sit around all day staring into the fire, or looking out of the window, brooding on his own thoughts. To the ultra-practical Sarah, who had 'a taste for formality and method', not to mention 'a love of order', this was downright laziness. For most of their time together, she harangued him mercilessly for loafing, urging him to get out onto the streets and look for work. 'You call yourself a writer?', she asked, 'Then get out there and find a publisher!'

That was probably why Hazlitt one day wandered into the office of a young publisher called John Murray, who earlier that year had reissued Hazlitt's *Eloquence of the British Senate* after Thomas Ostell's death.[24] Hazlitt had an idea. He proposed to Murray that he translate Jean-François Bourgoing's *Tableau de l'Espagne Moderne*, an account of the state of modern-day Spain, which he thought would enjoy some popularity given the brewing conflict there.[25] An exact contemporary of Hazlitt's, Murray was still finding his feet as a publisher. His most successful title so far was a cookery book published in 1805, and he awaited the emergence of Lord Byron and the poems that would make his fortune. Taking one look at Hazlitt he knew this was not the man. Besides which, Murray was only a year away from establishing the Tory *Quarterly Review*, a counterblast to the Whig *Edinburgh Review*, and may have sniffed something malodorous about Hazlitt's politics. He thanked the jobbing author for his interest and sent him on his way.

Hazlitt was under intense pressure to find employment, Sarah's frustration at his 'laziness' being equalled only by her contempt. Perhaps it was in an attempt to placate her that he worked on 'a collection of Verses chiefly amatory' which he claimed to be putting to press on 5 July,[26] perhaps a by-product of the 'amourous verses' and 'licentious ditties' he sang shortly after they fell in love.

But the romance was fast oozing out of their marriage, and the project seems never to have found a publisher.

He met Godwin on numerous occasions over the summer to suggest various proposals,[27] of which only one came to fruition: Hazlitt's *New and Improved Grammar of the English Tongue*, which he set about immediately. He always prided himself on his command on the language, partly because it was elemental to the dissenting culture out of which he had come. By the time he got to the Hackney New College, Hazlitt had certainly read Priestley's *Rudiments of English Grammar* (1761), *Theory of Language* (1762), and *Lectures on Oratory and Criticism* (1777), which offered the most progressive theory of linguistic usage to be offered during the eighteenth century.[28] As the beneficiary of its insights, he was well placed to set out what he had learnt in textbook form.

When their lease ran out at the start of November, the Hazlitts moved to Winterslow. Sarah was now six months pregnant. She put aside a workroom for her husband, which he decorated with prints of Claude Lorrain's landscapes. There he would write and paint, but spent most of his time contemplating Claude's 'Pastoral Capriccio with the Arch of Constantine and the Colosseum':

> It was the most graceful, the most perfect of all Claude's compositions. The Temple seemed to come forward into the middle of the picture, as in a dance, to show its unrivalled beauty, the Vashti of the scene! Young trees bent their branches over it with playful tenderness; and, on the opposite side of a stream, at which cattle stooped to drink, there grew a stately grove, erect, with answering looks of beauty: the distance between retired into air and gleaming shores. Never was there scene so fair, 'so absolute, that in itself summ'd all delight.'[29]

In this mood, Hazlitt returned to painting with renewed ambition. He would set out to Tytherley woods with his tools and, when he found a scene he liked, nailed his canvas to a tree and painted what he saw. Sometimes he took his lunch with him—two boiled eggs, bread, and cheese—and worked until teatime.[30] As always, it was his habit to gaze fixedly at the object he was painting until 'the very "light thickened" and there was an earthiness in the feeling of the air!'[31] On days when the weather was inclement, he remained at the cottage and worked on grander subjects—the story of Ugolino or the legend of Jacob's ladder. Hazlitt produced canvases very slowly, pondering each stroke before he applied it. And he found himself thinking on other topics as he did so. The rustic surroundings suited him for it was here, as William Jr pointed out years later, 'that most of his thinking was done'.[32]

None of which was much use to a woman anxious to start a family, and Sarah must often have reflected that she once intended to marry William Dowling, a local farmer who though less interesting was a reliable earner. Confinement gave her ample opportunity for such doleful observations, and she doubtless had cause to reprimand Hazlitt for his unproductiveness. These worries were exacerbated by others related to her pregnancy—she was, after all, in her thirties. The Lambs echoed these concerns. 'I hear of you from your brother but you do not write yourself,' Mary chided Sarah on 9 November, 'I beg that one or both of you will amend this fault as speedily as possible, for I am very anxious to hear of your health.'[33]

At 4.15 on the afternoon of 15 January 1809, Sarah gave birth to a son, William. Hazlitt loved children and would always be a doting father. The child brought home to him the importance of earning money, and he turned with renewed vigour to his pen, writing an article on metaphysics for the *Monthly Magazine*.[34] 'I will resume the subject in another letter,' he concluded,[35] but that promise was not kept, either because he was not paid enough, or at all. (The proprietor of the *Monthly Magazine*, Sir Richard Phillips, was shortly to be declared bankrupt.[36])

Nonetheless, the experience of writing it served to revive the idea of a *History of English Philosophy*—something Hazlitt was well qualified to write, and had meditated for some time. It was a natural spin-off from his *Essay*, and a further opportunity to expound his metaphysical discovery by conducting the reader through the tradition of philosophical argument on which it was based. Prior to his departure from London he discussed it with Godwin and attempted to find a publisher, but without success. The obvious solution was a subscription fund—the means by which his father's last book, *Sermons for the Use of Families* (1808), had been brought out by Joseph Johnson. Having been involved in its production, Hazlitt was aware of the mathematics: he needed advance sales of around 150 copies to cover costs. In order to generate that level of interest, he would publicize the volume with a prospectus—what we would call a 'flyer'.

Using the article he published in the *Monthly Magazine* as its basis, he composed a four-page teaser which he sent to Richard Taylor (who printed *Free Thoughts on Public Affairs* several years earlier). On 18 February 1809 Taylor produced 500 copies of 'Proposals for Publishing, in one Large Quarto Volume, a History of English Philosophy', the cost of which was borne jointly by Hazlitt and Basil Montagu.[37] It is clear, not just from the books he sent to Scarlett and Mackintosh, but from his part in this enterprise, that Montagu was one of Hazlitt's most helpful supporters. Taylor's records show that Montagu paid for successive reprintings of the flyer until 1812, and over the next few years he lent Hazlitt over £500.[38]

Hazlitt did his bit by sending copies to the likes of William Windham MP, Secretary of War to Pitt and the Ministry of All the Talents. Some have suggested that Hazlitt was misguided in targeting 'a panjandrum of the Tories',[39] but this is to do Windham an injustice. Years earlier, he supported the French Revolution and made his name not as a Tory but as Whig spokesman in opposition, supporting Catholic relief and repeal of the Test Act in Scotland, as well as opposing the slave trade. These were causes of which Hazlitt (and his father) approved. By the time Hazlitt contacted him, Windham had the reputation of a maverick; indeed, one commentator describes him as 'an unpopular, even slightly deranged, character'[40]—precisely the sort of politician to whom Hazlitt was drawn. It is even possible that Hazlitt had encountered him at political meetings in the 1790s, or at Horne Tooke's house in Wimbledon.[41] Perhaps he was aware that Windham had given Cobbett £600 to assist in the establishment of his *Political Register* and hoped he would help him similarly; apparently he did not.

The winter was abnormally hard. London flooded on 22 January and a hurricane hit the south of England a week later. In Salisbury, the waters were higher than at any period since records began. Winterslow was buffetted by the storms, but being on high ground Sarah's cottage was spared the worst of the floods, and they recovered more rapidly than many others. But the weather forced Hazlitt to stay within the confines of the cottage, and the couple soon found themselves getting on each others' nerves, a situation not helped by the added pressure of the baby. Sarah welcomed her husband's suggestion that he venture to London to seek more subscribers for the *History of English Philosophy* and catch up with the Lambs, simply because life without him was easier than the alternative. For Hazlitt the return to the metropolis was like a release from jail. He knew in his heart that his artistic career was going nowhere, and the strain of living with a shrewish wife who failed to see the point of his intellectual interests was beginning to depress him.

His visit to the Lambs at Mitre Court on the Ides of March was joyful.[42] The two friends smoked and drank into the small hours, telling each other stories while Mary laughed. This was the last time Hazlitt would see them here; the Lambs were preparing to move into rooms at 34 Southampton Buildings— 'Hazlitt's old lodgings',[43] which he had probably recommended to them.

Just over a week later, Thomas Holcroft died. His literary ambitions had met with scant success in recent years, and he had declined into impoverished obscurity, leaving behind an unfinished autobiography. A few days later there was a meeting of his friends, including Lamb and Godwin, to organize a subscription for his family. Hazlitt would probably have joined them had word not reached him that all was not well at Winterslow. He left London immediately. 'His child is expected to die,' Mary Lamb told a friend.[44] When he got to Winterslow, however, baby William was better, and Sarah said that if he had unfinished business in London he had better return. By the time he was back in late May, an ad hoc committee had been formed to commission Holcroft's *Memoirs* and Godwin offered Hazlitt the job of writing it. Holcroft's autobiography and diaries would comprise about half the text; Hazlitt would need to compose another 170 pages or so—'it will not be a hard job,' he thought, and accepted.[45]

During his absence, the Lambs had moved out of Southampton Buildings into new lodgings at Inner Temple Lane—'where I mean to live and die', Charles remarked.[46] They occupied two rooms on the third floor and five more on the fourth for a mere £30 a year. It was roomier than expected 'and all new painted'.[47] They were delighted with it. Hazlitt supped there with Godwin and Martin Burney on 29 May, when they drank a libation to the forthcoming *Memoirs of Thomas Holcroft, Esq*. There were other matters to discuss as well: Sarah had sent him to London partly in order to arrange the Lambs' visit to Winterslow, planned for July; Burney and Ned Phillips were also hoping to come down. Before anything could be settled, however, there were two disasters. Firstly, Mary Lamb had another of her periodic fits and had to be returned to the Hoxton madhouse. Hazlitt helped Charles through it as best he could, but before she could be released, he was summoned back to Winterslow as a matter of urgency.

Baby William died unexpectedly on 5 July at 8.30 in the evening, barely six months old; his parents were beside themselves with grief. Hazlitt summoned his sister, Peggy, to help them through it, and she was never to 'forget the look of anguish ... which at the first moment passed over his countenance'.[48] He found it almost impossible to discuss his feelings and grieved in silence. The experience of standing before the coffin on the day of the funeral was unbearable; his son's was the first dead body he had seen, and he never forgot it.

> The look was calm and placid, and the face was fair and firm. It was as if a waxen image had been laid out in the coffin, and strewed with innocent flowers. It was not like death, but more like an image of life! No breath moved the lips, no pulse stirred, no sight or sound would enter those eyes or ears more. While I looked at it, I saw no pain was there; it seemed to smile at the short pang of life which was over: but I could not bear the coffin-lid to be closed—it seemed to stifle me; and still as the nettles wave in a corner of the churchyard over his little grave, the welcome breeze helps to refresh me, and ease the tightness at my breast![49]

He was inconsolable as he accompanied the coffin to the graveyard of St Martin's church, Salisbury, where, four days after its death, the infant was interred in the same vault as its maternal grandfather, Lieutenant John Stoddart.

Hazlitt sublimated his grief by working hell-for-leather on the books Godwin had commissioned. He disappeared into his workroom for hours on end, much to his sister's dismay, who remembered how overwork nearly killed him years earlier. But she sensed this was a coping mechanism, and left him alone. The grammar book was done by mid-September, when he visited London to deliver it in person. He and Sarah were by now sufficiently recovered to entertain, and at the end of the month he dashed back to Winterslow to welcome the Lambs, who had managed finally to escape London for their visit. They were to enjoy 'nothing but sunshiney days & daily walks from 8 to 20 miles a day',[50] which took them as far afield as Wilton and Stonehenge. In the evenings they wolfed down meat suppers with toast. Not country-lovers by temperament, the Lambs normally hated being out of London. On this occasion, however, 'I never passed such a pleasant time in the country in my life,' Mary declared, confessing she was besotted with 'Winterslow, its woods & its sun flowers'.[51] It did Charles good too, for 'he neither smoked nor drank any thing but tea & small beer.'[52]

For their last ten days the Lambs were joined by Ned Phillips, 'a very good-natured card-playing fellow',[53] who partnered Sarah at cribbage. Hazlitt was fond of him, and told his father 'He is one of those kind of people who are always very much pleased with every thing, & it is therefore pleasant to be with him.'[54] Phillips paid his way by going out with his shotgun and bagging a hare and pheasant for dinner. He also collected beech nuts, delicious when roasted, some of which the Lambs took back to London.[55]

Part II: Beyond Xanadu

By this time his *New and Improved Grammar of the English Tongue* had appeared in Godwin's Skinner Street bookshop—though not in quite the form expected. During the summer, Godwin told his diary, 'I think I have made an entirely new discovery as to the way of teaching ye Eng. lang^e.'[56] This inspired him to write his own *Guide to the English Tongue*, which he 'spatchcocked'[57] within the same covers as Hazlitt's volume—a clumsy proceeding which did Hazlitt's work no favours. As Lamb observed, 'the grey mare is the better horse'.[58] Godwin mailed a copy to Archibald Constable, proprietor of the *Edinburgh Review*, declaring Hazlitt 'a man of singular acuteness and sound understanding' who had defined the parts of speech better than anyone else.[59] Constable recognized the name; he retailed copies of *The Eloquence of the British Senate* and was impressed by its author's versatility.

Joseph Johnson died at 3pm on 20 December 1809. He had been at the heart of a remarkable coterie of writers and artists associated with liberal causes, including Gilbert Wakefield, Mary Wollstonecraft, Thomas Paine, Henry Fuseli, William Cowper, Benjamin Franklin, and William Blake. He also nurtured the literary talents of the Reverend Hazlitt, whose publisher he remained to the end of his life. Hazlitt's son, too, was the beneficiary of Johnson's good judgement, which led to an advance of £80 for the *Abridgment* of Tucker. Both father and son were saddened by Johnson's passing. Godwin wrote the obituary which appeared in the *Morning Chronicle* on 21 December, praising Johnson for 'disinterestedness and a liberal feeling'. Both Hazlitts would have approved.

Hazlitt finished *Holcroft* and delivered it to Godwin on 9 January 1810. 'Holcroft had finished his life when I wrote to you', Lamb told Manning, 'and Hazlitt has since finished his life—I do not mean his own life, but he has finished a life of Holcroft, which is going to press.'[60] This was precipitate. Within days, Godwin decided Hazlitt's biography was unpublishable as it included comments about Mary Wollstonecraft and Gilbert Imlay (her lover) which he thought scandalous. This was understandable, sensitized as he was to anything that might revive the accusations of immorality that followed Wollstonecraft's untimely death in 1797. 'It will make you many bitter enemies,' he told Holcroft's widow. 'Many parts are actionable.'[61] This would have terrified anyone, but to Louisa Holcroft the removal of a potential source of income was an even worse prospect. She hastily consulted the committee that commissioned Hazlitt, hoping to find a solution, as Mary Lamb told Sarah: 'Mrs Holcroft still goes about from Nicholson to Tuthil & from Tuthil to Godwin, & from Godwin to Tuthil

& from Tuthil to Nicholson to consult on the publication or no publication of the life of the good man her husband. It is called the Life Everlasting.'[62] This was a source of amusement to the Lambs but an irritation for Hazlitt, whose hard work had led to nothing.[63]

Sarah was again pregnant, putting her husband under renewed pressure to earn. He wrote to Henry Crabb Robinson, recently retired as war correspondent for *The Times*, asking whether he knew of publishers willing to commission translation work: 'One more push I must make, & then I hope to be afloat, at least for a good while to come.'[64] Such optimism was unwarranted. Perhaps Hazlitt was buoyed up by the fact that he had completed the manuscript of his *History of English Philosophy*, for which he asked Robinson to find a publisher. Robinson was unable to help on either score, much as he wanted to.

On 6 March 1810, Sarah suffered a miscarriage. After the death of their baby this was a cruel blow and it is a good thing Hazlitt was at Winterslow when it happened. Despite their frayed relationship, he did his best to console Sarah, promising they would try for another child.

They were barely recovered when in mid-March Godwin wrote to ask whether Hazlitt would mind were he to 'abridge' the grammar book he had published the previous November. It had gone down badly with teachers and failed to sell; Godwin thought he could make it more palatable to them. Hazlitt said he was 'sorry to be dashed in pieces against the dulness of schoolmasters', adding: 'I can have no objection to the matter.'[65] Hazlitt had come to believe that his books had been 'suppressed', either by critical indifference or by his publishers—and to some extent had a legitimate grievance. The book in which he had invested most energy, the *Essay*, had produced a handful of reviews, mostly unfavourable, before disappearing, while the *Abridgement, Free Thoughts on Public Affairs*, and *Eloquence of the British Senate* vanished without trace. The only book that had so far enjoyed a reasonable sale was his *Reply to Malthus*, and even that was slow-burning. *Outlines of English Grammar* by 'Edward Baldwin' (Godwin's pen name) eventually appeared in June 1810; it sold barely a copy.

Sarah spent the month of April in London with the Lambs, leaving William in Winterslow. She needed their gaiety, the games and diversions they invented for themselves; it was the only way to get over the tragedies of past months. Moreover, she and William had suffered a tough winter and needed another break from one another.

During her London visit, Christie's held a major auction featuring paintings of Leonardo, Raphael, Van Dyck, Rembrandt, and Poussin, which Hazlitt hoped to view before it took place on 14 April.[66] Sarah sent him a catalogue but the weather was 'wet & uncomfortable'[67] and he remained at Winterslow instead, working on his painting of Jacob's ladder. 'I go on something like Satan', he told her, 'through moist & dry, sometimes glazing & sometimes scumbling as it happens, now on the wrong side of the canvas, & now on the right, but still persuading myself that I have at last found out the true secret of Titian's golden hue & the oleaginous touches of Claude Lorraine.'[68] Painting was to him an increasingly impossible quest to emulate masters whose vision and technique lay beyond his reach.

There were other distractions too. 'You are a good girl', he told his wife, '& I must be a good boy. I have not been very good lately.'[69] Sarah knew what that meant. There was a twenty-year-old peasant-girl in the village called Sally Baugh, who had recently thrown him into a 'frenzy'.[70] What was it that made him lose his head over women? The answer lies in the very quality that made him an artist. He had a tendency to fixate on the appearances of things—sometimes the smallest details—and to internalize them, possessing them in his mind. It was a compulsion he described when analysing Petrarch's love of Laura: 'For the purposes of inspiration, a single interview was quite sufficient. The smile which sank into his heart the first time he ever beheld her, played round her lips ever after: the look with which her eyes first met his, never passed away. The image of his mistress still haunted his mind, and was recalled by every object in nature.'[71] Whenever Hazlitt describes women with whom he was infatuated, he seizes on such things. Several years before, in his *Reply to the Essay on Population* (of all places), he described a girl with whom he had been in love 'who always wore her handkerchief pinned tight round her neck, with a fair face, gentle eyes, a soft smile, and cool auburn locks. . . . it was like a vision, a dream, like thoughts of childhood, an everlasting hope, a distant joy, a heaven, a world that might be.'[72] As with Petrarch's Laura, she is no longer herself, transformed by his imagination. This is what happened with Sally Baugh, and Sarah's absence only intensified his torments. He hated himself for succumbing, especially in the wake of Sarah's miscarriage, and wrote plaintively: 'My dear Sarah, I am too tired & too dull to be witty, & therefore I will not attempt it.'[73]

If he felt dejected, it was not without cause. Since arriving in Winterslow he had worked hard on two books, neither of which had added to their income. His efforts to continue his artistic career were going nowhere.

In July 1810 the Lambs returned for another Wiltshire summer, travelling to Salisbury on a night-coach because it was cheaper; they regretted it, for Lamb spent days recovering 'the deduction from my natural rest'.[74] However, once in Winterslow they had a wonderful time, as did the Hazlitts. By now, Sarah was pregnant again. The Wiltshire landscape seemed more idyllic when the Lambs were there and Hazlitt later remembered how 'I used to walk out at this time with Mr. and Miss Lamb of an evening, to look at the Claude Lorraine skies over our heads ... and to gather mushrooms that sprung up at our feet, to throw into our hashed mutton at supper.'[75] While the stew simmered, they gazed across the fields towards Salisbury, watching the sun go down, 'gemming the green slopes or russet lawns, and gilding tower or tree, while the blue sky gradually turning to purple and gold, or skirted with dusky grey, hung its broad marble pavement over all, as we see it in the great master of Italian landscape.'[76] Winterslow suited the Lambs, and Charles declared: 'I must devote myself to imbecility. I must be gloriously useless while I stay here.'[77] And so he was.

Shortly after arriving, Lamb decided he needed some new breeches, and they walked across the fields to the next-door village of Pitton, where Hazlitt knew of a 'little hunch-backed tailor ... with the handsome daughter, whose husband ran away from her and went to sea'.[78] When they went to collect Lamb's order, they found that instead of making the garment in a brown or snuff-coloured material as ordered, the tailor had decided it would look better in 'lively Lincoln-green', and changed the fabric accordingly. If Lamb was dismayed, he didn't let on: 'he rode in triumph in Johnny Tremain's cross-country caravan through Newbury, and entered Oxford "fearing no colours," the abstract idea of the jest of the thing prevailing in his mind (as it always does) over the sense of personal dignity.'[79]

The decision to return via Oxford took the Lambs out of their way, but enabled them to see a city they had long wished to visit. Hazlitt knew it well, and suggested he and Sarah accompany them. It was now the long vacation: the undergraduates had gone down, and the dons snoozed in their country retreats while Oxford roasted under the hot July sun. They had the city to themselves. It was a blissful, idyllic day, which would stay with them for years. Lamb fell in love with the place, and years later made Oxford in the vacation the subject of one of his finest essays.

Hazlitt enjoyed the role of guide: he 'descanted on the learned air that breathes from the grassy quadrangles and stone walls of halls and colleges'[80] while showing them Tom Quad, walking them through 'the groves of

Magdalen', and touring the Bodleian—which thrilled Lamb. 'What a place to be in is an old library!' Lamb was to write:

> It seems as though all the souls of all the writers that have bequeathed their labours to these Bodleians were reposing here, as in some dormitory or middle state. I do not want to handle, to profane the leaves, their winding-sheets. I could as soon dislodge a shade. I seem to inhale learning, walking amid their foliage; and the odour of their old moth-scented coverings is fragrant as the first bloom of those sciential apples which grew amid the happy orchard.[81]

The following day they walked to Woodstock to see Blenheim Palace and its collection of pictures. The Palace itself was, thought Hazlitt, 'Gothic, capricious, and not imposing—a conglomeration of pigeon-houses—"In form resembling a goose-pie"'.[82] They were shown round by a guide who 'pointed in vain with his wand to common-place beauties in matchless pictures',[83] leading Hazlitt first to correct him, and then to discourse on the paintings himself. This was as much a gesture of impatience as of respect for the collection: 'There is not a bad picture in it,' he remarked.[84]

Unaware that Blenheim had a Titian gallery, they did not ask to see it—'all naked pictures', Lamb heard from Henry Crabb Robinson when he got back to London, 'which may be a reason they don't show it to females'.[85] Titian was the god of Hazlitt's idolatry and he later returned on his own. It was, he thought, 'a glorious treat . . . nor do we know why it should not be shewn to every one.'[86]

Lamb suffered another unpleasant coach ride back to London, even though it took place during the day; the roads from Oxford to London were well worn, and the hot rays of the sun only increased their discomfort. And then, next day, disaster struck. Mary had another relapse and, as Charles told Hazlitt, 'she is now absent from home.'[87] It had something to do with their having been away, he noted, adding: 'I have lost all wish for sights.'[88] Sarah too suffered by the excursion: on 6 September she miscarried a second time. It was a terrible blow. She could not bring herself to record the details in her family chronicle, merely entering 'Ditto.' underneath her account of the previous miscarriage.[89]

CHAPTER 8

The youth is better than the old age of friendship.
Hazlitt, *Characteristics* ccxxix[1]

'**O** this is cruel! This is *base!*'[2] Coleridge shook his head, his skin ashen. Basil Montagu had just told him of Wordsworth's admonition: never to take Coleridge into his house, for his presence would be 'a serious injury' to him and his family, as Coleridge had been an 'absolute nuisance' to his.

'Not only that . . . ', said Montagu.

'What? Can there be more?'

'Wordsworth authorized me to tell you so!'

'To tell me?' Montagu nodded. Quivering with grief, Coleridge began to sob like a child.

In fairness to Wordsworth, Coleridge was a far from ideal houseguest. When not downing laudanum for his pet ailment, diahorrea, Coleridge drank gin. Not surprisingly, he often woke up in the middle of the night, screaming at the top of his voice, terrifying Wordsworth's family. And when in good shape, he couldn't resist dominating the conversation with interminable monologues about himself. Obsessed with Wordsworth's sister-in-law Sara Hutchinson, whom he was sure he had once seen in bed with Wordsworth, he appropriated her as his personal slave, making her transcribe screeds of prose while professing to her undying love. She found him repulsive and fled Grasmere on the brink of a nervous breakdown.

Having heard this from Wordsworth, Montagu fed it back to Coleridge in florid detail. 'Lies!' Coleridge wailed, 'Lies!'

'No, Samuel', said Montagu, kindly. 'It is the truth.'

Since 1798 Coleridge and Wordsworth had comprised the literary world's most fertile and productive partnership. Now it was over, and news of the break-up was a sensation. Hazlitt heard about it at first hand, for Coleridge had just become his next-door neighbour at Southampton Buildings. In January 1811

Hazlitt returned there, having been thrown out of Winterslow by his wife. The Hazlitts had spent the previous Christmas together but so infatuated was he with Sally Baugh, who had just announced her engagement to a local labourer, William Shepherd, that Sarah ordered him back to London. She had had enough, at least for the time being. It was not their first separation, nor the last.

At Southampton Buildings, the two men lived in adjacent houses—Hazlitt at number 34, Coleridge at 33. They sat up together into the small hours, Hazlitt puffing on his pipe while Coleridge ranted against the Grasmerians.[3] If Hazlitt listened politely to these wayward, drug-addled, and occasionally unhinged musings, it was not without sadness, for no one knew better the extent of Coleridge's potential. He later observed how Coleridge's yammerings gave rise to a 'giddy maze of opinions, started, and left, and resumed . . . He has a thousand shadowy thoughts that rise before him, and hold each a glass, in which they point to others yet more dim and distant. He has a thousand self-created fancies that glitter and burst like bubbles.'[4] Towards the end of March, Henry Crabb Robinson visited Hazlitt, only to find Coleridge there. 'Coleridge philosophized as usual,' he confided to his diary at the evening's end,[5] unable to keep the note of weariness from his voice. Hazlitt probably had Coleridge in mind when he wrote, years later: 'A person who talks with equal vivacity on every subject excites no interest in any.'[6]

There was no end to the threat Coleridge posed to the Lambs. On 9 March, Mary had a breakdown having heard him describe the death of a mutual friend, George Burnett, in a madhouse. Hazlitt told Robinson the Lambs were 'injured by Coleridge's presence in town and their frequent visits and constant company at home, which keep their minds in a perpetual fever.'[7]

Robinson proved a loyal friend when Hazlitt made a half-hearted attempt to set up, yet again, as portrait-painter, for he secured three commissions—one from his brother Thomas Robinson; another from Thomas Clarkson; and a third from his friend Mr Howel.[8] He also introduced Hazlitt to the work of another unknown and impoverished artist: William Blake. You could get hold of his books only if you went to his house, knocked on the door, and asked him to print one for you, a process that took weeks—for he and his wife illuminated each page by hand. One day in March, Robinson invited Hazlitt for tea and showed him *Songs of Innocence and of Experience*, which included such poems as 'The Chimney Sweep', 'London', and 'The Tyger'.[9] Hardly anyone knew these works because Blake's volumes were so scarce. Nor was their author well regarded: both his writings and personality gave the impression he was a 'decided madman'.[10] Here Hazlitt showed his mettle.

'They are beautiful,' he told Robinson, after the poems were finished. 'They are only too deep for the vulgar.'

'But the author—he is an odd man, is he not?'

'He has no sense of the ludicrous. He is ruined by vain struggles to get rid of what presses on his brain. He attempts impossibles.'

'He is like a man who lifts a burden too heavy for him,' suggested Robinson. 'He bears it an instant, it then falls and crushes him.'

'Yet "The Chimney Sweep" ... is a remarkable poem.'[11] In this, as in much else, Hazlitt was ahead of his time; it was not until the early twentieth century that critical opinion turned in Blake's favour.

While Hazlitt's critical faculties became sharper his artistic abilities declined. Earlier that month he was commissioned to paint a young man, but the portrait was returned by the sitter's mother with 'an abusive letter'.[12] The portrait of Mr Howel was, in Robinson's judgement, 'a good caricature likeness, but a coarse painting'.[13] As for the picture of Thomas, Henry Crabb's brother, Hazlitt refused to let anyone see it, leading Robinson to suspect he had destroyed it. Having already spent the fee, Hazlitt was now in the awkward position of being in Robinson's debt, which embarrassed no one more than Robinson himself. 'I fear poor Hazlitt will never succeed,' he confided to his diary, 'With very great talents and with uncommon powers of mind I fear he is doomed to pass a life of poverty and unavailing repinings against society and his evil destiny.'[14] The one portrait that satisfied its sitter was that of Thomas Clarkson, which his wife described as 'most beautifully painted & there is a freedom in the whole Picture very creditable to Hazlitt'.[15]

This encouraged Hazlitt to write to the Clarksons for a handout. When word of that reached Hazlitt's friends they were appalled; after all, the Lambs had introduced them only in a social context. 'By the bye', Henry Crabb Robinson told Catherine Clarkson, 'C[harles] & M[ary] Lamb feel as I do & express themselves strongly on the *indelicacy* (to use a *delicate* word) of Hazlitt's application to Mr. Clarkson—He is also an instance of great powers of intellect rendered worthless to their possessor from constitutional infirmities & moral obliquities!!!'[16] By 'obliquities', Robinson did not refer solely to the 'application'; he knew about the prostitutes who visited Hazlitt's rooms.

Hazlitt retreated to Winterslow in June 1811, in response to news that Sarah was pregnant; however, the impending arrival of another child can only have intensified the pressure to earn. He took the botched portrait of Thomas Robinson and put it on his easel—but, thinking he was in danger of 'doing away with what likeness there is',[17] turned the canvas reverentially to the wall and locked the door behind him.

William Hazlitt Jr was born on 26 September 1811 at 3.40 in the morning— 'that unfeather'd, two Leg'd thing, a Son'.[18] His parents were delighted, as were the Lambs. 'As we old women say, "May he live to be a great comfort to you",' Mary told Sarah. 'Delighted Fancy already sees him some future rich alderman or opulent merchant,' wrote Charles,[19] before composing an atrocious poem in celebration of 'The long expected One'.[20] Despite these good wishes, William's parents lived in constant fear he would suffer the same fate as their other children; fortunately these anxieties would prove hollow. William Jr grew up to become a journalist like his father, before training as a barrister. He was appointed registrar in the court of bankruptcy where he remained for thirty years, retiring in 1891.

Shortly after William's birth, Hazlitt realized he had an untapped income stream in his still-unpublished *History of English Philosophy*, the proposal for which had so far attracted only thirty subscribers. Why not turn it into lectures, which he could deliver at one of the learned institutions around London? Such courses were popular, and a good source of money for those who gave them, depending on the size of audience. It was also a good publicity vehicle for the book, should he manage to publish it. He set about the task of adapting it to the demands of the lecture hall, asking friends for help in making contact with potential venues. It must have been Sarah who contacted her brother, asking whether he could suggest anything. John Stoddart had long suspected the inability of his brother-in-law to look after his family, and felt a smug self-righteousness at the knowledge that Hazlitt needed his assistance. He wrote suggesting the Russell Institution in Great Coram Street, Bloomsbury. Thanks perhaps to Hazlitt's admirer James Scarlett, who was on its committee, the Institution commissioned him to deliver ten lectures on philosophy, beginning 14 January 1812.[21] Hazlitt paid a fee for hire of the venue; members of the Institution were admitted gratis, and he recouped his costs through ticket sales to non-members.

This put him in competition with Coleridge, who began a series on Shakespeare and Milton at the London Philosophical Society in November 1811, scheduled to run into January the following year. Although they were lecturing on different days of the week (Hazlitt on Tuesdays, Coleridge on Mondays and Thursdays), Coleridge took some of his audience. Admission to Hazlitt's lectures was probably thought to be costly at two guineas. Coleridge charged the same, but delivered fifteen lectures rather than ten, and had a reputation (though a dubious one) as a speaker. Hazlitt himself supported Coleridge, returning to London for the first of his lectures on 18 November. No one was satisfied with it, Robinson observing, 'I had heard the same things from Coleridge in private conversation, and frequently in a better style than in the lecture itself.'[22] If Coleridge failed to surprise those who knew him, it is not to be wondered at: two lectures a week would have strained even the most seasoned performer. At Lamb's on 27 November, the conversation revolved around him, Hazlitt dominating the proceedings with a characteristically incisive analysis that silenced everyone else.

'Mr Coleridge isn't competent to the task of lecturing on Shakespeare, for he is not well read in him', Hazlitt began. 'He knows little more than is in that school-text, the *Elegant Extracts*; indeed, I told him myself of many beautiful passages he had never before heard of. That's why he has not yet justified his arguments by reference to Shakespeare, and I doubt he ever will. No, his forte is Milton, of which his readings are very fine; his natural whine gives them effect. But this whine has grown over the years and is now disagreeable. Mr Coleridge has more ideas than any other person I have ever known. His failing is that he pushes his arguments until he is obscure to everybody but himself. He is like a man who, instead of cultivating and bringing to perfection a small plot of ground, attempts to cultivate a whole field; in his ambition, he digs up the ground only for the encouragement of weeds.'[23] Hazlitt looked round at the faces of Lamb's other guests—George Dyer, Ned Phillips, John Rickman, Martin Burney, and James Burney. They looked stunned.

'To put it another way', he continued, 'compare him with William Roscoe, my friend in Liverpool. Mr Coleridge is a man full of ideas but of no industry; the other is a man of great industry but no ideas. The merit of Mr Roscoe's *Life of Lorenzo de Medici* is that he collected with great labour all his materials and employed them to advantage; the mind of Mr Coleridge is chock-full of materials, but he lacks the perseverance to employ them and, fancying himself deficient, is constantly searching for more.'[24] Hazlitt's scepticism of his former mentor was justified. Coleridge was now so enslaved to opium that he could barely get himself to the lecture hall, and had been known to abandon the lectern without warning in mid-flow or to subside into catatonic silence. No one felt more acutely than Hazlitt the waste of talent brought about by Coleridge's addiction.

By the time Coleridge made his sixth appearance on 5 December 1811, he was charged with having plagiarized Schlegel—an understandable crime for someone whose abilities were increasingly impaired.[25] On that occasion, Hazlitt defended him: 'That must be a lie', he responded, 'for I myself heard Coleridge give the very same theory before he went to Germany and when he did not even understand a word of German.'[26]

Outside the lecture hall, Coleridge was in a censorious frame of mind: seeing Lamb and Hazlitt smoking together in Fleet Street, he told John Rickman that 'as long as Hazlitt remains in town I dare not expect any amendment in Lamb's Health...Were it possible to wean C.L. from the Pipe, other things would follow with comparative ease—for till he gets a Pipe, I have regularly observed that he is contented with Porter—& that the unconquerable Appetite for Spirit comes in with the Tobacco—the oil of which, especially in the gluttonous manner in which he *volcanizes* it, acts as an instant Poison on his Stomach or Lungs.'[27] Coming from an opium addict, this was hypocrisy on a grand scale. Perhaps he said something to Lamb, who 'expressed himself morally concerning both Hazlitt and Coleridge and *their* habits'.[28]

In the meantime Hazlitt drummed up interest in his own lectures, which would begin in the new year. Robinson obligingly got two friends to attend, but Hazlitt wanted their money in advance and 'wrote to beg [he] would pay for them'.[29] To make matters worse, he had no news concerning Thomas's portrait.

'What do you mean to do with it?' Henry Crabb asked.

'I will try to do something', mumbled Hazlitt, 'or else...I must...'

Once again, Robinson was embarrassed on his friend's behalf. 'I feel real compassion for the poverty into which a man of great powers of mind is cast,' he told his brother, 'The truth is that poor H. is so poor & so unhappy that I can't but feel more pity than displeasure.'[30]

Hazlitt was depressed because he was failing his family, which only fuelled Sarah's irritation with him. Back in Winterslow, she was dependent on her brother's annuity and her own modest income to make ends meet. The fact that the couple spent Christmas and New Year apart is symptomatic of the tension between them. But he had high hopes for the philosophy lectures, which he advertised in the *Times* and *Morning Chronicle*.[31] On 14 January 1812 he opened with an 'introductory' talk on Hobbes, attended among others by Lamb, Thelwall, and John Stoddart. It did not go well. Immediately before he stepped

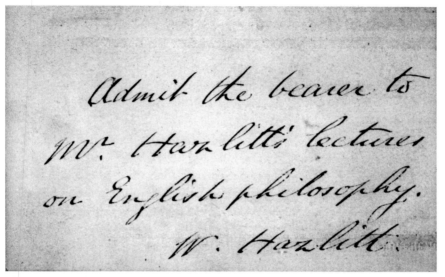

Fig. 12. Ticket of admission, in Hazlitt's hand, for his philosophy lectures.

up to the lectern, the Secretary of the Institution, George Hack, muttered to him: 'You will limit yourself to an hour, won't you? There's a good chap. Our lectures never go on for longer.'[32] His heart sank immediately at the knowledge that the script in his hands, read at his usual pace, would last about three hours. Shaking with nerves, he began reading quickly in a low, inaudible monotone, without looking up at his audience, whose enjoyment was not enhanced by the fact that the *History of English Philosophy* was so dense as to be incomprehensible. 'He read ill a very sensible book', Robinson thought, 'and, as he seems to have no conception of the difference between a lecture and a book, his lectures cannot possibly be popular, hardly tolerable.'[33]

Friends and acquaintances realized he had to be told. John Stoddart wrote him a long letter enumerating his faults in forensic detail, and the following day they had a fractious conversation that 'irritated [Hazlitt] greatly'.[34] Not surprisingly: this was the man on whose charity his family depended. For someone as proud as Hazlitt, Stoddart's condescension, however well meant, was a kick in the teeth.

The following evening Robinson bumped into Hazlitt at the Lambs', where the lecturer was playing cards in a semi-traumatized state. He told Robinson he was so depressed he was thinking of abandoning the series altogether. After

Hazlitt explained the manner in which he had been told of the one-hour time limit, Robinson felt a rush of compassion, and said so. Again, Hazlitt felt patronized and it was only by an effort of will he did not leave there and then.

He got over it. With less than a week to rewrite the next lecture (on Locke), Hazlitt knuckled down to the job, enlisting the help of Burrell, a friend of Stoddart's.[35] The night before it was due, he went to Basil Montagu's in Bedford Square and gave a dress rehearsal to some friends: it went well. The following evening, the audience at the Russell Institution found him a changed man: they had no difficulty hearing him, and he was more confident—almost, Robinson thought, to the point of arrogance.[36] They were delighted, and from time to time applauded. The following day, *The Times* praised him for being 'audible, distinct, and animated; and the felicity of his expressions very frequently excited applause'.[37]

This uncertain beginning behind him, Hazlitt was launched. Though never much of a showman, his performances were full of witty commentary and crammed with insights not found elsewhere. All the same, he struggled to retain his audience, perhaps because the subject-matter, though less congested, was still difficult. The series came to a halt on the day of the ninth lecture, postponed for lack of funds. 'I fear his debts oppress him so that he cannot proceed,' Robinson confided to his diary.[38] Hazlitt resumed at the end of March, adding an additional lecture to compensate listeners for the postponement. It took place on 28 April, and was a roaring success. In typically self-deprecating fashion, he concluded with the conceit that metaphysics were hardly worth the study:

> And yet there are persons who can find no better way of amusing themselves. There is an Indian legend of a Brahmin who was so devoted to meditation that he forgot to wash. For this he was turned into a monkey. But even as a monkey he retained his original propensities, for he kept apart from the other monkeys and did nothing but eat coconuts and read metaphysics. I, too, should be well contented to pass my life like this monkey, did I but know how to provide myself with a substitute for coconuts![39]

Coconuts were indeed the problem, and remained so for the rest of his life. With the conclusion of the lectures, a source of income dried up. But he had not wasted his time. He returned to his printer and asked him to reprint his 'Proposals for printing a *History of English Philosophy*', again with the assistance of Basil Montagu. As a teaser, Hazlitt also produced a 'Table of Philosophical Opinions' and circulated that too.[40] Copies were ready for distribution at the last two lectures, and many among his audience subscribed.[41] Indeed, he continued to reprint the 'Proposals' during the summer, producing 175 copies by 27 June. If ever there was a time for his *History of English Philosophy* to go to press it was now, and he knew it. He was on top of the material and in touch with a readership. Only the finances stood in his way. In July he borrowed £30 from Anthony Robinson to print more 'Proposals', promising repayment within a fortnight. But Robinson was not repaid, nor would the *History* reach the printing house.

It was a hot summer, and an eventful one. The Prime Minister, Spencer Perceval, was assassinated on 11 May by a businessman with a grudge against the Government, to be succeeded by Lord Liverpool, who had no more idea of how to deal with rising bread prices and popular discontent than his predecessor. On 26 May Daniel Isaac Eaton was made to stand in the pillory for having published *The Age of Reason*, Paine's deist critique of Christianity. Eaton's appearance was a triumph, for the crowd couldn't understand what he had done wrong and instead shouted their support. 'Pillory a man for publishing a book!! Fye, Fye!', they cried. 'Religious Liberty!', 'Liberty of Conscience!', cried others. Hazlitt may have been among them. Henry Crabb Robinson noted with pleasure that 'the feeling was so strong in favor of the man that a man who had dared to insult him would have suffered worse than a pillory himself.'[42]

Coleridge embarked on another lecture series, this time on drama, at Almack's, a fashionable club in St James's. Shortly before the course was to start, Wordsworth visited London to be reconciled with him after their falling-out. But they would never be on the same terms as before. Offered a ticket for Coleridge's lectures, Wordsworth testily observed it was 'a most odious way of picking up money, and scattering about his own and his friend's thoughts',[43] before disapproving of the way in which Coleridge turned acquaintances into ticket vendors.

There is no evidence that Hazlitt went to Coleridge's new series or saw anything of Wordsworth. Instead, he made a little money by writing for Basil Montagu an essay outlining the philosophical case against capital punishment. (It would not be published until after Hazlitt's death.[44]) Whatever he received was quickly spent, and he was soon in desperate need. Sarah brought baby William to London during the summer, probably staying with her brother whose quarters were more spacious than her husband's.

By the end of the summer Hazlitt was 'at his wits end for a livelihood'.[45] Then he came up with a plan. He asked Henry Crabb Robinson to ask John

Stoddart, now at *The Times*, to persuade its proprietor, John Walter II, to give him a job.[46] At the same time, he got Lamb to ask John Dyer Collier of the *Morning Chronicle* to put the same proposal to its proprietor, James Perry: 'I am sure I shall feel myself obliged to you for your exertions, having a great regard for [Hazlitt],' wrote Lamb.[47] The only person aware of both approaches was Hazlitt. Needless to say, this was to get him into trouble, for he risked causing offence to someone—not least the friends who made the applications in the first place. When Robinson heard what had happened, he felt insulted; we do not know how Stoddart reacted, though it would be reasonable to suppose the brothers-in-law had another fractious encounter.

On 4 October Robinson visited Catherine Clarkson to discuss Hazlitt.[48] What would become of him? They had their answer within the week when Robinson heard 'that Hazlitt has been engaged as a reporter by Perry. It is now in his power to live comfortably, if he be not altogether without the power of acting prudently.'[49] Finally, at the age of 34, Hazlitt was started.

He was jubilant, having managed to generate an income stream out of nothing! Yet he cannot have suspected this was the profession that would sustain him for the rest of his days. In all probability, he thought of it as a temporary solution to a temporary problem: lack of funds. Perhaps, when he was back on an even keel, he could return to his canvases. But journalism was a trade he would never give up, as he could never afford to do so. Why should James Perry, a hard-headed newsman of over three decades' experience, have taken him on? Hazlitt's curriculum vitae was not, after all, typical—that of a failed artist who was a stranger to the newspaper office. Perry was swayed by the testimonials. Lamb (who had contributed to the *Chronicle* a decade earlier) assured him that Hazlitt would make a good parliamentary reporter 'from his singular facility in retaining all conversations at which he has been ever present'.[50] That swung it. From Perry's perspective Hazlitt was a risk, but he needed new recruits, and would reserve the right to dismiss Hazlitt should he prove unsuitable. Perry put him on a salary of four guineas a week.

When the parliamentary session began on 24 November Hazlitt took his place on the reporters' benches—no sinecure. While journalists were tolerated in the chamber, they did not have the facilities available today. They were expected to sit in the back row of the crowded Strangers' Gallery and permitted to take no more than brief jottings as an aide-memoire.[51] They had no right of priority when gaining access to the gallery, and admission was not guaranteed on busy days when it was necessary to queue hours in advance. Besides being noisy, the crush of people in the corridor outside sometimes led to injury: the painter, Sir Thomas Lawrence, was nearly killed when trying to reach his seat. When in their places, reporters frequently found it difficult to get out; unable to leave, the poet Thomas Campbell developed a bladder infection which he never shook off.[52] Not a pleasant place in itself, the House of Commons was unventilated and when full the air grew foul. It was a job for the hale and hearty rather than the delicate and infirm.[53]

Perry had established his own 'system' for reporting which Hazlitt described in detail:

> several Reporters take the different speeches in succession—(each remaining an hour at a time)—go immediately, and transcribe their notes for the press; and, by this means, all the early part of a debate is actually printed before the last speaker has risen upon his legs. The public read the next day at breakfast-time (perhaps), what would make a hundred octavo pages, every word of which has been spoken, written out, and printed within the last twelve or fourteen hours![54]

There was a growing appetite for such reports. After the American and French Revolutions, working people (not to mention many of the middle class) had become aware that they had political power even if they did not have the vote, and the key to exercising that power was knowledge. For that, they needed information on the personalities and issues of the day. The Romantic period marked the moment at which the media came into its own.

Hazlitt's colleagues included the legendary Peter Finnerty, famous as antagonist of the Foreign Secretary, Viscount Castlereagh. In the late 1790s, Finnerty had been a member of the United Irishmen. As editor of their house-journal, *The Press*, he had known Robert Emmet and those involved in the rebellions of 1798 and 1803. Having somehow escaped serious punishment, he survived to be a thorn in the Government's side. After an article detailing Castlereagh's ruthless suppression of the Irish he was imprisoned in Lincoln gaol for eighteen months. When Hazlitt took up his post at the beginning of the new session, Finnerty had just been released and taken on as reporter by Perry.[55] A hard drinker, Finnerty used to take Hazlitt to the Cider Cellars in Maiden Lane (a few minutes' walk from the *Chronicle* offices at 143 Strand) and perhaps the more expensive Bellamy's chop-house, so close to the Commons that the division bell could be heard summoning bibulous members back to the Chamber.[56]

Hazlitt began his journalistic career at the top, writing for one of the most prestigious national dailies in one of its most sought-after posts. He quickly mastered his duties, his vice-like memory enabling him to retain an hour's debate in his head before writing it up at the *Chronicle* office. Despite his lack of journalistic experience, he discovered the requisite skills within himself: 'Something I did, *took*; and I was called upon to do a number of things all at once. I was in the middle of the stream, and must sink or swim.'[57] It was a good time to be in Parliament. In the spring of 1812 there had been violent Luddite outbreaks in Nottingham and Huddersfield for which three men would be hanged. Among those arrested (though not executed) was the reformer John Cartwright, whose complaints that his cause had been suppressed were presented by an exotic new member of the upper house—Lord Byron. To be thrown into the thick of this must have been intoxicating, and Hazlitt loved it. Celebrating at Lamb's on Christmas Eve 1812, Robinson found him 'in high spirits; he finds his engagement with Perry as Parliamentary reporter very easy, and the four guineas per week keep his head above water. He seems quite happy.'[58]

PART III

A Philosopher in Grub Street

CHAPTER 9

'We are nothing, if not critical.' Be it so: but then let us be critical, or we shall be nothing.

Hazlitt, 'The Periodical Press'[1]

THERE were certain speakers Hazlitt loved. Listening on 25 February 1813 to the Irish politician William Plunket, Hazlitt was so carried away 'that he omitted to take any notes at all'.[2] Plunket's 'eloquence swept along like a river, "Without o'erflowing, full." Every step told: every sentence went to account.'[3] Similarly, Sir Francis Burdett spoke in a manner 'I could not enough admire'.[4] Samuel Whitbread was a 'true parliamentary speaker. He had no artifices, no tricks, no reserve about him. He spoke point-blank what he thought, and his heart was in his broad, honest, English face.'[5]

Others he loathed. Castlereagh 'spouted without beginning, middle, or end—who has not an idea in his head, nor a word to say for himself...what shall I say of this inanimate automaton? Nothing!'[6] And he took against Sir Samuel Romilly for his 'oracular way of laying down the law in the House:— his self-important assumption of second-hand truths, and his impatience of contradiction, as if he gave his time there to humanity for *nothing*.'[7]

The ordeal of reporting from the Commons was leavened by visits to the local watering holes, which did Hazlitt's health no good.[8] More worryingly, the job lacked challenge. It was basically a memory test. Hazlitt's talent lay in his analytical firepower: 'I have no mind to have my person made a property of, nor my understanding made a dupe of.'[9] Few were better at spotting errors, internal contradictions, deliberate obfuscations or outright lies, and it was not long before he wanted to expose them. He asked Perry to let him move onto the leader columns but was given the brush-off, which only aggravated his mounting restlessness. The story of how he broke out of the straitjacket of parliamentary reporting bespeaks daring, wiliness, and wit.

On Friday 9 April 1813 the Whig Peer Richard Wellesley (brother of the Duke of Wellington) delivered what was by all accounts a dull, stupid speech in the Commons which it was Hazlitt's duty to report. It was not surprising that the Marquess Wellesley, having spent much of his career building up the East India Company, was hostile to government attempts to end its stranglehold on Indian trade. Hazlitt listened with contempt both for Wellesley's stumbling, incompetent manner, and the venality of his argument. As he made his way up Whitehall on his way back to the *Chronicle*, he simmered with rage at the prospect of reproducing it, infuriated at being made servant to Mammon. He was diligent in his work, capable of forging coherent sentences and logical trains of thought where none existed.[10] Having taken his copy to the printing house in the basement, he resorted to the Cider Cellars with Finnerty, who probably suggested the means by which he could take revenge with his first political commentary.[11]

First he sat down at a table in the Cider Cellars and drafted his observations— the work of ten minutes, if that. Out came all his fury at having to transcribe Wellesley's drivellings. Then, another drinking buddy was dispatched to *The Courier*, the evening paper edited by T. G. Street, submitting it as their own. Street ran it the following afternoon.[12] Its excoriation of Wellesley was all in a day's work—after all, the *Courier* was a government paper, and Wellesley was obstructing a flagship policy. Not only were his speeches 'prodigies of physical vigour and intellectual imbecility', but

> It was curious, though somewhat painful, to see this lively Nobleman always in the full career of his argument, and never advancing one jot the nearer; seeming to utter volumes in every word, and yet saying nothing; retaining the same unabated vehemence of voice and gesture, without any thing to require it; still keeping alive the hope and expectation of genius without once satisfying it; soaring into mediocrity with adventurous enthusiasm, harrowed up with some plain matter of fact, writhing with agony under a truism, and launching a common-place with all the fury of a thunderbolt.[13]

No one had previously seen anything like this: Hazlitt invented the political sketch as we know it today. Although newspapers had commented for decades, the bite was as sure as it was unprecedented. Hazlitt's portrait of 'this lively Nobleman' achieved in words what cartoonists such as Gillray did with the image. His long apprenticeship had paid off.

What he did next was a masterstroke that would gain an additional reader-ship. On Monday morning he took Saturday's *Courier* to Perry, claiming the article to be the work of John Wilson Croker. This in itself was newsworthy.

Secretary of the Admiralty, Croker had long abandoned hope of becoming a poet, preferring literary pursuits of a different kind. For reasons of malice and self-advancement he had, since 1809, contributed to Tory newspapers a fetid stream of articles smearing government critics. As he was known to write regularly for the *Courier*, the attribution was all too plausible. But this bitter denunciation of Wellesley was something else—Wellesley was, after all, a Peer of the realm. Perry reprinted it with a brief preamble that left no doubt of his reasons for so doing: 'The Treasury Journals complain of the harsh treatment shewn to Ministers—let us see how they treat their opponents. If the following does not come from the poetical pen of the Admiralty *Croaker*, it is a close imitation of his stile.'[14]

Hazlitt's first political commentary was therefore published twice, by rival newspapers. It ridiculed Croker and Wellesley, made fools of two editors—Perry and Street—and gave its author not one, but two, showcases for his talents. So proud of it was he that he would lay claim to it in his *Political Essays* (1819), giving it pride of place at the beginning of the volume. For the moment, however, its authorship remained secret. Perry now regarded his newest parliamentary correspondent in a different light, and began to allow him to write for other parts of the paper.

That evening, Hazlitt took baby William to be christened. He invited some guests—Mary Lamb, Martin Burney, and the artist Benjamin Robert Haydon—and met them at the church where for a while they passed the time agreeably enough. Then someone asked whether a clergyman had been invited. Hazlitt's face went ashen.

'Well', he said, 'I suppose there may be some slight probability of my having forgotten to give that piece of information.' In a moment, he was cursing himself, his stupidity, his neglect, before adding: 'Never mind; it is too late to correct my folly in this affair. Let us at all events enjoy the christening-dinner!'[15] They returned home, expecting to find a feast. Sarah had the 'flu, but in their absence had managed to produce an unappetising pile of potatoes and 'a bit of overdone beef, burnt, toppling about on seven or eight corners, with a great bone sticking out like a battering ram'.[16] The guests made their excuses and fled.

A month or so later, probably during May 1813, the Hazlitts moved into a new abode: Milton's house. It had been brought to their attention by another colleague on the *Chronicle*, Walter Coulson, who happened also to be the pro-tégé of the landlord, the Utilitarian philosopher Jeremy Bentham.[17] Bentham owned a string of properties in central London, including the house inhabited

Fig. 13. 19 York Street (now Petty France), formerly the home of Milton, Hazlitt's residence from 1813 to 1819.

by Milton from 1652 to 1660—19 York Street (in Milton's day, as ours, Petty France). During Milton's day it had been 'a pretty garden-house opening into St. James's Park';[18] alas, the aspect of the building had since changed. What was once the front was now its rear, so that instead of facing the park it over-looked grimy York Street, while the spacious garden under whose spreading oaks Milton dictated *Paradise Lost* had been appropriated by Bentham for his much grander residence in Queen Square Place round the corner, leaving it no more than a claustrophobic, bricked-in yard barely wide enough for a washing line. The impracticality of living there was underlined by the hefty rent—thirty pounds a year. But Hazlitt idolized Milton and could not resist it. Moreover, the property was in Westminster, one of the few constituencies where householders (or 'pot-wallopers') had the vote. For the first and last time in his life Hazlitt would exercise a right not generally available for decades.

Bentham delegated business to minions, preferring not to deal with tenants himself (indeed, he denied knowing this one's identity), while for Hazlitt, glimpses of his landlord were few and far between. On one occasion, William Bewick remembered Hazlitt pointing him out at the window, remarking: 'Ah! that is the great lawgiver, Bentham; a remarkable man: he would make laws for the whole universe, but, as sailors say, "he doesn't allow for the wind." '[19] It was a shrewd judgement—and Hazlitt's distrust of Utilitarianism would soon be the cause of difficulty.

Sarah was relieved when Hazlitt told her he had found them a home, but any such feeling soured when she saw what awaited her. During this time, that part of Westminster, known as 'the Rookery', was a warren of gloomy tenements thronged with beggars, cutpurses, and petty criminals. In 1808 they were said to be 'of the lowest order',[20] and the children of York Street were, recalled Hazlitt's son, 'rather a promiscuous circle'.[21] The previous tenant of the house, James Mill (father of John Stuart), another disciple of Bentham, found the area intolerable—or at least his wife had, as Bentham recalled: 'dirty, ragged, ill-looking children were frequently within her view: she was unhappy—she was continually in tears.'[22]

A dark, hazardous structure, 19 York Street was in frighteningly bad condition. On arrival, visitors had to contend with a rickety, ladder-like staircase rising to a dark first-floor landing, which opened onto a large, square, wainscotted room. This was where Hazlitt entertained such guests as P. G. Patmore, William Bewick, and George Ticknor, all of whom left vivid accounts of it. According to tradition, it was where Milton once kept his organ; now, the only furniture was a table and three chairs, untouched since their delivery by the removal men. There were no books or pictures, and the panelling had been painted a dull, grubby white. Round the mantelpiece where one might expect a mirror or picture, visitors found Hazlitt's jottings 'in good bold hand...and covering the whole space, all manner of odd conceits, of abbreviations,—words,—names,—enigmatical exclamations,—strange and queer sentences,—quotations,—snatches of rhyme,—bits of arithmetical calculations,—scraps of

Fig. 14. Leigh Hunt, drawn by Thomas Wageman, two years after first meeting Hazlitt, *c*.1815. Hunt's gaze speaks not only of his determination but of his shrewdness.

Latin,—French expressions,—words or signs by which the author might spin a chapter, or weave an elaborate essay.'[23] Sarah decided early on to abandon this room to her husband, declining even to put curtains up at the windows. It was symptomatic of her attitude to the entire house; as her own grandson recalled, she was 'one of the least domestic of her sex'.[24] Eventually Hazlitt was obliged to employ a housekeeper, the domineering Mrs Tomlinson.

During the parliamentary recess, when his pace of work eased, Hazlitt made the acquaintance of Leigh Hunt, then in Horsemonger Lane prison. In our own time, we have seen how government, in time of war, clamps down on journalists; in Hazlitt's day, the Government was even more anxious about the potential of the fourth estate to bring about revolution—a fear bolstered by the recurrent proximity of revolution on the other side of the Channel. With such high stakes, the Government (of which the monarch was head) took no chances, framing a law of libel by which anyone could be imprisoned regardless of whether what they wrote was factually correct. The Hunt brothers—Leigh and his brother John, who published *The Examiner*—fell foul of it for having described the Prince Regent (famous as a rake and debauchee) as an 'exciter of desire'. They went on to declare that 'this Adonis in loveliness was a corpulent gentleman of fifty!' He was also 'a violater of his word, a libertine over head and ears in debt and disgrace, a despiser of domestic ties, the companion of gamblers and demireps, a man who has just closed half a century without one single claim on the gratitude of his country or the respect of posterity!'[25]

At a time when the monarch had the power to appoint ministers, determine policy, and declare wars, it was inadvisable to pick fights with him: too thin-skinned to shrug off criticism, the Regent held all the instruments of power he needed to take revenge. His ministers rigged the trial they gave the Hunts, contriving prison terms of two years apiece to commence in February 1813.[26] Leigh managed to secure for himself a comparatively luxurious residence in the Surrey Jail, lining his cell with rose-trellis covered wallpaper, busts of Spenser, Milton, and Chaucer, a piano, and the contents of his library. There he played host to a throng of supporters including the Lambs ('in all weathers'[27]), Shelley, Byron, and, during the summer, William Hazlitt.

On his first visit, Hazlitt hung back in the corridor as if fearful of being shut in with the inmate. Hunt later recalled: 'I know not which kept his hat off with the greater pertinacity of deference, I to the diffident cutter-up of Tory dukes and kings, or he to the amazing prisoner and invalid who issued out of a bower of roses.'[28] Hazlitt demonstrated his solidarity with the prisoner by returning; here he met John Scott, editor of *The Champion* (another liberal paper), and on another occasion dined with Benjamin Robert Haydon and Thomas Barnes. He also met Hunt's brother John, who endured a less congenial stay at Coldbath Fields Prison and became a good friend. These contacts put Hazlitt at the centre of London's literary and intellectual world.

At the *Chronicle*, he made inroads into other areas of the paper. First he proposed to Perry a new kind of essay similar to those written by Montaigne, Bacon, Addison, and Steele: 'I have several papers of this kind by me, if they can be made any use, such as—On classical education—On advantages & disadvantages of Education in general—on love of posthumous fame—on taste & genius—on love of nature—on patriotism—causes of methodism—on envy among artists—characters of writers, painters, actors &c.'[29] These topics indicate not just the catholicity of Hazlitt's interests but his desire to communicate philosophical and political beliefs using a means at once direct, conversational, and intimate. He would combine serious analysis with prejudice, banter, and anecdote, reinventing the essay as a staple of modern journalism, giving rise to the plethora of columns and feature articles that fill our newspapers today.

Perry was intrigued by his new employee's enterprising spirit; indeed, for all the emphasis sometimes laid on their failure to get on, the evidence suggests mutual admiration. He agreed to a series of 'Common-Places'—the first of which, 'On the Love of Life', ran on 4 September.[30]

At the same time, Hazlitt proposed political commentaries. One of his best, on the appointment of Robert Southey as Poet Laureate, was published on 18 September. In purely personal terms, Hazlitt seems to have got on better with Southey than with any of the other Lake poets. At best, Hazlitt's relationship to Coleridge was that of a pupil, while Wordsworth always held him at arm's length (as he did most of his admirers); but his few meetings with Southey were genuinely congenial. This is not surprising. For one thing, being only four years his senior, Southey was closer in years to Hazlitt than either Coleridge or Wordsworth; for another, Southey was easier company than they were, as Percy Bysshe Shelley found when visiting him in Keswick in 1811. The fact is, Southey was almost completely lacking in side—something possessed by Wordsworth and Coleridge in industrial quantities. What's more, Southey enjoyed Hazlitt's company and had a genuine sympathy with Robert Emmet and the plight of the Irish: that's why they got on so well in 1803. Since then, however, Southey had undergone one of the most extreme changes of heart of the Romantic period. A decade after the Keswick debacle, he now opposed Catholic emancipation and wanted to ship refractory Irish to the colonies. As far as he was concerned, the poor were a constant threat to the political stability of the country, and he supported the execution of insurrectionists. Such writers as Cobbett and Hunt were, in his view, fifth columnists, enemy agents who wanted to soften up the populace for Revolution. In short, the fire-breathing republican of the 1790s had become, in middle-age, a government stooge.[31]

Southey's elevation to the Laureateship provided Hazlitt with his first opportunity to bait that most detested of animals—the turncoat. 'To *have been* the poet of the people may not render Mr Southey less a court favourite', Hazlitt wrote, 'and one of his old Sonnets to Liberty must give a peculiar zest to his new Birthday Odes'[32]—a reference to the demand that the Laureate celebrate the monarch's birthday with a hymn of praise. A week later, Hazlitt renewed the attack:

> Why have we not retained a Royal Jester as well as a Royal Poet? They both had their origin in times of equal rudeness and simplicity; and as much wisdom would have been displayed in abolishing the one as the other . . . Imagination, indeed, can hardly conceive a state of servitude more pitiable than that, to which a man of genius and taste is subjected, who condescends to twine the laurel wreath around his brows. As an office affording any thing like ample or adequate scope for the exercise of his talents, it would be ridiculous to mention it: and its stipend is too small to provide a just remuneration.[33]

There is a serious political point here. It is not just that Hazlitt was right to question an institution that was inherently corrupt, but that he identified the Laureateship as a weapon with which the establishment muzzled its critics. By succumbing to such blandishments, the turncoat (like any traitor) necessarily weakened his former comrades.[34] This was a point Hazlitt would make many times throughout his life.

When, in the new year, Southey produced the first poem of his Laureateship, *Carmen Seculare*, Hazlitt enjoyed himself with a review in which he compared it with various items that betokened its author's apostasy:

> a fancy birth-day suit, a fashionable livery worn inside out, a prince's feather with a sprig of the tree of liberty added to it,—the academy of compliments turned into quaint Pindarics,—is a sort of metaphysical rhapsody, chaunted by a gentleman-usher, and exhibits the irregular vigour of Jacobin enthusiasm suffering strange emasculation under the hands of a finical lord-chamberlain. It is romantic without interest, and tame without elegance. It is exactly such an ode as we expected Mr Southey to compose on this occasion. We say this from our respect for the talents and character of this eminent writer. He is the last man whom we should expect to see graceful in fetters, or from whom we should look for the soul of freedom within the *liberties of a court!*[35]

The impossibility of responding to such finely honed (and wholly justified) abuse infuriated Southey, and would irritate him for years to come.

Having broken out of the straitjacket of parliamentary reporting, Hazlitt now set his sights on the post of drama critic, which was already occupied by William Mudford—a dull, large, slow-witted man whose pedestrian musings made the theatrical column one of the paper's least enticing features. 'Mudford is like a man made of fleecy hosiery,' Hazlitt observed, alluding both to his penchant for thick undergarments and his stupidity.[36] In the middle of September, Mudford made the mistake of writing a brief essay on the lack of decent comedy, to which Hazlitt responded with a sophisticated analysis on the mechanism and effects of comic drama, concluding that Mudford's 'reasoning proceeds on a total misconception of the nature of the Drama itself.'[37] This brilliant performance was to reappear, with virtually no revision, as 'On Modern Comedy' in *The Round Table* (1817). Its clarity was as startling as its command, and readers of the *Chronicle* were astonished by it.

They included the 72-year-old Sir Philip Francis, who despite ill-health wrote to Perry, singling it out for praise:

> In the midst of incessant bodily pain, I think myself lucky when I find anything that furnishes me with a little relief or diversion. I did so, and more than I thought possible, in reading a letter in your paper of Friday last on the subject of comedy. I may say, as Longinus said of Moses, the author of it is no common man, and truly, whether it be yourself or anybody else, I should like to know his name.[38]

No one yet knew Francis as one of Hazlitt's favourite political writers, Junius. This giant of eighteenth-century culture now testified, on the basis of a single essay, that Hazlitt was 'no common man'. Perry's response was characteristic: he claimed authorship of the essay for himself, salving his conscience by giving Hazlitt a hundred pounds, with the words: 'Your writings have done more for this paper than all the rest put together.'[39] The more important consequence is that it prompted Perry to admit Hazlitt to the theatrical columns, running his reviews cheek by jowl with Mudford's. Hazlitt always came off best.

He was just in time to celebrate the most distinguished actress of the day— Catherine Stephens. He was present when she made her Covent Garden debut in Arne's *Artaxerxes* on 23 September 1813: 'A voice more sweet, varied, and flexible, was perhaps never heard on an English stage,' he wrote.[40] Years later, he recalled: 'Those were happy times, in which she first came out...Oh! may my ears sometimes still drink the same sweet sounds, embalmed with the spirit of youth, of health, and joy!'[41] It is a measure of the passion he brought to his new post that he fell in love with her and they had an affair.[42]

Hazlitt lived passionately and to the full. His days kept him in the West End, at the House of Commons, or in the theatre, while he immersed himself in affairs of state and of the heart, writing with equal intensity of both. At the

Fig. 15. Catherine Stephens, painted in 1822 by John Jackson. Hazlitt fell in love with her as soon as he saw her debut at Covent Garden in 1813.

time he fell in love with Stephens, his attention was caught by the essays of a young Turk in *The Times*, one Edward Sterling (father of John Sterling), who as 'Vetus' developed a line in trenchant attacks on Napoleon. By the autumn of 1813, Napoleon was increasingly embattled. The most decisive encounter of the war, the Battle of Leipzig, went against him in October, leading his exhausted army to retreat.

Hazlitt's unrelenting support of Napoleon, which amounted to hero worship, now seems the height of madness. But he was not alone. William Hamilton Reid, Lord Wycombe, John Thelwall, William Godwin, and William Cobbett also supported him, along with more Whiggish personalities such as Lord Melbourne, Sir John Soane, and Byron. 'I am a very moderate person—very moderate indeed', wrote Mary Russell Mitford, 'neither Whig, nor Tory, nor Reformer—nothing but a Buonapartiste—a simple Buonapartiste!'[43]

Part III: A Philosopher in Grub Street

The Allied victory at Leipzig gave rise to a debate about whether to sue for peace, allowing Napoleon to keep his conquests, or to invade France and restore the Bourbons. Vetus favoured continuation of the war: 'We have but one security,' he wrote, 'Let us keep all we conquer. Let our Allies keep all they can acquire.'[44] Hazlitt responded immediately: 'The serpent's hiss, the assassin's yell, the mowing and chattering of apes, drown the voice of peace; and Vetus, like the solemn owl, joins in the distance, and prolongs the dreary note to death!'[45] Throughout his responses to Vetus, Hazlitt took the view that the Allies should parley with Napoleon and leave the French monarchy in exile. So far as he could see, the Revolution had wrought advances which the Allies had no business reversing.

His arguments drew the fire not just of Vetus but of Sterling's editor at *The Times*—John Stoddart. After returning from Malta, Hazlitt's brother-in-law had drifted back into Grub Street and began writing leaders for *The Times* in 1812. By April 1814, its proprietor, John Walter II, had decided to make him editor.[46] Twenty years earlier, Stoddart was a republican who shaved his head and wore a red cap to declare his Jacobin sympathies; now, ambition drove him to the opposite extreme. His leaders were 'haughty & intemperate'[47] condemnations of the French—for their Revolution, their leader, and their culture. And as the war progressed, Stoddart became increasingly violent in his criticism, regarding Hazlitt as stupid beyond belief for his continuing attachment to the hopes of the Revolution. In that spirit, he ridiculed the 'true Jacobin' in his leader article of 29 January 1814: 'The Bank, the Institute, the Legion of Honour, the Emperor's profound policy, his matchless skill, his irresistible heroism! Thus they went on—puff! puff! puff!—and our silly Dottrels, who profess and call themselves "*The true Jacobins*," who peep at "a star over a cottage," and rail against "the wax-work and still life" of a Court which they never saw—they were and are of all men the most easily fooled by the magnificence of these rhetorical flourishes.'[48]

This was *war*. Never one to back down from a challenge, Hazlitt composed one of the most vituperative pieces he would ever publish—'Dottrel-Catching', in which he reminded Stoddart of his former radicalism, lamenting that now, 'for the smallest concession, [he] is prevailed upon to give up every principle, and to surrender himself, bound hand and foot, the slave of a party, who get all they want of him, and then—"Spunge, you are dry again!"'[49] This battle of words would drag on for years.

Fig. 16. Edmund
Kean, drawn by
Samuel Cousins in
1814, the year of his
triumph at Drury
Lane.

Hazlitt was increasingly isolated, even among friends. In mid-December he turned up at the Lambs' to find them toasting the Allies. He became angry and accused Henry Crabb Robinson of betraying his revolutionary convictions. This did not go down well, Robinson regarding him as 'overbearing and rude. . . . He mixes passion and ill-humour and personal feelings in his judgements on public events and characters more than any man I know and this infinitely detracts from the value of his opinions which, possessing as he does rare talents, would be otherwise very valuable.'[50]

New Year 1814 proved eventful, not least in the theatre. Edmund Kean made his first appearance at Drury Lane, playing Shylock, on 26 January. 'The boxes were empty, and the pit not half full,' Hazlitt would recall, 'The whole presented a dreary, hopeless aspect. I was in considerable apprehension for the result. From the first scene in which Mr Kean came on, my doubts were at an end.'[51] The actor was twenty-seven, with a reputation for offstage dissipation and onstage brilliance. His impact was explicable partly by his appearance: he was thin-featured with black hair, dark eyes, and a penetrating stare. 'For voice, eye, action, and expression, no actor has come out for many years at all equal to him,' said Hazlitt.[52] Rejecting the usual interpretation of Shylock as a comic grotesque, Kean portrayed him with the intensity usually reserved for Hamlet and Richard III: 'in giving effect to the conflict of passions arising out of the contrasts of situation, in varied vehemence of declamation, in keenness of sarcasm, in the rapidity of his transitions from one tone and feeling to another, in propriety and novelty of action, presenting a succession of striking pictures, and giving perpetually fresh shocks of delight and surprise, it would be difficult to single out a competitor.'[53] This was a delivery to match Hazlitt's own compelling manner—something akin to the impact of Marlon Brando's appearance in *A Streetcar Named Desire* in 1947, another performance that changed the way in which people thought about acting. At first, Perry questioned Hazlitt's opinion but the reviewer insisted 'it would last'.[54] And he was right. Kean knew how to draw an audience into his character's psychology, while looming over them in an almost threatening way. Playgoers were thrilled, and he played to packed houses. It was the beginning of the end of the Kemble 'religion'; from now on, everyone modelled themselves on Kean.

In ensuing weeks he came out as Richard III, Hamlet, Othello, and Iago, and on each occasion Hazlitt reviewed him. Sometimes Hazlitt was so inspired that he treated readers not just to an account of Kean's interpretation, but to a discussion of how the play worked. It was a tour de force of intellectual energy, all the more so for the circumstances of composition:

> Many of these articles (particularly the Theatrical Criticism) are unavoidably written over night, just as the paper is going to the press, without correction or previous preparation. Yet they will often stand a comparison with more laboured compositions. It is curious that what is done at so short a notice should bear so few marks of haste. In fact, there is a kind of *extempore* writing, as well as *extempore* speaking. Both are the effect of necessity and habit. . . . Where there is the necessary stimulus for making the effort, what is given from a first impression, what is struck off at a blow, is in many respects better than what is produced on reflection, and at several heats.[55]

None of this can have helped Hazlitt's home life; typically, he did not return to York Street until around 4am when the paper went to press.

For all their brilliance, his theatre reviews caused strains with his editor. As Mary Russell Mitford, a friend of Perry, recalled,

> Mr. Perry used to contemplate the long column of criticism—and how he used to execrate 'the damned fellow's damned stuff' for filling up so much of the paper in the very height of the Advertisement season. I shall never forget his long face. It was the only time of the day that I ever saw it either long or sour. He had not the slightest suspicion that he had a man of genius in his pay—not the most remote perception of the merit of the writing—nor the slightest companionship with the Author.[56]

Yet Mitford was aware of at least one reason for Perry's unappreciativeness. The previous year his wife Anne had gone to Lisbon to seek treatment for tuberculosis, and on her return voyage was captured by pirates and taken to Algiers. The experience had such a devastating effect on her health that soon after her release she died, aged 37. Anxiety over her fate is one likely cause of Perry's failure to acknowledge Hazlitt's talent.

As the year wore on, Napoleon's situation became desperate, and Hazlitt became more strident in his support of him in the leader columns. As late as 1 March, with the Allies marching on Paris, he trumpeted what he took to be Napoleon's resurgence: 'The march to Paris has been tried and has failed. . . . Alas! how chop-fallen the would-be heroes who with such big words called for nothing less than perpetual war, or the utter extermination of the BONAPARTEAN dynasty.'[57] But time was against both him and the doomed Emperor. On 3 April he published a lengthy condemnation of the war and the French royal family.[58] He could not have known that Paris had fallen several days earlier, the news reaching London only on 5 April. Celebrations began immediately, and four days later came news of Napoleon's abdication.

'We rejoiced at this great point being gained,' recorded Joseph Farington, the Royal Academician, in his diary.[59] 'Babylon the great is fallen!', gloated Stoddart in *The Times*, 'Paris, the proud city, the city of philosophy, has bowed her neck to the conqueror.'[60] Celebrations continued for months. London was lit up: the Crown and Anchor in the Strand (once a hotbed of radical protest) displayed 'A brilliant Star and Festoons', while one of Hazlitt's favourite haunts, Drury Lane Theatre, was 'entirely illuminated with the word PEACE, in letters of about four feet each, with an Imperial Crown'.[61] A 'Jubilee' in the London Parks featured fire-eaters, dancing dogs, and gingerbread stalls while a Chinese pagoda was constructed on a bridge in St James's Park and a 'Temple of Concord' erected in Green Park.

There were furious sessions in the Cider Cellars with a few intimates including Finnerty and John Black, the hard-drinking Scot on the foreign news desk. This self-destructive phase was precipitated by genuine disappointment, for with Napoleon's downfall it seemed that the Revolution had failed: the Bourbons would be restored to France and Spain, the Spanish Inquisition reinstated, and Europe carved up among the Allies. It was after one of these drinking bouts that the angry journalist stumbled into the Lambs' one evening in early April and lashed out at everyone, going so far as to inform his host 'he did not admire him on account of his infinite littleness'. Afterwards, Hazlitt was so appalled at his own conduct that he was 'ashamed to shew his face' there again.[62] His place at Lamb's table was henceforth occupied by Stoddart, puffed up, toad-like, with self-righteous satisfaction. After this dark point, Hazlitt's 'spirit refused to look abroad or be comforted'.[63] It was a profoundly undermining experience.

> To have all the world against us is trying to a man's temper and philosophy. It unhinges even our opinion of our own motives and intentions. It is like striking the actual world from under our feet: the void that is left, the death-like pause, the chilling suspense, is fearful.[64]

Hazlitt's ill-judged leader articles did his career no favours. Perry hated to find himself on the losing side, and to be labelled Napoleon's poodle was not something with which he had ever been comfortable. One night he hauled Hazlitt out of the Cider Cellars and ordered him to write an article on press freedom. 'Do it!' he ordered. He stood over Hazlitt while, bleary-eyed, he put pen to paper. After a few minutes Perry pulled the manuscript from his grasp and glanced at the opening sentences; sneering, he crumpled it into a ball and threw it at him. 'This is the most pimping thing I ever read!' he barked. 'If you cannot do a thing of this kind you won't do for me.' Hazlitt blamed this on the fall of Bonaparte, 'by which my articles were made in the event very unfortunate'.[65]

Matters worsened when Hazlitt reviewed the British Institution's summer exhibition in May. Sir Thomas Lawrence's portrait of Lord Castlereagh, he wrote, 'has a smug, smart, upstart, haberdasher look'.[66] Hazlitt had scant regard

Chapter 9

Fig. 17. James Perry, Hazlitt's first editor, as depicted by Sir Thomas Lawrence in 1814. Hazlitt was probably not aware that Lawrence was working on this portrait when he ridiculed the artist in the pages of Perry's paper.

for Lawrence whose portraits 'might do very well as mirrors for personal vanity to contemplate itself in'.[67] Nor did he care for its subject; after all, Castlereagh's brutal suppression of the rebellion of 1798 had cost the lives of many thousands. Unfortunately, it so happened that Lawrence (then one of the most fashionable artists in London) was at that moment painting Perry—who, upon reading Hazlitt's comments, inserted a response in the next available edition of the paper:

> We by no means agree with the observations of our Correspondent on the Portrait of Lord Castlereagh, in which the Critic seems to have mixed the ebullition of party spirit with his ideas of characteristic resemblance. Politics have nothing to do with the Fine Arts. It is universally agreed, that one of the best Portraits in the Exhibition, if not the very best, in every essential point of the art, is that of Lord Castlereagh.[68]

[165]

So far as I am aware, this is a unique example of an editor contradicting the judgement of his own art critic. By doing so, Perry drew more attention than ever to Hazlitt's comments, making himself look ridiculous into the bargain.

Mary Russell Mitford thought this was why Perry got rid of Hazlitt—and it is the usual explanation given by biographers.[69] But Perry had another axe to grind: 'Whether Hazlitt's offence was writing in other papers, I cannot tell,' reflected Henry Crabb Robinson.[70] Not only had Hazlitt been moonlighting at *The Examiner* and *The Champion*; he was implicated in attacks on Perry in at least one of them, for on 12 June 1814 Leigh Hunt castigated Perry in *The Examiner* for reporting falsely that the Prince Regent was applauded rather than hissed when he appeared in public:

> He is a party-man it is true; but what is very curious is, that his party feels with the public in this matter; and whether party-man or not, he has been accustomed to exhibit too much spirit and independence as a journalist to render this strange appearance on his part a matter of indifference.[71]

This cut Perry to the quick. He liked the company of lords, but wasn't a toady of the Prince Regent. As he mulled over the attack, he began to suspect that Hazlitt was responsible for it: he had to be the 'W.H.' over whose initials Hunt published 'On Hogarth's Marriage-a-la-Mode' in that very issue. He reacted accordingly.

> Perry said to him expressly that he wished Hazlitt to *look out for another situation*—the affronting language Hazlitt could not easily forget—as he was not fit for a reporter. Hazlitt said he could do miscellaneous things. Perry said he would think of it. However, when Hazlitt afterwards went to the office for his salary he was told Mr. Perry wished to speak with him. He went to Perry's room. Perry was not alone, and desired Hazlitt to wait. Hazlitt went to another room. Perry then seeing Hazlitt there, went out of the house. Hazlitt, in consequence, never called again.[72]

CHAPTER 10

To be in want of money, is to pass through life with little credit or pleasure; it is ... to be a law-stationer, or a scrivener or scavenger, or newspaper reporter.

Hazlitt, 'On the Want of Money'[1]

H AZLITT had no difficulty finding work elsewhere. For Leigh Hunt he embarked on one of his finest theatrical reviews, of Kean's Iago.[2] Now at the height of his powers, Kean opened in the part on 2 July: it was, Hazlitt thought, 'one of the most extraordinary exhibitions on the stage'.[3] Instead of acting the villain, Kean performed him as 'an excellent good fellow and lively bottle-companion'.[4] This 'completely foiled the critics' who hardly knew what to make of it.[5] But the audience did: they were spellbound.

However much Hazlitt produced for *The Examiner* and *The Champion*, there was still a shortfall in his earnings compared with what he made at the *Chronicle*. Sarah argued they should scale down and find somewhere cheaper to live—a suggestion given force by an unexpected piece of news. On 25 July 1814 Francis Place, the tailor and reformer, toured Bentham's garden with the architect James Bevans, who had been commissioned to design and build a 'Chrestomathic' school which would expound Utilitarian ideas. Milton's garden would be paved over and in its place would stand an octagonal building ninety feet in diameter that would accommodate 600 children who would enter through a gateway on the site of 19 York Street—which would be demolished.

> They propose to erect a Chrestomathic school, by cutting down some fine old trees on the classic ground where Milton thought and wrote, to introduce a rabble of children, who for the Greek and Latin languages, poetry, and history, that fine pabulum of useful enthusiasm, that breath of immortality infused into our youthful blood, that balm and cordial of our future years, are to be drugged with chemistry and apothecaries' receipts, are to be taught to do every thing, and to see and feel nothing.[6]

Part III: A Philosopher in Grub Street

It was not that Hazlitt was against education but that he saw a hideous irony to which the Utilitarians were blind: the trees under which Milton once composed the greatest poem in the English language stood on sacred ground. Its conservation would be a far greater tribute to the educative impulse than the erection of a Utilitarian academy could ever be. Indeed, Hazlitt saw the plan to destroy Milton's garden as symptomatic of the soullessness of the entire Utilitarian project. He felt as protective of the trees (to which he had no access) as he did of the house. But when he tried to reason with Place, he got nowhere.[7]

Hazlitt pointed out to Sarah that to move now would play into Bentham's hands. He was determined to stay, if only to preserve the house. Sarah was anxious to go, for she detested the building (already in a state of considerable decay) almost as much as she did the area in which it stood. It may have been at around this moment that she began to consider separating from her husband. Despite these pressures, Hazlitt was not to be deterred. As a show of defiance, he paid for a commemorative tablet to be embedded in the wall outside his study, overlooking Bentham's garden, reading 'Sacred to Milton, Prince of Poets'. Shortly after, Bentham ambled in its shade with 'some expatriated Patriot or Transatlantic Adventurer' and paused, 'for want of breath and with lack-lustre eye', to point out the stone to his guest.[8] To the philosopher, such gestures were futile sentimentalities, and he probably said as much.

July 1814 brought a literary sensation: Wordsworth's *Excursion*. Hazlitt probably read 'The Ruined Cottage' and 'The Pedlar' at Alfoxden in 1798; now, sixteen years later, they comprised part of the new nine-book poem.[9] It was published in the lavish quarto format—similar to what we call a coffee-table book—within the means only of the well-heeled. The first Hazlitt knew of it was when Martin Burney told him Lamb had received a presentation copy. He immediately asked Burney whether he could beg its loan on his behalf: he wanted to review the poem and could not afford to buy one. This was a tricky manoeuvre. Hazlitt had not yet re-established contact with Lamb having (as Lamb reported to Wordsworth) 'blowed us up about 6 months ago, since which the union hath snapt'.[10] Burney agreed to make the request and Lamb, who held no grudge, handed it over.

No one was better qualified to assess Wordsworth's achievement. Hazlitt knew what had been projected—a poem that aimed to change the moral and political constitution of the world forever, bringing about a new brotherhood of man. It was dreamed up by Coleridge and adopted by Wordsworth as his life's work. By no means the failure it has been claimed, *The Excursion* is in many respects a triumph. But to one who knew the ambitions of its conception, it could not help falling short. Originally intended to sweep away differences of class, wealth, and privilege, it was now dedicated to William Lowther, second Lord Lonsdale—a Tory Peer with a seat on the Treasury board.[11] Hazlitt saw what this signified: in the six years since their last meeting, Wordsworth had followed in the wake of Southey and Coleridge, becoming a government lackey. How were the mighty fallen!

Hazlitt's review appeared in three parts in *The Examiner* between 21 August and 2 October 1814.[12] It could hardly have begun more favourably: 'In power of intellect, in lofty conception, in the depth of feeling, at once simple and sublime, which pervades every part of it, and which gives to every object an almost preternatural and preterhuman interest, this work has seldom been surpassed.'[13] It went on to encapsulate the essential qualities of Wordsworth's poetry:

> the evident scope and tendency of Mr. Wordsworth's mind is the reverse of dramatic. It resists all change of character, all variety of scenery, all the bustle, machinery, and pantomime of the stage, or of real life—whatever might relieve or relax or change the direction of its own activity, jealous of all competition. The power of his mind preys upon itself. It is as if there were nothing but himself and the universe. He lives in the busy solitude of his own heart; in the deep silence of thought. His imagination lends life and feeling only to 'the bare trees and the mountains bare'; peoples the viewless tracts of air, and converses with the silent clouds![14]

'Ha!', Wordsworth exclaimed when this was read out to him, 'the dog writes strong.' But upon discovering the dog's name, he was thrown 'into a greater rage than ever'.[15] He had come to loathe Hazlitt, and could not accept his judgement, favourable or not. Wordsworth's antipathy is understandable: not only was Hazlitt the voice of a liberal conscience to which he had long turned a deaf ear, he was also an unwelcome reminder of the young man he had once been, and the radical principles he had disowned. What option was there but to discredit him?

Hazlitt had an investment in *The Excursion*, for he suspected that one of its main protagonists, the Solitary, through whom Wordsworth critiqued the French Revolution, was a thinly disguised portrait of their mutual friend Joseph Fawcett. This left an unpleasant taste in Hazlitt's mouth, for the despairing Solitary was not the Fawcett he remembered, nor did he resemble other radicals. Indignation led him to compose for the second part of the review one of the finest passages of prose he ever published, pledging fidelity to ideals Wordsworth had abandoned.

> ... yet we will never cease, nor be prevented from, returning on the wings of imagination to that bright dream of our youth; that glad-dawn of the day-star of liberty; that spring-time of the world, in which the hopes and expectations of the human race seemed opening in the same gay career with our own; when France called her children to partake her equal blessings under her laughing skies; when the stranger was met in all her villages with dance and festive songs, in celebration of a new and golden era; and when, to the retired and contemplative student, the prospects of human happiness and glory were seen ascending, like the steps of Jacob's ladder, in bright and never-ending succession. The dawn of that day was suddenly overcast: that season of hope is past: it is fled with the other dreams of our youth, which we cannot recall, but has left behind it traces, which are not to be effaced by birthday odes, or the chaunting of *Te Deums* in all the churches of Christendom. To those hopes eternal regrets are due: to those who maliciously and wilfully blasted them, in the fear that they might be accomplished, we feel no less what we owe—hatred and scorn as lasting.[16]

It is impossible to be unmoved by Hazlitt's belief in revolution and the knowledge that its failure was the great tragedy of his life. He had lived to witness the first step towards an egalitarian society only to see it swept away. The unelected monarchies of Europe would hold on to power by all means available, propped up by former republicans and regicides. That was why he cried as he read *The Excursion*, 'because he was disappointed, and could not praise it as it deserved.'[17]

The third part of the review contained a riff on the Cumbrian peasantry, raising the eyebrows of those who read it: 'All country-people hate each other,' he began. 'There is nothing good to be had in the country, or, if there is, they will not let you have it. They had rather injure themselves than oblige any one else. The common mode of life is a system of wretchedness and self-denial, like what you read of among barbarous tribes.'[18] He could have left it at that, but went on:

> The small-beer is sure to be sour—the milk skimmed—the meat bad, or spoiled in the cooking. You cannot do a single thing you like; you cannot walk out or sit at home, or write or read, or think or look as if you did, without being subject to impertinent curiosity. The apothecary annoys you with his complaisance; the parson with his superciliousness. If you are poor, you are despised; if you are rich, you are feared and hated. ... There is a perpetual round of mischief-making

and backbiting for want of any better amusement. There are no shops, no taverns, no theatres, no opera, no concerts, no pictures, no public-buildings, no crowded streets, no noise of coaches, or of courts of law,—neither courtiers nor courtesans, no literary parties, no fashionable routes, no society, no books, or knowledge of books.[19]

Whatever else can be said, this was a tour de force of invective, hugely entertaining in itself. And he did know something about country people, particularly those in the Lake District, who had run him out of Keswick in 1803. Wordsworth and his family realized this immediately. His wife, Mary, observed how Hazlitt 'declaims against the Poverty of the country,—That *nothing good* is to be got—speaks of the want of every thing that is intellectual and elegant, enumerates these wants, and amongst the items courtezans are found. A pretty comment upon these opinions would be to relate the story of the critic's departure [from] this unaccommodating country.'[20] When Hazlitt's review was read out by John Wilson, Wordsworth told him of the Keswick escapade and in so doing provided a malicious man with a powerful weapon he later used against Hazlitt.[21]

Shortly before 19 September 1814, Lamb retrieved his copy of *The Excursion* from 'detention', embarrassed at having lent it for a review that, he told Wordsworth, 'wore a slovenly air of dispatch and disrespect'.[22] Well, what else *could* he say? In fact, Hazlitt's review was one of the most sophisticated to appear, spelling out for the first time the principal arguments which readers of *The Excursion* have been debating ever since.

The Hazlitts attended their local church, St Margaret's, Westminster, on 26 September 1814, for the baptism of their son.[23] This time (probably because the occasion was arranged by Sarah) a priest was notified. St Margaret's had a colourful history. Hazlitt knew Milton was married here, but could not have known it was where Samuel Pepys arranged extramarital trysts, Pepys's diary not being published until 1825. The certificate records Hazlitt's profession as 'Gentleman', and the godfathers as Walter Coulson and Martin Burney. By now, Coulson was 'very intimate . . . with Mr. Hazlitt and Mr. Martin Burney'[24]—that is, they probably went drinking together. Burney, once described by Southey as 'the queerest fish out of water',[25] was a renowned eccentric, completely unlike his straitlaced father, Captain Burney, and got on famously with Hazlitt, often joining him for morose bouts in the Cider Cellars; for his part, Hazlitt loved him as a brother.

Part III: A Philosopher in Grub Street

The baptism can only have reminded Sarah that her husband was once more without a regular income. Under renewed pressure, he found work wherever he could. The departure of John Scott, editor of *The Champion*, for Paris in late September, gave him hope of a temporary post. Hazlitt met him while visiting Leigh Hunt in prison and Scott had the wisdom to acknowledge his talent. An Aberdonian who went to school with Byron, Scott had worked alongside Hunt at the War Office and since 1813 been owner and editor of *Drakard's Paper*, which became *The Champion* at the start of 1814. Irascible by nature, he made a bad impression on others; Robinson described him as 'a little swarthy man with rather an unpleasant expression in his countenance'.[26] By the time Hazlitt left the *Chronicle* he was contributing leaders to Scott's paper and was soon writing theatre and art reviews for him as well. In the months following Napoleon's defeat, France opened up and the English flocked there in droves. Hazlitt would have loved to return but lacked either the money or the leisure, and instead suggested to Scott, who was determined to go, that he cover editorial duties during his absence.

Scott agreed,[27] and while he was away *The Champion* carried Hazlitt's first front-page commentary,[28] a number of drama reviews, a leader article, and a series of essays on the fine arts, including one on Reynolds.[29] They included a four-part article, 'Fine Arts, whether they are promoted by academies and public institutions?', attacking the Royal Academy and the British Institution. Suspicion of official bodies was in Hazlitt's blood. His father's Unitarianism was an expression of contempt for the political and doctrinal abuses of the Church of England, and Hazlitt loathed the artistic establishment on similar grounds— their institutional interests were, he believed, antithetical to genuine creativity. His articles caught the approving eye of Catherine, second wife of Sir James Mackintosh, who sent him a letter of admiration to which Hazlitt responded. Before long, she had invited him for tea, over which they enjoyed a congenial conversation.

'Do you happen to know Mr Jeffrey?' she asked.

'You mean the editor of the *Edinburgh*?'

'Just so.' Lady Mackintosh had not written for the *Edinburgh Review*[30] but her husband had done so since November 1812.

'I do not, madam. But would like to.' Catherine Mackintosh smiled.

'Perhaps I might write him on your account.'

'I should be most grateful.'[31]

As favours went, this was a sizeable one. The *Edinburgh* was the opinion-former of the day, with a circulation of 13,000 and a readership of many thousands more.[32] Hazlitt would join the most distinguished stable of talents in the literary world, including Henry Brougham, Sydney Smith, and Thomas Moore. Its political complexion, as these names suggest, was Whig; that would do for him.

When Mackintosh discovered his wife had given Hazlitt a helping hand, he didn't like it. 'I was rather amused at the effrontery of Mr Hazlett', he told her, 'who abused me in the *Examiner* and who now employs you to procure him influence and income in the *Edinburgh Review*.'[33] He was sore at Hazlitt's essay, 'Why the Arts are not Progressive?', which lumped his forthcoming *History of Britain* alongside Miss Burney's new novel, Miss Edgeworth's tales, and Madame de Staël's next work, 'whatever it may be'.[34] This may seem innocuous to us, but to Mackintosh it was a source of humiliation.[35] How galling to find that his wife had just promoted the man responsible for it!

By then, Hazlitt was 'in a very flattering manner enrolled in [Jeffrey's] corps'[36]—an association of which he was proud, not just because it paid well (£25 per article), but for the journal's prestige. 'This has put Hazlitt in good spirits,' Robinson told his diary, 'he now again hopes that his talents will be appreciated, and become a subsistence to him.'[37] Hazlitt remained with the *Edinburgh* for the rest of his life; only his association with *The Examiner* would last so long.

A few days after Scott's return, a revolution took place at Blackfriars where John Walter II began to print *The Times* with mechanized steam presses, increasing production to over 1,300 copies an hour compared with 250 using the hand-powered Stanhope press. By 1818 production had risen to 2,000 an hour, and new methods of distribution meant the paper arrived in the furthest reaches of the kingdom within a day of publication.[38] Hazlitt would make fun of these new developments, saying the *Times* was a 'prodigious prosing paper...which seems to be written as well as printed by a steam-engine'.[39] But newspaper proprietors would have to invest in the new technology were they to survive. Demand for newsprint continued to grow, and Hazlitt was a beneficiary. In the past year he had managed to turn his fortunes around and was beginning to make his mark. He wrote what he wanted and published with whomever he chose. By that means, he preserved his independence. That was how he liked it.

Part III: A Philosopher in Grub Street

The Hunt brothers were released from jail on 2 February 1815. Leigh Hunt wanted to resume his usual editorial duties from the *Examiner* office in Maiden Lane, but the psychological effects of imprisonment led him to suffer a form of agoraphobia. For the time being he stayed with his old friend Thomas Massa Alsager at his home at Blackman Street, barely a minute's walk from the prison.[40] This was inconvenient not least because it stymied Hunt's plan of resuming the post of drama critic. He asked Hazlitt to write the first of several drama reviews and then, on 28 May, installed him as 'Theatrical Examiner', a post Hazlitt retained until October 1816, writing 65 reviews over 75 weeks. For the most part, this was less strenuous than his work for the *Chronicle* because *The Examiner* was a Sunday paper, giving him (in most cases) a day or two's grace before deadline. He would review several new productions each week, and late nights remained part of the job.

Another famous prisoner had just jumped the wall. News reached London of Napoleon's escape from Elba and landing at Fréjus on Friday 10 March. It was the beginning of the Hundred Days. Louis XVIII scuttled back to London and the Allies regrouped. Hazlitt followed Napoleon's progress as he marched north.

> Those days were jocund and jubilant—full of heart's ease and of *allegresse*. Its footsteps had an audible echo through the earth. Laughed eyes, danced hearts, clapped hands at it. It 'loosened something at the chest'; and men listened with delight and wonder (wherever such were to be found) to the unbarring and unbolting of those doors of despotism which they thought had been closed on them forever. All that was human rejoiced; the tyrant and the slave shrunk back aghast, as the clash of arms was drowned in the shout of the multitude.... Therefore Buonaparte seemed from his first landing to bestride the country like a Colossus, for in him rose up once more the prostrate might and majesty of man; and the Bourbons, like toads or spiders, got out of the way of the huge shadow of the Child Roland of the Revolution.[41]

Something of Hazlitt's mood is indicated by the fact that Sarah now became pregnant with a son, who would be born in the autumn. Hazlitt was not alone in such revived hopes: Thomas Moore was 'decidedly glad' of Napoleon's return, while Byron declared himself sickened by the Allies and the 'barking of the wardogs'.[42]

On the evening of 12 March Hazlitt wandered into the offices of *The Champion* to see its editor. Scott took him to the Cider-Cellars where they engaged in conversation on subjects other than work. Despite being married to one of the most beautiful women of the time, Caroline Colnaghi, Scott was a notorious wife-beater. He had been known to strike her when angry about nothing more than the colour of a carpet.[43] A chance remark about her led the unguarded Hazlitt to divulge revelations of his own, dropping hints about infidelities, peccadilloes, and *amours de voyages.*[44]

'Scott was an unhappy man and ill-used everybody he knew,' Haydon once said.[45] On the next available front page of *The Champion* Scott alleged Hazlitt was responsible for the immorality associated with *The Examiner.* Leigh Hunt was led astray by his theatre reviewer, he suggested, who encouraged in him 'a wayward and unmanly disregard of those observances which are necessary to render talent respectable'.[46] Hazlitt was upset and told Benjamin Robert Haydon, whom he had known since 1812, having been introduced to him by Northcote. Haydon was volatile, self-regarding, impecunious, devoutly religious, and fiercely intelligent. He alienated most of those he befriended, but for now was intrigued by this brilliant man who had failed as an artist. For his part, Hazlitt ruminated: 'I don't know what it is that attaches me to Haydon so much, except that he and I, whenever we meet, sit in judgment on another set of old friends, and "carve them as a dish fit for the Gods." '[47] Over the next few years they became good friends.

Haydon recorded in his diary that Scott 'made Haslitt tipsey, got out the secrets & weaknesses of his nature, & then assailed him the very next Sunday in an anonymous letter, touching on these very points.'[48] Hazlitt also told Leigh Hunt what had happened, who advised him to break with Scott. It was a painful course of action not just because of the betrayal, but because it shut off a much-needed source of income. Hazlitt would not return to *The Champion* until Joseph Clayton Jennyns took it over in August 1817.

He must have found it irritating not to be able to write commentaries during Napoleon's Hundred Days, but Hunt wrote the *Examiner*'s leaders, and Hazlitt was restricted to the drama column. His frustrations bubbled over in argument with Robinson on 15 April: 'Hazlitt retains all his hatred of kings and bad governments, and believing them to be incorrigible, he (from a principle of revenge) rejoices that they are punished. ... Hazlitt is angry with the friends of liberty for weakening their strength by going with the common foe against Buonaparte, by which the old governments are so much assisted.'[49] Hazlitt was right to be annoyed with the Whigs for abandoning Napoleon, the only chance the French people had of creating a democracy. But Robinson thought him 'wrong as well as offensive in almost all he said'.[50]

Part III: A Philosopher in Grub Street

His frustrations led him to smuggle political comment into whatever he wrote, sometimes with unfortunate consequences. Reviewing Fanny Burney's novel *The Wanderer*, Hazlitt denounced George III as a warmonger under whose reign 'our prose has run mad and our poetry grown childish'.[51] Burney's position as Keeper of the Queen's robes gave point to this observation—and Hazlitt went on to say that her female characters 'stand so upon the order of their going, that they do not go at all. . . . They would consider it as quite indecorous to run down stairs though the house were in flames, or to move off the pavement though a scaffolding was falling.'[52] Hilarious as this was to readers of the *Edinburgh Review*, it gave scant cheer to the novelist and her family. Indeed, she soon raised the matter with her brother, Captain James Burney. As it happened, he knew Hazlitt well, for he was one of those who regularly attended the Lambs' 'at homes'—and as the Lambs had recently opened their doors again to Hazlitt, the two men were once more playing whist together. Reading Hazlitt's ribaldries about his sister's novel, Captain Burney was barely able to contain himself. Friendship, it seemed to him, had to count for something, especially when it came to reviews. And if Hazlitt didn't like his sister's writings he could at least say so more respectfully. Were Burney to continue playing cards with the man, it would be seen as an endorsement. As he saw it, he had no choice: he set pen to paper in a reproachful letter that brought their friendship to an end.

> May 17th 1815
>
> Sir
>
> It would be strange, if not wrong, after years of intimate acquaintance, that cause of offence should happen between us, and be so taken, and be passed over in silence, and that acquaintance still continue. Your attack on my Sister's early publications dissatisfied me, and the more in coming from a quarter I had been in the habit of believing friendly. If I had seen it before publication, I should have remonstrated against some of your remarks because I think them unjust. Your publication of such a paper shewed a total absence of regard towards me, and I must consider it as the termination of our acquaintance—
>
> Jas Burney[53]

Hazlitt and Burney continued to coincide at the Lambs' for years, but never again exchanged a word.

When it became clear that Allied forces under Wellington were soon to confront Napoleon, anti-war demonstrators mounted protests in New Palace Yard, Whitehall, on 18 May and 15 June. Perhaps Hazlitt joined them; if so, he would have heard speeches by Major Cartwright, Sir Francis Burdett, and Henry 'Orator' Hunt. In that charged atmosphere, everything was politicized. A week before the Battle of Waterloo, on 11 June, Hazlitt reviewed *Comus* at Covent Garden, aware he was noticing the work of a republican who remained true to his principles even under Charles II.

> We have no less respect for the memory of Milton as a patriot than as a poet. Whether he was a true patriot, we shall not inquire: he was at least a consistent one. He did not retract his defence of the people of England; he did not say that his sonnets to Vane or Cromwell were meant ironically; he was not appointed Poet Laureat to a Court which he had reviled and insulted; he accepted neither place nor pension; nor did he write paltry sonnets upon the 'Royal fortitude' of the House of Stuart, by which, however, they really lost something.[54]

This was an undisguised attack on Southey and Wordsworth. The poem to which Hazlitt referred had just appeared for the first time in Wordsworth's *Poems* (1815), 'Now that all hearts are glad, all faces bright', a celebration of George III's 'regal fortitude' in the face of deepening insanity.

Now in London, Wordsworth was visiting mutual friends and acquaintances—Godwin, Lamb, Robinson, John Scott, and Haydon—while stipulating Hazlitt's exclusion from any gathering to which he was invited. Lamb was once again entertaining Hazlitt at his get-togethers and hated the idea of excluding him, but he obliged, as did everyone else.[55] When Wordsworth saw the review of *Comus* he was determined to take revenge. What was the paper? *The Examiner*. And who was its editor? Oh yes . . .

Having recovered from his agoraphobia, Hunt was now settled with his family at Maida Vale. Relations between him and Wordsworth had become cordial in recent months. Henry Brougham, a mutual friend, told the poet 'his writings were valued by Mr Hunt',[56] and just before Hunt's release from prison Wordsworth sent him a copy of his *Poems* (1815). The day Hazlitt's review was published there came a knock at Hunt's door. When told who it was, Hunt guessed at once the reason for his visit.

Wordsworth entered the drawing-room with his left hand lodged in his waist-coat pocket—a favourite pose. It was their first encounter. Hunt later recalled his 'dignified manner, with a deep and roughish but not unpleasing voice, and an exalted mode of speaking'.[57] As they shook hands a child's go-cart happened to pass in the garden.

'Would you like refreshment, Mr Wordsworth?', asked Hunt.

'Anything which is *going forward*', replied the poet, at which Hunt 'felt inclined to ask him whether he would take a piece of the cart'.[58]

Hunt later noted that Wordsworth's apparent intention was 'to thank me for the zeal I had shown in advocating the cause of his genius'[59] but he was well aware that the poet's actual mission was more serious. He made a pre-emptive strike and bravely put a copy of the morning's paper in his hand.

'Have you seen the paper of the morning?' he asked. 'If you have, I should consider your call as a higher honour.'[60] It was a masterstroke, and for a moment Wordsworth was dumbfounded. Hunt pointed out the review of *Comus*. But at that point his courage deserted him.

'Is this your work?', enquired Wordsworth.

'Not mine, sir', Hunt replied, 'but one of the more wilful contributors.'[61] It could only have been Hazlitt's. At this point Wordsworth did what he always did, ascribing Hazlitt's hostility to embarrassment at the Keswick escapade, which he now related in all its glory. For years to come, this was Wordsworth's response to accusations of political apostasy. But Hazlitt's claims were just. This was the poet who had advocated a new kind of poetry designed to address the concerns of working people and precipitate a more egalitarian society. This was the man who less than ten years earlier had declared the duty of the Government as being 'to give consideration to the people at large, and to have *equality* always in view'.[62] This was the pamphleteer who had once justified revolutionary violence. Now in his mid-fifties, Wordsworth was a changed man. Like Coleridge and Southey, he no longer believed in those things. He supported King and country, no longer willing to question the principles by which they claimed authority. He was, as Mary Godwin observed when she first read *The Excursion*, 'a slave'.[63]

Charles Lamb invited both Hazlitt and his wife to one of their 'at homes' on Saturday 17 June. Besides being one of the few occasions they went out together, it gave Sarah a break from the boredom of pregnancy. After four and a half months, she was eager to see old friends. All the same, noted Robinson, Hazlitt 'looked wild and uncomfortable',[64] probably because Sarah had ordered him not to get into arguments—a near impossibility given that the Allies were in the countryside outside Brussels preparing for the most decisive encounter of the war. Against the odds, Hazlitt managed to contain himself. His discomfort was not eased by Captain Burney, whom he now encountered for the first time since the letter of 'dissatisfaction'.

Chapter 10

The Battle of Waterloo took place on 18 June. Three nights later Haydon was walking across town late at night, having had dinner at John Scott's house. As he crossed Portman Square he ran into a messenger from the Foreign Office.

'The Duke has beat Napoleon, taken one hundred and fifty pieces of cannon, and is marching to Paris!', the man shouted. Haydon stared at him, stunned.

'Is it true?' he shouted back.

'True!' came the answer, as the man disappeared into the darkness. Delirious, Haydon sprinted back to Scott's. The house was dark; everyone was in bed. Haydon knocked loudly on the door.

'Who is it?', Scott shouted from the upstairs window. 'What do you want?'

'The Duke has beat Napoleon, taken one hundred and fifty pieces of cannon, and is marching to Paris!' Scott's mouth went dry; his journalistic instincts kicked in, and questions poured out of his mouth.

'None of your questions—it's a fact!' shouted Haydon.[65]

'Total Defeat of Bonaparte' read the headline in the next day's *Morning Chronicle*: 'We stop the press to announce the most brilliant and complete victory ever obtained by the Duke of Wellington and which will forever exalt the Glory of the British Name.' The mood of jubilation exceeded even that of the preceding year, for everyone knew this was the end of a two-decade-long conflict waged across the world. The cost in money and lives had been astronomical. Between 1793 and 1816 the British national debt rose from 273 to 816 million pounds; total war dead among European armies amounted to over three million. Here, it was hoped, was the end to blockades, press gangs, and the privations of war. Wellington was declared Prince of Waterloo by the King of the Netherlands, and chivalric orders of knighthood showered on him from Russia, Denmark, Naples, Saxony, and Bavaria. He was a hero to everyone but Hazlitt: 'I hate the sight of the Duke of Wellington for his foolish face, as much as for any thing else,' he told his friends, 'I cannot believe that a great general is contained under such a paste-board vizor of a man.'[66] On this occasion Lamb probably agreed with him; in later years he would compare 'the great moralist of Apsley House' with Punch.[67]

If disappointment at Napoleon's defeat in 1814 had been intense, that in 1815 was even more so. Meeting Hazlitt for the first time, a young lawyer, Thomas Noon Talfourd, found him 'staggering under the blow of Waterloo. . . as if he had sustained a personal wrong'.[68] Talfourd did not agree with Hazlitt's politics, but tried to engage him in philosophical discussion. All efforts to save Hazlitt were in vain. He was descending into a pit.

> As for Hazlitt, it is not to be believed how the destruction of Napoleon affected him; he seemed prostrated in mind and body: he walked about, unwashed, unshaved, hardly sober by day, and always intoxicated by night, literally, without exaggeration, for weeks; until at length wakening as it were from his stupor, he at once left off all stimulating liquors, and never touched them after. (Haydon, *Autobiography*)[69]

It was worse than any other episode he suffered. He cared as passionately about politics as did his father about his faith. He believed empowerment to rest in the hands of the populace, which had to free itself of monarchs, the landed gentry, and their tribe. To him, Napoleon's defeat represented 'the utter extinction of human liberty from the earth'.[70]

His columns in *The Examiner*, the only paper for which he wrote, became spasmodic and intermittent. Nor is it a coincidence that he now fell into arrears with local tax payments.[71] Sarah reminded him she was expecting a child in four months' time, and he needed to keep working. But he was too depressed to care. If it fell to one of his friends to take him in hand, Hunt is the most likely candidate. He had an interest in sobering him up—demand for fresh copy—and probably got him to Drury Lane for Kean's appearance in *Rule a Wife and Have a Wife* on 27 June, coaxing from him the review published in the next available issue of *The Examiner*. (Positioned on the back page, immediately after Hunt's leader, it was probably the last thing set before the paper went to press.)

'We went to see Mr Kean in Leon', Hazlitt began blearily, before regaining focus with a sharp, rigorous account of Kean's performance. The odd concluding sentence, with its heavily ironic manner, suggests Hazlitt heard someone rejoicing at the late victory, and responded with a rant about Wellington.[72] It is not hard to imagine uproar in the pit before the drama critic of *The Examiner* was ejected unceremoniously into the night.

But the binge was not over. For the next three weeks he made no appearance either in *The Examiner* or elsewhere; perhaps he consorted with the low-life figures of whom, from time to time, we catch glimpses in his lifestory—the pimps, prostitutes, badger-baiters, and billiard players of Regency London. Or perhaps he indulged in drinking sessions with his brother. He was always close to John Hazlitt who, now more than ever, would have been an ally. John's politics were, if anything, more radical than his own, and he would have shared Hazlitt's disappointment at Napoleon's downfall.

Then, as suddenly as he had disappeared, Hazlitt returned to the pages of *The Examiner*. We do not know how, or why, but we do know that he immersed himself in work, as if making up for lost time. Besides his weekly 'Theatrical Examiner', which noticed three or four openings a week, he published some of his best 'Round Table' essays during ensuing months. There is no evidence that he completely gave up drink but, as a rule, he moderated his consumption, and enjoyed a resurgence of energy that saw him through periods of frantic industry.[73]

For much of the late summer and early autumn of 1815 he was preoccupied with domestic matters. The York Street house cannot have been an easy or comfortable place in which to live. Hazlitt and Sarah were often at loggerheads, except on those occasions when they got drunk together; the rooms in which they lived were usually in a mess, as Sarah had little taste for housework; and there were the stresses and strains of managing the servants, something neither had much appetite for. It did not help when their housekeeper, Mrs Tomlinson, demanded that, with the impending arrival of another child, her daughter Becky move into York Street to lend a hand. The request seemed reasonable enough, and in any case neither of the Hazlitts wished to challenge it—but Becky was another mouth to feed and would mean an increase in the rates, calculated according to the number of inhabitants in each house. By 15 September Hazlitt's contributions to the poor rates were £3 16s 6d in arrears,[74] a debt that stood until the beginning of 1816. In the midst of such travails the great consolation was young William, now four. One day, while Hazlitt talked with Bewick in his office, he heard a scratching noise at the door, which slowly opened. In came William, on all fours. Hazlitt immediately jumped up, 'ran to him, and clasping his boy in his arms, hugged, and kissed, and caressed him, like some ardent loving mother with her first-born'.[75]

He continued to visit his brother, who needed his comradeship more than ever. Having put himself forward for an associateship of the Royal Academy, John Hazlitt failed to win a single vote. This was a reaction not only to his own radical politics, but to his brother's repeated attacks on the Academy itself—for Hazlitt had described Academicians as 'the worst judges of pictures'[76] and argued repeatedly that the Academy served only to vitiate the taste of the public.[77] Although Hazlitt's attacks were published without a byline, his identity was widely known within the Royal Academy.[78] With that failure, the alcoholism that blighted John's career began to worsen. Hazlitt visited him regularly, but was unable to halt his brother's decline.

On the evening of Monday 27 November Hazlitt was at Covent Garden theatre reviewing Frederick Reynolds' new farce *What's a Man of Fashion?*—'a question which it does not solve'.[79] It wasn't very good—at least, he commented that 'We do not think this farce a bit better than some we have lately noticed'[80]— but it did have one attraction: Lucia Elizabeth Mathews (better known as Madame Vestris), whom he liked. Perhaps he went to see her afterwards before returning home late; separated from her husband, the actress could boast numerous admirers.[81] Hazlitt returned home late and climbed into bed, only to be awakened in the small hours: his third and last son was born at 8.45 in the morning. He named him after his brother.

CHAPTER 11

*I do not think there is any thing deserving the name of
society to be found out of London . . .*
Hazlitt, 'On Coffee-House Politicians'[1]

*I went to Alsager's. There I met the Lambs, Hazlitt, Burrell,
Ayrton, Coulson, Sly, and Godson. I enjoyed the evening,
though I lost at cards, as I have uniformly done. Hazlitt was
sober, argumentative, acute, and interesting: I had no
conversation with him, but I enjoyed his conversation with
others. Lamb was good-humoured and droll, with great
originality, as usual . . .*
Henry Crabb Robinson, Diary, 9 December 1815[2]

THE sobriety was new—and Hazlitt better company as a result. That evening
he was enjoined to talk about the baby, which put him in buoyant mood.
He was probably prevailed upon to spend Christmas 1815 at home, but on Boxing Day he reviewed the pantomimes, perhaps taking young William with him,
now four, either to *George Barnwell* or (more likely) *Harlequin and Fortunio;
or The Poet's Last Shilling* at Covent Garden. It would have been William's first
glimpse of Grimaldi, of whom Hazlitt was an admirer:

> We were glad, right glad, to see Mr Grimaldi again. There was (some weeks back)
> an ugly report that Mr Grimaldi was dead. We would not believe it; we did not
> like to ask any one the question, but we watched the public countenance for the
> intimation of an event which 'would have eclipsed the harmless gaiety of nations.'
> We looked at the faces we met in the street, but there were no signs of general
> sadness; no one stopped his acquaintance to say, that a man of genius was no
> more. Here indeed he is, safe and sound, and as pleasant as ever. As without
> the gentleman at St Helena, there is an end of politics in Europe: so without the
> Clown at Sadler's Wells, there must be an end of pantomimes in this country![3]

Part III: A Philosopher in Grub Street

Hazlitt also got his first glimpse of the Indian jugglers at around this moment who, having arrived in September, took London by storm.[4] He was enchanted by their ability to keep four brass balls in the air at the same time, 'which is what none of us could do to save our lives'.[5] There were large rings on the jugglers' toes which, while they juggled, 'kept turning round all the time of the performance, as if they moved of themselves'.[6] Nor was this all. The jugglers specialized in sword-swallowing, terrifying their audiences, many of whom were seeing such feats for the first time; no one could have been more alarmed than Hazlitt: 'the police ought to interfere to prevent it,' he commented.[7]

He redoubled his efforts to make money. Besides theatrical pieces and 'Round Table' essays he was now writing regularly for the *Edinburgh Review*, which paid well. But that was not enough: the potential for real earnings lay in books. Throughout much of 1816 he composed *Characters of Shakespear's Plays*, drawing partly on his dramatic criticism, which would appear the following year. In addition, he worked on two other volumes—firstly, the *Memoirs of Holcroft*, which ran into the sand years before when Godwin took exception to his use of scurrilous passages from Holcroft's diary. He finally produced an acceptable manuscript and Longman was ready to put the book into production. The printer was John M'Creery, whose offices were in Black Horse Court off Fleet Street. M'Creery was a 'severe' Irishman from Burndennet near Strabane, County Tyrone, who had been part of the Roscoe circle in Liverpool years earlier, when Hazlitt was a struggling artist. He had liked Hazlitt then and was pleased to find himself working with him years later. Hazlitt would make regular journeys to his house in Stamford Street, Blackfriars, sometimes taking William Jr with him, where they supped while Hazlitt flirted with his host's two handsome daughters.[8] M'Creery was one of several printers with whom Hazlitt became intimate, others including Carew Henry Reynell and John Whiting. That he socialized with them indicates his close involvement in the typesetting process, when he would make last-minute alterations to his text. This collaboration was a happy one and Holcroft's *Memoirs* appeared on 20 April in an edition of 1,000. Just over half would sell; in 1818, the edition was remaindered.[9]

Hazlitt began immediately on something else—*The Round Table*, a collection of his and Leigh Hunt's *Examiner* essays in two volumes. Much was already written, printer's copy for volume 1 consisting of newspaper cuttings. In the week before Christmas 1815 he signed a contract with the Edinburgh publisher Archibald Constable, and sent the first pages to him early in February. Proofs,

Fig. 18. John M'Creery, the printer who probably had known Hazlitt in Liverpool during the 1790s, and who was to collaborate with him on the Memoirs of Holcroft. Despite his severity, Hazlitt seems always to have got on with him.

however, were slow in coming, and after a while Constable fell completely silent. Hazlitt began to worry and in a letter of 19 March wrote: 'I cannot help thinking the work would answer at least sufficiently to pay expenses & trouble as I know they are talked of in London, & the Examiner has received several inquiries to know if it was not intended to collect them into a separate publication.'[10] Constable proved dilatory, both as correspondent and as publisher. It wasn't that he disliked Hazlitt or his book but that, canny as he was, he suspected that (despite the enthusiasm of Hazlitt's friends) a collection of reheated newspaper pieces would attract little custom. Months would pass before publication. For someone like Hazlitt, who cared intensely about the quality of his work and its availability, this was by turns frustrating and depressing; it only deepened his suspicion that the fates were against him. Over the course of 1816 he wrote letter after letter to Constable, chivvying him along, only to be greeted, more often than not, with silence. 'May I ask what is become of the Round Table?', he enquired in June, 'I hope it is not broke down.'[11] His desperation was due partly to financial worries. '[I am] a poor author,' he told Constable in December,[12] when production of the volume had all but stalled—referring not to the quality of his work but to that of his purse. The experience was a grim lesson in the indignities of authorship and the inscrutable whimsicality of publishers, which made Hazlitt think twice before entrusting another book to Constable.

Financial need led him to accept commissions from Macvey Napier, who was recruiting contributors to the *Encyclopaedia Britannica*, of which he was editor. By 18 March Hazlitt had written 'Fine Arts', and in August he sent Napier an appreciation of the artist James Barry, which would be published (in much-shortened form) in 1817. Napier was so pleased with it he commissioned Hazlitt to write profiles of the philosopher Johann Bernhard Basedow, the scientist Johann Beckmann, and the Italian poet Xavier Bettinelli. 'I should like these in a month,' Napier stipulated.[13]

Leigh Hunt published *The Story of Rimini* in mid-February 1816. His most important long poem, telling the story of the incestuous lovers Paolo and Francesca from Dante's *Inferno*, was just the sort of thing to excite his friends' louche palates. 'It is full of beautiful and affecting passages,' Hazlitt told its author. 'You have I think perfectly succeeded. I like the description of the death of Francesca better than any. *This will do.* You are very metaphysical in the character and passion, but we will not say a word of this to the ladies.'[14] In the *Edinburgh* he summed up Hunt's life-affirming spirit:

> Mr Hunt...has mingled every tint of many-coloured life in the tissue of their story—blending tears with smiles, the dancing of the spirits with sad forebodings, the intoxication of hope with bitter disappointment, youth with age, life and death together. He has united something of the voluptuous pathos of Boccaccio with Ariosto's laughing graces. His court dresses, and gala processions he has borrowed from Watteau. His sunshine and his flowers are his own![15]

Hunt was delighted, remarking: 'If such men as Mr Hazlitt and Mr Jeffrey think well of it, and after the various adversities I have had, I can sit down to cultivate it quietly, and have my leg of mutton, and the run of the fields and the bookshops:—it is all I want in this world, my old friends included.'[16]

Hazlitt produced some of his best theatre criticism during the spring, thanks partly to Kean's continuing success: he appeared as Othello, Sir Giles Overreach, Shylock, and Sforza (in *The Duke of Milan*). By now, thespian and reviewer were on good terms, perhaps because they were habitués of the same dives and brothels. At the end of March Hazlitt invited him to York Street for dinner; Kean, however, was prevented from coming by a mishap (or so he claimed):

> Dear Hazlitt—I have met with an awkward accident. Having been hurled out of a gig, and got a dislocated arm (not to speak of diverse bruises and a severe shaking) I shall be unable to appear at your dinner or play for some nights in the Duke of Milan.[17]

This was not entirely accurate: in fact, he was suffering from a severe bout of alcohol poisoning. All the same, Hazlitt loyally defended him against accusations of drunkenness the following Sunday before launching a defence of the acting profession: 'A man of genius is not a machine. The neglected actor may be excused if he drinks oblivion of his disappointments; the successful one, if he quaffs the applause of the world, and enjoys the friendship of those who are the friends of the favourites of fortune, in draughts of nectar. There is no path so steep as that of fame; no labour so hard as the pursuit of excellence.'[18] No one knew the truth of that so well as Hazlitt. At Kean's next appearance, as Shylock on 1 April, the theatre was filled to the rafters, attracting even the Duke of Gloucester and Princess Sophia. His public were thrilled to have him back. Hazlitt commemorated the occasion with an appreciative notice.[19]

At around this moment he was introduced to Bryan Waller Procter by Lamb. Procter, a trainee solicitor, knew Hazlitt's contributions to *The Examiner* and regarded him as a genius. Years later he recalled Hazlitt's demeanour at their first meeting: 'His figure was indeed indifferent, and his movements shy and awkward; but there was something in his earnest irritable face, his restless eyes, his black hair combed backwards and curling (not too resolutely) about a well-shaped head, that was very striking.'[20] Years later, Hazlitt's grandson recorded an interesting physical attribute of Procter: he 'had a way of twitching his ears, and when he was courting Miss Skepper, who was reputed to have a will of her own, Hazlitt said that, when they were married, she would make him twitch his ears still more.'[21] Procter was just one of a number of lawyers attracted to Hazlitt, others including Thomas Noon Talfourd, Basil Montagu, and Charles Well, all of whom had literary pretensions.

Part III: A Philosopher in Grub Street

By late April Hazlitt had a little money in hand; there was the £50 from Longman as well as payments from Napier and other editors. Now was a good time to visit his parents who since his father's retirement had been dependent on irregular grants from the Presbyterian Fund. Perhaps he wanted to share with them what he had recently earned. After leaving Wem the family had moved first to Addlestone in Surrey[22] before settling at Combe Down, two miles to the south of Bath. Though 78, Hazlitt Sr was as eager as ever to enshrine his views in print: in 1816 he published four articles in the *Monthly Repository*.[23] It is not clear whether he was paid, though one hopes so. The need for money must have been what induced him to take a lodger into his household—Catherine Emmet, consumptive daughter of Christopher Temple Emmet, eldest brother of Robert Emmet, the United Irishman executed after the uprising of 1803. Orphaned as a child, Catherine (now aged 29) would have been grateful for the protection of the Hazlitts. In happier times, she had visited New York as the guest of her uncle, Thomas Addis Emmet, a veteran of the 1798 uprising, now a prominent Irish-American, and often reminisced with Peggy about the people and places she had known there. The two women became so close that on her death in 1824 she left Peggy the considerable sum of £500.[24] 'Most grateful do I feel for having met with a friend such as my dear Miss Hazlitt, who can feel and allow for all my weaknesses,' Catherine told her cousin Elizabeth:

> We are now, together with her good Father and Mother, residing on Combe Down near the town of Bath. The situation itself is most delightful, and the air is reckon'd uncommonly wholesome for all who have in their constitution anything of a consumptive tendency. . . . My dear Miss Hazlitt could tell you how often our conversation is of New York . . . As to company, we see none. Our enjoyments are totally of the domestic kind.[25]

Hazlitt would have encountered the new member of his father's household on this visit, probably for the first time. Perhaps he treated the family to a visit to the Theatre Royal in Bath, where Maria Theresa Kemble was playing Julio in Holcroft's *Deaf and Dumb* (which he saw on 4 May) and Bizarre in Farquhar's *The Inconstant* (7 May). It was a pleasure to see Charles Kemble's wife in the parts with which she made her name—her Julio, Hazlitt wrote, 'we should hope never to forget'.[26]

Back in London he attended the first performance of *Bertram* on 9 May. Perhaps Kean brought the play to Hazlitt's attention, for he was the driving force behind it, taking the part of the moody, passionate, diabolical Bertram. Byronic in character, Charles Maturin's play was staged at the urging of the noble Lord, who described it as 'a very extraordinary production—of great & singular merit as a composition'.[27] Its principal flaw, Hazlitt noted, was Maturin's rudimentary storytelling ability, but he adored its poetry: 'It is a *Winter's Tale*, a *Midsummer Night's Dream*, but it is not *Lear* or *Macbeth*.'[28] The playtext went through seven editions within a year, much to the delight of its publisher, John Murray.

Murray was riding high. Byron's fortunes had taken off, and with it those of his friends and investors. When in April 1816 Byron went into self-imposed exile on the Continent, public interest in him hit an all-time high as London gorged itself on tales of incest, choirboy sodomy, and marital infidelity. It was a good moment for Lady Caroline Lamb to fuel the flames with *Glenarvon*, a *roman-à-clef* which depicted Byron as the depraved Earl of Glenarvon and reprinted verbatim the letter he had sent her when ending their affair. Murray could not have jeopardized his friendship with Byron by publishing it; Henry Colburn, on the other hand, had nothing to lose. He paid its author £500 for the first edition and made a handsome profit, as he did out of the second and third editions published later that year.

Glenarvon appeared on 9 May, the day after another tale of tainted love, *Christabel*, which appeared in print for the first time with 'Kubla Khan' and 'The Pains of Sleep'.[29] Though drafted years earlier, these poems had remained in manuscript because Coleridge was unable to bring them to completion. Even if he had finished them, he was at a loss to decide whether 'Kubla Khan' was anything besides a 'psychological curiosity'. As for 'The Pains of Sleep', Coleridge knew it was a naked admission of the physical disorders attendant upon opium addiction—or, as he put it, 'a pandemonium of all the shames & miseries of the past Life from early childhood all huddled together, & bronzed with one stormy Light of Terror & Self-torture'.[30] If such misgivings, which had conspired to keep these works out of print for the best part of two decades, seem surprising in light of the fact that at least two of them are now ranked among the greatest poems in literary history, it is worth remembering that they simply did not conform to most readers' expectations. Even in 1816, poetry was a formalized art dominated by eighteenth-century conventions to which they did not comply. For years, however, 'Christabel' and 'Kubla Khan' had circulated in manuscript. The immediate instigator of their publication was Byron who, having heard Coleridge recite them at his house, urged Murray to issue them. Motivated largely by the desire to placate his best-selling poet, Murray agreed, paying Coleridge £80 for the copyright.

Hazlitt probably heard the first part of 'Christabel' in Somerset in 1798 and had been known to describe it as 'the finest poem in the language of its size';[31] now he took a different view. 'Christabel' contained 'a great deal of beauty, both of thought, imagery, and versification; but the effect of the general story is dim, obscure, and visionary. ... The faculties are thrown into a state of metaphysical suspense and theoretical imbecility.'[32] Worse still, 'Kubla Khan' proved that 'Mr Coleridge can write better nonsense verses than any man in England.' This was not obtuseness on Hazlitt's part; he knew the poems were works of genius, but didn't see why Coleridge should be given an easy ride. After all, here was the man who in 1798 had seemed capable of revolutionizing the world. All that potential had been smoked away in opium dreams and interminable monologues delivered in exchange for crumbs dropped from the hand of Sir George Beaumont. As soon as he had finished the *Examiner* article Hazlitt embarked on an even angrier one for the *Edinburgh Review*:[33] 'The lines given here smell strongly, it must be owned, of the anodyne,' he wrote of 'Kubla Khan', 'and, but that an under-dose of a sedative produces contrary effects, we should inevitably have been lulled by them into forgetfulness of all things.'[34] When he got to 'Christabel', he struck hard:

> The thing now before us is utterly destitute of value. It exhibits from beginning to end not a ray of genius. ... there is literally not one couplet in the publication before us which would be reckoned poetry, or even sense, were it found in the corner of a newspaper or upon the window of an inn. Must we then be doomed to hear such a mixture of raving and driv'ling, extolled as the work of a 'wild and original' genius, simply because Mr Coleridge has now and then written fine verses, and a brother poet chooses, in his milder mood, to laud him from courtesy or from interest?[35]

This was not as unfair as it now seems. Hazlitt had believed in Coleridge. He had placed his faith in the preacher he encountered at the Unitarian chapel in Shrewsbury in 1798, trusting that he had the power to lead mankind out of bondage through the combined force of poetry and philosophy. Nearly two decades on, that faith had resulted only in these fragmentary poems, one of which was described by its author as a 'psychological curiosity'. If Hazlitt was angry, it was with himself as much as Coleridge, for having been taken in by him. These articles were his revenge. Nor were they the end of it. During the next nine months he would be responsible for four separate attacks on *The Statesman's Manual* and one on *Biographia Literaria*.[36]

Chapter 11

The *Christabel* articles generated consternation within the Lamb circle, which included both poet and reviewer. Lamb in particular was troubled. He had been at school with Coleridge, and was the drinking companion of Hazlitt.

'There is more praise than abuse in it,' said Martin Burney one evening at Lamb's, defending Hazlitt.

'Rubbish!', said Lamb—who hardly ever shouted anyone down. 'No one will care or understand what little praise there is, and the satire will be universally felt. Such an article is like saluting a man: "Sir, you are the greatest man I ever saw", and then pulling his nose!'[37]

Shattered by the onslaught, Coleridge confided his feelings to Lamb, who was deputized to speak in confidence with Hazlitt.

'William, you should be ashamed of yourself,' said Lamb. 'Poor Coleridge was in tears—in tears!—as he read your review.'

'Damn him!', replied Hazlitt, '*I hate him*: FOR I am under obligations to him.'[38]

'But you once said you liked *Christabel*. I've heard you say so!'

'I grumbled part to myself, while I was writing—but nothing stings a man so much as making people believe lies of him.'[39] And that was all he had to say on the matter.

When Lamb relayed this to the aggrieved poet, Coleridge declared that Hazlitt

owes to me more than to his own parents—for at my own risk I saved perhaps his life from the Gallows, most certainly his character from blasting Infamy . . . You would scarcely think it possible that a monster could exist who boasted of guilt and avowed his predilection for it. All good I had done him of *every* kind, and never ceased to do so, till he had done his best to bring down infamy on three families, in which he had been sheltered as a brother, by vices too disgusting to be named—and since then the only wrong I have done him has been to decline his acquaintance. Thank God! I feel these things more philosophically than Catullus did.[40]

Coleridge had turned the Keswick ducking-party into a lynch-mob, and Hazlitt's misdemeanour into 'vices too disgusting to be named'. From this point onwards, Wordsworth and Coleridge dedicated themselves to the dismantling of Hazlitt's reputation, by fair means or foul.

It was sheer vindictiveness. Hazlitt's attacks were well founded. When first he met the Lakers, their declared aim was to realize the objectives of the French

[191]

Revolution by non-violent means. It had been abandoned at a time when ordinary people were more oppressed than ever. In 1815, thanks to the War, the national debt stood at £834 million. The following year income tax was repealed, shifting the burden entirely to indirect taxation, which fell disproportionately upon the poor. Bad harvests between 1816 and 1819 led wages to plummet at a time when unemployment was high and bread prices increased. At the same time, new technologies that led industrialists and landowners to lay workers off were introduced. These conditions created two million paupers in a country of nineteen million. Fearful of revolution, the Government used spies and agents provocateurs to ferret out those campaigning for workers' rights, who were tried and summarily executed. In these oppressive times Britain needed writers who believed in the egalitarianism of the Revolution, for political change depended on intellectual argument—as it had in France. Where were the idealists of 1798, who had spoken to Hazlitt of poems that would precipitate millennial change? They dedicated their outpourings to Tory Peers, accepted Poet Laureateships, and published their finest poetic achievements as 'psychological curiosities'. Poets are Tories by nature.

It was not true, as Haydon believed, that had Wordsworth allowed Hazlitt into his company 'his vanity would have been soothed, his virulence softened'.[41] That was to overstate Hazlitt's *amour propre*. Hazlitt was angry with Wordsworth for good reason: the poet had betrayed his principles. The man who once said his poems 'were written with a view to show that men who do not wear fine clothes can feel deeply'[42] had just published a poem commemorating Wellington's victories with the clunking line, 'Yea, Carnage is thy daughter',[43] implying that the bloodshed of the Napoleonic Wars was divinely sanctioned. Disgusted, Hazlitt quoted it as evidence of Wordsworth's apostasy.[44] 'Why do you so constantly let your temper get the better of your reason?', Northcote once asked Hazlitt. 'Because I hate a hypocrite, a time-server, and a slave,' he answered.[45] And he was right to do so.

Towards the end of May 1816, the Hazlitts' baby caught measles. Having struggled gamely for several weeks, the infant John Hazlitt died at 4am on Wednesday 19 June, and three days later was laid in the burying ground attached to St Margaret's Chapel, Westminster, in a brief ceremony performed by the curate, William Groves.[46] The child was seven months old; his mother recorded the corpse as 'two feet three Inches in length'.[47] Hazlitt was distraught, worse afflicted than at baby William's death in 1809. When he saw the corpse he cut a lock of hair from his head, wrapped it in paper, and wrote on it:

'My dear little John's hair, cut off the day he died.'[48] He carried it with him for the rest of his life. Grief did nothing for his marriage: not long after, John Stoddart described the Hazlitts as 'a worthy couple—they quarrel, fight, make it up over the gin bottle, and get drunk together.'[49] They could not go on like that indefinitely.

At this bleak moment it seemed to Hazlitt there was nothing to be lost by saying what he thought about the Utilitarians and their clique, one of whom included the philanthropic businessman Robert Owen, who ran his cotton mill in New Lanark along 'rational' lines, providing employees with free health care and education. Hazlitt had nothing against that, but when Owen published *A New View of Society* (1816), a hotchpotch of ideas filched from other thinkers, he denounced it. Owen was a charlatan, he argued. His book said nothing that was not better said by others and presented no real threat to the establishment; that was why his volume was dedicated to the Prince Regent. Hazlitt could not refrain from adding that New Lanark was a sort of brothel: 'Neither the great world nor the world in general care any thing about New Lanark, nor trouble themselves whether the workmen there go to bed drunk or sober, or whether the wenches are got with child before or after the marriage ceremony. Lanark is distant, Lanark is insignificant.'[50]

The Utilitarians were horrified: Bentham was one of Owen's business part-ners; Place and Owen had been good friends for years.[51] 'You have seen the two articles in the *Examiner* against Robert Owen,' Place told James Mill on 15 September 1816, 'they are as you will conclude by Hazlitt.'[52] There were no by-lines in *The Examiner*, and Place must have learnt this from an informant. It was typical of the spy-system by which Bentham monitored the troublesome tenant of York Street. Mill replied: 'I felt considerable indignation at the treatment of Owen in the *Examiner*. A man may differ from him—and a man may say he ascribes too much importance to his own opinions. But there is nothing about Owen [that] provokes hostility—I cannot think well of any man that shows it to him.'[53] Bentham shared his disquiet.

Hazlitt attacked the Benthamites again in 'On Commonplace Critics' on 24 November. Such a critic 'has something to say upon every occasion, and he always tells you either what is not true, or what you knew before, or what is not worth knowing'.[54] His aesthetic values were formed by Dr Johnson, Hume, and Adam Smith, which lead him to think 'Milton's pedantry a great blemish in his writings, and that *Paradise Lost* has many prosaic passages in it'.[55] As he itemized the foibles of the 'commonplace critic', Hazlitt let slip an identifying feature: 'He thinks Jeremy Bentham a greater man than Aristotle.'[56] Of course, the 'commonplace critic' could have been any of several people, but Place would have been struck by the resemblance to himself.

Hazlitt often saw the artist Benjamin Robert Haydon socially, but a major event in the cultural life of the country now drew them closer. The Elgin Marbles had been in the country for a decade, in a coalshed at Elgin's London residence, Burlington House; now they were offered for purchase to the Government, which set up a Select Committee to report on their value. Witnesses were called from the artistic academies, one of the most notable being the dilettante Richard Payne Knight, an expert on the sexual symbolism of ancient sculpture, particularly the phallus. Familiar only with Roman copies of Greek art, Knight lacked the ability to appreciate an ancient masterpiece like the Marbles and told the Committee it was of the 'second rank'.

To members of the Hunt circle, Knight represented everything that was wrong with the academic establishment. Haydon was particularly angry because he had been nominated as one of Elgin's witnesses but the Committee declined to summon him. That drove him to write a scorching denunciation of Knight for *The Examiner*. Central to his argument was the view that the Marbles were a truthful and accurate representation of 'flesh, bone, and tendon, from extension, flexion, compression, gravitation, action or repose'[57]—that is, they possessed what Hazlitt called 'gusto'. Haydon's essay was published as a pamphlet, translated into Italian and French, and distributed across the Continent. It caused uproar. A few months later, Hazlitt stoked the controversy, reiterating Haydon's line that the Marbles 'are in their essence and their perfection casts from nature,—from fine nature, it is true, but from real, living, moving nature'.[58]

Today, the Elgin Marbles are so highly regarded it is impossible fully to appreciate the intellectual leap Hazlitt and Haydon made when they constructed a coherent aesthetic by which they could be appreciated—locating them within a tradition extending from ancient times to the present. It is thanks partly to them that the Marbles were, after much debate, purchased for the nation.[59]

Haydon's regard for Hazlitt was enhanced by the vigour with which he attacked the satirical catalogue raisonné of the British Institution, published anonymously in summer 1816.[60] For the past two years, the Institution had been exhibiting the work of the Old Masters in an attempt to encourage a greater appreciation of them. The satirical catalogue, now thought to be by Robert Smirke RA, criticized the Institution for doing so, believing that it was at the expense of modern artists. For instance, in his introductory remarks, under the heading 'Staircase Rails and Velvet Hangings', Smirke asked: 'Who does not see that the Angelic Females in Rubens's Pictures, (particularly in that of the Brazen Serpent,) labour under a fit of the bile, twice as severe as they would do if they were not suffering on red velvet?—Who does not see, from the same cause, the Landscapes by the same Master, are converted into *brown studies*, and that Rembrandt's ladies and gentlemen of fashion look as if they had been on duty for the whole of last week in the Prince Regent's new Sewer?'[61] Hazlitt was particularly struck by this comment and cited it both in his review of the British Institution and the attack on the catalogue,[62] condemning its author for having only 'the low wit and dirty imagination of a paltry scribbler', while lacking any 'feeling of excellence in art, or of beauty or grandeur in nature'.[63] For Hazlitt, this affair and that of the Elgin Marbles were part of a larger critique of the artistic academy, of which he had been suspicious since his days as an artist: 'the marring of Art is the making of the Academy'.[64] In Smirke's uninspired prose he detected 'the same assumption of privilege, of self-complacent superiority, the same expression of brazen power in the world of art as he saw in the political world, in Legitimacy and the Tory party'.[65]

Haydon and Hazlitt concurred in their dislike of the Academicians, and their closeness encouraged Haydon to include Hazlitt's face in the crowd at the foreground of his masterpiece, 'Christ's Entry into Jerusalem'. On 3 November Hazlitt visited Pond Street, Hampstead, where Haydon had his studio, and sat for him, 'pouring out the result of a week's thinking'. This was exceptionally brave of him, for it was impossible to breathe freely in Haydon's cramped lodgings; the combined fumes of paint, stale food, and unwashed bedlinen led most people to become faint after a few minutes.[66] Haydon's diary records how he plied Hazlitt with wine, listening to tales of his early life, 'his weaknesses and follies'. It was always to be a bantering, blustering, spirited friendship because, despite being temperamentally well suited, the two men had very different opinions: Haydon was a Christian, Hazlitt an atheist. And Haydon supported Liverpool's government, telling one of his friends that 'my politics are very simple: I hate the French, wish England may get the better right or wrong, when she fights them—further in such matters I have no feeling.'[67] Hazlitt would have found that almost stupid. Indeed, it was probably in November 1816 that he let slip something so seditious Haydon could not bring himself to repeat it. Nonetheless, Haydon respected Hazlitt as 'a sincere good fellow at bottom, with fierce passions and appetites'.[68]

Fig. 19. John Keats in profile, sketched by Benjamin Robert Haydon in 1816, the year in which Keats met Hazlitt.

Hazlitt was sitting for Haydon one cold November day when there came a knock at the door. 'Come in!', said Haydon. It was a young, good-looking man with curly brown hair and glowing dark eyes. 'Mr Keats!', said Haydon, 'Meet Mr Hazlitt.' John Keats was still a student at Guy's Hospital and had just begun to write his finest poetry. 'On First Looking into Chapman's Homer' dates from October 1816—the first incontrovertible evidence of his genius. Charles Cowden Clarke read it within hours of composition and showed it to Hunt.

Hunt in turn showed it to Haydon, and soon afterwards introduced him to its author. The sonnet appeared in *The Examiner* on 1 December 1816.[69]

Keats knew Hazlitt from his reviews and essays; indeed, he incorporated elements from them into his thinking. Hazlitt is the source for Keats's famous definition of 'negative capability' as well as his musings on the subject of imagination.[70] For his part, Hazlitt was pleased to meet another admirer of the Elgin Marbles, Hunt's *Rimini*, and the cause of Art. But this young man was special. Everyone who met him experienced a 'strange personal Interest in all that concerns him', and came to see, as his publisher John Taylor put it, that he would one day be 'the brightest ornament of this Age'.[71] Hazlitt was one of the first to recognize Keats's gift, and after his death would say he 'gave the greatest promise of genius of any poet of his day. He displayed extreme tenderness, beauty, originality and delicacy of fancy.'[72]

What did they discuss? Probably, among other things, the Miss Dennetts—a popular turn in the afterpieces which followed the evening's entertainments at Covent Garden. Hazlitt never stopped praising them, with one of whom he was always a little in love.[73] They made their London debut on 11 September:

> They are quite charming. They are three kindred Graces cast in the same mould; a little Trinity of innocent delights; dancing in their 'trinal simplicities below'. They are like 'three red roses on a stalk'; and in the *pas de trois* which they dance twice over, they are as it were twined and woven into garlands and festoons of blushing flowers, such as 'Proserpine let fall from Dis's waggon.' You can hardly distinguish them from one another, they are at first so alike in shape, age, air, look; so that the pleasure you receive from one is blended with the delight you receive from the other two, in a sort of provoking, pleasing confusion. Milton was thinking of them when he wrote the lines
>
> > Whom lovely Venus at a birth
> > With two sister Graces more
> > To ivy-crowned Bacchus bore.[74]

Yet after all we have a preference, but we will not say which it is, whether the tallest or the shortest, the fairest or the darkest, of this lovely, laughing trio, more gay and joyous than Mozart's. 'But, pray, dear Sir, could you not give us a little bit of a hint which of us it is you like the very, very best?' Yes, yes, you rogue, you know very well it's you, but don't say a word of it to either of your sisters.[75]

CHAPTER 12

Once a renegado, and always a renegado.
Hazlitt, *Characteristics* cclvii[1]

COLERIDGE was recovering. Crippled for years by addiction, he had recently placed himself under the care of Dr James Gillman and his wife who, by regulating his consumption of opium, managed to get him to the point at which he could begin writing again. Never one to shrink from a challenge, he produced three Lay Sermons, the first of which, *The Statesman's Manual*, would appear in December 1816. Several months before this, in September, his publisher trailed it in the newspapers. Hazlitt decided to review it months before publication on the grounds that its contents were as predictable as the man himself.

> His mind is in a constant estate of flux and reflux: he is like the seahorse in the ocean; he is the man in the moon, the wandering jew. The reason of all this is that Mr Coleridge has great powers of thought and fancy, without will or sense. He is without a strong feeling of the existence of anything out of himself, and he has neither purposes nor passions of his own to make him wish it to be. Mr Shandy would have settled the question at once:—'You have little or no nose, sir.' All that he does or thinks is involuntary; even his perversity and self-will are so. They are nothing but a necessity of yielding to the slightest motive. Everlasting inconsequentiality marks all he does.[2]

This was a jaw-droppingly cruel remark and, once again, Hazlitt's friends were appalled. Henry Crabb Robinson told his brother that Hazlitt ('a man of the very finest talents & the worst heart of any man I know') had published an attack that was both 'magnificent & daemoniacal—He deserves flogging with a golden scourge'.[3] 'Have you read the review of Coleridges character, person, physiognomy &c. in the Examiner?' Charles Lamb asked Wordsworth, 'His features even to his *nose*—O horrible licence beyond the old Comedy.' Yet for all his loyalty to Coleridge, Lamb could not abandon Hazlitt, if only because 'I get no conversation in London that is absolutely worth attending to but his.'[4] All the same, Hazlitt's appearances at the Lambs' became increasingly strained, and his attacks on Coleridge probably explain an outbreak of violence one evening at their card table.

Hazlitt was playing whist with Lamb's brother John (a peaceable fellow), when he heard him say that Holbein's colouring was as fine as Van Dyck's. This was loose talk on John Lamb's part, inspired by little or no real knowledge, a naturally speculative nature, and one or two convivial drinks. But it wasn't the sort of thing you threw out in front of Hazlitt, who really cared about such subjects.

'If you don't hold your tongue, right now, I'll expose you in the newspapers!' threatened Hazlitt.

'And if you do', said John, excitably, 'I'll pound *you* into a mortar!'

Hazlitt swore, at which John lunged forward, punching him in the eye. The card table overturned, everyone jumped up in alarm, and Thomas Noon Talfourd (another guest) grabbed Hazlitt's arms to prevent him from retaliating.

'By God, sir!', Hazlitt said to Talfourd, 'you need not trouble yourself. I do not mind a blow, sir; nothing affects me but an abstract idea!'[5] It was true. He could take a punch or two from John Lamb, but the downfall of liberty had hurt him inwardly. And it was typical of him so readily to shake hands with Lamb's brother, even though he walked around London for the next two weeks with a black eye (something his enemies gossiped about for years).

More widespread unrest was about to bubble over. On 15 November Henry 'Orator' Hunt addressed some 10,000 people at Spa Fields, adjacent to Sadler's Wells, from the window of a public house, wearing a white top-hat symbolic of the 'purity of his cause'. They signed a petition demanding universal male suffrage, annual general elections, and a secret ballot (none of which then existed), which he wanted to present to the Prince Regent. The Regent had no intention of being doorstepped and simply refused to see him. Having been twice refused access, Hunt agreed to address a second meeting at Spa Fields on 2 December. But before he arrived, it degenerated into violence. Those involved were arrested and tried, though the prosecutions failed when it was discovered the trouble was instigated by a government spy.

Hazlitt followed these events avidly, aware they would increase the severity with which the Home Secretary dealt with future insurrection. Leigh Hunt allowed him to comment in *The Examiner*, in a series of articles condemning the Liverpool administration: 'The war has wasted the resources of the country in foolery, which the country has now to pay for in a load of taxes on its remaining resources, its actual produce and labour,' he complained,

> The tax-gatherer is a government-machine that takes sixty-five millions-a-year from the bankrupt pockets of the nation, to give to those who have brought it into that situation; who takes so much from the necessaries of life belonging to the poor, to add to the superfluities of the rich; who adds so much to the hard labour of the working part of the community, to 'relieve the killing languor and over-laboured lassitude of those who have nothing to do'; who, in short, out of the grinding poverty and ceaseless toil of those who pay the taxes, enables those who receive them to live in luxury and idleness.[6]

This was fighting talk—and dangerous, given the alarm with which the Government now viewed the press. Ministers viewed journalists as a principal source of insurrection, alarmed by the popularity of Cobbett's *Political Register*.

Hazlitt's views were related to his detestation of erstwhile radicals who had turned Tory. Accordingly, in an article on 22 December, he offered Wordsworth a sort of Christmas present—though not, perhaps, one he wished to receive:

> He sees nothing but himself and the universe. He hates all greatness, and all pretensions to it but his own. His egotism is in this respect a madness; for he scorns even the admiration of himself, thinking it a presumption in any one to suppose that he has taste or sense enough to understand him. He hates all science and all art; he hates chemistry, he hates conchology; he hates Sir Isaac Newton; he hates logic, he hates metaphysics, which he says are unintelligible, and yet he would be thought to understand them: he hates prose, he hates all poetry but his own; he hates Shakespeare, or what he calls 'those interlocutions between Lucius and Caius', because he would have all the talk to himself, and considers the movements of passion in *Lear*, *Othello*, or *Macbeth* impertinent, compared with the Moods of his own Mind; he thinks every thing good is contained in the *Lyrical Ballads*, or, if it is not contained there, it is good for nothing; he hates music, dancing and painting; he hates Rubens, he hates Rembrandt, he hates Raphael, he hates Titian, he hates Vandyke; he hates the antique, he hates the Apollo Belvedere, he hates the Venus de Medicis. He hates all that others love and admire but himself. He is glad that Bonaparte is sent to St Helena, and that the Louvre is dispersed for the same reason—to get rid of anything greater, or thought greater than himself. The Bourbons and their processions of the Holy Ghost give no disturbance to his vanity; and he therefore gives them none.[7]

All of this was true; at least, it was based on Hazlitt's encounters with Wordsworth. Reading it on the day of publication, Henry Crabb Robinson was disgusted yet again and, meeting Hazlitt that afternoon at Basil Montagu's, refused to shake his hand, instead asking whether he were its author.

'You know I am not in the habit of defending what I do,' Hazlitt replied. 'I do not say that all I have done is right.' Robinson then accused him of having used private confidences in his attacks.

'It may be indelicate, but I am forced to write an article every week, and I have not time to make one with so much delicacy as I otherwise should.' Hazlitt defended himself on the grounds that if someone held an opinion in private, they had no business advocating its opposite in public: 'It is useful to expose people who otherwise would gain credit by canting and hypocrisy.'

Hearing this, Montagu came to Hazlitt's assistance: 'It is difficult to draw the line in such cases. If I were in the House of Commons and I heard a man applaud a measure of government publicly which he had privately reprobated to me the day before, should I be censurable in rising up and declaring this?'

Four years before, Robinson lobbied to find Hazlitt work as a journalist. He had procured portrait commissions for him and helped find a publisher for *Eloquence of the British Senate*. Until now, despite Wordsworth's interdictions, they continued to socialize; but this was too much. He was mindful of Coleridge who the previous day declared Lamb 'ought not to admit a man into his house who abuses the confidence of private intercourse so scandalously'.[8]

Robinson broke with Hazlitt that evening and, though they would speak again, things could never be the same. Yet Hazlitt held no grudge. Years later, he told their mutual friend Mary Lamb: 'Robinson cuts me—but in spite of that I shall always have kind feeling towards him, for he was the first person that ever found out there was anything in me.'[9] Such generosity of spirit was typical. However harshly they judged him, Hazlitt always gave former friends their due.

Robinson related what had taken place to Wordsworth, who was delighted to hear that another of Hazlitt's associates had sent him to Coventry. He in turn wrote to Haydon: 'The miscreant Hazlitt continues, I have heard, his abuse of Southey, Coleridge and myself in *The Examiner*. I hope that you do not associate with the fellow, he is not a proper person to be admitted into respectable society, being the most perverse and malevolent creature that ill luck has ever thrown in my way. Avoid him—hic niger est[10]—and this, I understand, is the general opinion wherever he is known in London.'[11] Given the esteem in which he held Wordsworth, Haydon's response was robust:

Part III: A Philosopher in Grub Street

With respect to Haslitt, I think his motives are easily enough discernible. Had you condescended to visit him, when he praised your Excursion just before you came to Town, his vanity would have been soothed, and his virulence softened—he was conscious from what an emergency you had helped to rescue him—he was conscious of his conduct while in your neighbourhood—and then your taking no notice of his praise added to his acid feelings.—I see him scarcely ever and then not at my own house.[12]

Actually, Haydon often entertained Hazlitt at his house; he ignored Wordsworth's advice, and a few days later had Hazlitt to model for him. 'I never had so pleasant [a] sitter,' he recorded in his diary. 'He amused me beyond all description.'[13]

The unreliability of Hazlitt's health owed much to the effects of alcohol in earlier years. In July 1816 he began a note to Constable remarking that 'I have been & am exceedingly ill,'[14] and writing to his son in 1822 explained, 'my health is so indifferent, and I may not be with you long.'[15] So it was that, in the early days of 1817, he scrawled a note in a spidery hand to Francis Jeffrey:

> Dear Sir
> I have been exceedingly unwell, or I should have answered your former letter before, & have got something for the Review. I cannot get either of the long articles done which I spoke of, on literature and philosophy for the present number, but I will attempt an article, which you shall have by the twenty-first, on Mr Coleridge's Lay Sermon, if I do not hear from you to the contrary, it will be about a sheet, & enter into the skirts of the Kantean philosophy.
> I am, dear Sir, Yours faithfully
> W. Hazlitt
> 3rd Jany 1817[16]

He remained in uncertain shape for the first months of the New Year. His unremitting pace of work cannot have helped. To Jeffrey he complained he was 'writing for three newspapers at a time to the ruin of my health & without any progress in my finances'.[17] Nor was his the healthiest of lifestyles: he worked without respite for long hours in confined, airless rooms in a city polluted by smog.

He dragged himself out of bed to review the pantomimes for the first *Examiner* of 1817 and was a strong presence in the following week's paper to which he also contributed 'The Times Newspaper: On the Connection between

Toad-Eaters and Tyrants'—star exhibits of the toad-eating variety being Wordsworth, Coleridge, and Southey. This was a classic rant against those who tried 'to sneak over one by one to the side on which "empty praise or solid pudding" was to be got; they could not live without the smiles of the great (not they), nor provide for an increasing establishment without a loss of character; instead of going into some profitable business and exchanging their lyres for ledgers, their pens for the plough (the honest road to riches), they chose rather to prostitute their pens to the mock-heroic defence of the most bare-faced of all mummeries, the pretended alliance of kings and people!'[18] Not only was he right to denounce them, but he was one of the few people in a position to do so. For he knew better than most of his contemporaries how hot in the revolutionary cause these latter-day 'prostitutes' had once been.

In February a new theatrical talent hit town. A report having reached Covent Garden that a certain Junius Brutus Booth had attracted a following for his portrayal of Richard III, the management signed him up. With the same build and appearance as Kean, Booth mimicked his inflections down to the smallest detail. He appeared as Richard III on 12 February and enjoyed such acclaim he repeated it the following night. Covent Garden now had a secret weapon against Kean and offered Booth £8 a week for the rest of the season. Before he could sign, however, Booth received a counter-offer from Kean to play Iago with his Othello at Drury Lane. Could the imitator upstage his master? It was too good an invitation to decline: Booth accepted.

London was electrified. Booth was drawing full houses on the strength of a performance modelled on the man against whom he would now be playing. On the night of their first joint appearance the theatre was packed to the rafters; Hazlitt was in the pit. 'The two rival actors hunt very well in couple', he wrote, 'The original and the copy go together, like the substance and the shadow.'[19] It was clear to him that Booth was 'a very close and spirited repetition . . . the most spirited copy we ever saw upon the stage'[20]—but *not* the real thing. Nor was he the only one to see this. Bryan Waller Procter believed that Kean raised his game accordingly and appeared to be endowed 'with supernatural strength. His eye was glittering and blood-shot, his veins were swollen, and his whole figure restless and violent. It seemed dangerous to cross his path, and death to assault him.'[21] The play was scheduled again two nights later, but Booth said he was too ill to do it and returned to Covent Garden for the remainder of the season. Irritated by his refusal to partner Kean, audiences dropped off, and Booth eventually left the profession altogether.

The battle of the actors was played out against larger conflicts. Thanks to the Government's divisive policies, the country was now so polarized it was impossible not to take sides: you were either for or against reform, for or against the iniquity of the tax system, for or against popular protest. As Lord John Russell wrote: 'London is more absorbed in politicks than at any period I ever remember.'[22] In the wake of the Spa Fields riots, activists had returned to petitioning as a way of expressing their grievances. On 28 January 1817, the day of the State Opening of Parliament, Admiral Lord Cochrane, war hero and government critic, presented half a million signatures to the Palace of Westminster, accompanied by an estimated 20,000 people from all over the country. The Prince Regent set out from St James's Palace to be greeted by 'marks of disapprobation from the multitude' gathered outside. The corpulent 56-year-old had never been more detested than now, when so many were suffering deprivation and poverty, blame for which rested at his door. On his return to the Palace, 'gravel, stones, and other things were thrown at the royal carriage' and its window 'shattered in two places by stones or some missiles, from a hand unseen'.[23] The Regent claimed to have been fired on by someone hidden in the trees, though no bullet-holes were found and no one was arrested. Cobbett thought the entire thing had been staged to justify the backlash that followed.

The Government acted swiftly. They appointed two secret committees which declared there were plots afoot to cause insurrection. Habeas corpus was suspended on 3 March and public meetings declared illegal unless authorized by a magistrate—the same 'Gagging Act' introduced by Pitt in 1795 when one Samuel Taylor Coleridge regarded himself as its target.

Such measures weren't enough for the Poet Laureate, who spied a loophole. On 19 March 1817 Southey wrote a confidential 'memorandum' to Lord Liverpool, urging a clampdown on journalists critical of the Government. He had long desired this. In September the previous year, Henry Crabb Robinson noted a conversation in which Southey 'considers the government seriously endangered by the weekly papers—by Cobbett and still more by the *Examiner*. Jacobinism he deems more an object of terror than at the commencement of the French Revolution. . . . He would have transportation the punishment for a seditious libel!'[24] Southey was determined to impress this on the Prime Minister. Laws such as those recently passed, he argued, were 'altogether nugatory while such manifestoes as those of Cobbett, Hone, and *The Examiner*, etc., are daily and weekly issued, fresh and fresh, and read aloud in every alehouse where the men are quartered, or where they meet together'.[25] He urged Liverpool to employ the measure that so appalled Robinson: 'No means can be effectual for checking the intolerable license of the press but that of making transportation the punishment for its abuse.' Southey's biographers remain silent about this, implying that Hazlitt's attacks on him were unprovoked.[26] But were any justification required, this was it. The man who, two decades earlier, preached republicanism, was now using his position as Poet Laureate to urge the Prime Minister to suppress his former comrades-in-arms.

The Government proved responsive. On 27 March the Home Secretary ordered the Lords Lieutenant to arrest all printers, demagogues, and writers responsible for seditious, blasphemous, or libellous material. True or false, anything that wounded the feelings of ministers or brought contempt upon them was deemed 'libellous'. Cobbett ensured he and his family were on a ship bound for America later that day, not to return for over two years.

In the meantime, one of Southey's chickens had come home to roost. In the 1790s, the young republican had attacked Pitt's Tory government in a play about the fourteenth-century poll-tax rebel, Wat Tyler. He had since lost the manuscript and was now horrified to find it was 'to be published', according to the *Morning Chronicle* of 14 February 1817. Despite applying to the Lord Chancellor for an injunction, Southey was stunned when a dissenting minister named Winterbottom came forward, claiming to have been given the copyright in 1796. Southey was sure he was an imposter—'they have procured a man to perjure himself, & swear that I made a free gift of the manuscript', he told Coleridge.[27] But the Chancellor ruled that he was unable to prevent publication until Southey had proved his counterclaim, which he could not do. In that case, decreed Lord Eldon, publication could proceed. Southey was deeply disappointed. For all his loyalty to the Government, they had not protected him from the embarrassment of having his youthful indiscretions exposed. 'I have not heard who was the Resurrection-Man in Uncle Wats affair, it will come out in due time, & may very possibly be traced to the Old Serpent coterie', he remarked sourly[28] (meaning, by 'Old Serpent', the Unitarian circles he frequented in the 1790s[29]). Eldon's judgement left the way open to the pirates, and over the next decade twelve different publishers published seventeen different editions, selling an estimated 60,000 copies. *Wat Tyler* became Southey's best-selling work, from which he earned not a single penny.

This precipitated one of Hazlitt's finest pieces of political journalism. In a withering attack, he compared with the newly published play an article Southey had recently published in the Tory *Quarterly Review* condemning the cause of reform:

> The author of Wat Tyler was an Ultra-jacobin; the author of Parliamentary Reform is an Ultra-royalist; the one was a frantic demagogue; the other is a court-tool: the one maintained second-hand paradoxes; the other repeats second-hand common-places: the one vented those opinions which gratified the vanity of youth; the other adopts those prejudices which are most conducive to the convenience of age: the one saw nothing but the abuses of power; the other sees nothing but the horrors of resistance to those abuses: the one did not stop short of general anarchy; the other goes the whole length of despotism: the one vilified kings, priests, and nobles; the other vilifies the people: the one was for universal suffrage and perfect equality; the other is for seat-selling, and the increasing influence of the Crown: the one admired the preaching of John Ball; the other recommends the Suspension of the Habeas Corpus, and the putting down of the *Examiner* by the sword, the dagger, or the thumb-screw; for the pen, Mr Southey tells us, is not sufficient.[30]

Not so long ago, Southey had been 'shamefully hot with Democratic Rage as regards politics, and ... Infidel as to religion';[31] as recently as 1803 he had elegized Robert Emmet in the newspapers. Now he thought pauperism the result of 'misconduct' and dismissed the advocates of reform as 'some weak men, some mistaken or insane ones, and other very wicked ones'.[32] By drawing attention to Southey's 'disjointed opinions'[33] Hazlitt was merely stating the truth. Of the former radicals he had known, Southey was the most shameless in his betrayal and persecution of former comrades: 'Those who have undergone a total change of sentiment on important questions ought certainly to learn modesty in themselves, and moderation towards others; on the contrary, they are generally the most violent in their own opinions, and the most intolerant towards others.'[34]

On 14 March, during a debate on the Seditious Assemblies Bill (another attempt by the Government to suppress growing unrest), William Smith, MP for Norwich, stood up in the Commons and took a leaf out of Hazlitt's book by producing, from either pocket, the *Quarterly Review* and *Wat Tyler*. He then proceeded to read from each, declaring: 'He could not suppose for a moment that the same individual had written those two passages,' to cries of 'hear, hear, hear!'[35] However, he went on, 'what he most detested, what most filled him with disgust, was the settled, determined malignity of a renagado.'[36] Such humiliation in the highest forum in the land was more than Southey could bear, and in his own defence he composed *A Letter to William Smith*, published 26 April.

That day Hazlitt happened to pass Southey in the street. They hadn't seen each other since his last visit to the Lakes nearly fourteen years previously. Southey walked on without a glance; Hazlitt realized who it was only after he had passed by. He was sorry to have cut him, even inadvertently, and 'turned, and looked after him for some time, as to a tale of other times—sighing, as we walked on, *Alas, poor Southey!*' He then entered a bookshop and purchased a copy of *A Letter to William Smith*, 'which appeared the same day as himself, and this at once put an end to our sentimentality'.[37] Its defence was feeble, and he proceeded to make mincemeat of it. Southey's performance 'is a concentrated essence of a want of self-knowledge', he announced; it was (echoing Coleridge's Preface to 'Kubla Khan') a ' "psychological curiosity", a study of human infirmity'.

> Once admit that Mr Southey is always in the right, and everyone else in the wrong, and all the rest follows. . . . He is both judge and jury in his own cause; the sole standard of right and wrong. To differ with him is inexcusable, for 'there is but one perfect, even himself.' He is the central point of all moral and intellectual excellence; the way, the truth, and the life. There is no salvation out of his pale; and yet he makes the terms of communion so strict, that there is no hope that way. The crime of Mr William Smith and others, against whom this high-priest of impertinence levels his anathemas, is *in not being* Mr Southey.[38]

Southey was no match for this, and knew it. After reading it he complained to Wordsworth that 'Hazlitt's scurrility is so dressed up that all who are capable of understanding it must needs loathe it; to the ignorant it is almost as unintelligible as Coleridge's philosophy.'[39] In fact Hazlitt cut to the justice of the case—but that was too much for Southey to admit. Keats was typical of many when he revelled in it on 11 May: 'By the by, what a tremendous Southeyan article his last was.'[40] Hazlitt displayed courage in his comments: it was not he but Southey who had the ear of a Prime Minister whose recent legislation was designed to silence anyone the Government found irksome.

There is a twist in the tale. Southey believed his letter to the Prime Minister to be confidential; in fact, its contents were known to Hazlitt, for he quotes it in his review of the *Letter to William Smith*.[41] That he was aware of Southey's role in the passing of the new legislation, but continued to challenge him, underlines both his courage and his fidelity to his principles.

Part III: A Philosopher in Grub Street

The new year brought fresh acquaintances. The 24-year-old Percy Bysshe Shelley had returned from Geneva on 8 September 1816, having spent the summer months in the company of Lord Byron. That collaborative moment inspired a stream of writings including Byron's *Childe Harold's Pilgrimage* Canto III, Shelley's 'Hymn to Intellectual Beauty', and Mary Shelley's *Frankenstein*. Hazlitt must have read the third Canto of *Childe Harold* by the time he first met Shelley at Hunt's cottage in the Vale of Health on 26 January 1817. Also present were Godwin, Walter Coulson, and Shelley's friend Thomas Jefferson Hogg. Mary Shelley had arrived in London earlier that day, having married Percy a few weeks earlier. Hazlitt had known her since she was a girl.

Shelley and Hazlitt knew one another through their writings. Hazlitt read 'Hymn to Intellectual Beauty' when it appeared in *The Examiner* on 19 January,[42] while Shelley read Hazlitt's *Memoirs of Holcroft* the previous October[43] and had seen his recent theatrical reviews and political essays.[44] Before their meeting, Hazlitt had heard about Shelley's legal battle to gain custody of the children of his first marriage, his former wife having committed suicide by drowning herself in the Serpentine, for Shelley's lawyer was Basil Montagu. On 24 January none other than the Lord Chancellor, John Scott, Lord Eldon, decided that guardianship would be determined on the basis of whether the 'principles of Deism' in *Queen Mab* were truly dangerous or 'a mere effusion of the imagination'. Shelley would have to wait months for a decision, a process he and the children found unendurably painful—evidence of Eldon's essential inhumanity.[45]

Though temperamentally different, Hazlitt and Shelley had much in common: both detested the Government and the political system; both were religious sceptics; both loved philosophy and poetry, even though they had different ideas about it.[46] This was enough, at a first meeting, for them to get on. Four years later, Hazlitt wrote a controversial account of the younger man that looked back to early 1817: 'He has a fire in his eye, a fever in his blood, a maggot in his brain, a hectic flutter in his speech, which mark out the philosophic fanatic.'[47] Those remarks upset Hunt enough to cause a rift with their author. Yet at the time of their first meeting, Hazlitt marvelled at the dynamism of the young man who spoke with animation of the sufferings of the poor and necessity for political change. A few weeks later they met again. 'Several of Hunt's acquaintances come in the evening—music. After supper a discussion until 3 in the morning with Hazlitt concerning monarchy and republicanism,' Mary Shelley recorded in her diary on 9 February.[48] This was probably the evening Charles Cowden

Clarke heard 'a very warm argument in favour of the monarchy upheld by Leigh Hunt and Coulson, and in favour of republicanism by Shelley and Hazlitt'.[49] Now in his thirtieth year, Clarke was the son of the headmaster whose school Keats attended, with whom he remained a close friend. He wanted to pursue a literary life, and was often to be found in the company of Hunt and the Lambs— though few at this moment could have suspected he would one day become Hazlitt's publisher.

A week later on 16 February Hazlitt brought his wife to meet the Shelleys. In the evening, Hunt remembered, 'I showed them the verses of my young friend [Keats], and they were pronounced to be as extraordinary as I thought them. One of them was that noble sonnet "On first Reading Chapman's *Homer*", which terminates with so energetic a calmness, and which completely announced the new poet taking possession.'[50] There was also, according to Mary Shelley, 'Music'—probably a piano recital by Hunt.

Shelley probably discussed with Hazlitt his latest project, *A Proposal for Putting Reform to the Vote throughout the Kingdom*, in which he suggested that the Friends of Liberty organize a referendum on parliamentary reform. His agenda was moderate: he was not demanding revolution but called for annual parliaments and a limited extension of the electoral base. Hazlitt would have approved, urging only that Shelley go further. But Shelley wanted to see whether he could forge an alliance with the moderates. He published the *Proposal* at his own expense in March and sent copies to Cobbett, Francis Place, and Robert Owen, among others. In an *Examiner* editorial, Hunt praised it, commending 'the feelings of this noble nature, whom we have the honour and the happiness of knowing'.[51]

In July 1816 Hazlitt had been driven to ask Constable: 'May I hope to see some more Round Tables before I die?'[52] It was, he said, 'the only child of my brain that I ever had any affection for'.[53] *The Round Table*, jointly written by Hazlitt and Hunt, was finally published on 14 February 1817 at the princely sum of 14 shillings, having taken more than a year to emerge from the printing house. Hazlitt knew it was a breakthrough work, for it gave the reading public their first glimpse of his mature style. Here was a distinctive new voice— opinionated, fresh, fiercely intellectual—willing to marry high and low culture, slang and high-flown rhetoric, in the cause of a unified, fully realized vision. The years he had spent working out his philosophical understanding of human nature and applying it to political, social, and intellectual problems had paid off. To take one example: buried in the midst of these essays was 'On Gusto', which explained a cornerstone of his philosophical vision: 'Gusto in art is power or passion defining any object.'[54] Gusto is an index of the imaginative intensity with which the artist endows his work. It is, in the first place, a test of disinterestedness—the ability to transcend the self so as completely to apprehend the sensations of another object; in the second place, of the ability to communicate them through technical expertise; and, finally, of the disinterested gaze of the viewer, to whom the work of art transmits them. Thus,

> Rubens makes his flesh-colour like flowers; Albano's is like ivory; Titian's is like flesh, and like nothing else. It is as different from that of other painters, as the skin is from a piece of white or red drapery thrown over it. The blood circulates here and there, the blue veins just appear, the rest is distinguished throughout only by that sort of tingling sensation to the eye, which the body feels within itself. This is gusto.—Vandyke's flesh-colour, though it has great truth and purity, wants gusto. It has not the internal character, the living principle in it. It is a smooth surface, not a warm, moving mass. It is painted without passion, with indifference. The hand only has been concerned. The impression slides off from the eye, and does not, like the tones of Titian's pencil, leave a sting behind it in the mind of the spectator. The eye does not acquire a taste or appetite for what it sees. In a word, gusto in painting is where the impression made on one sense excites by affinity those of another.[55]

Hazlitt's ideas were completely new and were to influence such admirers as Keats, whose 'negative capability' derives from them.

For all Hazlitt's genius, Constable failed to recognize the importance of *The Round Table* and did not market it properly. Sales were sluggish, and years passed before its significance was acknowledged; nor was it reprinted during Hazlitt's lifetime.[56] Nonetheless, it won admirers. 'Never read the *Round Table*?', Mary Russell Mitford asked her friend Sir William Elford. 'I am sure you would like them—they are so exquisitely entertaining—so original—so free from every sort of critical shackle—the style is so delightfully piquant—so sparkling—so glittering—so tasteful—so condensed—the images & illustrations come in such rich & graceful profusion that one seems like Aladdin in the magic garden where the leaves were emeralds, the flowers sapphires, & the fruit topazes & rubies.'[57] Keats read it enthusiastically and asked Reynolds: 'How is Hazlitt? We were reading his [*Round*] *Table* last night—I know he thinks himself not estimated by ten People in the world—I wish he knew he is.'[58]

Hazlitt felt unappreciated with good reason: his work came under attack from the outset. The *Quarterly*[59] ridiculed his use of English (an irritating criticism for someone who had written a grammar-book) before alleging the essays were misanthropic:

> There is nothing in the world which he seems to like. . . . He writes an essay in eager vituperation of 'good nature' and good natured people: he abuses all poets, with the single exception of Milton (he, indeed, 'was an honest man; he was Cromwell's secretary'): he abuses all country-people: he abuses the English: he abuses the Irish: he abuses the Scotch. Nor is it simply abuse; it is the language of Billingsgate.[60]

The reviewer[61] knowingly fathered Hunt's facetious articles and slapdash style onto Hazlitt, who was derided for being at home among washerwomen (subject of one of Hunt's pieces).[62] The moral implication was clear, and successive reviewers repeated it. Such attacks hurt, and it was not in Hazlitt's nature to submit mutely to them. But for the moment he decided to press on with other projects.

Over the course of the last year, Hazlitt had been writing *Characters of Shakespear's Plays*. If *The Round Table* announced the arrival of a new talent, here was evidence that it was more than a flash in the pan. But he hesitated to surrender it to the prevaricating Constable, instead hatching a plan with his friend, the printer Carew Henry Reynell. Reynell bought the copyright for £100 and printed the volume 'with a title-page destitute of any indication where the book was to be had'.[63] Hazlitt then set about the job of promoting it: he got a friend to run the essay on Hamlet in *The Times* and asked Jeffrey to notice it in the *Edinburgh Review*: 'My friends may praise what I write, but I do not find that the public read it, & without that I cannot live.'[64] Godwin was reading it by 29 May, as were others in the literary world. The idea was that word of mouth would generate demand.

Not until early June did Hazlitt offer his new book to publishers, claiming it was written 'for a friend, who wishes to dispose of the edition of 1000 copies for 200 guineas'.[65] This would have yielded Reynell a profit of £120 (assuming he was to receive the full sum). Constable did not bite—but Rowland Hunter, who had taken over the business of Hazlitt's first publisher Joseph Johnson, did. Charles and James Ollier, who had published Shelley's *Proposal*, also took a share in the volume, which appeared in bookshops on 9 July with a new title page.[66]

Characters played to Hazlitt's strength—to articulate the motivations and morality of individuals in Shakespeare.[67] While Hazlitt was a shrewd psychologist, his judgements come from the viscera: 'we never could forgive the Prince's treatment of Falstaff'; Henry V is 'a very amiable monster, a very splendid pageant'; 'Portia is not a very great favourite with us'.

> The greatness of Lear is not in corporal dimension, but in intellectual; the explosions of his passion are terrible as a volcano: they are storms turning up and disclosing to the bottom that rich sea, his mind, with all its vast riches. It is his mind which is laid bare. This case of flesh and blood seems too insignificant to be thought on; even as he himself neglects it. On stage we see nothing but corporal infirmities and weakness, the impotence of rage; while we read it, we see not Lear, but we are Lear;—we are in his mind; we are sustained by a grandeur, which baffles the malice of daughters and storms; in the aberrations of his reason, we discover a mighty irregular power of reasoning, immethodized from the ordinary purposes of life, but exerting its powers, as the wind blows where it listeth, at will on the corruptions and abuses of mankind. What have looks or tones to do with that sublime identification of his age with that of *the heavens themselves*, when in his reproaches to them for conniving at the injustice of his children, he reminds them that 'they themselves are old!' What gesture shall we appropriate to this? What has the voice or the eye to do with such things?[68]

Previously, anyone wanting to read about Shakespeare would have gone to Johnson or Pope, whose commentaries were framed in eighteenth-century terms. Here was a new approach responsive to the Romantic fascination with psychology. And therein lies the key to Hazlitt's modernity. He saw that Shakespeare's gift lay in his understanding of the mind, and interpreted the plays in that light. It was a perspective that shocked and stimulated those who read it. 'Aye. This is it—most likely H. is right throughout,' Keats scribbled in his copy on the margin of page 159.[69] Another reader, Stendhal, was so excited he urged a friend to translate it into French.[70]

Early reviews were favourable, but Hazlitt was lambasted by the *Quarterly* for his snipes at Henry VIII. (He alluded to the monarch's 'gross appearance, his blustering demeanour, his vulgarity, his arrogance, his sensuality, his cruelty, his hypocrisy, his want of common decency and common humanity'.[71]) Another Tory journal, the *British Critic*, said the book was 'stuffed with dull, common-place, Jacobin declamation'.[72] It hardly mattered: the entire first edition of *Characters of Shakespear's Plays* sold out within six weeks,[73] benefitting from what Robinson described as a 'very puffing review' from Jeffrey in the *Edinburgh*.[74] It went to a second edition in 1818, and later that year was pirated by Wells and Lilly in Boston[75]—Hazlitt was beginning to build up a reputation in America. When, some years later, a friend showed him the Boston edition, Hazlitt 'evinced no vexation at the piracy, and only thought of the swift passage of his fame across the Atlantic'.[76]

Publication of a book rarely produces much income for the author, at least in the short term. In a letter of June 1817 Hazlitt complained to Jeffrey he was in debt, and in August wrote 'in *forma pauperis*' to beg an advance of £30 on an article projected on modern novels.[77] His financial situation was about to become more precarious still: Leigh Hunt wanted to reclaim the post of 'Theatrical Examiner' for himself, which would deprive Hazlitt of his one regular source of income. He needed a new job—fast.

CHAPTER 13

Let a man do all he can in any one branch of study, he must either exhaust himself and doze over it, or vary his pursuit, or else lie idle. All our real labour lies in a nut-shell. The mind makes, at some period or other, one Herculean effort, and the rest is mechanical.

Hazlitt, 'On Application to Study'[1]

The Times, Hazlitt declared on 22 December 1816, was a 'patent water-closet for the dirty uses of legitimacy: a leaden cistern for obsolete prejudices and upstart sophistry "to knot and gender in"'.[2] Not the kind of thing designed to curry favour with anyone on its staff, least of all its editor John Stoddart, who happened also to be Hazlitt's brother-in-law. Towards the end of the Napoleonic Wars, Stoddart distinguished himself for vigorously anti-Bonapartist leaders which opposed the making of peace with the man he denounced as 'a Corsican upstart',[3] 'the discomfited Tyrant',[4] and 'a monster redeemed from vice by no single virtue'.[5] Not content with that, he launched a full-frontal attack on Hazlitt and those who urged negotiation with the French:

> Oh, wilful and obstinate blindness! . . . Where was their jealous love of liberty, when that low creeping fog had actually spread over the whole continent of Europe, a small part of Spain and Portugal excepted? Did they not then act the pandars to base fear, and, like shrieking night-birds, predicting total eclipse, urge us to withdraw from the 'unprofitable' and 'hopeless' contest, and lie down unnerved in that more than Egyptian darkness and bondage?[6]

In return, Hazlitt published a series of attacks on a man he described 'hallooing as loud as he can among the indefatigable war-pack'.[7] More recently, he had amused himself by telling readers of *The Examiner* that his brother-in-law was 'a very weak and violent man . . . a very stupid, senseless, vulgar person'.[8] It wasn't just that Hazlitt didn't like Stoddart personally, but that he loathed his treachery, knowing that, once upon a time, he was as determined a jacobin as those he now sought to discredit.

Stoddart's boss, John Walter II, was equally tired of his editor's rabidly anti-Jacobin leaders, which made *The Times* appear little more than a government mouthpiece. After remonstrating vainly with him to tone them down, Walter decided to ditch him.[9] He began by appointing Thomas Barnes as Stoddart's 'deputy', authorizing him to 'correct' Stoddart's articles. This was a calculated humiliation and in April 1816 Stoddart complained his influence had dwindled to 'less than nothing'[10]—as Walter intended. Finally Stoddart stepped down in the summer of 1816, leaving editorship in the hands of Walter and Barnes.

Thirty-two years old, Barnes was educated at Christ's Hospital and Pembroke College, Cambridge, where he took the best degree of any Pembroke man between 1806 and 1810. Though briefly a candidate for a Fellowship, he moved to London to take up the post of drama critic for *The Times* before gaining Walter's favour and being promoted to that of parliamentary correspondent (coinciding with Hazlitt's spell at the *Chronicle*). In spring 1817 he heard Hazlitt was looking for work and, knowing what a good writer he was, expressed an interest in taking him on, were he of a mind to join the paper he had so energetically vilified.[11] By 25 April, Henry Crabb Robinson (a former *Times* war correspondent) could record in his diary that 'Walter has been recommended by Barnes to take H[azlitt] as Theatrical Reporter w[hi]ch on the account of both H[azlitt] & the paper I am glad of'. Robinson was consulted on the matter, and 'confirmed W[alter] in the project of retaining H[azlitt] as a writer, at the same time that I did not encourage him to form a personal intimacy with him'.[12] Barnes's motivation for hiring Hazlitt was partly political: Walter had not yet resolved to give him sole editorship; in the meantime Edward Sterling, the drama and opera critic, was also in the running. Barnes hoped that, were Hazlitt to be brought in, Sterling would be marginalized.[13]

Accordingly, Hazlitt met Barnes and Walter at the *Times* office, a long two-storied red-brick building in Printing-House Square, Blackfriars, south of Ludgate Hill. The editor's room was on the first floor, near the composing room. As Walter shook hands with the limp hand of the shy, querulous figure at the doorway, he must have wondered how such a feeble specimen could write such aggressive prose. For much of the meeting, Walter let Barnes do the talking; he tended to retreat in such situations, preferring to observe and listen.[14] Hazlitt's attacks must have been mentioned, especially given the curious fact he would be working alongside Sterling (though only Walter knew that Sterling was Hazlitt's old enemy, 'Vetus').[15] None of that mattered to Walter. He cared only about the quality of the paper, which meant securing the best available writers. Hazlitt admired his pragmatism, and Walter took him on; Hazlitt's earliest identifiable contribution to the *Times* appeared on 29 April 1817.[16] He later commended Walter's management: 'I would . . . advise any one who has an ambition to write, and to write *his best*, in the periodical press, to get if possible "a situation" in the *Times* newspaper, the Editor of which is a man of business, and not of letters.[17] He may write there as long and as good articles as he can, without being turned out for it'[18]—a swipe at Perry.

By moving to *The Times* Hazlitt took a step up in the journalistic world. The paper had a circulation of nearly 7,000 copies a day, twice that of the *Chronicle*.[19] This was thanks to Walter's far-sighted investment in the steam presses that, from 29 November 1814, produced 1,300 copies an hour compared with 250 using the old Stanhope Press—making *The Times* the first British newspaper to be produced on an industrial scale.

Hazlitt's reviews of new productions at Covent Garden and Drury Lane were thus read by more readers than those of any other daily paper. It was a demanding job. Where the 'Theatrical Examiner' had been composed over days, his *Times* articles were written while the play was in progress: 'I might set down nearly all I had to say in my mind while the play was going on. I know I did not feel at a loss for matter—the difficulty was to compress and write it out fast enough.'[20] It took him about twenty minutes to walk back to the *Times* offices; by the time he got there, the whole thing was done, though he had yet to put pen to paper. On some nights he would see the main play at one theatre and dash round the corner to catch the afterpiece at the other, before running down the Strand to the composing room where he would dictate copy to the printer.[21] As theatres changed their bills daily, he might do this several nights a week. It was probably at this period that he developed the capacity to judge a production on the basis of little more than 'a few hasty glances and a few half-heard phrases. From these he drew instant deductions that it took others hours of observation to reach, and as many more of labour to work out.'[22] The added pressure gave these pieces freshness and intensity: 'There may be less formal method, but there is more life, and spirit, and truth. . . . A number of new thoughts rise up spontaneously, and they come in the proper places because they arise from the occasion. They are also sure to partake of the warmth and vividness of that ebullition of mind from which they spring.'[23]

Chapter 13

Five days before starting on *The Times*, Hazlitt spent the evening with Keats's friend John Hamilton Reynolds, who recorded his impression of him:

> On Thursday last Hazlitt was with me at home, and remained with us till 3 o'clock in the morning! Full of eloquence—warm, lofty and communicative on everything imaginative and intelligent; breathing out with us the peculiar and favourite beauties of our best bards; passing from grand and commanding argument to the gaieties and graces of wit and humour, and the elegant and higher beauties of poetry. He is indeed *great* company and leaves a weight on the mind, which 'it can hardly bear'. He is full of what Dr Johnson terms 'good talk'. His countenance is also extremely fine—a sunken and melancholy face, forehead lined with thought and bearing a full and strange pulsation on exciting subjects, an eye dashed in its light with sorrow but kindling and *living* at intellectual moments, and a stream of coal-black hair dropping around all. Such a face, so silent and so sensitive, is indeed the banner of the mind. 'It is as a book, in which men may read strange things.' He would have become the pencil of Titian, and have done justice to the soul-fed colours of that bold and matchless Italian.[24]

Like Keats, Reynolds was influenced by Hazlitt's philosophy and was one of several writers he helped promote—in Reynolds' case by recommending him as an Edinburgh reviewer. (Keats later looked to Hazlitt for the same kind of assistance.[25]) At another soirée that August, Bryan Waller Procter was charmed by Hazlitt's 'quick, restless eye ... which opened eagerly when any good or bright observation was made, and I found at the conclusion of the evening that when any question arose, the most sensible reply always came from him. Although the process was not too obvious, he always seemed to have reasoned with himself before he uttered a sentence.'[26]

Other acquaintances of the moment included Charles Wells, one of several solicitors with literary aspirations. They got on because Hazlitt liked his high-spirited, witty personality, and he became one of the 'coffee-house politicians' with whom Hazlitt stayed up all night, probably at the Southampton Tavern in Holborn. Wells recalled that, every night over a three-year period, he and Hazlitt 'used to get very drunk together'.[27] Among other things, they chuckled over the lewd goings-on at Charles II's court, described by Count de Grammont: 'Jacob Hall's prowess was not forgotten, nor the story of Miss Stuart's garters.'[28] On one occasion, Wells turned to Hazlitt and announced his intention to give up the law and become a writer. 'I consider you to possess great original genius', said Hazlitt, 'aboriginal, it might be said,—and I strongly advise you to stick to your profession.'[29] This was the kindest way of putting it; Wells would publish two books, both of which were ignored by reviewers, and eventually stopped seeing Hazlitt because he 'had everything to learn from Hazlitt, and Hazlitt nothing from him'.[30]

The Government was busily exploiting its newly assumed powers to suppress journalists: T. J. Wooler, editor of *The Black Dwarf*, and William Hone, editor of the *Reformist's Register*, were arrested for sedition on 3 May; Richard Carlile, publisher and writer, would be detained on 20 August. An unexpected by-product was the forging of new alliances among persecuted radicals: hearing of Hone's arrest, John Hunt offered assistance to his wife, as he told his brother: '[Hone] is, I think, what is understood by the phrase, "a coarse man", and will (they say) do things in his trade of bookselling which are not thought respectable. But then he is poor. I understand that he is honest and consistent; and I felt so strongly when I heard he had been arrested, that I called immediately on his wife to inquire about him.'[31] John Hunt knew what it was to suffer imprisonment, having been incarcerated in 1813, when he was subjected to rigid discipline and stricken with sciatica at Coldbath Fields prison. His kindness was acknowledged by Hone in a letter from King's Bench Prison on 8 May: 'Your kind conversation with my wife on Monday sensibly affects me,' he told him, 'I am often backward in expressing acknowledgments of services but I am never insensible of them.'[32] Hone's three trials and ultimate victory over the Government would be a milestone in the fight for a free press.[33]

On 23 June John Philip Kemble made his farewell performance in the role of Coriolanus at Covent Garden. Having been inducted into the magic of the theatre by him over a quarter of a century earlier, Hazlitt noticed his last hurrah con amore, celebrating Kemble's 'intensity, in the seizing upon some one feeling or idea, in insisting upon it, in never letting it go, and in working it up, with a certain graceful consistency, and conscious grandeur of conception, to a very high degree of pathos or sublimity'.[34] There could be no higher praise.

A highlight of the season was the visit of the French actors François-Joseph Talma and Mademoiselle Georges (Marguerite-Josephine Weimer, formerly Napoleon's mistress), the end of the Napoleonic Wars having renewed the traffic of theatrical virtuosi across the Channel. Although Hazlitt thought Mademoiselle Georges 'large, and in some degree unwieldy', her acting was 'more quick, more extreme, and more unceasing' in tone and gesture than anything he had seen; of Talma 'we can hardly speak highly enough': 'He owes everything to the justness of his conception, and to the energy of his execution. His acting displays the utmost force of passion, regulated by the clearest judgement. It is the triumph of art, but of art still prompted and impelled, and kindled into the very frenzy of enthusiasm, by the inspiration of nature and genius.'[35] In short, he had gusto.

Another noteworthy Frenchman was in town that summer—Stendhal, who read one of Hazlitt's articles in the *Edinburgh Review* the previous year and was bowled over by it. In particular, he was taken by a passage which discussed Petrarch's love of Laura:

> The smile which sank into his heart the first time he ever beheld her, played round her lips ever after: the look with which her eyes first met his, never passed away. The image of his mistress still haunted his mind, and was recalled by every object in nature. . . . As our feelings become more ideal, the impression of the moment indeed becomes less violent; but the effect is more general and permanent. The blow is felt only by reflection; it is the rebound that is fatal.

Stendhal could not have known the name of the man whose words he was reading, but understood immediately what they signified: it was an uncannily accurate portrait of his own mind[36] and probably the work of someone who had undergone the same experience. He seized the nearest thing to hand—his copy of Molière—and scribbled in its margin: 'L'explication anglaise du caractère de Dominique: . . . it is the rebound that is fatal'[37] (Dominique being one of the names by which Stendhal referred to himself[38]). So completely did he identify with the passage that he reprinted it in his *Histoire de la Peinture en Italie* (1817) as 'Biography of the A[uthor]'.[39] And we know he studied Hazlitt's essay in detail because it is the source for sections of his discussion of Dante elsewhere in that volume.[40] He returned to Hazlitt's comments when putting to bed his *Rome, Naples et Florence* (1817), reprinting them as the book's epigraph.[41]

One reason for Stendhal's visit to London was to meet Henry Colburn, who would reprint *Rome, Naples et Florence* in November; another was to track down Hazlitt's contributions in back numbers of the *Edinburgh Review*, as he recorded in his journal: 'Nous allons chercher dans l'Oxford street l'*Edinburgh review*, que nous trouvons enfin pour 15 guinées'.[42] Stendhal took whatever issues he could find to his rooms at the Tavistock Hotel in Covent Garden, a short distance from the theatres Hazlitt attended daily. The two men should have met at this moment, but circumstances did not oblige: their acquaintance would have to wait.

In the midst of the July heatwave Hazlitt took his six-year-old son to visit John Black, who had just taken over editorship of the *Morning Chronicle*, a development that led him to write for it once more.[43] Black's house backed onto the Thames at Millbank, in those days a quiet riverside lane leading out of Westminster to Chelsea. While the grown-ups chatted, William Jr played in the garden, filling his bucket with water which he emptied onto the vegetable beds. On one of these sorties, he fell into the river. Unable to swim, he shouted for help, but the adults were too deeply embroiled in conversation to hear. Fortunately, Black's dog Platoff (named after the Russian commander) jumped in and hauled the youngster out.[44] Despite being a doting father, Hazlitt was absent-minded to the point of negligence. Such incidents bear out William Jr when, in his early seventies, he told his son that 'Your grandfather and grandmother were both of the kindliest nature, but with no more notion of managing children than the man in the moon, as I know to my Cost, & to that of my own family.'[45]

In October 1817 Bentham heard of Hazlitt's inability to keep up with his rent and instructed his factotum, John Herbert Koe, to 'distrain' him, saying he 'is no object of compassion: for that his gains are considerable, even ample, though his habits profuse and negligent.'[46] This disproves Bentham's claim not to have known his tenant's identity. Not only was he aware that Hazlitt was resident at York Street, but spies kept him informed of his tenant's 'gains' and 'habits'.

Reluctant to distrain immediately, Koe first consulted Basil Montagu. This was a clever move. Not only was Montagu Hazlitt's friend, but he had lent him money in the past, partly to help him out of such scrapes. Moreover, money problems were his speciality, as he published a four-volume *Digest of Bankruptcy Laws* in 1805-7. In the event, Montagu's advice was not very friendly: he suggested that Koe 'threaten [Hazlitt] very severely with legal proceedings if he does not pay'.[47] Koe did so but to no avail. Hazlitt simply did not have the money, and in any case did not take kindly to threats. In desperation, Koe returned to Montagu and asked him to intervene. Were he to fail, Koe would resort to Bentham's preferred option, which meant throwing Hazlitt and his family into the streets. Montagu assured Koe that Hazlitt would pay, and went to see him. During a lengthy conversation Hazlitt proved he had no means of producing the money. No wonder: his outgoings were considerable. Sarah's relaxed attitude to housewifery led them to depend on their housekeeper, Mrs Tomlinson. Knowing a good thing when she saw one, Mrs Tomlinson often entertained her two daughters at York Street, one of whom was married to a soldier who 'was frequently asked in by ... his affectionate mother-in-law'; on such occasions 'there was high festival below stairs'.[48] Which meant, more often than not, that Hazlitt's earnings fed seven people rather than three. The obvious solution would have been to sack Mrs Tomlinson, but she had a knack of making herself indispensable. She was also rather frightening: Hazlitt was 'crushed and confounded'[49] by her, while Leigh Hunt compared her with Queen Caroline.[50]

Montagu had a brainwave: he proposed that Koe ask John Stoddart for the money. Montagu probably knew of the annuity Stoddart settled on the Hazlitts at the time of their marriage, and realized he would pay their back rent. It was a solution embraced by Koe who reported to Bentham: 'I have got an introduction to him and intended to have gone there on Monday: but I have had some drawing which has kept me constantly here: but I hope to finish this night and I will certainly call there tomorrow so that you shall hear something about it by tomorrow's or Saturday's post: that is if I find him at home.'[51] The fact that the Hazlitts continued at York Street for another two years suggests that Stoddart obliged. But it was a mammoth humiliation to have to draw— yet again—on the largesse of a man he had publicly condemned, whose yearly allowance had maintained his family for years. Redemption at the hands of Dr Slop (the nickname Hazlitt and his friends gave to Stoddart) was almost worse than being distrained.

Only financial pressure can have led him to consider a return to lecturing. His previous experience of it had been mixed, but the publishing of *Characters of Shakespear's Plays* underlined the importance of advance publicity, and a lecture series would give his next project a good 'puff'. He visited the Surrey Institution on the other side of Blackfriars Bridge to meet its secretary, P. G. Patmore. Founded in 1808, the Institution possessed a newspaper room, reference library, and lending library, as well as a 'convenient Laboratory, furnished with the necessary apparatus affording every facility to Chemical and Philosophical Researches'.[52] Its rotunda featured lectures by the foremost experts in their fields, admission to which was included in the annual subscription of £3.3s.0d. This was the ideal venue for a series that would revolutionize the way in which people thought about literature; although, as Patmore recalled, his first encounter with their author was inauspicious.

> I saw a pale anatomy of a man, sitting uneasily, half on half off a chair, with his legs tucked awkwardly underneath the rail, his hands folded listlessly on his knees, his head drooping on one side, and one of his elbows leaning (not resting) on the edge of the table by which he sat, as if in fear of its having no right to be there.

His hat had taken an odd position on the floor beside him, as if that too felt itself as much out of its element as the owner.

He half rose at my entrance, and, without speaking a word, or looking at me, except with a momentary and furtive glance, he sat down again, in a more uneasy position than before, and seemed to wait the result of what I might have to say to him, with the same sort of desperate indifference with which a culprit may be supposed to wait the sentence of his judge, after conviction.[53]

As it was Patmore's job to approve the application, he was alarmed to find that Hazlitt's lectures were not yet written—indeed, 'they had been merely *thought of*'.[54] Moreover, the engagement was one that demanded punctuality over the period not just of weeks but months, and Hazlitt did not appear to have that kind of discipline. For all that, Patmore agreed to schedule his appearances for successive Tuesdays beginning 3 January 1818, and commissioned a prospectus for them.[55]

In the meantime, Hazlitt concluded his run of attacks on Coleridge with a thumper: *Biographia Literaria* was published in July 1817 and noticed in the *Edinburgh Review* (published in September). Coleridge claimed always to have been a Trinitarian in philosophy and an enemy of Jacobinism:[56] 'my principles of politics have sustained no change', he pleaded.[57] Hazlitt knew better. In response, he produced a tour de force of invective—over 10,000 words subjecting Coleridge to the meatgrinder of his powerful intelligence, before disposing of what remained in the incinerator; it paid 50 guineas.[58] Of all his attacks, this was the most focused, its theme being the betrayal of one's youthful beliefs for the sake of an egotistical, vain obsession with metaphysics:

the disease, we fear, was in the mind itself; and the study of poetry, instead of counteracting, only gave force to the original propensity; and Mr Coleridge has ever since, from the combined forces of poetic levity and metaphysic bathos, been trying to fly, not in the air, but under ground—playing at hawk and buzzard between sense and nonsense,—floating or sinking in fine Kantean categories, in a state of suspended animation 'twixt dreaming and awake,—quitting the plain ground of 'history and particular facts' for the first butterfly theory, fancy-bred from the maggots of his brain,—going up in an air-balloon filled with fetid gas from the writings of Jacob Behmen and the mystics, and coming down in a parachute made of the soiled and fashionable leaves of the Morning Post,—promising us an account of the Intellectual System of the Universe, and putting us off with a reference to a promised dissertation on the Logos, introductory to an intended commentary on the entire Gospel of St John.[59]

That was just the start. The central issue, of which Hazlitt never lost sight, was Coleridge's 'lamentable affectation of surprise at the otherwise unaccountable slowness of good men in yielding implicit confidence to a party ... who could with impunity, and triumphantly, take away by atrocious calumnies the characters of all who disdained to be their tools,—and rewarded with honours, places, and pensions all those who were'.[60] Once again, the true and rightful target of this review was the betrayal of beliefs once espoused by Wordsworth, Southey, Stoddart, and others. Finally, Hazlitt dismissed Coleridge in a single sentence: 'Till he can do something better, we would rather hear no more of him.'[61] Full of vengeful ire, Southey offered John Murray a response for the *Quarterly Review*, 'laying it on with a willing hand and a cat and nine tails',[62] but Murray declined: he detested 'personalities'.

In the space of just over a year, Hazlitt had written two devastating reviews of the *Christabel* volume, four of *The Statesman's Manual*, and one of *Biographia Literaria*, each centred on the charge that Coleridge had smoked away his early promise with opium; betrayed his youthful radicalism; and become so preoccupied with metaphysical quandaries as to have become an irrelevance. They appeared at some cost to Hazlitt and his friends: Lamb had lost his temper with Martin Burney; the normally peaceable John Lamb had punched their author in the face; and Robinson severed relations with him. But they were worth it, for they spoke only what was true.

Were any justification required, one need look no further than Coleridge's letter to Lord Liverpool of 28 July 1817. At Southey's urging, the Government had clamped down on its critics; now Coleridge wrote to express 'the strong feeling of respect, the inward honor, which I have been so long in the habit of connecting with your name',[63] as well as his 'support of those principles ... of the measures and means, which have at length secured the gratitude and reverence of the wise and good to your Lordship and your Lordship's fellow-combatants in the long agonizing contest'[64]—by which he meant the Government's suppression of dissident opinion. He encouraged the Prime Minister to use all necessary violence against protestors, observing that 'the system ends as it began in "physical force", as the sovereign people are sure to learn, where the minority happens to consist of a ruffian at the head of an army of ruffians'.[65] Coleridge wanted to give Liverpool a philosophical defence for his forcible suppression of 'ruffians'—that is, those agitating for reform. The majority, Coleridge noted, 'must either keep under or expel the minority',[66] the populace being 'but the sprigs and boughs in a forest tossed against each other by an agency in which their own will has the least share'.[67] He concluded with a Coleridgean piety: 'God grant that under the wise and temperate measures of your Lordship, and your Lordship's coadjutors in the British cabinet, the necessary process may be carried on in meekness and by individual collisions.'[68] This was an odd way to describe the measures Liverpool had enacted, which were anything but temperate, let alone wise. That Coleridge was hoping one of these 'collisions' might involve Hazlitt is implied by the concluding reference to the 'inveterate and pre-determined malignity' of 'literary and political guides'.[69]

Coleridge's apologists avoid this letter, and who can blame them? They prefer the firebrand of the 1790s who lectured against Pitt to the drug-addled Judas who, twenty years on, justified the use of violence against peaceful protest. What makes it worse is that Coleridge stood to gain nothing by it, being neither a State pensioner nor in search of a sinecure. He wrote unbidden, volunteering his support for government-sponsored injustice for its own sake. To those who accused him of apostasy, Coleridge replied, 'there is not a single political opinion which I held at five and twenty which I do not hold now.'[70] He was wrong. As a young man he would have deplored the measures taken by Liverpool's government, and despised the older self who curried favour with it in such obsequious prose. If we wish fully to understand Hazlitt's motives, we have only to remember that he had known Coleridge in 1798 when he heard him deliver a sermon which 'echoed from the bottom of the human heart'.[71] 'I could not have been more delighted if I had heard the music of the spheres,' he remembered, 'Poetry and Philosophy had met together, Truth and Genius had embraced, under the eye and with the sanction of Religion.'[72] And yet, even at the height of his disillusionment, Hazlitt was capable of acknowledging the promise of the man: a deleted passage in the manuscript of his *Lectures on the English Poets* admits: 'He is the earliest friend I ever had, and I will add to increase the obligation, that he is the only person from whom I ever learnt anything in conversation. He was the only person I ever knew who answered to my idea of a man of genius.'[73]

Coleridge was the subject of conversation when Hazlitt spent the evening of Sunday 12 October at Haydon's new house in Lisson Grove with Thomas Barnes. Talking of Coleridge's drug addiction, Haydon remarked, poetically: 'Let him be in a delusion and a sleep.'

'Yes', said Barnes, 'but he *kicks* in his sleep'.

'I don't know as to his kicking', said Hazlitt, 'but I know he talks and writes in his sleep.'[74] It was one of Hazlitt's favourite jokes that the fuzziness

Fig. 20. Hazlitt's inscription on the flyleaf of John Philpot Curran's copy of *Characters of Shakespear's Plays*. Hazlitt admired Curran as the defender of the United Irishmen, and was happy to 'stand upon a little punctilio' when dining at his house.

of Coleridge's recent writings (most of them dictated) reflected the influence of opium.[75]

John Philpot Curran died of a stroke on 14 October. Hazlitt was an occasional visitor to his house at Amelia Place, Brompton, during the last two years of his life. They had probably encountered each other at Horne Tooke's Wimbledon gatherings decades earlier, but the two men had become much closer with the passing of time. All the same, Curran was nearly three decades Hazlitt's senior, and the younger man always felt obliged to observe an eighteenth-century decorum when in his company. William Jr remembered his father 'thought it necessary to stand upon a little punctilio; as, for instance, when he dined at Mr. Curran's'.[76] Curran was a link with Hazlitt's Irish heritage, and something of a hero. A farmer's son from Newmarket, County Cork, Curran rose to become a leading Whig politician during the 1790s. As a lawyer he was renowned for his forensic demolition of evidence brought against Irish nationalists, particularly the United Irishmen. Notable clients included Hazlitt's former colleague Peter Finnerty, Lord Edward Fitzgerald, Wolfe Tone, and W. J. MacNeven.[77] Curran's daughter Sarah was involved with Robert Emmet. On his visits to Curran, Hazlitt would have wanted to question him about the many notables he had defended, and they must have talked more than once about the future of Ireland. Hazlitt's last visit appears to have been a few weeks before Curran's death, when he gave him a copy of *Characters of Shakespear's Plays*.[78]

October 1817 saw the appearance in *Blackwood's Edinburgh Magazine* of a devastating attack on Hunt. Its author, J. G. Lockhart, had Hazlitt in his sights too, alleging that Hunt begged Hazlitt to notice *Rimini*: 'The very culpable manner in which his chief poem was reviewed in the *Edinburgh Review* (we believe it is no secret, at his own impatient and feverish request, by his partner in the *Round Table*), was matter of concern to more readers than ourselves. . . . Mr Jeffrey does ill when he delegates his important functions into such hands as those of Mr Hazlitt.'[79] This was how the *Blackwood's* men operated, undermining their enemies with allegation and innuendo, however baseless. In this case the charge was damaging not just to Hunt but Hazlitt, who depended on the prestige and income provided by the *Edinburgh*. Hunt wrote immediately to Jeffrey to say that 'nothing can be falser than what is said respecting my having asked and pestered Mr Hazlitt to write an article upon my poem in the *Edinburgh Review*. I never breathed a syllable to him on the subject, as anybody who knows me would say for me at once, for I am reckoned, if anything, somewhat over fastidious and fantastic on such matters.'[80] Not long after, in early November, John Hunt visited the London agent of *Blackwood's* to tell him the article was objectionable, demanding to know its author's name. Blackwood said it was 'sent from London by a writer of great ability', the implication being that it was Coleridge's.[81] Lies and red herrings: that was Blackwood's stock-in-trade.

Lockhart and his cronies made further attacks on Jeffrey for employing Hazlitt; in July 1818, Lockhart wrote: 'It was indeed a fatal day for Mr Jeffrey, when he degraded both himself and his original coadjutors, by taking into pay such an unprincipled blunderer as Hazlitt. He is not a coadjutor, he is an accomplice. The day is perhaps not far distant, when the Charlatan shall be stripped to the naked skin, and made to swallow his own vile prescriptions.'[82] The aim was to bully Jeffrey into dismissing Hazlitt—in effect, to destroy Hazlitt's livelihood. But Jeffrey was unmoved, and stood by his contributor. Frustrated, the Blackwoodsmen sought a softer target—Keats.[83]

At around this time, John Hunt proposed the establishment of *The Yellow Dwarf*, which he invited Hazlitt to co-edit. There was a place, Hunt believed, for a paper that would speak its mind about the Government's depredations—something journalists were increasingly reluctant to do. The reading public needed a free press more than ever. In Derby on 7 November three men—Jeremiah Brandreth, Isaac Ludlam, and William Turner—were hanged, drawn, and beheaded for their part in the 'rising' of 8 June, fomented by Oliver, a government agent. Turner's last words were 'This is all Oliver and the government.'[84] Moreover, William Hone's three trials—scheduled for three consecutive days—concluded on 20 December. Against the odds, he won them all, persuading each jury that his conviction would be an injustice.

Fig. 21. William Hone defending himself during his three trials, as seen by his collaborator, George Cruikshank. If Hazlitt was not one of the many people who witnessed his triumph, he certainly celebrated when he heard about it. He would argue Hone's cause in the first number of *The Yellow Dwarf*.

Londoners celebrated for days. 'Wooler & Hone have done us an essential service,' Keats told his brother, referring also to T. J. Wooler, editor of *The Black Dwarf*, acquitted of libel in June.[85] In saying this, he articulated the thoughts of many moderates who believed the Government had gone too far. Henry Crabb Robinson shared in the jubilation, describing Hone's trials as 'inconceivable folly',[86] only to be told by one of his more straitlaced friends he was 'a mischievous character' for saying so.[87] Robinson reflected that much the same view would be taken by Southey, who feared 'the danger aris[in]g from the popular feeling a[gains]t the governm[en]t'.[88] As Hazlitt witnessed Hone's victory, he must have felt, more than ever, that he wanted to comment. It was decided that *The Yellow Dwarf* (so-called because it was printed on yellow paper) would open with a broadside attack on Government attempts to rig Hone's trial.[89]

Part III: A Philosopher in Grub Street

Toward the end of the year Basil Montagu introduced Hazlitt to Sir Anthony Carlisle who for nearly a quarter of a century had been surgeon at the Westminster Hospital and Professor of Anatomy at the Royal Academy since 1808. His patients had included Mary Wollstonecraft in her final days. It was not an ideal match: even Thomas Carlyle (no softy) found the Professor a 'hard-headed fellow . . . Utilitarian to the bone'[90]—hardly a sensibility Hazlitt would have found simpatico. However, they got on well enough for Carlisle to subscribe to Hazlitt's *History of English Philosophy*[91] and to invite him to his lectures at the Academy. Carlisle's performances were hugely popular, showbiz spectacles as much as academic events. On one occasion he introduced eight naked lifeguardsmen doing sword exercises so the audience could analyse their musculature. Another week he brought in the Indian jugglers to show off the flexibility of their joints. On the evening Hazlitt attended, Carlisle was in full court dress with curled and powdered bagwig, cocked hat, and lace ruffles down to the wrists. 'I should not have known my unpoetic acquaintance in that disguise,' Hazlitt said to his friend Bewick, who accompanied him, 'he seems like the owl peeping and winking in an ivy-bush upon some ancient turret, and I cannot conceive of such an arrant puppy finding anything good, or of *use*, or beauty in poetry. I now know *the man*.'[92]

Carlisle was discussing psychology, and asked: what is the difference between reason and emotion? His answer was to pass two dinner plates round the audience, one bearing a human brain, the other a heart. It was as articulate an expression of his insensitivity as Hazlitt could have desired. When the plates arrived before him, Hazlitt 'shrank back in sensitive horror, closed his eyes, turned away his pale, shuddering countenance, and appeared to those near him to be in a swooning state.' 'Of what use can all this be to artists?', he gasped, 'Surely the bones and muscles might be sufficient.'[93]

As new year approached, Hazlitt realized he had to resign from the *Times*. The combination of his forthcoming lectures, *The Yellow Dwarf*, and the articles he wrote for the *Edinburgh Review* and *The Examiner* were employment enough. Sarah would not have welcomed this; after all, *The Times* provided their only regular income. But Hazlitt had made up his mind. He handed his resignation to Walter, who responded by handing it back. He was too good a writer to lose. How much did he want? But Hazlitt had faced down his wife, and was immune to Walter's blandishments: he would leave *The Times* 'in spite of repeated and pressing remonstrances'.[94] Canny to the last, Walter accepted his resignation but insisted he work out his notice to the final day of the calendar month.[95]

Hazlitt was *not* invited to a memorable dinner party at Haydon's studio on the last Sunday of 1817, though many of his acquaintances were. It was to become known as 'the immortal dinner' because of those present—Keats, Lamb, and Wordsworth (at whose behest Hazlitt was excluded). At one point in the proceedings Lamb drunkenly teased Wordsworth for having called Voltaire 'dull' in *The Excursion*: perhaps, in an oblique sense, Hazlitt *was* present, for Lamb might not have said this had it not been for Hazlitt's review of Wordsworth's poem: 'We cannot however agree with Mr. Wordsworth that *Candide* is *dull*. It is, if our author pleases, "the production of a scoffer's pen", or it is any thing, but dull.'[96]

PART IV

The Plain Speaker

CHAPTER 14

In a note to Haydon about a week ago, (which I wrote with a full sense of what he had done, and how he had never manifested any little mean drawback in his value of me) I said if there were three things superior in the modern world, they were 'the Excursion,' 'Haydon's pictures' & 'Hazlitts depth of Taste'. So I do believe . . .

Keats to George and Tom Keats, 13 January 1818[1]

*T*he *Yellow Dwarf* opened on 3 January 1818 with a barnstorming performance in which Hazlitt analysed the three trials of William Hone—a factually based, investigative piece detailing legal abuses by the prosecution.[2] Over the course of its 21 issues Hazlitt would provide the new journal with some of his best political writing, including 'On Court-Influence', 'On the Clerical Character', 'What is the People?', and 'On the Regal Character' (all reprinted in *Political Essays*). Together they comprise a primer on the governmental system and its flaws—for which reason, decreed Wordsworth, *The Yellow Dwarf* 'ought to be instantly put down'.[3]

Hazlitt's copy of the paper, now at the British Library,[4] reveals he also provided brief paragraphs of wit and wisdom for the 'Miscellaneous' section—a task for which his wide range of reading equipped him. He was among the few in England to have read Baron de Grimm's *Correspondance Littéraire*, including volumes available only in French ('What a fund of sense there is in Grimm's Memoirs!' he would exclaim[5]). Thus, when Hunt wanted items with a Gallic theme, he could furnish them at a moment's notice.[6]

Despite having left *The Times* he could not slow down, having a mere ten days between launch of *The Yellow Dwarf* and that of his poetry lectures. At that moment P. G. Patmore received some surprising news: the editors of *Blackwood's Edinburgh Magazine* wanted him to report on the lectures. This was a weird thing to do in the light of the Cockney School attacks the previous October, though in keeping with *Blackwood's* policy both to praise and undermine their targets (Coleridge and Wordsworth were accorded similar treatment[7]).

Patmore was intimidated by the thought of visiting Hazlitt at home, feeling 'inexpressible horror and dread of his supposed personal character', their contact thus far having led him to regard him as 'little better than an incarnate fiend'.[8] What he found when he visited the York Street house was not what he expected.[9] After being made to wait 'a long interval' by Mrs Tomlinson, he was led up to Hazlitt's office which, like most visitors, he found oppressive. The windows looked upon 'some dingy trees' and although it was two in the afternoon the breakfast dishes were still on the table.[10] His reception, he thought, was 'not very inviting'—both Hazlitt and Sarah were there but neither rose to welcome him, both absorbed in work on the lectures.[11] Patmore told Hazlitt of his commission to review the series and persuaded Hazlitt to give him sight of the manuscripts.

It was six years since Hazlitt's last public lectures, and the fact he had not repeated the experiment speaks for itself. On 13 January 1818 at 7pm he entered the rotunda at the Surrey Institution as a man of substance, author of *The Round Table* and *Characters of Shakespear's Plays*. But he had reason to be nervous: his financial future rested on this series; it was, he later recalled, 'a case of life and death'.[12] Moreover, the very act of standing before an assembled multitude was terrifying for someone so shy. White as a sheet, he approached the table gripping his script tightly in his fist, while the audience gave him a round of applause. Seeing his nervousness, some shouted, 'Bravo, Hazlitt!' A silence finally descended on the hall, he laid out his papers, cleared his throat, and began tremulously to read. But as he did so the quavering tones of his own voice unsettled him. He stopped, looked up, and found himself gazing across a sea of faces, some of whom he recognized, some of whom he didn't. It was enough to strike fear into anyone. He put his hands as casually as he could into his waistcoat pockets, fidgeted a moment, then removed them. His body began to shake with fear. His mouth and throat were dry. There was only one thing to do. He collected his papers together, turned to his right, stepped smartly down from the lectern and strode rapidly towards the corridor. Luckily there were a number of friends at the door, including William Bewick, who seized hold of him and manhandled him back to the podium. By now the audience was applauding, cheering his name and shouting for him to come back. It was a friendly, encouraging sight, and with cries of 'Bravo, Hazlitt!' ringing

Fig. 22. The rotunda at the Surrey Institution, where Hazlitt delivered his successful lectures on the English poets in January 1818. He would return here for two more series of lectures in ensuing years.

in his ears, he climbed the steps back to the speaker's desk and began once more.[13]

After that one show of uncertainty, Hazlitt found his feet. His lectures were a roaring success. How relieved he was when word got round that, as Bewick declared, 'they are . . . the finest lectures that ever were delivered.'[14] Since his last such venture, his technique had improved. For one thing, he now understood that in order to give pleasure to his audience, he had to please himself. That was to prove his salvation. His technique, he later reflected,

is merely to read over a set of authors with the audience, as I would do with a friend, to point out a favourite passage, to explain an objection; or if a remark or a theory occurs, to state it in illustration of the subject, but neither to tire him nor puzzle myself with pedantic rules and pragmatical *formulas* of criticism that can do no good to any body. . . . In a word, I have endeavoured to feel what was good, and to 'give a reason for the faith that was in me' when necessary, and when in my power.[15]

[235]

Hazlitt's greatness as a critic resides in the truth of this self-effacing statement. He had no overarching theory of literature, and no wish to expound one. His approach was instinctive. Beginning with his own definition of poetry, he felt his way intuitively through the canon, applying his laser-like intelligence to the texts and authors before him.

At the end of that first evening, Hazlitt walked home with Patmore, who offered his arm. Hazlitt at first declined it, then 'pressed it ... and he then took it—but as if it had been a bar of hot iron—holding it *gingerly*, with the tips of his fingers, much after the fashion in which he used to shake hands with those friends who were inadvertent or absent enough to proffer that ceremony'.[16] Together they walked down Fleet Street and the Strand. Halfway down White-hall they were accosted by prostitutes who knew Hazlitt and addressed him familiarly, asking for money. A lesser man might have pretended not to know them, but Hazlitt replied cordially, regardless of Patmore: 'His forbearance and charity for the "unfortunate" persons in question were without limits; and he did not care if all the world knew it.'[17]

With the second lecture, on Chaucer and Spenser, Hazlitt hit his stride. Procter later described his delivery: 'He read his lectures in an abrupt yet somewhat monotonous voice, but they were very effective. If he failed in communicating, by his manner, the lighter graces of his authors, he established their graver beauties, and impressed on his auditors a due sense of their power. Keats, the poet, who used to go there to hear him, remarked to a friend of mine that he reminded him of Kean.'[18] Keats arrived just as everyone was leaving, only to be 'pounced upon' by 'Hazlitt, John Hunt & son [that is, Henry Leigh Hunt], [Charles] Wells, Bewick, all the Landseers, Bob Harris, Rox of the Burrough[19] Aye & more'.[20] Keats later said that 'I generally meet with many I know there.'[21] One prominent absentee was Leigh Hunt who 'refused to go near the place ... [because] it would seem a collusion if [he] said anything in favour after what [Hazlitt] had said of [him]'.[22] Stung by allegations that he pestered Hazlitt to review *Rimini*, Hunt stayed away, assuming Hazlitt would not mind—but he did, and it was among the charges levelled against him when they quarrelled in 1821.

Lamb (another absentee) heard that Hazlitt 'goes on lecturing against W[illiam] W[ordsworth] to give a zest to said lectures'[23]—probably from Henry Crabb Robinson, who was exasperated by that aspect of them. Robinson made no bones about the third lecture: '[Hazlitt] delighted me much with the talent he displayed, but I was equally disgusted with the malignant spirit that broke through in the covert attack on Wordsworth without naming him; he was very abusive, reproaching modern poets for their vanity and incapacity of admiring and loving anything but themselves.'[24] Why did Hazlitt have old acquaintances on his mind? Because that evening Coleridge opened a series of lectures at the London Philosophical Society, hoping to take Hazlitt's audience from him— but could he succeed? Not as well as he hoped: Coleridge began at 8pm, just as Hazlitt finished—which meant that if the athletic Hazlittian left the Surrey Institution ten minutes before the hour, there was time enough to dash across Blackfriars Bridge to join Coleridge's audience at Fleur-de-Luce Court off Fleet Street. A number managed it, including Robinson.

By comparison with Hazlitt, Coleridge was a bore, as even Robinson had to admit: on 24 February he noted 'much obscurity and metaphysics in the long introduction and not a little cant and commonplace in the short criticisms'.[25] Coleridge was also less easy on the eye. Besides objecting to 'the cloudiest language of German metaphysicians', James Mackintosh noted that 'The lecturer himself is become grotesque & unwieldy, the roundest mass of fat I have lately seen.'[26]

Robinson's attendance led to a momentary rapprochement with Hazlitt. Coinciding at Montagu's on 15 February, 'We did exchange a few words together', as Robinson recorded in his diary.[27] But Hazlitt's defiance of the laws of propriety proved too much. After the lecture two days later, Robinson observed that Hazlitt was 'almost obscene in treating of Prior', 'drew an ingenious but not very intelligible parallel between Swift, Rabelais and Voltaire, and even eulogised the modern infidel, so indiscreet and reckless is the man';[28] while on 24 February he was moved to hiss when Hazlitt criticized Wordsworth's *Letter to a Friend of Robert Burns*[29] ('as weak in effect as it is pompous in pretension'[30]). He did not return for the final lecture.[31]

For others, these lectures were the first sighting of a powerful new intellect. It was not just that Hazlitt exemplified a new sensibility but that he was one of the few capable of articulating it. It was a glimpse of the future, for Romantic ideas were beginning to shape the culture in a manner that continues to this day. Take, for instance, Hazlitt's portrait of Byron, which praises his 'depth of passion'—'always of the same unaccountable character, at once violent and sullen, fierce and gloomy. It is not the passion of a mind struggling with misfortune, or the hopelessness of its desires, but of a mind preying upon itself, and disgusted with, or indifferent to all other things. . . . It is like a cancer, eating into the heart of poetry. But still there is power; and power rivets attention and forces admiration.'[32] That description of poet as anti-hero foreshadows the pose struck by countless male icons over the succeeding two centuries.[33] Moreover, Hazlitt shocked his listeners by denying the widespread belief that Pope was the perfect poet, condemning 'those critics who are bigotted idolisers of our author'.[34] It is easy to understand how such declarations thrilled such listeners as Keats, who excitedly told Haydon that 'Hazlitt has damned the bigotted . . . how durst the Man?! he is your only good damner and if ever I am damn'd—I shoul'nt like him to damn me.'[35]

Hazlitt's modernity depends partly on his grasp of psychology. It is second nature for a twenty-first century reader to look at writers and their work with insights drawn from Freud, Jung, and their ilk; in 1818, prior to our science of the mind, such an approach was shockingly new. In that sense, Hazlitt is the father of modern literary criticism. No one in his own day took that view, of course; his contemporaries were as astonished by the perceptiveness of his thought as by the elegance of its expression but could not know the extent to which it would change the world.[36] All the same, there was no escaping their newness, as Mary Russell Mitford noted: 'He is a very entertaining person, that Mr Hazlitt, the best demolisher of a bloated unwieldy overblown fame that ever existed. He sweeps it away as easily as an east wind brushes the leaves off a faded peony. He is a literary Warwick—"a puller down of kings".'[37] The 'overblown fame' she saw Hazlitt sweeping away was that of Dr Johnson: the eighteenth century had given way to the nineteenth.

Hazlitt's lectures made him a star, and former colleagues took renewed interest in him—not least James Perry, his former employer at the *Chronicle*. Perry attended the lecture on Swift and reviewed it favourably: 'We know indeed of no author of the present day who excels Mr Hazlett in critical discernment— none whom it would in general be more safe to take as a guide and instructor in our native literature.'[38] Touched by Perry's attempt to make amends for his undignified departure from the *Chronicle*, Hazlitt sent him a ticket for the last of the series: 'Mr. Hazlitt presents his compliments & thanks to Mr. Perry, & incloses a card for his lectures, in case Mr. Perry or any friend should feel a disposition to look in.'[39] In return, Perry invited him to a grand dinner party where Hazlitt distinguished himself by his shyness, as Mary Russell Mitford recalled:

> M^r. Perry remembered him as an old acquaintance & asked him to dinner, & a
> large party to meet him, to hear him talk & to shew him off as the lion of the

day. The lion came—smiled & bowed—handed Miss Bently to the dining room—asked Miss Perry to take wine—said once Yes & twice No—& never uttered another word the whole evening. The most provoking part of this scene was that he was gracious & polite past all expression—a perfect pattern of mute elegance—a silent Lord Chesterfield—& his unlucky host had the misfortune to be very thoroughly enraged without any thing to complain of. Even Champaign failed to open his lips.—Not having been there I admire this piece of malice very much—If I had been present perhaps my opinion might have altered.[40]

Mitford did not realize that what she described was typical of Hazlitt's conduct among strangers. There was no malice in it; it was his way, for instance, to 'enter a room as if he had been brought back to it in custody; he shuffled sidelong to the nearest chair, sat himself down upon one corner of it, dropped his hat and his eyes upon the floor, and, after having exhausted his stock of conventional small-talk in the words, "It's a fine day" (whether it was so or not), seemed to resign himself moodily to his fate.'[41] Had there been any desire for revenge, Hazlitt would have declined to answer Perry's invitation; instead, he attended, behaving in what he thought the most appropriate manner given the strangeness of his surroundings—that is, with studied politeness. It was typical of him not to understand he was expected to shine. Afterwards, he must have known he had committed a gaffe: 'We may give more offence by our silence than even by impertinence,' he noted regretfully.[42]

His last lecture, 'On the Living Poets', on 3 March, was delivered to a house 'crowded to the very ceiling'.[43] Among the audience was William Godwin, who brought his wife, Mary Jane—grateful for a respite from ongoing disputes (over money) with their son-in-law, Percy Bysshe Shelley.[44] In this last lecture Hazlitt had some advice for Shelley's chum, Lord Byron—that he wished he would not write about Napoleon because he wrote 'both for and against him. . . . Why should Lord Byron now laud him to the skies in the hour of his success, and then peevishly wreak his disappointment on the God of his idolatry?'[45] Several audience members hissed their disapproval at this—not surprisingly, given the exiled Peer's cult status. Hazlitt reacted characteristically. He looked at them, repeated his words with emphasis, and added: 'If my Lord Byron will do these things, he must take the consequences; the acts of Napoleon Buonaparte are subjects of *history*, not for the disparagement of the Muse.'[46] Were proof needed that Hazlitt had arrived, this was it. His audience was tamed, and the lecture's conclusion was greeted by three successive rounds of applause and shouts of 'Bravo, bravo!'[47] The following evening, London was blasted by an apocalyptic storm, as if the flowering of his genius were acknowledged by the gods: houses were unroofed, chimney-stacks blown in, trees uprooted in St James's Park, and post-chaises smashed to smithereens.

He did not rest on his laurels. As he went along, he polished his texts, sending each chapter to his printing house when he was done with it. By the end of the lectures he was correcting proof;[48] his publishers needed to cash in on his fame with all haste. Nor was this the only book on the stocks. He had another ready to hit the presses, containing his collected theatre reviews. *A View of the English Stage* described a revolution in drama: the passing of the eighteenth century (symbolized by the retirement of John Philip Kemble) and advent of the new acting style of Kean. Hazlitt was among the few reviewers to have realized that Kean's intuitive interpretations were a glimpse of the future, the forerunner of a manner that prevails today. Kean's acting was the ideal complement to Hazlitt's equally instinctive approach to writing. 'My opinions have been sometimes called singular', he admitted in his Preface,

> they are merely sincere. I say what I think: I think what I feel. I cannot help receiving certain impressions from things; and I have sufficient courage to declare (somewhat abruptly) what they are. This is the only singularity I am conscious of.[49]

Though typically self-effacing, this is a good description of Hazlitt's technique in general. What singles him out is the sensitivity of his perceptions, matched by the consummate skill with which he analyses and records them. His respect for the actors on whom he sat in judgement is everywhere to be seen throughout this book. Indeed, he pays tribute to them at the outset, before going on to apologize to those of whom he may have spoken unfairly (several of whom he names)—a handsome gesture which I believe to be unique in theatrical criticism. *A View of the English Stage* is a remarkable volume, the best record we have of what it was like to join the audience in the pit of Drury Lane or Covent Garden to watch Edmund Kean, Catherine Stephens, Sarah Siddons, John Philip Kemble, and Eliza O'Neill. No other reviewer could have compiled such an evocative record of Regency drama from their cuttings file.

It was published on 29 April 1818 by Robert Stodart, a bookseller with radical sympathies. Unfortunately Stodart was a poor businessman and sales were slow; all the same, it had at least one admirer in Mary Russell Mitford: 'so much of Hazlitt is rather dangerous to one's taste', she told Sir William Elford, 'rather like dining on sweetmeats & supping on pickles—so poignant is he & so rich—every thing seems insipid after him'.[50] The reviewers were less enthusiastic. The *British Critic* prefaced its patronizing comments with the observation that the volume contained 'very little Jacobinism, and to the best of our belief, no blasphemy'[51]—as if such things were to be expected. The *British Review* framed its critique within the larger argument that Hazlitt's aim was to 'destroy the very foundations of morality and decorum, by a series of periodical attacks upon all received opinion, and by the systematic ridicule of every thing that is serious or respectable':[52] but that was published in 1819, by which time political enemies were using whatever means they could to destroy his reputation.

The advertisement leaf at the end of *A View of the English Stage* promised publication of *Lectures on the English Poets* 'This Day'—but it was not to be. Production of the *Lectures* stalled while Hazlitt wrote at white heat for *The Yellow Dwarf*. One of his most astute political essays, 'What is the People?', appeared in two parts on 7 and 14 March, with its incendiary message that 'nothing rouses the people to resistance but extreme and aggravated injustice'.[53] The point of the article was to launch an attack on the British constitution, especially the monarchy: 'The line of distinction which separates the regal purple from the slabbering-bib, is sometimes fine indeed,' Hazlitt commented, 'Any one above the rank of an ideot is supposed capable of exercising the highest functions of royal state.'[54] It was brave of him to write so trenchantly at a time when the Government was increasingly sensitive to criticism, and it is a wonder that he and John Hunt escaped prosecution. At last, copies of the *Lectures on the English Poets* were in circulation by late May, and in Taylor and Hessey's bookshop by 4 June.[55] It proved one of Hazlitt's most popular volumes, and within months an American edition had appeared in Philadelphia.[56]

Hazlitt repeated the poetry lectures at the Crown and Anchor Tavern in the Strand, beginning on Monday 23 March at 8pm. The Tavern had a sizeable meeting hall which could accommodate two thousand or more, long associated with radical politics: sympathizers of the French Revolution gathered here in the 1790s to commemorate the storming of the Bastille; now it was headquarters to Sir Francis Burdett and other reformers.[57] The decision to repeat the lectures was opportunistic, but Hazlitt had no choice, as Haydon observed: 'Haslitt is going to lecture at Crown & Anchor I am sorry for it, tho' he will get money, it is letting his talents down a little.'[58] This was jealousy on Haydon's part, not shared by Hazlitt's audience who greeted him with the 'warmest approbation';[59] they included Godwin (who missed all but the last lecture at the Surrey Institution), Amelia Curran, Thomas Massa Alsager, Charles Kemble, Martin Burney,

Part IV: The Plain Speaker

Basil Montagu and his wife, William Hone, the Lambs, John Soane, J. M. W. Turner, and Thomas Moore.

Moore attended the lecture on Burns and the old English ballads, and may have spoken with the lecturer afterwards; if so, he probably revealed that his patron was none other than Lord Lansdowne, whose father (when Prime Minister) had assisted Hazlitt's father when his life was threatened by British soldiers in Ireland in the 1780s. Hazlitt's junior by a year, the Dublin-born writer had been a literary star since publishing the mildly erotic *Poetical Works of the Late Thomas Little* in 1801, and now enjoyed widespread acclaim for his *Irish Melodies*, which had begun to appear in 1808. They liked each other and, shortly after the lecture, Hazlitt wrote a lengthy appreciation of Moore's humorous poem, *The Fudge Family in Paris*,[60] from which it is clear that he admired him both as a poet and a man.

> He is neither a coxcomb nor a catspaw,—a whiffling turncoat, nor a thorough-paced tool, a mouthing sycophant, 'a full solempne man', like Mr Wordsworth,—a whining monk, like Mr Southey,—a maudlin Methodistical lay-preacher, like Mr Coleridge,—a merry Andrew, like the fellow that plays on the salt-box at Bartlemy Fair,—or the more pitiful jack-pudding, that makes a jest of humanity in St Stephen's Chapel. Thank God, he is none of these—he is not one of the Fudge Family. He is neither a bubble nor a cheat. He makes it his business neither to hoodwink his own understanding, nor to blind or gag others. He is a man of wit and fancy, but he does not sharpen his wit on the edge of human agony, like the House of Commons' jester, nor strew the flowers of fancy, like the Jesuit Burke, over the carcase of corruption, for he is a man not only of wit and fancy, but of common sense and common humanity. He sees for himself, and he feels for others.[61]

Having read the review, Moore sent Hazlitt an autographed copy of *The Fudge Family in Paris* bearing the inscription: 'To William Hazlitt Esq', as a small mark of respect for his literary talents & political principles from the Author | April 27th. 1818'[62]—a rare contemporary acknowledgement of Hazlitt's achievement as a political writer. Perhaps Moore was reading *The Yellow Dwarf*.

Another member of the audience for the repeat performances of the *Lectures*, John Soane, has not previously figured in a biography of Hazlitt, and it is worth saying something here about him. He had long been famous as architect of the Bank of England, a national monument under construction since 1788 (when Hazlitt was ten), and on which Soane would continue to labour until 1833—three years after Hazlitt's death. He was also Professor of Architecture at the

Royal Academy, a post that inspired the project to convert his home at Lincoln's Inn Fields into a museum for architecture and the arts (a function it serves to this day).

Soane was also Vice President of the Surrey Institution and at the last of the lectures there had collared the speaker before he was carried away by friends.

'Sir, that was a wonderful lecture,' he said. 'I'm sorry I've been unable to attend the others. I understand they were just as good.'

'You are too kind, sir. But of course, you may hear them again, for I repeat them at the Crown and Anchor. Do you know it?'

'Why yes, Sir. Very well. When do you begin?'

'I will send you details.'

'Please do so, Mr Hazlitt. I should especially like to hear the lecture on Shakespeare. I understand you had much to say on him.'

'It was a condensed version of my book, Sir. You know it? *The Characters of Shakespear's Plays?*'

'No sir, I don't think I do.'

'I shall send you one.'[63]

A week or so later a note arrived at Soane's door:

Mr. Hazlitt incloses a ticket to his Lectures & begs Mr. Soane to accept his best acknowledgements for the favour and flattering attention he has shewn him. Mr. H. will leave a copy of the book on Shakespear, the instant the second edition is out, which will be this or the following week.
19 York Street, Westminster
Monday morning.[64]

Although the note was sent in March,[65] Soane did not get round to attending the repeat lectures until April, when he heard 'Burns and the Old English Ballads'[66] and 'On the Living Poets', as he recorded in his diary:

13 April
In the Eveng Mr. Turner etc drank Tea with me & we went to Mr Hazls Lecture—at Holyland 3s/6d
17 April
Went with Mr. Turner to Haslitts last Lect. Paid 0.3/6

'Mr. Turner' was J. M. W. Turner, Soane's friend since the early 1790s and a regular visitor to his home. Soane thus provides two occasions on which Hazlitt was introduced to the man described in *The Round Table* as 'the ablest landscape painter now living'.[67] As early as 1814, Hazlitt had declared that Turner's 'powers of eye, hand, and memory, are equal to any thing', and that his 'Dido and Aeneas' 'has all the characteristic splendour and confusion of an Eastern composition'.[68] He was exceptional in praising Turner, whose work usually attracted uncomprehending abuse.[69]

Turner was about the same height as Hazlitt (that is to say, short by modern standards) and spoke with a pronounced Cockney accent. Three years Hazlitt's senior, he had little in the way of formal education, having trained as an artist from an early age. But he loved poetry and theatre, and was stimulated by Hazlitt's judgements on the poets he discussed. If they talked about Turner's recent tour of the Low Countries and the Rhineland, Hazlitt would have been fascinated to hear of his adventures, and may even have wangled an invitation to see the sketches he made there.[70] At some point, however, it is clear that Turner said something that displeased him, because in later years Hazlitt said he disliked Turner 'as a man'. The probable explanation is that they got onto the subject of Napoleon who, according to Turner, was a murderer, tyrant, and butcher. If so, Hazlitt would have sprung to his hero's defence.[71]

Although Patmore fulfilled his promise to review Hazlitt's lectures favourably for *Blackwood's*, his comments were undercut by an anonymous poem in the same issue of the journal which referred to 'pimpled Hazlitt's coxcomb lectures'.[72] Hazlitt's non-existent pimples (a sign of addiction to gin) were a convenient way of smearing the Cockneys as a whole; it was repeated in *Blackwood's* until as late as 1829,[73] and picked up by other enemies. Patmore was embarrassed and sent an ill-advised reproof to Blackwood:

> By the bye, was it not a gratuitous piece of *imprudence* (to say the least of it) to admit that line in the last No about 'pimpled Hazlitt'? In consequence of being one of the Managers of a Literary Institution I have been led to form a slight personal acquaintance with Mr. Hazlitt, & I have reason to know that such notices as that to which I allude are exceedingly obnoxious to him—& I suppose your editor is not ignorant how tremendous his power is when he sets about to resent what he feels or fancies to be an injury.[74]

To Blackwood, this read as a threat—what 'power' could Hazlitt exert over him?—and he responded accordingly. He began by pooh-poohing the slur, with an additional untruth—'is it possible that he [Hazlitt], the most severe and slashing satyrist of the day, can care for an unmeaning expression in an unmeaning *jeu d'esprit*? Surely not'[75]—before a menacing display of nonchalance: 'I can have no wish to offend or irritate Mr Hazlitt. But neither have I the slightest fear of him.'[76] Blackwood did not make such declarations without taking careful note of their instigators, and that was Hazlitt's ill fortune: from now on, he would be marked out for special treatment by the Blackwoodsmen.

Recent attempts to humanize Blackwood have lacked conviction.[77] He was a malicious thug driven by greed and ambition with no loyalty to business part-ners and an utter hatred of competitors, especially Hazlitt's friend Archibald Constable. The measure of the man is illustrated by his reaction to a Mr Douglas from Glasgow who, on 13 May, stung by abuse in the latest *Blackwood's*,[78] got on the Edinburgh stage, found Blackwood in the streets of Edinburgh, and laid his whip lightly across his shoulders. Such behaviour, undertaken in a public place (known as horsewhipping), was taken to bestow dishonour on the individual at the receiving end, and sometimes led to duels. On occasion the whipping was severe; Peter Finnerty once received its full force across his face.[79] But Douglas's touch was light as a feather—all the redress he needed—and he walked off with-out leaving his name and address. Blackwood responded by heading straight for a shop to buy a large 'hazel sapling'. He hunted Douglas down (who was just about to board the Glasgow stage) and attacked him publicly, beating him 'as hard as he could', leaving him bruised and bleeding on the ground.[80] Not satisfied with that, Blackwood wrote to the *Glasgow Chronicle* with his account of the incident, boasting of his misdeeds. He was living proof of the maxim, 'Want of principle is power.'[81]

That was what Hazlitt was up against. The *Blackwood's* writers knew both that he wasn't pimpled, and that he seldom drank alcohol: that was the point. 'Had I really been a gin-drinker and a sot', he told Patmore, 'they would have sworn I was a milk-sop.'[82] Years later, he told Charles Brown: 'Of what use would it be were I publicly to convict them of untruth in this description of me?—of none whatever. They would then persuade their readers, far more to blame than themselves, that in their representation consisted the very marrow, the excellence of the jest:—nay, that the jest would be nothing if it *were* true.'[83] Hazlitt was confronted several times in his career with the disturbing truth that merely to allege something in print was sufficient to turn it into fact, and never stopped resenting the credulity of the reading public.

A man's reputation is not in his own keeping, but lies at the mercy of the profligacy of others. Calumny requires no proof. The throwing out malicious imputations against any character leaves a stain, which no after-reputation can wipe out. To create an unfavourable impression, it is not necessary that certain things should be *true*, but that they *have been said*. The imagination is of so delicate a texture, that even words wound it.[84]

Two years before his death, he summed it up as a pithy aphorism: 'Seeing is believing, it is said. Lying is believing, say I.'[85]

The charge received numerous rebuttals in succeeding years. John Scott would write that 'It is a hoax...to tell a man that he has pimples on his face when it happens to be clear, as Blackwood's men have done to Mr. Hazlitt.'[86] Hazlitt would deny it in 'A Reply to "Z"', when he told the anonymous author of the attack (Lockhart): 'I am *not* pimpled, but remarkably pale and sallow. You were told of this as a false fact, and you repeated and still repeat it, declaring to hundreds of persons individually and to the public that you not only do not care for the distinction between truth and falsehood, but that you are superior to being thought to care about it.'[87]

Hazlitt had a choice: to take legal action or do nothing. His friends counselled caution. After all, Blackwood's intentions were unclear, given publication of Patmore's favourable notice. And perhaps the attacks would stop; Blackwood's reply to Patmore gave grounds for so hoping: 'I know the powers of Mr Hazlitt and perfectly sympathize with your admiration of them.'[88] Moreover, they would have argued, what hope was there of finding the culprit? Hunt's repeated challenges for the author of the Cockney School essays to identify himself had been met with further anonymous attacks, including the charge that *Rimini* was 'vile, profligate, obscene, indecent, and detestable'.[89] Hazlitt wanted to take action, but the slipperiness of his opponents discouraged him.

Such attacks had the potential to kill sales of his work, as he discovered when two months later the *Quarterly* delivered a diabolical notice of *Characters of Shakespear's Plays*—possibly by its editor, William Gifford.[90] Unfortunately it was published on 9 June, shortly after the appearance of the book's second edition on 30 May. At first, his publishers were sanguine: 'Gifford may say what he will of him—they are old Enemies of each other,' John Taylor remarked.[91] But sales of *Characters* soon dried up. Hazlitt never stopped resenting the sensitivity of the reading public to bad reviews. Years later he recalled how the volume 'sold well—the first edition had gone off in six weeks—till that review came out. I had just prepared a second edition—such was *called* for—but then the *Quarterly* told the public that I was a fool and a dunce, and said that I was an evil-disposed person; and the public supposed Gifford to know best, confessed it had been a great ass to be pleased where it ought not to be, and the sale completely stopped.'[92]

He could not take the *Quarterly* to court, so produced an angry response in *The Examiner*, ridiculing Gifford for being 'low-bred' (the son of a glazier and a cobbler's apprentice) and of diminutive stature ('This little person'[93]). Personal or not, Hazlitt's charges were just: 'He insults over unsuccessful authors; he hates successful ones. He is angry at the faults of a work, more angry at its excellences.'[94]

Hazlitt's irritation was understandable because books were his livelihood. Not that his income from the lectures was anything to sneer at. They produced around two hundred guineas—which, as he told Jeffrey, 'is very well for ten weeks work'.[95] That, he must have hoped, would last—but it was quickly spent, and by July he was writing to Constable for an advance of £50.[96] What he had written of actors applied equally to himself: 'They live from hand to mouth: they plunge from want into luxury; they have no means of making money *breed*, and all professions that do not live by turning money into money, or have not a certainty of accumulating it in the end by parsimony, spend it.'[97] As that suggests, Hazlitt had an improvident side, to which he admitted in *Characteristics*: 'The secret of the difficulties of those people who make a great deal of money, and yet are always in want of it, is this—they throw it away as soon as they get it on the first whim or extravagance that strikes them, and have nothing left to meet ordinary expenses or discharge old debts.'[98] There would be no end to his indebtedness. Even after his decease, outstanding bills had to be paid off by friends. But against the charge of thriftlessness should be placed Hazlitt's life-long generosity: he spared nothing to take care of his son and wife, even after divorce; sent money to his parents; and did not hesitate to help friends in need. Moreover, it should be remembered that virtually everyone lived on debt in Regency times, when no stigma was attached to the borrowing of money.[99]

By early May Hazlitt was again in poor health and impoverished, as he complained to Jeffrey, who immediately responded: 'I am concerned to find that your health is not so good as it should be—and that you could take more care of it, if your finances were in better order—We cannot let a man of genius suffer in this way.'[100] With characteristic generosity, he enclosed a note for £100 even though Hazlitt was not then writing for him, promising more were it needed. Hazlitt also asked Jeffrey's opinion on a third rendition of the poetry lectures, this time in Edinburgh, but Jeffrey advised against it both from the extreme dissipation of the fashionable part of its population and from a sort of conceit and fastidiousness in all the middling classes which originating at least as much in a coldness of nature as in any extraordinary degree of intelligence makes them very ready to find fault and decry—Most lectures have accordingly failed entirely in this place . . . Estimating the merit of your lectures as highly as I am sincerely inclined to do I can by no means insure you ag[ains]t a total failure—but I think it much more likely that you might have about 30 or 50 auditors—not of the first rank or condition—and be abused as a jacobin and a raving blockhead by a great many more.[101]

Perhaps Jeffrey had in mind the abuse Hazlitt had received from *Blackwood's*; Hazlitt shelved the project of a Caledonian tour, at least for the moment.

Despite its quality, *The Yellow Dwarf* failed to find a readership large enough to sustain it and folded in June. In one respect that was a blessing, for it released Hazlitt from the treadmill of weekly publication. The experience was salutary: having acted as editor for the first time, he found it did not suit. Except for a brief spell in 1821, when he filled in at the *London Magazine*, he would not take the editor's chair again.

CHAPTER 15

Satirists gain the applause of others through fear, not through love.

Hazlitt, *Characteristics* lxxii[1]

H AZLITT still needed money. Patmore booked him into the Surrey Institution in October for a second series of lectures, this time on the English comic writers—a crowd-pleaser if ever there was one—while Hazlitt arranged publication rights with Taylor and Hessey who agreed to pay him £200 ('That is an improvement', he told Constable[2]). Now all he had to do was write them. It was July. London was sweltering, in the grip of a heatwave, said to be the hottest since 1779. He decided to go to Winterslow—on his own, a sign that his marriage had all but broken down. Sarah was leading an independent social life, turning up at the homes of such friends as Godwin and Lamb without him, and may already have moved out of York Street.

Before leaving, Hazlitt received a visit from Alexander Henderson, a Scot who approached him through Godwin; it may have been on this occasion that Henderson stayed for a week in Hazlitt's house. Hazlitt had no way of knowing his guest was one of Blackwood's spies, capable of declaring without shame that 'Mr Blackwood is a personal, & a kind, friend of mine'.[3] And if he knew that Blackwood ran an intelligence network collecting information for use in Cockney School attacks, informants including Alaric Watts, Eyre Evans Crowe, and other figures on the London literary scene, he never for a moment suspected Henderson's part in it.[4] Henderson was so plausible that Hazlitt sought out his hospitality in Edinburgh in 1822 and regarded him as a friend until the end of his life.[5] Henderson somehow gained his trust, and Hazlitt opened up. If Hazlitt had a fault, it was that he was too trusting of his acquaintances, revealing confidences at the drop of a hat—a quality that had already led to betrayal by John Scott. So it was that, during their conversations, Hazlitt said he couldn't tell the difference between Milton's Latin and Greek (in jest, surely?), and admitted he didn't know how many characters there were in the Greek alphabet.[6]

Part IV: The Plain Speaker

'I have seen some of your articles in the *Scots Magazine*, have I not?', asked Henderson. Indeed he had. Hazlitt's first contribution to the *Edinburgh Magazine* (also known as the *Scots Magazine*) had just that moment appeared in print—'On the Ignorance of the Learned'. Henderson was trying to confirm whether it was Hazlitt's, for it had appeared over the initials 'W. H.'

'Yes, I'm sorry to say,' replied Hazlitt, unwittingly providing Henderson with ammunition that would soon be used against him. 'The editors are ninnies, and their journal is a millstone round the neck of humanity. I regret having had anything to do with it, but I needed the money.'

'Money?', enquired Henderson. 'Why, Mr Hazlitt, you are so well employed, by such a range of editors—not least Mr Jeffrey—that I wonder at it.'

'Alas, I fear I may have been expelled from the *Edinburgh Review*, for Mr Jeffrey has not been in touch with me for months.'[7] Perhaps he feared that embarrassment over the numerous loans Jeffrey had made him might explain the editor's reluctance to commission him; if so, he did not say so to Henderson. He didn't need to. Henderson had more than enough for Blackwood's purposes, and soon transmitted the fruits of his skulduggery to his paymaster.

On Saturday, 8 August, Hazlitt set out for Winterslow on foot, a copy of Congreve's plays in his pocket. For the next three weeks he put party squabbles behind him. He walked first to Guildford, lodging probably at the White Hart Inn on the High Street (today the site of Sainsbury's supermarket), before heading for Farnham on Sunday, 39 miles south-west of London on what is now the A31, and then to Alton, 12 miles further on. He later recalled the pleasure of reading Congreve at one of the inns there:

> I was fairly tired out; I walked into an inn-yard . . . I was shown by the waiter to what looked at first like common out-houses at the other end of it, but they turned out to be a suite of rooms, probably a hundred years old—the one I entered opened into an old-fashioned garden, embellished with beds of larkspur and a leaden Mercury; it was wainscoted, and there was a grave-looking, dark-coloured portrait of Charles II hanging up over the tiled chimney-piece. I had *Love for Love* in my pocket, and began to read; coffee was brought in in a silver coffee-pot; the cream, the bread and butter, every thing was excellent, and the flavour of Congreve's style prevailed over all. I prolonged the entertainment till a late hour, and relished this divine comedy better even than when I used to see it played by Miss Mellon, as Miss Prue; Bob Palmer, as Tattle; and Bannister, as honest Ben.

Fig. 23. Winterslow Hut in 1893, much as it appeared to Hazlitt. He found it a congenial place in which to compose his essays and lectures, despite the strange looks he attracted from its staff.

This circumstance happened just five years ago, and it seems like yesterday. If I count my life so by lustres, it will soon glide away; yet I shall not have to repine, if, while it lasts, it is enriched with a few such recollections![8]

Were any evidence needed that Hazlitt knew *The Prelude*, it is provided by such passages as this—perfect variations on the Wordsworthian spot of time. He understood the concept well but, instead of going back into the depths of childhood trauma like Wordsworth, he domesticated it, finding inspiration in everyday experience.

The following day he walked to Winchester, and from there across country to Winterslow, probably taking the old Salisbury road—a journey of some 14 miles. He later remembered that 'On the road-side between Winchester and Salisbury are some remains of old Roman encampments, with their double lines of circumvallation (now turned into pasturage for sheep), which answer exactly to the descriptions of this kind in Caesar's Commentaries.'[9] He arrived in Winterslow on the afternoon of Monday 10 August 1818.

Part IV: The Plain Speaker

He would be based at Winterslow Hut, the inn on the main road between Salisbury and Andover, just over a mile's walk from Winterslow proper. As the Hut was a dropping-off point for the Salisbury Mail, he could communicate easily with his London friends and have books sent when needed. However, he was short of money. Past debts had eaten up his recent earnings so he turned to Archibald Constable who obliged with £50 in early August.

Winterslow was rejuvenating, as always; London air was 'impure, stagnant—without breathing-space to allow a larger view of ourselves and others'.[10] Here in Winterslow he could regain that space: it was to him what Grasmere was to Wordsworth. 'I laugh, I run, I leap, I sing for joy.'[11] This was literally true in a way it is not today—for pedestrians then had the run of Salisbury Plain, a vast open space across which Hazlitt loved to walk. He described 'the solemn, undefined impression of romantic pleasure he felt in watching here and there, like stars on the earth, a cottage light after nightfall, upon the huge walls of black, formed by the mountains in the background, and the sensations occasioned by his quitting some village on the borders of the vast plain, as their lights grew few, and the sounds of the rustling autumnal leaf were heard'.[12] There, his writing took on a different character: 'My style [in London] is apt to be redundant and excursive. At other times it may be cramped, dry, abrupt; but here it flows like a river, and overspreads its banks. I have not to seek for thoughts or hunt for images: they come of themselves, I inhale them with the breeze, and the silent groves are vocal with a thousand recollections.'[13] More to the point, London was a place of discomfort to Hazlitt—socially, politically, financially; Winterslow was a sanctuary. Here he was at ease even when, looking about himself, he saw ordinary people scraping a living: 'In the field opposite the window where I write this, there is a country-girl picking stones: in the one next to it, there are several poor women weeding the blue and red flowers from the corn: farther on, are two boys, tending a flock of sheep. What do they know or care about what I am writing about them, or ever will—or would they be the better for it, if they did?'[14] This reflective manner is characteristic of Hazlitt's Winterslow writing, and may owe something to the fact that he had an 'understanding' with at least one local woman, who served as his amanuensis: his description of Millamant (from *The Way of the World*), he later recalled, was 'transcribed by fingers fairer than Aurora's'.[15]

Any tranquillity he found in the country was soon disrupted by a raspberry from the Blackwoodsmen. Before leaving London he had been rash enough to acknowledge authorship of 'On the Ignorance of the Learned' to Henderson, who lost no time in communicating the fact to his Edinburgh colleagues. There was no reason why the essay should have offended them, for it did no more than criticize, in a general way, the kind of education Hazlitt had avoided by being tutored at home. The university man, he argued, may possess knowledge but is unfitted for life:

> He can hardly find his way into the next street, though he is acquainted with the exact dimensions of Constantinople and Peking. He does not know whether his oldest acquaintance is a knave or a fool, but he can pronounce a pompous lecture on all the principal characters in history. He cannot tell whether an object is black or white, round or square, and yet he is a professed master of the laws of optics and the rules of perspective. He knows as much of what he talks about, as a blind man does of colours.[16]

There is no hint that Hazlitt was thinking of Blackwood's lieutenants, J. G. Lockhart and John Wilson—nor could he have known they both attended Oxford and Glasgow universities. It thus took a sizeable degree of self-regard for them to assume they were his targets.

But then, Lockhart was a proud, spiteful, vengeful man, indifferent to the feelings of others. He revelled in the persona adopted in 'Translation from an Ancient Chaldee Manuscript', which appeared in *Blackwood's* in October 1817—the Scorpion 'which delighteth to sting the faces of men'[17]—and clung to the soubriquet for years. He was a cold fish and malign with it, and if Sir Walter Scott did not realize that when Lockhart married his daughter Sophia, he did later, for nothing else could explain his dying words: 'My dear, be a good man—be virtuous—be religious—be a good man.'[18] Lockhart's sidekick, John Wilson, had a startling appearance, as Lockhart himself pointed out: 'His hair is of the true Sicambrian yellow; his eyes are of the lightest, and at the same time of the clearest blue.'[19] Hazlitt later described Wilson as 'a mere swaggering bully' who attacked 'friend and foe alike; good at *slang*, solemn and wordy in his heroics; the bludgeon-man'.[20] Which was about right. Wilson's manipulation of idiom was a hallmark of his writing, and dealt violently with his opponents. He declared he would 'cut with a blunt knife the throat of any man who yawned while he was speaking to him' having first offered to 'smash his nose flat with the other features till his face was one mass of blood'.[21] Besides being a bully, Wilson was also a poetaster whose pale imitations of Wordsworth were 'laughed at, ridiculed & mocked', leading him to 'attack & pull down the reputation of all other poets whom he thought he could safely assail'.[22] Moreover, he was capable of hammering someone in print while expecting still to command their respect, being genuinely hurt when, visiting Edinburgh in 1822, Hazlitt failed to drop by.[23] All of which hints at mental instability, something confirmed by C. K. Sharpe, who said Wilson was 'as shifting as the Northern lights and stark mad to boot'.[24] Both Wilson and Lockhart possessed the kind of cleverness that coexists with sadism and arrogance, qualities they possessed in spades. Yet to those who complained, Blackwood testified they were 'of perfect good humour'.[25]

Regardless of the evidence, Lockhart and Wilson decided 'On the Ignorance of the Learned' was a personal attack, and Wilson decided to respond. 'Hazlitt Cross-Questioned' stated its case at the outset: 'He is a mere quack, Mr Editor, and a mere bookmaker; one of the sort that lounge in third-rate bookshops, and write third-rate books.'[26] Wilson posed eight questions designed to bear this out. Though crude, the attack was chillingly well informed, benefitting from information supplied by Wordsworth, among others. For instance, Wilson accused Hazlitt of having stolen his ideas from the poet and alleged that Hazlitt 'once owed your personal safety, perhaps existence, to the humane and firm interference of that virtuous man, who rescued you from the hands of an indignant peasantry whose ideas of purity you, a cockney visitor, had dared to outrage'[27]—a reference to Hazlitt's undignified retreat from Keswick in 1803. The mischief here lay in Wilson's vagueness: how had Hazlitt sullied the 'purity' of the Cumbrian peasantry? Readers were left to draw their own horrified conclusions. Wilson also knew of the recent conversations with Henderson, and pointed out that Hazlitt was 'expelled, as you deserved, from the Edinburgh Review, and obliged to take refuge in the New Series of the Scots Magazine', before recounting what Hazlitt had unwisely said about the *Scots Magazine* and its editors.[28] Hazlitt had told so many friends that Jeffrey had 'expelled' him that it was impossible to know who was Wilson's informant.[29] The irony is that, when quizzed on the matter, Jeffrey told him 'it is quite false that you have been expelled from the E.R.—Tho' as it is ag[ains]t our principle to proclaim or acknowledge any name among our contributors I cannot give you a formal consent for saying so.'[30] 'Hazlitt Cross-Questioned' was signed 'An Old Friend with a New Face', as if the article were by Coleridge. More smoke and mirrors.

Blackwood's was published in London on 1 September and its contents trailed in the newspapers—so it was not just readers of the journal who knew of the attack but anyone who saw the advertisement. The issue also contained a ruthless criticism of Keats's *Endymion*, under the Cockney School rubric. Having extracted the information from one of Keats's friends, Benjamin Bailey, that Keats abandoned his medical studies at Guy's Hospital in order to write, Lockhart made sickness its theme: Keats suffered from a 'case' of 'mania' brought on by a 'diuretic or a composing draught' which led directly to the 'phrenzy' of *Poems* (1817) and the 'calm, settled, imperturbable drivelling idiocy'[31] of *Endymion* (1818). 'It is a better and a wiser thing to be a starved apothecary than a starved poet; so back to the shop Mr John, back to "plasters, pills, and ointment boxes," &c.'[32] Taylor and Hessey, who published both Keats and Hazlitt, were quick to register what had happened. James Hessey wrote on 5 September to his partner that

> I sent thither for you Blackwoods Magazine which contains a cruel attack on poor Keats and some sad low abuse of Hazlitt.—It is really time these fellows were put down and I should like very much to see a severe philippick against them in some of our English Magazines—I have not seen Keats since the Mag. appeared, but Hazlitt has been here and he is very much moved—He thinks & so do I that he had better remain quiet and let them take their course.[33]

Hazlitt had broken off his sojourn in Winterslow to read the article and discuss it with friends. Though aware of his distress, Hessey counselled against legal action. Over the following two weeks Hazlitt discussed it with Godwin, Leigh Hunt, and Basil Montagu, all of whom thought Wilson's article 'beneath any kind of notice'.[34] But Hazlitt was not so sure. The attack, well informed and defamatory, gave him sleepless nights and caused agonies of embarrassment by day. He felt the injustice of Wilson's vague reference to the Keswick debacle, for it turned an episode which in his eyes reflected badly on Coleridge into one that portrayed him as a sexual deviant of unknown stripe.

He met Hessey on 16 September at his shop in Fleet Street. Hessey had the unpleasant job of telling him that his new course of lectures was no longer worth £200, which was what Hazlitt had been offered in July. The *Blackwood's* attack had begun to affect sales of his other books, and his publishers could no longer be sure of selling enough copies to recoup such a large advance. This was a terrible blow, and brought home in the most direct manner the fickleness of the public. 'Surely the public is an ass!', he would write. 'Hath it not a grave aspect that smileth not at a joke, and that is inapprehensive of the wisdom of a hoax?'[35]

He told Hessey there and then he would take legal action against both Blackwood and his London agent Murray—which, Hessey concluded, 'is the best thing he can do'.[36] As a show of solidarity, Hessey invited him to dinner with Keats, just back from his Scottish tour, but not a word was said about the impending prosecution—though, as Keats recorded, 'I understand [Hazlitt] is excessively vexed'.[37] When, not long after, they did discuss the *Blackwood's* attacks, Hazlitt found Keats as upset as he was. Although some biographers would have us suppose Keats bore Lockhart's sneers with stoic good cheer, that is not supported by the evidence. Benjamin Bailey wrote that 'Keats attributed his approaching end to the poisonous pen of Lockhart', and Keats apparently told his friend Charles Brown: 'If I die you must ruin Lockhart.'[38] That he said something similar to Hazlitt is implied by Hazlitt's later observation that to be 'convicted of cockneyism' was 'too much for one of the writers in question, and stuck like a barbed arrow in his heart. Poor Keats! What was sport to the town, was death to him.'[39] The same might be said of Hazlitt himself, who was just as sensitive, if not more so.

In mid-September Hazlitt wrote to Jeffrey, retaining him as his lawyer, who replied: 'I know you to be a man of genius—and I have no reason to doubt that you are a man of integrity moreover—and most certainly my good opinion of you is in no degree affected by the severities of the Blackwoods' publications.'[40] Such dependability from a man he had never met was greatly reassuring.

At the same time Hazlitt demanded from Blackwood the identity of the author of the attack 'in order that I may institute legal proceedings thereon'.[41] Blackwood's absurd one-sentence reply reads: 'Sir, I have just rec'd your letter of the 18th and have merely to say that from its strain I am not inclined to make any answer at present to the inquiry it contains.'[42] Hazlitt wrote immediately to 'follow an action of Damages at my instance before the Court of Session'.[43] The sum for which he would sue was £2,000. He told former colleagues on *The Times* what was going on and they reported it on 21 September, saying *Blackwood's* 'is a book filled with private slander'.[44]

John Murray was rattled; with a 50% stake in *Blackwood's* he had reason to be, and over the following weeks Blackwood attempted vainly to reassure him. 'I suppose this fellow merely means to make a little bluster, and try if he can pick up a little money,' Blackwood insisted on 22 September, adding that the next issue of the journal would contain a 'most powerful' article on Hazlitt (as if that were a solution).[45] Three days later he wrote again, boasting that 'My friends laugh at the idea of his prosecution.'[46] Blackwood's insouciance alarmed Murray further, whose repeated admonitions only elicited further expressions of confidence: 'For God's sake, keep your mind easy; there is nothing to fear,' Blackwood declared on 2 October.[47] A summons arrived at his office on 6 October, and he told Murray about it four days later, blaming his arch-enemy Archibald Constable who, he conjectured, was underwriting Hazlitt's expenses.[48] Blackwood's response was to issue more threats, saying he would get Sir Walter Scott to tell Constable 'that he must give up this system of urging on actions, else it will be worse for him'.[49]

Then, on 20 October, came an unexpected development: an anonymous pamphlet appeared in Edinburgh entitled *Hypocrisy Unveiled and Calumny Detected*, condemning *Blackwood's* for 'matchless impudence, and a total want of principle', not to mention 'a deep and settled malignity'.[50] Its author was Macvey Napier, editor of the *Encyclopaedia Britannica* (for which Hazlitt had been writing).[51] Somehow Napier learnt that Lockhart and Wilson were responsible for the Cockney School attacks and, in addition to criticizing Blackwood and Murray, he named the Scorpion and the Leopard. Not willing to take that lying down, Lockhart and Wilson responded in their own names, complaining to Napier's publisher about his 'villainous and lying pamphlet'.[52] Besides being an act of unbelievable stupidity, this was a major error, for the Blackwoodsmen had until now taken immaculate pains to conceal their identities. No one was supposed to know who they were, yet here were two of its ringleaders admitting to joint authorship of an article that had become the subject of legal action. Hypocrisy was indeed unveiled! Napier reprinted the entire correspondence in *The Scotsman* of 24 October and then in all subsequent editions of the pamphlet.[53] So much interest did the affair generate that Napier's pamphlet had run to a fourth edition by the year's end.

Murray was astonished by Wilson and Lockhart's 'palpable absurdity', telling Blackwood their 'exposure now is complete, and they must be prepared for attacks themselves in every shape'.[54] He was genuinely appalled by their editorial policy: 'In the name of God, why do you seem to think it *indispensable* that each number must give pain to some one or other. Why not think of giving pleasure to all? This should be the real object of a magazine.'[55] It was perhaps a little obtuse of him not to see the answer: he was in partnership with malevolent people who enjoyed inflicting pain on others. Blackwood wrote to mollify him: Lockhart and Wilson had made a 'lamentable mistake', he agreed, but they would 'recover triumphantly. . . . Out of evil cometh good', and so forth.[56]

In the midst of this, Hazlitt struggled with his lectures. By 22 October he had four completed and the rest sketched out. But he was once more in desperate need of money. With no regular writing assignments, he was living on nothing until the lectures were delivered. He turned to Hessey who reported to Taylor: '[Hazlitt] came for more money which I was obliged to give him.'[57]

On leaving Hessey, Hazlitt walked to Covent Garden with Keats, who sported the loosely knotted handkerchief and open-necked shift popular among liberal young men of a Byronic cast.[58] What did they discuss? *Endymion* had just received another punishing review, this time in the *Quarterly* from J. W. Croker (target of Hazlitt's first political commentary), who elaborated the 'mania' identified by Lockhart: '[Mr. Keats,] being bitten by Mr. Leigh Hunt's insane criticism, more than rivals the insanity of his poetry.'[59] Perhaps they discussed the review, or perhaps Keats took exception to Hunt, whose literary manner now seemed vulgar to him. 'It is a great pity that people, by associating themselves with a few things, spoil them. Hunt has damned Hampstead, masks, sonnets, and Italian tales.'[60] Besides that, Keats might have mentioned 'negative capability', his theory about the creative imagination,[61] or—most likely of all— his brother Tom, who would soon enter the final stages of tuberculosis before his death on 1 December, aged nineteen. At all events, the walk from Fleet Street to Covent Garden did not take long—fifteen minutes, if that—and Keats had other things to do. They parted at the Strand, and Hazlitt continued on to the fives court in St Martin's Street, Leicester Fields.

Throughout these years, Hazlitt was said to be a 'furious' player of the game, in which a ball is hit against a wall with a gloved hand in a manner not unlike squash—also called 'hand-tennis'. It is sometimes played with a wooden bat or racquet.[62] He excelled at both forms of the game, going at it for five or six hours straight,[63] often with men younger than himself—John Payne Collier (11 years his junior), for instance. He always attracted an audience because of his determination to win, which made him look 'more like a savage animal than anything human'.[64] As he admitted, 'I start up as if I was possessed with a devil'.[65] Like today's tennis players, Hazlitt was vocal on the court, as Bewick recalled: 'his sighs, groans, and lamentations left no doubt that he was becoming warm in the spirit of the game, and sad trouble he had to hitch up his trousers, it being his custom to be free of braces. . . . His ejaculations were interlarded with unintentional and unmeaning oaths that cannot be repeated, but may be imagined. In this way he would stamp and rave:—"Nothing but my incapacity,— sheer want of will, of power, of physical ability,—of the Devil knows what!" '[66] Patmore too recalled Hazlitt's frustration: 'I have seen him more than once, at the Fives Court in St Martin's Street, on making a bad stroke or missing his ball at some critical point of the game, fling his racket to the other end of the court, walk deliberately to the centre, with uplifted hands imprecate the most fearful curses on his head for his stupidity, and then rush to the side wall and literally dash his head against it!'[67] Collier claimed that Hazlitt 'once in my presence knocked a better player down by a blow on the forehead with his racket, because he could beat him in no other way.'[68] The physical and emotional release was sorely needed during the Blackwood affair, which 'put me nearly underground'.[69] No wonder. Such a sensitive man found the public humiliation and strain of dealing with lawyers intolerable.

Such was Blackwood's confidence that he made no preparation for the legal proceedings (as he admitted to Murray in November), leaving him little choice but to settle out of court. In the event of a settlement not being reached, he requested Murray to 'send down all Hazlitt's writings you can lay your hands on, with any information you can pick up'[70]—even at that stage, despite Murray's strictures, soliciting more intelligence for future attacks. There is no evidence Murray obliged.

When proposing an out of court settlement, Blackwood's face-saving measure was to tell Patmore that Hazlitt was being used by Constable to 'stir up actions against the Magazine', adding he was 'a scapegoat, through whose means they may vent all their malignity towards me.'[71] All the same, Blackwood was 'a reasonable man' and if Hazlitt could 'name a reasonable sum . . . the affair may be concluded in five minutes'.[72] It took a little longer than that. Hazlitt first demanded that Blackwood cover his expenses and make a donation to charity, which he declined to do; in the end Blackwood consented to pay Hazlitt's expenses and 'a trifle to Hazlitt himself privately' (£100).[73] This was in mid-December. By now, Murray was fed up with his business partner. It was true that London sales of *Blackwood's* had risen from 1,500 to 2,000 since Hazlitt began his action but Murray had come to detest the rag. Besides Hazlitt, it savaged William Gifford, editor of Murray's own house-journal the *Quarterly Review*, as well as Thomas Moore (an 'ungentlemanly and uncalled-for thrust', Murray called it), who was a friend, to whom he sent a written apology. Having told Blackwood that Wilson and Lockhart 'are not worth sixpence',[74] Murray ceased to co-publish in March 1819.[75]

But the attacks did not stop. Even as Hazlitt's representatives negotiated, the *New Monthly Magazine* published two articles 'On the Cockney School of Prose Writers' in October and December 1818. The anonymous author, who wrote under Lockhart's cipher, 'Z.', reproached Hazlitt for his 'imbecile ravings at Mr. Southey' and his 'idiot raving against the Dr.' [John Stoddart]: 'he is the

shabby petit maitre—the dirty dandy of literature!...a mere quack—a moun-
tebank; who has wriggled himself into public notice by spouting his creaking
prose in tavern halls'.[76] Its parting shot was to accuse Hazlitt of befriending
women who have 'sunk into the lowest depths of misery and iniquity', concluding he was a 'hardened and atrocious criminal'[77]—that is to say, a pimp.
Wilson's reference to the Keswick affair had given renewed impetus to character
smears, which would continue for many years to come.

On 3 November 1818 Hazlitt returned to the rotunda of the Surrey Institution
for his lectures on the comic writers of Great Britain. The *Blackwood's* business
was ongoing, and friends turned out to support him, including the Lambs,
the Godwins, Archibald Constable, and the Leigh Hunts. (Earlier that evening
Godwin invited Constable to his house with the irresistible words: 'We have
a quadruped for dinner at four, who, if he had lived till March, might have
gone mad, & we could accommodate you to the Lecture.'[78]) Hazlitt knew how
important it was to obtain favourable coverage, and arranged for John Hamilton
Reynolds to review the lectures in the *Scots Magazine*.[79] There was also a puff
in *The Examiner*:

> It is known in the literary world that attempts have recently been made by certain
> anonymous slanderers to depreciate the talents of this Gentleman. To those who
> may have been impressed by such attempts (if any such there be) we say, 'Go
> and hear him.'—As for the low revilers themselves, they had better stay away,
> for they would find in the satisfaction and approbation of Mr. Hazlitt's numer-
> ous auditors only so many additional reasons for the exercise of their depraved
> propensities.[80]

His previous success had made Hazlitt a star-turn, and when he began this
second outing it was with greater confidence than before. Not everyone was
a fan, however. During the second lecture (Shakespeare and Jonson) he allowed
himself a sneer at Gifford, his tormentor in the *Quarterly*, producing a combination of hisses and applause.[81] The uproar brought the lecture to a standstill
for several minutes but Hazlitt stood his ground, faced his audience down, and
recommenced. The incident was reported in *The Times*[82] and *The Examiner*.
'There are sometimes odd people connected with institutions of this sort',
Hazlitt afterwards told Bewick, 'committeemen, directors, and what not, consequential individuals, who, although civil or courteous to you in success, may
take offence.'[83] He omitted the remark from his published text.

That didn't discourage him from challenging his audience in other ways. 'He spoke of Congreve, Wycherley, Vanbrugh and Farquhar,' Henry Crabb Robinson recorded, 'making distinctions which may be true, but of which the evidence was not apparent, and betraying illaudable feeling, which he uttered in offensive epigrams—he seems to delight in gently touching the sore points of the saints—being always on the brink of obscenity and palpably recommending works of the most licentious character.'[84] For all that, Robinson found Hazlitt's wit irresistible. A week later he was reading *A View of the English Stage* in bed and recorded guiltily that it had 'amused me and stolen more time from me that I ought to waste on such books'.[85]

Keats was a notable absentee, nursing his brother Tom, who died on 1 December. After the funeral, Keats began to re-establish contact with friends: he visited Leigh Hunt and was disappointed by his egotism; was badgered for a loan by the tactless Haydon; and on 14 December called on Hazlitt at York Street. He found him at home with William Jr, of whom Keats had seen enough to think him a 'little Nero'.[86] William Jr, alternately spoilt and neglected, was increasingly prone to tantrums, and dictated terms to his long-suffering parents. He was turning out to be a truculent, demanding, uneasy young man. Keats wanted to read the manuscripts of Hazlitt's lectures and found his friend obliging: he left with that on the English novelists, which had yet to be performed. He was thrilled with it, copying several pages for his brother George, now in America, as 'a specimen of [Hazlitt's] usual abrupt manner, and fiery laconiscism' (*sic*).[87]

The last lecture, on comic writers of the last century, was delivered on 5 January. It contained a throng of witticisms, bon mots, and insights. The audience was in raptures and applauded Hazlitt long and loudly. But the moment of his triumph was soured by an unsettling encounter with an old friend. On his way out of the rotunda, applause ringing in his ears, he was approached by Anna Dorothea Benson Skepper Montagu, Basil Montagu's wife, who presided over their Bedford Square salon. She was a formidable literary hanger-on who had known Burns, flirted with Wordsworth and Coleridge, and hosted countless soirées. On this occasion she looked Hazlitt straight in the eye and said

'Mr Hazlitt, I did not like your lecture *at all!*'

Without missing a beat he smiled, bowed, and answered: 'Mrs Montagu, madam, allow me to compliment you upon the excellent *tea* you make in Bedford Square.' He understood her motives only too well; as he told Bewick, she wanted 'to prevent me becoming vain of that brawling popularity, blown so straight in my teeth, in this gentle way to put me down a peg. Indeed, I begin to think her not so handsome, and I laugh at her singularity, for, after all, what can she really know of so difficult a matter?'[88]

John Soane attended four of the lectures, enjoyed them as much as those on the English poets,[89] and invited their author to dinner on 25 January 1819. Hazlitt was aware that Soane's house at 12–14 Lincoln's Inn Fields was a museum of architecture and the arts, but could not have been prepared for the glories that lay within. It was literally stuffed with pieces of masonry, carvings, and statues from the ancient world, which Soane showed students from the Royal Academy, where he had been Professor of Architecture since 1806. Hazlitt admired the classical simplicity of the statues, rating them for their gusto. As they ascended the staircase to the first floor, Soane proudly showed him his shrine to the Bard, a large fresco depicting Shakespeare's characters. Upstairs, Hazlitt marvelled at the yellow drawing room, where Soane kept the eight paintings that comprise Hogarth's 'A Rake's Progress', which he had owned since 1802 (and which remain in the house today). Hazlitt was as delighted with them as he was by the bust of Napoleon that stood beneath.

Soane was even more proud of the grand library/dining room, to which they adjourned for their meal. He had demolished and rebuilt number 13 Lincoln's Inn Fields partly to realize his ambition of creating this room, which used a combination of hanging arches, glass and mirrors, to create the illusion of size. The walls were painted pompeian red—a deep, intense shade which Soane had discovered on a piece of plaster in Pompeii.

What did they discuss? It is possible that Hazlitt knew Soane's younger son George—journalist, playwright, and ne'er-do-well—for he reviewed a play by George in 1817, and would do so again in 1820, when he described him as 'a man of genius'.[90] Both moved in the same circles, and had written for *The Champion* under John Scott's editorship. Indeed, George's writings had been the cause of acrimony between him and his parents, for in 1815 he published two articles condemning his father's architecture—claiming, among other things, that the 'exceeding heaviness and monumental gloom' of 13 Lincoln's Inn Fields was 'intended to convey a satire upon himself' (that is, his father). This unfair attack was the indirect cause, Soane believed, of his wife's death a few months later. It may be that he suspected Hazlitt knew George, and wanted to consult him on a matter concerning him. Or perhaps it was Hazlitt who did most of the talking, urging Soane to subscribe to his *History of English Philosophy*, a prospectus for which he brought with him. It remains in Soane's library to this day[91]—though not, unfortunately, alongside the book it was designed to promote: Hazlitt's *History* remains one of the 'lost' titles of the Romantic period.[92]

After dinner, Soane took his guest to see another lecturer—Johann Heinrich Fuseli, his colleague at the Royal Academy and former associate of Sir Joshua Reynolds, James Barry, Joseph Johnson (Hazlitt's first publisher), Mary Wollstonecraft (who fell in love with Fuseli), Flaxman, and Blake. Though in his mid-seventies Fuseli still cut an impressive figure, with his lion's mane of white hair and long nose.[93] Hazlitt was impressed by the lecture: 'Mr. Fuseli has wit and words at will; and, though he had never touched a pencil, would be a man of extraordinary pretensions and talents.'[94]

Afterwards, Soane introduced them. Hazlitt was charmed by Fuseli's conversation which he found 'striking and extravagant':

> He deals in paradoxes and caricatures. He talks allegories and personifications, as he paints them. You are sensible of effort without any repose—no careless pedantry—no traits of character or touches from nature—every thing is laboured or overdone. His ideas are gnarled, hard, and distorted, like his features—his theories stalking and straddle-legged, like his gait—his projects aspiring and gigantic, like his gestures—his performance uncouth and dwarfish, like his person. His pictures are also like himself, with eye-balls of stone stuck in rims of tin, and muscles twisted together like ropes or wires. Yet Fuseli is undoubtedly a man of genius, and capable of the most wild and grotesque combinations of fancy. It is a pity that he ever applied himself to painting, which must always be reduced to the test of the senses. He is a little like Dante or Ariosto, perhaps; but no more like Michael Angelo, Raphael, or Correggio, than I am. Nature, he complains, puts him out ... Whatever there is harsh or repulsive about him is, however, in a great degree carried off by his animated foreign accent and broken English, which give character where there is none, and soften its asperities where it is too abrupt and violent.[95]

A near-contemporary of Fuseli, John Wolcot died on 13 January. Ten days earlier, Hazlitt paid tribute to 'Peter Pindar' in the last of his lectures on the comic writers, acknowledging their friendship: he 'is old and blind, but still merry and wise:—remembering how he has made the world laugh in his time, and not repenting of the mirth he has given'.[96] The heartiness of his laugh was something Hazlitt recalled as late as 1828.[97] We do not know how long the two men had known each other, but they dined together at Godwin's house as early as 15 March 1809, and probably met before that. Hazlitt honoured him not just because he was such a funny writer, but because of his audacity. The author of popular anti-royalist satires, he was fortunate in escaping legal action; in fact, the Government bribed him to desist, their offers including a pension of £300 a year (which he declined). The King and his ministers had reason to fear him: at the height of his fame Wolcot was more widely read than almost any other living poet. Even Wordsworth praised his 'spice of malignity': 'Neither Juvenal or Horace were without it, and what shall we say of Boileau and Pope, or the more redoubted Peter? These are great names.'[98] Wolcot's private life was no less colourful. In 1807, aged nearly seventy, he was taken to court by his landlady's husband for having an affair with his wife, but the case collapsed when Wolcot's solicitor argued the aged poet 'had no Pindaric fire—or any other *fire* whatsoever!'

On his last visit to Wolcot's cottage in Euston Square, Hazlitt found him drinking rum. 'Do you not think my head would make a fine bust?' Wolcot asked. For the first time, his hair was so close-shaven 'he looked like a venerable father of poetry, or an unworthy son of the church.'[99] As always, his conversation was 'rich and powerful (not to say overpowering)—there was an extreme unction about it, but a certain tincture of grossness',[100] much to Hazlitt's taste. After coffee, Wolcot led him to the parlour where he kept his paintings (like Hazlitt, he was a failed artist) alongside those of Richard Wilson, whom he had known. 'Though he could see them no longer, otherwise than in his mind's eye, he was evidently pleased to be in the room with them, as they brought back former associations.'[101] Wolcot 'spoke slightingly of his own performances (though they were by no means contemptible), but launched out with great fervour in praise of his favourite Wilson, and in disparagement of Claude'.[102] He was, Hazlitt remembered, 'one of the few authors who did not disappoint the expectations raised of them on a nearer acquaintance'.[103]

CHAPTER 16

The most efficient weapon of offence is truth.
Hazlitt, 'On Disagreeable People'[1]

...we are really under the government of the Sword.
Francis Place to Thomas Hodgskin, 8 September 1819[2]

O<small>N</small> the evening of 31 January 1819, three men met over dinner in the back room of a small house on Ludgate Hill.[3] One uncorked a bottle of wine, filled their glasses, and proposed a toast.

'To *Political Essays*!'

'*Political Essays*!' they cried in unison, laughing. It was a bold gesture. Seven days earlier, Hazlitt signed a contract giving William Hone publishing rights to his next book, which attacked the enemies of freedom—Lord Liverpool, the Prince Regent, George III, Wordsworth, Coleridge, and the Poet Laureate.[4] That evening he delivered printer's copy, which sat on the table as he celebrated with his publisher. The third guest was a mutual friend—John Hunt, to whom *Political Essays* was dedicated. Their conversation covered a range of subjects including Daniel Defoe, of whom Hazlitt and his new publisher were admirers, as Hone later boasted to his friend John Childs: 'Hazlitt is a De Foeite.'[5]

Hunt, Hone, and Hazlitt were three of a kind—opposed to the Government and determined to expose its depredations, regardless of the risk. They were literary outlaws, beyond Government favour, never to receive the rewards doled out to former comrades who abjured their principles. All would face difficulties in the future, but on that joyful evening they had the security of each other's company, pleased in the expectation of a book which attributed to Hazlitt, for the first time, a magisterial collection of essays bound to irritate the Government and its lackeys.

With Hone as publisher, Hunt as dedicatee, and M'Creery as printer, there was no doubt as to its pedigree: *Political Essays* was a work of dissent. It is one of Hazlitt's best, though it attracts less attention than it deserves. Within its pages the Holy Alliance was pilloried for restoring the Bourbons to the throne; the Government hammered for its use of spies; Coleridge, Wordsworth, and Southey roasted for apostasy; the institution of hereditary monarch held to be a 'millstone'[6] round the country's neck; and clerics denounced as self-serving hypocrites. Yet Hazlitt was no 'radical', at least in any sense his contemporaries would have understood; he was, rather, an independent freethinker, intolerant of cant, hypocrisy, and lies.

> I am no politician, and still less can I be said to be a party-man: but I have a hatred of tyranny, and a contempt for its tools; and this feeling I have expressed as often and as strongly as I could. I cannot sit quietly down under the claims of barefaced power, and I have tried to expose the little arts of sophistry by which they are defended. I have no mind to have my person made a property of, nor my understanding made a dupe of. I deny that liberty and slavery are convertible terms, that right and wrong, truth and falsehood, plenty and famine, the comforts or wretchedness of a people, are matters of perfect indifference. That is all I know of the matter; but on these points I am likely to remain incorrigible, in spite of any arguments that I have seen used to the contrary.[7]

'No man has lashed political apostasy with more severity', Hone remarked, 'nor given harder blows to tyranny and tyrants of all kinds, than Mr Hazlitt. His literary excellencies are unsurpassed by any living writer; especially in the just conception and masterly delineation of character. His volume is a Political Jewel House.'[8]

As well as repeating his lectures on the comic writers at the Crown and Anchor, Hazlitt was now proofing them for Taylor and Hessey, who would publish on 26 March. At the same time he sketched out a third series for the Surrey Institution, this time on 'the Age and Literature of Q. Elizabeth'.[9] Doubtless he wanted to get on with this new venture, but before he could do so his enemies took another swipe at him. On 2 February 1819 the *Quarterly Review* published a notice of *Lectures on the English Poets* that argued 'the greater part of Mr Hazlitt's book is either completely unintelligible, or exhibits only faint and dubious glimpses of meaning; and the little portion of it that may be understood is not of so much value, as to excite regret on account of the vacancy of thought which pervades the rest.'[10] This had nothing to do with the book itself; Hazlitt's crime was that he opposed the Government, and the *Quarterly* was a Government organ. Short of bribing their critics with sinecures, the only redress available to ministers was to discredit them in print—and that's what they did to Hazlitt for the remainder of his life.

Hazlitt responded with a counterblast aimed at William Gifford, editor of the *Quarterly*: 'Sir, You have an ugly trick of saying what is not true of any one you do not like; and it will be the object of this letter to cure you of it', he began, 'You say what you please of others: it is time you were told what you are.'[11] He proceeded to do this in a manner no one who reads this masterpiece of invective could ever forget.

> You are a little person, but a considerable cat's-paw; and so far worthy of notice. Your clandestine connexion with persons high in office constantly influences your opinions, and alone gives importance to them. You are the *Government Critic*, a character nicely differing from that of a government spy—the invisible link that connects literature with the police. It is your business to keep a strict eye over all writers who differ in opinion with his Majesty's Ministers, and to measure their talents and attainments by the standard of their servility and meanness. For this office you are well qualified.[12]

This was the prelude to a blistering exposure of Gifford as a creature operating 'under the protection of the *Court*'.[13] Hazlitt did not miss the opportunity of reminding his readers that the Regent and his ministers 'had powerful arts of conversion in their hands, who could with impunity and in triumph take away by atrocious calumnies the characters of all who disdained to be their tools; and reward with honours, places, and pensions all those who were.'[14] This was true. Gifford stood at the helm of a journal established for the sole purpose of arguing the Government's case: 'in plain English', as one of its contributors, Robert Southey, admitted, 'the ministers set it up. But they wish it not to wear a party appearance,—only to breathe at this time the right English *at-him-Trojan* spirit.'[15]

Hazlitt completed the 87-page *Letter to William Gifford, Esq.* just days after reading the *Quarterly*'s notice of his lectures. He put his name on its title page and paid for its publication out of his own pocket. On 1 March it appeared in a few select bookshops priced at three shillings.[16] The sale was modest and many surviving copies were given to friends including Leigh Hunt, Godwin,[17] and Martin Burney.[18] In private, Hunt described it as 'a most bitter γνῶθι σεαυτὸν [Know thyself] letter to Gifford',[19] and he wrote its only review—a two-parter in *The Examiner*, which hailed 'this quintessential salt of an epistle'.[20] Keats

Fig. 24. Hazlitt's antagonist: the tailor, reformer, and Benthamite stooge, Francis Place, as depicted by Samuel Drummond in 1833. He was to blame for Hobhouse's defeat in the 1819 Westminster election, for which Hazlitt never forgave him.

copied several pages for his brother George, commenting: 'The manner in which this is managed: the force and innate power with which it yeasts and works up itself—the feeling for the costume of society; is in a style of genius— He hath a demon as he himself says of Lord Byron.'[21]

Another admirer was John Cam Hobhouse, Byron's friend,[22] who had recently entered Hazlitt's orbit. One motive for Hazlitt's move to York Street was that ratepayers in Westminster ('potwallopers') had the vote, giving it the largest electorate of any borough in the kingdom—nearly 20,000, of whom many had radical sympathies. Hobhouse was adopted as the reform candidate on 17 November 1818, proposed by Sir Francis Burdett, the only politician Hazlitt thought 'a very honest, a very good-tempered, and a very good-looking man'.[23] (He may have known Burdett from Horne Tooke's Wimbledon get-togethers in the 1790s.)

There was no challenge from the Whigs, in order not to split the vote, making Hobhouse's victory certain. Then, on 9 February, less than a week before the polls opened, events took an unexpected turn: Francis Place presented a 'report' denouncing the Whigs as a 'corrupt and profligate faction'.[24] Enraged, they entered the fray after all, nominating as their candidate Sir George Lamb, brother of Lord Melbourne. This would make the seat harder for Hobhouse to win and overnight the campaign became the most hotly contested in years. Sir George enlisted the assistance of his sister-in-law, Lady Caroline Lamb (ex-lover of Lord Byron), to quaff ale with the potwallopers, exchanging kisses for votes.[25] Those kisses were also threats: shopkeepers knew they faced loss of custom were they to abandon the Whig cause.[26]

Voting took place between 15 February and 3 March, with hustings in Covent Garden on 24 and 27 February, at which both candidates spoke. Hobhouse's supporters were much in evidence, especially when Sir George stepped forward. 'No place-hunting Whigs!' they heckled, 'No Wolf in sheep's clothing—Baa!'[27] (Hazlitt was probably among the bleaters.) When Hobhouse spoke, Hazlitt cheered loudly enough for him to notice; they soon met, perhaps under the eye of Francis Place, and got on well. Perhaps Hazlitt knew already that Hobhouse was of a dissenting background, his father having been a noted Unitarian who, like the Reverend William Hazlitt, fought against the Test and Corporation Acts; at any rate, they soon discovered many acquaintances in common, although Hobhouse's career was much classier than his own (Hobhouse was educated at Westminster, then at Trinity College, Cambridge, graduating BA in 1808). But Hazlitt liked the younger man, and their political exchanges soon led him to mention the *Letter to Gifford*, a copy of which he gave him as a sort of good-luck present.

On 3 March, Sir George was declared the winner by a margin of less than 500 votes. Hobhouse declared the election a sham and it was later revealed that gangs of prizefighters had been hired to keep his voters from polling stations, an abuse to which local magistrates turned a blind eye. Hobhouse's supporters went on the rampage, engaged in running skirmishes with constables and horseguards. They were chased across St James's Park and down the Strand, and after smashing the windows of Sir George's campaign headquarters broke those of *The Morning Chronicle*, *The Courier*, and Lord Castlereagh's house in St James's Square. There were thirty arrests. Hazlitt shared their outrage and blamed Place, whose 'self-opinion is the first thing to be attended to'. Never one to keep his views to himself, Hazlitt rewrote the Preface to *Political Essays*, condemning the Benthamite master-tailor for his determination to 'make it an impossibility for any thing ever to be done for the good of mankind, which is merely the plaything of his theoretical imbecility and active impertinence!'[28] He named his target as 'Mr Place, of Charing-Cross' and for years cited him as one who 'mar[s] popular Elections'.[29] None of which improved his standing among the Utilitarians. Place reacted characteristically. Days after publication of *Political Essays*, he wrote to Hobhouse, warning him against Hazlitt: 'I draw no inference from his hurraing for Hobhouse—if I had it would have been that he was a crazy kind of fellow wholly impelled by his feelings.'[30] He could not resist adding that 'the devil wants money'—implying Hazlitt might ask him for a handout.[31] This ill-motivated smear campaign took place behind Hazlitt's back; indeed, he was never to find out what had happened, commenting as late as summer 1825: 'I have been whispered that [Hobhouse has]... conceived some distaste for me, [though] I do not know why.'[32]

His relations with Hobhouse were complicated by a dispute. Byron had been upset by Hazlitt's claim in *Lectures on the English Poets* that he blew hot and cold about Napoleon: 'Buonaparte's character, be it what else it may, does not change every hour according to his Lordship's varying humour.... Why should Lord Byron now laud him to the skies in the hour of his success, and then peevishly wreak his disappointment on the God of his idolatry?'[33] This was tantamount to calling Byron a hypocrite. Furious, Byron composed a long, self-justificatory screed protesting that 'I never flattered Napoleon on the throne—nor maligned him since his fall. I wrote what I think on the incredible antitheses of his character,' and so forth.[34] Having done that, he might have thought twice about publishing it, but remained so incensed he ordered Murray to include it as an appendix to the forthcoming *Don Juan* (which was supposed to be anonymous). Vetting proofs during the summer, Hobhouse advised Murray, 'I certainly would recommend this note not being inserted— Hazlitt is *beneath* notice. Besides—this shows an eagerness to reply to every paltry criticism—perpend I say perpend.'[35] Hobhouse prevailed, and Byron's essay was dropped. When in mid-August Hazlitt heard about this, it was his turn to be furious, for by then it was clear that *Don Juan* was to be one of the most popular (and scandalous) poems of its day. As he told Haydon, 'What a great service it would have been to have been attacked by Lord Byron!'[36] Quite right: such a widely read denunciation would have boosted sales of *Lectures on the English Poets* and stimulated those of his other titles. This fed back to Hobhouse, who recorded in his diary on 25 August 1819: 'Hazlitt is going to attack me for cutting out the notice against him in Don Juan—strange. He says I did it to sink him!! How came he to know it at all? What a scoundrel!!'[37]

Lectures on the English Comic Writers appeared on 26 March 1819 and received favourable comment in *The Examiner* (by Leigh Hunt), *The Scotsman* (William Ritchie), and the *Monthly Review* (William Taylor). Mary Russell Mitford thought it 'famous'.[38] The novelist and collector William Beckford liked it too: 'A richer vein of bold original criticism and sparkling allusions than is contained in these lectures is not to be found in any volume I am acquainted with,' he wrote.[39] But they were in a minority: nothing could undo the damage wrought by Hazlitt's critics. His reputation had gone into a steep decline from which nothing could redeem it. Although Taylor and Hessey advertised the new volume widely alongside *Lectures on the English Poets* and *Characters of Shakespear's Plays*, it failed to warrant a second edition.

That spring, George Ticknor arrived in town. The Smith Professor of French and Spanish at Harvard, still only 27, had been touring Europe for the past four years, and Britain was his last stop before returning home. During his stay he was taken up by the Holland House Whigs, including Sir James Mackintosh, Lord John Russell, and Sydney Smith—and while touring the north he encountered Scott, Southey, and Wordsworth. In April he visited Hazlitt at York Street and found him 'occupying the room where, tradition says, [Milton] kept the organ on which he loved to play'.[40] Like others before him, he noted the sparseness of the furnishings ('his table, three chairs, and an old picture') and marvelled at Hazlitt's scribbles on the wall. Ticknor later recalled that Hazlitt spoke 'in short sentences, quick and pointed, dealing much in allusions, and relying a good deal on them for success; as when he said, with apparent satisfaction, that Curran was the Homer of blackguards, and afterwards, when the political state of the world came up, said of the Emperor Alexander, that "he is the Sir Charles Grandison of Europe." '[41] When he realized where Ticknor was from, Hazlitt told him proudly of his family's American sojourn and his father's exploits among the Bostonians.[42]

Ticknor was invited to the Saturday Night Club at Hunt's house in York Buildings on what is now the Euston Road, close to Baker Street. It was the ideal setting in which to observe the Cockney School at play, 'for then Lamb's gentle humour, Hunt's passion, and Curran's volubility,[43] Hazlitt's sharpness and point, and Godwin's great head full of cold brains, all coming into contact and conflict, and agreeing in nothing but their common hatred of everything that has been more successful than their own works, made one of the most curious and amusing *olla podrida* I ever met'.[44] The Saturday Night Club changed venue each week, so that at some point the participants gathered at Hazlitt's.[45] Fortunately for him, these evenings did not include dinner; Hazlitt was no cook, and in any case could not have afforded to feed so many guests at once.

Those occasions when he did entertain met with mixed results. One evening, he invited Bryan Waller Procter for dinner who, despite his Tory affiliations, he thought 'a very good fellow'.[46] Procter arrived at York Street prepared for a slap-up meal only to find the menu limited to 'a couple of Dorking fowls' (which Hazlitt had been given) and some bread. Furthermore, Hazlitt 'drank nothing but water, and there was nothing but water to drink'.[47] Though Hazlitt offered to send out for porter, Procter declined 'and escaped soon after dinner to a coffee-house, where I strengthened myself with a few glasses of wine'.[48] He recounted this not as evidence of Hazlitt's meanness but to show that his host 'never thought of eating or drinking, except when hunger or thirst reminded him of these wants'.[49]

That is not to say that Hazlitt did not know how to enjoy himself: he did, but with close friends, chief among whom were the Reynells. Carew Henry Reynell was the printer with whom he hatched the plan to promote *Characters of Shakespear's Plays* and their acquaintance quickly blossomed into friendship. By now, the Reynell family was one of Hazlitt's principal 'sources of consolation and encouragement'.[50] They lived in Bayswater, then in the countryside, and Hazlitt would walk there from York Street. Connaught Place (close to what is now Marble Arch) then marked the western edge of the city; beyond it, there were only fields and scattered settlements. The Reynells' house was 'in a large fruit and flower garden, and commanded an unbroken view over the fields as far as Harrow'.[51] Hazlitt often took young William there, who years later remembered the hedge running along what is now the Bayswater Road, and the solitude of the walk.[52] (To someone as timid as Hazlitt, the possibility of meeting footpads or highwaymen in the countryside around London was a perpetual terror.)

By this time, Hazlitt and Sarah had separated. She had never liked York Street, and Hazlitt's incompetent management of rates, rent, and Mrs Tomlinson had exasperated her to the point at which she could no longer remain there. Her brother had a substantial residence in town, large enough to support her and William Jr for the time being (another humiliation for her husband), where they were resident throughout the spring and summer of 1819, the boy making frequent visits to his father at York Street. Sarah was now living an independent social life: Keats saw her and William Jr in the street on 13 February; on 11 May she was at Lamb's with 'some old female friends'; and on 18 July she supped at Charles Lloyd's.[53] Soon after, she moved to Winterslow, taking William Jr with her.

In June Hazlitt began to prepare the third series of lectures he would deliver in the autumn, his first thought being to secure a publisher. Relations with Taylor and Hessey were strained by their refusal to honour the verbal agreement to give him £200 for the lectures on the comic writers and, rather than deal with them himself, he commissioned Godwin as his agent. Godwin gave them a 'manuscript prospectus'[54] but they failed to make an attractive offer, explaining that Hazlitt's books were slow sellers.[55] Negotiations finally broke down on 14 June, when Godwin was 'so much discouraged . . . that I judge it most respectful to Mr Hazlit to drop it, & proceed no further'.[56] Hazlitt had Godwin to supper at York Street to discuss other possibilities. They decided to approach Constable, who declined on 25 June in an unendearingly pompous manner: 'engaged as we are in so many works at the present time, we regret we cannot meet your views'.[57] Eventually, Hazlitt struck a deal with Robert Stodart, who had published *A View of the English Stage* and retailed the *Letter to Gifford*. Of the three publishers they approached, he was the least desirable given those titles' small sale—but exhaustion had set in, and Hazlitt was tempted by Stodart's offer of £150.[58]

His acquiescence may have had something to do with the fact that Hazlitt and Stodart got on. Stodart had radical sympathies, and he and Hazlitt saw eye to eye on political matters.[59] Stodart liked him so much he invited him to dinner with some friends: Procter, Washington Irving, the actor William Farren, '& one or two others'.[60] Hazlitt had the time of his life. Irving was already famous as a storyteller, and Hazlitt thought him 'a most agreeable and deserving man',[61] while Farren had become a star the previous autumn for his portrayal of Lord Ogleby in *The Clandestine Marriage*, a popular comic turn: 'He plays the old gentleman, the antiquated beau of the last age, very much after the fashion that we remember to have seen in our younger days, and that is quite a singular excellence.'[62]

Having secured his advance from Stodart, Hazlitt left for Winterslow in late June, taking a small library to help him write the lectures on Elizabethan literature. These would be the hardest he had so far tackled because 'he knew little or nothing of the dramatists of that time, with the exception of Shakespeare'.[63] Before leaving, he spoke to Lamb and Procter, who were well informed on the subject and willing to lend him books: Lamb gave him his own *Specimens of English Dramatic Poets* while Procter handed over 'about a dozen volumes, comprehending the finest of the old plays'.[64] He remained at Winterslow Hut for about six weeks, where he immersed himself in his subject: 'I wish that I had sooner known the dramatic writers contemporary with Shakspeare,' he confessed, adding that the writing of these lectures 'almost revived my old passion for reading, and my old delight in books, though they were very nearly new to me'.[65] As Procter observed, it was a remarkable achievement so rapidly to have acquainted himself with 'the character and merits of the old writers more thoroughly than any other person'.[66]

That he was in the habit of using Winterslow Hut as a research library drew bemused stares from the local peasantry. 'Their rudeness, intolerance, and conceit, are in exact proportion to their ignorance: for as they never saw or scarcely heard of any thing out of their own village, every thing else appears to them odd and unaccountable.'[67] As he wrote those words,

> I hear a fellow disputing in the kitchen, whether a person ought to live (as he expresses it) by pen and ink; and the landlord the other day (in order, I suppose, the better to prepare himself for such controversies) asked me if I had any object in reading through all those books which I had brought with me, meaning a few odd volumes of old plays and novels. The people born here cannot tell how an author gets his living or passes his time; and would fain hunt him out of the place as they do a strange dog, or as they formerly did a conjuror or a witch.[68]

It was an isolating experience. But on his walks, the words of Dekker, Marston, Ford, and Webster provided an escape from his discomforts—as he recalled in the third of the lectures:

> there are neither picture-galleries nor theatres-royal on Salisbury-plain, where I write this; but here, even here, with a few old authors, I can manage to get through the summer or the winter months, without ever knowing what it is to feel *ennui*. They sit with me at breakfast; they walk out with me before dinner. After a long walk through unfrequented tracks, after starting the hare from the fern, or hearing the wing of the raven rustling above my head, or being greeted by the woodman's 'stern good-night,' as he strikes into his narrow homeward path, I can 'take mine ease at mine inn,' beside the blazing hearth, and shake hands with Signor Orlando Friscobaldo, as the oldest acquaintance I have. Ben Jonson, learned Chapman, Master Webster, and Master Heywood, are there; and seated round, discourse the silent hours away.[69]

At the end of July he detached himself from his labours to see *Political Essays* through the press; Hone published on 14 August, having sat on Hazlitt's copy since January. Its reception was disappointing: Gifford groaned in the *Quarterly* at having 'wasted more time on [Hazlitt] than he deserved'; the *Anti-Jacobin Review* called him an 'infidel caviller' who had produced 'a collection of trash'; while the *Edinburgh Monthly Review* shut the volume 'with feelings of unrelieved disgust'.[70] Sales were sluggish, and remainders thronged the bookshops as late as 1840. It went unnoticed by professional politicians, none of whom mention it in journals or reminiscences—perhaps because its appearance was overshadowed by a national tragedy.

'Outrage at Manchester', Godwin recorded in his diary on 16 August, the day before receiving his copy of *Political Essays*. Local magistrates had decided to send in the yeomanry to break up a peaceful demonstration of 60,000 people at St Peter's Field who gathered to hear Henry 'Orator' Hunt speak on behalf of universal suffrage. But the soldiers were inexperienced and one knocked down a woman, trampling her child underfoot. This created panic among the crowd, prompting the authorities to send in the hussars. They dispersed the demonstrators with a brutality that left eleven dead and over 400 seriously injured from sabre wounds, including more than a hundred women and children. The Government reacted with typical high-handedness. The Peterloo Massacre was publicly endorsed by Lords Sidmouth (the Home Secretary), Liverpool, and the Prince Regent. Southey drew up a petition congratulating the magistrates.[71] On the assumption that the hundreds of people killed or wounded by the hussars were the source of the trouble, the Government then framed even more legislation calculated to suppress protest. In December six 'Gagging Acts' were introduced, labelling any reformist meeting 'an overt act of treasonable conspiracy' and strengthening laws against blasphemy and sedition. That explains why the outcry in the press was muted, and why only one reference to the Peterloo Massacre appears in all 21 volumes of Hazlitt's collected writings.[72]

Hazlitt had troubles of his own. He was in desperate need because the bailiffs were pursuing him for a debt of £50: 'Another of the greatest miseries of a want of money, is the tap of a dun at your door.'[73] It was a sound he dreaded and too often heard. 'Oh! it is wretched to have to confront a just and oft-repeated demand, and to be without the means to satisfy it; to deceive the confidence that has been placed in you; to forfeit your credit; to be placed in the power of another, to be indebted to his lenity; to stand convicted of having played the knave or the fool; and to have no way left to escape contempt, but by incurring pity.'[74] He pleaded with them, begging for a little time in which to scrape together what he owed. They wanted their money by the end of the week or else they would have to detain him in the sponging house—and for how long? As the law demanded that debtors remain in prison until their debts were discharged, but under conditions that prevented them from continuing paid employment, people could disappear into confinement for years on end, even for comparatively minor sums. Hazlitt had to use what time he had to raise money. He approached Haydon, who he had helped in the past, and who claimed to admire the copies Hazlitt had made of two of Titian's paintings in the Louvre—the young Venetian nobleman with a glove and Ippolito de Medici. 'Esau sold his birth-right', Hazlitt told him, 'My copies in the Louvre & the recollections associated with them are all I have left that I care about.'[75] In desperation, he offered them to him for £40. Despite making appreciative noises, Haydon had little real regard for the paintings, which he thought 'heathen copies from the louvre Titians'.[76] He would not bite.

Hazlitt realized with terror there was no time left. Before the bailiffs could come for him, he disappeared back to Winterslow to complete his lectures, hoping to give them the slip. But they were cunning. Aware of his friendship with John Hunt, they threatened him with imprisonment were Hazlitt's debts not discharged immediately. When he heard this, Hazlitt was alarmed. Hunt was a good friend who had endured enough time in jail on his own account. He begged a loan from Procter, who finally paid off his creditors.[77] Grateful for Hazlitt's swift action, Hunt offered him the use of his cottage in Up Chaddon (now Upper Cheddon), three miles north of Taunton, as a sort of thank-you present—'You can have my little parlour to write in, which is a snug place for the purpose, being hung round with prints after Raphael, Titian, Correggio, and Claude, and looking over a piece of grass into a fine orchard'[78]—but Hazlitt preferred Winterslow, at least for now, despite the sidelong glances of the peasantry and the mounting debts. That was unwise: it may be that Mrs Hine, landlady at Winterslow Hut, got wind of his money problem, for she was soon demanding immediate payment of the tab he had run up over past months. Hazlitt decided, reluctantly, to write to Francis Jeffrey, begging him for £100 'to parry an immediate blow'.[79] Not for the last time, Jeffrey obliged and the lectures were finished by the third week of September, when Leigh Hunt congratulated their author on having 'broken the neck of the Elizabethan poets'.[80]

Hazlitt's problem was cash flow. His political enemies had seen to that. Despite his industry, his book sales had slumped because the reading public had been told he was a disreputable person. As a result he was dependent on handouts from friends. The stomach problems that dogged him throughout his life were exacerbated by his irregular diet—the result not of fastidiousness but of poverty. 'It is hard to go without one's dinner through sheer distress, but harder still to go without one's breakfast.'[81] Hazlitt knew both humiliations. The depth of his present difficulties was underlined by the nasty surprise awaiting him in London. Bentham had put 'an execution'[82] on his house: he was to be evicted for rent arrears. The bailiffs would be sent in on 25 December—a festival that, to a Utilitarian, was as suitable for an eviction as any other day of the year. Realizing what was afoot, the servants had fled, taking household items in lieu of unpaid wages. The whole thing was overseen by Francis Place, still smarting over the Preface to *Political Essays*.

Hazlitt had just heard the news when Haydon dropped by, who found him 'in great distress'.[83] He was in tears, as anyone would have been. His enforced removal from what had once been a family home must have seemed emblematic of the ruin of his life. Guilty at not having responded to his earlier appeal, Haydon told him his paintings were worth £50 rather than 40, and agreed to take them in exchange for a promissory note (rather than cash).[84] On the surface this might seem an act of generosity, especially for someone as mean-spirited as Haydon; in fact, it was 'the malice of a friend'. It was hugely insensitive at a moment like this to deprive Hazlitt of those things he most valued,[85] particularly given that Haydon thought the paintings 'not artistic'.[86] Hazlitt had lost virtually everything, and was now compelled to surrender the last tokens of his youthful ambition to someone who despised them. Such was the pain of separation that for years Hazlitt would visit Haydon's house solely to gaze at them. It would have been kinder to have lent him £50. In 'On the Want of Money' Hazlitt described with unerring precision the psychology of someone in his position:

> All the variety of pecuniary resources which form a legal tender or the current coin of the realm, are assuredly drained, exhausted to the last farthing before this time. But is there nothing in the house that one can turn to account? Is there not an old family-watch, or piece of plate, or a ring, or some worthless trinket that one could part with? nothing belonging to one's-self or a friend, that one could raise the wind upon, till something better turns up? At this moment an old clothes-man passes, and his deep, harsh tones sound like an intended insult on one's distress, and banish the thought of applying for his assistance, as one's eye glances furtively at an old hat or a great coat, hung up behind a closet-door. Humiliating contemplations! Miserable uncertainty![87]

Hazlitt begged his landlord for mercy, to which Bentham replied 'he had never heard of my name'[88] and knew nothing about the eviction.[89] Lies. He knew exactly who Hazlitt was, and had done so from the moment he moved in. During the past seven years, Place had been at his side, informing him of Hazlitt's doings; now he urged Hazlitt's removal.[90]

Though eccentric, Bentham was not so far gone as to be unaware of how badly this reflected on him. His calloused sensibility is indicated as much by the 'lacklustre eye' with which he gazed at the plaque Hazlitt embedded in the wall of York Street, reading 'Sacred to the Prince of Poets', as by his reaction two years later to the request from an American Miltonist for a souvenir of the house once occupied by the author of *Paradise Lost*: Bentham's response was to rip out its staircase ('a mass of matter, of not insupportable bulk') and ship it across the Atlantic.[91] Bentham was, moreover, a devious man. It was no more than the truth when, in *The Spirit of the Age*, Hazlitt wrote of him: 'The favoured few, who have the privilege of the *entrée*, are always admitted one by one. He does not like to have witnesses to his conversation.'[92] The aged philosopher thus disowned all knowledge of the eviction and took what steps he could to distance himself from it.

Hazlitt was right to feel betrayed by those 'friends' who could have petitioned Bentham on his behalf—an urge they preferred to resist. 'Oh, it was an understood thing, the execution, you know,' said Henry Leigh Hunt (John Hunt's son), when Hazlitt mentioned it to him.[93] Walter Coulson brought the house to Hazlitt's attention in the first place and had influence with Bentham, but did nothing. (Even Bentham noted Coulson's 'coldness': 'a good sound judgment but no affections public or private'.[94]) And these were his friends![95] No wonder Hazlitt detested the Utilitarians. They called themselves reformers but their actions revealed them to be as unfeeling as Bentham himself; it would be hard to imagine a better justification for Hazlitt's credo: 'I believe in the theoretical benevolence, and practical malignity of man.'[96]

Since the beginning of the year Keats had written 'The Eve of St Agnes', 'La Belle Dame Sans Merci', his great Odes, and 'Lamia'. This final burst of creativity owed something to his love of Fanny Brawne, to whom he declared, 'I cannot exist without you.'[97] Shortly before Hazlitt's return to London, Keats moved to 25 College Street, to the immediate south of Westminster Abbey, less than ten minutes' walk from York Street. He was thinking of taking up reviewing and wanted to talk to 'Hazlitt, who knows the market as well as any one'.[98] Perhaps he hoped for an introduction to Jeffrey: 'If I can get an article in the "Edinburg", I will. One must not be delicate,' he told Charles Brown.[99]

Not having seen Hazlitt for some time, Keats was horrified by what confronted him at York Street. The house had been stripped of furniture, its sole tenant huddled in the corner of the study attempting to work. When Hazlitt explained, almost in tears, what had happened, Keats shook his head, sadly. 'I came to ask you about my own future. I want to be a journalist. To follow your path.'

A wry smile crossed Hazlitt's face. 'Look around you,' he said, gesturing at the empty rooms. 'My professional standing is undermined by "Z" and his clan; I have no money; the bailiffs are overdue; my wife and child gone; and the few objects I most value in Mr Haydon's hands. If you have poems ready, try the press once more.'[100]

Hazlitt began his last series of lectures at the Surrey Institution on the evening of Friday 5 November 1819. Though he suffered little nervousness, financial difficulties caused minor problems: 'he hitched up his knee-britches continually in a very distressing manner, for they kept slipping over his hips through the want of braces, and disclosing bits of shirt.'[101] He expected to see Keats in the audience, who failed to turn up; the poet had just moved to Hampstead, seven miles away, and the journey may have seemed too much.[102] All the same, Hazlitt paid his respects by incorporating into his discourse a line from 'Sleep and Poetry'.[103] ('Hazlitt has begun another course of Lectures,' Keats proudly told his brother George, 'I hear he extractd me.'[104]) The opening performance drew an admiring review from John Hunt, commending Hazlitt's 'usual deep feeling for humanity, its weaknesses, and its powers'.[105]

He invested himself fully in his performances. At the fifth lecture on 3 December, he recited the song from *Gammer Gurton's Needle*, with its repeated final line: 'Of jolly good ale and old' (as in: 'I stuff my skin so full within | Of jolly good ale and old'[106]). On reaching the last word 'he dwelt upon it, till it seemed to vibrate in the air, after it had left his lips, thus—"Jolly good ale and OLD".'[107] He had not lost his sense of fun.

The last lecture took place on Christmas Eve, the night before the execution. He knew it would be the trickiest because he had never completely worked out how to resolve the series. Back in July, when roughing out the lectures on the back of an envelope, he described the concluding fixture as 'German Drama and its connection with modern Philosophical paradoxes, contrasted with the Drama of the Elizabethan Age'[108]—a theme which, were he to attempt it, would take him some distance from the others. In the event, he focused on 'Ancient and Modern Literature', cannibalizing an essay on Greek drama written for the *Edinburgh Review* in 1816. While not his finest hour, he had done well to finish at all.[109]

For those who sat in the rotunda at the Surrey Institute that cold evening in 1819 there was a reward at the end. Hazlitt concluded innocently enough, honouring the writers he had discussed. 'I have done: and if I have done no better, the fault has been in me, not in the subject,' he declared, with typical modesty. 'If I have praised an author, it was because I liked him: if I have extractd a passage, it was because it pleased me in the reading: if I have spoken contemptuously of any one, it has been reluctantly.'[110] When it seemed that all scores were settled and he was ready to step down, he continued, just for a moment. His audience knew he was done, but he had one final insight which they knew would be worth the hearing.

> In youth we borrow patience from our future years: the spring of hope gives us courage to act and suffer. A cloud is upon our onward path, and we fancy that all is sunshine beyond it. The prospect seems endless, because we do not know the end of it. We think that life is long, because art is so, and that, because we have much to do, it is well worth doing: or that no exertions can be too great, no sacrifices too painful, to overcome the difficulties we have to encounter. Life is a continued struggle to be what we are not, and to do what we cannot. But as we approach the goal, we draw in the reins; the impulse is less, as we have not so far to go; as we see objects nearer, we become less sanguine in the pursuit: it is not the despair of not attaining, so much as knowing that there is nothing worth obtaining, and the fear of having nothing left even to wish for, that damps our ardour and relaxes our efforts; and if the mechanical habit did not increase the facility, would, I believe, take away all inclination or power to do any thing. We stagger on the few remaining paces to the end of our journey; make perhaps one final effort; and are glad when our task is done![111]

PART V

The New Pygmalion

CHAPTER 17

The truth is, a man in love prefers his passion
to every other consideration, and is fonder of his
mistress than he is of virtue. Should she prove
vicious, she makes vice lovely in his eyes.

Hazlitt, *Characteristics* cccl[1]

Iɴ the last months of 1819 preparations were afoot for *The London Magazine*, to be launched under the editorship of John Scott. During the five years since he and Hazlitt last worked together, Scott had come to regret the conduct which led Hazlitt to break with him. When they were reunited at Haydon's on 16 January 1820, his feelings of guilt 'were quite punishment enough'.[2] They made up, but Hazlitt knew Scott could not be trusted—'I suspect he is at me again,' he would tell Haydon in August.[3]

As its first editor, Scott made the *London* one of the leading periodicals of its day. This was possible because its publisher, Robert Baldwin, paid up to a guinea per printed page—a rate that secured the talents of Lamb, John Hamilton Reynolds, Procter, Patmore, and John Clare. For the time being, Hazlitt was less pressured by money-worries than in preceding years. As the *London* published monthly, its deadlines were less punishing than those of a daily paper, making Hazlitt amenable to the post of drama critic. The challenge became more interesting when the death of George III on 29 January led to immediate closure of the theatres. Hazlitt's solution was to write themed essays based on a lifetime's theatregoing.

It was the harshest winter for years, and conditions were atrocious. The Serpentine and Thames froze over and temperatures were well below zero for much of January. The West Country, where his parents lived, was badly hit. Five children died of cold during the first two weeks of the year, and on Dartmoor farmers reported the snow to be deeper than in 1814. Not surprisingly, his father's health faltered, and Hazlitt rushed to his bedside, fearing the worst. His parents were now settled at Crediton in Devon at a house called Winswood, 'a commodious, rambling place of the old-fashioned stamp, with a good garden'.[4] In recent years his father had become something of an eccentric, and from this period date stories of his 'being once nearly killed by a swan; of his love for snuff and barley-sugar, and of his keeping both in the same waistcoat pocket; of his occasional playfulness, and of his wife's little jealousies'.[5] Now eighty-three, he was 'feeble and broken'.[6] 'I saw Death shake him by the palsied hand & stare him in the face,' Hazlitt was to write.[7]

If his parents had not been told of his separation from Sarah, he told them now. They were saddened and worried, for they wanted to stay in touch with William Jr. There was no cause for alarm: Sarah remained on good terms with them and continued to visit, bringing their grandson with her.

After a week or so, his father's health took a turn for the better, and Hazlitt grew restless. The weather had eased, making it easier to get around. Though eager to move on, he was in no rush to return to the metropolis—where, in any case, the theatres remained shut. First he took up John Hunt's invitation to visit Up Chaddon, and after a few days there went south-east to Ilminster and Hindon—'a dreary spot' where at the Lamb Inn he drafted his April essay for the *London Magazine* (a reminiscence of favourite actors), 'sitting in an arm-chair by a sea-coal fire'.[8]

He knew he was a bare 26 miles from Winterslow, on the old road between Taunton and Salisbury, and headed in that direction. During the next two weeks, which he spent at the Hut, he composed more essays for the *London*. He had been given the go-ahead to write something besides reviews, for he now embarked on a new venture—his *Table Talks*. Unbuttoned and argumentative, these essays were the pinnacle of his achievement and would comprise *Table Talk* (1821–2) and *The Plain Speaker* (1826), justifying his claim to the title of the British Montaigne. The first of them, 'On the Qualifications Necessary to Success in Life', has the fluency of the Winterslow manner,[9] and its subject— meetings with remarkable men (Horne Tooke and Godwin)—was easier to approach from that vantage point.

Robert Stodart published *Lectures on the Dramatic Literature of the Age of Elizabeth* on 3 February. For once, reviews were largely favourable as neither the *Quarterly Review* nor *Blackwood's* saw fit to notice it. Critical comment came principally from John Scott in the *London*, who launched into a dia-tribe about how Hazlitt's writing 'is in general, neither complete nor exactly proportioned'.[10] This cannot have given the lecturer much cheer and was the first sign, were any needed, of his editor's duplicity. In the *Edinburgh Review*, Thomas Noon Talfourd was closer to the mark when he observed that Hazlitt expressed 'the intense admiration and love which he feels for the great authors on whose excellences he chiefly dwells.'[11] None of this was much help: though the book was widely advertised, sales were disappointing.

On 25 March Hazlitt was at the Egyptian Hall in Piccadilly for the private view of Haydon's painting, 'Christ's Entry into Jerusalem', which incorporated portraits of the artist's friends (including Wordsworth, Keats, and Hazlitt). One of the most popular events in the London social calendar, it came perilously close to disaster—for at first the reaction to the painting, on which Haydon had been working for the past five years, was lukewarm. One of those who came to see it was Sarah Siddons, who had made the last of her numerous farewell appearances in June 1819. But she had lost none of her glamour, or her sparkle. Dressed in a flamboyant silk dress, the 64-year-old emerged from the throng, swanned up to the canvas, turned and declared to the crowd, in her finest Shakespearean manner: 'It is decidedly successful! and its paleness gives it an awful & supernatural look!'[12] That was all the endorsement Haydon needed, and from then on the evening was a triumph. His friends were there to witness the appearance of his personal *deus ex machina*, and he later remembered 'Keats and Hazlitt...up in a corner, really rejoicing'.[13] Hazlitt enjoyed the occasion, and wrote kindly but honestly of Haydon's 'ardour and energy', saying that with 'Christ's Entry' he 'laid the groundwork, and raised the scaffolding, of a noble picture; but no more. ... It is the foundation, not the superstructure of a first-rate work of art. It is a rude outline, a striking and masterly sketch.'[14]

Haydon wrote to thank Mrs Siddons for her good offices and struck up an acquaintance warm enough to invite her for dinner; recalling Hazlitt's admiration of her acting he invited him too. 'I shall *not* come', Hazlitt replied, 'for I have been accustomed to see Mrs Siddons only on the stage, and to regard her as something almost above humanity; and I do not choose to have the charm broken.'[15] Though a strange response, it is consistent with his review of her Lady Macbeth in 1817, when he complained that each time she made a comeback her performance seemed 'inferior to what it used to be', and on those grounds suggested she 'either return to the stage, or retire from it altogether'.[16] He wanted to retain in imagination the memory he cherished of her, fearing it would be dispelled were they to meet.

Haydon's success did not give pleasure to everyone: Sir James Northcote hated him so much it brought about 'a retention of urine'. When Haydon dropped by, Northcote received him with the equivalent of a raspberry. 'What d'ye call on me for?' he barked, 'I wonder why you call on me. I wish ye widden call on me.'[17] Northcote later boasted that 'he had not seen [Haydon's] large picture now exhibiting, neither does he admit him into his house'.[18] A number of reviewers had reservations about the picture, centred mostly on what is now regarded as its weakest feature—the figure of Christ. But overall the response was positive and Robert Hunt was typical in commending Haydon's 'high capability of Genius in Art'.[19] It drew many thousands of viewers, and on 10 June was accompanied by Géricault's 'The Raft of the Medusa', imported from Paris, which attracted favourable, if not effusive, reviews.[20] In months to come Haydon toured his painting to the Midlands, Scotland, and Ireland. In Edinburgh and Glasgow alone it attracted crowds of over 50,000 who paid nearly £5,000 in admission fees.

Hazlitt returned to Winterslow in April, taking Joseph Farington's *Life of Reynolds*, which he would review for Jeffrey. Farington's text 'is in bungling open stitch', he told his editor, with 'plenty of loop-holes for aperçus on the subjects of patronage, public taste, portrait painting, & the grand style of art as pursued in this country by Barry, West, Fuseli, Haydon, &c.'[21] Hearing he was to review it, Haydon bade him 'put forth your strength'.[22] Hazlitt needed no encouragement, filling the article with so many *apercus* as to occasion Jeffrey's complaint, 'you are too fond of paradoxes.'[23] He began by describing Farington's as a 'superfluous publication'[24] before quoting the most contentious passages and refuting them: Farington's account of the state of painting, for instance, 'is no less accurate than it is deplorable'.[25]

Horrified to find himself the vehicle for Hazlitt's ribaldries, Farington complained bitterly to Sir Thomas Lawrence, President of the Royal Academy. Lawrence soon identified the culprit and soothed his colleague's frayed nerves: 'No man reading the article can leave it without knowing that it cannot have been written by a Mind of high Rectitude or Delicacy of Feeling, but by a coarse and worldly Man, whose Perceptions have been narrow'd by selfishness and Scepticism. Democracy is fit Companion to them, and I understand he is one of the most violent of her Disciples.'[26] There was no love lost between him and Hazlitt; Lawrence had often been the butt of his mockery, and would be again.

On 17 May Hazlitt attended the premiere of *Virginius*, written by his old friend James Sheridan Knowles. William Macready had been cast in the title role, and took charge of rehearsals early on. His conscientiousness brought success, and Hazlitt thought it 'the best acting tragedy that has been produced on the modern stage'.[27] That evening, Knowles introduced Hazlitt to Macready over supper at a coffee-house in Covent Garden (salmon and a boiled leg of mutton). Hazlitt had reviewed Macready's Othello in 1816—'and though it must be in favourable terms, it cannot be in very favourable ones'[28]—but Macready bore no grudge: he had a high regard for Hazlitt, and was eager to make his acquaintance. It proved a lively evening. 'Hazlitt was a man whose conversation could not fail to arrest attention,' Macready later remembered. Unable to contain his excitement, Knowles entertained them with what Macready described as 'boisterous boyish sallies'. 'Don't play the fool, James,' said Hazlitt. 'At least not at table.' Macready admired Hazlitt's benevolent indulgence of the playwright: Knowles, he thought, was 'a very child of nature, and Hazlitt, who knew him well, treated him as such'.[29]

Virginius filled the theatre night after night, and Macready kept it in his repertoire for the rest of his career. 'It really is a good thing,' wrote Leigh Hunt in *The Examiner*, 'It has faith in nature and the human heart.'[30] Thanking Hunt for his kind words, Knowles paid tribute to Hazlitt: 'Yes indeed, Mr. Hunt,—when all my other friends would have discouraged me from writing—he cheered me on—pointed out what were good or bad—read to me examples of good composition from good Poets—and spared no pains to give my little talent the happy direction which has led to such a recompense as appeared in last Sunday's Examiner.'[31] Hazlitt noticed the play in the July *London Magazine*, describing Virginius as Macready's 'best and most faultless performance'.[32]

By the time Keats's last book of poems was published on 1 July 1820, its author was a dying man, enduring painful and futile treatments for tuberculosis. As soon as copies were available, he sent one to Hazlitt with an inscription: 'To Wm Hazlitt Esquire with the Authors sincere esteem'.[33] It contained his most accomplished poetry, including 'Isabella' (of which Hazlitt 'thought highly'[34]), 'The Eve of St Agnes', and 'Ode to a Nightingale'—all of which, as Keats's first anthologist, Hazlitt would include in *Select British Poets*.

Hazlitt's father fell ill in mid-July. Peggy sat up with him through the night as he 'went on talking about glory, honour, and immortality'.[35] 'He made as good an end as Falstaff,' Hazlitt would write. 'After repeating the name of his R[edeemer] often, he took my mother's hand, & looking up, put it in my sister's, & so expired. There was something graceful & gracious in his nature, which shewed itself in his last act.'[36] Hazlitt's father had lived to see the death of Joseph Priestley who, he once believed, would change the world for the better. Neither of his sons became servants of the faith, and that must have been a terrible disappointment—particularly in William's case. But Hazlitt had tried to make up to his father for that dereliction; first by constructing a secular philosophy designed to ratify his father's optimistic view of human nature, then by pursuing a literary career in which he continued to expound it. In his own idiosyncratic way, he had tried to live up to his father's hopes, even if he could not do so as a minister.

The old man died on 16 July at 7am; he was eighty-four. Hazlitt was not there, but heard about it later—much later. He had gone to Winterslow to write more 'Table Talk' essays,[37] leaving no forwarding address with his landlady in London. Only when Sarah visited Winswood eleven days later did Peggy know where to find him.[38] Hazlitt's mother Grace was unable to write; she was grief-stricken, having also just lost her own mother, who died aged 99.[39] None of which would have made the news easier to absorb. Hazlitt adored his father, and his enduring regret was to have failed him.[40] He knew what pain he had caused. His mother passed on the request that he write an obituary for the *Monthly Repository*, for which his father had written almost to the end of his life,[41] but he could not do even that, perhaps because he was too upset. In any case, he had already paid tribute to him and his generation in 'On the Clerical Character', published in *The Yellow Dwarf* several years earlier:

> They were true Priests. They set up an image in their own minds, it was truth: they worshipped an idol there, it was justice. They looked on man as their brother, and only bowed the knee to the Highest. Separate from the world, they walked humbly with their God, and lived in thought with those who had borne testimony of a good conscience, with the spirits of just men in all ages. . . . Their sympathy was not with the oppressors, but the oppressed. They cherished in their thoughts—and wished to transmit to their posterity—those rights and privileges for asserting which their ancestors bled on scaffolds, or had pined in dungeons, or in foreign climes. Their creed too was 'Glory to God, peace on earth, good will to man.' This creed, since profaned and rendered vile, they kept fast through good report and evil report. This belief they had, that looks at something out of itself, fixed as the stars, deep as the firmament, that makes of its own heart an altar to truth, a place of worship for what is right, at which it does reverence with praise and prayer like a holy thing, apart and content: that feels that the greatest being in the universe is always near it, and that all things work together for the good of his creatures, under his guiding hand. This covenant they kept, as the stars keep their courses: this principle they stuck by, for want of

knowing better, as it sticks by them to the last. It grew with their growth, it does not wither in their decay. It lives when the almond-tree flourishes, and is not bowed down with the tottering knees. It glimmers with the last feeble eyesight, smiles in the faded cheek like infancy, and lights a path before them to the grave!— This is better than the life of a whirligig Court poet.[42]

The Reverend William Hazlitt was remembered in the 'Deaths' section of *The Examiner*, which described him as a having been 'through his whole life a friend to truth and liberty'.[43] Though few in number, those words did him justice, and were probably chosen by his son.

On 14 August, Hazlitt returned to London and moved back to Southampton Buildings, where he had lived when starting out. One reason for returning was its convenience. Fleet Street was five minutes to the south; the Strand, home to the principal daily and weekly newspapers, half a mile to the west; the theatres were nearby, and he was surrounded by booksellers, printers, and publishers— Taylor and Hessey in Fleet Street, M'Creery in Took's Court, William Hone on Ludgate Hill. Holborn was also a major terminus for coaches heading west: in one letter he refers to 'the Old Salisbury or Mail from Holborn',[44] handy for Winterslow.

Fifty feet from his front door, the Southampton Coffee-House stood at the Chancery Lane end of Southampton Buildings:[45] 'it stands on classic ground, and is connected by local tradition with the great names of the Elizabethan age.'[46] This became Hazlitt's unofficial office. For several years James End, its proprietor, reserved Hazlitt's table in the 'little dingy wainscoted coffee-room . . . in his favourite box on the right-hand side of the fireplace'.[47] He would resort there at night, having had nothing to eat since breakfast, to order 'cold roast beef or rump-steak and apple tart; for he rarely tasted anything else but these—never by choice, unless it were a roast fowl, a pheasant, or a brace of partridges, when his funds happened to be unusually flourishing'.[48] Here he brooded over his thoughts until joined by other 'coffee-house politicians', some of whom were lawyers working close by. Besides Martin Burney, Talfourd, and Procter, they included George Mounsey, the 'good-natured, gentlemanly man' he had met years earlier.[49] Mounsey was well-to-do, with an estate near Carlisle, and a huge number of cats who shared his Staple Inn chambers, which were 'remarkable for their unsavouriness'.[50] When he visited the Southampton, he was 'much addicted to nips of ale and gin'.[51] Hazlitt admired him for being the oldest frequenter of the place, the latest sitter-up, well-informed, inobtrusive, and that sturdy old English character, a lover of truth and justice. I never knew Mounsey approve of any thing unfair or illiberal. There is a candour and uprightness about his mind which can neither be wheedled nor brow-beat into unjustifiable complaisance. He looks strait-forward as he sits with his glass in his hand, turning neither to the right nor the left, and I will venture to say that he has never had a sinister object in view through life.[52]

With his other cronies, Hazlitt was (Patmore recalled) 'always more or less ready to take part in that sort of desultory "talk" . . . in which he excelled every man I have ever met with'.[53] Patmore remembered carousing there with him and Hone, thinking how well suited Hone's 'joyousness of spirit'[54] was to 'the simple, natural, and *humane* cast of Hazlitt's mind'.[55] Here, during the autumn of 1820, they sat with the artist George Cruikshank, planning 'the next Political squib for Hone, & Cruikshank was wont to pour out some ale on the table & draw a sketch on the table with the outpoured beer.'[56] One such squib may have been *The Queen's Matrimonial Ladder*, in which Hone and Cruikshank poked fun at George IV's attempt to divorce Queen Caroline on grounds of infidelity (quite a charge from a renowned bigamist and rake).[57]

Patmore recalls Hazlitt as teetotal though, when someone ordered some ale (or 'grog'),

> It was his frequent and almost habitual practice, the moment the first glass was placed upon the table after supper, to take it up as if to carry it to his lips, then to stop for a few moments before it reached them, and then to smell the liquor and draw in the fumes, as if they were 'a rich distilled perfume.' He would then put the glass down slowly, without uttering a word; and you might sometimes see the tears start into his eyes, while he drew in his breath to the uttermost, and then sent it forth in a half sigh, half yawn, that seemed to come from the very depths of his heart.[58]

Hazlitt's rooms at 9 Southampton Buildings were two floors up at the back of the building, facing west. He brought with him his trunk of clothes, his bust of Napoleon, and his earliest portrait—that of an old woman ('I have it by me still,'[59] he wrote in 'On the Pleasure of Painting', composed in August).[60] The building was occupied by the family of Micaiah Walker, a tailor four years Hazlitt's senior.[61] His wife Martha let rooms on the upper floors mainly to bachelors—though, during Hazlitt's tenancy, other rooms were occupied by a pharmacist called Griffiths and a married couple, the Folletts.

Chapter 17

On the morning of 16 August (a date he was to remember for the rest of his days[62]), Sarah, the second of the Walker girls, brought the new lodger his breakfast. She was rather plain in looks but the unnatural smoothness of her movements seized his attention immediately. Procter also testified to the peculiar way in which she carried herself: 'I never observed her to make a step. She went onwards in a sort of wavy, sinuous manner, like the movement of a snake.'[63] As she was leaving his room, Hazlitt later told her, Sarah 'turned full round at the door, with that inimitable grace with which you do every thing, and fixed your eyes full upon me, as much as to say, "Is he caught?" '[64] Of course he was. Within days, 'you sat upon my knee, twined your arms around me, caressed me with every mark of tenderness consistent with modesty; and I have not got much farther since.'[65] Hazlitt had experienced this kind of obsession when he fell for Sally Baugh in Winterslow, and wrote about it in the article that so fascinated Stendhal: 'The smile which sank into his heart the first time he ever beheld her, played round her lips ever after: the look with which her eyes first met his, never passed away. The image of his mistress still haunted his mind, and was recalled by every object in nature.'[66] Working from that sketch, Stendhal put a name to the process: 'by *crystallization* I mean a certain figment of the brain which renders unrecognizable an object which is generally a very ordinary one, and makes it a thing apart.'[67]

Hazlitt's imagination transformed into something ethereal what to others was mundane, even distasteful; Procter described Sarah's face as 'round and small, and her eyes were motionless, glassy, and without any speculation (apparently) in them. . . . She was silent, or uttered monosyllables only, and was very demure. Her steady, unmoving gaze upon the person whom she was addressing was exceedingly unpleasant.'[68] Hazlitt knew from an early stage that his feelings were not reciprocated. 'You are to me every thing, and I am nothing to you.'[69] From the first, it was a game.

> The next morning, S. brought up the tea-kettle as usual; and looking towards the tea-tray, she said, 'Oh! I see my sister has forgot the tea-pot.' It was not there, sure enough; and tripping down stairs, she came up in a minute, with the tea-pot in one hand, and the flageolet in the other, balanced so sweetly and gracefully. It would have been awkward to have brought up the flageolet in the tea-tray, and she could not well have gone down again on purpose to fetch it. Something therefore was to be omitted as an excuse. Exquisite witch! But do I love her the less dearly for it? I cannot.[70]

He spent all his time with her, giving her a gold locket in the shape of a heart containing a lock of his hair—'*A gold chased heart. A chased* heart indeed, but not given for a *chaste* heart!', he would later comment.[71]

Sexual obsession caused Hazlitt's rate of production to slow down. His drama column was absent from the *London Magazine* in October and November, and he soon resigned the post altogether, his valedictory notice appearing at the end of 1820. He spent Christmas and New Year with his mother and sister at Crediton—to maintain his sanity as much as anything else. Besides which, there was business outstanding from his father's death which he needed to sort out.

From there he travelled to Winterslow Hut, where he set to work on the *Table Talk* essays he was stockpiling for the book he would publish in the spring. In one of them he describes the Arcadian existence he enjoyed at the edge of Salisbury Plain: 'I never was in a better place or humour than I am at present for writing on this subject. I have a partridge getting ready for my supper, my fire is blazing on the hearth, the air is mild for the season of the year, I have had but a slight fit of indigestion to-day (the only thing that makes me abhor myself), I have three hours good before me, and therefore I will attempt it.'[72] As he regained his fluency, he could not suppress the memory of Sarah Walker, who managed to infuse his every thought—as in this apostrophe to Tytherley Woods:

> Ye woods that crown the clear lone brow of Norman Court, why do I revisit ye so oft, and feel a soothing consciousness of your presence, but that your high tops waving in the wind recal to me the hours and years that are for ever fled, that ye renew in ceaseless murmurs the story of long-cherished hopes and bitter disappointment, that in your solitudes and tangled wilds I can wander and lose myself as I wander on and am lost in the solitude of my own heart; and that as your rustling branches give the loud blast to the waste below—borne on the thoughts of other years, I can look down with patient anguish at the cheerless desolation which I feel within! Without that face pale as the primrose with hyacinthine locks, for ever shunning and for ever haunting me, mocking my waking thoughts as in a dream, without that smile which my heart could never turn to scorn without those eyes dark with their own lustre, still bent on mine, and drawing the soul into their liquid mazes like a sea of love, without that name trembling in fancy's ear, without that form gliding before me like Oread or Dryad in fabled groves, what should I do, how pass away the listless leaden-footed hours?[73]

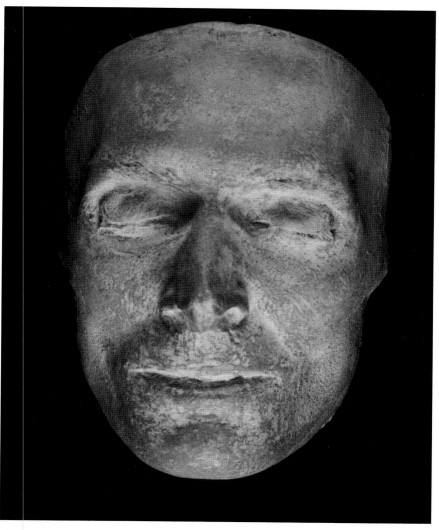

Plate 1. Hazlitt's Death-Mask. As taken by the sculptor from Sarti's, summoned to Hazlitt's Frith Street lodgings by Charles Wells and Richard Henry Horne. Horne was horrified to see 'that a portion of the eye-brows had been accidentally carried into the cast'.

Plate 2. John Hazlitt, self-portrait, painted during the 1790s. John Hazlitt loved his younger brother and kept an eye on him when he first came to London. They remained close throughout Hazlitt's life.

Plate 3. Mary Peirce Hazlitt, wife of John Hazlitt. Descended from dissenting minister James Peirce, Mary Hazlitt won the respect of Lamb and Coleridge, and brought her children up well despite her husband's alcoholism.

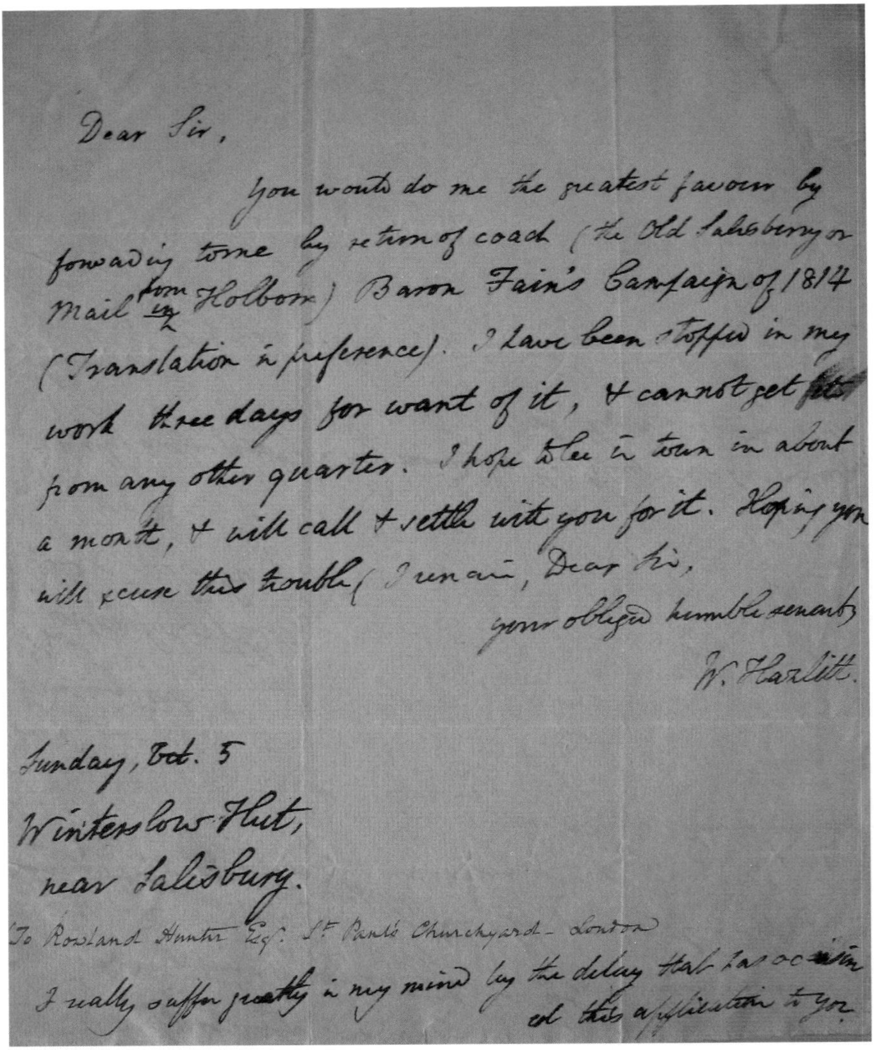

Dear Sir,

You would do me the greatest favour by forwarding to me by return of coach (the Old Salisbury or Mail by Holborn) Baron Fain's Campaign of 1814 (Translation in preference). I have been stopped in my work three days for want of it, & cannot get it from any other quarter. I hope to be in town in about a month, & will call & settle with you for it. Hoping you will excuse this trouble, I remain, Dear Sir,

your obliged humble servant,

W. Hazlitt.

Sunday, Oct. 5

Winterslow Hut,
near Salisbury.

To Rowland Hunter Esq. St. Paul's Churchyard — London

I really suffer greatly in my mind by the delay that has occasioned this application to you

Plate 4. 'I really suffer greatly in my mind by the delay that has occasioned this application to you'. Writing from Winterslow Hut to a London bookseller, Rowland Hunter, Hazlitt here requests a copy of Baron Fain's memoirs, an essential source for his *Life of Napoleon*. This is one of several, hitherto-unknown letters discovered during the course of research on this volume (MS in the possession of the author).

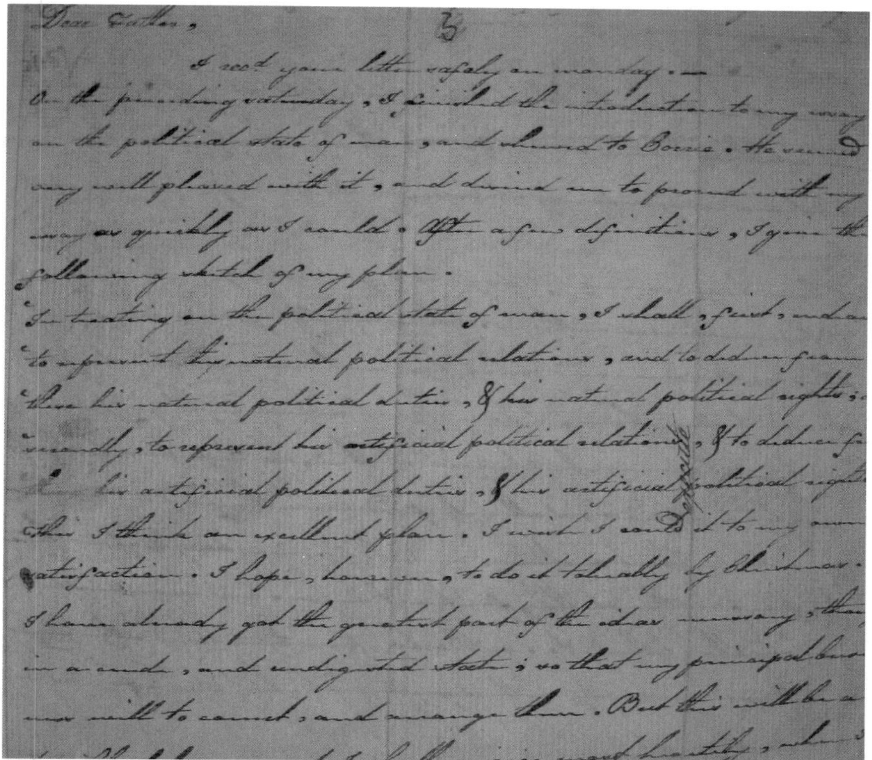

Plate 5. 'Dear Father, I recd. your letter safely on monday.—' Hazlitt writing to his father from Hackney New College, October 1793; young Hazlitt's neat handwriting was the labour of many hours. This is one of several manuscripts discovered during the course of work on this volume (MS in the possession of the author).

Plate 6. Hazlitt as a boy, painted in America by John Hazlitt. The brothers' affection for each other is evident in this early portrait; as their sister remarked: 'while they lived, their bond of brotherly love was never broken'.

Plate 7. Margaret Hazlitt by John Hazlitt. Hazlitt's sister remained with their parents throughout her life. Like her parents, she always had a soft spot for her younger brother.

Plate 8. William Hazlitt by John Hazlitt.

Plate 9. Charles Lamb by William Hazlitt. This was the finest portrait of Hazlitt's artistic career. It portrays his good friend Charles Lamb in the Titianesque guise of a Venetian senator— hardly one to which the diffident Lamb was suited. All the same, he co-operated good-humouredly with the artist, sporting a forbearing half-smile on his face.

The more she shunned him, the more she haunted him. It hardly mattered that her locks were not hyacinthine—his imagination made them so. He possessed a good editorial instinct that would keep the more effusive front-line reports on his emotional state from the printing house, but this one slipped through.

When he returned to London she found new ways of tormenting him, telling him of a former lover for whom she had 'the sincerest affection', who would not marry her because of 'pride of birth'.[74] This changed Hazlitt's 'esteem into adoration';[75] yet he remained tortured by the knowledge that her feelings were skin-deep, despite her willing involvement in protracted kissing sessions. It was as if, from the outset, she possessed an instinctive ability to cause sensations both of pleasure and the most acute pain. To someone as sensitive as Hazlitt this was no joke: it had the effect of making him doubt himself and his life's work. 'What abortions are these Essays!' he wrote one day. 'What errors, what ill-pieced transitions, what crooked reasons, what lame conclusions! How little is made out, and that little how ill!'[76]

He was distracted from her by an event that had consequences for everyone connected with the *London Magazine*. The issue for December 1820 contained an article entitled 'The Mohock Magazine' in which John Scott rebutted the claim that Hazlitt was pimpled, named Lockhart as *Blackwood's* editor, and alleged Sir Walter Scott's involvement in the journal ('several offensive articles have been composed under his roof'[77]). The fact that Scott's charges were true only exacerbated the humiliation felt by Lockhart and his distinguished father-in-law; Lockhart declared that Scott's article had distressed him 'very much, not on account of myself, but of [Sir Walter] Scott, of whose hitherto unprofaned name such base use was made in it'.[78] According to the chivalric code by which Sir Walter lived, there was only one thing Lockhart could do. 'I am sorry for it, John', advised the novelist, 'but you cannot do otherwise, you must fight him.'[79] For his part, Hazlitt counselled his editor not to let them off lightly: 'Don't hold out your hand to the Blackwoods yet, after having knocked those blackguards down.'[80]

Lockhart travelled to London and began a series of intricate negotiations with Scott, which culminated in ... nothing, somehow reaching a point at which neither was humiliated by not challenging the other to a duel. Lockhart was relieved. He was terrified of the prospect, and having effectively made peace with Scott returned to Scotland. Everything looked set to rest there until Sir Walter intervened. Visiting London in February 1821, he urged Lockhart's friend Jonathan Christie to publish his own 'declaration' against John Scott. It was such a powerful, unanswerable document that Scott had little option but to fight.[81] And fight he did.

It was a cold, foggy evening when the two men met at the Chalk Farm Tavern on the night of Friday 16 February 1821. Having ordered a bottle of wine, Scott and Christie sat at a corner-table and drank each others' health, with a wry smile on their faces. But it was impossible to talk in a friendly manner in the knowledge of what they were about to do and, mindful that their seconds were waiting outside, they quickly downed their drink and left.

Scott was seconded by Patmore, who wore a white greatcoat to ensure he wasn't shot by mistake. The four men walked half a mile across the heath and stopped a short distance from a clump of trees. At 9 pm their seconds loaded their pistols and handed them to each combatant. As Scott and Christie stood back to back, holding their weapons, they could sense each others' terror. The seconds counted the paces: 'One . . . two . . . three . . . four.' When the count reached ten, they turned, peered into the darkness, and fired—first Scott, then Christie. Neither was hit. They were relieved. With so much fog, there was no shame in neither bullet having found its mark.

The matter could have ended there, but it had been agreed in advance they would fire a second time. The pistols were reloaded and the combatants took up their positions. They heard the order to fire. Patmore saw a flash of gunpowder to his right followed by a shriek of pain to his left. It was Scott. Christie's bullet had torn an inch-wide hole in his right side, between the ribs and the hipbone, penetrating ten inches to lodge on the far side of his abdomen. It was a horrific wound, but Patmore judged he had a chance of survival. Scott was rushed to a doctor.

After a hideous operation to remove the bullet, Scott received what then passed as post-operative care—a vigorous application of leeches. For the moment, he was out of trouble. It happened that the March issue of the *London Magazine* needed just then to be dispatched to the printing house. Most of the work was done, except for the editorial, which appeared under the banner of 'The Lion's Head'. Hazlitt stepped in at Baldwin's request and composed it in Scott's absence: 'The spirit which animates the Lion's Head being necessarily absent this month, its mouth must be closed. But the tidings will be received with as much satisfaction as they are announced,—that the danger which was at first apprehended is considerably diminished.'[82] For Scott had rallied, and appeared convalescent. Alas, it was too early to be sure: the leeches went about their business, quietly and methodically, and soon undermined his constitution. John Scott died on 27 February.

Reaction divided along party lines. Sir Walter told Lockhart: 'It would be great hypocrisy in me to say I am sorry for John Scott. He has got exactly what he was long fishing for.'[83] Southey was equally harsh: 'he deserved *winging*', he told his brother Herbert, 'There was something about Scott that I did not like, he was a very able man, and in the way of becoming a very mischievous one.'[84]

Scott's friends were horrified. Hearing of events in Ravenna, Byron donated £30 to a subscription for Scott's widow.[85] 'He died like a brave man,' he wrote, 'and he lived an able one. . . . He was a man of very considerable talents—& of great acquirements.'[86] On 3 March Henry Crabb Robinson found that 'Lamb seems to have felt acutely poor Scott's death.'[87] Sir Walter led a conciliatory visit to London, where he sought to mend relations with the Cockneys, breakfasting with Haydon and Lamb, among others; it was probably on this occasion Scott said of Lockhart: 'He is so mischievous, he is like a monkey in a china shop.'[88] Lamb's renowned gentleness has led him to be thought immune to anger, but Sir Walter's excuse-making enraged him, and he responded by telling the novelist of 'his metropolitan preference of houses to rocks, and citizens to wild rustics and highland men'.[89] Soon after, Lamb composed his anti-Caledonian masterpiece, 'Imperfect Sympathies'—perhaps the greatest of his essays.[90]

Baldwin now sought a replacement editor for the *London*. For a while Talfourd thought of applying, only to be told by Lamb and Robinson that it was 'incompatible with his profession' (of lawyer).[91] They were probably concerned that he too would become embroiled in altercations with Lockhart. And perhaps they were aware that there was another candidate in the wings. On 5 March Baldwin told Hazlitt: 'I must not any longer neglect to avail myself of your kind offer to assist in filling up the chasm made by the death of our lamented friend.'[92] For the two months of Hazlitt's editorship, the *London Magazine* thrived. But the only reason he took it on was the money. He had no wish to assume editorship permanently. He had done his stint as editor—on *The Yellow Dwarf*—and wanted no more. In any case, he had other irons in the fire.

The first volume of Hazlitt's *Table Talk* was published by John Warren on 6 April. This was a major publication which revealed his powers at their peak, in which he ranged from art ('On the Pleasure of Painting') to psychology ('On Thought and Action') to politics ('Character of Cobbett'). It was the first of the four volumes that make up Hazlitt's masterpiece—comprising *Table Talk* and *The Plain Speaker*. He took advantage of his editorship of the *London* and commissioned a review from Talfourd who declared there was 'no other living writer who can depict the intricacies of human character with so firm and masterly a hand'.[93] Elsewhere, the book was greeted with opprobrium. The *British Critic* misquoted it so as to ridicule him, while the *Quarterly* attacked it as rabble-rousing.[94] Worse than either of these, however, was an affronted letter from Leigh Hunt: 'I think, Mr Hazlitt, you might have found a better time, and place too, for assaulting me and my friends in this bitter manner.'[95] Hunt's irritation at being included as one of Hazlitt's 'people of one idea' was as nothing to his outrage at the description of Shelley as a 'philosophic fanatic': 'though a man in knowledge, he is a child in feeling',[96] Hazlitt had written. This was not unwarranted (as the women in Shelley's life had reason to know). But Hazlitt did not stop there: 'Egotism, petulance, licentiousness, levity of principle (whatever be the source) is a bad thing in any one, and most of all, in a philosophical reformer.'[97] Oh dear.

'In God's name', demanded Hunt, 'why could you not tell Mr. Shelley in a pleasant manner of what you dislike in him? If it is not mere spleen, you make a gross mistake in thinking that he is not open to advice, or so wilfully in love with himself and his opinions.'[98] Hunt reproved him for 'getting ready the proof-sheets of such a book as this—preparing and receiving specimens of the dagger which was to strike at a sick head and heart, and others whom it loved'.[99] Hazlitt was doubtless at fault. Throughout his life he expected friends to accept his strictures with the same disinterestedness with which he entertained theirs—not, perhaps, an entirely realistic approach to human nature.

'I have no quarrel with you, nor can I have,' he told Hunt. 'You are one of those people that I like, do what they will: there are others that I do not like, do what they may.'[100] Honest as ever, he admitted to being 'sick of friendship and acquaintanceship',[101] giving a catalogue of the wrongs inflicted on him by Hunt and his circle over the years. He concluded his letter by commissioning Hunt to 'write a character of me for the next number' of the *London*, as 'I want to know why everybody has such a dislike to me.'[102]

Hunt's response was to declare 'a sort of irrepressible love for Hazlitt, on account of his sympathy for mankind, his unmercenary disinterestedness, and his suffering'.[103] However, he remarked again that the attack on Shelley was 'outrageous, unnecessary, and even, for its professed purposes, impolitic'.[104] 'I wrote him an angry letter', Hunt told Shelley, 'the first one I ever did; and I believe he is sorry: but this is his way.'[105]

Chapter 17

Hazlitt never did explain his slighting references to Shelley, saying only that 'I do not hold myself responsible to him.'[106] All the same, Hunt came to appreciate the extent to which Hazlitt had been treated unjustly, and saw why he felt abandoned—separated from his wife and child, surrounded by fairweather friends, subject to constant attack. No writer was more reviled, and none were less deserving of it. Perhaps he was at fault for expecting from others the same disinterested attention which he gave their strictures, but as a personal failing this was less venal than the selfishness, deceit, and ingratitude which so often came his way. His fallings-out with such good men as Hunt and Lamb speak of the cost of a life in dissent; their essential quality is shown by the fact that, whatever passed between them, they made it up, accepting Hazlitt for what he was, and loving him all the more for it.

CHAPTER 18

The truth is, I seem to have been hurt in my mind
lately, & continual effort to no purpose is too much for
any patience; & mine is nearly exhausted. My dear
Talfourd, if you have a girl that loves you & that you
have regard for, lose no time in marrying, & think
yourself happy, whatever else may happen.

Hazlitt to Thomas Noon Talfourd, 1 December 1821[1]

T HE summer of 1821 brought unwelcome tidings. Robert Stodart, whose
stock included the *Letter to William Gifford*, *A View of the English Stage*,
and the third series of Hazlitt's *Lectures*, was gazetted bankrupt. He was shattered in body and mind, and in August M'Creery reported: 'Stodart is gone
mad he has attempted to destroy himself several times lately.'[2] M'Creery was
£100 out of pocket,[3] and Stodart's stock was sold to assignees, who disposed
of it to the highest bidder. That was how Hazlitt's books found their way into
John Warren's shop (which ran into difficulties in November[4]). When Stodart
recovered, he attempted to make amends; that much is implied by the note he
sent Hone on Boxing Day, asking: 'Will you do me the favor to dine with me on
Tuesday next to meet Mr Hazlitt & *no one else*?'[5] If he could not repay Hazlitt,
he could at least offer him dinner with an old friend.[6]

There were other changes in the pipeline. On 26 April Robert Baldwin sold
the *London Magazine* to Taylor and Hessey, and Hazlitt handed editorship
to John Taylor. He was content to do so; two months at the helm was long
enough. He fled to Winterslow in the first week of June, but felt listless, unable
to get Sarah Walker out of his system. After two weeks he complained he was
'labouring a long article to no purpose, [and] did not feel myself in spirits to
begin a new one.'[7] He headed back to Southampton Buildings at the beginning
of July only to find one of his best friends, John Hunt, in prison. Hunt had committed the crime of saying, in *The Examiner*, that the House of Commons was

filled with 'venal boroughmongers, grasping placemen, greedy adventurers, and aspiring title-hunters, or the representatives of such worthies—a body, in short, containing a far greater portion of public criminals than public guardians'.[8] True or not, his strictures fell foul of the libel laws. The sentence was harsh: a year in the notoriously strict Coldbath Fields prison. So much did Hazlitt love Hunt that, when visiting him, he lent him his cherished portrait of an old woman. Hunt thanked him with tears in his eyes. Among other things, they discussed the forthcoming coronation of George IV on 19 July. Both took a dim view of it and with reason. For one thing, the ceremony and ensuing banquet at Westminster Hall would cost the taxpayer £250,000. 'What does it all amount to?' Hazlitt exclaimed, 'A shew—a theatrical spectacle! What does it prove? That a king is crowned, that a king is dead! What is the moral to be drawn from it, that is likely to sink into the heart of a nation? That greatness consists in finery, and that supreme merit is the dower of birth and fortune!'[9] For another thing, news of the coronation coincided with that of Napoleon's death, which had occurred as long before as 5 May.[10]

For as long as he lived, Napoleon was a symbol of revolutionary aspiration; now those hopes were dead. Hunt and Hazlitt were deeply saddened. They could hardly be blamed for regarding the Hanoverian succession with bitterness; the new monarch was, after all, the overweight debauchee and bigamist whose own factotum referred to him as The Great Beast. Hazlitt decided to spend the eve of the coronation at the fives court in Canterbury, as a show of contempt.[11] Editing *The Examiner* from jail, Hunt compiled a special issue, its front page bearing a portrait of the Emperor framed by a black border. 'The age has lost its greatest name,' it lamented.[12] They were not alone. Byron declared that Napoleon's 'overthrow, from the beginning, was a blow on the head to me. Since that period, we have been the slaves of fools.'[13] Thomas Noon Talfourd went into mourning for a month. 'I am fully persuaded that Bonaparte was not only a splendid warrior & politician; but a very kind-hearted man,' he told Mary Russell Mitford, another Bonapartist, 'It is in the little traits of character—not in great wholesale projects—that the heart is really known; & I have heard many annecdotes of beautiful feeling of the late Emperor.'[14] As a tribute, Hazlitt collaborated with Hone on *Memorial of Napoléon*, a broadside bearing five rakish illustrations of their hero, framing Hazlitt's commemorative text, which began: 'He put his foot on the neck of Kings, who would have put their yoke upon the necks of the People.'[15]

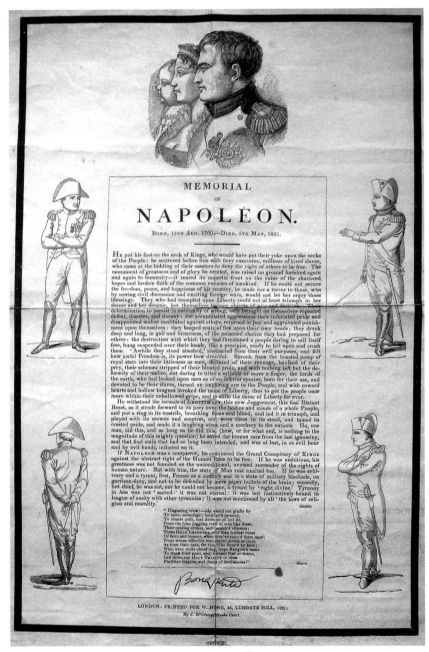

Fig. 25. Hone and Hazlitt collaborated on this broadside, *Memorial of Napoléon*, an elegy to the man they regarded as a hero.

Chapter 18

Otherwise, Hazlitt frittered his time away with Sarah Walker, declaring to her his love, only to receive teases in return. She permitted him few liberties, always leaving him frustrated, so that when she had gone he would arrange an appointment with a prostitute who Sarah would direct to his rooms. His unfulfilled passion for her was drawing him deeper and deeper into a black hole, but he could not help himself. His work rate slowed almost to nothing, and failure to produce set him thinking guiltily of William Jr. The night after the coronation he spoke affectionately of the boy, leading Henry Crabb Robinson, with whom he was back on speaking terms, to reflect that 'his fondness for his child (though it is a troublesome and forward child) is a good feature in his character.'[16]

A few days later he received a visit from James Hessey. Although it was mid-afternoon, Hazlitt had only just got up and Hessey found him breakfasting (that is to say, sipping black tea). Hessey wanted to commission from him a piece for the *London Magazine* in the 'Living Authors' series—a monthly profile of contemporary writers. Hazlitt peered coyly at the publisher from behind his tea-dish. It was a nice idea, but . . . relations with Taylor and Hessey had been strained ever since they rejected his last series of *Lectures*—an affront compounded by their recent rejection of 'Guy Faux' (which claimed the Catholic incendiary to be 'no hypocrite', 'neither knave nor coward'[17]).

Hazlitt reminded Hessey of this. 'I confess that if "Guy Faux" be not inserted I should never write a line with pleasure for the Magazine.'[18]

'But sir,' Hessey responded, 'those passages in praise of its subject are improper. The man was a traitor.' Hessey didn't want to end up in prison like John Hunt.

'Those are the passages for which I feel the greatest affection, sir, and it is for them I insist on publication. Perhaps they might be qualified by a note of some sort, exonerating the publisher from responsibility.'[19]

'Sir, please understand me—'

'We understand one other perfectly. The *London* is a fine magazine, sir. I feel the greatest affection for it and would happily see it write down its rivals by superiority of talent. I wish to assist in that good work by all the means in my power. All I ask is to have my liberty in the *Table Talks*. In all else I am willing to do as you and Mr Taylor ask.'[20]

As Hessey left Southampton Buildings he glanced back at its soot-stained exterior. He was genuinely sorry things had turned out like this. Not only did he like Hazlitt personally, but thought him one of their best contributors. That was why he took away with him the manuscript of 'Guy Faux', which he had agreed to re-read—but, as he told Taylor, they could not 'with any regard to our own safety insert the Article'.[21] It lauded Fawkes for having 'an object always in view dearer to one than one's-self...this is the true *ideal*, the high and heroic state of man'[22]—justification for 'terrorist' activity of any kind.[23] Hessey returned it with an apologetic note and instead John Hunt ran it in *The Examiner* in November, without getting into trouble. Hazlitt had now fallen out with Taylor and Hessey twice. They would not fall out a third time for he began gradually to shift his loyalties to other publications. Although he continued to contribute to the *London* until 1823, his principal employer soon became the *New Monthly Magazine*, recently acquired by Henry Colburn. By now one of the most successful publishers of the day, Colburn was also one of the more mysterious. No one seemed to know where he came from. It was said he was the illegitimate son of Lord Lansdowne or the Duke of York.[24] Whatever the case, the injection of capital from an unnamed benefactor helped him set up a Circulating Library in 1806 and then his own publishing house, which went from strength to strength. One reason for his prosperity was his innovative use of advertising space in newspapers and journals, the cost of which he passed on to his authors. He was, recalled W. C. Hazlitt, 'an early master in the art of puffing', and one of the first publishers to send reviewers advance copies of his books.[25]

As Hazlitt's productiveness decreased, he experienced more cash flow problems. Not for the first time, he wrote to Jeffrey requesting an advance on future work. So much had he borrowed that the Scotch advocate was concerned for him, as he revealed on 23 October:

> If you really want £50 you shall have it—but I want to see you regular and independent—and some times think it would be better if I were a little more strict with you—Besides I have really been rather imprudent in my advances to contributors of genius—at this moment I am out of pocket a good deal more than £1000—Do not however misunderstand this—You shall have the money next week, if you seriously think upon reflection that it would be better for yourself thus to encrease your debt to me...but still I cannot help wishing that you had some other employment than writing for printers and playing fives—[26]

The delicacy with which Jeffrey managed to pledge continuing support while at the same time expressing anxiety speaks volumes for his generosity. His fears were well founded, for Hazlitt would never find financial security. That much was evident after John Warren went bust in November 1821, terminating sales of three more Hazlitt titles (the third series of *Lectures, A View of the English Stage*, and *Table Talk* volume 1). More in debt than ever, Hazlitt was now pursued by bailiffs eager to confine him to the sponging house. John Clare remembered him 'with his eyes in his hands as it were throwing under gazes round at every corner as if he smelt a dun or a thief ready to seize him by the collar and demand his money or his life'.[27]

Around 27 October, a young solicitor, John Tomkins, moved into 9 Southampton Buildings. Sarah Walker went into a frenzy: 'she flung herself at his head in the most barefaced way, ran breathless up stairs before him, blushed when his foot was heard, watched for him in the passage, and was sure to be in close conference with him when he went down again.'[28] The effect on Hazlitt was equally violent. Until now, his only competition had been Griffiths (not a serious prospect); from this moment, he recalled, 'my mad proceedings commenced.'[29] For months to come, he was tormented by thoughts of unsuitability as Sarah's lover.

> Oh! thou dumb heart, lonely, sad, shut up in the prison house of this rude form, that hast never found a fellow but for an hour & in very mockery of thy misery, speak, find bleeding words to express thy thoughts, break thy dungeon-gloom, or die [& wither of pure scorn!] pronouncing the name of thy [Infelice] Clarissa.[30]

The next day he took his son to Godwin's for dinner. William Jr, now ten, observed the state to which his father had descended; Hazlitt, indeed, had no thought of concealing it. On the contrary, he poured out his frustrations, oblivious to his son's growing distress. It cannot have made it any easier that the boy had encountered Sarah Walker;[31] despite being a loving father, Hazlitt was too self-absorbed to realize how damaging this must have been. His negligence is reflected in the habit of taking William to the fives court—far from ideal surroundings for a youngster as it was a pick-up joint for prostitutes. Worse still, he thought nothing of introducing him to the 'strumpets' he brought back to his lodgings. It says much for the boy's strength of character that William Jr was once so appalled by the noises coming from his father's bedroom that he 'either kicked or abused them away'.[32] When Hazlitt's wife heard about this she was furious, and reproached him for 'carrying [William] out with him when he went picking up the girls on the town: it was likely to corrupt and vitiate him, and bring him up to like such ruinous practices'.[33] That he thought such people suitable company for his son may seem extraordinary, but it is worth remembering that childhood as we know it is a Victorian construct, and Hazlitt wanted William (however misguidedly) to learn the ways of the world under his supervision rather than alone, or with schoolfriends.

At all events, Sarah Hazlitt had recovered from the shock of these unsavoury revelations when, meeting her husband in the street one day, she asked how he was.

'Very well, thank you. I was just looking about for my dinner.'

'Well, mine is just ready, a nice boiled leg of pork—if you like William to have a slice?' So they dined together.[34] It would have been a good moment to break news of their divorce, assuming he had not already discussed it with her. Hazlitt knew of the attempt of his former colleague at the *Morning Chronicle*, John Black, to obtain divorce from his wife in Scotland, where it was more accessible than south of the border.[35] Now Hazlitt wanted to follow suit, having taken advice from Black on how to pursue it. For he was intent on proposing marriage to the great love of his life—Sarah Walker. His situation was distinct from Black's in that, despite their incompatibility as a couple, the Hazlitts seemed always to get on. At heart, Sarah had a genuine affection for the man who had fathered her son, while he never stopped being able to enjoy her conversation. If this was the first time she heard of his desire to obtain a divorce, she may have been upset, but there was no malice in her, and she had no desire to stand between him and married bliss.

Divorce gave him a motive to increase his rate of production again, for he would need money to finance it. In early December 1821 he heard about a fight that was to take place between two of the most important boxers of the day: Tom Hickman versus Bill Neate. Its whereabouts were kept secret until the last moment because boxing had been outlawed since 1750. Stripped to the waist, armed only with bare fists and 'bottom' (or courage), prizefighters would engage in combat until one or the other was knocked out. It was a brutal, bloody sport with a following drawn from all classes; indeed, some aristocrats were known to stage fights in their homes (what else was a ballroom for?). The Fancy, as boxing aficionados were known, included Hazlitt's friend Procter, a keen amateur fighter who trained with Tom Cribb. And Hazlitt himself referred to Bill Richmond as 'my old master'.[36] 'A man of colour, and a native of America',[37] Richmond came to England in 1777 with the Duke of Northumberland and began fighting in 1805. He was now a noted trainer, and Hazlitt was one of his pupils. Besides being an amateur boxer, Hazlitt loved to watch fights, probably at the fives court in St Martin's Street,[38] and his comments on Cribb and Tom Belcher ('the most elegant of sparrers'[39]) indicate he was an admirer of both.[40]

Chapter 18

Although fights were reported in the press, Hazlitt realized it might be possible to write an essay about the occasion that would not only do it justice, but say something about the culture that produced it. He checked with Henry Colburn, who told him the *New Monthly* would welcome the piece.[41]

On 10 December 1821 at 6.30 pm, Hazlitt slipped into the Hole in the Wall in Chancery Lane, a few minutes from Southampton Buildings—which, besides being a convenient refuge from duns, was a good place to discover the location of the fight the following day. The owner of the tavern, ex-prizefighter Jack Randall, was a veteran of thirteen fights, having knocked out his last opponent in a round lasting a mere eight minutes. Randall told him it was to held at Hungerford in Berkshire, seventy miles away. 'You had better get cracking!', he shouted after him.

Hazlitt went straight to Holborn only to find he had missed all the scheduled coaches, but managed to catch a ride with the Bath mail, which would drop him off at Newbury. By a stroke of luck he found himself travelling with 'my friend Thirtle'[42]—a prime example of the kind of shady character with whom Hazlitt sometimes rubbed shoulders. John Thurtell was proprietor of a tavern, the Black Boy in Long Acre, where he entertained so many brawling, disreputable customers that his licence was revoked. Thurtell now made his living as an organizer of 'sporting events'—bear and badger baiting, billiards, and fight-fixing. His career subsequent to this brief encounter would implicate him first in arson, then in the murder of William Weare, a former waiter and professional gambler. Thurtell apparently shot Weare at point-blank range before slitting Weare's throat and jamming the pistol into his skull—for which he was executed in January 1824. This was the man Hazlitt was pleased to encounter that evening.

At Newbury he met up with another friend, the lawyer Joseph Parkes,[43] and together they sat up at the Crown Inn listening to a 'tall English yeoman'[44]—a figure straight out of Chaucer. The following morning they walked the remaining nine miles to Hungerford. Fights were usually held in the open air in parts of the countryside round London. That morning, the roads from Gloucester, Newbury, Reading, Winchester, Bristol, and Southampton were jammed with coaches, gigs, carts, horses, and mobs of pedestrians—'open carriages were coming up, with streamers flying and music playing, and the country-people were pouring in over hedge and ditch in all directions'.[45] An estimated 25,000 attended, quite a number for those days.

Hazlitt's description of the match is a virtuoso display of technique, the like of which had not previously been seen; he even coined a phrase now known to every sports fan around the world: 'In the first round every one thought it was all over.'[46] The challenge he gives himself is: can I replicate in words the cut and thrust of a fist fight? He did so magnificently, in a manner sportswriters have imitated ever since.

> Neate seemed like a lifeless lump of flesh and bone, round which the Gas-man's blows played with the rapidity of electricity or lightning, and you imagined he would only be lifted up to be knocked down again. It was as if Hickman held a sword or a fire in that right-hand of his, and directed it against an unarmed body. They met again, and Neate seemed, not cowed, but particularly cautious. I saw his teeth clenched together and his brows knit close against the sun. He held out both his arms at full length straight before him, like two sledge-hammers, and raised his left an inch or two higher. The Gas-man [Hickman] could not get over this guard—they struck mutually and fell, but without advantage on either side.[47]

Sports events were reported in newspapers, but in dry, mechanical, formulaic terms. Hazlitt does something different: he takes us into the ring with the combatants so we can smell the sawdust, hear the crowd, and feel the impact of the blows as they are landed.

> Neate just then made a tremendous lunge at him, and hit him full in the face. It was doubtful whether he would fall backwards or forwards; he hung suspended for a second or two, and then fell back, throwing his hands into the air, and with his face lifted to the sky. I never saw any thing more terrific than his aspect before he fell. All traces of life, of natural expression, were gone from him. His face was like a human skull, a death's head, spouting blood, the mouth gaped blood. He was not like an actual man, but like a preternatural, spectral appearance, or like one of the figures in Dante's *Inferno*.[48]

We are used to vivid accounts of sporting events, but no one before Hazlitt had the vision to attempt anything like this; perhaps only someone who had studied the fine arts and pondered the extraordinary power of Titian and Raphael could have worked out how to do it. For Hazlitt's account of the fight works precisely because it succeeds in enshrining, like the paintings of the Italian masters, 'passion or power defining any object'—in this case two men slugging it out to the bitter end. And perhaps only Hazlitt could have realized that such a subject, for all its vulgarity, could be made as grand and glorious as Ippolito de Medici or the St Peter Martyr.

When he returned to London he was shattered, unable to stop thinking of Sarah and her infatuation with Tomkins.[49] It made life in Southampton

Buildings intolerable. The knowledge that he had settled on divorce and would soon be able to propose marriage was the one thing keeping him sane. For a while he considered renting *all* available rooms in the Walkers' house for £100 so as to cast his rivals into the street.[50] Shortly after he was alarmed by a bawdy conversation he overheard in the Walkers' living room as he stood on the staircase. The participants were Sarah Walker, her sister Elizabeth ('Betsey'), her brother Micaiah, and their mother; they were discussing another lodger, Griffiths.

> *Betsey*. Oh! if those trowsers were to come down, what a sight there would be.
>   (*A general loud laugh*.)
> *Mother*. Yes! he's a proper one: M[r]. Follett is nothing to him.
> *Caiah* (aged 17). Then, I suppose he must be seven inches.
> *Mother*. He's quite a monster. He nearly tumbled over M[r]. Hazlitt one night.
> *Sarah*. (At that once, that still & ever dear name, ah! why do I grow pale, why do
>   I weep & forgive?) said something inaudible, but in connection.
> *Caiah* (Laughing) Sarah says . . .
> *Sarah*. I say, M[r]. Follett wears straps—[51]

'Can there be a doubt, when the mother dilates in this way on codpieces & the son replies in measured terms, that the girl runs made for size?' Hazlitt wondered,

> Miss is small, & exaggerates dimensions by contrast. Misjudging fair! Yet it is she whom [I have] spared a hundred times from witnessing this consummation devoutly wished by the whole kitchen in chorus, after she has been rubbing against me, hard at it for an hour together thinking to myself, 'The girl is a goo[d girl], &c. & means no harm—it is only [her fond]ness for me, not her lech after a man'.[52]

In this distracted state he took longer than usual to complete 'The Fight', but when finally it was done he sent it to Colburn for the *New Monthly Magazine*. Its editor, Thomas Campbell, hated Hazlitt because in his lectures he said Campbell stole one of the best lines in his poem *The Pleasures of Hope* from Blair's *The Grave*.[53] Although this was true, and not meant as criticism, Campbell thereafter loathed him. Even Cyrus Redding, Campbell's assistant, admitted: 'It was difficult to imagine how Campbell at that time writhed under a few remarks that could not do him the slightest injury.'[54]

When 'The Fight' arrived in the office, Campbell racked his brains to think of some reason for rejecting it.

'The subject', he told Redding, 'is thoroughly blackguard! It gives currency to a disgraceful, demoralising species of vulgar exhibition that brands England just as the bull-fight does Spain with disgrace in the sight of all civilised nations.'

In the end, Redding persuaded him to run it on the grounds that rejection 'might be charged to his personal dislike of the writer',[55] reminding him that, whatever his opinion, publication was expected by Colburn.[56] It duly appeared, and is now regarded as one of Hazlitt's masterpieces.

He made final arrangements for divorce in January on a flying visit to Winterslow where he liaised with his wife. If Sarah accepted them, Hazlitt's mother and sister were outraged. 'We are so distressed about this shocking affair that I know not what to say,' Grace Hazlitt told her daughter-in-law, condemning her sons: 'God grant things may take a diffirent turn!! and that they may commence a moral quiet life!!' Margaret was more outspoken still: 'I hope you will not be perswaded to [go] to Scotland on any such errand. & I think you need put your self in the power of a madman. . . . have some one to take care of you . . . for my part I think he is mad I cant account for his conduct else.'[57]

On return to London he took Sarah Walker and her mother to see Macready as Romeo—an attempt to establish his suitability as prospective son-in-law. Two nights later, on the eve of departure for Scotland, he sat with Sarah and discussed their future; she was, he would recall, 'shy'[58] and it turned out to be one of those occasions on which 'little YES and NO' (as he called her) gave scant encouragement, at first taking the line that she would not marry him even after his divorce.

'Could you not come and live with me as a friend, a sister?' he asked.

'I don't know: and yet it would be of no use if I did, you would always be hankering after what could never be!'

'Would you live with me in your own house? All day? Just as dear friends and nothing more?'

'I can make no promises. You will always find me the same.' This was the kind of response that seemed to generate in him both hope and despair.

'Would you go with me to the play and let it be understood that I was paying addresses to you?'

'Not as a habit. My father is strict and would object.'[59]

'If you have no particular regard for me, you must behave as familiarly with everyone as you have done with me; if you had a genuine liking to me from the first, why refuse me now with scorn and wilfulness?' At this, Sarah coloured.

'I am obliged to you for letting me know the opinion you have always entertained of me.' She stood up and went to the doorway.

'Sarah!' he cried, running towards her. She turned. 'Sarah! I have to know: your conduct towards me, your liking for me . . . was it because I look like your old friend? The man you relinquished?'

'No, none—but there *was* a likeness, to . . .'

'To whom?' She glanced at the bust on his mantelpiece. 'You mean . . . your previous lover looked like Bonaparte?' he asked.

'All but the nose.'

'And the figure?'

'He was taller.'

Not half an hour earlier, he told Sarah's mother he would clear his room because he did not want to leave anything that would compel his return to Southampton Buildings; now Sarah engineered a reason for undoing that plan. He went to the bust, took it from the mantelpiece, and placed it in her hands. 'Would it give you pleasure to own it?'

'I will keep it for you,' she said.[60]

This was, he would tell Sarah, a 'delicious parting, when you seemed never weary of repeating the proofs of your regard and tenderness, and it was with difficulty we tore ourselves asunder at last!'[61]

Early next morning, he boarded a coach bound for the Great North Road. In his pocket he had Byron's *Sardanapalus, Cain and the Two Foscari*, three closet dramas published the previous month,[62] which he was to review for Jeffrey. Before he could settle to it, however, he had to get something off his chest. He broke his journey for a few days at Stamford, ninety miles north of London, where he purchased a red leather account book for two shillings. Inside the front cover he wrote 'Stamford, Jany. 29. 1822',[63] and began to enter the 'conversations' he had had with the woman called 'the statue'.

He arrived in Edinburgh on 4 February 1822. It was a clear, sunny, Caledonian afternoon, a propitious moment for his first sight of the Athens of the north. The Edinburgh we know today was just taking shape. The Old Town, extending to the east of the Castle, boasted many buildings dating from the medieval period, as well as its warren of wynds, pends, and alleyways with names like Bull's Close and Jackson's Entry. On the far side of the Nor'Loch, the glen to the north of the castle, the New Town was under construction, an enlightenment scheme of town-planning by which the city extended across a grid. By 1822 it was complete at its centre and undergoing expansion northwards. This was the occasion of much civic pride, and only months before Hazlitt's arrival the city had been lit for the first time by gaslamp. Comparisons with Athens sprang up not just for its architecture, but its intellectual culture. Hazlitt was in no mood to appreciate either: ' "Stony-hearted" Edinburgh! What art thou to me? . . . Thy cold grey walls reflect back the leaden melancholy of the soul.'[64]

He took lodgings at the heart of the New Town at 10 George Street, nearly opposite the Corinthian columns of St Andrew's church, thus beginning the forty-day residence requirement necessary for divorce, which he would prove with bills from his landlady, Mrs Dow. The next day he appointed a solicitor and made contact with Mrs Knight, madam of a brothel at James Street where for the purposes of the divorce he was to be discovered committing adultery.

He then composed his review of Byron's *Sardanapalus*. The play concerned a King (Sardanapalus) whose tragedy lay partly in his love for his mistress (Myrrha). Hazlitt praised its hero as 'one of the most truly good-humoured, amiable and respectable voluptuaries to whom we have ever been presented. . . . a sanguine votary of pleasure, a princely epicure'.[65] The parallels between his own circumstances and those of Byron's characters were so compelling he told Patmore about them: 'In my judgment Myrrha is just like S.W., only I am not like Sardanapalus!'[66] And to Sarah, he wrote:

> When I think of the thousand endearing caresses that have passed between us, I do not wonder at the strong attachment that draws me to you; but I am sorry for my own want of power to please. I hear the wind sigh through the lattice, & keep repeating over and over to myself two lines of Lord Byron's Tragedy—
>
> > So shalt thou find me ever at thy side
> > Here & hereafter, if the last may be—
>
> applying them to thee, my love, & thinking whether I shall see thee again. Perhaps not—for some years at least—till both thou & I are old—& then, when all else have forsaken thee, I will creep to thee, & die in thine arms.[67]

On 10 February Hazlitt walked out to Renton Inn. He needed some peace if he was to write. The first coaching house to the south (convenient for mail) was 'a lone inn, but on a great scale, thirty miles from Edinburgh. It is situated on a rising ground (a mark for all the winds, which blow here incessantly)— there is a woody hill opposite, with a winding valley below, and the London road stretches out on either side.'[68] Now a private house, it still stands, at the

Fig. 26. Renton Inn, the first coaching inn on the Great North Road to the south of Edinburgh. Hazlitt retreated here soon after arriving in Scotland in order to complete work on *Table Talk* volume 2.

easternmost edge of the Lammermuir Hills. Here, Hazlitt worked furiously, 'without ceasing & like a tyger',[69] composing eleven essays between 11 February and 7 March[70]—an astonishing rate of production.

At Renton he was subject to a more acute isolation than any he had previously known. The violent, squally weather that lashed north-west Europe during these weeks darkened his mood further.[71] 'The wind raves like ten demons at the window, has broke a pane in one of them, blown out the candles, and I think will blow the cook's lover away if he does not make haste,' he told Sarah on 5 March.[72] But he could not make light of disturbed dreams which spoke to him of loss; in one he found himself back in the Louvre: 'I looked for my favourite pictures, and found them gone or erased. The dream of my youth came upon me; a glory and a vision unutterable, that comes no more but in darkness and in sleep: my heart rose up, and I fell on my knees, and lifted up my voice and wept, and I awoke.'[73] On another occasion he dreamt he was reading *La Nouvelle Héloïse* to an old friend. Coming unexpectedly upon a passage that reduced him to tears when he first read it, he 'seemed to live these twenty years over again in one short moment!'—'Trop heureuse d'acheter un prix de ma vie le droit d'aimer toujours sans crime et de te le dire encore une fois, avant que je meurs!'[74]

Sarah's businesslike responses to his declarations of love[75] left him so distressed that he asked her to 'transmit me no more letters'.[76] It had begun to dawn on him that despite his feelings for her she would slip through his fingers. 'I want an eye to cheer me, a hand to guide me, a breast to lean on', he declared in one of his essays, 'all which I shall never have, but shall stagger into my grave without them, old before my time, unloved and unlovely, unless ——. I would have some creature love me before I die. Oh! for the parting hand to ease the fall!'[77] But he could not accept the worst—not yet. On 5 March he told Patmore 'I suspect her grievously of being an arrant jilt, to say no more, yet I love her dearly,'[78] and that evening composed another love letter, telling her 'You are my little idol—the dear image in my heart, as "that little image" on the mantelpiece (or somebody like it) is in thine.'[79]

He completed the manuscript of *Table Talk* volume 2 on the morning of Thursday 7 March 1822. Sitting at his desk at Renton Inn, he gazed at the storm outside. There was no sense of achievement, only fatigue. He picked up his pen. 'Well done, poor wretched creature!', he scribbled to himself on the final page.[80] He bound it in ribbon and dispatched it to his publisher, declaring: 'I thank God for my escape, & have now done with essay-writing for ever.'[81] As his publisher read those words in his London office, Colburn smiled—for he knew, as well as their author, that any such hope was futile.

CHAPTER 19

A woman may be modest, and a rake at heart.

Hazlitt, *Characteristics* cclxxv[1]

ULL of anticipation, Hazlitt returned to Edinburgh. His wife would soon
arrive and legal proceedings could begin. He wanted to get it over with so
he could return to London to propose to Sarah, and was in buoyant mood. Two
unwelcome pieces of news awaited him, however. The first was that his wife was
delayed: William Jr's half-term was within sight, and she would not come north
until it was over—mid-April at the earliest. The entire thing was originally to
have concluded in six weeks; he realized with a sinking heart he would be in
Scotland for at least another month on top of that. He had to find work, if only
to meet his expenses, and wrote to Taylor and Hessey, offering reviews for the
London Magazine.[2]

That was as nothing to the other piece of news delivered in a letter (now lost)
from Patmore, who revealed that Sarah Walker had declared a wish not to see
him again.[3] At first, in the small, dark room he rented on George Street, he
could not believe what he was reading. He re-read Patmore's letter—again, and
then again. Tears began to flow uncontrollably from his eyes, and sobs came
from the depths. He collapsed, and remained in his room for days after, unable
to function. The news precipitated a breakdown so complete as to make his
mood in preceding weeks seem placid by comparison. For a while he wanted
to kill himself, but something detained him—some small, persistent kernel of
hope. He lay in bed sobbing day and night, alarming his landlady. He was still
in distress when, at the end of March, he managed to tell Patmore 'I have been
in a sort of Hell, & what is worse, I see no prospect of getting out of it. I would
put an end to my torments at once; but I am as great a coward as I am a fool.'[4]
He was beginning to realize what a mess he was making of his life: 'I sit & cry
my eyes out . . . O I feel like one of the damned. To be hated, loathed as I have
been all my life, & to feel the utter impossibility of its ever being otherwise while
I live—take what pains I may!'[5]

Time did not heal the wound; on the contrary: 'By Heaven, I doat on her,' he told Patmore a week later. 'The truth is, I never had any pleasure, like love, with any one but her.'[6] In the same letter, he described his situation as being 'glued to a bitch, a little damned incubus, sucking in her soul & her breath',[7] before urging Patmore to visit Southampton Buildings to seduce her, testing the theory she was 'a common lodging-house drab. All she wants is to be tickled & go all lengths but the last—to be thrown on the floor & felt & all & still resist & keep up the game.'[8]

He was right. Sarah was a game player with no power besides the attraction she exerted over the men passing through her parents' boarding house. It would transpire that she had become intimate with Hazlitt and Tomkins at about the same time, bringing Tomkins his breakfast and spending an hour with him before doing the same thing with Hazlitt. The story of a former lover was a lie, used to distract each man from the other. Her deception was monstrous, and begat monsters.

It would have been better had Patmore not responded to Hazlitt, for he seemed to relish the role of Iago, on this occasion advising him to trust Sarah. Hazlitt was anxious to go along with him. 'I kiss the rod not only with submission but gratitude,' he answered, 'Your rebukes of me & your defences of her are the only things that save my soul from Hell. She is my soul's idol, & believe me those words of yours applied to the dear creature, "To lip a chaste one & suppose her wanton,"[9] were balm & rapture to me.'[10] Patmore persuaded him the divorce was worthwhile: 'When I sometimes think of the time I first saw the sweet apparition, August 16, 1820, & that perhaps, *possibly* she may be my wife before that day two years, it makes me mad with incredible joy & love of her.'[11]

Hazlitt met Francis Jeffrey, his employer and benefactor, for the first time, in March 1822. There were class differences of which both were conscious. Jeffrey had been educated at Edinburgh University and The Queen's College, Oxford, and was recently elected Lord Rector of the University of Glasgow. Hazlitt was of a distinctly less exalted stable, being from a dissenting background and educated at home.

For all that and all that, Jeffrey never declined his assistance when asked for money, and commissioned reviews from Hazlitt even when ridiculed by *Blackwood's* for doing so. He invited him to his home, Craigcrook, on the eastern slope of Corstorphine Hill, three miles to the north-west of Edinburgh, with views to Perth and Stirling. Hazlitt found his benefactor's conversation 'lively, various, and instructive';[12] indeed, 'His only difficulty seems to be not to speak,

Fig. 27. Edinburgh as seen from Corstorphine Hill, a view similar to the one that Hazlitt enjoyed when he lunched with Francis Jeffrey and his wife in March 1822. This was their only known meeting.

but to be silent.'[13] In this, they complemented each other, Hazlitt's tendency being to keep his mouth shut: only the previous month he advised his son not to lead the conversation, but to listen and 'Keep some opinions to yourself.'[14] That afternoon he sat with Jeffrey and his wife on their patio, looking towards Edinburgh, which glimmered in the afternoon sun. Among other matters, Jeffrey probably discussed the political situation, which he thought deplorable.

'These are bad days, Mr Hazlitt, bad for us all.'

'What do you mean, sir?'

'The King, out of humour with his ministers, has a rooted horror at all liberal opinions; and the Duke of York, with more firmness and cold blood, is still more bigotted. And consider the people. They are so poor, and their prospects so dismal, that it is easy to stir them up to any insane project of reform. The dread of this makes the timid rally round those who are for keeping order by force, and neutralises the influence of the Whigs.'[15]

'Ah yes.' Hazlitt would not have risked offending Jeffrey by saying what he thought of them, for he knew he was an *habitué* of Holland House. Yet Hazlitt genuinely liked him, judging him 'the best-natured of men . . . in his disposition there is nothing but simplicity and kindness.'[16]

Part V: The New Pygmalion

'Have you ever met Sir Walter Scott?' asked Mrs Jeffrey. She had taken a liking to the shy, awkward man who gazed abstractedly into the distance.

'No, madam. But I admire him greatly.'

'Would you like to meet him, sir?' asked Jeffrey. He and Scott had been friends since childhood and remained on cordial terms, despite political differences. Hazlitt looked at Jeffrey and his wife. Scott was 'the most popular writer of the age'[17] and no one gained more pleasure from his work than Hazlitt. However . . .

'I should be willing to kneel to him, sir, but I could not take him by the hand.'[18] He spoke apologetically, then looked away. Jeffrey glanced at him, then nodded. His wife cleared her throat. Both were aware of Scott's connections with *Blackwood's* and *The Beacon*—a newspaper established to counter the unpopularity of George IV by undermining his critics.[19]

'I'm sorry, sir, if I seem dull and out of spirits.' Hazlitt hardly ever apologised to anyone; his emotional state must have been glaringly obvious.

'I cannot perceive it, sir,' replied Jeffrey—but he was being polite. Not long after, he would say that Hazlitt 'reminds me of the tired ass in the desert, without occupation, profession, or pursuit'[20]—recollecting his guest's lacklustre mood. Nonetheless, their meeting was a pleasant one, and Hazlitt never forgot Jeffrey's kindness. 'I have seen the great little man', he told Patmore afterwards, '& he is very gracious to me—*Et sa femme aussi!*'[21]

Another acquaintance of the moment was the 41-year-old William Ritchie. The son of a flax dresser, Ritchie helped found *The Scotsman* in 1817 and was responsible for its coverage of literature and the arts. He admired *Characters of Shakespear's Plays* and published enthusiastic reviews of that and subsequent volumes.[22] Not only did Ritchie engage Hazlitt for *The Scotsman*, but he invited him to his home on 17 April, a week after Hazlitt's forty-fourth birthday.[23]

That evening Ritchie introduced him to three friends: J. R. M'Culloch, political economist and editor of *The Scotsman*; former naval officer Thomas Hodgskin; and George Combe, lawyer and phrenologist. On the face of it, these were men whose company Hazlitt might have enjoyed, M'Cullough and Hodgskin both having been pilloried by the Tory press. But, as he soon realized, none of them saw things quite as he did. A disciple of David Ricardo, M'Cullough was attached to principles of 'moderate reform'; Hodgskin thought M'Cullough 'a deep sensible man, but there is an apparent want of openness about him, he is more ready to gather than to give,—I mean information.'[24] Even if Hazlitt had not felt contempt for M'Cullough's moderation in politics, he would have sensed his 'want of openness', and remained tight-lipped in response. The two men could never have hit it off: M'Cullough possessed an arid sensibility to which Hazlitt could never have warmed, despite their having a mutual friend in Macvey Napier.

An Englishman who yearned to become an Edinburgh reviewer, Hodgskin was a friend of John Black, Hazlitt's old colleague on the *Chronicle*. Unfortunately he was also a Benthamite Utilitarian[25] who since 1817 had been one of Francis Place's circle of informants. Perhaps he was unaware of Hazlitt's tenancy of York Street, for he was vocal in his recognition of Hazlitt's genius even when talking to Place, saying he wished he had 'the wit of a Haslitt'.[26] It can be no accident that, two days after their meeting, Hodgskin declared, 'I am very strongly tempted by the prospect of obtaining a reporters place,'[27] probably in the hope that Hazlitt would give him an introduction to Jeffrey.

Combe must have strained Hazlitt's patience the most, for Hazlitt had just written two essays rubbishing the 'science' of which he was an exponent.[28] In that (as in much else) Hazlitt was ahead of his time, for phrenology, though discredited today, was then seriously regarded, particularly in Scotland. Hazlitt politely held his peace when Combe examined his cranium, as reported in his *System of Phrenology*: 'Hazlitt's head, which I have seen, indicates a large development of Ideality [the organ of imagination], and the faculty glows in all his compositions.'[29] Quackery in its purest form: you didn't need to be a phrenologist to see that Hazlitt had imagination. Combe also judged him 'a well-bred man, [who] does not monopolize conversation, listens with attention and interest to any one who speaks, and affects nothing. He is quite a gentleman in his manners and did not utter one sentiment which the most delicate and scrupulous female might not have listened to.'[30] This observation, almost a jibe, may owe something to the fact that Hazlitt declined alcohol, explaining 'he had hurt himself by drinking too freely and had given up strong potations', preferring 'an enormous quantity of tea'.[31] To Scotsmen this was absurd.

The conversation spilled into the small hours and was still in progress when Combe left at 1.30 am. Again, this is evidence of Hazlitt's scrupulous manners, for he could hardly have been at his ease with three hobby-horsical rationalists—'fearful odds against one poor metaphysician!', he later remarked. 'Their machine of human life, I confess, puts me a little in mind of those square-looking caravans one sometimes meets on the road in which they transport wild beasts from place to place.'[32] He probably had them in mind when, in *Characteristics*, he noted: 'The conversation of a pedantic Scotchman is like a canal with a great number of *locks* in it.'[33] His eventual departure from Ritchie's house must have felt like early release from prison.

When the *New Monthly* appeared at the beginning of March it contained Hazlitt's 'On Great and Little Things'. Though drafted the year before, he revised it prior to publication and was unable to resist a direct address to Sarah Walker: 'But shouldst thou ever, my Infelice, grace my home with thy loved presence, as thou hast cheered my hopes with thy smile, thou wilt conquer all hearts with thy prevailing gentleness, and I will shew the world what Shakespear's women were!'[34] Such outbursts were exactly what his enemies wanted. He would claim the essay was published 'by mistake'[35] but did not hesitate to reprint it in the second volume of *Table Talk*, which contained no less than five explicit references to Sarah Walker.[36] Perhaps, by putting his feelings into print, he felt closer to the act of possession.

Weeks slipped by, and still his wife did not come for the proceedings. He was preparing to travel south to beg her to make the journey when, walking down Leith Walk, he met a friend who told him: 'I saw your wife at the wharf. She has just paid her passage by the Superb.'[37] Sarah Hazlitt arrived in Edinburgh on 21 April 1822 after a week at sea. She showed courage in doing so, having been warned against it by Peggy, whose view was that her brother was dangerous—'don't go alone, but have some one to take care of you'.[38]

The divorce ground slowly into motion. Firstly, the annuity John Stoddart covenanted to the couple just before their wedding was revised, Hazlitt renouncing all further claim in his son's favour. From now on, William Jr would receive an annual income of £150. The new document was drawn up by Stoddart's solicitor in London and signed by Hazlitt two days after Sarah's arrival.[39] This was Hazlitt's last direct dealing with his detested brother-in-law. In the years since his departure from *The Times*, Stoddart had first established *The Correspondent*, a journal designed to encourage contacts between British writers and the French ultras, which soon failed,[40] before editing another daily, *The New Times*, where he continued his rabidly pro-government leaders, earning the ridicule of radical journalists as 'Dr Slop'; in 1820, for instance, William Hone and George Cruikshank issued a mock newspaper entitled *A Slap at Slop*, which advertised such squibs as *Royal Red Hot Slop* and *The Origin of Dr Slop's Name*. Hazlitt's loathing of the jacobin-turned-Tory was salved by his pleasure at witnessing (and possibly contributing to) these assaults. At long last he was now released from the ongoing humiliation of being Stoddart's pensioner, by which his son would receive a measure of financial security. In this, he and his wife were at one: her motive in divorcing him, she told Hazlitt, was 'to secure something to *his* child, as well as mine'.[41]

On 24 April he was 'discovered' at the James Street brothel in the arms of a prostitute, Mary Walker.[42] It must have felt unsettling when he realized that the prostitute bore the same surname as his inamorata, but he tried not to allow it to assume an undue significance. His wife's solicitor, James Gray, questioned Walker and the madam, Mrs Knight, who testified that Hazlitt 'was seen or known to be in bed with such women one or more, and to be shut up with them privately in a room or other apartments, and to have carnal and adulterous intercourse and dealings with them'.[43] Afterwards Gray spoke privately with his client.

'Well, Mrs Hazlitt', he said to Sarah, 'I was never more astonished than when I visited the establishment at James Street.'

'Why, sir?'

'The people, madam, the people were the lowest, abandoned blackguards I have ever met with. They would not say a word till I had treated them with mulled port! And it was only when they were half-intoxicated that I got out of them sufficient for the purpose.'

'I see.'

'The appearance of the house, the people, and everything about it was more infamous than anything I have ever known existed in Edinburgh at the present day.'[44]

'I am not at all surprised at it', said Sarah. 'For those are exactly the sort with whom Mr Hazlitt associates in London. He has a taste that way.'

'Well, madam—it is a very depraved one.'[45]

The sudden flurry of legal activity put Hazlitt under increased financial pressure. An obvious solution was to do some lecturing and with that in mind he contacted James Sheridan Knowles, who was now principal of an elocution school in Glasgow.

A principal British port generating wealth from imports of sugar, rum, and tobacco, Glasgow's culture was distinct from that of Edinburgh. Local politicians were radicalized, and the populace had come close to insurrection two years earlier, something averted only by an increased military presence.[46] Hazlitt had a sentimental reason for coming here. He wanted to roam the Inner and Outer Quadrangles of the Old College—the University on the High Street, founded in 1451, where his father had once listened to Adam Smith and assisted in the experiments of James Watt. As he did so, he must have wondered what the Old College was like in those far-off days, when the local Synod policed professors for evidence of heresy—Arianism, Arminianism, Socinianism, or worse. Such institutions were the cradle of the Unitarian faith in which he had been raised, and as he stood at the ornate gatehouse[47] facing the street he shed tears for its fragile but determined optimism.

Hazlitt's lectures would be managed by Knowles, with whom he probably stayed. They would take place at the Andersonian Institution (precursor of the University of Strathclyde) in John Street, which boasted a circular lecture theatre holding up to 500 people. He attracted only a hundred or so for the first, scheduled for 6 May, on Shakespeare and Milton. It went down well, one of his audience writing to the *Glasgow Sentinel* to say that Hazlitt 'is a genteel sort of a man to look at; and he entered upon his lecture more with the appearance of a gentleman amateur . . . than with that of an accustomed orator.'[48]

The next day Hazlitt and Knowles set out on a walking tour to Loch Lomond—which, he wrote, 'comes upon you by degrees as you advance, unfolding and then withdrawing its conscious beauties like an accomplished coquet'[49] (another echo of Sarah Walker). They crossed the Loch to Inversnaid but were prevented from climbing Ben Lomond by fresh snowfalls. Pushing on to the Trossachs, they returned to Glasgow via Callander and Stirling. His hope was to shake off his anxieties but he could not forget Patmore's worrying letter about Sarah's inconstancy. Despite the beauty of the bleak Scottish countryside, his emotions remained in turmoil: 'the air was damp and chill: the river winded its dull, slimy way like a snake along the marshy grounds: and the dim misty tops of Ben Leddi, and the lovely Highlands (woven fantastically of thin air) mocked my embraces and tempted my longing eyes like her, the sole queen and mistress of my thoughts! . . . I wept myself almost blind, and I gazed at the broad golden sun-set through my tears that fell in showers.'[50] He longed to be buried 'in one grave with her . . . while worms should taste her sweet body, that I had never tasted!'[51]

After his concluding lecture in Glasgow, from which he made £56, he returned to London by steamboat, convinced that the only cure was to see her. 'As the vessel sailed up the Thames, the air thickened with the consciousness of being near her, and I "heaved her name pantingly forth." '[52] He landed on Friday evening, 17 May, and sprinted from Blackwall docks to Southampton Buildings, full of anticipation. His room awaited him, but Sarah was curiously reluctant to emerge, and he went to bed unable to sleep. The next day he brought William Jr to meet her and she softened immediately. Delighted by her renewed friendliness, he caught sight of the bust of Napoleon which she had placed on the mantelpiece and declared: 'I gave it to you; nay, I have given you all—my heart, and whatever I possess, is yours!'[53] She smiled politely, bowed, and swept out of the room without comment, leaving him in renewed agitation.

When the boy had gone, he was desperate to see her again and cornered her outside his rooms, gripping her hand. He declared his love and explained his hurt at her silence, hoping he had not offended her. She answered coldly but politely, making him more attentive than ever. 'You look like a queen, my love, adorned with your own graces!'[54] He offered to kiss her, but she drew back, causing him as much pain as if someone had stabbed him in the heart. He could not help but imagine other suitors, other temptations. Before he could say anything more, she scampered downstairs to join her family.

He returned to his rooms, shaking with desperation. It was as if she had taken his entire world and crumpled it in her fist. 'I was made the dupe of trick and cunning, killed with cold, sullen scorn; and, after all the agony I had suffered, could obtain no explanation of why I was subjected to it. I was still to be tantalized, tortured, made the cruel sport of one, for whom I would have sacrificed all.'[55] Screaming, he seized the bust of Napoleon and hurled it to the ground, stamping on the fragments, then retreated to his bedroom, sobbing. A moment later Sarah's parents rushed upstairs, alarmed by his screams.

'She's in there! He's got her in there!' Mrs Walker cried. Hazlitt appeared in the doorway to his bedroom, tears coursing down his face.

'No, no!' he cried, '*She's* in no danger from *me*! 'Tis I must fear *her*. Don't you see? She has murdered me! She has destroyed me for ever!'[56] With that, he ran from the house.

This was a turning point. Hazlitt's destruction of the bust was symbolic not only of the devastation of his youthful aspirations (something confirmed by Napoleon's demise) but of hopes of a married life with Sarah. Though he continued to oscillate between idolatry and distress, his mood henceforth resolved into disillusioned resignation.

When he had calmed down he returned to the house and explained everything to Sarah's father, who (astonishingly) knew nothing of the affair. Mr Walker listened sympathetically, agreeing that if his daughter wanted to marry the lodger, he would not stand in her way. This filled Hazlitt with renewed hope and before returning to Scotland he managed to engineer a rapprochement, though once again she managed to give encouragement while plunging him into despair. At first she denied the existence of rivals (which cheered him greatly) but then, asked whether she would marry him, replied she could make no promises. 'My head reeled, my heart recoiled within me. I was stung with scorpions; my flesh crawled; I was choked with rage; her scorn scorched me like flames; her air (her heavenly air) withdrawn from me, stifled me, and left me gasping for breath and being.'[57]

In this disturbed, volatile condition he boarded the steamboat for Edinburgh on Wednesday 29 May and wrote Patmore one of the most *distrait* of the *Liber Amoris* letters.

> Dear P. What have I suffered since I parted with you? a raging gnawing fire in my heart & in my brain that I thought would drive me mad. The Steam-Boat seemed a prison, a Hell, & the everlasting waters and unendurable repetition of the same idea, my woes, the abyss was before me, & her face where all my peace was centered, all lost! I felt the eternity of punishment in this world. Mocked, mocked by her in whom I placed my hope & withering, writhing in misery & despair, caused by one who hardens herself against me. I wished for courage to throw myself into the waters, but I could not even do that, & my little boy too prevented me, when I thought of his face at hearing of his father's death, & his desolation in this life.[58]

When the ship docked at Scarborough he dashed on shore to post the letter, before reboarding to write another describing Sarah Walker as

> a regular lodging-house decoy, who leads a sporting life with every one who comes in succession, & goes different lengths according as she is urged or inclined. This is why she will not marry, because she hankers after this sort of thing. She has an itch for being slabbered & felt, & this she is determined to gratify upon system, & has a pride in making fools of the different men she indulges herself with & at the same time can stop short from the habit of running the gauntlet with so many.[59]

Hazlitt has come in for much criticism over this relationship, but his disenchantment with Sarah was justified. She was as manipulative as he imagined, the being he described in *Characteristics*: 'An accomplished coquet excites the passions of others in proportion as she feels none herself. Her forwardness allures, her indifference irritates desire. She fans the flame that does not scorch her own bosom, plays with men's feelings, and studies the effect of her several arts at leisure and unmoved.'[60] He was right to suspect that the woman for whom he was willing to sacrifice everything 'wanted to be courted not as a bride, but as a common wench'.[61] How could he release himself from her? The only way, he told Patmore, was to discover whether 'she was a whore, *flagranti delicto*, it would wean me from her, & burst my chain. Could you ascertain this fact for me, by any means or through any person (E. for example) who might try her as a lodger?'[62] Seduction by proxy was, perhaps, a step too far, but he could not expel the idea from his disordered mind. 'TRY HER through someone / anyone E. for example who will satisfy my soul', he repeated to Patmore several weeks later.[63]

Publication of *Table Talk* volume 2 on 15 June 1822 hardly registered with him. Once again, it showed Hazlitt's talents at their peak with such essays as 'On Coffee-House Politicians', 'On Going A Journey', 'Why Distant Objects Please', and 'On the Picturesque and Ideal'. The collection ended with one of his greatest works, 'On the Fear of Death', which reflected the growing awareness that his time was limited.

> The pleasures of our existence have worn themselves out, are 'gone into the wastes of time', or have turned their indifferent side to us: the pains by their repeated blows have worn us out, and have left neither spirit nor inclination to encounter them again in retrospect. We do not want to rip up old grievances, nor to renew our youth like the phoenix, nor to live our lives twice over. Once is enough. As the tree falls, so let it lie.[64]

Its virtues remained invisible to those who reviewed the volume, most of whom professed disgust at Hazlitt's references to Sarah Walker. Eyre Evans Crowe led the charge in *Blackwood's*, describing it as 'one gaping sore of wounded and festering vanity':[65] 'Your dirty imagination, Mr Hazlitt, is always plunging you into some dirty scrape. It is sickening to hear an old fellow like you talking at table, and before ladies too, perhaps, about "fulsome advances,"—"buds and promises,"—"casting off," and all that long etcetera of the vocabulary of vapid pollution.'[66] This was an outright falsification; Hazlitt nowhere used such terms. This was, on the contrary, one of his most accomplished works—a miracle given the circumstances under which it was produced.

On his return to Edinburgh he visited his solicitor to be told that the divorce was further delayed until Wednesday 17 July. The endless waiting drove an already distracted man into the mouth of madness. Like Othello, Hazlitt wanted 'ocular proof' of Sarah's infidelity: 'she's gone & my revenge must be—to love her—damn her, the little sorceress, the cruel, heartless destroyer!'[67] Were she seduced by a third party, it 'would lift my soul from Hell. . . . *You* may try her, if you like,'[68] he urged Patmore.

On 6 July he went with his friend Alexander Henderson to a tourist attraction, Dalkeith Palace, the grandest of Scottish Classical Houses, renowned for its collection of paintings. One of these, Luca Giordano's 'Truth Finding Fortune in the Sea', showed the nude figure of Fortune—Sarah Walker as he imagined her. It burnt itself into his memory, and for a while he became obsessed by it. By coincidence, they bumped into Hazlitt's wife as they left, for she too had come to view the paintings. Two days later he dragged another friend, John Robertson Bell, through six miles of heavy rain to feast upon the image a second time, for 'it drove [me] mad'.[69]

On Saturday 13 July he met his wife in the street and told her of his impatience. 'The more I try to hurry the lawyers, the more they delay. It is beyond endurance.'

'William, it will be over on Wednesday!'

'Let us hope there will be no further delay. I want to be off.'

'You need not worry about bumping into me on the steamboat back to London, for I won't be using it. By the way, did you think that a good collection of pictures at Dalkeith?'

'No, very poor. There were only two that were tolerable: one a Claude, though in bad condition; the other a female figure on the waters, probably a copy of some good picture.'

'I remarked it myself', she replied, 'and thought the figure exceedingly good!'[70] Sarah would not forget this.

Three days later Hazlitt wrote to Patmore in desperation: 'Tomorrow is the fatal day that makes or mars me.'[71] He was 'somewhat in the dumps', fearing his 'reception with [Sarah Walker] is doubtful'. Patmore was recently engaged, and Hazlitt told him: 'The hearing of your happiness has made me melancholy. It is just what I proposed to her to do. But on my forehead alone is written "*Rejected of women.*"'[72] In past months his passion had led him from the sublimest love ecstasy to the depths of near-suicidal despair, moderated only by violent, gut-wrenching fits of jealousy. A personality so profoundly undermined can surely be forgiven the occasional bout of self-pity.

At 11am on the morning of Wednesday 17 July he appeared in court. The case was heard, witnesses were called, the process concluded, and Hazlitt left (to use his words) 'a free man'.[73] The divorce, though valid, had been the result of collusion between Hazlitt and his wife, and was thus illegal according to the strict letter of the law. But only they were aware of that. The decree was pronounced at the cost of £25 10s 9d, no small sum for Hazlitt. That would not be the only cost. In a memorandum drawn up in April, he agreed to pay Sarah's expenses during her stay in Scotland and for William Jr's upkeep and education. In return, Sarah would always be a welcome guest at Crediton with Grace and Peggy, and never spoke otherwise than kindly of her former husband. This was a consolation to their son, who would not be made a pawn in a game of emotional blackmail. Yet for all the care with which his parents proceeded, William Jr found the divorce a harrowing experience. Such things were a rarity in those days and marked him out among his contemporaries. The endlessly repeated stories of his father's liking for prostitutes (which he knew to be true) were doubtless used against him in the schoolyard, and can only have compounded his defensiveness.

Hazlitt ran back to his lodgings at 10 George Street and packed his trunk. Not having sealed the letter he had written Patmore the previous day, he added a postscript:

Dear P. It is all over, & I am free: I could not stay here any longer, & have taken my place outside by the Mail tonight, so I shall be in town (please God, & thank God) on Saturday evening. W.H. If I am knocked up, I must stop a day or two on the road.[74]

Having written those words, he sat down for tea one last time. It was 4pm, and there was a knock on the door. It was his ex-wife, who joined him for a conversation, their last of any substance.[75]

'Did you know, Sarah, that my landlady, Mrs Dow, wanted me to marry her daughter?'

'Oh really? What does she look like?'

'An ill-favoured creature with bad teeth and a foul mouth.' They both laughed.

'Is it true Mr Patmore seduced Miss Walker?'

'Not to the best of my knowledge,' he replied. 'Patmore has never seen her above twice, and that was when he came to visit *me* at Southampton Buildings. Her conduct seems quite inexplicable to him and everyone I have told it to. She professes the greatest affection and esteem for me, and for the last year and a half has made a constant practice of sitting on my knee for two or three hours every day, with her arms around my neck, kissing me and expressing the greatest love and attachment. I have done everything but go to bed to her. And yet, though I made the warmest love to her, she either has no passions, and her fondness is all deceit, or she has the most astonishing control over them—for there she stopped short.'

'Your feelings for the woman, William, are most strange. After all, she is not handsome.' This was not jealousy. All witnesses agreed Sarah's looks were unexceptional.

'Aye, her eyes are the worst feature, for they bespeak hypocrisy and design, and have a poor slimy watery look. Yet she is well made with handsome arms.'

'But not the sort you used to admire', said Sarah, 'which is plump; *she* is as thin and bony as a scrag-end of mutton, like the woman in the picture at Dalkeith.'

'Fortune in the sea? Indeed, I fancy it *is* her.'

'But nearer my form in the thighs, the fall of the back, and the contour of the figure.'

'Yes, Sarah, you *are* very fine, very fine indeed.' That they were able to exchange such pleasantries immediately after obtaining their divorce indicates an astonishing lack of bitterness and genuine mutual affection.

'I can't wait to return to her,' Hazlitt told his ex-wife. 'She understands me perfectly. Do you know, neither she nor her family have any objection to visitors?' He meant prostitutes. 'Sarah greets them when they call for me, and directs them to my room. They call her a "nice girl". Yet she tortures me with her damned wilfulness. I don't know what she wants! She is never the same from one moment to the next: little yes and no.' Before he could say more, tears began to course down his cheeks and sobs poured out of him.

'William!' said Sarah. He looked into her face.

'I am determined to ascertain the true state of things in that house. I will lodge there, and watch her narrowly, and perhaps I will kill her and myself too, when I get there!'

'This is like your frenzy about Sally Baugh,' said Sarah.

'*That* was but a flea-bite, nothing at all to this, for she never pretended to love me; indeed, she declared she did not. This is the only person who ever really seemed to be fond of me. I'm sorry I did not ravish her the first week I came into the house. I shall set off for London by the mail-coach tonight, though I think I might be detained by illness or die on the road. Either way, the mere getting out of Scotland would be a blessed release.'

Hazlitt did not, in the end, return by mailcoach; instead he took the 8am steamboat the next morning, arriving in London in the early morning of Saturday 21 July. He had managed to convince himself that, with his divorce,

Sarah would feel differently towards him—that she would embrace him as her betrothed. But what was that sense of foreboding in the pit of his stomach? Where had that come from?

Once again, he sprinted from Blackwall to Holborn and reclaimed his rooms. Sarah was nowhere to be seen but he was told she would be in later. He lay on his bed, listening for the sound of her footfalls outside his door. The minutes passed with glacial slowness, and after several hours he stepped onto the landing to see whether he could hear her voice. As soon as he opened the door he saw her descending the stairs beneath him. 'Sarah! Sarah! My love!'

She froze and glanced up, a look of impassivity on her face.

'Is everything all right?' he asked.

She turned away and slowly continued downstairs. He sprang towards her.

'Sarah, I am a free man! I am free!' But she was backing away from him. 'What is it? Why do you flinch?' In desperation, he cried out: 'Can we not at least be friends? Cannot we be more than friends?' Without warning, she burst into tears, ran down the stairs, and disappeared into her parents' living room.

He was horrified; it had been his intention to propose marriage. Now everything for which he had fought was thrown into question. He left his door open throughout most of Sunday, looking out onto the landing from time to time in the hope of catching her as she passed, but she never did. He was in a state of mounting anguish. He didn't know quite what to think, but his darkest fears began to run riot. There was no chance of working; all he could think was where he might have gone wrong. By Monday evening he still had not seen her and was tormented by anxiety. Then he heard her voice downstairs followed by the front door slamming shut. He rushed down the staircase only to be told by her sister that Sarah had gone to visit her grandmother in Somers Town. On an impulse, he set off in her wake and, within minutes, as he proceeded up King Street to the south-east of Bloomsbury Square, found himself walking towards her: she was arm-in-arm with 'a tall, rather well-looking young man'.[76] It was Tomkins.

He passed them without a word, stopped and looked back, only to see them do exactly the same thing. Then they walked on. Dazed, he wandered aimlessly for a while before heading back to Southampton Buildings. Then, as he looked up from the path, he found himself again walking straight towards them; they looked away as he approached and passed without a word. It was like a scene out of some nightmarish vision. Twice had he crossed paths with them, but with no explicit acknowledgement of the fact. His throat rasped. He did not need to exchange words to know what this signified.

Part V: The New Pygmalion

When Sarah returned to the house he was sitting by the front door, waiting for her. 'I always suspected there was something between you two, but you denied it lustily', he said, 'why did you not tell me about it at the time, instead of letting me suffer?'

> I told her I hoped I should not live to see her come to shame, after all my love of her; but put her on her guard as well as I could, and said, after the lengths she had permitted herself with me, I could not help being alarmed at the influence of one over her, whom she could hardly herself suppose to have a tenth part of my esteem for her!! She made no answer to this, but thanked me coldly for my good advice, and rose to go. ... We parted friends, however, and I felt deep grief, but no enmity towards her.[77]

Could that last comment be true? It resolves *Liber Amoris*, but there is no evidence that the letter of which it claims to be part was ever posted or even written as an item of correspondence. Instead he remained in a disturbed state, as when on 8 August he called on Haydon 'in a state of absolute insanity about the girl who has jilted him'.[78] Six weeks later he remained 'full of his Sally Walker',[79] wandering about town, telling anyone who would listen—even total strangers— about his humiliation, in the most grotesque terms. One day he told no less than five people, entering 'into minute details of his love story'.[80] Another time, he went to look for new lodgings in Pimlico. After discussing the rent with the landlady, she looked at him oddly and said: 'I am afraid you are not well, sir?' 'No, ma'am,' he replied, 'I am not.' And without more ado he recounted the entire tale from beginning to end.

Perhaps he *was* behaving like a madman but, given the stress he was under, it is hardly surprising. We know from his own account that the *Blackwood's* affair nearly destroyed him; close on its tail, he had suffered a painful, expensive, and humiliating divorce for a woman who took a malicious pleasure in exerting her influence over him. He had loved her passionately but she proved to be exactly what he feared: a snake, a succubus, a lodging-house decoy. The experience of laying everything at her feet would not kill him, but did leave him shattered in mind and body, and marked him for the rest of his days.

Accusations of Hazlitt's 'sexual harassment' are a testimony to the stupidity of modern literary criticism, which has led some to argue for his exile from the syllabus. Not only do such critics know nothing of the social and sexual norms of Hazlitt's day, but they fail to recognize the anachronism inherent in the application of twenty-first-century American values to the English lower middle class in early-nineteenth-century London. Sarah did not think of herself as harassed or would surely have reported Hazlitt's conduct to her parents, which she never did. Nor is there cause to question Hazlitt's meticulous documentation of his dealings with her, which shows that she encouraged and teased him, leading them to have sexual contact of various kinds short of intercourse. He complained of her refusal to let him go further, but without ever compelling her to do so.

The knowledge that he was not to marry her plunged him into a deep inner darkness from which he was slow to emerge. Worse still, his imagination continued for years to be dominated by her; he admitted as much when he remarked: 'She is dead to me; but what she once was to me, can never die!'[81] He did not commit suicide but the obsession diminished him, undermining his constitution. Writing to Jeffrey in the third week of August, he apologized for 'any oddnesses I might [have been] guilty of while in Edinburgh', saying 'I am better a good deal, but feel much like a man who has been thrown from the top of a house.'[82]

CHAPTER 20

*Persons of talent and reputation do not make
money, because they do not keep it; and they do not
keep it, because they do not care about it till they feel
the want of it—and then* the public stop payment.

Hazlitt, *Aphorisms on Man* xl[1]

*William Hazlitt . . . was in his day the best abused man
in Great Britain; it was dangerous to be his companion,
so many stones were always flying about his ears.*

Chambers's Journal (1866)[2]

IN July 1822 Hazlitt moved into the heart of Mayfair, which retained the unofficial status of a village within the West End, having its own shops, marketplace, and amenities. From his doorstep on Chapel Street West he could see Chesterfield House, the Palladian-style mansion built in 1748 for Philip Stanhope, 4th Earl Chesterfield, author of one of Hazlitt's favourite books, *Letters to his Son*. It brought to mind the Revolutionary period, as he observed: 'Here, as I look down Curzon-street, or catch a glimpse of the taper spire of South Audley Chapel, or the family-arms on the gate of Chesterfield-House, the vista of years opens to me, and I recall the period of the triumph of Mr. Burke's "Reflections on the French Revolution", and the overthrow of "The Rights of Man"!'[3] Residents of nearby Curzon Street included the inoculator Edward Jenner (a subscriber to the *History of English Philosophy*[4]) and sculptor Sir Francis Chantrey. Here, decayed gentlefolk could scrape by, the most appropriate abode for Becky Sharp in chapter 36 of *Vanity Fair*, 'How to Live Well on Nothing a Year'.

From his new rooms he arranged publication of *Liber Amoris*. It is unlikely he thought long about whether to put it into print: he was dependent on his writing for a living, and the experience it described, though ruinous, was the ideal subject. What's more, composition was largely complete. Part I (his conversations with the statue) was done; Part II comprised his letters to Patmore;[5] he had only to write Part III, which used the epistolary manner, *a la Rousseau*, to resolve the narrative. The deciding factor was money.[6] John Hunt, recently freed from Coldbath Fields,[7] offered him £100 for it. Divorce had emptied his pockets, and that was too good to turn down. If anything, his resolve was hardened by the review of *Table Talk* volume 2 in the *Monthly Literary Register*, which declared: 'Let us have no more of his landlord's daughter in italics.'[8] There was only one response, as Hazlitt told Northcote:

> When one is found fault with for nothing, or for doing one's best, one is apt to give the world their revenge. All the former part of my life I was treated as a cipher; and since I have got into notice, I have been set upon as a wild beast. When this is the case, and you can expect as little justice as candour, you naturally in self-defence take refuge in a sort of misanthropy and cynical contempt for mankind. One is disposed to humour them, and to furnish them with some ground for their idle and malevolent censures.[9]

Any reservations about whether to publish would have centred on its story. But he 'saw no harm, no impropriety, in the contents. They were nothing more than the rhapsody which he had poured into the ear of everybody whom he met for a year or more.'[10] Indeed, it was inconceivable that anyone could object to an act of self-analysis, as serious in design as Wordsworth's *Prelude*. That was why it described his emotions with brutal honesty, refusing to pander to vanity or self-regard. And therein lay its greatness. Byron's comment on *Don Juan* comes to mind: 'it may be bawdy—but is it not good English?—it may be profligate—but is it not *life*, is it not *the thing*?'[11]

John Hunt told Hazlitt about his new venture: *The Liberal*, a journal his brother Leigh had planned to edit with Shelley in Genoa. But Shelley's death changed all that—the poet drowned in the Gulf of Spezia on 8 July, his boat making its way in full sail through a violent storm.[12] Leigh had instead to collaborate with Byron, with whom relations were never easy. The need for new contributors was urgent and, in a letter to his brother, Leigh requested that Hazlitt and Lamb be approached; on 26 October he asked more insistently, 'Is Hazlitt preparing anything yet? Have you made my request to Lamb? Lord B. admires Hazlitt's writings, and both likes and admires Lamb.'[13]

This wasn't true: Byron hated Hazlitt. 'Speaking of Hazlitt', Henry Muir recorded at this moment, 'Lord B. expressed himself in the most bitter terms, and would not allow that he could write good English.'[14] Nor would he shift from that position. As Hunt realized, Byron 'was afraid of Mr Hazlitt; he admitted him like a courtier, for fear he should be treated by him as an enemy.'[15] From Byron's point of view, Hazlitt was jumped-up, a lower-middle-class dissenter with little formal education. He set no value on Hazlitt's writings and, had they ever met, would not have hesitated to say so. But Hazlitt knew nothing of that. Instead, Hunt thought the invitation to contribute to *The Liberal* could succeed only were Hazlitt persuaded of Byron's good opinion and the opportunity to cultivate it. But that was to overstate Hazlitt's vanity: in fact he detested the 'double aristocracy of rank and letters' represented by Byron, a man who 'regards the House of Peers with contempt as a set of dull fellows; and . . . his brother authors as a Grub-street crew. A king is hardly good enough for him to touch: a mere man of genius is no better than a worm.'[16]

In early November Hazlitt agreed to contribute, probably out of loyalty to John Hunt, to whom he owed many favours. Hunt transmitted the news to Italy within days. 'Remember me to Mr. Hazlitt, & say how glad I am to hear of his joining us with his artillery,'[17] Leigh replied. Hazlitt was at the peak of his powers and in coming months would contribute some of his best work to *The Liberal*.

On 2 October he apologized to Jeffrey for not having said goodbye before leaving Edinburgh because '*I hated the sight of myself* & fancied every body else did the same.'[18] He wanted to take up Jeffrey's suggestion that he survey the newspaper and periodical press, saying 'I am better than I was, & able to work.'[19] The article he turned in—one of his funniest—serves as retrospect to his career as journalist; Robinson described it as 'very piquant!'[20] Hazlitt flattered no one, but was even-handed and forgiving. There were kind words for the *Morning Chronicle*, though he could not resist saying Perry 'was a little of a coxcomb, and we do not think he was a bit the worse for it.'[21] Angry at being ignored, the Tory *John Bull* claimed to be 'the WHOLE, SOLE, and EXCLUSIVE object contemplated from beginning to end'[22]—a shot across his bows.

The bailiffs were still looking for him, anxious to collect, and he laboured frantically over Christmas to pay them off.[23] The best he could do for his son was give him an inscribed copy of his own *New and Improved Grammar of the English Tongue*.[24] Despite his industry, he failed to satisfy his creditors and in February 1823 was driven to beg from Taylor and Hessey an advance on his picture-gallery pieces, promising three more within the fortnight: 'I hope you oblige me in this.'[25] But they did not, believing he had cheated them in the past;

unfortunately, they lacked the moral courage to say so to his face, though news of it leaked out to Blackwood and his spies.[26] Their treachery delivered him into the hands of the duns who, on the morning of Wednesday 12 February, ran him to ground.

'Mr Hazlitt, is it?' As he looked into the man's face, Hazlitt's heart stopped. This was what he had long feared. There were three of them: they always came in threes—one to serve the warrant, the others to ensure the unfortunate victim did not resist. Hazlitt heard the horses as the cab drew up alongside him; it had been following for several minutes. As its door swung open he noticed a shadowy figure inside. The man who addressed him was John Brock, Serjeant at Mace to the Sheriffs of London.[27]

'Sir', said Brock, doffing his hat with an unpleasant smile. He gestured towards the interior of the cab.

The arrest was made by the firm of Walbancke and Whittle, based at 5 Coleman Street Buildings,[28] just round the corner from the Guildhall. Brock took him straight to their offices and told him the initial detention was preparatory to an enforced stay at one of city 'compters'—jails for those who were to appear before the Sheriff. The first thing Hazlitt did was ask for a piece of paper. On one side of the sheet he wrote, 'Mr. Hazlitt presents his c[ompliments]'—but stopped in mid-sentence, realizing this hardly communicated the absolute terror he felt at the predicament in which he found himself. He turned the paper over and began again, with no pretence at social niceties:

My dear Sir,
  I have been arrested this morning & am at a loss what to do. Would you give me a call to talk the matter over, & see if your influence could procure me any terms of accommodation? I am sorry to plague you about my troublesome affairs. Believe me very truly

> your obliged friend
> and servant,
> W. Hazlitt

5 Coleman Street
Buildings, Feb. 12.[29]

He addressed it to Thomas Noon Talfourd and gave it to one of the messengers in the office. 'Poor men always use messengers instead of the post. Who has not had their letters, with the wafers wet, and the announcement that a person is waiting in the hall?'[30]

Talfourd was by now an accomplished and well-respected lawyer, having been called to the bar in 1821. He married in September 1822, just as Hazlitt was emerging from the Sarah Walker debacle. We do not know whether Hazlitt was invited to the nuptials; if so, it is doubtful whether he was in the mood for them. Five months later, his first thought was to contact Talfourd, who, as a barrister, could navigate the legal intricacies.

Upon receiving the note, Talfourd went straight to Walbancke and Whittle. He was one of the few who recognized Hazlitt's genius, describing him in after-years as 'one who was my great Master in the Art of Thinking, and the recollection of whose society is dearer to me than the enjoyment of that of my dearest living friends'.[31] His mere presence gave Hazlitt comfort. Talfourd prevented the legal process going further, and somehow engineered his friend's release. The next day, Hazlitt wrote to his creditors promising what he owed 'the instant I have the money at command'.[32] Not for the last time, he had escaped imprisonment by the skin of his teeth, but was badly shaken: the experience 'never passed from his mind'.[33]

On 1 March he probably attended the private view at the Egyptian Hall in Piccadilly of 'The Raising of Lazarus'—Haydon's largest canvas yet, for which William Bewick modelled as Lazarus.[34] Hazlitt was not the only one whose finances were precarious: on 13 April the picture was seized, the exhibition shut down, and (on 21 April) the artist arrested. 'I am ruined, infallibly, inextricably ruined', Haydon declared.[35] His possessions were sold off and the painting knocked down for a mere £350 to an upholsterer in Grosvenor Square. Haydon spent the next three months in the King's Bench Prison. He found the experience deeply traumatic and suffered nightmares for months after.[36] Hazlitt visited him on 25 June and 'shewed feeling throughout'.[37] Northcote was less sympathetic: 'Why, he ought to be *hung*,' he remarked.[38] 'The Raising of Lazarus' is now at Tate Britain, but rolled up—a mournful fate for a work now regarded as 'among the few masterpieces of historical painting in this country'.[39]

Hazlitt had been recovering from the Sarah Walker affair but his brush with the law set him back. He began to obsess once more about whether she was a 'lodging-house decoy' and in early March persuaded a friend, known to us only as 'Mr. F.',[40] to move into Southampton Buildings with the intention of seducing her. Between 4 and 16 March he kept a diary of F's time there, recording that, after barely a week, F had appeared naked before Sarah and kissed her on several occasions. The diary in which Hazlitt documented these events is a rough, furtive, near-illegible manuscript, a direct emanation of the irrational obsession by which he was still gripped. It shows that F's advances were entertained by Sarah with the same willingness she had shown Hazlitt's. Among other things, F told her 'he could bear to live by himself [if] he could [have] something to kiss & fondle & muss', before asking her to have sex. 'We should make good company', he told her.

'Would it be proper?' she asked.

'Hang propriety!' replied F.

'What, you would not hang propriety? Would it be seemly?'

'As to seemly, there is nobody to see us but ourselves.'

It was strange enough that F was Hazlitt's agent, but stranger still that Hazlitt recorded F's encounters with Sarah in such lurid detail. 'In lighting F. upstairs she waits for him to go first, & on his insisting on her leading the way, they had a regular scamper for it, he all the way tickling her legs behind. Yet she expressed no resentment nor shame. This is she who murdered me that she might keep every lodger at a proper distance.'[41] These sour insights in Sarah's character both pained and soothed him. 'I am exculpated by all this,' Hazlitt confided to the diary one evening, before meeting F at the Southampton Arms.[42]

'Would you like to take her into keeping?' Hazlitt asked him. 'I'll pay you half a guinea a week to take her as your whore.'

F laughed. 'No thanks', he replied, 'for that kind of money you can get girls that have some conversation in them, and she has none. I thought at first she was unable to talk, but now I'm convinced she is too stupid. If I ask her to go to bed with me, and she agrees, what would you have me do?'

'Why, you had better proceed.' But Hazlitt saw the doubtful look on F's face and realized at once what it signified. 'I suppose', he said, 'you do not wish to have a child by a monster.' F nodded.

'That is my feeling.'[43]

It was a squalid postscript to the Sarah Walker affair, establishing beyond doubt the true nature of the woman he had elevated to the status of a goddess, to whom he remained enslaved in his imagination. 'I also am her lover & will live & die for her only, since she can be true to any one,' he concluded.[44] The thorn had penetrated his flesh so deeply he could never extract it. It was killing him. 'Decoy!' he shrieked at one point—then, turning on himself: 'Damned, treble damned ideot! When shall I burn her out of my thoughts?'[45]

Part V: The New Pygmalion

In January 1823 his article 'On the Scotch Character' described the malice of the Scots as 'cold-blooded, covert, crawling, deliberate, without the frailty or excuse of passion. They club their vices and their venality together, and by the help of both together are invincible.'[46] This irritated his old antagonist John Wilson, now Professor of Moral Philosophy at Edinburgh University,[47] who once again assumed on the basis of no evidence at all that it was aimed at him. Wilson responded with a variation on the usual allegations about Hazlitt's private life by claiming he did Byron's 'dirty work . . . after the manner of pimps and purveyors', waltzing with 'washer-women and bar-maids, and used-up kept-mistresses'.[48]

This was worse than any previous attack for it cast Hazlitt as Byron's pander. It threw Hazlitt into a state of near-hysteria. He wrote to Thomas Cadell, who had taken over from Murray as *Blackwood's* London publisher, threatening to 'commence an action against you for damages sustained from repeated slanderous & false imputations in that work on me'.[49] Brief though it was, his note made Cadell 'somewhat uncomfortable'[50] and Cadell forwarded it to Blackwood, who responded by promising to bear his legal expenses. However, declared Blackwood, fear not! The despised Hazlitt would not bring an action, 'for he is such a character as would come with a very bad grace claiming damages from an English jury. . . . Besides the public will be completely on the side of the Magazine for attacking such a nest of infidels and profligates as Hazlitt, Hunt, Byron & Co. who are daily outraging not only private character, but every thing sacred & civil. So far therefore from there being any thing discreditable in the Magazine having attacked such a vile person as Hazlitt it will rather be considered as the reverse.'[51] But he was wrong. Several weeks later *The Examiner* reported: '*Cadell*, the London publisher of the *Blackguard Magazine*, has had an action commenced against him for some slander contained in that worthless publication. People were much surprised when they first heard that Mr. Cadell had degraded himself by becoming the agent of such a publisher as *Blackwood*.'[52]

The legal process was soon overtaken by events.

John Hunt published *Liber Amoris* on 9 May 1823, the engraved title page of which bore a portrait of Sarah Walker taken from a sketch by the author. The volume carried no authorial attribution though a Preface claimed it for 'a native of North Britain' who had died in the Netherlands. This was unlikely to fool anyone; Hazlitt's essays had been alluding to Sarah for months, and reviewers knew the book was his before it reached the bookshops. The reviewer in the

New European Magazine set the tone for what followed when he described it as 'the actual history of a man who sets himself up as a critic, a moralist, a judge of human nature, and,—*horresco referens*,—a reformer of the morals and politics of the people!', going on to ask:

> But what will the majority of his countrymen now think of this virtuous Essayist? Will they not regard him with all the horror and detestation which he deserves? Will they not, when they hear even his name mentioned, shudder at the sound, and pray to Heaven that their children may die ignorant of his existence? ... He will pass away from the earth, leaving only a scorned name, and a long catalogue of well-remembered evil-doings ... [53]

Scenting blood, other reviewers went in for the kill. The *Literary Register* attacked 'this precious record of vulgarity and nastiness ... in all the nakedness of his conceit, selfishness, slavering sensuality, filthy profligacy, and howling idiotcy';[54] the *Literary Gazette* ridiculed Hazlitt for being '*worreted* about a light lodging-house wanton, who permitted the fool to take every indecent liberty with her, and humbugged him preciously',[55] while *Blackwood's* claimed that *Liber Amoris* 'HAS EXPOSED AND RUINED THE COCKNEY SCHOOL'.[56] The worst onslaught appeared in the *John Bull*, which managed to obtain a love letter Hazlitt sent Sarah from Renton Inn, publishing it in full. 'You are my little idol', Hazlitt had written, thinking of Napoleon's bust, 'Little did I think, thou glorious lovely girl, when I once gave it thee to kiss, what I was doing. Keep it, cherish it in thy breast, as I would cherish thee for ever, and bless thee with my latest breath.'[57] This would have been humiliating enough among friends, but Hazlitt had to endure its appearance in a national newspaper[58]—an ordeal to a man for whom, 'if he entered a coffee-house where he was known, to get his dinner, it was impossible (he thought) that the waiters could be doing anything else all the time he was there, but pointing him out to other guests, as "the gentleman who was so abused last month in 'Blackwood's Magazine.' " '[59] Hazlitt believed the culprit was John Wilson Croker, target of his first political commentary, and responded with a 'half-length' portrait of this 'Jack-pudding in wit, a pretender to sense, a tool of power'.[60] The actual author of his disgrace was probably Theodore Hook, editor of *John Bull*.[61]

There was no question of proceeding with the action against Cadell, as the furore made it impossible to persuade a judge Hazlitt still had a reputation worth defending. Accordingly, no journal rejoiced more in his disgrace than *Blackwood's*, which rubbed his nose in it for years, as in 'Noctes Ambrosianae

No. XII' by Wilson and Lockhart, in which 'Timothy Tickler' is made to say: 'Pygmalion is so brutified and besotted now, that he walks out into the public street, enters a bookseller's shop, mounts a stool, and represents Priapus in Ludgate Hill.'[62]

Yet *Liber Amoris* has always had its supporters. Mary Russell Mitford declared Hazlitt's to be 'a fine passion, and therefore affecting'.[63] Thomas De Quincey said it 'greatly raised him in my opinion, by shewing him to be capable of stronger and more agitating passions than I believed to be within the range of his nature'.[64] As the direct descendant of Rousseau's *La Nouvelle Héloïse*, which has in common its frank treatment of sexual relationships, *Liber Amoris* was culturally alien to the broad mass of reviewers.[65] Yet it was vilified not on that account but for ideological reasons: by discrediting its author, Tory journalists deprived liberalism of its most articulate spokesman.[66] There was soon no question of the low esteem in which he was universally held. Everyone took it for granted that he was a filthy, middle-aged, sex-obsessed fool who consorted with pimps, petty thieves, fight-fixers, and other members of the criminal underclass. Hazlitt-bashing was soon an established subgenre of literary journalism at which all were expected to try their hand. For such a sensitive man it must have been a terrible thing to be on the receiving end of it. At around this time 'Two half-friends of mine, who would not make a whole one between them, agreed the other day that the indiscriminate, incessant abuse of what I write was mere prejudice and party-spirit, and that what I do in periodicals and without a name does well, pays well, and is "cried out upon in the top of the compass." '[67] So it would be for the remainder of his life. It was a principal cause of his continuing impoverishment.

Hazlitt's friends and acquaintances were largely unsupportive. Joseph Parkes observed to William Hone: 'I see that semi-Lunatic Hazlitt has published his designs & John Bull commented upon it.'[68] Henry Crabb Robinson thought *Liber Amoris* 'disgusting', 'low and gross and tedious and every way offensive. It ought to exclude the author from all decent society.'[69] Eight years after Hazlitt's death, it was what Wordsworth had in mind when he commented that 'the wreck of his morals was the ruin of him'.[70] And in an age of political correctness, it continues to generate controversy. Tom Paulin describes it as an 'exploration of imaginative extremity which never in all its sequence of dead surprises achieves an authentic image or cadence even for a moment'.[71] Feminists invoke it as evidence of 'sexual harassment', leading them to propose Hazlitt's exclusion from the canon, a recent textbook relegating him to a few pages.[72] 'There is either a good deal of bigoted intolerance with a deplorable want of self-knowledge in all this; or at least an equal degree of cant and quackery.'[73]

His crime was honesty, and in that he was more ahead of his time than in any other respect. *Liber Amoris* continues to alienate readers by its candid depiction of human frailty, revealing its author in the least flattering light. Society wasn't ready for it, and still isn't. One day, *Liber Amoris* will be given its due as a classic of Romantic prose alongside other works that examine the psychology of obsession—*Frankenstein*, *The Picture of Dorian Gray*, *Heart of Darkness*, *Moby Dick*, and *Fitzcarraldo*.

In summer 1822, William Beckford decided to sell Fonthill Abbey, having run out of funds to maintain it. A cross between St Pancras Station and Salisbury Cathedral, the Abbey was constructed on the ridge of Hinkley Hill in Wiltshire. Its maintenance had become impossible. Thanks to woefully inadequate foundations, its 300-ft tower collapsed no less than four times, on one occasion destroying the kitchens immediately after Beckford's Christmas dinner. The eccentric writer was renowned for his extensive collection of paintings, books, and *objets de vertu*; his louche Gothic novel *Vathek*; and his relationship with William Courtenay, allegedly the most beautiful boy in England. Beckford was also the subject of constant press speculation (the Abbey was said to be full of dwarves; Beckford refused to handle coins unless they were washed).

Wishing to escape this, he agreed with Christie's they could sell Fonthill and its contents; it was opened to the public and a catalogue published. Crowds thronged the road from London, including Wellington, Lord Holland, and Sir Francis Burdett. Hazlitt went too, and described Fonthill as 'a desart of magnificence, a glittering waste of laborious idleness, a cathedral turned into a toy-shop, an immense Museum of all that is most curious and costly, and, at the same time, most worthless, in the productions of art and nature.'[74] He reviled Beckford's taste for novelty over originality, cabinet pieces over gallery pictures, high finish and minute detail over the grander conceptions to be found in works of artistic imagination.

But the sale of 1822 never happened. It was halted when Beckford unexpectedly sold the Abbey—lock, stock, and barrel—for £330 to a Mr Farquhar, East India Merchant. Farquhar promptly sacked Christie and decided to turn a profit by mounting a much larger sale through another auctioneer, Phillips. Having bulked out Beckford's collection with the gleanings of junk shops, fleamarkets, and remainder bookshops, Phillips now needed someone who could puff the event to as wide a readership as possible—a public relations man. With his press contacts, Hazlitt was the ideal candidate. It was a humiliating function to serve, but he needed the money: his fee would be fifty guineas,[75] which he calculated would get him to the end of the year. Living expenses would be low because he would be allowed to reside at Fonthill; otherwise he could stay at Winterslow, where the living was cheap, continuing to write Table Talks for the *New Monthly*, Picture-Gallery essays for the *London*, and book reviews for the *Literary Examiner*.[76]

Before leaving London he visited the Caledonian Chapel in Hatton Garden to hear a dynamic new preacher from Scotland—Edward Irving. Though recently appointed, Irving was already a celebrity, admission to his sermons being by ticket only. Everyone flocked to hear the charismatic, tall Scot with black hair and piercing dark eyes, including the Basil Montagus who welcomed him to their Bedford Square salon. Hazlitt described him in the fourth and final number of *The Liberal* on 30 July 1823 as 'the most accomplished barbarian, and the least offensive and most dashing clerical holder-forth we remember to have seen.'[77] He had 'the free swing, the *bolt upright* figure of an Indian savage, or a northern borderer dressed in canonicals. . . . He crosses Piccadilly, and clears Bond-street of its beaux!'[78] Though complimenting him as 'an able and attractive expounder of Holy Writ',[79] Hazlitt regarded his sermons as incompatible 'with sound reason or with history'.[80] All of which went down like a lead balloon *chez* Montagu. Hazlitt had attacked mutual friends in the past and the friendship had survived; now, the Montagus decided enough was enough. Perhaps the embarrassment of having in their midst the man responsible for *Liber Amoris* strengthened their resolve. He was cast into outer darkness beyond Bedford Square, no longer to be admitted to their *conversazioni*.[81]

Hazlitt remained in London long enough to see *Characteristics* through the press. This slim, 152-page volume is the neglected masterpiece of Hazlitt's career, if not the Romantic period as a whole, concentrating the wisdom of a lifetime into over 400 aphorisms. To that extent, it may be read as condensed autobiography, boasting analysis as intense as anything in his more discursive essays. Few things, for instance, are more resonant than his observations on women, which (though unfair) bespeak a disillusionment understandable in the light of recent events: 'A coxcomb is generally a favorite with women'; 'Personal pretensions alone ensure female regard'; 'Women never reason, and therefore they are (comparatively) seldom wrong'; 'Women have as little imagination as they have reason. They are pure egotists.'[82] The book throngs with commentary on friends, past and present: 'I am always afraid of a fool. One cannot be sure that he is not a knave as well'; 'The true barbarian is he who thinks everything barbarous but his own tastes and prejudices.'[83] Typically, Hazlitt reflects not just on himself but on his art: 'It is not easy to write essays like Montaigne, nor Maxims in the manner of the Duke de la Rochefoucault.'[84] He was too modest; so completely did he master the knack of writing in this condensed form that even after *Characteristics* appeared he was unable to desist, continuing to maxim-ize under such titles as 'Common Places' and 'Trifles Light as Air'. His *Aphorisms on Man* appeared posthumously in the *Monthly Magazine*.

Characteristics was the last volume on which he collaborated with John M'Creery, the printer with whom he had produced Holcroft's *Memoirs* over a decade previously, and who had probably known him since Liverpool years. M'Creery remained a 'special Sunday resource . . . earmarked for pleasant early suppers'[85] and his kindly support was appreciated at this dark period. When *Characteristics* was published by Simpkin and Marshall on 5 July 1823, without its author's name on the title page, the 'prejudice and party-spirit' of his reviewers was exposed in short order. William Jerdan in the *Literary Gazette* declared the anonymous volume the work of 'a sensible and acute man, conversant with the world . . . a student in "the noblest study of mankind," and altogether a person of good moral feeling'.[86] Quite right too—but starkly at odds with the judgement Jerdan reached six weeks earlier, when he concluded his account of *Liber Amoris* by saying that 'a greater blockhead or sillier creature never wrote himself down an ass in the face of a despising and hissing public'.[87] It proved his judgements to be politically motivated, and Hazlitt commented that 'even Mr Jerdan recommends the volume of CHARACTERISTICS as an excellent little work, because it has no cabalistic name in the title-page'.[88] The error was quickly acknowledged, and a week later the *Literary Register* made up for it with the ludicrous theory that *Characteristics* was a commentary on *Liber Amoris*: 'it is really pitiable to see a man possessed of any thing like talent so utterly lost to every feeling of shame, as to be thus the bare-faced proclaimer of his own profligacy and disgrace.'[89] This was rubbish, but the best they could manage. No matter: Hazlitt's name was dirt, and *Characteristics* sold few copies.[90]

* * *

Dark woods waving over Pembroke's princely domain crown the heights to the left; a clear chrystal stream winds its pebbly or its sedgy course almost the whole way; and groves, hills, and valleys, glitter in the sun and showers. A neat little inn by the roadside, called the French Horn, with its painted bow-window and flaunting geraniums, reminds the passenger strongly of the old-fashioned prints in 'Walton's Angler.'

Hazlitt, 'Fonthill Abbey', *The Examiner*, 10 August 1823[91]

On arrival at Fonthill, he gave a handsome tip to Beckford's former footboy, Tom, who took him for a lord in disguise and treated him accordingly. There was virtually anything he would have done for Hazlitt, including steal the best fruit from the hothouses, harness white ponies to the phaeton so as to conduct him round the estate, or procure 'an inordinate quantity of cream for his breakfast and tea'.[92] It was a glimpse of life independent of the pen: this was, he declared, 'an Eden rescued from a desart'.[93] But it did not come without cost. To be charged with puffing the contents of Fonthill (effectively an enormous junk shop) was arduous for one whose tastes were formed on Titian and Raphael: at least, when he had visited the previous summer, Beckford's collection was intact; now it was diluted with oddments culled from the rag-and-bone shops of south London. His tactic would be to focus on the few items he liked—for instance when he commended Meiris's 'Lady with a Parrot': 'The parrot is above all praise and all price. He holds his head down, and you almost expect to hear him speak.'[94]

Hazlitt enjoyed Beckford's extensive library. Here, too, Phillips' men had been at work, but some interesting volumes remained, including a first edition of James I's *Daemonologie* and Walpole's *Life of Charles James Fox*, all the more interesting for Beckford's marginalia, including (in the latter case) his anecdotes of Fox.[95]

Hazlitt ventured into the crowded salerooms only to be nauseated by the self-styled art experts still to be encountered in such places today. He satirized them in 'The Science of a Connoisseur', a dialogue between an elderly 'connoisseur'[96] and unfortunate 'friend'. The old man 'wriggled up to the Metzu like a crab, sideways',[97] we are told, before expatiating on the virtues of the cabinet picture. No one bothers with Andrea del Sarto now, he says, 'for the spectator has been dazzled by the dear little Mieris's, Netschers, and G. Dows, those minions of the fancy, and darlings of the eye, till history becomes cold, barren, and repulsive.'[98] Hazlitt ridicules the language of preciosity as much as the opinions expressed—'a very mummy and petrifaction of criticism'.[99]

Chapter 20

'Why don't you marry some girl with a small independence & let the Fine Arts go to Hell—the best place for them?', he asked Bewick on 23 August.[100] As well as revealing something of his own mood, the question hints at the need for a wealthy spouse. News of his quest spread far and wide. Passing through Paris on her way to London, Mary Shelley heard that 'whereas formerly [Hazlitt] thought women silly, unamusing toys, & people with whose society he delighted to dispense—he was now only happy they were & given up to the admiration of their interesting foibles & amiable weaknesses. He is the humble servant of all marriageable young ladies.'[101]

It was at this moment he met Isabella Bridgwater, widow of the former Chief Justice of Grenada, Henry Bridgwater, who died of yellow fever in 1820, seven years into their marriage. She met Hazlitt on a stagecoach as he travelled to one of the picture galleries he was reviewing for the *London*—probably Hampton Court, close to where she was staying. Recognizing his name, she 'fell in love with him on account of his writings'.[102] His interest in her may have had something to do with her £300 annuity, inherited from her first husband. But there were difficulties. In August Hazlitt told an acquaintance she 'had relations— [the] kind of people who ask after character, & as mine smacks, sir, why it was broken off'.[103] The most obdurate was her brother, Alexander Mackenzie Shaw, a member of the 17th Light Dragoons, of whom Hazlitt remarked to Haydon: 'Officers, you know, are awkward fellows to deal with!'[104] Something of the strain between them is indicated in one of Hazlitt's aphorisms: 'An officer in a Scottish marching regiment has always a number of very edifying anecdotes to communicate: but unless you are of the same mess or the same clan, you are necessarily *sent to Coventry*.'[105] Nonetheless, Isabella proved more headstrong and persistent than either Hazlitt or her brother expected.

While in London, Hazlitt visited Patmore and his family in Fulham, where he received a pleasant surprise. When Haydon was imprisoned for debt, his possessions were sold, including Hazlitt's copies of Titian which Haydon had purchased several years earlier. Patmore bought them from Haydon's creditors and now had them on his wall. He valued them highly, and was moved by Hazlitt's reaction: 'he would stand and gaze on them with a look of deep sadness, not unmixed with pleasure, and almost with tears in his eyes—as one may imagine a fond parent gazing on the grave of his buried hopes'.[106] Patmore wanted to return them to him, but the matter was a delicate one as he did not wish to suggest they were unappreciated. One day, Hazlitt ventured to ask whether he 'would like to part with them', because—if he did—'I think I can get you a good sum for them.'[107] 'No', replied Patmore, 'but *you* may have them if you like.' He agreed to take a promissory note of ten pounds, which Hazlitt made good shortly after.[108] The paintings remained in Hazlitt's possession till the day he died.

He spent the autumn and early winter in Winterslow where he began two new projects. *The Spirit of the Age* is probably the greatest of his books—an analysis of the politicians, writers, wits, and thinkers of his time, most of whom he had either known or met. His second major project was a biography of Napoleon. This was a way of piecing together the fragments of the bust he destroyed at Southampton Buildings, and so resurrecting the ideals of his youth. It was, he believed, the most important work of his life albeit one that, from the outset, required extensive research. In the wake of the Emperor's death, a throng of memoirs, histories, and biographies had begun to pour out of presses on both sides of the Channel. He became panicky about it immediately, and contacted Rowland Hunter, one of his publishers, asking him to send research materials: 'I really suffer greatly in my mind by the delay that has occasioned this application.'[109]

A few weeks later he saw the October *London Magazine*. It contained two things of interest. The first was unsettling: a short article by Thomas De Quincey which borrowed without acknowledgement the arguments in Hazlitt's *Reply to Malthus* (1807), reprised in *Political Essays* (1819). Hazlitt was entitled to some irritation. After all, Malthus and his supporters had retaliated—and, he wrote in a letter to the *London*, 'as I have been a good deal abused for my scepticism on that subject, I do not feel quite disposed that any one else should run away with the credit of it.'[110] It is typical of his generosity of spirit that he took care not to accuse De Quincey of plagiarism, contenting himself by saying only that 'our ingenious and studious friend the *Opium-Eater* agrees with me'.[111] In the next number of the *London*, De Quincey published a graceless self-justification in which he wriggled and squirmed but was compelled to admit to what he termed a 'coincidence with Mr. Hazlitt'.[112] No one likes being found out, and De Quincey never forgave him what he thought a calculated humiliation (though it was nothing of the kind). The opium-guzzler eventually took revenge with the unflattering, lying 'portrait' he drew of Hazlitt in 1845.[113]

The second item of interest in that month's *London* was a source of comfort: Lamb's 'Letter of Elia to Robert Southey, Esquire', which reproached the Laureate for having lamented the lack in Lamb's writings of 'a saner religious feeling'.[114] Given his own mental history (not to mention that of his sister), Lamb had cause to take such comments personally and administered a rebuke in the course of which he praised Hazlitt, whom he had not seen for years:

> What hath soured [Hazlitt], and made him to suspect his friends of infidelity towards him, when there was no such matter, I know not. I stood well with him for fifteen years (the proudest of my life), and have ever spoke my full mind of him to some, to whom his panegyric must naturally be least tasteful. I never in thought swerved from him, I never betrayed him, I never slackened in my admiration of him, I was the same to him (neither better nor worse) though he could not see it, as in the days when he thought fit to trust me. . . . But, protesting against much that he has written, and some things which he chooses to do; judging him by his conversation which I enjoyed so long, and relished so deeply; or by his books, in those places where no clouding passion intervenes—I should belie my own conscience, if I said less, than that I think W.H. to be, in his natural and healthy state, one of the wisest and finest spirits breathing. So far from being ashamed of that intimacy, which was betwixt us, it is my boast that I was able for so many years to have preserved it entire; and I think I shall go to my grave without finding, or expecting to find, such another companion.[115]

This would have been an extraordinary tribute in normal circumstances, but its appearance at this moment made it exceptional. What was more, it enjoyed wide circulation, being reprinted in the *Morning Chronicle* of 4 October, and the *Examiner* on 5, 12, and 19 October.[116] By writing it, Robinson observed, Lamb 'exposed himself wilfully to obloquy'.[117] Lamb didn't care: he loved Hazlitt—and showed himself a true friend by standing alongside him at a time of need. Hazlitt communicated his gratitude through his ex-wife, still a regular visitor to the Lambs. 'I am pleased H. liked my letter to the Laureate',[118] Lamb replied. Hazlitt's official response came in 'On the Pleasure of Hating', in which he remarked: 'I think I must be friends with Lamb again, since he has written that magnanimous Letter to Southey, and told him a piece of his mind!'[119] He would do exactly that. In August 1823 the Lambs moved to Colebrooke Cottage, Islington—the first house they had to themselves—and Hazlitt visited them before the year's end.[120] This was one of the happier developments of Hazlitt's final years, for he and Lamb remained fast friends until his death.[121]

PART VI

Mr Hazlitt's Grand Tour

CHAPTER 21

If an author, baulked of the goddess of his idolatry,
marries an ignorant and narrow-minded person,
they have no language in common: if she is a
blue-stocking, *they do nothing but wrangle.*

Hazlitt, *Aphorisms on Man* liv[1]

Hazlitt put some coins in the driver's hand and got in the chaise. His new wife was smiling, and he smiled back.

'Where to, sir?', asked the coachman. Hazlitt looked quizzically at the man. Where to? The question took him by surprise, for he had given no thought as to where they might spend their honeymoon, only to finding the church at Coldstream in the Border country. Looking round, he saw two pointed hills in the distance.

'Where's that?', he asked.

'Melrose, sir.'

'Then take us there.'

It was a fortuitous choice. Melrose is one of the most beautiful spots in the Lowlands, the perfect place for Hazlitt and Isabella to spend the rest of the month. In such rural Scottish towns, well away from the main coaching routes, Londoners with long curling hair were something of a spectacle. Hazlitt astonished the good people of Melrose when first he walked down the main street, crowds gathering to stare at him 'like so many idiots'.[2] His reaction was typical. Instead of smiling good-naturedly, he stood in the middle of the road and shouted: 'What the devil do you see in me, you staring hawbucks? Cannot a stranger walk quietly through your town without exciting this vacant and impertinent curiosity? What is there for you to see? You gaping Scotch ninnies!'[3] Which made them stare even more, convinced he was mad.

Isabella had just married a middle-aged man whose finances and reputation lay in tatters. Why? Because this was a woman who since childhood had nursed unfulfilled artistic longings and who, having grown up in a remote part of the Scottish Highlands, had been married off to a lawyer who took her to Grenada in the West Indies, where his principal concerns lay with boundary disputes, blackguardism, and other parish-pump issues.[4] Compared with him, Hazlitt cut a glamorous figure, enough to make the thirteen years' age gap less significant than the sixteen that separated her and Henry Bridgwater. How could she resist a writer, the associate of Charles Lamb, Mary Shelley, and Benjamin Robert Haydon—to all of whom he introduced her? She restored to him a degree of sanity and self-esteem; as Haydon observed, 'his whole nature seems altered; he goes about the World with a gay Lothario expression.'[5] Hazlitt and Isabella were old enough to know these things would not last, but perhaps hoped their feelings for each other would deepen.

Money was always a problem—her possession of it and his lack of it. She was certainly not mean, but had seen profligacy enough to wish to conserve what she had. At some point she realized she had to make her husband an allowance (without which the situation would have been intolerable), but did not want to support his first wife and child. So throughout their marriage Hazlitt continued to write. As soon as they arrived in Melrose he corrected proofs of *Sketches of the Principal Picture-Galleries of England*, which Taylor and Hessey were to publish in May.[6] He also joined the local library from which he borrowed the Duc de Sully's *Memoirs*—further preparation for his biography of Napoleon.[7]

Towards the end of April, James Sheridan Knowles came down from Glasgow to join them for a few days. Knowles was revising his play, *Alfred the Great*, which he hoped would be as successful as *Virginius*, and asked Hazlitt for advice: 'You can do more for me than any man alive,' he told him.[8] They were soon joined by William Bewick, who was struck by Knowles's 'bright blue eyes and sunny smile, buoyant with health and exuberant spirits', as he returned from a day's fishing in the Tweed.

A week later, Bewick drew a chalk portrait of Hazlitt, now one of the best-known images of him, emphasizing the luxuriant curls of his hair. 'Is my hair really like that?' Hazlitt asked.

'It is exactly your own hair, my dear,' replied Isabella.

'It puts me in mind of some of Raphael's heads in the cartoons,' said Hazlitt. 'It is something to live for, to have such a head as *that*.'[9]

He must have realized, as soon as they reached Melrose, that Abbotsford, home of Sir Walter Scott, was a mere two miles to the west. Hazlitt loathed

Scott's politics but was generous enough to defend him from those who sniped at him on political grounds. 'Scott's large heart rises above party prejudices,' he told Bewick, 'and he is a fine, hale, hearty creature, full of genius and romance—who tells a story, a legend, a ballad, a plot inimitably. As a man, I am told, he is frank, free, and open-hearted, simple and natural in his manners, and ready to grant every one his meed of praise and justice. Such a fine character is rare in these selfish and oppressive times.'[10]

Bewick knew Scott, and wanted to see his famed abode. He visited Abbotsford alone and was shown round by the novelist, who insisted he stay the night. Over breakfast the next morning, the conversation turned to Hazlitt.

'Is it true he is at Melrose?' asked Scott.

'Yes', said Bewick.

Scott looked bemused. 'What is he doing there?'[11]

Bewick told him, and Scott responded: 'Mr Hazlitt is one of our most eloquent authors, and a man, as far as I can judge, of great natural and original genius. It is a great pity such powers are not concentrated upon some important work, valuable to his country, literature, and lasting to his fame.'[12] Scott was not aware that both he and Hazlitt were at work on biographies of Napoleon; nonetheless, his was a kindly assessment.

Hazlitt may never have known of Scott's remarks because, by the time Bewick returned to Melrose, he and Isabella had left for London. The Hazlitts took a house at Down Street, two minutes from Chapel Street West: Mayfair evidently suited them. Then, just over a week after their return, news of Byron's death reached London. The poet had been dispatched by over-enthusiastic leeching administered during a bout of tick fever, contracted while fighting in the Greek War of Independence; the doctors relieved him of no less than 2.5 litres of blood—43% of his total volume—enough to kill him with or without infection. Hazlitt was a keen reader of *Don Juan* which, as he said in *The Spirit of the Age*, 'has great power',[13] and his immediate response was to lament the passing of a writer who was also a friend of liberty:

> Greece, Italy, the world, have lost their poet-hero; and his death has spread a wider gloom, and been recorded with a deeper awe, than has waited on the obsequies of any of the many great who have died in our remembrance. Even detraction has been silent at his tomb; and the more generous of his enemies have fallen into the rank of his mourners. But he set like the sun in his glory; and his orb was greatest and brightest at the last; for his memory is now consecrated no less by freedom than genius.[14]

Byron was mourned as a popular hero partly because he was associated with the cause of revolution. The crowds that turned out to watch the cortege as it made its way from Westminster to Hucknall Torkard churchyard in Nottinghamshire were so overwrought that at one point they came close to rioting. It was one of the first displays of mass hysteria, made possible by the new print media and cult of celebrity. Standing among the mourners, the poet John Clare, on a visit to London, noted that the streets were lined with people from 'the commonest and the lowest orders', by comparison with whom the better-off, watching from windows, 'thought more of the spectacle than the poet'.[15] As the procession passed by, the girl next to Clare sighed, 'Poor Lord Byron.' He gazed at her: she 'was dark and beautiful, and I could almost feel in love with her for the sigh she had uttered for the poet'.[16]

Shortly after, on 5 July, Clare and Hazlitt met for the first time at one of the occasional dinners thrown by the *London Magazine* for its contributors, guest of honour at which was none other than Samuel Taylor Coleridge. The white-haired, 57-year-old, self-styled 'Sage of Highgate' had succeeded in making for himself the life he had always wanted. Dr and Mrs Gillman pandered to his every need as he held forth from his bed, to the extent of acting as amanuenses. He got precious little exercise and had put on much weight, as Carlyle noted when describing him a week or so earlier as 'a fat, flabby, incurvated personage, at once short, rotund, and relaxed, with a watery mouth, a snuffy nose, a pair of strange, brown, timid, yet earnest looking eyes, a high tapering brow, and a great bush of grey hair'. He added that he was 'full of religion and affection and poetry and animal magnetism'[17]—which gives some idea of the kind of evening Hazlitt and Clare were in for. Clare kept an eye on Hazlitt as Coleridge rattled away, thinking him 'a silent picture of severity . . . his eyes are always turned towards the ground except when one is turned up now and then with a sneer that cuts a bad pun.'[18] Years later, he captured Hazlitt's demeanour with a phrase of dazzling aptness—'his fox like eyes looking directly at nothing and yet seeing all'.[19] Hazlitt had long bidden farewell to his former mentor, and must have felt only sadness at the pitiful spectacle to which Coleridge was reduced. This was the man who, once upon a time, was set to change the world! Who could imagine him to pose the slightest threat to the order of things now?

Fortunately, there were happier distractions in London that summer. The National Gallery collection originated from the acquisition of 38 paintings formerly in the possession of the banker John Julius Angerstein. After Angerstein's death in 1823 the paintings were purchased by the House of Commons for

£6,000 and remained at his house, 100 Pall Mall, where from 10 May 1824 they went on show to the public. Hazlitt was well acquainted with the collection having described it in 1822 as the 'finest gallery, perhaps, in the world'.[20] Once, hearing someone describe it as 'a heap of trash', he exploded: 'You betray in this a want not of taste only, but of common sense, for this collection contains some of the finest specimens of the greatest masters, and *that* must be excellent in the productions of human art, beyond which human genius, in any age or country, has not been able to go.'[21] He loved Angerstein's collection so much he provided his own catalogue for it in his *Picture-Galleries of England,* the only instance in which he did so. He was thrilled with its acquisition for the nation and, from the moment it opened, was a regular visitor.[22] Here he could gaze at paintings that were to him old friends—including Raphael's portrait of Pope Julius II, Rembrandt's woman taken in adultery, and Hogarth's *Marriage a la Mode* (all of which remain at the National Gallery today).

Hazlitt persuaded Isabella they should go to the Continent where he could begin work in earnest on his biography of Napoleon; she agreed.[23] More fashionable than ever, the Continent would, over the next year or so, attract droves of tourists including John Cam Hobhouse, John Wilson Croker, Sir Francis Burdett, Jeremy Bentham, and the Duke of Wellington.[24] Someone else happened to be on her way there: Sarah Stoddart, who called on Down Street at the end of June.[25] If Isabella was taken by surprise, she kept her composure, for Sarah confessed herself 'much taken with her successor'.[26] Her aim was to collect money for their son's maintenance; Hazlitt gave her what he had, promising to send more.

Sarah left William Jr at Down Street, where Hazlitt and Isabella would look after him until it was time for him to go to his new school in Exeter. Isabella found her stepson difficult. He was thirteen—an awkward age—and his parents' divorce had not made him any less diffident. Worse still, it was hard for him to regard Isabella as anything other than The Enemy, such was his loyalty to his mother. Hazlitt did all he could to smooth things over but it was hard going. There was no escaping the relief on everyone's part when, finally, it was time for William to leave. Having seen him off in Holborn, Hazlitt visited Godwin and shed tears at the knowledge of the mess he had made of his son's life.

Now in his sixty-eighth year, Godwin was a broken man.[27] In April 1822 he and his family had been evicted from their home in Skinner Street to be saved from imprisonment only by the donations of friends, including Lamb. He was now struggling to repay his creditors—a fight he would lose, for he was declared bankrupt in 1825. In August 1824 Hazlitt became a frequent visitor to Godwin's lodgings above his bookshop at 195 Strand; Godwin wanted him to promote his forthcoming *History of the Commonwealth* in the *Edinburgh Review*.[28] Hazlitt hesitated, for he found Godwin a tedious historian. 'His style creeps', he told friends, 'and hitches in dates and authorities.'[29] However, he had written something else for the *Edinburgh* that would be of interest, and took care not to conceal it from him.

The July number of the *Edinburgh* carried Hazlitt's notice of *Posthumous Poems* by Percy Shelley (Godwin's late son-in-law), edited by Godwin's daughter Mary. Hazlitt had enjoyed himself at Shelley's expense in the past and was not prepared to temper his severities just because he was dead:

> Mr. Shelley's style is to poetry what astrology is to natural science—a passionate dream, a straining after impossibilities, a record of fond conjectures, a confused embodying of vague abstractions,—a fever of the soul, thirsting and craving after what it cannot have, indulging its love of power and novelty at the expense of truth and nature, associating ideas by contraries, and wasting great powers by their application to unattainable objects.[30]

That was only the start.

> He shook off, as an heroic and praiseworthy act, the trammels of sense, custom, and sympathy, and became the creature of his own will. He was 'all air', disdaining the bars and ties of mortal mould. He ransacked his brain for incongruities, and believed in whatever was incredible. Almost all is effort, almost all is extravagant, almost all is quaint, incomprehensible, and abortive, from aiming to be more than it is.[31]

To be fair, he added that Shelley, 'with all his faults, was a man of genius', 'an honest man' who 'practised what he preached—to his own sufficient cost'.[32] He went on also to commend 'Julian and Maddalo' for its 'thoughtful and romantic humanity'[33] but thought 'The Triumph of Life' 'filmy, enigmatical, discontinuous, unsubstantial'.[34]

When Hazlitt showed this to Godwin, Mary Shelley was also present, then visiting her father. There were no bylines in those days, so Hazlitt could have palmed it onto someone else, but it was typical of him to come clean. After all, Godwin had been a friend for nearly three decades, and Hazlitt had known Mary for most of her life. Recently returned to England, Mary can hardly have found Hazlitt's strictures pleasant, but she found it impossible to hold a grudge.

'I do not know whether he meant it to be favourable or not,' she told Marianne Hunt, 'I did not like it at all—but when I saw him I could not be angry—I was never so shocked in my life, [for he was] gau[nt] and thin, his hair scattered, his cheek bones projecting—but for his voice & smile I sh[oul]d not have known him—his smile brought tears into my eyes, it was like a sun-beam illuminating the most melancholy of ruins—lightning that assured you in a dark night of the identity of a friend's ruined & deserted abode.'[35] She had cause to notice the difference, not having seen Hazlitt since 1818. At all events, his visits both before and after publication of the review ensured the survival of the friendship.[36] He also showed Godwin his *Spirit of the Age* profile, so the aged philosopher would not be surprised when it appeared in print.

When Hazlitt took Isabella to meet the Lambs in Islington, a discussion ensued about the Shelley article—when, among other things, he was heard to say: 'Many are wiser and better for reading Shakspeare, but nobody was ever wiser or better for reading Shelley.'[37] His point was that Shelley's poetry was so divorced from reality that for all its good intentions it had no hope of improving the world. He also took Isabella to meet John Hunt and his wife, who were charmed by her: '*This* Mrs Hazlitt seems a very pleasant and ladylike person,' Hunt told his brother, still in Italy. 'She was the widow of a Barrister, and possesses an independence of nearly 300*l*. a-year.'[38]

In the last week of August Hazlitt and Isabella said their goodbyes to friends and acquaintances and began to make preparations for their year-long tour of the Continent. Hazlitt's recent publishing ventures having failed to produce much income, he approached Taylor and Hessey for an advance of £50 on articles promised for the *London Magazine*, but they declined.[39] He then visited his old friend John Black, editor of the *Morning Chronicle*, and proposed something different: he would file regular reports on his journey. Black was delighted by the idea and agreed. By this means, Hazlitt earned a modest income along the way. What was more, his reports could be collected as a book. Again, he tried to sell the idea to Taylor and Hessey but they declined, perhaps recalling the unsold copies of his *Lectures* in their warehouse.[40]

During his last days before departure, he made plans for one other volume which lack of time prevented him from completing. For the best part of a decade he had been working intermittently on an anthology, *Select British Poets*. Since 1817 he had worked closely with a printer, James Whiting of Lombard Street, in an attempt to ensure the poetry was correctly rendered, and before leaving for the Continent handed the entire thing over to Lamb, asking him to finish the proofs and put it to bed.[41] Shortly after Hazlitt's departure a problem arose: its selections from Wordsworth, Coleridge, Keats, Lamb, Byron, and Shelley were still in copyright and an injunction was threatened.[42]

At that point Thomas Tegg stepped in. A Dickensian character, Tegg was the closest thing in the booktrade to a rag-and-bone man. In his time, he had been a bookseller, an author, a publisher of street literature, and provincial book auctioneer. He also made a living out of remainders, picking unsold titles out of the warehouses and selling them on—he was, he boasted, 'the broom that swept the booksellers' warehouses'. 'I fear he proposes to publish books he can have without paying for,' observed Talfourd,[43] and Tegg probably picked up the entire run of Hazlitt's *Select British Poets* gratis. He sold it to William C. Hall, an American importer, who shipped it to New York where it went on sale on 4 October 1824. For this reason, it has always been unavailable in Britain but comparatively easy to find in America, where throughout the nineteenth century it was an invaluable resource for the general reader. Hazlitt's selection is both discriminating and representative; besides giving readers the best of Chaucer, Shakespeare, Spenser, Sidney, Drayton, Samuel, and Milton, he provided an astute selection of Romantic poetry including 'The Rime of the Ancient Mariner', 'Tintern Abbey', 'She Walks in Beauty', 'Hymn to Intellectual Beauty', 'Ode to the West Wind', 'The Eve of St Agnes', and 'Ode to a Nightingale'. Few people at the time were knowledgeable enough to select so many works now regarded as exemplary, and this proved one of the most successful publications of Hazlitt's career. The sad irony was that he made nothing from it, nor learnt of its fate for months to come.[44]

'As we entered Brighton in the evening, a Frenchman was playing and singing to a guitar.'[45] It was an auspicious beginning to their tour. Hazlitt and Isabella took rooms in a hotel, admired the Royal Pavilion (John Nash's redesigns were completed only two years earlier) and quizzed the sun-worshippers. The following morning they walked to the end of the new chain pier, completed December 1823, and boarded a cross-channel steamboat, the *Rapid*. 'Not a cloud, not a breath of air; a moon, and then star-light, till the dawn, with rosy fingers, ushered us into Dieppe.'[46]

After twenty years away, he now observed the French with affectionate curiosity. He was shaved at Dieppe by a barber 'who inserted a drop of citron juice in the lather I was to shave with, and converted it into a most agreeable perfume'.

Fig. 28. Brighton's chain pier was constructed in 1823 as a landing-stage for the steamboats that plied their way back and forth across the Channel, and was where Hazlitt and Isabella boarded the *Rapid*.

He was uneasy about this because it was 'a false refinement, to which I had not been accustomed, and to which I was averse.'[47] But the diligence that took them to Rouen the next day was a different matter: unlike the stagecoaches back home, 'it is roomy and airy, and remarkably easy in its motion.'[48]

In Paris they occupied a suite at the Hotel des Etrangers, rue Vivienne, a more luxurious establishment than he was used to. Staying there in 1796, Wolfe Tone called it an 'infernal extorting mansion...as dear as the devil'; it was no cheaper in 1824, as Hazlitt's first wife observed when she dropped by, anxious for more maintenance. Hazlitt, Sarah told their son, was 'splendidly situated...and gets his food cooked in the English way, which is a very great object to him; but, as may be supposed, it is terribly expensive.'[49] Isabella must have been rattled by Sarah's second visit, and probably expressed her disinclination to maintain Hazlitt's first family. If so, there were cross words between them. It was a problem that would not go away.

Hazlitt soothed Isabella by taking her to the Louvre, where most of his time had been spent in 1802—and where he returned often in his memory.

[357]

There was one chamber of the brain (at least) which I had only to unlock and be master of boundless wealth—a treasure-house of pure thoughts and cherished recollections. Tyranny could not master, barbarism slunk from it; vice could not pollute, folly could not gainsay it. I had but to touch a certain spring, and lo! on the walls the divine grace of Guido appeared free from blemish—there were the golden hues of Titian, and Raphael's speaking faces, the splendour of Rubens, the gorgeous gloom of Rembrandt, the airy elegance of Vandyke, and Claude's classic scenes lapped the sense in Elysium, and Poussin breathed the spirit of antiquity over them. There, in that fine old lumber-room of the imagination, were the Transfiguration, and the St Peter Martyr, with its majestic figures and its unrivalled landscape background. There also were the two St Jeromes, Domenichino's and Correggio's—there 'stood the statue that enchants the world'—there were the Apollo and the Antinous, the Laocoon, the Dying Gladiator, Diana and her Fawn, and all the glories of the antique world—

> There was old Proteus coming from the sea,
> And aged Triton blew his wreathed horn.[50]

So deeply were those images burnt into his memory, he 'had never been absent from them'.[51] He was lucky he arrived when he did, for a week later the Louvre closed after the death of Louis XVIII.

French culture fascinated him because it was so literary. He liked the way in which even an apple seller could be found 'sitting at a stall with her feet over a stove in the coldest weather, or defended from the sun by an umbrella, reading Racine or Voltaire'.[52] And he enjoyed scouring bookstalls that contained 'neatly-bound, cheap, and portable editions of all their standard authors'.[53] He even noticed a Café Byron—though not a Café Wordsworth.[54]

The idea of publishing here must have occurred before leaving London, for he had often passed the branch office of the Galignani brothers in the Strand. There was a flourishing market for English books in France, and the Galignanis were its principal suppliers: perhaps it was no accident that his hotel was a few doors from their Paris shop. Jean-Antoine Galignani, born 1757, with his sons Anthony and William (born 1796 and 1798, respectively) made a handsome living out of two publications—*Galignani's Messenger*, which reprinted articles from London newspapers, and a successful tourist book, *The New Paris Guide*. They also pirated British authors including Scott, Wordsworth, Coleridge, Byron, Shelley, and Keats.

Hazlitt met them to propose revised editions of *Table Talk* and *The Spirit of the Age* (not yet published in London). Terms were agreed and production commenced. Progress, however, was painfully slow. Apparently the Galignanis saw little prospect of either title doing much business, and were content for them to crawl through the press at a snail's pace. As a result, Hazlitt was compelled to delay his departure for Italy. He had originally intended to leave by mid-October, but was still there a month later when, in exasperation, he wrote: 'M'. Hazlitt would esteem it an extreme favour if M'. Galignani would hurry the work through the press in order that he may see it before he goes.'[55]

The autumn did not go to waste. He renewed contact with Dr William Edwards, a fellow-student at the Hackney College three decades earlier, now resident at rue du Helder, ten minutes' walk away. 'It is wonderful how friendship, that has long lain unused, accumulates like money at compound interest. We had to settle a long account, and to compare old times and new.'[56] They talked about literary society in Britain, and Hazlitt 'had some difficulty in making him understand the full lengths of the malice, the lying, the hypocrisy, the sleek adulation, the meanness, equivocation, and skulking concealment, of a *Quarterly Reviewer*, the reckless blackguardism of *Mr. Blackwood*, and the obtuse drivelling profligacy of the *John Bull*.'[57]

'What of the Revolutionary patriots of the 1790s,' Edwards asked him, 'those who were so hot, desperate, and noisy in the year 1794? Where are *they* now?'

'I cannot tell,' Hazlitt replied with a smile. 'Perhaps you might ask Mr Southey for an account of them.'[58]

Edwards and his French wife, Marie-Angélique, held literary gatherings every Wednesday, and there Hazlitt met Marie-Henri Beyle, known to us as Stendhal. Not yet the great novelist he would become (*Le Rouge et Le Noir* being six years hence), Stendhal was a prickly, eccentric man, exactly the sort of person to whom Hazlitt warmed. They had much in common: both were radical in politics, despised hypocrisy, and admired Napoleon. They also shared a love of the Waverley novels, *La Nouvelle Héloïse* and *Don Quixote* (which 'made me die laughing', Stendhal wrote[59]). Hazlitt's 'Sir Walter Scott, Racine and Shakespear' was inspired partly by their conversations.[60] Stendhal's tales of Napoleon, for whom he had worked in Moscow, would have fascinated Hazlitt. Years earlier, Stendhal told Byron tales of Napoleon's depression when pulling out of Russia; of Prince Major-General Berthier who, 'having pulled down his breeches for his occasions, could not button them again'; of dysentery among the soldiery—'45,000 men who were half a day at stool'; and of the Emperor of Austria's passion for sealing wax and his 'employ in painting eyes at the bottom of ladies' chamberpots, to which he gave a regard frippon'.[61] Most of this was rubbish, but they were entertaining stories, and Stendhal may have entertained Hazlitt with them too.

It was in matters of love that the two writers were most similar, for both were subject to the obsessive psychology that led Stendhal to fall for Elena Dembowski almost to the extent of committing suicide. Realizing this, Stendhal gave Hazlitt a copy of his most recent publication, *De L'Amour*, which sold a mere handful of copies. It analysed the process by which a man enslaved himself to a woman, also the subject of *Liber Amoris*: 'how Hazlitt's hair must have stood on end as he turned over those burning pages; how he must have marvelled at this French sympathiser who understood his predicament with Sarah so much better than his own countrymen; and how he must have concealed the volume from his new sedate wife.'[62]

Hazlitt was so impressed by *De L'Amour* that he quoted several pages from that 'charming little work'[63] in one of his Continental reports in the *Chronicle*, which by now were attracting comment. On 2 November Mary Russell Mitford exclaimed: 'How very amusing Hazlitt's letters are, with their good things and their bad things!'[64] A week later, Henry Leigh Hunt, John Hunt's son, now managing his father's business, wrote with the news that he wished to publish the book-length version of them.[65]

As winter closed in, Hazlitt and Isabella were impatient to continue to Italy. 'M\u02b3. Hazlitt presents his compliments to Mr. Galignani', the frustrated author wrote in December, '& wishes to state that his time here is limited. If the work does not proceed faster than it has hitherto done, he cannot possibly stay to superintend it.'[66] On 28 December he wrote again: 'I am exceedingly disappointed at the work not being ready as I was promised, but as it is, I cannot stay to see it through the press.'[67] It was the holiday period, and the Galignanis were content to slumber.

Not so in London where, on 11 January 1825, Henry Colburn published *The Spirit of the Age*—Hazlitt's masterpiece. Hazlitt once defined the 'spirit of the age' as 'the progress of intellectual refinement, warring with our natural infirmities'[68]—which gives the game away. As Hazlitt looked back over the course of his life, he saw great hope (in the form of revolution) followed by crushing failure (the downfall of Napoleon). And throughout the profiles of eminent personages that fill his book, he pursues the idea that human weakness had somehow outweighed the aspirations of youth: once 'tossed in the revolutionary tempest',[69] Godwin was now forgotten; Scott is 'the most popular writer of the age' but condemned for indifference to 'the future good of mankind';[70]

Byron criticized for hating the people and despising the court;[71] while the hero of abolition, William Wilberforce, is convicted of fighting only when it is 'safe and advantageous to himself!'[72] Hazlitt's most painful sentiments concern the Lake Poets: Southey's radical past is evoked ('he was an enthusiast, a fanatic, a leveller'[73]) in order to compare it with the 'by no means natural or becoming character of poet-laureat and courtier';[74] Wordsworth's poetry is praised as 'one of the innovations of the time' only for its author to be revealed as 'the God of his own idolatry!';[75] while for Coleridge, Hazlitt reserves one of his most heartfelt expressions of disappointment:

> Alas! 'Frailty, thy name is Genius!'—What is become of all this mighty heap of hope, of thought, of learning, and humanity? It has ended in swallowing doses of oblivion and in writing paragraphs in the *Courier*.—Such, and so little, is the mind of man![76]

Yet *The Spirit of the Age* stands as a monument to its time because, for all his disillusionment, Hazlitt still values the hope, thought, learning, and humanity which he persists in crediting to those about whom he writes, even those who have undermined him: Wordsworth possesses 'a peculiar sweetness in his smile',[77] Jeffrey has 'not been tempted by power',[78] Burdett is praised for 'his integrity and independence',[79] Southey for being 'correct, exemplary, generous, just'.[80] It is in such redeeming details, as much as in Hazlitt's catalogue of failure, that the importance of his book resides. For it is the most eloquent defence we have of the cultural movement now called Romanticism—characterized by the desire to create a better, fairer world. Hazlitt was the only man who could then have described it through an analysis of those by whom it was shaped, for he either knew personally those of whom he wrote, or had informants close to them. Moreover, he is uniquely un-partisan in his perspective. Unlike those who attacked him, he was capable of assessing his enemies without prejudice. He is judgmental, certainly, but always with reason, and a keen awareness of the social, political, or cultural context in which they lived—something requiring an almost godlike perspective which he was alone in possessing. That's why *The Spirit of the Age* is important—not just as cultural history, but as a reminder of where the modern age began. It explains why we are who we are, with portraits of individuals that have become archetypes of our own era—that of Byron, for instance, is of the first aristocrat to cause mass hysteria among the British people; that of Scott describes a man with the creative potential to change the world for the better, but who has decided merely to entertain; that of Gifford a man of letters who 'has all his life been a follower in the train of wealth and power'.[81] In such figures Hazlitt discerned the shape of the future, while composing the first, and probably still the best, introduction to the Romantic period.

On Friday 14 January the Hazlitts sped out of Paris on the diligence heading south, leaving the rest of Galignani's proofs unseen. It was nearly three weeks before they reached Florence, and in the meantime there were hard winter roads ahead. They booked tickets on the Lyonnais, the 'Swift-sure of Diligences' which was advertised in hyperbolic terms—'It was to arrive ten hours before any other Diligence; it was the most compact, the most elegant of modern vehicles'; it was 'a thing of life', 'a minion of the fancy'.[82] Unfortunately it was also badly run, and arrived four hours late with no one else on board. Two of the horses, they were told by the conducteur, had dropped dead on the road. Relays were raised along the way, with the conducteur bargaining furiously with innkeepers to save a few sous, the peasants quizzing them 'as a shabby concern'.

They arrived in Lyons at 11 pm on Tuesday 18 January 1825, exhausted after a miserable journey through the cold and wet. At the Hotel des Couriers they were given supper by a brown, dark-haired gypsy from the south of France, whose over-familiarity unnerved Isabella. It had nothing offensive in it, Hazlitt noted, 'any more than the good natured gambols and freedoms of a Newfound-land dog'.[83]

In the morning they went sightseeing and found Lyons a 'fine, dirty town'. The streets were high and narrow, 'like sinks of filth and gloom', while the shops 'are mere dungeons'.[84] Two days later they set out for Turin over Mount Cenis in a French stagecoach in which all six places were occupied, 'a very purgatory of heat, closeness, confinement, and bad smells. Nothing can surpass it but the section of a slave-ship, or the Black-hole of Calcutta.'[85] They travelled overnight and stopped for breakfast at Pont Beau-Voisin, frontier town of the King of Sardinia's dominions, where the border guards inspected their possessions. In those days it was possible to travel without a passport, although many of Hazlitt's contemporaries preferred to obtain travel documents before setting out, as possession of them put to rest fears of one's being a spy or troublemaker. Hazlitt probably didn't even apply for one, assuming he would either be refused or his movements traced by the authorities.[86] As a result, he and Isabella were routinely subject to questionings and searches when crossing borders. The guards had no problem with Isabella's trunk and waved it on, but when they opened Hazlitt's, they quickly became alarmed—for it contained books!

Books were the corrosive sublimate that eat out despotism and priestcraft—
the artillery that battered down castle and dungeon-walls—the ferrets that fer-
reted out abuses—the lynx-eyed guardians that tore off disguises—the scales that
weighed right and wrong—the thumping make-weight thrown into the balance
that made force and fraud, the sword and the cowl, kick the beam—the dread of
knaves, the scoff of fools—the balm and the consolation of the human mind—the
salt of the earth—the future rulers of the world![87]

The trunk contained such inflammatory items as Bacon's *Advancement of
Learning, Paradise Lost*, an *Edinburgh Review*, and several *Morning Chroni-
cles*, all of which were confiscated.

Finally they were waved on to be compensated by their first sight of the Alps,
the sun glinting on their summits. They peered into terrifying precipices and
saw rivers and streams pouring off the mountains. Here, thought Hazlitt, the
vanity of the egoist would be chilled and shrunken up; but anyone capable of
being raised up by the immensity of the natural world was in for a treat. 'It gives
one a vast idea of Buonaparte to think of him in these situations.'[88]

Italy was a revelation. For one thing, the climate was noticeably different—
more like spring than winter. 'It was as if I had to begin my life anew.'[89] Hazlitt
fell in love with Turin, describing it as 'a city of palaces' made all the more
wondrous by the chain of mountains behind it.[90] There they boarded a voiture
for Florence, where they arrived on Saturday 5 February 1825. This was the city
of Michelangelo, Galileo, Machiavelli, and Boccaccio. If that was not enough to
intrigue him, the Carnival was in progress and, as they got out of the carriage,
they were greeted by masked revellers. Upon checking into the Hotel of the Four
Nations, they were delighted to find they could order a pudding for dinner, not
to be had in France.[91] That was it. They were staying—at least for the next few
weeks.

CHAPTER 22

*It is well to be a citizen of the world, to fall in, as
nearly as we can, with the ways and feelings of others,
and make one's self at home wherever one comes.*

Hazlitt, 'Travelling Abroad'[1]

THEIR first visitor was Leigh Hunt, who had known for months that Hazlitt and his new wife were heading in his direction. He had come to Italy in June 1822 to help Shelley and Byron edit *The Liberal*—which, despite the calibre of its contributors, had attracted poisonous reviews and folded after four numbers. When Byron left for Greece in summer 1823, Hunt had come to Florence and was now resident at Maiano, a small village several miles to the north.

Hunt liked their 'little comfortable English-looking room', and was delighted with Isabella, with whom he flirted. 'I like her much,' he commented, 'She seems gentle & affectionate, & loves to hear him talk.'[2] Hunt's expatriate friends included Charles Brown, who toured Scotland with Keats and put him up at Wentworth Place in Hampstead. Brown retired while still in his twenties, having inherited £10,000 from his brother, and was now a 'convivial, corpulent, bearded, balding gentleman of property and leisure, an epicure, and something of a ladies' man'.[3] He was also a venal, self-important blackguard, as is evident from his private life. He married Abigail O'Donoghue, his housekeeper ('our irish servant', as Keats called her), in a ceremony of questionable legality in August 1819. A son, Carlino, was born in July 1820, whom his mother secretly baptized a Catholic; on discovering this, Brown took Carlino from his mother and emigrated to Italy, where he befriended Byron, Hunt, Edward Trelawny, and Joseph Severn. He never liked Hazlitt, later telling 'anecdotes of Hazlitt's personal cowardice, as well as of his slovenliness', adding 'he was the worst-tempered man he ever knew.'[4] Most of this was lies; moreover, he thought *Liber Amoris* 'a pitiable work. Talk of love indeed, why it was nothing more than a bad (I won't say venereal) disease; and the Girl, one would imagine, would have been smoked in five minutes by such a man as Hazlitt, for the first five pages of his account of her made me smoke her—tongue, hams, and all.'[5]

One of the first things Hunt discussed with Hazlitt was an ongoing dispute with his brother. He had ceased to edit *The Examiner* when he moved to Italy, and now John was passing his publishing house onto his son, Henry. A bitter dispute between the Hunts ensued, and by now they were communicating only through Brown, whose mediation proved disastrous. Although Brown made a genuine attempt to sort things out, he could not help taking Leigh's side, and soon found an intractable situation becoming more so. Soon after Hazlitt's arrival Brown summoned him to his house, explained the affair in laborious detail, and reported to John Hunt that Hazlitt's judgement 'perfectly coincides with mine'.[6]

Another lie. Hazlitt would never have taken sides against John Hunt, who was one of his closest friends. Hunt gave him shelter and support when the world condemned him; looked after William Jr during the Sarah Walker affair; and was a man of principle, having been twice imprisoned in Coldbath Fields prison and then paying a fine of £100 for having published Byron's *The Vision of Judgement* in *The Liberal*. It was John who kept the Hunts' business afloat, as he told Leigh the previous year: 'At the moment I write, I am obliged to be soliciting loans to enable me to go on with credit; and you may gather from one fact the situation in which I am placed—that, solitary as my nature is, I have been obliged to admit a widower and his three children to board and lodge in my house.'[7] Lacking any sense of the complexities of the matter, Brown bungled it so comprehensively that the Hunts were not reconciled until 1840.

He offered to introduce Hazlitt to another man of letters, Walter Savage Landor, resident in Florence since 1821 when he began his *Imaginary Conversations*, a series of invented dialogues between eminent figures living and dead (Henry VIII and Anne Boleyn, Washington and Franklin, Milton and Marvell). Reviewing it the previous year, Hazlitt had been even-handed: 'It displays considerable originality, learning, acuteness, terseness of style, and force of invective—but it is spoiled and rendered abortive throughout by an utter want of temper, of self-knowledge, and decorum.'[8] Though his comments have been thought unfavourable,[9] Hazlitt went out of his way to commend Landor's 'strength of thought, and vigour and variety of style ... He is excellent, whenever excellence is compatible with singularity.'[10] And he was right. *Imaginary*

Conversations was as weird a piece of writing as anyone could have produced, and its author an eccentric with such a loathing of uninvited guests that no one called on him unannounced.

Hazlitt saw that were he to accept Brown's offer of an introduction, Landor would suspect him to be hiding under Brown's skirts. Instead, he chose a bright spring day, walked four miles to Landor's home, the Palazzo Medici in Fiesole, and knocked boldly on the door. Opening it, Landor found a man with brown curly hair, wearing a dress-coat and nankeen trousers halfway up his legs, which left his stockings visible over his shoes[11]—an odd get-up, even for an Englishman. He was intrigued.

'S-sir', Hazlitt stammered. 'L-let me apologise, sir . . .'

'Apologise?', said Landor.

'Indeed sir. I apologise, both for my unheralded arrival and—er—my . . . my . . .'

'Yes?'

'Review!'

'Your *review*, sir?'

'Yes sir!'

Hazlitt began awkwardly to apologise for his review of *Imaginary Conversations*, confessing he had indeed said Landor wrote 'for knaves and fools'.[12]

'Knaves and fools, sir?'

'Knaves and fools; indeed, sir. That's exactly what I said, sir.'

Far from being irritated, Landor was amused and the foundation laid for a congenial friendship. This was remarkable because Landor was as difficult, spiky, and fiercely intelligent as anyone Hazlitt had ever encountered—'an enthusiastic friend; and as far as sound, violence, and unmeasured denunciation went, a bitter hater. . . . He had a warm feeling for all men of literature, and would have nurtured genius in whatever obscure nook he found it lurking. Self-satisfied under all circumstances, he was without personal ambition or the desire of aggrandisement.'[13] Hazlitt and Landor did not always see eye to eye (particularly on the subject of Napoleon) but they enjoyed some energetic discussions and quickly took to each other.

Three years Hazlitt's senior, Landor had been an undergraduate at Oxford until being rusticated for firing a shotgun at another student from the window of his rooms. Like Hazlitt, he ventured into France during the Peace of Amiens in 1802, when he saw Napoleon at close quarters. He too had known Southey, but unlike Hazlitt remained on friendly terms with him, despite their political differences. It was typical of Landor that he should have fought alongside the Spanish freedom-fighters against the French in 1808, rounding up his own private army: like Byron he did not merely speak the language of freedom, he backed it up with action. For most of his literary career, Landor had published plays and poems (some in Latin), none of which had been successful, until 1824 when Taylor and Hessey had agreed to publish *Imaginary Conversations.* Five publishers had already turned it down, and only after the intervention of a mutual friend had John Taylor been persuaded to take it. Its runaway success came as a pleasant surprise to all concerned.

On that first visit Landor asked whether Hazlitt knew Wordsworth. 'I have a strong desire to meet the man,' he explained.

'Well, sir, you never saw him then?' said Hazlitt. 'You have seen a horse, I suppose?'

Landor raised his eyebrows. 'Of course, sir.'

'Well, sir, if you have seen a horse, sir—I mean his head, sir—you have seen Wordsworth.'[14] When, years later, Landor did meet Wordsworth he could not help reflecting that 'There was *equinity* in the lower part of his face: in the upper was much of the contemplative, and no little of the calculating.'[15]

Before long, Hazlitt was able to say things no one else could have got away with. 'Mr Landor, I like you, sir,' he would say, 'I like you very much, sir—you're an honest man, sir; but I don't approve, sir, of a great deal that you have written, sir. You must reform some of your opinions, sir!'[16] Landor thought this hilarious. They became so close that Hazlitt even told him of the circumstances of his 'discovery' in the Edinburgh brothel that precipitated his divorce, embellishing the tale in a way that did himself no credit: 'Well, sir, down I lay, and the folding-doors opened, and in walked Mrs Hazlitt accompanied by two gentlemen. She turned to them, and said: "Gentlemen, do you know who that person is in that bed along with that woman?" "Yes, madam," they politely replied, "'tis Mr. William Hazlitt." On which, sir, she made a curtsey, and they went out of the room, and left me and my companion *in statu quo.* She and her witnesses then accused me of adultery, sir, and obtained a divorce against me, which, by gad, sir, was a benefit to both!'[17] This kind of remark has sometimes been cited to Hazlitt's detriment, but that would be a misjudgement. Such trenchant self-criticism provided a means of coming to terms with what must now have seemed a futile, expensive, sordid, and embarrassing episode.

In short, Hazlitt 'was made much of by the royal animal'[18]—so much that Landor drafted a note in his honour, instructing Taylor and Hessey to insert it into the second edition of *Imaginary Conversations*. In passing, Landor revealed to Hazlitt the terms on which Taylor and Hessey had first published it—that he share with them the profit or loss. Hazlitt realized Landor had been exploited and told him so, saying it was usual that, were the author to share profits, the publisher took *all* the risk. Moreover, as Landor further revealed, Taylor and Hessey paid him only eighty pounds for the first edition (now sold out) and had so far failed to render the final account.

What then occurred reveals Landor's combination of wilfulness and pride. He wrote a letter prohibiting Taylor and Hessey from publishing the second edition and instructed his cousin Walter Landor of Rugely to demand immediate settlement from them. This arrived at Taylor and Hessey's offices in the Strand at the same time as the note in praise of Hazlitt; it did not take a genius to see the connection. Taylor blamed the entire thing on Hazlitt, believing he had poisoned Landor against them because of their refusal to give him an advance prior to his departure for the Continent, and said so to Hessey. Landor's high opinion of Hazlitt was mistaken, he claimed, adding that when 'Hazlitt treats him as he has done others, the Re-action will be terrible, for Hazlitt will betray him unless he is deterred by a consciousness of Landor's vast superiority of Genius.'[19] This was sour grapes. The terms they had offered Landor *were* unfair; Taylor and Hessey *were* dilatory in settling Landor's account, and knew they were in the wrong. Not for the first time, Hazlitt became a scapegoat: he had done no more than dispense the kind of advice any disinterested party would have volunteered. Landor's account with Taylor and Hessey was promptly settled and the second edition transferred to Colburn (at Hazlitt's suggestion).[20]

Leigh Hunt now saw Hazlitt regularly for the first time since publication of 'On Paradox and Common-Place' over five years earlier, in which Hazlitt was responsible for ruderies about Shelley, including the claim he was a philosophical fanatic with maggots in his brain. Since then, Hazlitt had pelted Shelley with rotten eggs in his review of the *Posthumous Poems*, while Hunt responded in the *Literary Examiner* by saying that Hazlitt 'lost' some of the books he had lent him, concluding that, 'in spite of his offences against me and mine (not to be done away by his good word at intervals) I pardon the irritable patriot and metaphysician, who would give his last penny to an acquaintance, and his last pulse to the good of mankind.'[21] In that spirit of unresolved pique he invited the Hazlitts to Maiano for dinner. The countryside around Hunt's farmhouse home was ravishing and, on arrival, Hazlitt told Hunt 'that it was a sight to enrich the eyes.'[22]

Chapter 22

Hunt turned to Isabella and said: 'I have something to show Hazlitt, but will not let him see it till after dinner, as it might spoil his appetite.'

'Oh!' said Isabella. 'It will do him good. Show him now.'

That was encouragement enough. Hunt placed a sheaf of papers in her husband's hands—an unpublished essay on Hazlitt's follies and foibles. Isabella watched with mounting apprehension as her husband read in silence. On reaching the end, Hazlitt looked at its author and remarked: 'By God, sir—there's a good deal of truth in it!'[23]

With that, they were reconciled, and after dinner Hunt showed the Hazlitts his hair collection. In an era without photography, the cutting of hair was the most effective way of memorializing others—more authentic, somehow, than the painting of a portrait. He began by showing them a lock of Milton's taken while an undergraduate at Cambridge, 'remarkable for its excessive and preternatural fineness', which corroborated Milton's claim to be 'Lady of the College'.[24] He hoped to impress Hazlitt with a lock of Napoleon's hair, which had come via the Emperor's barber. Hazlitt held it reverently, turned it in his palm, and said: 'I cannot get up a sensation about it. Memorials of this kind do not touch me, perhaps from a defect of imagination.'[25] Hunt was disappointed, but Hazlitt's eye was caught by another specimen, glinting in the light of the dying sun. 'Whose is this?', he asked.

'Lucretia Borgia's', Hunt answered. It was given him by Byron. Hazlitt was spellbound, and described it in one of his dispatches to the *Morning Chronicle*—'calm, golden, beautiful, a smiling trophy from the grave!'[26] Hunt could not resist the temptation of asking Hazlitt for a lock of his own—'a good thick ring, smooth and glossy, and almost black'.[27]

Though Hunt had been resident in Maiano for over 18 months he had not encountered Landor, despite his proximity to Fiesole. So Hazlitt introduced them.[28] Hunt took as readily to him as Hazlitt had done, finding him 'lively and unaffected, as full of scholarship or otherwise as you may desire, and dashed now and then with a little superfluous will and vehemence, when he speaks of his likings and dislikes'.[29] Hunt in turn introduced Hazlitt to Henry Augustus Dillon-Lee, 13th Viscount Dillon, owner of Ditchley Park in Oxfordshire and author of two pamphlets on Catholic emancipation and a novel, *Sir Richard Maltravers*. But for 'some twist in his brain', Hazlitt thought, he 'would have been a clever man'. Dillon's technique was 'to pin you in a corner; and, when once there, you might as well attempt to get out of chancery. I went to dine with him—the only time I ever dined at a lord's table. He had all the talk to himself: he never waits for an answer.'[30] Among other things, Dillon discoursed on sex changes which happened, '*au sens contraire*, in our time'.[31] Knowing what eccentrics they both were, Hazlitt introduced Dillon to Landor, and his matchmaking proved fortuitous, for they got on well. Uncharacteristically, Dillon paid courteous attention to Landor, and sometimes gave advice, but so diplomatically as not to offend him; Landor thought 'Lord Dillon's smiling handsome fair face was like a ray of sunshine in Florence.'[32]

Though cool when they arrived, Florence soon warmed up, 'like April weather in England'.[33] By now, Hazlitt and Isabella knew the city and its inhabitants well. Hazlitt loved the main square, the Piazza della Signoria where, among other things, Michelangelo's David stood alongside Cellini's Perseus. The delight he took in this public space did not stop him being rude about it: Perseus, he wrote, 'smells of the goldsmith's and jeweller's shop', while 'The David is as if a large mass of solid marble fell upon one's head, to crush one's faith in great names. It looks like an awkward overgrown actor at one of our minor theatres, without his clothes: the head is too big for the body, and it has a helpless expression of distress.'[34] A copy of David is now in the square, while Perseus has been moved to the Loggia dei Lanzi gallery.

By the time he got to the Pitti Palace, Hazlitt was in his element: the Venus de Medici was 'a little too much like an exquisite marble doll'; the Apollo Belvidere was 'positively bad, a theatrical coxcomb, and ill-made'. On the other hand, Raphael's Fornarina (clad in little more than shadows, now at the Palazzo Barberini in Rome) was 'full to bursting, coarse, luxurious, hardened . . . a bouncing, buxom, sullen, saucy baker's daughter',[35] and Hazlitt was pleased to be reunited with Titian's Ippolito de Medici; gazing at it, he shed tears for the young artist who once copied it so scrupulously, to whom the world had offered so much.

By the third week of February, Hazlitt and Isabella were preparing to move to Rome, where they wanted to spend the next two months, but were waiting for proof-sheets of the Paris *Table Talk*. In the meantime, Brown wrote a letter of introduction to Joseph Severn, the painter who sailed with Keats on his last voyage, now resident in Rome. Brown revealed what a snake he was, unable to refrain from saying that 'an Edinburgh Reviewer is a formidable sort of person, and his pen is not one of the finest nibbed.'[36] The suggestion was that Hazlitt was their inferior. Social class was important to Brown, who 'spoke highly of Hazlitt's wife as a gentlewoman'.[37]

Fig. 29. Raphael's
La Fornarina,
painted between
1518 and 1520.
Hazlitt thought her
'full to bursting,
coarse, luxurious,
hardened . . . a
bouncing, buxom,
sullen, saucy baker's
daughter'.

On 11 March Hazlitt complained to Galignani that 'The proof-sheets have
never come' and, as an aside, asked: 'What is the Select Poets of Great Britain
I see advertised at the end of your last month's Magazine?'[38] The enterprizing
Thomas Tegg had just published in London a new version of *Select British Poets*
minus the copyright texts, which was thus no longer susceptible to prosecution.
It bore Hazlitt's name on its title page, reprinted his Preface, and its spine
bore the rubric 'Hazlitt's Select Poets of Great Britain'. The new volume did
respectable business, assisted by what was left of Hazlitt's literary reputation—
though (needless to add) Tegg paid him not a penny for it.

Hazlitt had not received an answer to his question when they finally set out for Rome. He left his books with Brown, probably to pay a debt,[39] and bade farewell to Landor and Leigh Hunt. The journey south took them through Sienna, which he thought 'more like a receptacle of the dead than the residence of the living',[40] and Aquapendente, which was 'old, dirty, and disagreeable'.[41] San Lorenzo, he remarked, 'looks like a town that has run away from the plague and itself, and stops suddenly on the brow of a hill to see if the Devil is following it'.[42]

They had been a week on the road when, on the morning of 18 March, they saw, rising from the plain, the dome of St Peter's. Continuing downhill, they crossed the Tiber and entered the northern gate of Rome, bringing them straight into Piazza del Popolo with its obelisk and twin churches. After a brief stay at Franks's Hotel, which Hazlitt didn't like, they moved to Salvator Rosa's former house at 33 via Gregoriana, 'which overlooks the town, and where you can feast the eye and indulge in sentiment, without being poisoned by bad air'.[43] The association with Rosa must have given him pleasure, though he may have heard about the house from Stendhal, who stayed there in 1823. (It was demolished in 1888 to make way for the Palazzo Stroganoff, now the Bibliotheca Herziana.[44]) Standing at the top of the Spanish Steps, just in front of Trinità dei Monti, number 33 was ideally placed to afford Hazlitt, as he lay in bed, a view of countless streets, palaces, and churches across the city. He must have wished never to rise. But rise he did.

His reports make sniffy remarks about Rome, as if he felt obliged to express dissatisfaction with it. But it is clear, reading between the lines, that the city worked its charm on him. For one thing, he and Isabella were ideally located for a walk down the long road that runs in a south-easterly direction from the top of the Spanish Steps towards the Esquiline hill—the via Sistina, which turns into via delle Quattro Fontane. His description reminds us that the city in his day was quieter than now, containing pockets of rural life.

> As we loitered on, our attention was caught by an open greensward to the left, with foot-paths, and a ruined wall and gardens on each side. A carriage stood in the road just by, and a gentleman and lady, with a little child, had got out of it to walk. A soldier and a girl were seen talking together further on, and a herd of cattle were feeding at their leisure on the yielding turf. The day was close and dry—not a breath stirred. All was calm and silent. . . . The daisy beneath our feet—the fruit-trees blossomed within the nodding arches.[45]

There are no daisies along it today, and the fruit-trees have long been felled. Instead, cars are jammed night and day along one of the busiest thoroughfares in central Rome.

They enjoyed the grander ruins, of which the Coliseum was 'the noblest': 'As you pass under it, it seems to raise itself above you, and mingle with the sky in its majestic simplicity, as if earth were a thing too gross for it; it stands almost unconscious of decay, and may still stand for ages.'[46] The domed Pantheon 'has the most perfect unity of effect', he thought, with 'a simplicity and grandeur like the vaulted cope of Heaven'.[47] And on Easter Sunday they visited St Peter's, crowded with pilgrims who had come to see the Pope give his benediction. 'The rich dresses of the country people, the strong features and orderly behaviour of all, gave this assemblage a decided superiority over any thing of the kind I had seen in England.'[48] Hazlitt watched the Pope washing the pilgrims' feet and thought him 'a harmless, infirm, fretful old man'.[49]

He visited as many picture galleries as he could, including Palazzos Rospigliosi, Doria, Borghese, and Corsini. His judgement on them, as on the city, was that they 'disappointed me quite'.[50] This was because he had been told Rome possessed a dozen galleries 'equal to the Louvre'—which it clearly did not;[51] all the same, some paintings would remain in his memory forever. At the Villa Farnesina in Trastevere he feasted upon the sight of Raphael's Galatea: 'If any thing could have raised my idea of Raphael higher,' he wrote, 'it would have been some of these frescoes.'[52] And he fell in love with the three Graces in the Loggia of Cupid and Psyche: 'The fine flowing outline of the limbs, the variety of attitudes, the unconscious grace, the charming unaffected glow of the expression, are inimitable.'[53] At Palazzo Rospigliosi he admired Guido's Andromeda which 'has all the charm and sweetness of his pencil, in its pearly tones, its graceful timid action, and its lovely expression of gentleness and terror.... Raphael's women are Saints; Titian's are courtesans; Correggio's an affected mixture of both.'[54]

In his view the Palazzo Borghese had only four pictures worth seeing: Domenichino's *Diana and her Nymphs*; Raphael's *Deposition* ('pregnant expression and careful drawing'); Raphael's portrait of Cesare Borgia ('splendid'); and Titian's *Sacred and Profane Love* ('full of sweetness and solemnity'[55]). He also liked the Laocoön in the Vatican, not least 'for the workmanship, for the muscular contortions of the father's figure, and the divine expression of the sentiment of pain and terror in the children'.[56]

Fig. 30. Raphael, *Christ's Deposition*; Domenichino, *Diana and Her Nymphs*; Titian, *Sacred and Profane Love*. Hazlitt had a low opinion of the Borghese gallery, but picked these pictures out as star attractions.

And he admired the Sistine Chapel, where Michelangelo's Adam reminded him of Theseus in the Elgin Marbles. The faces of those near the bottom of the Last Judgement, however, 'are hideous, vulgar caricatures of demons and cardinals, and the whole is a mass of extravagance and confusion'.[57]

By now, the Galignanis had published *Table Talk* and *The Spirit of the Age*. Copies were sent to Florence, and received by Charles Brown in Hazlitt's absence.[58] Hazlitt requested that the Paris *Spirit of the Age* be sent to Landor, who wrote to say how 'pleased' he was with it. 'Somebody ought to like it', Hazlitt responded, 'for I am sure there will be plenty to cry out against it.'[59] How right he was. A book so far ahead of its time was bound to generate hostility. To Henry Crabb Robinson it consisted of 'violent praise and very ill-natured sneers strangely jumbled together'.[60] Hobhouse, reacting to the essay on Byron, thought it 'miserable, ill-written, ignorant and affected'.[61] Charles Brown thought it 'atrocious'—'I have learnt to detest, to loathe his "Spirits of the Age"'.[62] Even Lamb advised friends 'to borrow it rather than buy it'.[63] Godwin was in a minority, thinking it 'written with admirable temper & fairness, except perhaps the article of Gifford'.[64] Perhaps its ambition was a source of embarrassment to Hazlitt's contemporaries; yet, it is that very quality that has established it as Hazlitt's greatest work.

Expatriate circles were less welcoming in Rome than Florence; prominent among them was Joseph Severn. Now in his mid-thirties, Severn remained in the city where he nursed Keats in his last days, pursuing his career as an artist. Hazlitt thought little of his artistic abilities, thinking Rome such an incestuous backwater that anyone settled there would 'become, like other *cockneys*, ignorant, conceited, and superficial'.[65]

One reason for their failure to hit it off was that Hazlitt's bohemian manners seemed undignified to the younger man. 'Did you ever play tricks on Hazlitt?', Brown later asked Severn, 'Did you make him kneel down in a procession, while you stood behind him laughing? Why was he refused admittance in the Sistine chapel? Was it not because he was shabbily dressed?'[66] Brown confessed he was guilty of laughing at Hazlitt behind his back— 'and that's no great crime', he declared.[67] Hazlitt took revenge in 'English Students at Rome', published three years later: 'there is nothing that may not be expected from an English student at Rome who has not become an idler, a *petit-maître*, and a busy-body!'[68] This was probably directed at Severn, whose talents led not to artistic greatness but to the British consulship.[69]

Severn told him about Keats's grave, and Hazlitt made the journey to the non-Catholic cemetery at Testaccio—then a secluded, pastoral spot on the southern edge of the city—where Shelley's ashes were also interred.[70] Seeing their last resting places, he could not help reflecting that he had known both men in their prime. What, he must have wondered, would succeeding generations make of their work, or his own? He was glad to return with Isabella to the bustle of the city.

By now, summer was fast approaching, when everything would shut down. They hurried back to Florence and called on Leigh Hunt at Maiano. Only now did they realize what a reluctant traveller Hunt was. Though resident in Italy for several years, he hadn't been to Rome, Venice, Bologna, or Naples. And despite having passed through Paris, he hadn't visited the Louvre. He was 'moulting' in Florence, Hazlitt later said, 'dull as a hen under a pent-house on a rainy day'.[71] They offered to take him to Venice at their expense, but he declined. 'I'll take you to Rimini,' Hazlitt offered, supposing the author of *The Story of Rimini* would be keen to see where his poem was set.

'No', replied Hunt, 'Rimini the town isn't *Rimini* the poem.'[72]

The Hazlitts proceeded on their way. Venice delighted them—'magical, dazzling, perplexing'.

> You enter its narrow, cheerful canals, and find that instead of their being scooped out of the earth, you are gliding amidst rows of palaces and under broad-arched bridges, piled on the sea-green wave.... You land, and visit quays, squares, market-places, theatres, churches, halls, palaces; ascend tall towers, and stroll through shady gardens, without being once reminded that you are not on *terra firma*.[73]

They continued north, passing the Borromee Isles, with which they were 'utterly disappointed',[74] the paintings in the Isola Bella turning out to be 'trash', and two days later began their ascent of the Simplon Pass—'The eagle screams overhead, and the chamois looks startled round.'[75] It was a perilous experience. The mountains were shrouded in fog and they encountered driving sleet on the precipices. It was with relief they descended into Switzerland and travelled on to Vevey. At Sion Hazlitt was reminded, by a trail of smoke, of Rousseau's visit to the iron foundry to look for employment. They stopped at the local inn so he could ask whether the philosopher had ever been there. The waiter did not know, but went to ask the manager, and came back with the answer: 'M.

Rousseau never lived here, but passed through about fourteen years ago on his way to Italy, when he had only time to stop to take tea!'[76]

It was raining when on 7 June they arrived at Vevey, where they remained for the next four months. They rented a cottage half a mile from the town in an idyllic spot surrounded by vineyards, backing onto an orchard with a stream that fed into Lake Geneva. Across the water they could see the rocks of Meillerie, where Julie confessed her love to St Preux in Rousseau's *La Nouvelle Héloïse*. Not only was it picturesque, but the living was cheap: mutton threepence a pound, trout to be caught in the lake for nothing, wine threepence a bottle. Hazlitt spent afternoons in the orchard and, when the heat began to wane, he and Isabella took a walk until the moon came up. It would be pleasant to suppose that the couple here took a holiday from the squabbles that seem to have punctuated their married life, inspired mainly by unequal finances. Certainly, Hazlitt found a measure of peace here that he would experience only at Winterslow. One afternoon in the orchard, he described himself

> sitting in the open air in a beautiful valley near Vevey: Clarens is on my left, the Dent de Jamant is behind me, the rocks of Meillerie opposite: under my feet is a green bank, enamelled with white and purple flowers, in which a dew-drop here and there still glitters with pearly light—
>
> And gaudy butterflies flutter around.
>
> Intent upon the scene and upon the thoughts that stir within me, I conjure up the cheerful passages of my life, and a crowd of happy images appear before me. No one would see it in my looks—my eyes grow dull and fixed, and I seem rooted to the spot, as all this phantasmagoria passes in review before me, glancing a reflex lustre on the face of the world and nature.[77]

Hazlitt seldom had much opportunity for leisure reading, but now indulged himself: 'I should like to devote a year's entire leisure to a course of the English Novelists; and perhaps clap on that old sly knave, Sir Walter, to the end of the list',[78] he had written a few years previously. He borrowed from the local library the Galignani editions of *Ivanhoe*, *The Fortunes of Nigel*, and *The Heart of Mid-Lothian*, and settled down with them.[79] 'No one admires or delights in the Scotch Novels more than I do,'[80] he commented.

A few weeks later they were visited by a cousin of Shelley's, 'Captain' Thomas Medwin, author of the first of many bodice-rippers about the super-star of the Romantic period, *Conversations of Lord Byron*, which sold in huge quantities and was pirated by the Galignanis, who distributed it across Europe.

Besides being a best-selling author, Medwin was a social climber who had married a Swedish baroness whose fortune he was in the process of squandering. Supposing himself a man of letters, he sought Hazlitt out as soon as he heard he was in the area, hoping to turn their encounter into an article.

Their talk revolved around literary figures whom, from what he is claimed to have said, Hazlitt despised. According to Medwin, Hazlitt attacked Byron for being mean with money; Scott for being a bad writer; and Washington Irving simply for being successful, by which time he had reduced Medwin to such a state of distress he 'knew not what to say to calm him'.[81] All of which was untrue. It was Medwin who was aggrieved: John Cam Hobhouse had just denounced him as a liar for his memoir of Byron. It was he, not Hazlitt, who was upset, leading the older man to offer him solace: 'Write a pamphlet in response,' Hazlitt suggested. In a manuscript note, Medwin admitted that Hazlitt's advice 'took the sting out of the envenomed shafts of my remorseless enemy'.[82] It was typical of Hazlitt to have done this good turn, and bad luck that Medwin was the liar Hobhouse claimed him to be. Instead of admitting that his outpourings led Hazlitt to relate his own misfortunes (which was what happened), Medwin pretended his host was so embittered as to be unhinged. The interview was published in 1839, by which time Hazlitt was an easy mark, there being no one to set the record straight.

Hazlitt was keenly aware of the literary associations of the place in which he was settled. He always felt a close connection with Rousseau, who died in 1778, the year of his own birth, and cannot have failed to recall he once proposed to bring Sarah Walker here, 'to sail on sunny seas, to bask in Italian skies ... and to have repeated to her on the spot the story of Julia and St Preux'.[83] With Isabella, he explored the country in which Rousseau had set *La Nouvelle Héloïse*, visiting Clarens, where Julie was born, as well as those places where Rousseau sited the central events of his novel.

In the Alps they saw Mont Blanc, 'an image of immensity and eternity', and Hazlitt remembered Shelley's poem, which led him to indulge similar musings: 'You stand, as it were, in the presence of the Spirit of the Universe, before the majesty of Nature, with her chief elements about you; cloud and air, and rock, and stream, and mountain are brought into immediate contact with primeval Chaos and the great First Cause.'[84] They passed through the Vale of Chamouni and headed north to Geneva, 'where the living was luxurious, and the expence was comparatively trifling'.[85] Hazlitt paid tribute to his hero by visiting Rousseau's birthplace at 40 Grand Rue. There he came across the

Edinburgh Review for April, which contained an unpleasant surprise: Jeffrey's review of *The Spirit of the Age*.

Jeffrey was among those profiled in Hazlitt's volume and hadn't liked what he read. Perhaps he detected a note of satire in Hazlitt's calling him a 'sprightly Scotchman',[86] or felt it would be wrong on grounds of principle to deliver anything besides a negative judgement. He began by saying Hazlitt was a 'very clever man, who has read and thought a great deal—but observed both less extensively, and with far less accuracy', before rehearsing his old charge that 'a perpetual hunting after originality, and a determination to say every thing in a strange manner, lead him into paradox, error, and extravagance'.[87] Hazlitt took this hard—and not surprisingly. Opinions of him were so starkly polarized that anyone who criticized him in print was, in effect, siding with his enemies. He had expected better of Jeffrey, and could only put it down to the vehemence of *Blackwood's* recent attacks. He would write no more for the *Edinburgh Review* during Jeffrey's editorship, instead responding with a poem, 'The Damned Author's Address to his Reviewers',[88] published in Galignani's *London and Paris Observer* on 18 September, a sort of epitaph on their friendship. Its opening lines, rebutting Jeffrey's central charges, allude to the Scottish economist J. R. M'Cullough, whom he had encountered in Edinburgh in 1822:

> The rock I'm told on which I split
> Is bad economy of wit—
> An affectation to be thought
> That which I am and yet am not,
> Deep, brilliant, new, and all the rest:
> Help, help, thou great economist
> Of what thou ne'er thyself possest,
> Of financiers the ruthless Moloch,
> Dry, plodding, husky, stiff Macullough![89]

'Teach me, great Jeffrey, to be dull!', he concluded. He was right: it was an absurd presumption for rationalistic Scotsmen to 'correct' him. History gives him the last laugh, for it is not the essays of M'Cullough or Jeffrey that are today reprinted in paperback and read by lovers of good writing.

Hazlitt and Isabella headed home on 20 September. They travelled north to Germany and at Rastatt dined on what Hazlitt described as *chiffrons* but which, when he enquired, were said to be wood partridges, more highly esteemed than the field ones. 'So delicately do they distinguish in Germany!'[90] Mannheim was

Fig. 31. Rubens,
*Christ's Descent from
the Cross*, in the
Cathedral of Our
Lady, Antwerp.
Rubens installed the
painting in the
cathedral, where it
remains to this day.

splendid, the houses 'too fine to live in ... only made to be looked at'.[91] They sailed north on the Rhine, where they saw Coblentz and the grand fortress of Ehrenbreitstein towering over it. 'It was like a brilliant dream; nor did the mellow winding notes of the horn, calling to the warders of the drawbridges as we passed along, lessen the effect.'[92] No wonder they were struck by the flatness of Holland: 'All the way from Utrecht to Amsterdam, to the Hague, to Rotterdam, you might fancy yourself on Clapham Common.'[93] Amsterdam was 'a kind of paltry, rubbishy Venice', but they enjoyed the Hague, which 'is Hampton-Court turned into a large town'.[94]

Instead of sailing home from Rotterdam they took a more roundabout route through Ghent, Lille, and Antwerp—where they visited the Cathedral of Our

Lady to see Rubens's magnificent *Christ's Descent from the Cross*, which Hazlitt had seen in the Louvre over two decades before.

'It is the finest picture in the world,' the guide said to them. Hazlitt looked at him. The man clearly had no idea to whom he was talking. This was the kind of remark for which Hazlitt had been known to get into fights. Fearing the worst, Isabella placed a warning hand on his forearm and glared sternly.

'*One* of the finest,' Hazlitt said, after a pause.[95]

From Calais, they took the steamboat to Dover where they arrived on 16 October. After all they had seen, London looked to their eyes 'like a long, straggling, dirty country-town'.[96] They returned to Down Street and re-established contact with old friends. Much had changed in their absence. At the end of March (seven weeks after his fiftieth birthday) Charles Lamb was discharged on grounds of ill health from the office job he had held for the past 33 years. It was a joyous development, for he and his sister would live comfortably on his yearly pension of £450: 'I have left the damned India House for ever!', he told Henry Crabb Robinson.[97] For the first time in their lives the Lambs were financially secure and without responsibility. But retirement proved more demanding than expected. Lamb's initial euphoria was followed by illness during the summer—a 'nervous attack', he called it[98]—and in the early autumn Mary too had a relapse. They were receiving visitors again by the second week of October, and Hazlitt and Isabella visited them then.

On 10 November Haydon called at Down Street and stayed for hours, listening to tales about Leigh Hunt's reluctance to travel—'we roared with laughter, and made more noise with our laughing than all the coaches, waggons, and carts in Piccadilly.'[99] Haydon thought Hazlitt looked ill, but found him improved in other ways, not least his wife. 'She is a very well-behaved superior woman,' he told Mary Russell Mitford, 'and will make him a decent being in regard to washing his face and hands (etcetera). He was breakfasting to-day as a gentleman should, and seemed to be living "cleanly", as a gentleman ought. I like Hazlitt, in spite of all: everybody must.'[100] This was a rare word of praise from Haydon, whose money troubles had made him unstable and prone to outbursts against virtually everyone—not least Hazlitt, whom he thought so depraved he would not allow his wife anywhere near him or Isabella.[101]

Leigh Hunt returned to London on 14 October and soon called on Hazlitt. Among other things, they discussed the rift that now divided Leigh from his brother, thanks to Brown's mismanagement of their dispute. Isabella was a sympathetic listener, and she once more impressed Hunt by her kindness. He later told Hazlitt that 'I am more at ease with you in your own house, than any where else; & have felt so comfortable there both in Florence and Down Street, that I wish to please you by saying what I do, & think you should be pleased, because it is true.'[102] His brother had retired to Cheddon Fitzpaine near Taunton, weary of financial anxiety and government prosecution, transferring editorship of *The Examiner* to his son, Henry Leigh Hunt, who took as partner Keats's old friend Charles Cowden Clarke. These two younger men thought Hazlitt one of the greatest writers of the age and were eager to secure his next book: they soon agreed terms for *Notes of a Journey through France and Italy*, which would be published in June 1826.

Hazlitt could look back on a remarkable year. He had enjoyed a momentous tour of the Continent, had a major collection of essays in the pipeline, and was meditating his next big project in which Henry Leigh Hunt now expressed an interest: his life of Napoleon.

CHAPTER 23

Why is it that the French are so delighted with
themselves? They never quit Paris.

Hazlitt, 'Travelling Abroad'[1]

Godwin was in for an unpleasant surprise. One day in early May 1826 he read in the paper that Hazlitt's new collection, *The Plain Speaker*, contained 'anecdotes' about him. Irritated, he wrote to its publisher, Henry Colburn:

> In the larger announce of 'The Plain Speaker,' I find my name among others, as one of the persons of whom the author thinks proper to retail his anecdotes. No curiosity can be more natural, & few desires more venial, than the wish to know what sort of anecdotes respecting one's self any one of the lounging public may be amused with, that chuses it. . . . Would you then oblige me with the loan of the book? I will promise not to detain it more than a week.[2]

Godwin felt humiliated at being compelled to beg for a volume which, if his friendship with its author meant anything, he should have seen months earlier. Such niceties had been abandoned, and he probably guessed why. The answer was to be found in Hazlitt's essay 'On the Qualifications Necessary to Success in Life', part of which he copied out in his neatest hand.

> The well known author of the 'Enquiry concerning Political Justice' in conversation has not a word to throw at a dog; all the stores of his understanding or genius he reserves for his books, and he has need of them, otherwise there would be *hiatus in manuscriptis*. He says little, and that little were better left alone, being both dull and nonsensical; his talk is as flat as a pancake, there is no leaven in it, he has not dough enough to make a loaf and a cake; he has no idea of any thing till he is wound up, like a clock, not to speak, but to write, and then he seems like a person risen from sleep or from the dead.[3]

He knew Hazlitt well and knew what he was capable of. And there had certainly been times when Hazlitt had come close to upsetting him in the past. But this was too much. The impression given by Hazlitt was that he was a robotic airhead. Godwin was incensed. On 24 May he composed what he described as 'Notes on Hazlit':

> I have certainly been a capital colloquial debater—Ask Mackintosh. . . . My art of debate was, to be a good listener, & then to answer straight to what was alleged against me
>
> As to general conversation, I will merely say, that Hazlit has five or six times taken my stories from my lips, &, having marred a plain tale in the telling, has thought them worth putting in print
>
> How came Curran, Canning, Holcroft, & twenty more to take a fancy to me? From my powers of conversation
>
> How did I win the hearts of the cleverest women I knew? By the effect of my talk
>
> Many of the best passages of my books were talk at first—I gave spontaneous utterance to my thoughts, & as soon as I was alone, put down what I had said[4]

Hazlitt's offence was worse than Godwin realized: the essay had been in print for nearly six years, having appeared in the *London Magazine* for June 1820.[5] Since then, the two men had met on countless occasions, often at Godwin's home. Their friendship was more than three decades old, and the family connection went as far back as Godwin's Wisbeach childhood when Hazlitt's mother (then a girl) played with him on Saturday afternoons. As a seventy-year-old, he was protective of old friendships, but Hazlitt had ridiculed him in front of Colburn (who happened also to be his own publisher) and the 'lounging public'. It was one humiliation too many.

Why did Hazlitt do it? He had long believed that 'We do not like our friends the worse because they sometimes give us an opportunity to rail at them heartily. Their faults reconcile us to their virtues.'[6] It was a token of comradeship, he believed, to confront them with their failings: 'we never have much esteem or regard, except for those that we can afford to speak our minds of freely'.[7] But this makes more sense in an informal context, and hardly justifies the publication of such harsh judgements, especially in the case of an old friend like Godwin, who had a right to expect better. Hazlitt should have understood that—and perhaps would have done so in other circumstances. But these were extreme times. Despite the stability Isabella brought him, he felt himself to be on the fringes of society. So bemired was his name that no publisher printed it on his own books lest it damage sales, while everything he wrote became the occasion for further attack. He felt at every turn that he had nothing left to lose. When you are constantly set upon, he told Northcote, 'you naturally in self-defence take refuge in a sort of misanthropy and cynical contempt for mankind'. The best way of doing that was to give enemies 'some ground for their idle and malevolent censures'.[8] That self-destructive instinct took hold the day he humiliated Godwin in *The Plain Speaker*. It was a terrible miscalculation, and he would live to regret it—but only when it was too late. With so many mutual acquaintances, they found it impossible to avoid each other and, when they coincided, as at Northcote's house on 4 February 1829,[9] exchanged not a word.

Even so, Hazlitt's last collection of essays was a tour de force of intellectual brilliance which, together with the two volumes of *Table Talk*, stands as a monument to his creative genius. *The Plain Speaker* actually grew out of *Table Talk*. Many of its component essays originally appeared in periodicals under the 'Table Talk' rubric, and were at an early stage projected as component parts of volumes 3 and 4 of that work. (Indeed, a number of them appeared in the Paris edition of *Table Talk* (1825) prior to their British publication.[10]) Plain speaking was part of Hazlitt's heritage—not just as the son of an Irishman, but as the inheritor of a dissenting creed that placed a premium on honesty and forthrightness. The theme permeates the volume in such essays as 'On the Prose Style of Poets', 'On the Conversation of Authors', 'On Reason and Imagination', 'On Londoners and Country People', and 'Whether Genius is Conscious of its Powers?', to name a few. The archetypal plain speaker is Hazlitt himself, and the submerged theme of the book is the theory and practice of his craft, even down to his attitude towards the finished work: 'I never begin one of these *Essays* with a consciousness of having written a line before; and having got to the end of the volume, hope never to look into it again.'[11] He must have known, even as it was published, that *The Plain Speaker* was the summation of a remarkable career. Not that any of the reviewers acknowledged that—only sneers and insults greeted his work these days, killing sales and deminishing his literary reputation further: 'literary prostitution', lamented *The Atlas*; a 'wild and unsparing effusion of egotism', wailed the *Monthly Review*; a 'collection of trash', shrieked *The Star Chamber*.[12] There was no point in persisting. He would continue to publish books, but never again as an essayist.

Henry Leigh Hunt wanted to lure him back to *The Examiner* as drama critic, and made him 'Theatrical Examiner' on 7 May 1826. Hazlitt agreed on a one-off basis, and enjoyed himself with a paean to Caroline Brocard, a ballet dancer with whom he was in love, then stunning theatregoers with *La Naissance de Venus*. 'Even when she sits down or merely walks across the stage', he wrote, 'the stretching out of her hands, the motion of her neck, her dimpled smiles, seem a thrill of pleasure, or to be awakened by some heavenly harmony. . . . It is a dream of grace and beauty.' He concluded with a compliment: 'We should add, that we do not think that Venus should have dark hair, and that Mademoiselle——has very pretty eyes!'[13]

Hazlitt was working on proofs of *Notes of a Journey*, published 1 June. Hunt and Clarke objected to putting his name on the title page, but he pointed out that most of the book had already appeared in the *Morning Chronicle* and its author's identity was well known. Hunt and Clarke relented, but the title page was already printed so a printer's devil went through the entire run stamping Hazlitt's name on each copy. It made no difference: 'coarse and vulgar', said *La Belle Assemblee*; 'puerile', said the *Monthly Review*; while *The Atlas* accused him of 'John Bull prejudices'.[14]

He had been researching his life of Napoleon for some time, though not in a very serious way. Since at least the summer of 1825 he had known Walter Scott was at work on the same subject, but now the interest of Hunt and Clarke decided him: it was time to get the thing done. Why do it at all? To defend Napoleon against the misrepresentation expected from Scott. Napoleon was 'the child and champion of the Revolution', 'a thorn in the side of kings'. He had kept an entire people from 'being handed over, like a herd of cattle, to a particular family, and chained to the foot of a legitimate throne'.[15] 'I felt pride', Hazlitt said, 'to think that there was one reputation in modern times equal to the ancients, and at seeing one man greater than the throne he sat upon.'[16] For the next two years he concentrated on what he regarded as his greatest enterprise.

This was not the best moment for a project that would span four volumes. In 1825 a series of banking failures precipitated what we would call 'natural wastage' in the publishing industry, the most spectacular example being that of Hazlitt's friend Archibald Constable, whose bankruptcy brought down his business partners, including Scott. Overnight, Sir Walter turned from being one of the wealthiest authors in the kingdom to a pauper, liable for £86,000—a debt he laboured vainly to pay off until the end of his days.[17] William Hone was also caught in the downturn. His creditors were Hunt and Clarke, who had him arrested and detained at the King's Bench, where he remained with his family the next two and a half years. Even publishers unaffected by the crisis exercised caution.

Fig. 32. Rue de la Chausée-d'Antin in Paris, *c.*1860. Though taken three decades after Hazlitt's death, this photograph shows the road in which Hazlitt and Isabella lodged in 1826, much as it would have appeared to them.

As Napoleon's biographer, Hazlitt needed to consult reference sources available only in Paris, and decided to return there.[18] In July he and Isabella took a house on the fashionable rue de la Chausée-d'Antin. (Its pre-Revolutionary name had been restored in 1815, but Hazlitt insisted on calling it by the name it took during the Napoleonic Wars—rue Mont-Blanc.) It was central, had a spacious garden, and was ten minutes from the Galignanis in rue Vivienne. By now, Paris was the home of Balzac (born 1799) and Baudelaire (born 1821), and was fast becoming a haven for artists and writers, where Hazlitt's instinctive

[387]

bohemianism found greater acceptance than in London. The difference between British and French attitudes to the arts is indicated by Haydon's second imprisonment in the King's Bench for debt in June 1827. Although a public subscription won him liberty after a month, his detention caused him 'suffering & anxiety not to be described'.[19]

Money problems dogged Hazlitt too—not surprisingly, as he lived in one of the most expensive areas of Paris. The strain took its toll on his marriage: over the last year Isabella had ample opportunity to note her husband's improvidence, on which she did not hesitate to speak her mind. On 8 August Hazlitt told Patmore he was 'damnably off here for money', adding he got 'into nothing but rows & squabbles'.[20] Isabella was increasingly disillusioned with him. She realized that the creative genius she had married would always be dependent on her for financial help, and that his contribution to their living expenses would always be minuscule. It did not help that *The Plain Speaker* and *Notes of a Journey* were doing poor business, thanks partly to the recession. He proposed to Galignani an anthology of selections from sixteenth- and seventeenth-century plays.[21] This was not an original idea—Charles Lamb had edited *Specimens of English Dramatic Poets* as long before as 1808—and it smacked of desperation. Galignani was not tempted.

At this difficult moment Hazlitt composed what was to be a masterpiece, 'On the Feeling of Immortality in Youth'—the first of the sequence which, as Stanley Jones observes, forms 'a kind of prose elegy—the true prose-poems of English romanticism'.[22] Hazlitt knew that the increasing fragility of his stomach meant his remaining time would be shorter than he once hoped, his health having been undermined by drink, the stress of the *Blackwood's* case, the Sarah Walker affair, and, more recently, friction between him and Isabella. It led him to reflect on the nature of human life in a manner that recurs more frequently in his work from this point onwards. 'No young man believes he shall ever die,' he began, before one of the greatest descriptions in literature of what it is to grow old:

> While the spirit of youth remains unimpaired, ere the 'wine of life is drank up,' we are like people intoxicated or in a fever, who are hurried away by the violence of their own sensations: it is only as present objects begin to pall upon the sense, as we have been disappointed in our favourite pursuits, cut off from our closest ties, that passion loosens its hold upon the breast, that we by degrees become weaned from the world, and allow ourselves to contemplate, 'as in a glass, darkly,' the possibility of parting with it for good.[23]

As so often in his essays, he reflected also on his present situation, surrounded by objects that reminded him how far he had come:

> As I was writing out this passage, my miniature-picture when a child lay on the mantle-piece, and I took it out of the case to look at it. I could perceive few traces of myself in it; but there was the same placid brow, the dimpled mouth, the same timid, inquisitive glance as ever. But its careless smile did not seem to reproach me with having become a recreant to the sentiments that were then sown in my mind, or with having written a sentence that could call up a blush in this image of ingenuous youth![24]

Had he betrayed that early promise? Not in the least, for he had remained true to his principles—unlike some he could name—and it was symptomatic of his ability to live with himself that he could think about how to die.

> If we can slip out of this world without notice or mischance, can tamper with bodily infirmity, and frame our minds to the becoming composure of *still-life*, before we sink into total insensibility, it is as much as we ought to expect. We do not in the regular course of nature die all at once: we have mouldered away gradually long before; faculty after faculty, attachment after attachment, we are torn from ourselves piece-meal while living; year after year takes something from us; and death only consigns the last remnant of what we were to the grave. The revulsion is not so great, and a quiet *euthanasia* is a winding-up of the plot, that is not out of reason or nature.[25]

He must have known his time was limited, but there remained many demands from the living—not least Isabella, who ordered that he increase his contribution to their outgoings. He composed several more essays before asking Patmore to extract from Colburn an advance of £20 on 'Manuscript to that amount';[26] Patmore succeeded, and in return Hazlitt sent 'On the Want of Money', which describes the sundry humiliations of poverty: 'It is hard to be without money. To get on without it is like travelling in a foreign country without a passport—you are stopped, suspected, and made ridiculous at every turn, besides being subjected to the most serious inconveniences.'[27]

He also began a series of pieces for the *New Monthly* that would sustain him in future months.

> Called on Mr. N——; had, as usual, an interesting conversation.[28]

Landor's *Imaginary Conversations* made the dialogue a fashionable form, and Hazlitt included one between himself and Sir James Northcote in *The Plain*

Speaker ('On Envy'). Northcote was one of his oldest friends. They had known each other since at least 1802 when the Royal Academician, 32 years his senior, encouraged him to visit the Louvre. Now, during the summer of 1826, Hazlitt began work on 'Boswell Redivivus',[29] the implication being that he immortalized Northcote's bon mots in the same spirit as Dr Johnson's recording angel.

But Hazlitt made no pretence to accuracy; indeed, many of the witticisms attributed to Northcote were his own. He explained his method from the outset: 'I differ from my great original and predecessor (James Boswell, Esq. of Auchinleck) in this, that whereas he is supposed to have invented nothing, I have feigned whatever I pleased. I have forgotten, mistaken, mis-stated, altered, transposed a number of things. All that can be relied upon for certain is a striking anecdote or a sterling remark or two in each page.'[30] As a result, the conversations were full of interest—scurrilous, gossipy, occasionally rude, but always entertaining—more so than real life. Northcote was thrilled with them. 'It's beautiful!' he exclaimed when he first saw them, 'My God! It brought me to life.'[31]

The opening number set the tone for what followed. Northcote was quoted as saying that Fuseli thought 'Nothing was good enough for him that was not a repetition of himself.' He claimed to have told Fuseli about a 'very fine Vandyke', to which he replied: 'And what is it? A little bit of colour. I wouldn't go across the way to see it.'[32] In the second dialogue, Hazlitt described Northcote trying to paint himself, 'prying into the glass like a monkey, to see if the portrait was like. He had on a green velvet-cap, and looked very like Titian.'[33] (Did Northcote suspect mockery? Possibly not.) As for gossip, readers interested in the Johnson circle were not disappointed. The third dialogue described how, when *She Stoops to Conquer* was first staged, Goldsmith 'was so choked all dinner-time that he could not swallow a mouthful'.[34] In the sixth dialogue Northcote claimed that Sir Joshua Reynolds tolerated Burke only because he wanted him to write his biography: 'Indeed, Miss Reynolds used to complain that whenever any of Burke's poor Irish relations came over, they were all poured in upon them to dinner. . . . He thought no more of the person who actually did write it afterwards [Northcote] than he would have suspected his dog of writing it.'[35] Hazlitt combined this with debates on artistic reputation, historical versus portrait painting, and the nature of genius.

Given his magpie-like memory, it was only to be expected that 'Boswell Redivivus' included verbatim quotations. The first in the series was full of outrageous remarks about Byron ('a flat and *commonplace* person'[36]), mostly by 'G's daughter' (Mary Shelley) and someone called 'F——'. There were a number of clues to F's identity: he had little regard for Byron's powers as a conversationalist; 'had been a little spoiled by flattery when he was young', and when he first saw Byron in Italy did not recognize him because he had 'grown so fat, like a great chubby school-boy'.[37] Anyone with the least knowledge of literary London would have recognized Leigh Hunt, who promptly complained to the *New Monthly*'s editor, Thomas Campbell.

Long an enemy of Hazlitt, Campbell used this as an excuse for arguing for his permanent removal from the journal, having first written Hunt a letter lamenting 'this detestable passage in Hazlitt's paper' for which, he said, 'I am, as I deserve to be, visited with much regret.'[38] Campbell copied it to Colburn, who pooh-poohed him, sending him back to the printing house with a few patronizing words. What appeal 'Boswell Redivivus' had, it gained from its indiscretions: the series would continue. Campbell seethed. For its author, it was a crucial source of income; in early September 1826 Hazlitt wrote to his friend Thomas Allsop, asking him to squeeze another advance out of Colburn: 'Say I am very much pushed & shall be for some weeks.'[39]

During the summer, the Hazlitts were joined at rue de la Chaussée-d'Antin by William Jr.[40] It was an emotional reunion. Hazlitt had always wanted his son to 'make yourself master of French, because you may find it of use in the commerce of life',[41] and now could ensure he did. He would be the architect of William's education, just as his father had been of his—but at a price, for the decision to take care of him amounted to a declaration of 'no confidence' in his marriage. He was well aware that Isabella found William hard work, and that William regarded her as an usurper. He was aware too that Isabella had spoken repeatedly of the fear that she would end up taking care of his family—which, with William's introduction into the household, was fully realized. Perhaps he deluded himself into believing he could smooth the waters, enabling them to live harmoniously together; if so, he was a fool. William remained with his father and stepmother for most of the next year. How they got through it we can only imagine, but there must often have been raised voices and frayed tempers. From this point onwards, the breakdown of Hazlitt's marriage became a matter of time.

The advanced state of Scott's nine-volume biography of Napoleon placed additional pressure on him. Scott now abandoned the good opinion he once held of his colleague, remarking to his lawyer: 'I understand Hazlitt is trying to cut in before with a life of Boney on which subject I shall only say He be damned.'[42] Hazlitt expressed no such animus, even when Scott visited Paris for three weeks at the end of October. They coincided at Galignani's reading room on 30 October, but did not speak. Scott walked in without ceremony, sat down, and started to read. No one had any idea that the best-selling novelist of the day was in the building—except Hazlitt, for whom Scott's 'red face and scarlet waistcoat' was reminiscent of Cobbett's 'florid face and scarlet gown': 'The one is like an English farmer, the other like a Scotch *laird*. Both are large, robust men, with great strength and composure of features.'[43] A week later, Scott was presented to the French King, Charles X, but Hazlitt did not begrudge him that, so impressed was he by his unassuming demeanour: 'If we were to describe the secret of this author's success in three words, we should say that it consists in the *absence of egotism*.'[44]

Hazlitt again sought out Dr Edwards, his old friend from Hackney, with whom he visited the fruit and flower market, and who took him to a levee thrown by the Duchesse de Noaille, who received her guests 'in her bed-room, sitting at a card-table near her bed, a four-post one with a good deal of gilding about it'. The adjoining apartments were crowded with hangers-on, playing cards. Hazlitt liked the casualness of it, for there was 'none of the stiffness of an English ceremony of the same class'. He was introduced to the Duchess, and remained until he was tired.[45] Through Edwards, he again met Stendhal, whose two-part analysis of Romanticism, *Racine et Shakespeare* (1823, 1825), defined the spirit of the age in a characteristically provocative manner:

> Le *romanticisme* est l'art de présenter aux peuples les œuvres littéraires qui, dans l'état actuel de leurs habitudes et de leurs croyances, sont susceptibles de leur donner le plus de plaisir possible.
>
> Le *classicisme*, au contraire, leur présente la littérature qui donnait le plus grand plaisir possible à leurs arrière-grands-pères.[46]

This would have given them lots to talk about, not least because Stendhal's pamphlet ran variations on Hazlitt's essay, 'Sir Walter Scott, Racine, and Shakespear', from *The Plain Speaker*.

Hazlitt talked with him about *De L'Amour*, informing him (among other things) of a fault in his writing: 'Le grand défaut de cet écrivain, défaut bien rare, c'est *l'abondance des pensées*':

> A force d'ellipses hardies, son style tombe souvent dans ce défaut. Il doit expliquer ses pensées et allonger ses phrases dans sa seconde édition. Il doit renvoyer beaucoup des pensées qu'il *indique*, plus qu'il ne les exprime, à quelque autre ouvrage sur les passions.[47]

According to Stendhal, this was 'Said by M. Hazlitt', and when revising *De L'Amour* in 1826 he took his advice, elucidating his thoughts at greater length. He was right to do so. Hazlitt correctly saw the book as an 'ouvrage sur les passions', and its author as someone with more to say about the workings of the mind. He may have known Stendhal would do so through fiction, for at this moment the Frenchman was writing *Armance*, about a young man, Octave de Malivert, and his cousin—the gorgeous, half-Russian Armance de Zohiloff. The protagonists spend most of the novel discussing their feelings for each other before Octave rushes off to take part in the Greek War of Independence (like Stendhal's hero, Byron), only to kill himself with a mixture of opium and digitalis. Stendhal may have discussed it with Hazlitt, who would have been fascinated by its protagonist.

Early in 1827 the Hazlitts were visited by George Huntly Gordon, a distant relative of Isabella's. He had known her when she was nineteen, shortly before she went to Grenada. Hearing she was in Paris made him 'desirous of renewing my acquaintance with my former flame of one day!—and to see Mr. H. many of whose works I had read with much delight.'[48] A slightly eccentric figure, Gordon was hard of hearing and carried a 'speaking-tube'. He arrived at six in the evening and did not leave till two in the morning. Over dinner he met William Jr, whom he liked so much he helped him in a professional capacity years later.[49] During the meal Hazlitt ate nothing but drank 'some 3 or 4 basins of Tea!'[50] At the end of the evening, recalled Gordon, Isabella observed her husband 'had taken a prodigious "fancy" for me and my *tube*!'[51]: speaking down it 'gave a new sort of *fillip* to his thoughts'.[52]

A few days later Hazlitt gave him a guided tour of the Louvre. They met at ten in the morning and remained there until four in the afternoon, Hazlitt barking his dissertation on Titian and Raphael into Gordon's tube, to the astonishment of passing Parisians. He was, thought Gordon, 'better than any book I had ever read on the *Art Pictorial*'.[53] Theirs was a genuinely congenial acquaintance, and they would meet again.

Hazlitt was more of a man about town here than in London where, for reasons of class, he had been accepted only by a circumscribed social network. He preferred Paris where they 'do not ask what a man is worth, or whether his father is owner of a tin-mine or borough—but what he has to say, whether he is amiable and *spirituel*. In that case (unless a marriage is on the *tapis*) no one inquires whether he has come in his carriage or on foot.'[54] This was appealing to Hazlitt, and it is a mark not only of his desirability within French society, but of the esteem in which he was held as a writer by Parisians, that he should have been invited to dinner by such exalted figures as the Marquis de Lafayette. By March 1827 Lafayette was in his seventieth year, a hero of both the American and French Revolutions and still a man of substance in the political arena. Other guests that evening included Alexander von Humboldt, Prussian naturalist and explorer, one of the most famous men in Europe; Benjamin Constant, politician and political theorist; Sir Edward Sabine, British army officer and physicist; and the American novelist James Fenimore Cooper, famous for *The Last of the Mohicans* (1826).

Sabine evidently held forth, Hazlitt later noting he was 'listened to with some attention as a *marked character*'.[55] Hazlitt took advantage of the occasion to quiz Constant and Lafayette about Napoleon, whom they had known, and their testimony appears in his *Life*. Cooper, however, failed to impress him: 'his looks and manners seemed to announce a much greater man. He strutted through the streets with a very consequential air; and in company held up his head, screwed up his features, and placed himself on a sort of pedestal to be observed and admired, as if he never relaxed in the assumption nor wished it to be forgotten by others, that he was the American Sir Walter Scott.'[56] Nonetheless, he was sufficiently intrigued to borrow *The Last of the Mohicans* from the Galignanis,[57] and liked it enough to read *The Pilot* as well, which he thought 'a master-piece in its kind'.[58] A few years later he would write a characteristically perceptive critique of Cooper's fiction, complaining that

> He is not so much the master of his materials as their drudge: he labours under an epilepsy of the fancy. He thinks himself bound in his character of novelist to tell the truth, the whole truth, and nothing but the truth. Thus, if two men are struggling on the edge of a precipice for life or death, he goes not merely into the vicissitudes of action or passion as the chances of the combat vary; but stops to take an inventory of the geography of the place, the shape of the rock, the precise attitude and display of the limbs and muscles, with the eye and habits of a sculptor.[59]

Meanwhile Hazlitt continued the 'Boswell Redivivus' series, which was about to precipitate further trouble. In the sixth of the dialogues, published March 1827, he attributed to Northcote the story of 'old Mr Mudge' (the Revd Zachariah Mudge) who had 'run away from the Academy where he was brought up, because Moll Faux, the housemaid, would not have him'.[60] Incensed, Mudge's family complained to Northcote, who was acutely embarrassed because he had actually said this. Shame turned to anger, and anger to cunning: Northcote saw he could wriggle out of his predicament by blaming his gaffe on Hazlitt.

Northcote summoned Colburn to his house, intending to declare his horror at the liberties taken in his periodical. Sensing trouble, Colburn declined to make the (ten-minute) journey to Argyll Place, crumpling the artist's note into a very small ball and aiming it at the fireplace. When Northcote realized he had been treated with 'neglect and contempt'[61] he was enraged and stormed across the road to the publisher's office in New Burlington Street, demanding to see Colburn instanter. Not to be intimidated, Colburn simply told his secretary to say he was busy. Twice humiliated, twice frustrated, Northcote slunk back to his lair and devised another way of making his point. He may have been aware of Campbell's hostility towards Hazlitt; it was certainly no secret. Realizing Colburn had no motivation to assist in his project, he saw that Campbell probably would—out of sheer malice. Good. A bag of poison waiting to spurt, he sent Campbell a lengthy denunciation of Hazlitt, which began by deploring the title of the dialogues, with its implied casting of himself as Dr Johnson—'Good God! do you not feel this to be dreadful?'—before proceeding:

I have often in my vain moments said, that I should be pleased to receive morning visits at times from the Devil, because I might be amused by his knowledge of the world, and diverted by his wit, and should be sufficiently on my guard to avoid his snares. This impious desire has indeed been granted to me and Boswell Redivivus is the consequence. You will scarcely pity a calamity which my presumption has brought upon myself; I have at these times in the Closet indulged in idle conversation, not knowing who I was with, in all the confidence of Friendship. I thought no more of what was said by either of us afterwards concluding that it had passed off in air. But I now find to my sorrow that this despicable and worthless trash has been treasured up and is proclaimed at the Market Cross where my family connections and dearest friends are brought forward to publick inspection with their names at full length properly spelt in order to prevent any possible mistake being made; and things uttered in idle merriment now stamped in everlasting print, not as I represented them, but as speeches of cold, dry and hateful malignity, and grossly different from my meaning; and I am now kept in perpetual torture not knowing what each new month may bring forth. Good God! do you not think such a situation terrible?[62]

Northcote found in Campbell a more receptive audience than he had in Colburn. Without losing a beat, the editor donned sackcloth and wrote a letter more grovelling than the one sent to Leigh Hunt the previous year. He was, he said, 'afflicted beyond measure at finding my own inattention to have been the means of wounding the feelings of a venerable Man of genius' and asked only that Northcote 'Dictate the form and manner of my attempting to atone for having unconsciously injured you if I can make you any atonement.' 'The infernal Hazlitt', he promised, 'shall never more be permitted to write for the New Monthly.'[63]

The entire correspondence was an exercise in disingenuousness. Northcote's claim to have spoken in an unbuttoned mood, 'not knowing who I was with', was a lie; he was thrilled to see himself lauded as a latter-day Johnson and proud to advertise the fact—as indeed he continued for years to do; he gossiped endlessly about the Johnson circle with all and sundry, and had no regard for the long-departed Zachariah Mudge, piping up only because he was caught out and had to blame someone else. His insincerity is borne out by his response to Campbell, declining the offer of a printed apology.[64]

Likewise, Campbell cared nothing for Northcote, but exploited his outpour-ings out of dumb spite, so much did he detest Hazlitt. He made the most of it, threatening Colburn with resignation unless the boil was lanced. The pragmatic Colburn saw no point in losing his editor over such a triviality and gave way—at least for the moment. It was a cynical decision, the product of duplicity, moral cowardice, and vindictiveness. The only one to suffer by it was Hazlitt, whose run of publications came to a halt for two months—a lengthy hiatus for someone in financial need. So worried was he that in May he decided to go to London to find out what was going on, leaving Isabella and William Jr together at rue de la Chausée-d'Antin—a mistake, for his son and wife detested each other, and relations between them could only deteriorate further in his absence.

When he arrived in London he went directly to Colburn's office to find out what had happened to the backlog of contributions he had sent for the *New Monthly*. Colburn did what he could to reassure his star writer, alluding to Northcote's conduct and Campbell's reaction to it. However, he assured him he would soon return to the journal. Hazlitt must have realized what had hap-pened, but there was nothing to be gained by making an issue of it, particularly when a swift return was promised. 'The soul of the jest is in the threefold fact that Mr. Hazlitt and Mr. Northcote saw just as much of each other as before; that Mr. Hazlitt took notes of Mr. Northcote's conversations, with the artist's perfect privity, as before; and that these conversations were printed, as Mr. Hazlitt chose to send them in, in Colburn's *New Monthly*, as before!'[65]

Hazlitt took advantage of this London visit to deliver the first volume of his *Life of Napoleon* to Hunt and Clarke, which went straight into production. With Scott's nine-volume opus already in print, whatever he could do to publicize his own work would be advantageous. He persuaded John Black to report delivery of the manuscript in the *Morning Chronicle* on 11 June:

> NAPOLEON.—A literary gentleman, of high attainments, who has been residing in Paris for some time, for the purpose of collecting authentic documents and facts to enable him to write the Life of Napoleon, is just returned with a considerable portion of his manuscript, ready for the press. We understand the work will extend to four octavo volumes.[66]

That was one in the eye for Scott. Hazlitt hoped it would fuel what he assured Hunt and Clarke was mounting disillusionment with Scott's Tory interpretation of history. From now on, Hazlitt made sporadic attacks on his competitor's *Life*, the first of which appeared in *The Examiner* on 2 September: 'Sir Walter by this work has not invalidated the definition of a Tory,—that it is a person who is guided by selfishness and servility to sacrifice truth and reason to malice and prejudice on all occasions. He should have put his own name to the work, not that of the "Author of Waverley," who is a delightful dealer in fiction, not a paltry retailer or insinuater of untruths.'[67]

There was an urgent need to find an additional source of income, Hazlitt realized, as Colburn could no longer be depended on to safeguard his interests. He alerted his friends and was soon contacted by three young men: the eccentric traveller James Silk Buckingham, editor of the *Oriental Herald*, and his colleagues David Lester Richardson and James Augustus St John (26 and 31 years old, respectively). Richardson and St John had met on the *Oriental Herald* but were about to set up their own paper, the *London Weekly Review*. They were part of a new generation of literary journalists who regarded Hazlitt as a genius; Richardson thought him 'the best critic on the Fine Arts that England has produced'.[68] Several years earlier, Richardson was invalided out of the Bengal army on grounds of ill health. St John was a Welshman who contributed to *Sherwin's Weekly Political Register* and from August 1819 wrote for Richard Carlile's *The Republican*, taking over editorship during Carlile's jail term in November and December of that year.

Hazlitt met all three at Buckingham's house in Cornwall Terrace, the first of the grand terraces to be built at the edge of Regent's Park.[69] Richardson was surprised to find his literary hero a shy, middle-aged man with a slouching gait and slovenly attire. He was fascinated by his mode of speech, which he later recalled was 'impeded by sudden breaks and difficulties' as if he 'seemed to labour with his meaning—to have a painful consciousness of his inability to express it fully'.[70] Buckingham attempted to lure Hazlitt into the pages of the *Oriental Herald* at half the usual rate.

'After all, my dear sir', said Buckingham, 'the journal is of such quality that one guinea from me is worth two from any other!'[71] Hazlitt laughed but would not budge, Buckingham having received him with 'a little too much "au grand Seigneur"'.[72] Richardson, by contrast, realized he could secure the services of his literary hero only by rewarding him well, and was prepared to do so. Hazlitt agreed to join the *London Weekly Review*, appearing in the very first number, and his loyalty to it was indicative of the enthusiasm of these young men for his writing.[73] Indeed, he was the only contributor to remain with it after its purchase by Colburn.

His first contribution was a review of Wordsworth's collected poems. It includes a vintage account of the poet's essential qualities:

> He murmurs about the domestic hearth—about cottage doors—about flower-beds—about infancy—about the calm joys of far retirement, repose, security, contemplation. He shuns the mighty struggles and untameable passions of daring men—the voice of war, whether raised by Freedom or by Oppression, scares him; he has no hymn for Liberty; no denunciations of wrath, revenge, or retribution, to pour out of the poetic vial upon the disturbers of the earth; no tale, instinct with energy, to tell, illustrative of any truth of vital importance to mankind, or engendering hatred or contempt of their oppressors.[74]

Hazlitt went on to amuse himself with the thought that Wordsworth 'never kicks against the pricks of authority', and 'might be poet-laureate, to-morrow, to the Shah of Persia, were his feelings towards despotism only consulted, for he entertains no malice in the world against that species of government'.[75] These charges did not preclude Hazlitt from affirming Wordsworth's genius, and he concluded with the entire text of one of his favourite poems, 'Laodamia'. Not long after this was printed, Hazlitt dined with Richardson, who was unaware that Hazlitt's chronic stomach condition allowed him to consume no meat besides mutton chops. A hint was dropped just as he arrived. 'I was vexed to discover that there was not on the table the only sort of meat he could venture upon,' Richardson later recalled[76]—but he had a quick word with his housekeeper and, by the time dinner was served, Hazlitt found a splendid chop awaiting him.

As his first assignment was the review of Wordsworth, it is not surprising that their conversation dealt with Hazlitt's relations with the poet, as Richardson remembered: 'He told me that Wordsworth considered it presumptuous in any one to criticise his writings, however gently.'[77] They also talked about the *Life of Napoleon*, now preparing for publication: it was, Richardson believed, Hazlitt's 'greatest performance'.[78]

CHAPTER 24

She parted on account of the ill-conduct of the boy.
Henry Crabb Robinson, diary entry for 7 October 1830[1]

T HERE was trouble brewing at home. Now fifteen, William Jr had been in Paris nearly a year. Never an easy child, he was once described by Keats as 'that little Nero',[2] and loyalty to his mother (who he thought 'had been ill-used'[3]) prevented him finding a modus vivendi with Isabella. Not only was he 'very pointed and severe in his remarks' to her,[4] but his own son said he 'was much distressed and hurt at the second marriage' (an understatement), indicating a permanent disinclination to accept her.[5] By the time Hazlitt returned to Paris in July 1827, the friction between them was intolerable, not eased by the fact that Isabella paid for the boy's upkeep and education.

The resulting stress on the marriage led to its collapse, as Hazlitt's essays attest. In 'On Disagreeable People', published 1 August, he wrote that 'Gallantry to women (the sure road to their favour) is nothing but the appearance of extreme devotion to all their wants and wishes.... The slightest indifference with regard to them, or distrust of yourself, are equally fatal.'[6] A few weeks later, in 'The Main-Chance', he condemned the 'lady of fortune' whose mind is 'intelligent and well-informed'[7] though twisted by stinginess—a quality that has 'taken refuge in the petty provincial towns, or in old baronial castles in the North of Scotland, where it is still triumphant'.[8] Isabella was Scottish.

' "Have I not seen a household where love was not?" says the author of the Betrothed; "where, although there was worth and good will, and enough of the means of life, all was imbittered by regrets, which were not only vain, but criminal?" '[9] The answer was 'yes'—Hazlitt's own.

The decision to return to Venice was a last-ditch attempt to save the marriage.[10] A family holiday, he argued, was their only chance. And he had an ulterior motive for taking the boy to Italy, which he mentioned to William Bewick: 'if he had to express his greatest ambition, it would be that his son should become a great painter, as he himself had unfortunately not become. . . . To be a great painter he thought above all other divine inspirations!'[11] Where better for William Jr to bear witness to the glories of the Italian renaissance than Titian's home town? With these expectations, the unlikely threesome—the 49-year-old essayist, his 36-year-old wife and 16-year-old son—travelled southwards.

They stayed at the Hotel Danieli, one of the most opulent hotels on the Grand Canal, the silk curtains of which (that most Proustian of impressions) remained in William Jr's memory for the rest of his life.[12] Here his father composed the great, elegiac 'On a Sun-Dial': 'For myself, as I rode along the Brenta, while the sun shone hot upon its sluggish, slimy waves, my sensations were far from comfortable'[13]—due less to the sun, perhaps, than the apprehension of impending crisis.

Their return journey was slow and uncomfortable, and seemed to take forever. By the time they got back to rue de la Chausée-d'Antin, tempers were frayed and William Jr as truculent as ever. Something untoward was said, which caused 'a bit of an explosion'[14]—doubtless an understatement. Hazlitt realized he had no choice but to separate Isabella and his son, at least for a brief while, until both had calmed down. He took William Jr back to London and left him with Sarah Stoddart (now resident there[15]). It was safe, he thought, to let Isabella simmer down for a while; eventually he would return to Paris and they could talk things over in peace. Perhaps they would go on holiday together. He was sure he could persuade her to give William Jr a second chance. He wrote, proposing they discuss, coolly and calmly, what they wanted from their marriage, and awaited her reply. Days passed, then a week, then two weeks, and before he knew it a month had gone by without a word. When finally she responded she was in Switzerland, and informed him 'they had parted for ever!'[16]

It is hard to know how he reacted, for he seems to have written about it only obliquely.[17] Hazlitt was a romantic. That was his flaw. He was all too prone to lose his head over women, and during their short time together formed an attachment that transcended the mere fact of her wealth. But love of his writing was not, perhaps, the best foundation for her interest in him—as a man, he lacked the elegance and energy of his prose manner. Her disillusionment can only have exacerbated the 'imbitterment' caused by William Jr's occupation of the Paris house—a problem to which Hazlitt was blinded by his unshakeable love for his son. The news, when it came, may have been a relief, but it was another blow to his faltering constitution.

He moved to Half Moon Street, 'a street of lodgings or, rather, apartments'.[18] Boswell had resided here in the eighteenth century, and the author of 'Boswell Redivivus' was mindful of the association. Soon after moving in, he left the manuscript of volume 2 of his *Life of Napoleon* on the dresser and went to bed. In the middle of the night some burglars tried to break in, having run into Half Moon Street from Shepherd's Market. The incident put him in such 'a great state of terror' that, next morning, he took the manuscript to one of the newspaper editors for whom he worked and asked that it be kept under lock and key until the printer called for it. 'You know, sir', he remarked, 'I had no watch, and they wouldn't have believed I had no watch and no money; and, by God, sir, they'd have cut my throat!'[19]

Shortly after, George Huntly Gordon invited him to dinner—which consisted of tea, several bowls of which kept him going all evening. Gordon knew Hazlitt was partial to the finest lapsang souchong from Robinson's in Piccadilly,[20] and ensured a good stock. As a result, Hazlitt was in fine fettle: 'Knowing he was a first rate Metaphysician, and having myself a fancy for that abstruse science I drew him out—and he was again as luminous and perspicacious as he had been on Pictures.'[21] Besides which, Hazlitt delivered 'a long, eloquent, & enthusiastic dissertation on Salisbury Plain'.[22]

He was thinking of Winterslow because he planned to return there. London had changed much in recent years. The redevelopment that carved out fashionable Regent Street was completed in 1825. St James's Park, to which he was once a near-neighbour, had just been remodelled—the canal reshaped, trees planted, new walks laid out—while Buckingham House was being turned from a townhouse into a palace. Carlton House, the opulent residence built by George IV, was demolished, and in 1827 work began on Nash's magnificent Carlton House Terrace, finished five years later. Further changes were in store. The area to the north-east of Carlton House had been occupied by a workhouse and the Royal Mews, much decayed and used as a stables; it was to be cleared for another project of Nash's—Trafalgar Square, the new National Gallery, and the redevelopment of Charing Cross.[23] More deracinating still, Hazlitt's London friends were no longer so numerous or accessible as once they were. Godwin declined his visits, while Lamb had just moved to Enfield, a good ten miles out of town—far enough for friends to regard him as gone 'into the country'.[24]

Chapter 24

Hazlitt had no investment in this new city, and Winterslow was the least costly alternative.

Once there he set about the third and fourth volumes of the *Life*, as well as more essays for *The Examiner*, the first of which was an attack on Scott's biography of Napoleon—or, as he put it, 'that rag-fair, puppet-shew performance' which proved that 'The rights of the people, or the public good ... are cant-phrases which only excite [Scott's] incredulity or spleen.'[25] It was a just criticism[26] but Hazlitt was mistaken in supposing that, by articulating it, he could reduce sales of Scott's volume. The sheer fact of its being by Scott was enough to guarantee its appeal. All 8,000 copies sold when it published in June 1827, and the second edition would do as well in November. It succeeded on a scale he could but envy.

The peace and calm of Winterslow encouraged the self-reflection that produced one of the best of the late essays, in November 1827. 'On the Shyness of Scholars' is the first of a series of meditations that, taken together, represent a kind of *apologia pro vita sua*. Here he explained why he did not shine in 'the gay, laughing circle' or 'come off with applause in the retailing of anecdote or the interchange of repartee':[27] 'he who is repeatedly found in situations to which he is unequal (particularly if he is of a reflecting and candid temper) will be apt to look foolish, and to lose both his countenance and his confidence in himself—at least as to the opinion others entertain of him, and the figure he is likely on any occasion to make in the eyes of the world.'[28]

When referring to the 'shattered, sickly frame and trembling nerves'[29] of the scholar he had himself in mind; though only in his fiftieth year, his digestive problems had been exacerbated by financial hardship and marital disaster, and left him a physical wreck, able to consume little more than tea and rice.[30] It did not help that he was suddenly under pressure to proof-read volumes 1 and 2 of the *Life of Napoleon*, working 'double tides' into the night.[31] He was malnourished, frail, and susceptible to infection. One day, he told Charles Cowden Clarke, having walked fifteen miles in the mud, he got into a stagecoach 'with an old lady who would have the window open. Delicacy, moderation, complaisance, the *suaviter in modo*, whisper it about, my dear Clarke, these are my faults and have been my ruin.'[32] Upon reaching Winterslow Hut, he took to his bed and nearly died. His greatest fear was to 'leave the world "rough" copy' of the last two volumes of his *Life of Napoleon*.[33] As he recuperated, he joked about his brush with the 'shadowy world' and composed a typically self-deprecating epitaph: 'Hic jacent reliquiae mortales Gulielmi Hazlitt, auctoris non intelligibilis: natus Maidstoniae in comitatu Cantiae, Apr. 10, 1778. Obiit Winterslowe, Dec. 1827.'[34]

He celebrated Christmas Day with a letter to the Galignanis proposing a French translation of his *Life of Napoleon*. He would not hear from them until late February, when they sent the disappointing news that Scott's *Life* had overprinted, there were three other biographies besides, and the French booksellers 'will not hear of a fifth'.[35] This heart-sinking response was the first hint that his magnum opus was too late to market, and spurred him to promote it. He had previously declined the terms and conditions of the miserly James Silk Buckingham, but now saw little alternative. Hunt and Clarke sent Buckingham an advance copy, an extract from which appeared in the first number of *The Athenaeum*, 2 January 1828, of which Buckingham was editor.[36] At the same time, Hazlitt wrote an attack on Scott's *Napoleon* which Buckingham published in his other journal, *The Sphynx*,[37] for which no payment was remitted. Henry Leigh Hunt had warned him of this. 'I am not surprised at what you tell me', Hazlitt answered, 'but drowning men catch at Buckinghams.'[38] They did not realize Buckingham too was in trouble—'shattered, harassed, & desponding',[39] another victim of the continuing recession. *The Sphynx* folded in April 1829, and his financial interest in *The Athenaeum* ceased within the year. The problems experienced by publishers had consequences for Hazlitt—who, in his foolhardy way, continued to assist others in need. 'I would to God you could let me have 5£ more on account by return of post', he wrote to James Augustus St. John, his editor at the *London Weekly Review*, 'I am pressed to death on another person's account not my own'.[40] We do not know which of his friends he had helped, but such generosity, regardless of his own needs, was typical of the man.

The first two volumes of Hazlitt's *Life of Napoleon Buonaparte* appeared on 11 February 1828 at a price of 30 shillings.[41] Its reception was underwhelming. The worst notice appeared in the *Literary Gazette*, which described it as 'wild-goose foolery' that 'has offended grammar, taste, sense, feeling, and judgment'. Even friends were unenthusiastic. 'Hazlitt's speculative episodes are capital; I skip the Battles,' Lamb told its publisher.[42]

There was justice in this. The narrative was a mishmash of set-pieces lifted from other sources, interspersed with Hazlitt's commentary. But for those willing to wade through it, there are rewards. His attacks on the French for their vanity, theatricality, and inconstancy are shrewd and often funny; he is frank in his judgement of Britain and her allies, and razor-sharp in his critique of monarchical government.[43] Hazlitt's biggest disappointment concerned the

Preface, composed in Paris, where it was considered 'a masterpiece, the best and only possible defence of Buonaparte, and quite new *there*!'[44] Hunt and Clarke felt differently. It was, they thought, 'impolitic', and therefore dropped— a shame, because it declared his convictions with a candour not found elsewhere:

> It is true, I admired the man; but what chiefly attached me to him was his being, as he had been long ago designated, 'the child and champion of the Revolution.' Of this character he could not divest himself, even though he wished it. He was nothing, he could be nothing but what he owed to himself and to his triumphs over those who claimed mankind as their inheritance by a divine right; and as long as he was *a thorn in the side of kings* and kept them at bay, his cause rose out of the ruins and defeat of their pride and hopes of revenge. He stood (and he alone stood) between them and their natural prey. He kept off that last indignity and wrong offered to a whole people (and through them to the rest of the world) of being handed over, like a herd of cattle, to a particular family, and chained to the foot of a legitimate throne. This was the chief point at issue—this was the great question, compared with which all others were tame and insignificant—Whether mankind were, from the beginning to the end of time, born slaves or not? As long as he remained, his acts, his very existence gave a proud and full answer to this question.[45]

Anyone who cannot understand Hazlitt's support of Napoleon should look no further than this and reflect on its fidelity to ideals long abandoned by his former comrades in return for sinecures. It was the same fidelity as that shown by his father when, in the face of opposition from the Presbyterians of Philadelphia and the Episcopalians of Boston, he continued to preach the virtues of a Unitarian God. It was too late for Hazlitt to heal whatever wounds he had inflicted on his father, but he could at least follow his lead by remaining faithful to his principles. And perhaps Hazlitt has had the last laugh, for the fairer society he once envisaged has begun to evolve. Although Britain still has a hereditary monarchy, its powers are greatly curtailed compared with those enjoyed by George IV, and the people more empowered. That was a prospect which Wordsworth, Coleridge, and Southey could not have envisaged in 1828.

The *Life* retains its power to stimulate and startle. No mere history, it is opinionated as only Hazlitt can be, and there have always been readers who appreciate its quality. Henry Crabb Robinson thought it better than Scott's— 'His remarks, for instance, on the death of Louis XVI, on Robespierre and his ferocity, on Buonaparte's adoption of the Concordat and his conduct towards the Catholic religion are excellent'[46]—as did Basil Montagu's wife who, within two weeks of publication, told Jane Welsh Carlyle: 'Do not forget to read Hazlitt's Life of Buonaparte, how entirely has he beat Sir W. Scott out of the field.'[47] Years after being cut for his acerbities about Irving, Hazlitt was readmitted to the Montagu circle.

Northcote's *One Hundred Fables* was published shortly before the *Life*. The aged artist had been working on it for years. He had composed his versified Aesop in rhyming couplets—but Northcote, for all his ambition, was no Dryden. Hazlitt went through it with a fine tooth-comb, sharpening his text.[48] The published volume was eccentric but charming, as collaborative a work as their published conversations, though Hazlitt's name appeared nowhere on it. Northcote had a second volume of *Fables* on the stocks and needed help with that too. He pledged in his will to bequeath Hazlitt £100, which he hoped would provide the necessary incentive.[49]

On 20 February 1828, Hazlitt composed 'A Farewell to Essay-Writing'. He had long 'hated writing, and would never have penned a line, and indeed never did so, till his necessities compelled him to do so'.[50] In truth, he could not afford to give it up, and would compose much more before his death two and a half years hence. He knew his time was short and needed to acknowledge his loosening grip on the world. In his reverie of a solitary walker, he paid tribute to the Wiltshire lanes he so loved:

> I have no need of book or companion—the days, the hours, the thoughts of my youth are at my side, and blend with the air that fans my cheek. Here I can saunter for hours, bending my eye forward, stopping and turning to look back, thinking to strike off into some less trodden path, yet hesitating to quit the one I am in, afraid to snap the brittle threads of memory. I remark the shining trunks and slender branches of the birchtrees, waving in the idle breeze; or a pheasant springs up on whirring wing; or I recall the spot where I once found a wood-pigeon at the foot of a tree, weltering in its gore, and think how many seasons have flown since 'it left its little life in air'.[51]

It was really a farewell to Winterslow. And by the time it appeared in print, at the end of March, he was back in London. The bucolic life was very well, but he needed one last trip to Paris to consult sources for his *Life of Napoleon*, funded by a ferocious burst of writing assignments in London.

He took rooms at 38 Gloucester Street, south of Queen Square, Bloomsbury, and offered his services to Henry Leigh Hunt. From 16 March to 15 June 1828 he attended the theatre during the week and reviewed it for the Sunday *Examiner*. Among other things, he was delighted by a company led by French comedian Adrien Perlet, whose genius he acknowledged with a pun: 'Monsieur Perlet is certainly a pearl of an actor. He does every part well, and every part varied from another.'[52] At the end of March he caught up again with Caroline Brocard, the ballerina over whom he rhapsodized in May 1826. He was no less besotted with her now, because she reminded him of Sarah Walker:

> To compare the varied graces of her movements, the voluptuous, yielding flexibility of her form, the thrill of pleasure, the soul of harmony, when she sits enthroned as Venus, or quits her throne 'to look a Goddess and to move a Queen,' to the gentle, smiling undulation of the elements from which she sprung, to the waving of a branch of a tree fanned by the zephyr's breath, to the mingled tints of the rainbow, to the glancing colours in the neck of Venus' doves, to anything most exquisite—to try in vain (oh! how much in vain) to describe her slender throat, and make a merit of the failure,—to follow her through the mazes of the dance, and still to distinguish her amidst the dazzling throng by that elegant turn of the head, the Guido air of enchantment, to drop a mysterious, bare-faced allusion to one other person in the world that was like her, peerless and alone, and end in a pensive sigh. Spirit of affectation! aid me.[53]

In the passion with which he reacted to the world, Hazlitt was as young as ever, whatever the state of his health.

Even before Leigh Hunt's *Lord Byron and some of his Contemporaries* was published in January 1828, it came under attack, not least for Hunt's criticism of Byron's meanness.[54] The Byronists were infuriated. Foremost among them, Thomas Moore was preparing his own memoirs, and had a vested interest in discrediting competitors. He published a satirical poem in *The Times*, which portrayed Hunt as a dog looking enviously at a lion:

> Nay, fed as he was (and this makes a dark case)
> With sops every day from the Lion's own pan,
> He lifts up his leg at the noble beast's carcase,
> And—does all a dog, so diminutive, can.[55]

From the Tories, there was worse. In the *Quarterly*, J. G. Lockhart described Hunt's memoir as 'the miserable book of a miserable man: the little airy fopperies of its manner are like the fantastic trip and convulsive simpers of some poor worn out wanton, struggling between famine and remorse, leering through her tears.'[56]

Knowing how ill-motivated this was, Hazlitt defended Hunt against the accusation that he was 'cockney': 'Pray, did it never strike you that Lord Byron himself was a cockney-writer, if descending from the conventional to the vernacular is to be so?'[57] And in *The Examiner*, he ticked off the *Quarterly* for its anonymous diatribes: 'the disguise of a Quarterly Reviewer is as complete (and, no doubt, as proper) as that of a footpad.'[58] In return, Hunt promoted *The Plain Speaker* in his new journal, *The Companion*, praising 'these masterly essays' over the course of one and a half issues.[59] Hazlitt responded with a favourable notice of *The Companion* in the *London Weekly Review*, beginning: 'There is no one, with the least grain of good sense, who does not relish Leigh Hunt's essays.'[60]

Their renewed closeness disproves the contention that Hazlitt alienated those around him. Despite past differences, the two men ended on better terms than ever. Leigh Hunt was 'my most excellent friend', said Hazlitt, 'I like his foibles (if he has any) better than the best virtues of many others.'[61] And it was more than merely verbal: they helped each other out with food parcels. In February 1828 Hazlitt sent 'the most agreeable of biographers' a hare and some Wiltshire bacon,[62] and in March 1829 Hunt sent a hamper to Hazlitt's lodgings.[63] One of Hunt's shirts was in Hazlitt's possession at his death.[64]

The Atlas had been prominently anti-Hazlittian since its establishment in 1826, as befitted one of the foremost Benthamite papers on the newsstands. But in late June its editor, R. S. Rintoul, resigned, believing the proprietor wanted to 'vulgarize and betwaddle'[65] it, taking the entire editorial staff to form *The Spectator*. An Irishman, Robert Bell, took over at a moment's notice, replacing staff with friends and acquaintances, including several *Examiner* journalists.[66]

So far as we know, Bell had not previously met Hazlitt, but someone told him he should. Summoned from the *Examiner* office, Hazlitt cut his usual unprepossessing figure, as Bell recalled:

> you were disappointed or astonished to meet an individual nervous, low-spoken, and feeble, who lived on tea as a regimen. There was not a particle of energy about him ordinarily. His face, when at repose, had none of the marks of extraordinary intellect, or even of animation. The common expression was that of pain, or rather the traces left by pain. It was languor and inertion. But when he kindled, a flush mantled over his sunken cheeks, his eyes lighted up wildly, his chest expanded, he looked like one inspired, his motions were eloquent, and his whole

form partook of the enthusiasm. This is commonly the case with men of genius, but it was so in a remarkable degree with him.[67]

Hazlitt contributed to the first *Atlas* edited by Bell[68] and appeared in its pages more than in any other journal between now and the end of his career. This was because Bell gave him complete freedom: besides waging war on old bugbears (the Utilitarians, phrenology, Coleridge), he ranged across contemporary politics and the visual arts. *The Atlas* would publish his last notice of the British Institution and a sizeable chunk of the *Conversations of James Northcote*. He reviewed theatre in its pages almost to the last, including some of the best pieces he ever wrote on the subject.[69] This was one of the happiest engagements of his career.

In January he had begun a sentence with the words, 'If I should go to Paris in the spring'.[70] He cannot have gone then; if he did go, it was not until mid-July.[71] The biggest argument against his having made the trip is the difficulty of paying for it—but he was working at breakneck speed, and may have scraped together the means to snatch a final glimpse of a country he loved. The review of a new guidebook to the Père Lachaise cemetery, published by the *London Weekly Review* at the end of August, suggests he may by then have been in Paris, where he would have remained several weeks.[72] If so, he would have caught up with Patmore, then writing about French theatres for the *New Monthly*,[73] and was reunited with Dr Edwards who in August received a prize from the Academie des Sciences for his work on the respiration of crabs.[74] Perhaps they visited the fruit and flower markets of Paris together, as in former years.

From the moment of his return to London he was as prolific as at any time in his life, partly because he was paying off debts. Typically, he published up to four or five pieces in each issue of *The Atlas*, while contributing to the *London Weekly Review*, *The Examiner*, and the *New Monthly Magazine*—a marvel of physical and mental endurance, especially given his uncertain health. It was at this time that David Lester Richardson took him to a watercolour exhibition in Suffolk Street, which he ridiculed with a play on the names of two artists: 'He repeated an old pun, declaring that he disliked *Westall* even more than *all West*.'[75] Then they walked round the corner to the house of the late philanthropist John Julius Angerstein in Pall Mall, where the National Gallery's collection was temporarily housed. 'Now I am at home!', Hazlitt exclaimed, as they entered, for the paintings were so well known to him as to be friends.

Richardson later remembered how 'The living, breathing, speaking portrait of Gevartius on his right—the rich allegorical landscape by Rubens directly facing him—the Claudes, Poussins, and other immortal works glowing on the walls on every side of us, seemed to hold his faculties in enchantment.'[76]

On the way home they passed a print shop displaying two large engravings by Turner. Hazlitt stopped and stared, remembering his encounter with the artist a decade earlier. 'I once thought', he remarked to Richardson, 'that Turner would have been a second Claude. But he has disappointed me. There is something imposing in his style, but there is no repose in it. It is theatrical, fluttery, flaunting—it is anything but Claude-like now. I dislike him, too, as a man.'[77]

It is good that Hazlitt had some new friends in London, for he began to spend more time on his own. Lamb lived outside the city, other friends had died, and others still were estranged. He had never had any difficulty being solitary, and spent hours gazing into the fireplace, thinking of the past. 'My mind to me a kingdom is,'[78] he had often declared to himself, in such moments, as imaginary vistas opened up in the mind.

> Sometimes, as I gaze upon the dying embers in my room, the ruddy streaks and nodding fragments shape themselves into an Italian landscape, and Radicofani rises in the distance, receding into the light of setting suns, that seem bidding the world farewell for ever from their splendour, their pomp, and the surrounding gloom! Or Perugia opens its cloistered gates, and I look down upon the world beneath, and Foligno and Spoleto stretch out their dark groves and shining walls behind me! You seem walking in the valley of the shadow of life; *ideal* palaces, groves, and cities (realised to the bodily sense) everywhere rise up before you— 'The earth hath bubbles as the water hath, and these are of them!'[79]

Earlier that year, he feared he might never return to Winterslow, but he was to be granted one more taste of the countryside he loved. There had been arguments over money with Mrs Hine, landlady of Winterslow Hut,[80] so on this occasion he stayed in the village proper, one and a half miles to the south of the Andover road. He had seen many autumns there, and followed the passing of 1828 with an attentiveness that amounted to adoration. He rose late, made tea, wrote some pieces for *The Atlas*, then walked along the Roman Road that led directly into Salisbury where at the Woolpack Inn he ensured his writings were carried by the Old Salisbury to the Bell and Crown in Holborn. That done, he enjoyed the sights and sounds of the town before walking home. It was a way of life that agreed with him, and he held to it as long as he could.

But he was not free of worry. Surviving correspondence from this moment testifies to the straits in which he found himself. At the end of October he wrote to Hunt and Clarke begging an advance on the last two volumes of his *Life:* 'Could you discount me a ten or twenty pound note of hand of my own. I have nearly done my work.'[81] (He was five chapters from the end of volume 4.) He could not know that Hunt and Clarke were in debt, and any advance came out of funds they did not have. On 19 September their problems worsened with the bankruptcy of William Hone who, for the past two and half years, had been labouring on their behalf at the King's Bench. The beneficiary was that old vulture Thomas Tegg, who promptly assumed the rights to Hone's books and commissioned more. Such was Tegg's business acumen that he was now lord of the largest mansion in Cheapside, formerly the official residence of the Lord Mayor of London.

Hazlitt spent the festive season with Sarah and William Jr in Winterslow. It was to be their last Christmas together. The divorce had been traumatic for everyone, not least William Jr who, years after his father's death, testified how 'painful [it was] to me'.[82] But Hazlitt had done his utmost to support him and his mother; Sarah continued to visit his mother and sister in Devon, and was in close contact with the Lambs. Hazlitt saw more clearly than ever that she and William were his first and only family. He probably did not stay in her cottage but found lodgings a short walk away, where he remained into the new year. The bills he was sent for tea, cream, bread, and butter are probably evidence of his entertaining Sarah and William.[83]

In January 1829, he began to make occasional trips to London. *The Atlas* needed another theatre reviewer, and he took up the slack. But the strain of travel took a heavy toll on health and purse. Towards the end of February Hazlitt moved back to London. His health was faltering; nothing speaks more eloquently of his sense of mortality than the recollections he now published in *The Atlas*. They included anecdotes of his time as a parliamentary reporter alongside Peter Finnerty, whose defiance of Castlereagh he recounted with relish: 'Lord Castlereagh either dreaded or admired his boldness, which was of the very vulgarest and most uncompromising description; his lordship always bowed to Peter in the lobby of the House, a condescension the latter used to acknowledge as a proof of the ascendancy of his own character.'[84] In another piece he remembered Mark Supple, a legendary Irish reporter whose 'way was the hyperbole; a strong vein of Orientalism with a dash of the *bog-trotter*'.[85] There were articles, too, on Joseph Priestley, Coleridge, and Curran.[86]

On Good Friday, 17 April 1829, disaster struck: Hunt and Clarke were gazetted bankrupt. Neither was any good as a businessman, their publishing list was ill-chosen, and, with Hone's bankruptcy, their own had become inevitable.[87] This was the 'most awkward failure'[88] the trade had known, though Henry Leigh Hunt was unsurprised; he had seen it coming, but poor Cowden Clarke had been kept in the dark and was blameless—which explains why Hazlitt remained on good terms with him. For Hazlitt, this was a disaster. Henry Leigh Hunt had knowingly made him dependent on the firm for his continuing existence. They had pledged £500 for the *Life of Napoleon*, which he had already spent. Hazlitt had promissory notes for £140 of that sum, now worth nothing. In short, he was more deeply in debt than ever. Calculations revealed he owed his creditors two hundred pounds; however hard he worked, his earnings were barely sufficient to sustain him, let alone pay them off. Walter Scott had also been ruined by his publisher, but his selling power was huge. By contrast, Hazlitt's name was a deterrent to potential readers; he could never have discharged his debts through book sales. He became more elusive than ever in a bid to elude the bailiffs, moving from one address to another without warning.

PART VII

London Solitude

CHAPTER 25

*He who has learned how to die has unlearned how to be a
slave. Knowing how to die frees us from all subjection and
constraint.*

Montaigne, 'That to philosophize is to learn to die'[1]

B Y July 1829 Hazlitt occupied the first floor of 3 Bouverie Street, a small
terraced building to the immediate south of Fleet Street, looking down
towards the river.[2] He could not have guessed that in 1845 an admirer by the
name of Charles Dickens would issue *The Daily News* from number 19—or that,
just over a century later, *The Sun* and *The News of the World* would publish
at number 30. Bouverie Street was then, as for years to come, at the heart of
the newspaper world, a good vantage point from which to witness the carnage
caused by the recession. Some papers went out of business while others, such
as *The Examiner* and *The London Weekly Review*, changed hands. Even that
Midas of publishers Henry Colburn was not immune to difficulty. Nearly half
the novels published in Britain bore his imprint, but were no longer selling; in
fact, he was so far in debt to his printer that he could continue only by making
a partner of him. Accordingly, on 1 September 1829 they printed a circular,
a copy of which they probably sent to Hazlitt, announcing that 'in future the
Business will be carried on in the joint names of HENRY COLBURN and RICHARD
BENTLEY.'[3]

During the summer, William Jr, now eighteen and no longer at school, moved
in with his father as an assistant. Hazlitt was still making regular visits to Argyll
Place to make notes for the ongoing *Conversations of James Northcote, Esq.*,
and William sometimes accompanied him. One day, Northcote asked whether
they could help with his biography of Titian. Despite having been on the stocks
since 1822,[4] Northcote had little besides 'a mass of extremely unconnected
manuscript'.[5] Over the next few months Hazlitt and his son resolved it into
something like order and bulked out the second volume with their translation
of Ticozzi's life of Titian.[6]

In the meantime, Hazlitt was reconciled with Francis Jeffrey, having broken with him several years previously. Hearing that Jeffrey had just resigned editorship of the *Edinburgh Review* to become Dean of the Faculty of Advocates, he wrote an article praising him as a 'staunch Whig': 'Those who know Mr. Jeffrey at a distance admire him: those who are better acquainted with him love and respect him; all will be glad of a distinction grateful to his feelings, and which has been merited neither by servility nor faction, but by an union of firmness with moderation.'[7] Seeing this in *The Atlas*, Macvey Napier, the new editor of the *Edinburgh*, got in touch,[8] and Jeffrey asked Napier to convey his regards. 'Tell Mr. Jeffrey I am much pleased by his kind recollection of me,' Hazlitt responded.[9] Relations with Napier became so cordial that, when he visited London the following month, Hazlitt felt able to request an advance: 'I would not thus early appear in *formâ pauperis*, but the loss of 200£ on my Life of Napoleon through the failure of Messrs. Hunt & Clarke has driven me to great straits at the present moment.'[10]

Napier's response was to put Hazlitt on the payroll of the *Edinburgh Review*, commissioning from him a review of Walter Wilson's biography of Defoe. A friend of Hone and former colleague of Lamb's, Wilson heard from both that Hazlitt was to notice his book.[11] This was enough to strike terror at the heart of even the most confident author, and he forwarded a copy with trepidation. 'I have no doubt he will make a good article,' he told Hone, with the caveat: 'I wish he could train his mind to write with less asperity.'[12] Hone took the volume to Hazlitt and reported to Wilson that his friend would 'set to work upon it kindly'.[13] Wilson need not have worried. It was a bravura performance, paying fulsome tribute to Defoe's literary and political career.

A fire in Bouverie Street that summer precipitated panic: Hazlitt ordered William Jr to save his paintings, directing they be stored in the Sussex Coffee-house across the road. When William pointed out that several nearby houses were already in flames and he would be in mortal danger if he entered, Hazlitt became cross, even though 'he himself did nothing but act the bystander with great success'.[14] Fortunately, their lodgings survived, and they were soon able to move back in.

A few weeks later, William Jr began walking out with Catherine Reynell, daughter of Hazlitt's old friend Carew Henry Reynell. There was an age difference—at 24, Kitty was six years older than William, but they had been friends for years, and it was not surprising they were attracted to one another. Many of Kitty's memories of Hazlitt date from this moment. On one occasion

Chapter 25

Fig. 33. Covent Garden theatre, which by 1829 was almost a second home to Hazlitt, and where he discovered Fanny Kemble. He had a favourite seat at the back of the auditorium from where he loved to listen to her voice.

he had just eaten pheasant for dinner when she arrived at Bouverie Street. He had been at a loss as to what to order, he said, and had chosen this, even though it was expensive.

'How much was it?', she asked.

'Ten shillings apiece.'

'Don't you think it was a rather a lot to pay?'

'Well, I don't know but what it was, Kitty', he said, blinking in his distinctive manner, and tucking his chin into his shirt-collar. On another occasion they met in Piccadilly, and she found him more out of spirits than ever. 'Well, you know', he said, 'I've been having some hot boiled beef for my dinner, Kitty—a most *uncomfortable* dish.'[15] She remembered these incidents not as evidence of his improvidence, but for what they revealed of his inability to take care of either his health or finances.

Hazlitt was saddened when Covent Garden theatre was threatened with closure after an unsuccessful season. The bailiffs had begun to size up its assets and a sale was announced. 'We sincerely hope that this theatre will not only open, but *keep open*,' he commented in *The Atlas*. 'Sorry should we be to have to wander through the Piazzas as a deserted cloister; to have that well-known avenue to so many bright visions and charming traditions closed up—"for ever silent and for ever sad"—and not a hope left to qualify the scent of rotten cabbage-stalks and soften the din of electioneering mobs!'[16] Desperate times precipitated desperate measures. At his wits' end, its manager Charles Kemble (a friend of Hazlitt) took the biggest gamble of his professional life: on Monday 5 October 1829 his daughter, Fanny, stepped onto the stage in the role of Juliet. Although it was her first outing she was an instant success—and Hazlitt was there to see her. For the next nine months he followed her through the repertoire, reviewing her for *The Atlas*.[17] Not everyone perceived her quality, but Hazlitt did so from the outset. Sitting 'in my beloved corner' of the theatre, he loved to listen to her voice, 'trembling at its own beauty, and prolonging its own liquid tones, like the murmur of the billowy surge on sounding shores!'[18]

On 16 October another actress made her London debut: Louisa Macnamara (whose stage name was Miss Mordaunt) appeared at Drury Lane in Andrew Cherry's *The Soldier's Daughter*. From that moment on, according to Charles and Mary Cowden Clarke, Hazlitt 'was "fathoms deep" in love with her, making us the recipients of his transports about her; while we, almost equal fanatics with himself, "poured in the open ulcer of his heart her eyes, her hair, her cheek, her gait, her voice," and "lay in every gash that love had given him the knife that made it." '[19] It may have been Macnamara to whom John Payne Collier referred when he noted 'Hazlitt's attachment to one of the Girls of the Theatre. She was passée, not handsome. He owned [she] had thin cuisses &c but was infatuated. Made her presents of necklaces, &c.'[20] This is further proof, were any needed, of Patmore's observation that 'he was always in love with somebody or other'.[21] It was true that Hazlitt loved women, right until the end of his life, and saw nothing wrong in the presence of streetwalkers in the theatres. When a group of puritans attempted to ban them from the upper gallery of Covent Garden, he wrote indignantly to Charles Kemble, describing the move as 'downright & wilful destruction', vowing to do what he could to suppress the 'moral battery'.[22]

He remained as sociable as ever. In November he visited Thomas Noon Talfourd at 2 Elm Court, Temple, and partook of a hare Talfourd had been given by John Mitford, the literary scholar and clergyman.[23] At around the same time he entertained the Cowden Clarkes at Bouverie Street, where he showed them 'a copy he had made of Titian's "Ippolito de Medici", and conversed finely upon Titian's genius'.[24] And a few days later he visited the Lambs at Enfield.[25]

Chapter 25

Catching sight of an essay Lamb was writing on Punch and Judy, he offered to draft a few sentences for it:

> Punch is a fellow possessing as little of the faculty of reason as possible without being ideotic. Many madmen have much more, even when not in lucid intervals. His actions denote no 'foregone conclusions,' and he has no sense of consequences. He is a striking instance (and a stricken one, as often) of a person who learns nothing from experience. It only serves as an irritation to his will.[26]

The two friends crowed with laughter as Hazlitt read this out.

One of the last things he did in 1829 was find a publisher for volumes 3 and 4 of his *Life of Napoleon*. Effingham Wilson (a friend of William Hone, who would publish Tennyson's first volume in June 1830) and Chapman and Hall (who later published Dickens and Thackeray) purchased remaining stock of the first two volumes and reissued them with the new ones. One evening in December he took the manuscript to James Whiting, the printer at Beaufort House in the Strand who printed the first two volumes, sat down and finished work on them. Among other things, he reinstated his controversial Preface, which now appeared in volume 3. The next morning he handed the manuscript to Whiting. His great work was done.[27]

It was a satisfactory way to end a difficult year. No wonder he took refuge in the theatre, where he had free admission: 'let the boxes be filled with innocence and beauty like beds of lilies on the first night of Isabella or Belvidera'[28]—as indeed they were when on Wednesday 9 December he saw Fanny Kemble's first appearance in *Venice Preserved*. Her Belvidera was 'highly creditable', he reported in *The Atlas*, adding that 'the applause was long and rapturous'.[29] If perfection was not attainable in life, it could be glimpsed, however fleetingly, in art.

He lived in the artists' quarter when first he came to London, and returned to it in early 1830. Frith Street in Soho had long been associated with all branches of the arts. A lifetime before, in 1764, a young prodigy named Wolfgang Amadeus Mozart stayed at number 20 with his father and sister. More recent denizens included Horne Tooke (1804) and John Constable (1810–11). Mary Russell Mitford stayed at number 45 in 1826. Number 6 is one of several houses built in 1718, and is today, as the Hazlitt Hotel, the oldest in the street. One of Hazlitt's favourite comedians, Joseph Munden, lived here in 1795.[30] In January or February Hazlitt moved into a small room on the second floor, looking onto

Fig. 34. 6 Frith Street as it is today, in the heart of London's Soho. It was once home to one of Hazlitt's favourite actors, Joseph Munden.

the building behind. This was not quite the step up some have suggested, though his landlady, Mrs Stapleton, would have been pleased to think it so. Admittedly, Soho Square remained prestigious, the residence of such luminaries as Sir Anthony Carlisle. But by the time Hazlitt moved in, Frith Street was home to a brothel at number 21, as the area cheerfully began to acquire its reputation as a red-light district.[31]

If (as W. C. Hazlitt claims[32]) Hazlitt moved in early January, it was an inopportune moment, to say the least: the weather was horrendous. On New Year's Day there were four feet of snow on the Bristol Road and the Thames was frozen over. In those days, before the macadamizing of central London thoroughfares, such conditions generated enormous lakes of mud, slush and snow, which made it impossible to get around. Cheapside and Fleet Street were in an appalling state and remained so for weeks. Hurricane-force winds battered the country during the second week of January, damaging ships moored on the Thames, and the following week it was minus 22°F on Hampstead Heath, with mail coaches reporting obstructions on approach roads into the capital.

Meaning only to be helpful, William Hone introduced Hazlitt to an accountant who promptly cheated him. The result was that in mid-February Hazlitt found unwanted visitors at the door: three gentlemen sent by Walbancke and Whittle, one to hold open the door of the cab, the others to help him into it. Once again, he found himself at Coleman Street Buildings, asking for a sheet of paper with which to write to Talfourd. 'Poor Hazlitt has been arrested on one of those detestable Bills of that detestable firm of Hunt & Clarke for £150, all honestly earned by him, & is at a Lock-up-House,' Talfourd told Mary Russell Mitford on 18 February 1830.[33] This was wholly unjust, Hazlitt being the innocent victim of others' misdeeds. He found the 'Lock-up-House' more traumatic than anything he had previously experienced and afterwards (according to his grandson) his 'strength and spirits were completely shattered'.[34] Talfourd kept him out of the Sheriff's court and debtors' prison,[35] enlisted the assistance of Basil Montagu, and secured his release.

But there was a catch. Hunt and Clarke's administrators agreed to let him go only on condition that he remit weekly payments in default of which he would be subject to further arrest. Liberty under such conditions was as good as the treadmill and there must have been occasions when he found it difficult to find the required sum, putting him in terror of the bailiffs.

Something of his mood as he embarked on this passage may be gathered from one of the first of the Frith Street essays—'London Solitude', published towards the end of March. It is a minor masterpiece which shows how, in his last days, he had begun to compose a kind of prose poetry drawn *de profundis*.

In London anything may be had for money; and one thing may be had in perfection without it. That one thing is solitude. . . . But in the mighty metropolis, where myriads of human hearts are throbbing—where all that is busy in commerce, all that is elegant in manners, all that is mighty in power, all that is dazzling in splendour, all that is brilliant in genius, all that is benevolent in feeling, is congregated together—there the pennyless solitary may feel the depth of his solitude. From morn to night he may pensively pace the streets, envying every equipage that sweeps by him in its pride, and coveting the crusts of the unwashed artificer.

And there shall pass him in his walks poets that musically sing of human feeling, priests that preach the religion of mercy, the wealthy who pity the sorrows of the poor, the sentimental whose hearts are touched by the tale of woe—and none of these shall heed him; and he may retire at night to his bedless garret, and sit cold and hungry by his empty grate; the world may be busy and cheerful and noisy around him, but no sympathy shall reach him; his heart shall be dry as Gideon's fleece while the softening dews of humanity are falling around him.[36]

An opportunity to make amends occurred with publication of Godwin's latest novel, *Cloudesley*, which Colburn and Bentley issued on 4 March 1830. Having obtained a copy, Hazlitt proposed to Napier that he 'make an article of it whether as a failure or successful';[37] Napier agreed, knowing he would be a fool to do otherwise—Hazlitt on Godwin was an excellent topic. Without telling him, Hazlitt also reviewed *Cloudesley* for *The Atlas*.[38] He did not usually notice the same book twice, but this was a final opportunity to pay tribute to an old friend, and he made the most of it.

Both reviews are consistent in declaring that *Cloudesley* lacked the 'molten passion' of Godwin's first novel, *Caleb Williams*.[39] Instead Hazlitt composed an appreciation of its author, arguing that Godwin's mind was 'essentially active',[40] that he 'has never betrayed his cause, or swerved from his principles'[41] (by contrast with one or two others he could name). He then launched into an account of Godwin's precarious livelihood (as well as his own):

He lies 'stretched upon the rack of restless ecstasy:' he runs the everlasting gaunt-let of public opinion. He must write on, and if he had the strength of Hercules and the wit of Mercury, he must in the end write himself down:

> And like a gallant horse, fallen in first rank,
> Lies there for pavement to the abject rear,
> O'er-run and trampled on.

He cannot let well done alone. He cannot take his stand on what he has already achieved, and say, Let it be a durable monument to me and mine, and a covenant between me and the world for ever! He is called upon for perpetual new exertions, and urged forward by ever-craving necessities. The *wolf* must be kept from the door: the *printer's devil* must not go empty-handed away. He makes a second attempt, and though equal perhaps to the first, because it does not excite the same surprise, it falls tame and flat on the public mind. If he pursues the real bent of his genius, he is thought to grow dull and monotonous; or if he varies his style, and tries to cater for the capricious appetite of the town, he either escapes by miracle or breaks down that way, amidst the shout of the multitude and the condolence of friends, to see the idol of the moment pushed from its pedestal, and reduced to its proper level. . . . With all his efforts, he builds no house, leaves no inheritance, lives from hand to mouth, and, though condemned to daily drudgery for a precarious subsistence, is expected to produce none but works of first-rate genius.[42]

Perhaps he hoped this might lead to a rapprochement; if so, he was disappointed. Godwin read both reviews,[43] but did not renew contact.

Hazlitt was already in precarious financial straits and sensed worse ahead. Since his arrest his stomach problem had become chronic, and his spells in bed battling acute pain were more frequent. He developed a strategy designed to see him through periods of enforced rest: in addition to his regular theatre reviews for *The Atlas*, he stockpiled occasional pieces reworking themes discussed in earlier years, such as his views of the public, the unreliability of friends, and people with one idea.[44] He was also continuing work on Northcote's behalf, finishing the fair copy of their collected conversations (which were also appearing in *The Atlas*), while polishing off the *Fables* and Northcote's *Life of Titian*, both well advanced.[45] Besides his uncertain health, these multifarious labours were motivated by a larger ambition: to leave his son enough money to enable him to lead a leisurely existence.[46] But he found Northcote a hard taskmaster. Despite having at his disposal the best writer in London, Northcote abused him unmercifully, as is clear from a conversation one fine spring day in 1830.

By now, the area that was to become Trafalgar Square had been cleared of buildings and surrounded by hoardings. It was alongside one of them—probably in Cockspur Street, to the south-west of the square—that Hazlitt bumped into his old friend, the artist William Bewick.

'My dear fellow, where have you come from? Where have you been? I have lost sight of you for an age!', exclaimed Hazlitt.

'I have been in the sunny clime', Bewick replied (meaning Italy), 'and am just on my way to Northcote to show him my "Jeremiah".'

'Ah! I am so glad you are just come as my redeeming star—my credit is at this time very low with him; you must know I am editing his *Fables*—I may say writing them—and he is just now very peevish and impatient at my not sending him some copy. I shall be ready tomorrow. Now if you see him today and put him in a good humour, which you will do by showing him your "Jeremiah"—you must speak of me, tell him you have just seen me, and that I shall see him tomorrow with more copy, and then you can tell me how his pulse beats.'[47]

Hazlitt was anxious not just because of the pace of work on the *Fables*; in one of their conversations he had once more made reference to the amorous propensities of Zachariah Mudge, having Northcote say that Mudge was 'always falling in love, and making out his favourites to be such paragons'.[48] Within weeks of its appearance in the *Court Journal*, Northcote received a letter from Bartholomew Dunsterville, a Plymouth Alderman, who wrote to 'assure you that those Conversations are very offensive and said to be yours and written by Hazlitt'.[49] Northcote responded with an old-fashioned raspberry: 'You also threaten me with more thundering letters which if they come I shall throw them into the Fire unanswered as I have nothing to do with Newspapers nor ever had, it is impossible for me to explain their nonsense therfore pray do not torment me any more about what is not my business to attend, as at present my great age and load of infirmities render me unfit for such silly matters.'[50] If Northcote was capable of ranting at such pompous fools as Dunsterville, he was equally prone fustian against his ghost-writer-in-chief.

On 28 May Hazlitt attended Fanny Kemble's last outing of the season, as Lady Townly in *The Provoked Husband*. This was her first stab at comedy and she proved her mettle in a manner which, he judged, was 'extremely beautiful and true to nature'.[51] Not only had an inexperienced actress turned in a series of deft performances in classic roles, but she had saved her father's business: 'She has passed in a single season through a trying ordeal with honour and applause; she has stayed, if not redeemed, the fortunes of the theatre; and, for the present, we take our farewell of her, confident that she will go on improving her intellectual capacity until her efforts are rewarded by that eminence in her profession, to which we think she is, of all our actresses, alone entitled.'[52] This was inspired partly by gratitude that he had lived to see it. His health had held out, and the series of reviews in which he followed her progress stands alongside those of Kean as a unique record of a new theatrical talent.

Now nineteen, William Jr wanted to be a singer and study with John Braham, whose 'noble simplicity and fervour' Hazlitt had praised in 1815.[53] Aware that his father really wanted him to be an artist, William Jr asked his mother to persuade him to agree to this change of direction. This was a tall order. Realizing she would get nowhere if she tried it, Sarah first asked Martin Burney to intervene but he refused, saying Hazlitt would never consent. She then tried Lamb, who sat his friend down in early June and broached the possibility that

William Jr be allowed to follow his own path. At that point Hazlitt expressed 'such horror and aversion to the idea of [William's] singing in public' that Lamb declined to 'meddle' further.[54]

To us, Hazlitt's refusal may seem tyrannical, but it would not have seemed so in those days, when a parent's wishes often overrode those of the child. From Hazlitt's perspective, his son's fidelity to the visual arts was a way of compensating for his own failure to fulfil his youthful ambitions. He was at fault, doubtless, for failing to see that he was projecting his own ambitions onto his son—but is not alone among parents in that. Such intransigence would lead to disappointment for both him and William Jr. Just as the Reverend Hazlitt had disappointed his Calvinist father by becoming a dissenter, and the essayist disappointed his father by abandoning the faith altogether, so William Jr would fail to become an artist, opting to become first a man of letters, then a man of law. Denial of the opportunity to sing never ceased to be a source of disappointment to him.

By mid-July, proof copies were available of Hazlitt's *Conversations of James Northcote, R.A.*, which Colburn and Bentley were readying for publication. This coincided with a brief letter to Northcote from Richard Rosdew, threatening legal action were the *Conversations* to include 'any of the false and libellous accounts of the Mudge family which have appeared in the New Monthly Magazine'.[55] Northcote was a calculating man whose essential cowardice emerged when confronted with force—probably what Fuseli had in mind when he observed that Northcote 'looks like a rat that has seen a cat'.[56] True to form, Northcote displayed his talent for disingenuousness in a response that condemned 'those *Cursed* papers which have cost me so many Hours of Agony and which I have not been able to suppress by all my endeavours.'[57] Hazlitt did what he could to put his mind at rest, deleting the comments that caused trouble in 1826 and devoting part of 'Conversation Twenty-Second' to Northcote's anxiety—'I ought to cross myself like the Catholics, when I see you,' Northcote begins, 'You terrify me by repeating what I say.'[58] But this was not sufficient. Northcote demanded cancellation of several pages more, to which Hazlitt replied that 'the present subdued tone of the Conversations may be the means of depriving the world of another masterpiece.'[59] He knew Northcote was attempting to deflect blame so that when writs began to fly, none landed at his door.

When Rosdew visited Northcote he was treated to a word-perfect performance: 'He called Hazlitt a papist, a wretch, a viper, whom he would stab if he could get at him. He said, when he first read [it], he thought for three days it would have killed him: in short, he said so much, and so warmly, that I pitied him, and left him with as warm feelings of regard as before.'[60] Yet it did not escape Northcote's friends that, for all his protestations, he continued to entertain Hazlitt as work continued on the second volume of *Fables* and *Life of Titian*. When this got back to Rosdew, he concluded that 'Ingratitude, envy, meanness, and inordinate self-conceit, together with falsehood, have marked the painter's conduct respecting the Mudges. To these I may add extreme vanity, to gratify which he would sacrifice any thing—not excepting his money!'[61] Northcote's hypocrisy was observed also by Alexander Dyce, who noted that the artist 'professed himself angry—occasionally very angry—with Hazlitt for having printed his *Conversations*: but, I believe, that in his heart he was gratified by the notoriety which that entertaining miscellany had given him.'[62]

Caught up in this whirl of publishing activity, it is hard to believe that Hazlitt had time for essays, yet at this moment he was writing some of his greatest. In 'The Free Admission' (composed June 1830) Hazlitt wrote con amore of one of the principal pleasures of his life:

> Quaffing these delights, inhaling this atmosphere, brooding over these visions, this long trail of glory, is the possessor of a Free Admission to be blamed if 'he takes his ease' at the play; and turning theatrical recluse, and forgetful of himself and his friends, devotes himself to the study of the drama, and to dreams of the past? By constant habit (having nothing to do, little else to think of), he becomes a tippler of the dews of Castaly—a dram-drinker on Mount Parnassus. He tastes the present moment, while a rich sea of pleasure presses to his lip and engulfs him round. The noise, the glare, the warmth, the company, produce a sort of listless intoxication, and clothe the pathos and the wit with a bodily sense. There is a weight, a closeness even, in the air, that makes it difficult to breathe out of it. The custom of going to the play night after night becomes a relief, a craving, a necessity—one cannot do without it. To sit alone is intolerable, to be in company is worse; we are attracted with pleasing force to the spot where 'all that mighty heart is beating still.' It is not that perhaps there is any thing new or fine to see— if there is, we attend to it—but at any time, it kills time and saves the trouble of thinking. O, Covent Garden! 'thy *freedom* hath made me effeminate!'[63]

The arrest in February had undermined Hazlitt's constitution and placed him under unremitting pressure to repay creditors. It was not surprising that his stomach problems, which were now causing occasional haemorrhages and constant pain, began to worsen. Towards the end of June, he was confined to bed and prescribed opium by his doctor (in those days the only available treatment). Though laid up, he continued to work, composing (against the odds) one of his most powerful essays, 'The Sick Chamber'.[64]

> I see (as I awake from a short, uneasy doze) a golden light shine through my white window-curtains on the opposite wall:—is it the dawn of a new day, or the departing light of evening? I do not well know, for the opium "they have drugged my posset with" has made strange havoc with my brain, and I am uncertain whether time has stood still, or advanced, or gone backward.[65]

His condition did not seem life-threatening, though he was weak and needed to build himself up. William Jr visited Frith Street to nurse him, and together they finished Northcote's *Life of Titian*, which would publish in the autumn. Including the *Conversations* and the last two volumes of the *Life of Napoleon*, he had no less than three books in the pipeline. Surely there were better times to come.

This hope was bolstered by news of the July Revolution. Since accession in 1824, Charles X of France had been determined to reinstate the autocratic power structure of the *Ancien Régime*, believing in an absolutist monarchy rather than a parliamentary one. His attempt to impose a series of ordinances suspending liberty of the press and dissolving the Chamber of Deputies led to three days of violent conflict—*les trois glorieuses*, 27–9 July (today commemorated by the colonne de Juillet in the Place de la Bastille). Artisans manned the barricades in Paris, battling royalist troops—and won. The Tuileries and the Louvre fell on the third day of fighting. 'I would rather saw wood than be a King of the English type,' Charles declared. He soon got his wish. He abdicated on 3 August and fled to Britain. Radicals were jubilant: a tyrant had been ousted—yet uncertainty remained. Would the country become a republic again under Lafayette, or a new monarch be appointed? For the moment, no one knew.

Hazlitt was thrilled: it had been his dearest wish to see the downfall of the Bourbons, and the last of their line had just defenestrated himself. The July Revolution, he wrote, was 'a resurrection from the dead, [which] showed plainly that liberty too has a spirit of life in it; and that the hatred of oppression is "the unquenchable flame, the worm that dies not." '[66] He could not resist a jibe at an old adversary: 'Two suns in one day, two triumphs of liberty in one age, is a miracle which I hope the Laureate will hail in appropriate verse.'[67] But he had seen revolutions come and go, and when one of the Reynell brothers expressed pleasure at what had taken place, he replied: 'Ah! I am afraid, Charles, things will go back again.'[68] He was right. On 9 August the Chamber of Deputies met in Paris and voted to install Louis-Philippe as King.

For a while it seemed Hazlitt was on the mend, but in August he succumbed to a 'species of cholera'[69] which had assailed him before; in his weakened state, it was hard to shake off. William Jr continued to look after him, now supported by friends. Charles Lamb moved temporarily into town and made regular visits to Frith Street to share nursing duties. Other visitors included Basil Montagu, who commissioned Dr Darling to tend him. Darling was a respected physician, having treated John Scott, Keats, Sir Thomas Lawrence, and Haydon.

Fearing time might be short, Hazlitt asked to see his mother. But she was old and frail, and could not make the journey from Devon; nor could Peggy leave her to come on her own. He would have to make do with friends. Charles Cowden Clarke came and sat at his bedside talking in an undertone, hoping to cheer him up. Clarke was pained beyond endurance that the financial failure of his publishing firm had contributed to Hazlitt's decline, and looked fondly back on the thirteen-odd years during which he had enjoyed his friendship. After a while, Hazlitt interrupted and whispered: 'My sweet friend, go into the next room and sit there for a time, as quiet as is your nature, for I cannot bear talking at present.'[70] The delicacy of these words moved Clarke almost to tears.

Conversations of James Northcote, R.A. was published on 26 August[71] and, at about the same time, proofs of Northcote's *Life of Titian* arrived at Frith Street. Hazlitt oversaw William's correction of them and they were completed by early September.[72] At that moment his old friend Bryan Waller Procter, a contributor to the *London Magazine* in its heyday, visited Hazlitt and, not having seen him for some time, was shocked by his condition—'ghastly, shrunk, and helpless', though his mind was as 'safe and as strong as ever'. Hazlitt presented him with copies of his first book, *An Essay on the Principles of Human Action* (1805), and his most recent, the newly published *Conversations*.[73] But he was too weak even to lift his hand from the coverlet, and his voice was no more than a 'hoarse whistle, resembling the faint scream that I have heard from birds'.[74]

Even now Hazlitt continued to publish, having left with Robert Bell a backlog of essays to be issued, week by week, in *The Atlas*. It was part of a deliberate strategy to ensure a flow of money; unfortunately, with doctor's and solicitor's bills to pay, it was not enough. He wrote to Montagu begging a loan of £15 'to prevent law expences, which I dread',[75] and with Edmund Kean, recently retired from the acting profession, pleaded for £50, which was refused.[76] Martin Burney was one of those who now shared nursing duties, and one day Hazlitt told him he needed to dictate a letter. Burney agreed, and Hazlitt whispered the words: 'Dear sir, I am dying; can you send me 10*l*., and so consummate your many kindnesses to me? W. Hazlitt.'[77] He ordered Burney to address it to 'Francis Jeffrey, Edinburgh'. Burney was both moved and astonished. It was typical of his friend not to flinch at the imminence of his own demise—but to say these things in a begging letter? He balked, hoping Hazlitt would change his mind, but was forced to promise to send it, and send it he did.

One way of making money was to continue writing, and Hazlitt was sufficiently desperate to believe that, even now, he could write an appreciation of a young novelist whose work he admired, Edward Lytton Bulwer (as he was then known), and got Longman to send copies of his novels—*Falkland* (1827), *Pelham* (1828), *The Disowned* (1828), *Devereux* (1829), and *Paul Clifford* (1830). Although they never met,[78] Bulwer was a strong admirer of Hazlitt's work, and years hence declared that 'When Hazlitt died, he left no successor.'[79] William Jr probably read several of the novels to his father, but in the end Hazlitt accepted he could not compose the article, and on 6 September dictated a note to Longman: 'Mr. Hazlitt is very sorry that he has been obliged to keep the Pelham, &c., but he was not quite sure as to whether he had to write an article respecting them. He has been some time confined to his bed, dangerously.'[80] This was an understatement. He had been ill-served by Dr Darling, whose administration of purgatives and a magical 'blue pill' had only weakened him. Another physician, John Carlyle (brother of Thomas Carlyle), was summoned.[81] As soon as he stepped into the bedroom he knew it was too late. Even though the cholera was now a lesser threat than Hazlitt's old stomach complaint, the fundamentals of his constitution were so fragile there was little he could do to help.

Lamb stopped by on Monday 13 September. Hazlitt had been too ill to see him the previous day, but now (he told Montagu) he found him 'lying in bed as bad as man can be that is alive. His complaint is spasms, he has been violently vomiting blood, and nothing stays upon his stomach. I consider him in danger, & am afraid he cannot afford a nurse. Some male friends have been sitting up with him, since the servant of the house was nearly exhausted. I think it right to let you know. I believe he wants to see you.'[82]

James Hessey, Hazlitt's erstwhile publisher, visited later that day. Since their last dealings he too had been declared bankrupt. He was horrified by Hazlitt's condition. Disease had aged his old friend. The eyes were sunken, the face and body skeletally thin, the hair grey. Worse still, Hazlitt was frantic with anxiety, but lacked the strength to explain its cause. Hessey was so upset he had to leave, but returned later and tried to visit a third time the following day, only to be told his friend could not receive guests. 'Poor Hazlett is very ill indeed—I fear on his death bed,' he told John Clare: 'I saw him twice on Monday, but yesterday he was too ill to see me. I fear his Mind is quite as ill at ease as his body.'[83] Another visitor at this moment, W. H. Reynell, saw 'he had *something in his mind*, which would kill him if he did not dispel it.'[84]

What was it that so agitated him? It seemed to relate to Basil Montagu, whom he wanted desperately to see once more. Stories later circulated about attempts to borrow money on behalf of 'a worthless woman by whom Hazlitt was at the last fascinated'. As Maclean notes, this was as much the product of malice as the equally dubious story that Hazlitt 'died a beggar'.[85] That said, it is true he wanted to borrow more money, and equally so that Montagu would not oblige. When he had gone, Hazlitt is alleged to have made a number of 'infamous slanders against Mr. M. touching money matters'.[86] As Montagu's son-in-law, Procter was put out: 'He owed much gratitude & some money to Mr. Montagu, & ought to have spoken very differently.'[87]

On Friday 17 September, Hazlitt felt 'much better'[88] and William Jr sent word of it to friends. The next day his 'recovery' continued, and William wrote more letters saying his father 'was in no danger'.[89] At some point during the morning of 18 September, he uttered what were to be his last words, which were to prove as controversial as any other aspect of his life: Arnold Bennett thought them 'grossly untrue—a piece of bravado in the menacing face of death'.[90] Maclean declined to quote them because they 'have a touch of *panache*, very foreign to Hazlitt', while Grayling says they astonished those who heard them.[91]

It would not be hard to conjecture that, as the sun rose in the sky early that Saturday, William Jr told his father he was soon to be engaged to Kitty Reynell, and that the 'idea gave him pleasure'.[92] Hazlitt could then have turned to his son and remarked, 'Well, I've had a happy life.'[93] But for anyone who knows Hazlitt, there is no need to invent such a scenario. As Stanley Jones observed, 'it was what he would have said. He *had* had a happy life, and the proof is to be found everywhere in the essays.'[94] Hazlitt's last words were uttered in the same spirit in which, at one of the darkest points in his life, he celebrated the inner freedom in which he had flourished:

I have had nothing to do all my life but to think, and have enjoyed the objects of thought, the sense of truth and beauty, in perfect integrity of soul. No one has said to me, *Believe this, do that, say what we would have you*; no one has come between me and my free-will; I have breathed the very air of truth and independence. Compared with this unbiassed, uncontrouled possession of the universe of thought and nature, what I have wanted is light in the balance, and hardly claims the tribute of a sigh. Oh! Liberty, what a mistress art thou! Have I not enjoyed thee as a bride, and drank thy spirit as of a wine-cup, and will yet do so to my latest breath![95]

At around lunchtime everything changed. His stomach suddenly pained him worse than ever, so badly that his son was forced to give him enough opium to induce unconsciousness—a state from which he would not emerge. Decline was mercifully rapid. William Jr summoned the three friends who had indicated their desire to attend him in his last hours—Charles Lamb, his friend Edward White, and James Hessey. At around four o'clock Hazlitt's breath grew shallow and less than half an hour later he stopped breathing altogether, so quietly that no one realized he was dead until a minute or two had passed.

Sunday 18th September 1830 at about half past four in the afternoon, died at his lodgings No 6 Frith Street Soho William Hazlitt aged 52 years, five months and eight days.
Mr Lamb, Mr White, Mr Hessey, and his own son were with him at the time.

Sarah Stoddart Hazlitt, MS note[96]

EPILOGUE

'HAZLITT dies', Godwin recorded in his diary on 18 September 1830, having heard the news from Lamb. Later that day, Coleridge composed the epitaph which, in his view, his former friend deserved:

W.H. Eheu!
Beneath this Stone doth William Hazlitt lie.
Thankless for all, that God or man could give,
He lived like one who never thought to die,
He died like one who dared not hope to live.[1]

The following morning, Sunday 19 September, two essays appeared in *The Atlas*—'Watch-Words' and 'Friends', both by Hazlitt[2]—and at the same time Jeffrey's letter arrived at Frith Street containing fifty pounds in response to Hazlitt's request for ten. It was sorely needed. Hazlitt owed Mrs Stapleton rent in arrears and his friends would have to pay off the debt. There was also a desire to make an *ex gratia* payment to one of the maids: 'For my own part I care far more about rewarding the Servant Girl than anything else & she is the first person that I shall consider,' Procter told Patmore.[3]

On Monday 20 September, Godwin visited his old friend Sir James Northcote. As they sat in the drawing room at 8 Argyll Place, they reminisced about the man who was both friend and fiend. Northcote remarked with undisguised satisfaction that the £100 set aside for Hazlitt in his will could now be reallocated.[4] Neither that, nor publication of the *Conversations* ('a delightful book',[5] in Robinson's opinion) and the *Life of Titian* (praised by one reviewer as 'full of calm good sense, and just feeling'[6]) made him any better disposed to the dead writer. When John J. Ruskin, father of the artist and critic, congratulated him on the *Conversations*, Northcote replied that 'Hazlitt, although a man of real abilities, yet had a desire to give pain to others.'[7] Having maligned him in life, there was no reason to stop now that he was dead: not for nothing did Hazlitt's grandson describe Northcote as 'an ill-conditioned, malevolent, mean-spirited person, for whom nobody probably ever entertained any real regard'.[8]

Epilogue

Godwin and Northcote had probably seen Leigh Hunt's tribute on the front page of that day's *Tatler*, hailing Hazlitt as 'one of the profoundest writers of the day, an admirable reasoner (no one got better or sooner at the heart of a question than he did), the best general critic, the greatest critic on art that ever appeared (his writings on that subject cast a light like a painted window), exquisite in his relish of poetry, an untameable lover of liberty, and with all his humour and irritability (of which no man had more) a sincere friend, and a generous enemy.'[9] This was no less than Hazlitt deserved. Even *Blackwood's* admitted him to be 'the ingenious author of numerous works, and an extensive contributor to the periodical literature of the day',[10] though *The Times* was less forthcoming: 'Mr Hazlitt, the author of several well-known publications, died on Saturday.'[11]

Readers of the death notices included John Clare, who told James Hessey he had read them twice

> before I dare believe it was Hazlitt that I had met & whose writings I had read with much gratification & it shocked me much to think another acquaintance had made a blank on our memorys & in our esteem for the tallents of Hazlitt was of no every day matter—what I have read are the works of a man of original Genius & it seems that he died in the character of Genius—neglected & forgotten—when will the cant & hypocrasy of trifling be put aside & the sterling merit of superior minds be so valued as to be considerd worthy of universal reward & the humbug of party cavils & party interest by done away with—I doubt never[12]

A few days later, Lamb threw a small dinner party in Enfield, inviting Thomas Noon Talfourd, James Sheridan Knowles, and the publisher Edward Moxon.[13] They drank to an incorrigible personality who, for all his faults, never deserted the principles he held dear.

Unfortunately, they were in a minority, most of the literary world regarding Hazlitt as did Thomas Carlyle when speaking of Cockney writers—'they are not red-blooded *men* at all; they are only *things* for writing "articles" '.[14] Henry Crabb Robinson, then in Florence, was informed of Hazlitt's passing by Landor on 2 October. He condemned him for having been 'a gross sensualist' but admired his 'honesty' in politics, adding: 'His prose writings I have always read with great delight.'[15] In subsequent days Robinson met Charles Brown, who still had the books Hazlitt left him five years earlier: 'They are of no value,' Brown remarked.[16]

Other readers of the obituaries included Charles Wells, Hazlitt's former drinking companion. He had published two books, neither of which attracted much attention, pursued his profession as a solicitor, and married Emily Hill. Though he had seen little of Hazlitt recently, his admiration never wavered. On the Tuesday or Wednesday after his death, Wells took his wife and a friend, Richard Henry Horne, to pay their respects. Only in his late twenties, Horne had been at school with Keats, at whom he had once thrown snowballs.[17] After a career as midshipman in the navy, he pursued a literary career. He was one of many young men who concurred with Leigh Hunt's assessment of Hazlitt but had been shy of making his acquaintance. In 1844 he would write *A New Spirit of the Age*, profiling Dickens, Tennyson, and Browning on Hazlitt's model.

On arrival at Frith Street, they saw a 'Room to Let' notice at the window. They knocked, were admitted by Mrs Stapleton, and tipped her for the privilege of viewing Hazlitt's remains. According to some accounts, she hid the coffin underneath the bed when showing potential occupants the room, but on this occasion it was where it should have been—on trestles alongside the bed, covered with a tablecloth. Wells, Emily, and Horne stood in silence looking at the body. Wells said he regretted having seen less of him in recent years, adding he 'had everything to learn from Hazlitt, and Hazlitt nothing from him; and so the over-ripe intimacy had dropped off.'[18] After a while Mrs Stapleton looked in and delivered a commentary on her tenant's last hours. As she spoke, they gazed round the room: Hazlitt's few books sat mournfully on the shelves (she would hold them hostage until his debts were paid[19]); Horne was moved by the sight of his hat and gloves. Before leaving, they had an idea, and asked Mrs Stapleton whether they could come back. She agreed.

They decided to commission a death mask and went to Sarti's, which sent an Italian artist to Frith Street to get the job done. Halfway through, Horne was 'somewhat dismayed on perceiving that a portion of the eye-brows had been accidentally carried into the cast. The countenance was grandly calm. It had a latent smile, not unlike that which gradually dawns upon one after gazing for a time at some of the faces of the Egyptian sculptures.'[20]

The funeral took place at 4pm on Thursday 23 September at St Anne's Church, Soho, a few minutes' walk from the lodging house in Frith Street. Hazlitt had been here for his brother's wedding years before, and must often have passed it on his walks round London. The occasion was arranged by Lamb who, besides family, invited only Patmore.[21] There were two young men in the churchyard he failed to recognize: Horne and Wells, who had taken some liberties on the deceased's behalf. At that time, there was feverish interest in phrenology and craniology, for which corpses were regularly disinterred and the heads removed. To protect Hazlitt from that indignity, Horne paid the sexton to dig five feet deeper than usual, watching over him to ensure it was done. When the grave was filled in, he arranged for trusses of straw to be layered in every foot or so, as an obstacle to graverobbers. Horne and Wells also paid for a stone to be placed over the tomb, bearing an epitaph by Wells.[22]

Here rests
WILLIAM HAZLITT
Born April 10, 1778. Died 18 September, 1830.
He lived to see his deepest wishes gratified
as he has expressed them in his Essay
'On the Fear of Death.'
Viz.:
'To see the downfall of the Bourbons,
And some prospect of good to mankind':
(Charles X
was driven from France 29th July 1830).
'To leave some sterling work to the world':
(He lived to complete his 'Life of Napoleon').

His desire
That some friendly hand should consign
him to the grave was accomplished to a
limited but profound extent; on
these conditions he was ready to depart,
and to have inscribed on his tomb,
'Grateful and Contented.'

He was
The first (unanswered) Metaphysician of the age.
A despiser of the merely Rich and Great:
A lover of the People, Poor and Oppressed:
A hater of the Pride and Power of the Few,
as opposed to the happiness of the Many;
A man of true moral courage,
Who sacrificed Profit and present Fame
To Principle,
And a yearning for the good of Human Nature.
Who was a burning wound to an Aristocracy,

That could not answer him before men,
And who may confront him before their Maker.

He lived and died
The unconquered Champion
of
Truth, Liberty, and Humanity,
'Dubitantes opera legite.'

This stone
is raised by one whose heart is
with him, in his grave.

Two days later, *The Examiner* ran a review of the *Conversations of James Northcote, R.A.*, criticizing Hazlitt's view of Utilitarianism.[23] It was probably by Albany Fonblanque, now allied to the Benthamites. The article was prefaced by a disclaimer saying it was written 'before the death of Mr. Hazlitt, but we see no reason for omitting or altering it'[24]—a graceless way for the paper to bid farewell to one of its finest writers.

The Atlas (also a Sunday paper) paid more respectful tribute under the heading, 'The Fate of Genius':

> On Thursday last the body of WILLIAM HAZLITT was borne beneath our windows; till that moment we were not aware that a man of genius, a popular writer— the author of no less able a work than the *Life of Napoleon*, which, alas! closed his literary labours—and an amiable man, had been our next door neighbour for months, enduring sickness, and at length dying in indigence. We boast of our national generosity, glory in the flourishing state of our literature, and thunder forth the power of the press, the palladium of our liberties; in the meanwhile 'the spirit which is life' is allowed to burn itself out in penury and privation. Publishers sport their carriages, or fail for a hundred thousand pounds; and those by whom they become publishers die for want of a dinner.[25]

Elsewhere in the same issue Bell included the last of the essays Hazlitt left with him, 'Gravity'.[26] Others would appear posthumously in the *Monthly Magazine*—further evidence of Hazlitt's anxiety to guarantee himself an income in the event of illness. Years before, Hunt's *Literary Examiner*, to which Hazlitt was a contributor, published a short item entitled 'The Ruling Passion Strong in Death': 'The celebrated Bayle died as he had lived, in the uninterrupted habits of composition; for with his dying hand, and nearly speechless, he sent a fresh proof to the printer.'²⁷ Hazlitt's ruling passion was no less strong, whatever his physical condition, and he would have been proud to reflect that, with the issuing of proofs and drafts from his rooms almost up to the day of his death, he had followed Bayle's example. At all events, 'Gravity' gave *Atlas* readers a final glimpse of the unique sensibility of a man who, in his last days, found himself in an 'insular situation'; it was as distinctive as anything he ever composed, not least in its concluding sentences:

> Look at your poultry, your geese, your chickens, and your turkeys; all of them are perfectly serious and grave. You may talk about the lively song of the lark; but look at the owl—there is gravity enough in that bird of wisdom to make up for the levity of a whole sky-full of larks. Every thing is in favour of gravity; we have the majority on our side; cows, sheep, asses, horses, dogs, cats, pigs, ducks, geese, *cum multis aliis*, keep us in countenance. Besides, if we wish to give any account of our pre-eminent gravity, we might quote for illustration our insular situation, and our consequent familiarity with fish. They are the gravest of all animals and the quietest withal. True, they may now and then make a frolic leap out of the water; but then they are like Englishmen at a carnival—they are out of their element. What can be graver than a cod's head and shoulders? What are you laughing at, Monsieur?²⁸

William Jr settled a few minutes' walk from Frith Street at number 15 War-dour Street, and after marrying Kitty Reynell in June 1833 moved to Charlotte Street, just round the corner from where his father and uncle had begun their London careers. His wife would prove one of the blessings in his life, softening the impact of his disappointments. Charles Wells, who must have liaised with William Jr about the inscription on Hazlitt's grave, became an occasional visitor to their home until his departure for France, where he was to die in 1879.²⁹ William Jr was assisted in his legal career by G. Huntly Gordon and Henry Brougham (who his father once commended as 'a striking instance of the versatility and strength of the human mind'³⁰), both of whom helped him achieve a degree of success that compensated for the thwarted desire to sing. He published his father's *Literary Remains* in 1836, a scholarly achievement which set forth the case for Hazlitt's importance both as a critic and a philosopher—though not, unfortunately, to much effect. One of the literary figures called upon to introduce it, Thomas Noon Talfourd, praised Hazlitt for evoking the 'predominant feeling' of the things he described so that 'they seem to glide in review before us':

Thus, his paper on 'Actors and Acting' breathes the very soul of abandonment to impulse and heedless enjoyment, affording glimpses of those brief triumphs which make a stroller's career 'less forlorn', and presenting mirrors to the stage in which its grand and affecting images, themselves reflected from nature, are yet further prolonged and multiplied.[31]

William Jr remained scarred by his parents' divorce and the circumstances surrounding it: the biography of his father in *Literary Remains* says that any 'other reference than a bare record of the fact is as unnecessary to the reader as it would be painful to me', before noting that the cause of the divorce was 'an imagined and most unfounded idea, on my father's part, of a want of sympathy on that of my mother'.[32] Beyond that, he remained tight-lipped on the matter even with his own son, William Carew Hazlitt. Nor was it easy to live with the knowledge that he failed to fulfil either his own dreams or those of his father. He ended his professional life as registrar of the court of bankruptcy—an exalted position, though not what he had hoped for.

William Jr lived to see the deaths of many of those whom Hazlitt called 'friend': Lamb and Coleridge in 1834, Godwin in 1836, Southey in 1843, Mary Lamb in 1847, Wordsworth in 1850, Martin Burney in 1852, John Stoddart in 1856. His mother died in her sixty-sixth year, in 1840.[33] As the common-law wife of John Tomkins, Sarah Walker had a son, Frederick, in 1823 or 1824.[34] She died in 1878. Conscious of the neglect into which his father's reputation had fallen, William Jr edited a 'new and uniform series' of his works, projected in 34 volumes. Of these only twelve were to appear. His own son, William Carew Hazlitt, attempted another edition, of which seven volumes were produced. For all their efforts, Hazlitt's reputation remained in the doldrums, the main explanation being the Sarah Walker affair which led many to regard his death as a divine judgement.[35] Calling at 6 Frith Street one day in 1846, one of his few admirers asked the then-inhabitant, 'Have you heard anyone mention Mr Hazlitt?' 'Hazlitt—Hazlitt?' came the reply. 'Was he a tailor?'[36]

By comparison with the wealth of material published on Lamb and De Quincey, interest shown in Hazlitt was pitifully sparse. His champions tended to be other men of letters. Bulwer Lytton—the novelist whose work Hazlitt read during his last illness—was one of many younger writers whose regard knew no bounds: 'I confess that few deaths of the great writers of my time ever affected me more painfully than his,' he wrote.[37] Dickens too was an admirer, and probably said as much to William Jr, alongside whom he worked on the

Morning Chronicle, reporting from Parliament, just as Hazlitt had done decades earlier. In March 1848 Dickens made a pilgrimage to Winterslow Hut in Hazlitt's honour, mindful that it was the 'birthplace of some of his finest essays'.[38] Robert Louis Stevenson was another 'fervent Hazlittite'[39] and in early 1882 researched a biography which he failed to write. Four years later Stevenson told George Saintsbury that Hazlitt was 'the greatest of essayists', adding that his oeuvre 'entitles him to a place apart as a splenetic, eager, tasteful, unjust man, filled with gusto and revolt; his reflective papers (when they were good) are genuine literature; their like has not been seen; they are the man's proper own.'[40] Oscar Wilde too was drawn to Hazlitt, especially *Characters of Shakespear's Plays* and *Table Talk*—and learned from his playfully aphoristic manner.[41]

With the advent of a more enlightened century, Hazlitt emerged from the shadows. Two scholars, Alfred Rayney Waller and Arnold Glover, produced an edition of collected writings in 13 volumes between 1902 and 1906 for Dent. As publisher of the Everyman series, Dent reprinted some of them as inexpensive volumes for working men and women. In that form Hazlitt was read by writers such as Edward Thomas, who fell in love with Winterslow, which he thought 'a romantic invention, and by association appropriate to Hazlitt'.[42] And yet, for all its qualities, Waller and Glover's edition was incomplete. As their correspondence with W. C. Hazlitt reveals, they scrambled right up to the last moment to trace uncollected essays.[43]

At the same time a French scholar, Jules Douady, was working on the first biography by someone outside the family. Douady's research extended to a trip to Winterslow where he scoured its lanes and byways for traces of the writer. He too was in touch with Hazlitt's grandson, now in his seventies, and on 16 August 1905 wrote excitedly to tell him he had just walked to Winterslow 'along a rustic path which Hazlitt must have followed many a time, for it runs along the park of Titherley'. Douady made a friend of the local schoolmaster, Mr Whittle, who showed him what remained of the cottage owned by Sarah Stoddart and accompanied him to Winterslow Hut—

a white spot in the middle of the vast plain. I will not make any attempt at describing a place you are particularly well situated to know: suffice it to say the landlord very kindly showed me through all the rooms of the inn, from top to bottom. There is not a cellar, not a nook that we left unexplored. As we were taking leave of our good natured host, he pursued me with an old farthing that he had formerly found, with some other coins, in a corner of the old inn.[44]

Epilogue

Douady's biography was published in Paris in 1906—a remarkable work, full of intuitions that resonate to this day. Nor was that all. Like Waller and Glover, the Frenchman was aware that Hazlitt published more than had been acknowledged, and another strand of his labours embraced the most comprehensive listing of his writings to date, the magisterial *Liste Chronologique des Oeuvres de William Hazlitt* (Paris, 1906). In that astonishing book, a mere 52 pages long, Douady attributed to Hazlitt many items overlooked by Waller and Glover. Two decades later, P. P. Howe revised the *Works* and with Douady's assistance added seven volumes to make a 21-volume 'Centenary Edition' published in 1930–4 which even now remains the critical standard. The most important of the growing number of volumes by and about Hazlitt was also one of the smallest: Howe's *The Best of Hazlitt*. First published in 1924, his selection of fourteen essays became a standard school-text for the next five decades, the principal means by which successive generations of children encountered Hazlitt's writing.[45]

The most perceptive of his early-twentieth-century critics were other writers, not least Somerset Maugham, who commended him as 'vivid, bracing, and energetic; he has strength and liveliness',[46] and Virginia Woolf who, on the centenary of Hazlitt's death, told readers of the *Times Literary Supplement* that

> His essays are emphatically himself. He has no reticence and he has no shame. He tells us exactly what he thinks, and he tells us—the confidence is less seductive— exactly what he feels. As of all men he had the most intense consciousness of his own existence, since never a day passed without inflicting on him some pang of hate or jealousy, some thrill of anger or pleasure, we cannot read him for long without coming in contact with a very singular character—ill-conditioned yet high-minded; mean yet noble; intensely egotistical yet inspired by the most genuine passion for the rights and liberties of mankind.[47]

Hazlitt's popularity has fluctuated over the years, but never completely waned, nor is there reason to think it will ever do so. When on Thursday 10 April 2003 a crowd of several hundreds gathered in the churchyard of St Anne's, Soho, to witness the unveiling by Michael Foot of a new tombstone over Hazlitt's grave, it was clear that his appeal was as enduring as ever. Contributors to the new memorial, which preserves Charles Wells's inscription, included journalists, businessmen, academics, artists, songwriters, and poets, many of whom had read Hazlitt's work and fallen in love with the sensibility behind it. His contemporaries might have found him difficult, but his life and work speak to us because he was so acutely aware of his own flaws, and applied to himself the same rigorous, clear-sighted vision he brought to everything else. He bore witness to the passing of his father's generation and the birth of the new age they made possible—the revolutionary concepts contained in the poetry of Wordsworth, Coleridge, Shelley, and Keats, whom he had known. In that sense, he glimpsed the future. Though a child of the Revolution, he understood that revolutions often sour and that the hopes that inspire them may come to nothing. But that did not make him any less attached to the aspiration to a fairer world; if anything, it made him prize 'the day-star of liberty' more than ever. That made him acutely sensitive to the changes wrought by his contemporaries, which were an articulation of that impulse, turning him into the most acute analyst of the cultural ferment we now call Romanticism. In that role he speaks to us of ourselves, our passions and anxieties. That, and the intensity of his engagement with the moment, the here and now in which he lived, gives his writing the power to transcend the strife from which it came.

> I look out of my window and see that a shower has just fallen: the fields look green after it, and a rosy cloud hangs over the brow of the hill; a lily expands its petals in the moisture, dressed in its lovely green and white; a shepherd-boy has just brought some pieces of turf with daisies and grass for his young mistress to make a bed for her sky-lark, not doomed to dip his wings in the dappled dawn— my cloudy thoughts draw off, the storm of angry politics has blown over—Mr Blackwood, I am yours—Mr Croker, my service to you—Mr T. Moore, I am alive and well.[48]

NOTES

The standard edition of *The Letters of William Hazlitt*, edited by Herschel Moreland Sikes with the assistance of Willard Hallam Bonner and Gerald Lahey, is (as
Stanley Jones observed) 'incomplete, inaccurate, and perfunctory'. Even at the time
of its publication (1978) a number of letters were known to exist which are not there
included; texts are inaccurately rendered; annotations throng with errors; recipients of
letters are incorrectly identified; and what might constitute an item of correspondence
not consistently applied ('On the Conduct of Life' and the letters to James Sheridan
Knowles in *Liber Amoris* Part III are not in my view eligible for inclusion).

However, the scholar has little option but to consult Sikes's edition, at least in the first
instance. But throughout this volume I have preferred, wherever possible, to render
all quotations from the appropriate copy-text, whether MS or printed source, rather
than Sikes. There have been occasions when the MS was either too fragile to handle or
otherwise unavailable, but in most cases throughout this volume the original source has
been examined, transcribed, and cited.

Annotations to Hazlitt's letters throughout this book therefore provide the appropriate page reference in Sikes alongside full references for the quotation—giving location of
MS, shelfmark, and folio number for manuscripts, or page reference for printed books.
I provide additional pieces of information not consistently provided by Sikes, including
watermark and postmark details. Editorial principles when rendering Hazlitt's MSS are
straightforward. Unlike Sikes I recognize ampersands where they occur, and provide
deleted or heavily crossed out words within square brackets. The pointing of the
original is preserved unless it requires emendation for ease of comprehension. Readers
will find Sikes's datings corrected frequently, and on several occasions I have had cause
to reassign recipients of letters. These matters are explained fully in my notes. During
my research I have discovered five new MSS letters of Hazlitt, two of which were
not previously known in any form, quotations from which appear during the course
of the book. I have had no hesitation citing and quoting *New Letters* and Gates as
their scholarly standards are beyond reproach. Wherever possible, I have conducted
my own survey of the MSS consulted by them, and provide further information in
notes.

Throughout this book I have tried to base direct speech on documentary sources,
rewriting principally to resolve obscurity. On occasion, it has been necessary to infer
some conversations which must have taken place, but which appear nowhere in the
record. Such conversations are usually flagged in a note.

Notes

Preface
1. Bewick i. 120.
2. Wu ix. 95.
3. Wu iv. 5.
4. Wu vi. 163.
5. Howe xvii. 219.

Prologue
1. Wu ix. 131.
2. In 'My First Acquaintance with Poets', the principal source for this episode, Hazlitt's published text announces that 'I rose one morning before day-light, to walk ten miles in the mud, and went to hear this celebrated person preach' (*The Liberal* 2 (1823), 25). As Stanley Jones has pointed out, the correct reading is as follows: 'I rose one morning before day-light, to walk ten miles in the mud and wet to hear this celebrated person preach' (Wu ix. 96). See 'A Hazlitt Anomaly', *The Library* 7 (1985), 60–2.
3. Wu ix. 96.
4. Ibid.
5. Ibid.
6. Wu ix. 97.
7. Ibid.
8. Wu ix. 99.
9. S. T. Coleridge to John Thelwall, 13 May 1796; Griggs i. 216.
10. Wu ix. 99.
11. Wu ix. 99–100.
12. S. T. Coleridge to the Revd. John Edwards, 20 March 1796; Griggs i. 192. It is true that this remark was made two years before the meeting with Hazlitt, but Coleridge remained just as critical of Priestley in 1798, if not more so.
13. Wu ix. 100. This is confirmed by Coleridge's letter to Joseph Cottle of 24 January 1798: 'The moment I received Mr Wedgewood's letter, I accepted his *offer*' (Griggs i. 380).
14. This was not the judgement of everyone in the Unitarian community. Joshua Toulmin told Hazlitt's father that Coleridge's appointment to Shrewsbury 'would have been very injurious. He is too eccentric and volatile and changeable to become a fixed Dissenting minister: a *genius* is not to be kept with the trammels of rules, customs and habits' (*Hazlitt Papers* 763).
15. In 'My First Acquaintance', Hazlitt has the card read: 'Mr Coleridge, Nether-Stowey, Somersetshire'. My reading is taken from the card itself, see p. 5.
16. From Beaumont and Fletcher's *Philaster*. The quotation is applied to Coleridge in 'On Going a Journey' (Wu vi. 164).
17. Although neither Coleridge nor Hazlitt scholars acknowledge it, this observation is corroborated by a notebook entry which must date from around this period; see Coleridge, *Notebooks*, ed. Kathleen Coburn and Anthony J. Harding (5 vols., Princeton, 1957–2002), i. 327.
18. Wu ix. 101.
19. Ibid.

20. It was family lore that Hazlitt's father took the family to America 'on account of being connected with the United Irishmen'. This is unlikely to have been the case because the United Irishmen were not yet formed in 1783; however, there is reason to suppose that the connection existed later. See Samuel Hazlitt to W. C. Hazlitt, July 1866; BL Add. MS 38899, 74r.
21. See Tom Paulin, *The Day-Star of Liberty* (London, 1998), 67.
22. Rousseau, *La Nouvelle Heloise*, tr. Judith H. McDowell (University Park, PA, 1968), Part IV, chapter 6, p. 286.
23. Wu vi. 167.
24. Ibid.
25. Wu vi. 166.
26. Howe xviii. 296.
27. Wordsworth, *The Thirteen-Book Prelude*, x. 692–3.
28. Howe x. 230.
29. Wu vi. 167. This is the version he gives in 'On Going a Journey'. In 'My First Acquaintance' he places this incident at Tewkesbury. I have preferred the earlier memory on the grounds that it is more likely to be accurate.
30. Wu ix. 103.
31. A footnote to the earliest version of 'This Lime-Tree Bower my Prison'; see Griggs i. 335.
32. Sara Coleridge to John Kenyon, 7 March 1845; Dr Williams's Library, Henry Crabb Robinson papers.
33. S. T. Coleridge to Joseph Cottle, 7 March 1798; Griggs i. 391.
34. S. T. Coleridge to Joseph Cottle, *c*.8 July 1797; Griggs i. 330.
35. *De Quincey* xi. 53.
36. S. T. Coleridge to Joseph Cottle, *c*.8 July 1797; Griggs i. 330.
37. Ibid.; Griggs i. 331.
38. Wu ix. 103.
39. Ibid.
40. Wu ix. 104.
41. William Wordsworth to Charles James Fox, 14 January 1801; *The Letters of William and Dorothy Wordsworth: The Early Years 1787–1805*, ed. Ernest de Selincourt revised Chester L. Shaver (Oxford, 1967), 315.
42. Wu ix. 105.
43. Ibid.
44. Ibid.
45. Ibid.
46. Cottle, though little studied, was an interesting man. He was later to compose an epic poem in 23 Books on the subject of *Alfred*; see the present author's 'Cottle's *Alfred*: Another Coleridge-Inspired Epic', *Charles Lamb Bulletin* NS 73 (January 1991), 19–21.
47. Wu ix. 105.
48. Wu ix. 106.
49. These lines are from a notebook kept by Wordsworth at Alfoxden; see *William Wordsworth: Lyrical Ballads, and Other Poems, 1797–1800*, ed. James Butler and Karen Green (Ithaca, NY, 1992), 114–15.
50. This is, at least, the view of most scholars; see, for instance, Duncan Wu, *Wordsworth's Reading 1770–1799* (Cambridge, 1993), p. 14; *Wordsworth's Reading 1800–1815* (Cambridge,

Notes

1995), 261–2. It is a rather important point when considering the differences between Hazlitt and Wordsworth.

51. Wordsworth and Coleridge's criticisms are inferred on the basis of Hazlitt's comments in his *Letter to William Gifford* (Wu v. 377). Hazlitt does not there attribute the criticisms specifically to Wordsworth and Coleridge, but I have argued elsewhere that they are their source; see my article, 'The Road to Nether Stowey', *Metaphysical Hazlitt: Bicentenary Essays* (Abingdon, 2005), 85–6.

52. Howe ix. 4.

53. Wordsworth, 'The Tables Turned', 25–8.

54. See my article, 'The Road to Nether Stowey', *Metaphysical Hazlitt: Bicentenary Essays* (Abingdon, 2005), 83–97.

55. That Hazlitt does not, in 'My First Acquaintance', mention any further encounter with the Wordsworths tends to support my account of the philosophical argument. However, it is unlikely that he did not see them further during his three-week sojourn in Somerset. It all goes to underline the fact that 'My First Acquaintance' is a very partial and incomplete recollection, being written over two decades after the events it describes, at a difficult time for its author.

56. S. T. Coleridge to George Coleridge, 10 March 1798; Griggs i. 397.

57. Ibid.; Griggs i. 395.

58. See Nicholas Roe, *Wordsworth and Coleridge: The Radical Years* (Oxford, 1988), 260–2.

59. S. T. Coleridge to Joseph Cottle, early April 1798; Griggs i. 403. Years later, Wordsworth denied all this: 'The facts mentioned by Coleridge of a spy, &c, came not to my knowledge till I had left the neighbourhood. I was not refused a continuance. I never applied for one' (*Barron Field's Memoirs of Wordsworth*, ed. Geoffrey Little (Sydney, 1975), 29).

60. Hazlitt nowhere says he first heard 'Kubla Khan' in 1798, but it is almost certain he did so during the three weeks he spent in Stowey at that time. My account of this first reading, though invented, draws on the earliest MS of the poem, now in the British Library, and Coleridge's explanatory note to it.

61. Wu viii. 323.

62. S. T. Coleridge to Thomas Poole, 16 October 1797; Griggs i. 354.

63. Wu v. 10–11.

64. Wu vii. 103.

65. Richard Warner, *A Walk through Some of the Western Counties of England* (Bath, 1800), 108.

66. See Tom Mayberry, *Coleridge and Wordsworth in the West Country* (Stroud, 1992), 108.

67. In 'My First Acquaintance' Coleridge is made to say Thomson was 'a great poet, rather than a good one' (Wu ix. 107); the epithets are transposed. Hazlitt wouldn't have constructed Coleridge's sentence as he did unless what he actually meant him to say was that he was 'a good poet, rather than a great one'. This is corroborated by Coleridge's remarks elsewhere, for instance in his *Table-Talk*, which do not suggest he thought Thomson a great poet in any sense. Stanley Jones reminds us that Hazlitt's 'My First Acquaintance' contains a number of errors. This is yet another example, though not previously noted. See Stanley Jones, 'A Hazlitt Corruption' and 'A Hazlitt Anomaly', *The Library* 33 (1978), 235–8, and 7 (1985), 60–2.

68. Wu ix. 107.

69. Wu ix. 108.

70. WH to William Hazlitt Sr, 10 June 1798; *Four Generations* i. 79 (*Letters* 71). Sikes's text is from *Four Generations*; the MS is at present untraced.
71. Wu ix. 95.
72. These comments appear in the MS of *Lectures on the English Poets*; see Wu ii. 379.

Chapter 1

1. *Haydon Table Talk* ii. 401–2. Haydon does not date the statement, but it presumably post-dates the demise of Hazlitt's father in 1820, and the sentiment is one that would fit Hazlitt's mood after the Sarah Walker debacle, 1823.
2. Howe xx. 283.
3. Hazlitt said he 'gave some time to Physic' (Moyne 33). He remained fascinated by physics for the rest of his life, and probably discussed these experiments with Benjamin Franklin.
4. Hazlitt probably attended lectures on which Smith's *Theory of Moral Sentiments* (1759) would be based. Smith's attendance certificates for Hazlitt are now at the State University of Victoria, Melbourne, Australia. They are dated 19 May 1758 and 23 April 1759. Texts of both appear in Harold Love, 'An Early Version of Margaret Hazlitt's Journal', *AUMLA* 43 (May 1975), 24–32, 32 n 5.
5. For more detailed treatment, see my article, ' "Polemical Divinity": William Hazlitt at the University of Glasgow', *Romanticism* 6.2 (December 2000), 163–77, esp. 171–2.
6. Wu vi. 279.
7. Wu ii. 155.
8. Moyne 34.
9. In later years Hazlitt would not have a high regard of his first publication, even though such colleagues as Joshua Toulmin would take pains to seek it out; see *Hazlitt Papers* 705.
10. Moyne 37.
11. A full listing of Hazlitt's contributions may be found in my 'William Hazlitt (1737–1820), The Priestley Circle, and *The Theological Repository:* A Brief Survey and Bibliography', *Review of English Studies* 56 (2005), 756–66.
12. Hazlitt and Priestley were corresponding by 1772, when Priestley cited one of Hazlitt's letters when writing to Theophilus Lindsey; see J. T. Rutt, *Life and Correspondence of Joseph Priestley* (2 vols., London, 1831–2), i. 161.
13. Joseph Priestley, *Autobiography* (Bath, 1970), 117.
14. I thank James N. Green of the Library Company of Philadelphia for this information.
15. Rutt, *Life and Correspondence of Joseph Priestley*, i. 175.
16. Priestley thought him 'the very first character in this kingdom' (Priestley to Richard Price, 21 July 1772; Bodleian Library, Eng. misc. c. 132, 19r).
17. The house was just off Bullock Lane; see *Hazlitts* 17 and J. B. Barnhill to W. C. Hazlitt, n.d. (postmarked 3 February 1899); BL Add. MS 38908, 27r. According to W. C. Hazlitt, the rent was £12.
18. *Hazlitts* 17. Hazlitt's father condoned baptism because it was performed by Christ; presumably it took place at the Unitarian chapel (rather than at the parish church—see Samuel Joy to W. C. Hazlitt, 4 February 1899; BL Add MS 38908, 28r).
19. This detail is given by Margaret Hazlitt (Moyne 39); Howe supposed the dispute to concern the American War of Independence, but that had been in progress for four years by 1780, and Hazlitt's views would by then have been known to his congregation (see Howe 2). He is followed by Grayling (Grayling 7).

20. See Joseph Hunter's MS notebook; BL Add. MS 36527, f. 158.

21. Further information on this episode, along with transcripts of the Reverend Hazlitt's articles, can be found in Ernest J. Moyne's article, 'The Reverend William Hazlitt: A Friend of Liberty in Ireland during the American Revolution', *The William and Mary Quarterly* 21 (April 1964), 288–97.

22. Richard Price to William Hazlitt Sr, 28 June 1782; private collection. This letter does not appear in the standard edition of Price's letters and is unpublished.

23. Moyne 46.

24. Ibid. 47–8.

25. Wu ii. 100–1.

26. Jeremy Belknap, 'Remarks on ye City of New York' (MS); Massachusetts Historical Society.

27. Foremost among the ministers who opposed Hazlitt were James Sproat, pastor of the Second Presbyterian church, famous for being the last clergyman to appear in public in cocked hat and wig, and George Duffield, pastor of the Third Presbyterian Church, who fought so doggedly against the British during the war that they put a £50 bounty on his head.

28. John Ewing, [untitled article beginning 'Fellow Citizens'], *Pennsylvania Packet*, 26 February 1785. This article was composed as part of an ongoing dispute arising from Hazlitt Sr's unsuccessful application to the Principalship of Dickinson College, an episode related by Ernest J. Moyne, 'The Reverend William Hazlitt and Dickinson College', *The Pennsylvania Magazine* 85 (1961), 289–302.

29. Moyne 50.

30. Ewing, [untitled article beginnning 'Fellow Citizens']. Ewing probably buried both children in his cemetery, but there are no burial records for his church at this period in the Presbyterian Historical Society in Philadelphia, and I am unable to confirm this conjecture.

31. Moyne 52.

32. Howe xix. 320–4. See also Bromwich 406–7.

33. This is reported by Moyne 145 n 26.

34. An Old Unitarian [William Hazlitt], 'An Account of the State of Rational Religion in America', *Monthly Repository* 3 (1808), 302–7, esp. 305.

35. William Hazlitt Sr to Richard Price, 19 October 1784; MS, American Philosophical Society.

36. Howe xvi. 367.

37. Moyne suggests that the farmers were sent by Hugh Henry Brackenridge, author of *Modern Chivalry*, who had settled in Pittsburgh in 1781 and was instrumental in founding the Presbyterian congregation there.

38. Moyne 56.

39. According to John Eliot—see John Eliot to Jeremy Belknap, 6 February 1784; MS, Massachusetts Historical Society.

40. Jeremy Belknap to Ebenezer Hazard, 16 August 1784; MS, Massachusetts Historical Society.

41. Moyne 57.

42. He did not reside there for long, having made the error of remaining loyal to George III throughout the war; after being placed under house arrest he was imprisoned in Connecticut shortly before the signing of the Declaration of Independence (to which his father was signatory).

43. Moyne 57.

44. Ibid. 57–8.

45. Ibid. 58.

46. Ibid. The old man was probably Samuel Shakespeare, born in Coventry, England, in 1731, which would have made him 53 years old. He was a baptist and was buried at the Welsh Tract Church, Iron Hill, Delaware, in 1793.
47. Ibid.
48. For further details on these and other events, see E. Wilder Spaulding, *New York in the Critical Period 1783–1789* (New York, 1932).
49. This is the listing for Moses Gomez in the 1786 New York City Directory.
50. Moyne 59.
51. Ibid.
52. Ibid.
53. Ibid. 60.
54. Ibid. 60–1.
55. Ibid. 61.
56. In his classic study, *The Unitarian Conscience*, Daniel W. Howe observes that 'Any student of Harvard Unitarianism quickly learns that it was—and was considered in its day—the religion of an elite. The moral philosopher in Cambridge was spokesman for a socially and culturally distinct class, centered in and around Boston' (*The Unitarian Conscience: Harvard Moral Philosophy, 1805–1861* (Middletown, CT, 1988), 7).
57. 'Harvard College was theirs. They controlled nearly all the old Puritan churches. One hundred and twenty churches, including the Pilgrim Church at Plymouth and the First Churches of Boston, Salem, Dorchester, Roxbury, and so on, were in their hands' (William H. Lyon, *Charles Chauncy: Minister of the First Church in Boston 1727–1787* (London, 1903), 19).
58. An Old Unitarian [William Hazlitt], 'An Account of the State of Rational Religion in America', *Monthly Repository* 3 (1808) 302–7, esp. 303.
59. Ibid.
60. The congregation expected Freeman 'to read the service of the Church twice every Sunday, and also on Saints' days; to deliver a sermon of your own composing as often as is convenient; and at other times to read such other sermons as are most approved by you' (King's Chapel records; MS, Massachusetts Historical Society).
61. The first objective was to dispense with the Trinitarian liturgy and replace it with a Unitarian one (as Hazlitt had proposed at Centreville). Hazlitt probably obtained from Theophilus Lindsey a copy of the Unitarian liturgy he used at the Essex Street Chapel. While he was at it, Lindsey sent Joseph Johnson's recent publications as well as some money; see Lindsey's letter to Hazlitt, 21 January 1785 (*Hazlitt Papers* 507). In a letter to William Tayleur of 1 December 1785, now at the John Rylands Library in Manchester, Lindsey says he has just sent £10 to Hazlitt; I am grateful to Grayson Ditchfield for this information. Hazlitt Sr also wrote a series of articles for the *American Herald* which argued that Christianity was corrupted by those who, 'under the assumed title of God's viceregents, frame, and impose upon others, as terms of christian communion, laws of their own'—that is, Bishops. It was a typically brave and uncompromising gesture, one that would do himself no favours at all, for the Bishops soon learnt his name and became determined to thwart the career of the man who dared challenge their authority.
62. Wu iv. 222.
63. Moyne 57. This may also have had something to do with a remark Hazlitt made to his congregation: in a letter of May 1785 Samuel Vaughan told Hazlitt that 'I was informed that

an indiscreet act of your own had prevented your being chosen at Brattle Street' (Samuel Vaughan to William Hazlitt Sr, 17 May 1785; *Hazlitt Papers* 698).

64. Hazlitt 'is in trouble', his friend John Eliot recorded in August 1784, 'His Wife & family are now come & put themselves upon him' (John Eliot to Jeremy Belknap, Boston, 26 August 1784; MS, Massachusetts Historical Society).

65. Philalethes [William Hazlitt Sr], 'For the American Herald', *The American Herald*, 1 November 1784, 1.

66. An Old Unitarian [Hazlitt], 'An Account of the State of Rational Religion in America', 306.

67. Hazlitt Sr arrived in Boston with a letter of introduction to Hancock from Professor James Davidson of the University of Pennsylvania, commending him as 'truely Xtian' (James Davidson to John Hancock, 31 May 1784; Ms 263, Boston Public Library). Hazlitt approved Hancock's support for widows, orphans, and the needy, and throughout his time in Boston was a frequent visitor to the governor's mansion.

68. Moyne 61.

69. Ibid. 62.

70. Ibid. My attempts to find documentary confirmation of this sighting have failed.

71. WH to William Hazlitt Sr, 12 November 1786; *Letters* 43. I have not been able to consult this MS.

72. Moyne 62.

73. Ibid.

74. This exchange is adapted from Mary Smith Cranch to Abigail Adams, 6 November 1784; *Adams Family Correspondence*, ed. L. H. Butterfield et al. (6 vols., Cambridge, MA, 1963–93), v. 479–80.

75. Moyne 62.

76. Ibid. 64

77. Ibid. 64.

78. Ibid.

79. Ibid. 65.

80. Ibid. 63. My attempts to trace this painting have proved fruitless; I wish to thank Professor Jules D. Prown and Professor David Bjelajac for their kindly assistance in this matter.

81. Wu vi. 232.

82. Cotton Tufts recorded in his diary for 5 December, 'Revd. Mr Hazlot preached', and on 12 December, 'Clear & cold Mr Hazlot preached'; the original MS is at the Massachusetts Historical Society—a copy of *Thomas's Massachusetts, Connecticut Rhode-Island, New-Hampshire and Vermont Almanack* (Worcester, MA, 1784) with a home-made paper wrapper bearing the inked inscription 'Dyary for 1784'.

83. Moyne 76.

84. Mary Smith Cranch to Abigail Adams, Braintree, 19 July 1785; *Adams Family Correspondence*, vi. 233–4.

85. Ibid.

86. John Quincy Adams to Abigail Adams, 19 September 1785; *Adams Family Correspondence*, vi. 369–70.

87. Hazlitt was to recall this portrait when the Sarah Walker affair reached its crisis; see Wu vii. 31.

88. The Archive of King's Chapel contains a receipt for the printing of a 'prayer Book for the Chapel', dated 1 October 1785; MS, Massachusetts Historical Society.

89. He may have had a hand in the letter enclosed with it, declaring that in separating themselves from the Church of England, the congregation believed 'Truth is the real object of their pursuit; and Truth they trust they are sincerely disposed to study & follow'; see Thomas Bulfinch and Shrimpton Hutchinson to Bishop Seabury, 1 October 1785; Ms. N-1867, Correspondence Box 1, Folder 20, King's Chapel Archive, Massachusetts Historical Society.

90. Moyne 73.

91. See Joseph B. Felt, *Annals of Salem* (2nd edn, 2 vols., Salem, 1849), ii. 605. The dating is provided by Margaret Hazlitt (Moyne 81). Hazlitt had been invited by the minister at Salem, William Bentley, and later commended the congregation as 'unprejudiced'; see William Hazlitt Sr to James Freeman [n.d., but *c*.March 1788], as quoted James Freeman to William Bentley, 21 April 1788; Houghton Library, bMS Am 1569.5(2).

92. Kirk Boott to William Hazlitt Sr, 24 June 1790, as quoted in William Hazlitt Sr to WH, 31 July 1790; Beineke Library (text published in *The Hazlitts* 389–93; incomplete text in *Memoirs* ii. 14–16).

93. James Freeman to William Hazlitt Sr, 20 November 1787; *Hazlitt Papers* 17.

94. Freeman's correspondence with Bentley is now at the Houghton Library, Harvard. Bentley's portrait was painted by John Hazlitt.

95. James Freeman to Theophilus Lindsey, 7 July 1786; as quoted in Thomas Belsham, *Memoirs of the Late Reverend Theophilus Lindsey* (London, 1812), 240 n.

96. James Freeman to Theophilus Lindsey, June 1789; as quoted in Belsham, *Memoirs of the Late Reverend Theophilus Lindsey*, 240 n.

97. WH to Macvey Napier, 21 July 1829; BL Add. MS 34614, f. 127 (*Letters* 366). The letter bears a receipt postmark of 23 July. Those dependent on Sikes for knowledge of this letter do so at their own risk; as Jones notes, Sikes's text is defective (Jones 4 n 11).

Chapter 2

1. Wu vi. 229.

2. For more on the tea gardens and the nursery, see John H. Harvey, 'An Early Garden Centre: South London in 1789', *The Garden History Society Newsletter* 13 (1 May 1971), 3–4, and Jim Gould, 'James Maddock, the Walworth Garden and "The Florist's Directory"', *Garden History* 19 (Autumn 1991), 155–62.

3. Wu vi. 230–1.

4. Moyne 82.

5. Ibid. 102.

6. Ibid. 106.

7. Wu viii. 208.

8. Ibid. vi. 231.

9. Ibid. vi. 231.

10. Joseph Hunter, MS notebook entitled 'Biographical Notices of some of my Contemporaries who have gained some celebrity, chiefly in the literary world, especially of such matters as have fallen under my own observation. By Joseph Hunter F.S.A.'; BL Add. MS 36527, ff. 158–9. Hunter is gossipy and not always accurate, but I see no reason to query him on this point.

11. See BL Add. MS 74782A, B; opposite page 54.

12. *Remains* Vol. i, p. v.

13. WH to John Hazlitt, March 1788; SUNY at Buffalo, Goodyear Collection (*Letters* 45).
14. Ibid. It is an index of his growing sense of superiority that he was unable to refrain from describing a classmate as 'a great dunce' (WH to John Hazlitt, March 1788; SUNY at Buffalo, Goodyear Collection (*Letters* 46)).
15. Howe xvii. 88.
16. There were two such episodes. Margaret Hazlitt refers to the first 'an year or two' after Hazlitt began to learn Latin (that is, in 1788 or 1789); see Moyne 89. The second occurred when he was fifteen (in 1792); see Moyne 105.
17. WH to John Hazlitt, March 1788; SUNY at Buffalo, Goodyear Collection (*Letters* 45).
18. Moyne 89.
19. Howe xvii. 91.
20. Theophilus Lindsey to William Hazlitt Sr, 31 August 1789; *Hazlitt Papers* 756.
21. Howe xvii. 255.
22. Ibid. 258.
23. Ibid. 261.
24. In his memoir of the Hazlitts, Joseph Hunter says it was at about this time that William ceased to 'attend the devotions of the family. He would not go to the chapel. He would shut himself up from the rest of the family: be seen by no one during the day' (BL Add. MS 36527, ff. 158–9).
25. Moyne 105.
26. WH to Grace Hazlitt, 9 and 13 July 1790; *Four Generations* i. 68 (*Letters* 47).
27. WH to William Hazlitt Sr, 19 or 20 July 1790; *Remains* Vol. i, p. xxii (*Letters* 52). Sikes dates the letter 'July, 1790', but I have preferred the more specific dating proposed by Jones, review of Sikes, *The Library* Series 6, 3 (1980), 356–62, esp. 358.
28. WH to William Hazlitt Sr, 19 or 20 July 1790; *Remains* vol. i, p. xxiii (*Letters* 52).
29. Kemble's adaptation was first acted at Drury Lane theatre on 8 March 1790.
30. Storace's opera adapted Grétry, Harrington, Pleyel, and Giordani. It was first performed 16 April 1790.
31. WH to William Hazlitt Sr, 19 or 20 July 1790; *Remains* vol. i, p. xxii (*Letters* 51).
32. Wu iii. 178.
33. Ibid. iii. 209–13.
34. Ibid. viii. 177.
35. William Hazlitt Sr to WH, 31 July 1790; Beineke Library, Yale University.
36. See Joseph Hunter in his 'Biographical Notices' who, it must be admitted, is not always reliable (BL Add. MS. 36527, ff. 158–9).
37. WH to Grace Hazlitt, 9 and 13 July 1790; *Four Generations* i. 69 (*Letters* 49).
38. For more detail concerning this episode see Jenny Uglow, *The Lunar Men* (London, 2002), 441–5.
39. George Eyre Evans, *Vestiges of Protestant Dissent* (Liverpool, 1897), 252.
40. John Ralph to William Hazlitt Sr, 23 July 1791; *Hazlitt Papers* 702–3.
41. This was probably the local paper of choice for the Hazlitts. It was a literary paper, and though attached to the Church of England was tolerant of dissenters.
42. WH to the editor of the *Shrewsbury Chronicle*, 2–9 November 1791; *Letters* 58. Sikes dates it '[Summer] 1791'; I have preferred the more accurate dating proposed by Jones, review of Sikes, *The Library* Series 6, 3 (1980), 356–62, esp. 358. The contents alone indicate a dating after the publication of letters critical of Priestley in October.

43. Thomas Milner to William Hazlitt Sr, 20 November 1791; *Hazlitt Papers* 704. Milner had been a member of Hazlitt's Maidstone congregation and the source for one of the articles Hazlitt published in the *Boston Magazine* in 1784; see my 'The Journalism of William Hazlitt (1737–1820) in Boston (1784–5): A Critical and Bibliographical Survey', *Review of English Studies* 57 (2006), 221–46, esp. 229.

44. Howe xix. 302.

45. Ibid.

46. Wu viii. 208.

47. This was first elaborated by Stanley Jones, 'Hazlitt's Quotations from *Hudibras* and *Don Quixote*', *Review of English Studies* 43 (1992), 488–97.

48. Wu viii. 208–9.

49. See the Minutes of the Board of the Presbyterian Fund, vii. 491; Dr Williams's Library.

50. WH to William Hazlitt Sr, 6 October 1793; BL Add. MS 70949, f. 159 (Charnwood Collection on deposit at the BL, Loan 60, II/31 (3)) (*Letters* 60).

51. Moyne 105.

52. Marrs i. 267.

53. Quoted H. W. Stephenson, *William Hazlitt and Hackney College* (London, 1930), 1.

54. Ibid. 4.

55. Ibid. 9.

56. He did not, apparently, retain a knowledge of shorthand into adulthood. The notebook he used when reporting parliamentary debates many years later, now preserved at the Berg Collection, NYPL, contains notes in longhand only.

57. Wu ii. 84.

58. WH to William Hazlitt Sr, 6 October 1793; BL Add. MS 70949, f. 159 (Charnwood Collection on deposit at the BL, Loan 60, II/31 (3)) (*Letters* 62). Sikes takes his text from W. C. Hazlitt, *Lamb and Hazlitt* (London, 1900), without reference to the MS.

59. WH to William Hazlitt Sr, 6 October 1793; BL Add. MS 70949, f. 159 (Charnwood Collection on deposit at the BL, Loan 60, II/31 (3)) (*Letters* 60).

60. Ibid.

61. This is probably why, on his visits to the Continent, William declined to apply for a passport.

62. WH to William Hazlitt Sr, 22 October 1793; MS in the possession of the author (*Letters* 63). Sikes takes his text from Hazlitt, *Lamb and Hazlitt*. The postmark, not previously reported, shows the letter was posted on 22 October 1793, when it was probably written.

63. WH to William Hazlitt Sr, undated; *Letters* 65. I have not been able to discover the location of the MS and none is given by Sikes, whose text is from *Lamb and Hazlitt*. Sikes's conjecture, 'November 1793', is possible.

64. WH to William Hazlitt Sr, undated; Houghton Library, *74M-23 (*Letters* 67). Sikes takes his text from Hazlitt, *Lamb and Hazlitt*, without reference to the MS. The Houghton catalogue indicates a date of composition of *c.*1794, but from the contents of the letter Sikes is closer to the mark with 'Late Autumn 1793', and I would hazard a conjecture of November or December that year.

65. Ibid.

66. Howe xx. 237.

67. Ibid. 236.

68. Ibid. 236–7.

69. Ibid. ii. 262.

70. *De Quincey* xi. 98.
71. The manuscript title page of the pamphlet is reproduced in the present author's *Wordsworth: An Inner Life* (Oxford, 2002), 81.
72. See *The Prose Works of William Wordsworth*, ed. W. J. B. Owen and Jane Worthington Smyser (3 vols., Oxford, 1974), i. 38.
73. It seems very likely that Wordsworth submitted the MS to Joseph Johnson, who did in fact go to prison in 1799 for having published a pamphlet by Gilbert Wakefield. Wordsworth's 'Letter' did not appear in print until 1876, in Grosart's edition of the *Prose Works*.
74. Robert Southey to Grosvenor Charles Bedford, 22 November 1793; as quoted in Nicholas Roe, *The Politics of Nature: William Wordsworth and Some Contemporaries* (2nd edn, Houndmills, 2002), 52. Roe helpfully discusses Southey's reading of Godwin.
75. Howe xi. 24.
76. Nicholas Roe, *Wordsworth and Coleridge: The Radical Years* (Oxford, 1988), 162. For details of Godwin's contact with Thelwall and Holcroft, see William St Clair, *The Godwins and the Shelleys* (London, 1989), 128 ff.
77. Wu vi. 133 n.
78. Ibid.
79. William Godwin, *Cursory Strictures* (London, 1794), 24.
80. Quoted from Hazlitt, *Memoirs of Thomas Holcroft* (3 vols., 1816), ii. 180.
81. Wu vii. 118.
82. William St Clair, *The Godwins and the Shelleys* (London, 1989), 132.
83. Andrew Kippis, Minutes of the Meetings of the Board of the Presbyterian Fund, vii. 506 (minutes for 5 December 1794); Dr Williams's Library.

Chapter 3

1. Howe xx. 333.
2. Godwin's part in this is vouched for by W. C. Hazlitt; *Four Generations* i. 158.
3. Howe iii. 171 n 1.
4. Milton, *Comus* 251–6.
5. Wu vi. 201.
6. *The Fenwick Notes of William Wordsworth*, ed. Jared Curtis (London, 1993), 80.
7. Howe iii. 171 n 1. Against this passage in his copy of Hazlitt's *Memoirs of Holcroft*, Godwin placed two lines in the margin; see Godwin's copy in the Pforzheimer Library, NYPL, ii. 247.
8. Howe iii. 155.
9. Wu iii. 29.
10. Ibid. 44.
11. Ibid. 81.
12. It is calculated that there were up to 50,000 prostitutes in London alone in 1813.
13. Howe xvii. 263.
14. The phrase is that used by Antony E. Simpson, 'The Ordeal of St Sepulchre's: A Campaign against Organized Prostitution in early Nineteenth-Century London and the Emergence of Lower Middle-Class Consciousness', *Social and Legal Studies* 15 (2006), 363–87, esp. 367. For a factual analysis of prostitution during Hazlitt's lifetime, see A. D. Harvey, *Sex in Georgian England* (London, 1994), Chap. 5.

15. Shelley scholars point to the tendency for Etonians to frequent brothels near the school. Kenneth R. Johnston hints that Wordsworth visited prostitutes at Cambridge; see *The Hidden Wordsworth: Poet Lover Rebel Spy* (New York, 1998), 128–30. As for Keats, he seems to have caught venereal disease from prostitutes in London and Oxford; see Andrew Motion, *Keats* (London, 1997), 196–7.

16. Charles Lamb to Thomas Manning, 29 November 1800; Marrs i. 248.

17. Charles Lamb to Thomas Manning, 27 February 1801; Marrs i. 277.

18. Charles Lamb to William Wordsworth, 30 January 1801; Marrs i. 267. There is a good deal more to be said on Lamb's sex-life; further evidence includes the story of how a prostitute blundered up the wrong staircase in the Temple, knocked on a respectable door, and asked for him.

19. Wu i. 42.

20. The open-minded Unitarians of Hackney would not condemn it; even Priestley regarded it as containing 'a great quantity of original thinking'.

21. S. T. Coleridge to John Prior Estlin, 1 March 1800; Griggs i. 577.

22. Quoted H. W. Stephenson, *William Hazlitt and Hackney College* (London, 1930), 48.

23. Ibid. 51.

24. Morley i. 6.

25. Andrew Kippis to William Hazlitt Sr, 14 August 1795; *Hazlitt Papers* 763.

26. Andrew Kippis, Minutes of the Meetings of the Board of the Presbyterian Fund, vii. 539 (minutes for 2 May 1796); Dr Williams's Library.

27. Theophilus Lindsey to John Rowe, 26 June 1795; John Rylands University Library of Manchester. I thank Grayson Ditchfield for drawing this letter to my attention and supplying me with his text.

28. See *The St James's Chronicle* no. 5958 for 27 February to 1 March 1796, published 1 March 1796, p. 2, cols. 1–2, 'Mr Burke's Letter on his Pension'. It includes Burke's memorable reference to 'the principle of Evil himself, incorporeal, pure, unmixed, dephlegmated, defecated Evil', occasionally invoked by Hazlitt.

29. Howe xvi. 222.

30. Wu viii. 213.

31. By a curious twist of fate, Sir Philip Francis (now generally regarded as the author of Junius's *Letters*) was to be one of Hazlitt's earliest admirers; see Wu (2007) i, pp. xxxiii–iv and p. 158 above.

32. Wu viii. 213.

33. For a powerful analysis of Burke's influence on Hazlitt, see Bromwich 288–300.

34. Wu viii. 209.

35. Ibid.

36. Wu ix. 99.

37. WH to William Hazlitt, Sr, 23 October 1796; W. C. Hazlitt, *Lamb and Hazlitt* (London, 1900), 46. Sikes takes his text from W. C. Hazlitt, but gets the page reference wrong: it should read pp. 46–9, not 44–7 (see *Letters* 69). The location of the MS is not known.

38. WH to William Hazlitt, Sr, 23 October 1796; Hazlitt, *Lamb and Hazlitt*, 47.

39. Richard Brinsley Knowles, *The Life of James Sheridan Knowles* (privately printed, London, 1872), 10.

40. 'It is a great many years since I saw Richer, the famous rope-dancer, perform at Sadler's Wells' (Wu vi. 69).

41. James Sheridan Knowles to Leigh Hunt, n.d., no postmark; BL Add. MS 38524, 165v.
42. Knowles, *The Life of James Sheridan Knowles*, 10.
43. Anon., 'Our Portrait Gallery.—No. LXVIII. James Sheridan Knowles', *Dublin University Magazine* 40 (October 1852), 428–35, esp. 429.
44. Wu vi. 29.
45. Howe iii. 127–8.
46. Wu ix. 100.
47. Ibid.
48. Wu vi. 29.
49. Ibid.
50. Wu vii. 247.
51. Ibid. viii. 186.
52. For more on Tooke's acquaintance with Wilkes, see Arthur H. Cash, *John Wilkes: The Scandalous Father of Civil Liberty* (New Haven, 2006).
53. Wu vii. 16.
54. Howe ix. 194.
55. Wu iv. 121.

Chapter 4

1. Wu vi. 11.
2. The exhibition opened on 26 December 1798 and ran to the end of July 1799. The Dutch and Flemish part of the Orleans Gallery had exhibited at 125 Pall Mall in April 1793, but there is no evidence that it was seen by Hazlitt; see BL 7805e5/44.
3. Howe x. 9. In Hazlitt's text 'heart' appears in the plural (both in Howe and his copy-text); this can only be a typographical error, and I have emended accordingly.
4. Ibid. 10.
5. Ibid. 31.
6. Ibid. 33.
7. Wu ii. 80.
8. Ibid. 11.
9. [Leigh Hunt], 'The Wishing-Cap. No II. A Walk in Covent-Garden', *The Examiner* (4 April 1824), 211.
10. Howe xi. 291. Hazlitt commends the painting also in an article of 1814 for *The Champion* (Ibid. xviii. 36).
11. Ibid. xi. 318.
12. Jones 13.
13. Charles Lamb to S. T. Coleridge, 8–10 June 1796; Marrs i. 22.
14. It is a peculiar fact that Wordsworth used Martha Ray's name for the protagonist of 'The Thorn'.
15. Howe iii. 199.
16. Ibid. 192.
17. From Henry Crabb Robinson's notes on the lectures; Robinson correspondence volume 1, f. 122; Dr Williams's Library.
18. James Mackintosh to George Moore, 6 January 1800; BL Add. MS 78763, 186v.
19. Wu vii. 155.
20. Ibid. 156.

Notes

21. William Pitt to James Mackintosh, 2 January 1799; BL Add. MS 78763, 191r–v.
22. William Godwin to James Mackintosh, c. June 1799; BL Add. MS 52451B, 32r–v. A number of acquaintances felt similarly. Coleridge told Wordsworth to write a poem addressed to 'those, who, in consequence of the complete failure of the French Revolution, have thrown up all hopes of the amelioration of mankind' (Griggs i. 527). In response, Wordsworth included in the earliest version of what was to become *The Prelude* a passage deploring that 'good men | On every side fall off we know not how, | To selfishness' ('The Two-Part Prelude' ii. 481–3). (It was widely believed that Mackintosh was angling for a government post.) Most striking of all was Lamb's angry epigraph, included in a letter to Manning of 22 August 1801 (see Marrs ii. 13).
23. This is based on William St Clair's analysis of Godwin's character at this time; see his *The Godwins and the Shelleys* (London, 1989), 280.
24. Henry Crabb Robinson to Thomas Robinson, endorsed '1799'; Robinson correspondence, vol. 1, Dr Williams's Library.
25. Henry Crabb Robinson, Reminiscences 1790–1809, f. 114; Dr Williams's Library.
26. Henry Crabb Robinson, Reminiscences 1809–1817, f. 24; Dr Williams's Library.
27. Hazlitt indicates their meeting at this time in a footnote to one of the *Political Essays*; see Wu iv. 171 n. May 1799 is the only time when such a meeting might have occurred prior to Southey's departure for Portugal in April 1800.
28. Godwin or Holcroft may also have introduced them, as Southey had known both in earlier years and declared his intention of seeing them in a letter of May 1799 (Curry i. 195).
29. See in particular Frere and Canning's 'The Friend of Humanity and the Knife-Grinder'; *Parodies of the Romantic Age*, ed. Graeme Stones and John Strachan (5 vols., London, 1999), i. 19–22.
30. S. T. Coleridge to William Godwin, 21 May 1800; Griggs i. 588.
31. WH to William Hazlitt Sr, 16 December 1799; Pforzheimer Library, NYPL (*Letters* 72). Stanley Jones thought 'Lea Hills' more likely to read 'Clent Hills', although Sikes's reading at that point is also to be found in *Shelley Circle* i. 220. My own examination of the MS leads me, regrettably, to doubt Jones's proposal, but the reading given by Sikes cannot be regarded as unimpeachable as the script is unclear.
32. Wu vii. 94.
33. Joshua Toulmin to William Hazlitt Sr, 20 March 1802; *Hazlitt Papers* 762.
34. Wu vi. 6.
35. *Four Generations* i. 235. The painting is now at the Maidstone Museum and Art Gallery.
36. Howe xvii. 180.
37. Ibid.
38. Wu vi. 17.
39. Howe xi. 200.
40. Ibid.
41. Wu vi. 279.
42. Ibid. 9.
43. For further discussion, see Tom Paulin, *The Day-Star of Liberty* (London, 1998), 83–4.
44. Ibid.
45. Wu i. 233.
46. Although Margaret Hazlitt said that Hazlitt made copies of ten paintings (Moyne 108), Wardle insists that Hazlitt copied only five (Wardle 68 and n 1). Wardle's judgement is trumped

by Hazlitt's own list of the ten paintings he copied, now in a private collection. See p. 84 above.

47. He was instrumental also in promoting the volume; see Wu (2007) i. 51–63.
48. WH to William Hazlitt Sr, 16 October 1802; *Remains* i, p. xl (*Letters* 75).
49. Wu vi. 169.
50. William Wordsworth, *The Thirteen-Book Prelude*, ed. Mark L. Reed (2 vols., Ithaca and London, 1991), vi. 407–8.
51. WH to William Hazlitt Sr, 16 October 1802; *Remains* i, p. xxxix (*Letters* 74).
52. Howe x. 108.
53. Wu vi. 12.
54. Ibid.
55. Howe x. 225.
56. WH to William Hazlitt Sr, 20 October 1802; *Remains* i, p. xlii (*Letters* 77). The text was emended by W. C. Hazlitt to read 'the [young man in] black' (*The Hazlitts* 414), and the emendation passes straight into Sikes. However, as Maclean points out, this cannot be right as Hazlitt had not at this time copied Titian's portrait. The whereabouts of the manuscript of this letter is not at present known, but my guess would be that, when it turns up, Hazlitt's phrasing at this point will be found not to require emendation (see also Maclean 591 n 121).
57. Wu viii. 309–10.
58. Ibid. 95.
59. The date of Fox's first visit to the Louvre is given in the standard edition of his correspondence: *Memorials and Correspondence of Charles James Fox*, ed. Lord John Russell (4 vols., London, 1853–7), iv. 455–6. He left Paris on 11 November 1802 (ibid. iii. 201).
60. Wu viii. 256.
61. Howe i. 171.
62. Ibid. There is an element of guesswork here; it is possible that Hazlitt merely witnessed other Englishmen congratulating Fox.
63. WH to William Hazlitt Sr, 10 December 1802; *Remains* i, p. xlvii (*Letters* 83).
64. WH to William Hazlitt Sr, 10 December 1802; *Remains* i, p. xlviii (*Letters* 83).
65. Farington v. 1819 ff.
66. Wu viii. 87.
67. Ibid.
68. Howe x. 254.
69. Ibid.
70. This document is now in private hands but is published in *Lamb and Hazlitt* 55–6. It is dated 'le 12 Pluviose an 11' according to the French Revolutionary calendar, which has been variously translated. Wardle gives 3 January 1803, a dating followed by Grayling (Grayling 80), which is not correct. It is in fact 1 February 1803, as Stanley Jones was the first to note.
71. Wu vi. 271.

Chapter 5

1. Wu ii. 337.
2. Ibid. ix. 109.
3. Howe places the meeting in 1804, a year too late (Howe 74–5). This was apparently followed by Maclean (Maclean 206), but rectified by Baker (Baker 153 n).
4. Lamb seems to have become friendly with Godwin in 1799, but may have known him before that; see William St Clair, *The Godwins and the Shelleys* (London, 1989), 223.

5. Charles Lamb to William Wordsworth, 20 March 1822; Lucas ii. 319.
6. They saw little of each other immediately after the dinner because two days later Mary Lamb suffered one of her attacks and had to be hospitalized, leaving her brother 'cut to the Heart'. (According to Coleridge's letter to his wife of 4 April, the attack occurred the 'Thursday before last'; that is to say, Thursday 24 March, two days after Godwin's dinner; see Griggs ii. 941.)
7. S. T. Coleridge to William Godwin, 4 June 1803; Griggs ii. 949–50.
8. I am mindful of Uttara Natarajan's account of Tucker's influence on Hazlitt; *Hazlitt and the Reach of Sense* (Oxford, 1998), 147–50.
9. Farington vi. 2271.
10. It is worth noting that Hazlitt's brother John had already painted Coleridge the previous year; see Morton Paley, *Portraits of Coleridge* (Oxford, 1999), 27–8.
11. Wu vi. 285.
12. Thomas West, *A Guide to the Lakes* (3rd edn, London, 1784), 209.
13. Richard Warner, *A Tour through the Northern Counties of England, and the Borders of Scotland* (2 vols., Bath, 1802), ii. 100–1.
14. 'He thought little of Junius as a writer' (Wu ix. 107).
15. These criticisms are abstracted from Coleridge's marginalia in his copy of *Junius*; see Coleridge, *Marginalia*, ed. H. J. Jackson and George Whalley (6 vols., Princeton, NJ, 1980–2001), iii. 226.
16. Wu viii. 116.
17. Morley i. 24. This episode goes some way toward explaining Hazlitt's growing ambivalence towards his mentor. Coleridge's copy of Junius at the British Library reveals a range of marginalia indicating both admiration and contempt; see Coleridge, *Marginalia*, iii. 220–8.
18. Morley i. 24.
19. S. T. Coleridge to Sir George and Lady Beaumont, 1 October 1803; Griggs ii. 1000 ('My opinions were the Drivel of a Babe').
20. Hazlitt's words, as quoted by Coleridge in a letter to Wordsworth, 23 July 1803; Griggs ii. 958.
21. S. T. Coleridge to William Wordsworth, 23 July 1803; Griggs ii. 957.
22. *The Prose Works of William Wordsworth*, ed. W. J. B. Owen and Jane Worthington Smyser (3 vols., Oxford, 1974), i. 124.
23. Maclean writes: 'This cannot have been his first visit to Grasmere as he had already painted a side-portrait of Wordsworth, and he never could paint except when he had the sitter before him' (Maclean 185). It is likely that Hazlitt passed through Grasmere on his way to Keswick; indeed, the Ambleside road obliged him to do so. If so, he may have stopped at Dove Cottage on his way north. However, he might just as well have continued on his way, and in the absence of the 'side-portrait', which is not now to be found, I see little option but to follow Hazlitt's other biographers in taking the view that it was not until he retraced his steps and returned to Grasmere from Keswick that Hazlitt met Wordsworth for the first time since 1798.
24. They turned up in 'On Novelty and Familiarity' (Wu viii. 281).
25. This was how Wordsworth refers to it in a letter to Hazlitt of 5 March 1804; Shaver 447.
26. Wordsworth, *The Two-Part Prelude*, i. 130–4. Quotation from the Cornell Wordsworth Series volume, ed. Stephen M. Parrish. That Wordsworth showed him the poem is confirmed by his readiness to share with him the news that, during the spring of 1804, he had composed 1200 lines more; see Shaver 447.

27. See Wu ii. 61 and 311 n 28.

28. Wordsworth, *The Borderers* (1797–9 text), III. v. 60–5. Quotation from the Cornell Wordsworth Series volume, ed. Robert Osborn.

29. It was cited in his lecture on poetry in general (Wu ii. 178, 370), and the English novelists (Wu vi. 118), and again in *The Spirit of the Age* (Wu vii. 166–7). Maclean has written helpfully of Hazlitt's exposure to Wordsworth's poetry at this moment (see Maclean 186–7). In later years Hazlitt was aware of passages from *The Thirteen-Book Prelude*, specifically the Arab dream (v. 49–165) and the climbing of Snowdon (xiii. 1 ff). As these were composed in 1804, he cannot have seen them on this occasion, and may have known them only by hearsay; see also Mark L. Reed, *Wordsworth: A Chronology of the Middle Years 1800–1815* (Cambridge, MA, 1975), 216 n 15. As he revised *The White Doe of Rylstone* in the early 1830s, Wordsworth stumbled upon one of the various occasions when Hazlitt recalled these lines, and was so surprised he commented on it; see *William Wordsworth: The White Doe of Rylstone*, ed. Kristine Dugas (Ithaca, NY, 1988), 158 n.

30. See, among other sources, Dorothy Wordsworth, *The Grasmere and Alfoxden Journals*, ed. Pamela Woof (Oxford, 2002), 161–2.

31. The word in London in 1806 was that Wordsworth was 'strongly disposed towards Republicanism' (Farington vii. 2785). His principal motive was to visit his former French girlfriend Annette Vallon and meet for the first time their daughter Anne-Caroline—none of which he revealed to Hazlitt.

32. Wordsworth, 'Calais, August 15th 1802' ('Festivals have I seen that were not names'), published 26 February 1803 in the *Morning Post*. Quotation from the Cornell Wordsworth Series, *Poems, in Two Volumes*, ed. Jared Curtis.

33. Wu viii. 331–2.

34. This conversation is based on remarks cited by Hazlitt in 'A Reply to "Z"'; Howe ix. 5.

35. 'Chaucer is another prime favourite of his, and he has been at pains to modernise some of the Canterbury Tales' (Wu vii. 166). Wordsworth's translations from Chaucer were begun in 1801; see *Translations from Chaucer and Virgil*, ed. Bruce Graver (Ithaca, NY, 1998), 12.

36. Dryden, *Alexander's Feast* 51–2.

37. This criticism is attributed to Wordsworth in *The Spirit of the Age* (Wu vii. 166), and is presumably the passage which Hazlitt admitted he took from Wordsworth's conversation for his *Lectures on the English Poets* (see Howe ix. 5, Wu ii. 240).

38. Wu viii. 190.

39. See Wu vi. 289, vii. 167. For Wordsworth and Coleridge on Daniel's poem, see my *Wordsworth's Poets* (Manchester, 2003), 171–5.

40. Wu vii. 167.

41. See my *Wordsworth's Reading 1770–1799* (Cambridge, 1993), 120–1.

42. Wu ix. 103.

43. William Wordsworth to Julius Charles Hare, 28 May 1838; *The Letters of William and Dorothy Wordsworth VI The Later Years Part 3 1835–1839*, ed. Ernest de Selincourt, rev. Alan G. Hill (2nd edn., Oxford, 1982), 594.

44. The scenario given here is conjectural, on the basis of De Quincey's testimony (*De Quincey* xi. 103). Biographers question whether Hazlitt ever proposed: Maclean doubts it (Maclean 592 n 133(b)); Baker finds it 'an interesting if implausible match' (Baker 135); Wardle thinks De Quincey's testimony 'at least suspect' (Wardle 78 n 19). The principal motive given for doubting it is malice on De Quincey's part, though I can see little for him to have gained

at the time he published this (in April 1839—nearly a decade after Hazlitt's death). The fact is, Hazlitt was a libidinous young man, capable of falling in love with women at a moment's notice. On balance, it is more likely that De Quincey was telling the truth on this occasion than otherwise.

45. S. T. Coleridge to Thomas Wedgwood, 16 September 1803; Griggs ii. 990–1.

46. See Grayling 86.

47. From the manuscript version of 'The Pains of Sleep' sent to Southey on 11 September; Griggs ii. 983.

48. For something of Coleridge's state at this time, see Molly Lefebure, *Samuel Taylor Coleridge: A Bondage of Opium* (London, 1977), 383–7; Richard Holmes, *Coleridge: Early Visions* (London, 1989), 356. Rancid lust for Sara Hutchinson culminated in the belief that he had seen Wordsworth in bed with her; see *Coleridge Notebooks* ii. 3148 f. 45v. See also, for my discussion, *Wordsworth: An Inner Life* (Oxford, 2002), 275–6.

49. See Louise Guiney to W. C. Hazlitt, 22 December 1903; BL Add. MS 38910, 63v.

50. Catherine Emmet lived with the Hazlitt family from 1816 until the end of her life in 1825 (five years after the death of Hazlitt's father). She contributed a small income to the household.

51. S. T. Coleridge to Sir George and Lady Beaumont, 1 October 1803; Griggs ii. 999.

52. Robert Southey to John May, 15 November 1803; *The Letters of Robert Southey to John May 1797 to 1838*, ed. Charles Ramos (Austin, TX, 1976), 84.

53. See Curry i. 331 and n; W. A. Speck, *Robert Southey: Entire Man of Letters* (London, 2006), 103. Godwin cherished a manuscript of the speech Emmet delivered at his trial, which included the defiant words: 'You tell me, My Lord, that I am accountable for all the blood that has been, and will be shed in this business—I do not fear to approach the Omnipotent Judge, and answer for the conduct of my short life. But were it possible to collect all the innocent blood that you have shed, in one great reservoir (Great indeed would it be) Your Lordship might swim in it' (Bodleian Library, Abinger Papers, Dep. c. 810/2, 3v).

54. *Coleridge Notebooks* i. 1577.

55. He had published an article over the summer (18 July and 20 August) but nothing since; see Coleridge, *Essays on His Times* ed. David V. Erdman (3 vols., Princeton, NJ, 1978), i 422–36.

56. *Coleridge Notebooks* i. 1610.

57. Hazlitt later remembered having seen Southey do this, and the most likely time for such an occasion would be 1803; see Wu iv. 171. In a letter of October 1803, Southey speculated that 'my gift is in singing songs, not writing them'; see *Selections from the Letters of Robert Southey*, ed. John Wood Warter (4 vols., London, 1856), i. 244.

58. It is not certain that Southey talked about Emmet with Hazlitt, but their shared interest in him, and the proximity of his execution, make him a likely topic of conversation. Southey's words are drawn from his letter to John King, 28 September 1803; BL Add. MS 47891, 6r.

59. Robert Southey to Richard Duppa, 14 December 1803; *The Life and Correspondence of the Late Robert Southey*, ed. Charles Cuthbert Southey (6 vols., London, 1849–50), ii. 238.

60. *Coleridge Notebooks* i. 1610.

61. Ibid. 1616.

62. Ibid.

63. Ibid.

64. Ibid.

65. *Coleridge Notebooks* i. 1618.
66. Hazlitt's philosophy reflected aspects of his Unitarian upbringing, but was essentially godless. Nature, imagination, and artistic gusto stood in for what Coleridge termed the Divine Wisdom. For more on this, see Uttara Natarajan, *Hazlitt and the Reach of Sense* (Oxford, 1998), 46–8.
67. *Coleridge Notebooks* i. 1619.
68. Ibid. 1622.
69. Ibid. 1623.
70. Patmore iii. 141.
71. Pope ii. 470. Haydon's informant is Wordsworth. Recollections of this incident date from later years when Wordsworth's dislike of Hazlitt was fully developed. Hazlitt's crimes, according to him, included such 'abominable & devilish propensities' as that of whipping a woman 'for not yielding to his wishes' (Morley i. 169). The more extreme accusation of rape, never brought by Wordsworth and Coleridge, has long been discounted; see Jones 298–300 and Michael Foot, 'Hazlitt's Revenge on the Lakers', *The Wordsworth Circle* 14.1 (Winter 1983), 61–8.
72. Southey's involvement is confirmed by a letter he wrote years later; see Curry ii. 92–3.
73. In later years, when Hazlitt had begun attacking him in print, Coleridge exaggerated what had happened, claiming that he saved him 'from the Gallows', adding that Hazlitt was guilty of 'vices too disgusting to be named' (Griggs iv. 693). In another letter he claimed that 'there were not less than 200 men on horse in search of him' (Griggs iv. 735). Corroboration that Hazlitt was on the run from nothing worse than a ducking-party is provided by Wordsworth, via Lamb and Robinson (see Marrs iii. 125 and Morley i. 169).
74. S. T. Coleridge to Francis Wrangham, 5 June 1817; Griggs iv. 735.
75. Morley i. 169.
76. Southey seems not to have mentioned it in any of the letters he wrote between now and the end of the year. Coleridge proposed that 'dear Southey will be so kind as to overlook the man', referring to Hazlitt in a letter of early January 1804 (Griggs ii. 1024 and n), while Wordsworth's letter to Hazlitt of 5 March 1804 refers to the fact that 'No body durst venture to seize your clothes or box', left behind at the time of the escapade (Shaver 447).
77. Charles Lamb to William Wordsworth, 28 December 1814; Marrs iii. 125.
78. S. T. Coleridge to William Wordsworth, 23 July 1803; Griggs ii. 958.
79. Ibid.
80. William Wordsworth to Sir George Beaumont, 3 June 1805; Shaver 594.
81. Wu ix. 97. Paley records a note in the National Portrait Gallery archive in which the portrait is said to describe a painting of 'Coleridge by Hazlitt, rather "Spanish" looking' (*Portraits of Coleridge*, 29).
82. William Wordsworth to Charles Lamb, 21 November 1816; *The Letters of William and Dorothy Wordsworth VIII A Supplement of New Letters*, ed. Alan G. Hill (Oxford, 1993), 161–2.
83. Robert Southey to S. T. Coleridge, 11 June 1804; *Life and Correspondence of the Late Robert Southey*, ii. 291.
84. This is confirmed by Paley, *Portraits of Coleridge*, 31.
85. S. T. Coleridge to William Wordsworth, 23 July 1803; Griggs ii. 958.
86. Robert Southey to Richard Duppa, 14 December 1803; *Life and Correspondence of the Late Robert Southey*, ii. 238.

87. William Wordsworth to Charles Lamb, 21 November 1816; *Letters of William and Dorothy Wordsworth VIII A Supplement of New Letters*, 161.
88. As he told Charles Lamb; see preceding note. There is no reason to doubt Wordsworth's claim that the portrait was destroyed, despite recent claims to the contrary.
89. William Wordsworth to William Hazlitt Jr, 23 May 1831; *Memoirs* i. 103 n. The MS of this letter appears to have disappeared from sight.

Chapter 6

1. Howe xx. 345.
2. *Gentleman's Magazine* 74 (1804), 185.
3. William Wordsworth to WH, 5 March 1804; Shaver 447.
4. See Marrs ii. 200.
5. David Bromwich usefully observes that Wordsworth is cruel to his characters 'in proportion as they bring to mind elements of himself which he now wants to banish' (Bromwich 171).
6. Howe iii. 171 n.
7. Priestley died on 6 February 1804 at his Pennsylvania home.
8. Godwin is the nameless friend referred to by W. C. Hazlitt; *Memoirs* i. 111.
9. The phrase is Coleridge's; see Griggs i. 553. Godwin had himself been brought up by an enthusiastic disciplinarian, the Sandemanian preacher Samuel Newton.
10. William Godwin to unknown correspondent, 18 October 1806 (deleted passage); Bodleian Library, Dep b. 227/3.
11. Marrs ii. 149.
12. One of the printers who worked on the Lambs' volume was Richard Taylor, who was also to work with Hazlitt; see 'Correcting the Lambs' *Tales*: A Printer's Records', *The Charles Lamb Bulletin* NS 140 (October 2007), 150–1.
13. Howe xx. 42.
14. 'The costume was the painter's whim, and must be said to detract from the effect of the whole' (*Memoirs* i. 113).
15. It may have been the 'Portrait of a Gentleman' which Hazlitt exhibited at the RA in 1805. There were, apparently, two copies of the picture; for further information see Scott McEathron, 'Hazlitt's Portrait of Lamb: An Early Institutional History', *The Charles Lamb Bulletin* NS 103 (July 1998), 74–89.
16. 'The volume had a very small circulation' (Keynes 1). Worldcat lists 20 copies, some of which may have been given away by the author during the course of his lifetime. That in my possession formerly belonged to Bryan Waller Procter and was, I believe, given him by Hazlitt; its title page is the frontispiece of *Metaphysical Hazlitt: Bicentenary Essays*, ed. Tom Paulin, Uttara Natarajan, and Duncan Wu (Abingdon, 2005).
17. *Memoirs* i. 112.
18. Howe xvii. 312.
19. See my *Wordsworth's Reading 1800–1815* (Cambridge, 1995), 104, and *Barron Field's Memoirs of Wordsworth*, ed. Geoffrey Little (Sydney, 1975), 66 n 110.
20. W. C. Hazlitt says Stoddart sent Scarlett a copy, but means that Montagu did so (*Four Generations* i. 92). Stoddart was in Malta, and it is far-fetched to think that he would from there have acted as Hazlitt's publicity agent. Montagu is more likely to have been responsible for this kindness, and certainly did his best to promote Hazlitt in subsequent

years. He probably sent a copy to Mackintosh, as they were good friends, and Montagu was in the habit of sending him books, including Hazlitt's. In September 1804 Mackintosh even suggested that Montagu apply to practise at the bar in Bombay; see BL Add. 78765, 35r.

21. *Memoirs* i. 112.
22. *Four Generations* i. 92–3.
23. WH to William Godwin, 5 January 1806; *Letters* 88.
24. Wu vi. 10.
25. Wordsworth, *The Thirteen-Book Prelude* x. 934–5. As this poem was unpublished until 1850, it is unlikely that Hazlitt knew these lines. My quotation is from the Cornell Wordsworth Series text, ed. Mark L. Reed (1991).
26. *Annual Review* 4 (1805), 657–64, esp. 658.
27. See Wu i, p. iv.
28. Howe xvii. 312.
29. Raymond Martin and John Barresi, *Naturalization of the Soul: Self and Personal Identity in the Eighteenth Century* (London, 2000), 139. The bicentenary of Hazlitt's *Essay* was commemorated with a collection of critical appreciations in *Metaphysical Hazlitt*, ed. Paulin, Natarajan, and Wu.
30. WH to William Godwin, 5 January 1806; *Letters* 88–9.
31. Charles Lamb to WH, 15 January 1806; Marrs ii. 199–200.
32. Charles Lamb to WH, 7 January 1806; Marrs ii. 199.
33. Charles Lamb to WH, 15 March 1806; Marrs ii. 223.
34. This had begun in earnest around 1798; see William St Clair, *The Godwins and the Shelleys* (London, 1988), pp. 196–7.
35. Lamb believed Hazlitt paid for its publication; see Marrs ii. 233.
36. Taylor's check-books, now at St Bride Printing Library, show that he printed the works of a number of dissenters, including those of Thomas Belsham, Theophilus Lindsey, Amelia Opie, Thomas Clarkson, John Disney, and John Prior Estlin. Taylor remained a friend of Godwin until the end of his life.
37. At a cost of £1.15.0 (Richard Taylor, Check-Book No.1, f. 65; St Bride Printing Library).
38. Very few copies survive; Keynes says that it is 'exceedingly rare at the present time' (Keynes 5). Worldcat lists three. There is another in my possession.
39. For their frequenting of brothels, Lamb's account of the girl they visited in the letter to Wordsworth of 26 June 1806 can hardly refer to anything else—though Lamb misjudged Wordsworth if he thought the poet would find it at all amusing; see Marrs ii. 233.
40. Ibid. 228.
41. It is clear from Mary Lamb's letter of 2 June 1806 that Sarah already knew John: 'William Hazlitt the brother of him you know is in town' (ibid.).
42. This commonplace book is now at the Berg Collection, NYPL.
43. William Hazlitt of Mauritius to William Hazlitt Jr, 31 December 1883; BL Add. MS 38904, 37r.
44. Her grandson described her as 'plain, downright, impervious' (*Memoirs* i. 166).
45. Charles Lamb to WH, 15 January 1806; Marrs ii. 200.
46. W. C. Hazlitt, BL Add. MS 74782B (formerly C.133.g.10), p. 38.
47. Stoddart Sr's profession was established by the late Robert Woof, 'John and Sarah Stoddart: Friends of the Lambs', *The Charles Lamb Bulletin* NS 45 (January 1984), 93–109, esp. 97.
48. *Memoirs* i. 166.

49. Ibid., italics mine.
50. See Woof, 'John and Sarah Stoddart: Friends of the Lambs', 105.
51. However, it should be borne in mind that Stoddart was by then a hostile witness, as was Southey, to whom the story was told; see Curry ii. 144–5.
52. Mary Lamb to Sarah Stoddart, 30 May to 2 June 1806; Marrs ii. 228.
53. Mary Lamb to Sarah Stoddart, 27 June to 2 July 1806; Marrs ii. 237.
54. Charles Lamb to William Wordsworth, 26 June 1806; Marrs ii. 233.
55. 'Abend bey Clarkson Charles Lamb und Schwester Er amusirte mich witzig in Gesprach W. Hazlitt ähnlich' (HCR diary, 10 June 1806; HCR bundle 6.VIII, Dr Williams's Library).
56. Coleridge was at that moment in Livorno in a near-suicidal state. Within the next two weeks he set sail for England.
57. Charles Lamb to William Wordsworth, 26 June 1806; Marrs ii. 233.
58. This has not previously been reported. The source is Robinson, who got the news from Anthony Robinson: 'Abend bey A.R. Er erzahte mir dass Hazlitt 80£s fur seinen Ausgng & Search von Johnson bekommen hatte—Das freuete mich' (HCR diary, 6 July 1806; HCR bundle 6.VIII, Dr Williams's Library).
59. Again, this has not been previously reported and is based on Henry Crabb Robinson's 1806 diary: 'A.R. sonnte sich mit W.H. dadurch dass er eisig für Wordsworth sprach' (HCR diary, 26 July 1806; HCR bundle 6.VIII, Dr Williams's Library).
60. This series of events is different from that usually given by biographers; for the background and rationale see 'Hazlitt's *Essay on the Principles of Human Action*: A Bibliographical Note', in *Metaphysical Hazlitt*, ed. Paulin, Natarajan, and Wu, pp. xv–xvi.
61. The dating is provided by Henry Crabb Robinson: 'Mit Hazlitt der durch A.R. einen kaufer fur sein vorgeschlagenes Buch uber Parliamentarische redner gefunden hat' (HCR diary, 21 July 1806; HCR bundle 6.VIII, Dr Williams's Library).
62. This is a logical inference consistent with the evidence.
63. This is documented by Coleridge himself.
64. See Molly Lefebure, *A Bondage of Opium* (London, 1974), 447.
65. Mary Lamb refers to Coleridge's 'pleasant Segar' in her letter of September 1806; Marrs ii. 240.
66. The terminal date is 5 December 1806 when Lamb told Manning that Rickman and Burney 'assemble at my house pretty regularly of a Wednesday, a new institution' (Marrs ii. 247).
67. Ibid.
68. Howe xvii. 123.
69. Charles Lamb to Thomas Manning, 5 December 1806; Marrs ii. 247.
70. *Monthly Literary Recreations* 1 (December 1806), 488.
71. Morley i. 9.
72. 'ich war unzufrieden mit dem Empfang gieng nachher zu Lamb um ihn zu Trösten' (HCR diary, 10 December 1806; HCR bundle 6.VIII, Dr Williams's Library).
73. Mary Lamb to Catherine Clarkson, 23 December 1806; Marrs ii. 253.
74. Wu vi. 208.
75. WH to William Hazlitt Sr, 'Tuesday'; *Four Generations* i. 97 (*Letters* 90). Sikes takes *Four Generations* as copy-text, mistranscribing 'pork' as 'port'. His dating is 'Early in January 1807', which appears to be correct.
76. It is clear from the exchange of letters between Lamb, Hume, and Hazlitt following the suicide hoax of early 1808 that it was taken for granted Hazlitt was given to 'wenching' (see

Lamb and Hazlitt 92, 95). This was regarded as cause for mirth; see for instance Hume's letter to Lamb of 12–13 January 1808: 'That he should frequent the stews! It makes me stew to think on it' (Beineke Library, Yale University; Osborn Files Folder 7747, 2v).

77. *Four Generations* i. 146.

78. Anthony Robinson to Henry Crabb Robinson, 19 April 1807; Dr Williams's Library, HCR Correspondence Vol. 4, f. 85.

79. Keynes says it is 'very uncommon at the present time' (Keynes 7), and Worldcat records 34 copies.

80. There was, however, at least one appreciative reader: Sir James Mackintosh. Having received a copy from Basil Montagu he was to recommend it as one of his 'Useful' books. See Sir James Mackintosh to Mr R., 18 September 1807; BL Add. 78765, 113v. He divided his favourite books up under the headings Necessary, Useful, and Curious. Basil Montagu sent the book on 26 August 1807; see BL Add. 52452, 20r ('Search has been abridged, and I am told very well, by some Person unknown to me: You will receive it with this letter').

81. It was advertised in the *Morning Chronicle* on that date. There was a second advertisement on 21 August and another on 16 October.

82. Keynes says that the first edition is 'exceedingly scarce' (Keynes 11), though Worldcat lists 23 copies at the time of writing.

83. It is just possible he was introduced to Cobbett by John Philpot Curran, who also introduced Cobbett to Godwin.

84. In none of his references does Hazlitt date or place the encounter, but 1807 is the most likely time.

85. Wu vi. 51 n.

86. Howe xi. 238–9.

87. It is my inference that Hazlitt's articles about Malthus grew out of a conversation on the subject with Cobbett.

88. A. O. [William Hazlitt], 'Poor Laws', *Cobbett's Political Register*, 14 March 1807, cols. 397–403, esp. 397.

89. Ibid.

90. Howe i. 275, 233.

91. Longman Archive; Reading University Library. I wish to thank Mike Bott of Special Collections at Reading for giving me access to the archive. Keynes says the first edition is 'very uncommon' (Keynes 9), though Worldcat lists 53 copies. It was first advertised in the *Morning Chronicle* on 6 August, and again on 12 August and 19 September (with the addition of the author's name). The growing confidence of publishers to invest in Hazlitt is signified by John Murray's reissue of *The Eloquence of the British Senate* in 1808 (Keynes 12). Sir James Mackintosh was among Hazlitt's readers, but this time with less enthusiasm, confiding to his diary that 'It contains some true & powerfully stated observations. . . . But it is perfectly disgraced by declamation & personality which render it tedious & obscure as well as offensive.' He later thought its 'unnecessary acrimony' the work of Coleridge. See Sir James Mackintosh, diary for 1808 (BL Add. MS 52436B, 50r–v) and Sir James Mackintosh to Richard Sharp, 8 October 1808; BL Add. MS 52451A, 60v.

92. Howe i. 340 n.

93. William Godwin to WH, 4 August 1807; Bodleian Library Dep.b.214/6. This appears to be the actual letter; a draft is also to be found at Dep.b.227/3.

94. WH to William Godwin, postmarked 6 August 1807; Bodleian Library Dep.b.214/6 (*Letters* 93–4).
95. William Godwin to WH, not dated [but probably 7 August 1807]; Bodleian Library Dep.b.227/3. Although Hazlitt has not previously been identified as the recipient, this letter cites the contents of Hazlitt's letter of 6 August. The manuscript is a draft.
96. 'I met my old flame in the street' (WH to Sarah Stoddart, [*c.*January 1808]; *Letters* 104).
97. *Memoirs* i. 167.
98. WH to Joseph Hume, 11 January 1808; *Letters* 100, *Lamb and Hazlitt* 78.
99. Mary Lamb to Sarah Stoddart, 28 November 1807; Marrs ii. 261.
100. Ibid.
101. Mary Lamb to Sarah Stoddart, 21 December 1807; Marrs ii. 263–4.
102. On this matter, see Hume's note to Lamb, *Lamb and Hazlitt* 92.
103. She was bequeathed a house in St Ann Street, Salisbury, by her father; see J. Rogers Rees, 'Hazlittiana', *Notes and Queries* 10th Series, 10 (1908), 61–3.
104. The settlement was revoked at the time of Hazlitt's divorce; see BL Add. 62943, ff. 23–4. Stoddart was prone to make gifts of various kinds to his sister; see Jones 38.

Chapter 7

1. WH to Sarah Stoddart, January 1808; SUNY at Buffalo (*Letters* 104). Sikes's transcription is flawed, and he fails to report the dispatch postmark dated January 1808.
2. Lamb wrote a fake newspaper report about it; see Marrs ii. 265.
3. Such things, Jones writes, 'served his fissured personality as a protective device, an amateurish psychiatric homoeopathy, following on his mother's terrible death' (Jones 24).
4. WH to Joseph Hume, 11 January 1808; *Lamb and Hazlitt* 78 (*Letters* 100). Sikes takes *Lamb and Hazlitt* as copy text.
5. Mary Lamb to Sarah Stoddart, 21 December 1807; Marrs ii. 264.
6. WH to Sarah Stoddart, January 1808; SUNY at Buffalo, Goodyear collection (*Letters* 102).
7. See for instance WH to Charles Baring Wall, 30 November 1821; Gates 654–5.
8. William Hazlitt Jr., Preface to *Winterslow* (London, 1902), p. v.
9. Moyne 110.
10. Howe x. 56.
11. Wu vi. 10.
12. Ibid. viii. 112.
13. *Memoirs* ii. 308.
14. Wordsworth's visit is sometimes dated to mid-April (Wardle 110, Grayling 124) because that is when he described it. However, that letter was written after his return to Grasmere, and is a recollection of something that had occurred in previous weeks; see *The Letters of William and Dorothy Wordsworth: The Middle Years Part 1: 1806–1811*, ed. Ernest de Selincourt, rev. Mary Moorman (Oxford, 1969), 221. Wordsworth was in London from *c.*27 February to 3 April 1808.
15. See Kenneth R. Johnston, *The Hidden Wordsworth: Poet Lover Rebel Spy* (New York, 1998), 125–6. Johnston also suggests that Wordsworth went to prostitutes at Cambridge—something that, while impossible to prove, is not easily ruled out; ibid. 130–4.
16. William Wordsworth to S. T. Coleridge, 19 April 1808; *Letters of William and Dorothy Wordsworth: The Middle Years Part 1: 1806–1811*, 221–2.

17. Ibid. 222.
18. Even the admiring Henry Crabb Robinson, who first met Wordsworth this year, found him brittle and intolerant: 'W. ist ein unbigsamen, vielleicht und intolleranter Mann aber immer gegen das Schlechte nur' (HCR diary, week beginning 14 March 1808; HCR bundle 6.VIII, Dr Williams's Library).
19. Marrs iii. 181.
20. *Hazlitts* 343.
21. Mary Lamb to Sarah Stoddart, 12 February 1808; Marrs ii. 269.
22. *Hazlitts* 343.
23. Mary Lamb to Sarah Stoddart, 12 February 1808; Marrs ii. 269.
24. The reissue brought Hazlitt for the first time to the attention of Archibald Constable, to whom Murray sent 14 copies of *Eloquence of the British Senate* in May 1808 (John Murray Archive).
25. See WH to John Murray, [?3 September to 26 November 1808]; John Murray Archive (Robinson 9–10). Napoleon deposed Spain's head of state in April, replacing him with his brother Joseph. As Spain was an ally, the British moved to expel the French in August.
26. Charles Lamb to George Dyer, 5 July 1808; BL RP 334 (Marrs ii. 284). Marrs takes Lucas as copy text, despite the existence of the copy of the MS in the BL, from which I take my quotation.
27. According to Godwin's diary, there were meetings on 20 May, 4, 6, 10 June, 3, 12, 15 July, and 22 August.
28. For more on Priestley's contribution to this subject, see Thomas P. Miller, 'Where Did College English Studies Come From?', *Rhetoric Review* 9 (Autumn 1990), 50–69, esp. 58–9.
29. Howe x. 54.
30. Moyne 109.
31. Wu vi. 5.
32. William Hazlitt, *Winterslow: Essays and Characters Written There* (London, 1902), Preface by William Hazlitt Jr, p. vi.
33. Mary Lamb to Sarah Stoddart Hazlitt, 9–10 December 1808; Marrs ii. 286.
34. It is not included in Howe; see Wu (2007) i. 3–13.
35. Ibid.
36. All the same, the next issue carried a letter from Capel Lofft beginning: 'I am glad to find the metaphysical subject revived by W.H.' (See 'To the Editor of the Monthly Magazine', *Monthly Magazine* 27 (1809), 132–3, esp. 132.)
37. For the scholarly sources, see Wu *Library* 27–9.
38. See ibid. 29–30. It was thanks partly to Montagu that Coleridge found sufficient subscribers to publish his periodical *The Friend*, many drawn from Montagu's colleagues and associates. (A number of them appear also on Hazlitt's subscription list.) Baker is mistaken in saying that no one subscribed to Hazlitt's volume (Baker 171); the subscription list is published in Wu *Library* 44–62.
39. Baker 171.
40. David Wilkinson in his essay on Windham in the *New DNB*.
41. Were there any doubt of his admiration, one need only consult *The Eloquence of the British Senate*, which includes one of his speeches; see William Hazlitt, *The Eloquence of the British Senate* (2 vols., London, 1807), ii. 575–81.

42. 'Bey Chas Lambe W Hazlitt da' (HCR diary, 15 March 1809; HCR bundle 6.VIII, Dr Williams's Library). According to Godwin's diary he dined with him and John Wolcot that evening.
43. See Marrs iii. 7.
44. Mary Lamb to Louisa Martin, 28 March 1809; Marrs iii. 7.
45. WH to William Hazlitt Sr, 5 November 1809; Massachusetts Historical Society (*Letters* 113). The MS bears an Andover frank and a dispatch postmark of 7 November. Besides Sikes, this letter is available at Gates 649–51 and in Ernest J. Moyne, 'An Unpublished Letter of William Hazlitt', *PMLA* 77 (1962), 341–2.
46. Charles Lamb to Thomas Manning, 28 March 1809; Marrs iii. 3.
47. Charles Lamb to S. T. Coleridge, 7 June 1809; Marrs iii. 12.
48. Moyne 109.
49. Wu vi. 292. Howe says this is a description of John Hazlitt who died in 1817. Wardle differs, observing that the phrase 'years ago' hardly accords with an essay composed by 1822, and adds: 'his grief at the death of his first and only son must have been even more poignant than at that of his third, when his second son survived. . . . Evidently he refused to look at the body of one of the two dead children. If so, it would more likely have been the second, especially if he had found his first experience so shattering' (Wardle 115). His reasoning is sound, and is followed by Grayling (Grayling 130).
50. Charles Lamb to S. T. Coleridge, 30 October 1809; Marrs iii. 26.
51. Mary Lamb to Sarah Stoddart Hazlitt, 7 November 1809; Marrs iii. 30–1.
52. WH to William Hazlitt Sr, 5 November 1809; Massachusetts Historical Society (*Letters* 113). Sikes fails to note the Andover postmark of 7 November. Presumably the letter was put on a coach at Winterslow Hut, went to Andover, and was from there directed to Wem.
53. Ibid.
54. Ibid.
55. Mary Lamb to Sarah Stoddart Hazlitt, 7 November 1809; Marrs iii. 31.
56. William Godwin, diary for 1809, entry for 29 July; Bodleian Library Dep. e. 210.
57. The term is Jones's; see his exemplary 'The "Suppression" of Hazlitt's *New and Improved Grammar of the English Tongue*: A Reconstruction of Events', *The Library* Series 6, 9 (1987), 32–43, esp. 34.
58. Charles Lamb to Thomas Manning, 2 January 1810; Marrs iii. 37.
59. William Godwin to Archibald Constable, 23 November 1809; Thomas Constable, *Archibald Constable and his Literary Correspondents* (3 vols., Edinburgh, 1873), ii. 53.
60. Charles Lamb to Thomas Manning, 2 January 1810; Marrs iii. 35.
61. William Godwin to Louisa Holcroft, n.d., no postmark, but written prior to 22 January 1810, and probably in the week before that; Bodleian Library, Dep.b.215/2.
62. Mary Lamb to Sarah Stoddart Hazlitt, 30 March 1810; Marrs iii. 50.
63. There must have been some agreement concerning payment, or Hazlitt would not have taken the job on. However, it is worth noting that, when the volume finally appeared in 1816, he received nothing; see David McCracken, 'Hazlitt and a Case of Charitable Journalism', *Keats–Shelley Journal* 28 (1979), 26–7.
64. WH to Henry Crabb Robinson, 26 February 1810; Dr Williams's Library (*Letters* 117).
65. WH to William Godwin, n.d.; Houghton Library, Harvard, *65M-10 (*Letters* 108). A copy is also to be found at Bodleian Library Dep.b.214/9, Sikes's copy text. The actual letter is at the Houghton. Neither MS carries either postmark or date. Sikes conjecturally dates it to the

'Latter part of June 1809'; there is, however, no reason to quarrel with Jones's dating of 30 March 1810 (Jones 37).

66. Further information about the sale may be found in Jones's 'Hazlitt and the Walsh Porter Sale', *Etudes Anglaises* 26 (1973), 452–4.

67. WH to Sarah Stoddart Hazlitt, *c.*16 April 1810; Houghton Library, *42M-1289F (*Letters* 120). Sikes's dating of '(PM: April) [1810]' is less than helpful; the postmark clearly reads 'Salisbury 17 APR 1810'.

68. WH to Sarah Stoddart Hazlitt, *c.*16 April 1810; Houghton Library, *42M-1289F (*Letters* 120).

69. Ibid.

70. Bonner 247. Sally Baugh remained a mystery in Hazlitt scholarship until her identity was uncovered by Jones (Jones 52–4).

71. Howe xvi. 45.

72. Howe i. 283.

73. WH to Sarah Stoddart Hazlitt, *c.*16 April 1810; Houghton Library, *42M-1289F (*Letters* 120).

74. Charles Lamb to Basil Montagu, 12 July 1810; Marrs iii. 53.

75. Howe xvii. 320.

76. Wu vi. 6.

77. Charles Lamb to Basil Montagu, 12 July 1810; Marrs iii. 52.

78. Howe xvii. 66.

79. Ibid. 66–7.

80. Wu vi. 168–9.

81. Charles Lamb, *Elia and Last Essays of Elia*, ed. Jonathan Bate (Oxford, 1987), 11.

82. Howe x. 71.

83. Wu vi. 169.

84. Howe x. 71.

85. Charles Lamb to WH, 9 August 1810; Marrs iii. 54.

86. Howe x. 73.

87. Charles Lamb to WH, 9 August 1810; Marrs iii. 54.

88. Ibid.

89. See BL Add. MS 38898 3r.

Chapter 8

1. Howe ix. 201.

2. S. T. Coleridge to William Wordsworth, 4 May 1812; Griggs iii. 400. Coleridge's claim that these remarks were his only criticism of Wordsworth is unlikely to be true.

3. There is no documentary evidence that Coleridge told Hazlitt about Wordsworth's treatment of him, but as he told most of their mutual friends it is likely he did; as Robinson recorded on 13 March, 'He alluded to sufferings endured *from* the north' (Morley i. 26).

4. *Edinburgh Review* 27 (December 1816), 446.

5. Morley i. 28.

6. Howe ix. 194.

7. Morley i. 24–5.

8. 'By W. Hazlitt having procured Mr Howel to sit for him for his picture'; HCR diary, 23 March 1811; Dr Williams's Library. Not in Morley.

9. Robinson probably showed Hazlitt transcriptions, though may have shown him the copy from which they were taken—that belonging to Flaxman. See G. E. Bentley Jr., *Blake Books* (Oxford, 1977), 384.
10. Morley i. 40–1.
11. Morley i. 25. This conversation is abstracted from Robinson's journal entry for 10 March 1811.
12. Morley i. 30.
13. Ibid.
14. Ibid.
15. One onlooker said it made Clarkson look like Oliver Cromwell; see Catherine Clarkson to Henry Crabb Robinson, August 1811; Dr Williams's Library, HCR Correspondence, Vol. 5, f. 50. Baker dates it 21 July 1811 (Baker 182 n).
16. Henry Crabb Robinson to Catherine Clarkson, 13 December 1811; Dr Williams's Library, HCR Correspondence, Vol. 5, f. 65.
17. Ibid.
18. Dryden, *Absalom and Achitophel* 170, one of Hazlitt's favourite quotations.
19. Mary and Charles Lamb to Sarah Stoddart Hazlitt and William Hazlitt; Marrs iii. 77.
20. See *Lamb and Hazlitt* 110.
21. For full details of the Russell Institution and its deliberations, see Wu *Library 33–5*.
22. Morley i. 51.
23. This is based on the entry for Wednesday 27 November 1811 in John Payne Collier's MS autobiography (Folger Shakespeare Library, M.a.222, f. 178).
24. Ibid. f. 180.
25. Foakes says Coleridge did not acquire his own copy of Schlegel until 'a day or two before he gave Lecture 9 of the 1811–12 series'; that is to say, shortly before 16 December 1811 (although that fact on its own does not obviate the possibility of plagiarism). See Foakes i., p. lxii.
26. As quoted by S. T. Coleridge in a letter to James Perry, 5 February 1818; Griggs iv. 831.
27. S. T. Coleridge to John Rickman, 26 October 1811; Griggs iii. 340.
28. Morley i. 50.
29. Henry Crabb Robinson to Thomas Robinson, 16 December 1811; Dr Williams's Library, HCR Correspondence, Vol. 5, f. 66.
30. Ibid.
31. See *The Times*, 4 January 1812; *Morning Chronicle,* 7 January 1812.
32. Morley i. 58. Morley incorrectly renders the Secretary's name 'Flack'.
33. Morley i. 57. It should be added that in an unpublished entry for 17 January, Robinson recorded calling on his friend Mr Porden, who 'was pleased by Hazlitt's lecture'; see HCR Diary, vol. 2, 23v; Dr Williams's Library.
34. Morley i. 58.
35. For more on Burrell, see Wu *Library* 46. Jones says he was an unsuccessful barrister (Jones 66).
36. Morley i. 60.
37. *The Times*, 23 January 1812, p. 3 col. 1. The author may have been Henry Crabb Robinson.
38. Morley i. 65.
39. Adapted from Morley i. 70.

40. No copy of this work appears to have survived, and it is known only from the records of Richard Taylor; see Wu *Library* 36.

41. For details see Wu *Library* 36.

42. Henry Crabb Robinson, Diary 2, 83v; Dr Williams's Library. This passage is not in Morley.

43. William Wordsworth to Mary Wordsworth, 2 May 1812; *The Letters of William and Dorothy Wordsworth VIII A Supplement of New Letters*, ed. Alan G. Hill (Oxford, 1993), 55.

44. See Howe xix. 368.

45. Charles Lamb to John Dyer Collier, dated 4 October 1812 by Marrs; Marrs iii. 85. The MS is at the Folger Shakespeare Library (Yd 341 (100)) and is undated, though someone has endorsed it 'about 1812 or 13'.

46. Entry for 21 September 1812–Robinson, Diary 2, 139r; Dr Williams's Library. This entry is not in Morley.

47. Charles Lamb to John Dyer Collier, dated 4 October 1812 by Marrs; Marrs iii. 85.

48. Robinson does not actually mention Hazlitt in his diary entry for this date, but the fact that Clarkson sent news of Hazlitt's appointment within the week suggests that he figured in their conversation of that day.

49. Morley i. 110.

50. Charles Lamb to John Dyer Collier, ?4 October 1812; Marrs iii. 85–6.

51. Note-taking had been prohibited in the House of Commons since a resolution of the Long Parliament in 1642, but restrictions had been relaxed since John Wilkes and his associates challenged them in 1771. See, for an account of this, Arthur H. Cash, *John Wilkes: The Scandalous Father of Civil Liberty* (New Haven, 2006), 280–2.

52. See Wu (2007) i, p. xxxii.

53. A lengthier account of the reporting 'system' established by Perry may be found in Wu (2007) i, pp. xxx–xxxiv.

54. Howe xvi. 224.

55. He apparently went to Perry with a letter of introduction from his lawyer, John Philpot Curran; see Ivon Asquith, *James Perry and the Morning Chronicle 1790–1821* (Ph.D. thesis, London University, 1973), 105.

56. See Wu (2007) ii. 218–26.

57. Howe xi. 288.

58. Morley i. 116.

Chapter 9

1. Howe xvi. 213.
2. *Memoirs* i. 196.
3. Howe xvii. 13.
4. *Memoirs* i. 196.
5. Howe xvii. 9.
6. Ibid. xvii. 14.
7. Ibid. 17.
8. His grandson reports that Hazlitt's career in the Commons was terminated 'by the injury which his constitution suffered from the use of stimulants, in which he followed what was an universal propensity in his day among members of the press' (*Memoirs* i. 196).
9. In the Preface to *Political Essays* (Wu iv. 5).

10. For Hazlitt's report of the debate, see Wu (2007) i. 31–45.
11. Finnerty's role in this affair is inference, but it is reasonable to suppose that Hazlitt took the advice of experienced colleagues before embarking on his plan. Not only was Finnerty one of the most experienced of his colleagues, he was also one of the most cunning.
12. For the *Courier* text, see Wu (2007) ii. 431–3.
13. Ibid. 432–3.
14. Ibid. 433.
15. Bewick i. 120–1.
16. Pope i. 303. Haydon's account of this dinner is not to be trusted; see Jones 94–5.
17. See *Four Generations* i. 105. Coulson was a frequent visitor to the Hazlitts and took a shine to Sarah, whose side he would take when the couple separated. He lived just round the corner in an apartment constructed from Bentham's stable (BL Add. MS 74782B (formerly C.133.g.10), p. 4).
18. Quoted Barbara K. Lewalski, *The Life of John Milton: A Critical Biography* (Oxford, 2000), 260. Hazlitt would always be amused by the local tradition that 'one Mr *Milford*, a celebrated poet, formerly lived there!' (Howe x. 283).
19. Bewick i. 117.
20. Jones 99.
21. *Memoirs* ii. 18.
22. Jeremy Bentham to Francis Place, 16 June 1831; BL Add. MS 37949, 252r.
23. Bewick i. 118.
24. *Memoirs* i. 214.
25. 'The Prince on St Patrick's Day', *The Examiner*, 22 March 1812, 177–80, esp. 179.
26. A full account of the offending article and ensuing trial is given by Nicholas Roe, *Fiery Heart: The First Life of Leigh Hunt* (London, 2005), 160–79.
27. Morpurgo 246.
28. Ibid.
29. WH to James Perry, n.d., but written shortly after 21 July 1813; Houghton Library, MS Hyde 76 (4.3), 226.2 (*Letters* 135). Sikes conjectures a dating of 'August 1813'; however, the postscript strongly indicates a dating of shortly after 21 July. The MS is watermarked 1809.
30. For a text, see Wu (2007) ii. 434–6.
31. See W. A. Speck, *Robert Southey: Entire Man of Letters* (New Haven and London, 2006), 120, 141–2, 179.
32. Wu iv. 22–3.
33. Wu (2007) i. 72–3.
34. It is significant that, shortly after Southey's appointment was announced, he congratulated Thomas Moore for declining the Laureateship; see Wu (2007) i. 74–5.
35. Wu iv. 23.
36. Ibid. vi. 176.
37. Howe xx. 9.
38. Sir Philip Francis to James Perry, 19 October 1813; *Memoirs of Sir Philip Francis, K.C.B.*, ed. Joseph Parkes and Herman Merivale (2 vols., London, 1867), ii. 374. Parkes was a friend of Hazlitt in the early 1820s and is mentioned in 'The Fight'. See p. 305.
39. Morley i. 153. This was reported to Robinson by Hazlitt some time after the event, and not there connected with Francis's letter (which Perry did not wish to show him). However, the two things are almost certainly connected.

40. Wu iii. 23.
41. Ibid. vi. 261–2.
42. Though speculative this was first advanced by Stanley Jones, who was cautious in his thinking; see Jones 112.
43. Mitford Letters, vol. iii f. 371.
44. *The Times*, 12 November 1813, p. 2 col. 1.
45. Wu iv. 32.
46. Stoddart's contract, dated 3 April 1814, is still to be found in the News International Archive (Walter Papers, folio 55). It reveals, among other things, that Stoddart received a salary of £1,400—a handsome sum.
47. The phrase is to be found in a letter from one 'O'Donnel' to John Walter II, 10 January 1819; News International Archive, Walter Papers folio 69.
48. *The Times*, 29 January 1814, p. 3 col. 3.
49. Wu (2007) ii. 451–2. This text is the original form in which Hazlitt meant 'Dottrel-Catching' to be read.
50. Morley i. 133.
51. Wu iii. 4.
52. Ibid. 9.
53. Ibid.
54. Ibid. vi. 262.
55. Howe xvi. 222 n.
56. Mary Russell Mitford to Sir William Elford, 28 December 1818; Reading Central Library, Mitford Letters, vol. iii, f. 356.
57. Wu (2007) i. 149. The would-be heroes are Vetus and Stoddart.
58. Scott was wary of it. He published it under the title, 'A Correspondent's Observations on the Motives and Principles of those who are for Maintaining Everlasting war against Revolutionized France', and prefaced it with a disclaimer: 'There are several important points of difference between our sentiments and those of our correspondent, as conveyed in the following article.—We think he extends too much indulgence to the French ruler, when he refers his inordinate appetite for conquest to the interference of other states with the right of the French people to choose their government. But as his communication generally, will give us an opportunity of making a few observations on several matters that are at present contested, we shall keep back a more particular specification of our dissent, for an article which will probably appear next week.—*ed.*' (*The Champion*, 3 April 1814, p. 105 col. 3.)
59. Farington xiii. 4483.
60. *The Times*, 6 April 1814, p. 3 col. 4.
61. *The Morning Chronicle*, 10 June 1814.
62. Morley i. 142.
63. Patmore ii. 290.
64. Howe xvii. 311.
65. Morley i. 154.
66. *The Morning Chronicle*, Tuesday, 3 May 1814, p. 3 col. 4. Hazlitt would repeat his insults in his 1816 essay on the British Institution (Howe xviii. 108).
67. Howe xi. 257.
68. *The Morning Chronicle*, Thursday, 5 May 1814, p. 3 col. 1.
69. See for instance Baker 194–5, Wardle 144, Grayling 175.

70. Morley i. 154.
71. *The Examiner*, 12 June 1814, p. 377.
72. Morley i. 154. A more detailed account of Hazlitt's involvement in the *Examiner*'s criticism of Perry may be found in Wu (2007) i, pp. xxxviii–xxxix.

Chapter 10

1. Howe xvii. 186.
2. Hazlitt was so pleased with it that he reprinted it in both *The Round Table* and *A View of the English Stage*; see Wu ii. 17–20, iii. 41–51.
3. Wu ii. 17.
4. Ibid. 19.
5. Ibid. 17.
6. Ibid. viii. 232.
7. For more on the background to Place's project, see my article, 'Hazlitt, Francis Place, and the Bentham Circle: New Findings', *The Charles Lamb Bulletin* NS 132 (October 2005), 95–103.
8. Wu vii. 78. This is Hazlitt's testimony, though it is worth noting that his grandson said: 'I have heard that [Bentham] would make his visitors do obeisance to the tablet in honour of Milton' (*Four Generations* i. 134 n).
9. For more on Hazlitt's understanding of the 'Recluse' poetry in 1798, see 'The Road to Nether Stowey', *Metaphysical Hazlitt: Bicentenary Essays*, ed. Tom Paulin, Uttara Natarajan, and Duncan Wu (Abingdon, 2005), 83–97.
10. Charles Lamb to William Wordsworth, 19 September 1814; Marrs iii. 112.
11. Lonsdale was instrumental in obtaining for Wordsworth the post of Distributor of Stamps for Westmorland and part of Cumberland.
12. David Bromwich notes it was 'the first serious discussion of Wordsworth's poetry by a critic who could claim to be neither an advocate set up by the poet himself nor a spokesman for fashionable literature' (Bromwich 158).
13. Wu ii. 325.
14. Ibid. 327.
15. Ibid. 322.
16. Ibid. 334.
17. Morley i. 202.
18. Wu ii. 337.
19. Ibid. 338.
20. Mary Wordsworth to Dorothy Wordsworth, 29 October 1814; *The Letters of Mary Wordsworth 1800–1855*, ed. Mary E. Burton (Oxford, 1958), 24.
21. For more particulars, see Jones 158–9.
22. Marrs iii. 112.
23. The certificate is now to be found in BL Add. MS 38898 f. 1.
24. William Coulson to G. Huntley Gordon, 3 June 1867; BL Add. MS 38899, 390v.
25. *The Life and Correspondence of the Late Robert Southey*, ed. Charles Cuthbert Southey (6 vols., London, 1849–50), ii. 292.
26. From Robinson's entry for Sunday 18 June 1815, not included by Morley; see Robinson diary, vol. iv, 124r; Dr Williams's Library.
27. This is the view of Scott's principal biographer; see Patrick O'Leary, *Regency Editor: Life of John Scott* (Aberdeen, 1983), 56.

28. 'Whether the Friends of Freedom Can Entertain Any Sanguine Hopes of the Favourable Results of the Ensuing Congress?', signed H.
29. 'Character of Sir Joshua Reynolds' (Howe xviii. 51).
30. As suggested by Jones 161; the author of the article which he attributes to her was, according to the *Wellesley Index*, James Mill.
31. This conversation is speculative, but is based on Stanley Jones's supposition that her 'recommendation is likely to have been more Hazlitt's idea than her own'; see Jones (1966) 264. Henry Crabb Robinson's version of events in his letter to his brother Thomas of 29 November 1814 is more or less sound, except in terms of who provided the introduction: 'William Hazlitt has been received into the Corps of Edinburg Reviewers in a manner flattering to him. The attention of Lady Mackintosh was drawn to some fine articles by him in the Champion on the influence of Institutions & Academies in the fine arts; And thro' Sir James's introduction he became known to Jeffrey' (HCR Correspondence, vol. v, f. 117; Dr Williams's Library).
32. The circulation of the biggest Whig daily, the *Morning Chronicle*, was seldom more than 3,500; for that reason the *Edinburgh* was always of far greater importance as an opinion-former. See William St Clair, *The Reading Nation in the Romantic Period* (Cambridge, 2004), 573, and Ivon Asquith, *James Perry and the Morning Chronicle 1790–1821* (Ph.D. thesis, London University, 1973), 299.
33. James Mackintosh to Catherine Mackintosh, letter-journal of 22 August to 24 December 1814, BL Add. MS 52441, 120r–v.
34. Howe xviii. 10.
35. He told his friend John Allen that for 'personal & political reasons the slight of the Morning Chronicle surprized me', and asked whether he could find out who was responsible. He was horrified to hear that it was 'the Critic in the Examiner who is I believe one of two bad writers on either of whom it would be easy & very proper to inflict condign punishment.' See James Mackintosh to John Allen, endorsed '?11 or 18 January 1814'; BL Add. MS 52182, 53r and James Mackintosh to John Allen, 19 January 1814; BL Add. MS 52182, 55r.
36. Morley i. 153.
37. Ibid.
38. [*The Times*], *A Newspaper History 1785–1935* (London, 1935), 139–40.
39. Wu iii. 146.
40. For more on Alsager, see D. E. Wickham, 'Thomas Massa Alsager (1779–1846): An Elian Shade Illuminated', *The Charles Lamb Bulletin* NS 35 (July 1981), 45–62.
41. Howe xv. 229–30. News of Louis XVIII's departure from Paris reached London on 23 March.
42. *The Letters of Thomas Moore*, ed. W. S. Dowden (2 vols., Oxford, 1964), i. 357; Marchand iv. 295.
43. See Haydon as quoted by O'Leary, *Regency Editor*, 83.
44. Pope ii. 315.
45. Ibid.
46. *The Champion*, 19 March 1815, p. 1 col. 2.
47. Wu viii. 122.
48. Benjamin Robert Haydon, diary; Houghton Library fMS Eng 1331 (13) vol. x, p. 26. I have referred here to the original rather than Pope because Jones queried the wording but was unable to check it. Pope's readings were correct. See Jones 168 and n 25.
49. Morley i. 164.
50. Ibid.

51. Howe xvi. 20.
52. Ibid. 22–3.
53. Captain James Burney to William Hazlitt, 17 May 1815; Morgan Library, MA 38. The letter is quoted also by Howe 166–7.
54. *The Examiner*, 11 June 1815, p. 382.
55. Morley i. 170.
56. See *The Letters of William and Dorothy Wordsworth: The Middle Years 1806–20*, ed. Ernest de Selincourt, rev. Mary Moorman and Alan G. Hill (2 vols., Oxford, 1969–70), ii. 195.
57. Morpurgo 254.
58. Ibid.
59. Ibid. 253.
60. Morley i. 169.
61. This exchange is inferred. It is clear that Hunt unmasked Hazlitt as the author of the review, in an attempt to curry favour with Wordsworth, and that this was the first he had heard of the Keswick escapade.
62. Farington vii. 2785.
63. See *The Journals of Mary Shelley 1814–1844*, ed. Paula R. Feldman and Diana Scott-Kilvert (2 vols., Oxford, 1987), i. 25. In 'To Wordsworth', Percy Bysshe Shelley lamented Wordsworth's 'desertion' of 'Songs consecrate to truth and liberty'.
64. Morley i. 170.
65. *Life of Benjamin Robert Haydon*, ed. Tom Taylor (2nd edn, 3 vols., London, 1853), i. 301.
66. Wu viii. 91.
67. Wu (2007) ii. 418–19.
68. Thomas Noon Talfourd, *Final Memorials of Charles Lamb* (2 vols., London, 1848), ii. 170.
69. Ibid. i. 303.
70. Patmore ii. 323.
71. City of Westminster Archives, E2875 Rate Books. Hazlitt appears as 'Azlett'. The debt had been cleared by the end of 1815.
72. 'The morality of this excellent comedy is very indifferent; and having been prompted by the observations of some persons of fashion near us, we got into a train of agreeable reflections on the progressive refinement of this our age and country, which it was our intention to have communicated to our readers, but that we dropt them in the lobbies!'
73. Stanley Jones is correct to point out that 'there are instances after 1815 of his taking drink of other kinds', which he enumerates (Jones 179). This flies in the face of W. C. Hazlitt, who argues that 'it was about 1815 that he resolved, in obedience to medical advice, to abstain wholly from all fermented liquors for the future' (*Memoirs* i. 222). W. C. Hazlitt was, of course, attempting to quell rumours of his grandfather's drunkenness.
74. Absey Division, Petty Session of 19 September 1815, City of Westminster Archives.
75. Bewick i. 118.
76. Wu ii. 79.
77. See Howe xviii. 46.
78. Farington xiv. 4937.
79. Wu iii. 94.
80. Ibid.
81. These included the Prince Regent. For this period in her life, see Charles E. Pearce, *Madame Vestris and Her Times* (London, n.d.), 39–42.

Notes

Chapter 11

1. Wu vi. 182.
2. Morley i. 178.
3. *The Examiner*, 31 December 1815, p. 843.
4. The troupe was from Seringapatam, and was first advertised in *The Times* on 15 September 1815. They inspired a letter to *The Examiner*, 17 December 1815, p. 813.
5. Wu vi. 67.
6. Ibid. 68.
7. Ibid.
8. See *Hazlitts* 169. For more on M'Creery, see J. R. Barker, 'John McCreery: A Radical Printer, 1768–1832', *The Library*, 5th series, 16 (1961), 81–103. M'Creery and Hazlitt had a mutual friend in Godwin (whose diary records visits from M'Creery on 21 September 1809 and 21 February 1810).
9. Longman Divide Ledger No. 2, Longman Archive, Reading University Library.
10. WH to Archibald Constable, 19 March 1816; National Library of Scotland, MS 674 (Constable papers), 132v (*Letters* 155). This letter was written on the same day as number 53 in Sikes's edition, misdated 9 February 1816 (*Letters* 152).
11. WH to Archibald Constable, 7 June 1816; Gates 652. Not in Sikes.
12. WH to Archibald Constable, 15 December 1816; National Library of Scotland, MS 7200, 128r. Not in Sikes. Hazlitt had been compelled to take as an advance the £50 which his contract stipulated he was entitled to six months *after* publication, as Longman reported to Constable on 4 April 1816: 'We inclose you some sheets of the Round Table which Mr. Hazlitt left with us last night. As he was *particularly* pressed for money we were prevailed on to pay him the £50 which he was to receive for the edition of the work in *Cash*.' See Thomas Norton Longman to Archibald Constable, 4 April 1816; Longman I, 99, no. 194, Reading University Library.
13. Macvey Napier to WH, 24 August 1816; National Library of Scotland, MS 674 (Constable papers), 69v.
14. WH to Leigh Hunt, postmarked 15 February 1816; Wordsworth Library, WL MS Foot 12 [1998.71.2] (*Letters* 153–4). Note the variation on the opening sentence of Jeffrey's review of *The Excursion*, 'This will never do.'
15. Wu (2007) i. 181.
16. Leigh Hunt to Archibald Constable, 19 August 1816; National Library of Scotland, MS 674 (Constable papers), 228r. The reading of this letter given by Gates is somewhat different (Gates 79). Haydon also liked *Rimini*, and wrote to congratulate its author: 'I have read, and reread your exquisite pathetic tale, till my Soul is cut in two—and every nerve about me pierced with trembling needles—I can say no more till we meet—but that it is the sweetest thing of the time, and that the World must think so.' See Benjamin Robert Haydon to Leigh Hunt, 21 February 1816; BL Add. MS 38108, 155r.
17. Edmund Kean to WH, n.d. This letter appears in Sotheby's catalogue of 26 February 1906. It is not mentioned in Sikes, and is at present untraced. See Maclean 352, Howe v. 400, Wardle 167 n 22.
18. *The Examiner*, 31 March 1816, p. 203; Wu iii. 125. These remarks (effectively a defence of himself) would find their way into 'On Actors and Acting' when it appeared in *The Round Table* (Wu ii. 156).
19. Wu iii. 126–8.

Notes

20. Procter (1830) 469.
21. W. C. Hazlitt, *The Hazlitts Part the Second: A Narrative of the Later Fortunes of the Family* (Edinburgh, 1912), 18.
22. This was an odd place for them to have gone; see Jones 113.
23. A full accounting of Hazlitt's contributions to this journal can be found in 'William Hazlitt (1737–1820) and the *Monthly Repository*: A Bibliographical Study', *The Charles Lamb Bulletin* NS 136 (October 2006), 133–43.
24. See David A. Quaid, *Robert Emmet: His Birthplace and Burial* (Dublin, 1902), 46. In a letter to W. C. Hazlitt of 13 June 1903, Louise Guiney comments: 'I am quite sure that if this annuity was paid promptly to Peggy Hazlitt, her mother and her brother John shared it. Miss Emmet, like all her family, was a person of great character and charm, and the bequest shows how well she could appreciate her friend' (BL Add MS 38910, 31r).
25. Thomas Addis Emmet, *Memoir of Thomas Addis and Robert Emmet* (2 vols., New York, 1915), i. 192.
26. Wu iii. 100.
27. Marchand iv. 336.
28. Wu iii. 137.
29. The announcement was made in the *Morning Chronicle* of that date.
30. Coleridge, *Notebooks*, ed. Kathleen Coburn and Anthony J. Harding (5 vols., Princeton, NJ, 1957–2002), ii. 2091.
31. See S. T. Coleridge to R. H. Brabant, 5 December 1816; Griggs iv. 693.
32. *The Examiner*, 2 June 1816, p. 349; Howe xix. 33.
33. The review though published in the September number of the *Edinburgh* did not appear until 12 November; the journal was often published behind time. Hazlitt's review has been variously attributed to Jeffrey, Thomas Moore, and others, but recent scholarship has accepted the sole attribution to Hazlitt. For further discussion see Wu (2007) i. 203–6.
34. *Edinburgh Review* 27 (September 1816), 58–67, esp. 65; Wu (2007) i. 215–16.
35. *Edinburgh Review* 27 (September 1816), 66–7; Wu (2007) i. 217–18.
36. These attacks are analysed in greater depth in my article, 'Rancour and Rabies: Hazlitt, Coleridge and Jeffrey in Dialogue', *British Romanticism and the Edinburgh Review: Bicentenary Essays*, ed. Massimiliano Demata and Duncan Wu (Houndmills, 2002), 168–94.
37. Morley i. 197.
38. Griggs iv. 693.
39. Ibid.
40. Ibid. 692–3.
41. Benjamin Robert Haydon to William Wordsworth, 15 April 1817; quoted Robert Woof, David Blayney Brown, and Stephen Hebron, *Benjamin Robert Haydon 1786–1846* (Grasmere, 1996), 40.
42. Shaver 315.
43. 'Ode. The Morning of the Day Appointed for a General Thanksgiving', 282. This frightful (but interesting) poem is presented in no less than three reading texts by the edition of the Cornell Wordsworth Series, Carl H. Ketcham.
44. See for instance Wu i. 126; iii. 181; iv. 90 n, 133; viii. 347.
45. Wu viii. 92–3.
46. See Baptism register for St Margaret's Church, Westminster, Westminster Archives.
47. BL Add. MS 38898, 3r.
48. *Memoirs* ii. 225.

49. Curry ii. 144–5.
50. Wu iv. 96.
51. 'A few interviews made us friends', Place recorded; see BL Add. MS 27791, ff. 264–8; on Bentham and Owen see BL Add. MS 33553, ff. 189–99.
52. Francis Place to James Mill, 15 September 1816; BL Add. MS 35152, 214r.
53. James Mill to Francis Place, 8 October 1816; BL Add MS 35152, 220r.
54. Wu ii. 136.
55. Ibid. 137.
56. Ibid. 138.
57. Benjamin Robert Haydon, 'On the Judgment of Connoisseurs being Preferred to that of Professional Men,—Elgin Marbles, etc.', *The Examiner*, 17 March 1816, p. 163.
58. Howe xviii. 100.
59. This was at some cost; President of the Royal Academy, Sir Thomas Lawrence, told Haydon that his article 'has saved the Marbles, but it will ruin you' (*The Autobiography and Memoirs of Benjamin Robert Haydon*, ed. Tom Taylor (2 vols., London, 1926), i. 232).
60. For Haydon's opinion see ibid. i. 263.
61. [Robert Smirke], *A Catalogue Raisonee of the Pictures now Exhibiting at the British Institution* (London, 1815), 9–10.
62. Wu (2007) i. 241; Wu ii. 140.
63. Wu ii. 141.
64. Ibid. He felt so strongly about it that he didn't hesitate to reprint his attack on the catalogue in *The Round Table*.
65. Jones 256.
66. *The Autobiography and Memoirs of Benjamin Robert Haydon*, ed. Taylor, i. 260.
67. Benjamin Robert Haydon to unknown correspondent, 4 November 1820; Bodleian Library, MS. Don. c. 63, 5r.
68. Pope ii. 64–5.
69. See Hunt, 'Young Poets', *The Examiner*, 1 December 1816, pp. 761–2.
70. See for instance David Bromwich, *Hazlitt: The Mind of a Critic* (Oxford, 1983), chapter 11, and Uttara Natarajan, *Hazlitt and the Reach of Sense* (Oxford, 1998), 107–19.
71. John Taylor to Sir James Mackintosh, 5 December 1818; BL Add MS 78766, 166r.
72. *Select British Poets* (London, 1824), p. xv; Howe ix. 244–5.
73. At least one reader was sickened by it: on 4 January 1817 one 'Candidus' wrote to the Tory *Courier* quoting Hazlitt's most recent riff on them, with the comment: 'Now, Sir, what namby pamby stuff is this! What an impotent attempt at mock description!' Candidus was irritated by the purple prose into which Hazlitt had slipped, and decreed 'that prose ought not to be poetry, and that even poetry ought to be sense' (*The Courier*, Saturday, 4 January 1817, p. 3 col. 4).
74. Milton, *L'Allegro*, 14–16.
75. *The Examiner*, 27 October 1816, p. 682.

Chapter 12

1. Howe ix. 204.
2. *The Examiner*, 8 September 1816, 571–2.
3. Henry Crabb Robinson to Thomas Robinson, 16 December 1816; HCR Correspondence, vol. v, f. 133a; Dr Williams's Library.

4. Charles Lamb to William Wordsworth, 23 September 1816; Marrs iii. 224–5. When Robinson protested to the Lambs that they continued to welcome him to their at homes, Mary answered: 'We have few pleasures & few friends & cannot afford to give up H.' (Henry Crabb Robinson to Wordsworth, *c.*1816; HCR Correspondence, vol. v, f. 135; Dr Williams's Library).

5. This account is drawn from Haydon iii. 319–20.

6. Wu iv. 102.

7. *The Examiner*, 22 December 1816, p. 803.

8. Morley i. 200–1.

9. Henry Crabb Robinson, Reminiscences, vol. 4 1834–43, f. 468; Dr Williams's Library.

10. 'He has a black heart'; from Horace, *Satires* I. iv. 85.

11. William Wordsworth to Benjamin Robert Haydon, 7 April 1817; *The Letters of William and Dorothy Wordsworth III. The Middle Years Part 2 1812–1820*, ed. Ernest de Selincourt, rev. Mary Moorman and Alan G. Hill (Oxford, 1970), 377.

12. Benjamin Robert Haydon to William Wordsworth, 15 April 1817; Wordsworth Library, WL MS A, f.9.

13. Pope ii. 110.

14. WH to Archibald Constable, 24 July 1816; National Library of Scotland, MS 7200, 140r. As Jones notes, the text at *Letters* 162 is inaccurate (Jones 227).

15. WH to William Hazlitt Jr, February or March 1822; *Remains* ii.73 (*Letters* 216). I doubt whether this has any right to be regarded as a letter at all; it is in effect an essay. No MS has survived, but it probably never existed as an item of correspondence. As Sikes includes it in his volume, I have treated it as a letter in order to make it possible for the reader to locate it.

16. WH to Francis Jeffrey, 3 January 1817; National Library of Scotland, MS 5319, 280r (*Letters* 164).

17. WH to Francis Jeffrey, 20 April 1817; William Hazlitt collection GEN MSS 33, Box 1, Folder 1, Beineke Library, Yale University (Baker 214, *Letters* 171).

18. Wu iv. 137–8.

19. Ibid. iii. 190.

20. Ibid.

21. Procter, quoted Jeffrey Kahan, *The Cult of Kean* (Aldershot, 2006), 19.

22. Lord John Russell to Francis Horner, 21 February 1817; BL Add. MS 72844, 34r.

23. Quoted from reports in *The Examiner*, 2 February 1817, p. 66.

24. Morley i. 189.

25. Charles Duke Yonge, *The Life and Administration of Robert Banks, Second Earl of Liverpool, K.G.* (3 vols., London, 1868), ii. 298. Coleridge also wrote to Liverpool at this moment, but Liverpool found his missive all but incomprehensible (see Griggs iv. 757–63).

26. It is not mentioned by W. A. Speck in his excellent *Robert Southey: Entire Man of Letters* (2006) or by Mark Storey, *Robert Southey: A Life* (1997), to take the two most recent examples.

27. Robert Southey to S. T. Coleridge, 21 March 1817; unpublished MS, quoted in Sotheby's catalogue for auction of 13 December 2007, p. 71.

28. Ibid.

29. Throughout their letters and notebooks, Coleridge and Southey referred to the Unitarian poetess Anna Laetitia Barbauld as an old serpent.

30. Wu iv. 158.

31. The testimony of Thomas Poole's brother John, *c.*1794; see Mrs Henry Sandford, *Thomas Poole and his Friends* (2 vols., London, 1888), i. 103.
32. As quoted in Speck, *Robert Southey: Entire Man of Letters*, 174.
33. Wu iv. 158.
34. Ibid.
35. *The Times*, Saturday, 15 March 1817, parliamentary report, p. 2, col. 2.
36. Ibid.
37. Wu iv. 193–4.
38. Ibid. 175.
39. Curry ii. 156.
40. Rollins i. 144.
41. Hazlitt took the phrase 'vigour beyond the law' from Southey's advice to the Prime Minister: 'I beseech you do not hesitate at using that vigour beyond the law...which your own personal safety requires as much as the vital interests of the country' (see Yonge, *Life and Administration of Robert Banks*, ii. 299).
42. He must have liked it because he included it in his suppressed *Select British Poets* (London, 1824), 750–1.
43. See *The Letters of Percy Bysshe Shelley*, ed. Frederick L. Jones (2 vols., Oxford, 1964), ii. 476.
44. He probably did not know that Hazlitt had been responsible for the damning review of 'Christabel' (a favourite poem of his) in the *Edinburgh*, about which he told Byron: 'In my opinion the *Edinburgh Review* is as well qualified to judge of the merits of a poet, as Homer would have been to have written a commentary on the Newtonian System' (Ibid. i. 514).
45. This is the quality Hazlitt underlines in his *Spirit of the Age* portrait: 'In the whole of his public career, and with all the goodness of his disposition, he has not shewn "so small a drop of pity as a wren's eye" ' (Wu vii. 210).
46. The convergence of their interests is indicated by Shelley's regard for Peter Finnerty, Hazlitt's former colleague at the *Morning Chronicle*, to whose support fund Shelley contributed and on whose behalf he published his *Poetical Essay on the Existing State of Things* in 1811. The only known copy of the pamphlet surfaced in July 2006; see H. R. Woudhuysen, 'A Shelley Pamphlet Come to Light', *TLS* 14 July 2006, p. 12, and 'The Shelley Pamphlet', *TLS* 21 July 2006, p. 17.
47. Howe viii. 148.
48. *The Journals of Mary Shelley 1814–44*, ed. Paula R. Feldman and Diana Scott-Kilvert (2 vols., Oxford, 1987), i. 163.
49. Charles and Mary Cowden Clarke, *Recollections of Writers* (London, 1878), 26. This provides the earliest evidence we have of an encounter between Clarke and Hazlitt (cf. *Four Generations* i. 174).
50. As *Poems* (1817) was not published until 1 March, they must have been reading it from manuscript. See Leigh Hunt, *Lord Byron and Some of His Contemporaries* (2 vols., London, 1828), i. 410.
51. *The Examiner*, 2 March 1817, 139.
52. WH to Archibald Constable, 24 July 1816; National Library of Scotland, MS 674 (Constable papers), 140r (*Letters* 162).
53. WH to Archibald Constable, 7 June 1816; Gates 652. Not in Sikes.
54. Wu ii. 79.
55. Ibid. 79–80.

56. Keynes supposed from its uncommonness that 'the edition consisted of a relatively small number of copies', though the run was 1,000. The Longman accounts at Reading University Library indicate that sales were slow and had more or less dried up completely by 1819.
57. Mary Russell Mitford to Sir William Elford, 28 December 1819; Mitford Letters, vol. iv, f. 394.
58. John Keats to John Hamilton Reynolds, 21 September 1817; Rollins i. 166.
59. Though dated April 1817 it was actually published in September.
60. *Quarterly Review* 17 (April 1817), 154–9, esp. 157–8.
61. The reviewer may have been John Taylor Coleridge, though it is very likely to have been Gifford. See the 'Quarterly Review Archive' online: http://www.rc.umd.edu/reference/qr/index/33.html
62. When Robinson caught up with this, he was struck by the unfairness of it: 'I suspect some friend of the Laureate's wrote with laboured malice to avenge his friend. The severity of the criticism has defeated its object in a great measure, I have no doubt. The *Quarterly* exceeds the *Edinburgh* in acrimony and vulgarity' (Morley i. 210).
63. *Four Generations* i. 118. See also *Memoirs* i. 228.
64. WH to Francis Jeffrey, 28 April 1817; Beineke Library, Yale University (*Letters* 171, Baker 214). Sikes and Baker date the letter to 20 April but it is actually dated 28 April at the end of the text. It bears no postmark. The attribution of the *Times* piece was first argued by Jones (1966) 274, and repeated by Charles E. Robinson, 'Percy Bysshe Shelley, Charles Ollier, and William Blackwood: The Contexts of Early Nineteenth-Century Publishing', *Shelley Revalued: Essays from the Gregynog Conference*, ed. Kelvin Everest (Leicester, 1983), 183–226, 189.
65. WH to Archibald Constable, 29 May 1817; National Library of Scotland, MS 7200, ff. 141–2 (*Letters* 173).
66. The new title page bore the names of its publishers; see Keynes 28.
67. See Jonathan Bate, *Shakespearean Constitutions: Politics, Theatre, Criticism 1730–1830* (Oxford, 1989), 150–1.
68. See Wu i. 193, 195, 230, 180.
69. Hazlitt, *Characters of Shakespear's Plays* (London, 1817); Houghton Library, *EC8.K2262.Zz817h.
70. See Stendhal to Baron de Mareste, 14 April 1818: 'J'embrasse le Vicomte et Smidt. Ce dernier est-il en pied? Que ne traduit-il Hazlitt ou Shakspeare, ou le catéchisme parlementaire de J. Bentham.' Stendhal, *Correspondance 1800–42* ed. Henri Martineau (10 vols., Paris, 1933–4), v. 124.
71. Wu i. 213.
72. *British Critic* 9 (January 1818), 15–22, esp. 19.
73. *Memoirs* i. 228.
74. Morley i. 210.
75. A copy of this edition is to be found at the Houghton Library, *83-271.
76. *Memoirs* i. 229. W. C. Hazlitt does not say who brought the Boston edition to York Street; George Ticknor is a likely candidate. The copy given to Hazlitt was formerly in the possession of his grandson, but is not now to be found.
77. WH to Francis Jeffrey, *c.*10 August 1817; Beineke Library, Yale University (*Letters* 176). The letter is not dated but bears a receipt postmark of 12 August (although there is a dispatch postmark, it is too smudged to be legible).

Notes

Chapter 13

1. Wu viii. 56.
2. Howe xix. 356.
3. *The Times*, 12 October 1813, p. 2 col. 2.
4. *The Times*, 7 December 1813, p. 3 col. 4.
5. *The Times*, 14 December 1813, p. 3 col. 2.
6. Ibid. p. 3 col. 3.
7. Wu iv. 34. This spat culminated in the recently attributed letter by 'No Star-Gazer', published in the *Morning Chronicle* on 3 February 1814 (Wu (2007) i. 129–32).
8. Wu (2007) i. 219, 221.
9. This must have taken place after consulting Stoddart's contract, which appointed him permanently; see Walter Papers 55, News International Archive.
10. Quoted Derek Barnes, *Thomas Barnes of The Times* (London, 1943), 27.
11. It was probably Hazlitt's earlier criticism of *The Times* that led Barnes to criticize him when he dined with Robinson on 26 January 1817: 'B[arnes] left us soon after dinner. He was bitter & contemptuous speaking of Hazlitt—with little reason surely—for it was less the morals than the talent of H[azlitt] which he attacked. And B[arnes] is certainly very inferior to him' (Robinson diary, vol. v, 127r for Sunday, 26 January 1817; this entry is not in Morley).
12. Robinson diary, vol. v, 161r for Friday 25 April 1817. This entry is not in Morley.
13. These machinations took place in secret; no one was supposed to know the editor's identity, as Hazlitt's grandson recalled: 'Without being so constituted, the organ possessed an official authority. Its statements were judicial. A good deal of this superstition (for superstition it was) proceeded from the consummate tact of the management. The *Editor of the Times* was impersonal; no one was supposed to know who he was; the public had as distinct a notion of his individuality as of the Cumaean Sibyl or the Grand Lama of Tibet' (BL Add. MS 74782B (formerly C.133.g.10), 162).
14. This was the opinion of John Dyer Collier, whose MS autobiography records: 'Mr Walter's mode of address was particularly quiet, but not perfectly easy' (Folger Shakespeare Library, M.a.230, f. 60).
15. The News International archive contains a letter by Walter of 14 December 1812 in which he assures Sterling he will not reveal him to be the author of Vetus's letters: 'for the sake of mere formality, rather than from any belief that you can entertain any doubts of my firmness, I beg you will keep this as a record of my assurance, that nothing whatever shall induce me to disclose, either directly or by implication, the author of V[etu]s' (Walter papers, f. 44).
16. The item in question is a newly attributed review of 'Mr Dowton's Mrs Malaprop'; see Wu (2007) i. 225. This was why, writing to Jeffrey ten days earlier, Hazlitt said that he was 'writing for three newspapers at a time'—*The Times*, *The Examiner*, and the *Edinburgh Review*. See WH to Francis Jeffrey, 28 April 1817; Beineke Library, Yale University (*Letters* 171, Baker 214). Sikes and Baker date the letter to 20 April but it is actually dated 28 April. Fenner is not correct in restricting Hazlitt's employment with *The Times* to May–June 1817 (Fenner 52).
17. Barnes and Walter were sharing editorial duties; Hazlitt is referring here to Walter.
18. Wu iii. 4.
19. The circulation of the *Chronicle* was stable at around 3,500 to 4,000 throughout the second decade of the nineteenth century because of Perry's failure to invest in Koenig's new steam press.

Notes

20. Howe xi. 289.
21. An example may be found in Wu (2007) i. 264–70.
22. Patmore ii. 318.
23. Wu viii. 56–7.
24. J. H. Reynolds to Mary Leigh, 28 April 1817; Keats House KH 521 (London Metropolitan Archive).
25. See Rollins ii. 177.
26. Procter (1877) 176.
27. Paul F. Matthiesen, 'Gosse's Candid "Snapshots" ', *Victorian Studies* 8 (1965), 329–54, esp. 352 n, 353.
28. Wu vi. 179. Jacob Hall was a rope-dancer; Charles II was in love with Frances Stewart, whose legs were (he said) more handsome than those of any other woman, 'and she, to prove the truth of his majesty's assertion, immediately showed her leg above the knee'. Hazlitt is confusing this with the story of Lady Chesterfield's green stockings; see Anthony Hamilton, *Memoirs of Count de Grammont* (2 vols., London, 1818), ii. 42.
29. R. H. Horne, 'Charles Wells', *The Academy*, Saturday, 19 April 1879, 349–50, esp. 350.
30. Ibid. 349.
31. John Hunt to Leigh Hunt, n.d., though endorsed in pencil 1817; BL Add. MS 38523, 41r.
32. William Hone to John Hunt, 8 May 1817; BL Add. MS 38108, 189r.
33. It has been told most recently by Ben Wilson, *The Laughter of Triumph* (London, 2005).
34. Wu iii. 213.
35. Howe xviii. 236. Hazlitt was probably responsible for a piece about Talma that appeared in the *Chronicle* as early as March 1814 (see Wu (2007) i. 156–8).
36. In *The Life of Henry Brulard*, Stendhal recalls that the women he loved 'were my passionate preoccupation. . . . I was not promiscuous, not enough so; I was preoccupied only by the woman I loved, and when I wasn't in love I pondered the spectacle of human affairs or read with delight Montesquieu or Walter Scott' (*The Life of Henry Brulard*, tr. John Sturrock (New York, 2002), 20).
37. Robert Vigneron, 'Stendhal et Hazlitt', *Modern Philology* 35 (1938), 375–414, 376. Vigneron's article remains an invaluable source for anyone working on this topic.
38. Others include Louis Alexandre Bombet, Lisio Visconti, Cornichon, le chef de bataillon Coste, Timoléon du Bois, and William Crocodile.
39. See Stendhal, *Histoire de la Peinture en Italie* ed. Paul Arbelet (2 vols., Paris, 1969), ii. 144 n; the note appears at the end of chapter 130.
40. Victor Del Litto, *La Vie Intellectuelle de Stendhal* (Paris, 1959), 528–32.
41. Though it has to be said that the recent French editions of this work which I have been able to consult, as well as the English translation, disregard the epigraph of 1817. I have explored the ramifications of these connections at greater length in 'Stendhal and the British Romantics', *British and European Romanticisms*, ed. Christoph Bode and Sebastian Domsch (Trier, 2007), 37–49.
42. Entry for 12 August 1817; Stendhal, *Journal 1800–23*, ed. Henri Martineau (5 vols., Paris, 1937), v. 319. On 28 September 1816 he told his friend Louis Crozet that 'le jour où ils m'ont donné le moyen de lire *the Edinburgh Review* sera une grande époque pour l'histoire de mon esprit' (Stendhal, *Correspondance 1800–42*, ed. Henri Martineau (10 vols., Paris, 1933–4), iv. 370).

43. *Memoirs* is vague about the dating, but 1817 is made likely by the fact that Hazlitt began contributing to the *Morning Chronicle* during June in the wake of Perry's retirement.
44. See *Memoirs* i. 213 n.
45. William Hazlitt Jr to W. C. Hazlitt, 22 March 1884; BL Add. MS 38904, 45v.
46. *The Correspondence of Jeremy Bentham*, vol. ix: January 1817 to June 1820, ed. Stephen Conway (Oxford, 1989), 91.
47. Ibid. 113.
48. *Memoirs* i. 215–16.
49. Patmore ii. 306.
50. Leigh Hunt to WH, 22 September 1819: 'Nunc scio quid sit *Majestas*. I do not allude to M^{rs}. Tomlinson, though she certainly ought to be called Caroline' (SUNY at Buffalo). The letter appears at *Memoirs* i. 254 and Gates 101–2.
51. *Correspondence of Jeremy Bentham*, ix. 118.
52. Quotations from a document issued by the Institution dated October 1816, in a bound collection of miscellaneous papers relating to it at British Library 822i9.
53. Patmore ii. 250–1.
54. Ibid. 251.
55. The unique copy of the Prospectus for the series is now at the Cambridge University Library; reproduced at Keynes pp. xxii–iii.
56. See chapter 10 in particular; Coleridge, *Biographia Literaria*, ed. James Engell and Walter Jackson Bate (2 vols., Princeton, NJ, 1983), i. 180, 184–5.
57. Ibid. ii. 208.
58. Morley i. 209.
59. *Edinburgh Review* 28 (August 1817), 488–515, esp. 491; Howe xvi. 118.
60. *Edinburgh Review* 28 (August 1817), 488–515, esp. 493; Howe xvi. 120.
61. *Edinburgh Review* 28 (August 1817), 488–515, esp. 515; Howe xvi. 138. The run of reviews with which this concluded is the subject of a fascinating critical study: Robert Keith Lapp, *Contest for Cultural Authority: Hazlitt, Coleridge, and the Distresses of the Regency* (Detroit, 1999).
62. Robert Southey to John Murray, 4 September 1817; Curry ii. 171. As a schoolboy, Southey had opposed the use of capital punishment in *The Flagellant*, for which he had been expelled from Westminster School.
63. S. T. Coleridge to Lord Liverpool, 28 July 1817; Griggs iv. 757.
64. Ibid. 758.
65. Ibid. 761–2.
66. Ibid. 761.
67. Ibid. 762.
68. Ibid. 763.
69. Ibid. 763. He mentioned Hazlitt's 'pre-determined Malice' in the letter he had written to John Murray several months earlier (Griggs iv. 707).
70. S. T. Coleridge to Daniel Stuart, c.2 April 1817; Griggs iv. 719.
71. Wu iv. 120.
72. Ibid. 121.
73. Ibid. ii. 379.
74. Pope ii. 134.

Notes

75. For more on this, see my 'Rancour and Rabies: Hazlitt, Coleridge and Jeffrey in Dialogue', *British Romanticism and the Edinburgh Review: Bicentenary Essays*, ed. Massimiliano Demata and Duncan Wu (Houndmills, 2002), 168–94, esp. 179.

76. *Memoirs* ii. 148.

77. MacNeven is mentioned in a late essay of Hazlitt's on Peter Finnerty; see Wu (2007) ii. 225.

78. This copy is now in the Berg Collection, New York Public Library. It bears the inscription, 'The Right Honourable J. P. Curran | From the Author.' Hazlitt also knew the eldest of Curran's daughters—Amelia, an artist. She attended the lectures on the English poets in March 1818, and later dined with Hazlitt and Godwin. In 1819 she would paint the best-known lifetime portrait of Shelley.

79. Z. [J. G. Lockhart], 'On the Cockney School of Poetry No. I', *Blackwood's Edinburgh Magazine* 2 (October 1817), 38–41, esp. 41.

80. Leigh Hunt to Francis Jeffrey, '1817'; Gordon i. 271 n 1. No other date is given besides the year, and its present whereabouts is not known. But the date of composition must be shortly after publication of Lockhart's 'Cockney School' attack—that is, *c.* October 1817.

81. As quoted P. P. Howe, 'Hazlitt and "Blackwood's" ', *Fortnightly Review* 112 (1919), 603–15, esp. 605.

82. Z. [J. G. Lockhart], 'On the Cockney School of Poetry No. III', *Blackwood's Edinburgh Magazine* 3 (July 1818), 453–6, esp. 456. They tried the same tactic on other editors. William Maginn later ridiculed Thomas Campbell, editor of the *New Monthly Magazine*, for employing Hazlitt: 'Let me ask you, Mr Thomas Campbell, why you permit Mr William Hazlitt, the modern Pygmalion, to fill your pages with gross, scurrilous, and low-lived abuse of people, whom such a man should not be permitted to name' (William Maginn, 'Letters of Timothy Tickler No. IX', *Blackwood's Edinburgh Magazine* 14 (September 1823), 308–12, esp. 309.

83. Like Hazlitt, Keats knew they were coming for him. 'There has been a flaming attack upon Hunt in the Edinburgh Magazine,' he told Benjamin Bailey in November. 'I never read anything so virulent, accusing him of the greatest crimes, depreciating his wife, his poetry, his habits, his company, his conversation. These philippics are to come out in numbers called "the Cockney School of Poetry". . . . In the motto they have put Hunt and Keats in large letters' (Rollins i. 179–80).

84. 'Execution of Brandreth, Turner, and Ludlam', *The Examiner*, 9 November 1817, 716–17, esp. 717.

85. John Keats to George and Tom Keats, 22 December 1818; Rollins i. 191.

86. Robinson diary, vol. vi, 61r for Saturday, 20 December 1817. Not in Morley.

87. Robinson diary, vol. vi, 62r for Sunday, 21 December 1817. Not in Morley.

88. Ibid.

89. This important article has recently been attributed to Hazlitt; see Wu (2007) i. 290–3.

90. Thomas Carlyle, *Reminiscences*, ed. J. A. Froude (2 vols., London, 1881), i. 232.

91. See Wu *Library* 47.

92. Bewick i. 142.

93. Ibid. 141–2.

94. 'Remarks on a Paragraph in the Times', *The Examiner*, 7 September 1823, 582.

95. Howe proposed that Hazlitt's last review was published on 19 December (Howe xviii. 270–1), but recent scholars suggest otherwise; see Wu (2007) i. 289.

96. Wu ii. 330. The evening is the subject of a book; see Penelope Hughes-Hallett, *The Immortal Dinner* (London, 2000).

Notes

Chapter 14

1. Rollins i 204–5.
2. This article has only recently been identified as his; see Wu (2007) i. 290 ff. It is sufficiently well informed to indicate that Hone and Hazlitt were known to one another. Hone would attend one of Hazlitt's lectures in March 1818 as a way of paying his respects (Jones 282).
3. Wu iv. 238. Mackintosh, who came in for criticism in its pages, regarded it as 'a democratical weekly Paper printed at 2d in which the opposition is much abused.... What I said on Scotch Reform is called "the Creed of Holland House" & I to be the Oracle of "The Hol[lan]d House Cabal". It does not disturb me' (Diary of James Mackintosh, entry for 3 May 1818; BL Add. MS 52443B, 66v–67r).
4. It is described in detail by Wu (2007) ii. 497–8.
5. Wu viii. 29.
6. Wu (2007) i. 315–18.
7. For example, Henry Crabb Robinson recorded in his diary for 31 December 1817: 'Mem: At Surry Institution looked over Blackwoods Mag: The publisher had written cringing letters to W[ordsworth] & then published letters of sheer vulgar abuse with[ou]t any criticism or knowledge of any kind whatever' (Robinson diary, vol. vi, 58r). Not in Morley.
8. Patmore ii. 260.
9. The date of Patmore's visit was shortly after 20 January 1818, on which date Hazlitt agreed to 'let you have a sight of the Lecture' (WH to P. G. Patmore, 20 January 1818; Connecticut Historical Society). This note is not in Sikes nor so far as I am aware is it in print anywhere. It is addressed to Patmore 'care of the Surry Institution' and was evidently sent by hand. I thank Barbara Austen of the Connecticut Historical Society for this information.
10. Patmore ii. 261–2.
11. Sarah helped Hazlitt by copying many of the lengthy quotations; see, for instance, the manuscript of Lecture II, now at the State Library of Victoria, Melbourne, that of Lecture III, at the Folger Shakespeare Library, Washington DC, or that of Lecture IV, in the Gluck Collection at the Buffalo and Erie County Public Library.
12. WH to Leigh Hunt, 21 April 1821; *Letters* 204.
13. This is adapted from the account given in Bewick i. 143–4.
14. William Bewick to John Bewick, 11 February 1818; Bewick i. 41.
15. Wu v. 281.
16. Patmore ii. 275. Hunt also testified to Hazlitt's reluctance to shake hands: 'His fingers, half coming out, and half retreating, seemed to think that you were going to do them a mischief; and when you got hold of them, the whole shake was on your side' (Leigh Hunt, 'Shaking Hands', *The Indicator* 40 (12 July 1820), 314–15, esp. 315).
17. Patmore ii. 276. Patmore's coyness in his account of their meeting with the 'sundry petitioners' does not make it any easier to work out what happened, but I follow Jones in assuming them to be streetwalkers (see Jones 52).
18. 'My Recollections of the Late William Hazlitt', *New Monthly Magazine* 29 (November 1830), 469–82, esp. 473.
19. Mr Rokes of the Borough was an undertaker. His claimed presence is a sort of joke meaning that everyone in London was there—as much as to say, 'Uncle Tom Cobbley and all'.
20. John Keats to George and Tom Keats, 23 January 1818; Rollins i. 214.

21. John Keats to George and Tom Keats, 21 February 1818; Rollins i. 237. David Bromwich notes that 'Keats was in the habit of conversing freely after the lectures, with Hazlitt and his circle' (Bromwich 367).

22. WH to Leigh Hunt, 21 April 1817; *Letters* 204.

23. Morley i. 218.

24. Ibid.

25. Ibid. 220.

26. The Diary of Sir James Mackintosh, entry for 20 February 1818; BL Add. MS 52443A, 72r–v.

27. Robinson diary, vol. vi, 86r. Not in Morley.

28. Morley i. 219.

29. Ibid. 220.

30. Wu ii. 283.

31. Contrary to Grayling, Robinson was not present at the last of the lectures (see Grayling 228).

32. Wu ii. 306.

33. Camille Paglia compares Byron with Elvis Presley; see *Sexual Personae* (London, 1992), 361–2.

34. Wu ii. 234.

35. John Keats to B. R. Haydon, 21 March 1818; Rollins i. 252.

36. It gave his first readers a new kind of literary pleasure, as John Clare told his publisher John Taylor: 'I like Hazlitts Lectures uncommon—his style is the most pleasing of any living prose writer I have met with—the treat is delicious I have began them all & know not which to finish' (John Clare to John Taylor, *c.*3 April 1821; Storey 178).

37. Quoted Jones 284.

38. *The Morning Chronicle*, 23 February 1818, p. 3 col. 2.

39. WH to James Perry, n.d. [23 February 1818]; National Library of Scotland, MS 15953, 60r. Not in Sikes. This is the fragment recorded by Jones (1977) 339, who explains the rationale for its dating.

40. Mary Russell Mitford to Sir William Elford, 'Bertram House', 28 December 1818, endorsed 'January one 1819'; Reading Central Library, Mitford Letters, vol. iii, f. 356.

41. Patmore ii. 305–6.

42. Howe ix. 193.

43. 'Mr Hazlitt's Lectures on Poetry', *The Examiner*, 8 March 1818, 154.

44. See William St Clair, *The Godwins and the Shelleys: The Biography of a Family* (London, 1989), 444–5.

45. Wu ii. 307.

46. Bewick i. 148. For his part, Byron was incensed when he read what Hazlitt had said about him; see my 'Talking Pimples: Hazlitt and Byron in Love', *Romanticism* 10.2 (2004), 158–72.

47. *The Examiner*, 8 March 1818, 154.

48. See James Augustus Hessey to John Taylor, 6 March 1818; *Keats Circle* i. 13 (the original is at the Morgan Library, MA 215, 29). John Hamilton Reynolds requested proofs of the first lecture to read through that month; see Wu ii, p. xvi.

49. Wu iii. 5.

50. Mary Russell Mitford to Sir William Elford, 28 December 1818, endorsed 'January one 1819'; Reading Central Library, Mitford Letters, vol. iii, f. 356.

51. *British Critic* 10 (October 1818), 441–5, esp. 441.

52. *British Review* 13 (May 1819), 313–39, esp. 313–14.
53. Wu iv. 258.
54. Ibid. 254.
55. The evidence for dating publication is given at Wu ii, p. xvi.
56. A copy is to be found at the Houghton Library, *EC8.H3394.818lb. A second London edition came out the following year. Like the first, it was brought out by Taylor and Hessey. Entirely reset, it incorporated verbal alterations by the author; see Keynes 40.
57. It was also the meeting place of the 'King of Clubs', the Whig dining fraternity of which Mackintosh, Hobhouse, Burdett, Kinnaird, and Byron were members.
58. B. R. Haydon to Keats, 25 March 1818; Houghton Library, MS Keats 4.7.9 (Rollins i. 259).
59. *Morning Chronicle*, 25 March 1818.
60. Two days after its appearance, Moore thanked Hazlitt, enclosing a copy of the third edition bearing an inscription expressing respect 'for his literary talents & political principles'. This is now at the Wordsworth Library, Grasmere. Hazlitt's review was reprinted by the *Morning Chronicle* on 11 May.
61. Wu iv. 266.
62. This volume is in the Michael Foot collection at the Wordsworth Library, Grasmere. The inscription appears on the recto of the half-title.
63. This exchange is conjectural, based on the note from Hazlitt to Soane.
64. WH to Sir John Soane, n.d. [16 or 23 March 1818]; SM Priv. Corr. I.H.11.1; Sir John Soane's Museum. Not in Sikes. There is no postmark, and the note was probably conveyed by hand.
65. For the rationale in my dating of the note, see Wu *Library* 40.
66. Thomas Moore was also there, as was Owen Rees of the firm of Longman, Hurst, Rees, and Orme.
67. Wu ii. 78. As Howe noted, 'We may gather . . . that Hazlitt knew Turner' (Howe xii. 396), but until now it has not been known when.
68. Howe xviii. 14, 19.
69. Turner may have known the *Round Table* essay, and had certainly read two of Hazlitt's articles on the Fine Arts for *The Champion* (though apparently without being aware of their authorship); see *Collected Correspondence of J. M. W. Turner*, ed. John Gage (Oxford, 1980), 58.
70. For the best available summary account of that tour, see Cecilia Powell, *Turner in Germany* (London, 1995), 20–9 and *Turner's Rivers of Europe* (London, 1991), 20–36. For more on this subject, see my 'When Hazlitt Met Turner', *Turner Society News* 99 (May 2005), 8–10.
71. For this conjecture I am grateful to Cecilia and Nicholas Powell.
72. *Blackwood's Edinburgh Magazine* 2 (March 1818), n.p.
73. See Alan Lang Strout, 'Pimpled Hazlitt', *English Literary History* 4 (June 1937), 154–9, esp. 157.
74. P. G. Patmore to William Blackwood, 'London', 16 April 1818; National Library of Scotland, MS 4003, f. 200.
75. William Blackwood to P. G. Patmore, 20 April 1818; Champneys ii. 437.
76. Ibid.
77. See for instance Emily Lorraine de Montluzin, 'William Blackwood: The Human Face Behind the Mask of "Ebony" ', *Keats–Shelley Journal* 36 (1987), 158–89.
78. Douglas was mentioned in 'Nicol Jarvie's Letter to the Author of Rob Roy' in *Blackwood's* for January and March 1818.

79. On 22 June 1817 *The Courier* reported that Finnerty was horsewhipped across the face by V. G. Dowling.
80. Gordon i. 278.
81. Howe ix. 197.
82. Patmore ii. 314–15.
83. *Keats Circle* ii. 58–9.
84. Howe ix. 197.
85. Ibid. vii. 308.
86. John Scott, 'The Mohock Magazine', *London Magazine* 2 (December 1820), 666–85, esp. 667.
87. Howe ix. 10. The slander remained a bone of contention even after his death. When William Jr was preparing his father's *Literary Remains*, Basil Montagu wrote to say that his wife 'particularly desires that it may be noticed, somewhere or other, that Blackwood's Magazine described your father as drinking daily, and with a *red spotted face* at the time when he had abstained for some years from fermented liquor of any kind, and that he was always remarkable for the marble paleness and clearness of his complexion' (Basil Montagu to William Hazlitt Jr, *c.*1836; BL Add. MS 38523, 153r).
88. William Blackwood to P. G. Patmore, 20 April 1818; Champneys ii. 437–8.
89. J. G. Lockhart, 'Letter from Z. to Mr. Leigh Hunt', *Blackwood's Edinburgh Magazine* 2 (January 1818), 414–17, esp. 416.
90. The Quarterly Review archive says 'William Gifford, possibly'; see http://www.rc.umd.edu/reference/qr/index/36.html
91. John Taylor to James Taylor, 4 June 1818; quoted in Edmund Blunden, *Keats's Publisher: A Memoir of John Taylor* (London, 1936), 54. The present whereabouts of this letter is not known.
92. John Dix, *Lions: Living and Dead; or, Personal Recollections of the Great and Gifted* (London, 1852), 38. See also Wu vi. 86. Hazlitt's detestation of the public dates from this moment, and inspired him up to the moment of his death; see for instance 'The Public', Wu (2007) ii. 385–9.
93. This suggests that Hazlitt had seen Gifford, who lived in nearby James Street, a few minutes' walk to the west of York Street.
94. William Hazlitt, 'The Editor of the Quarterly Review', *The Examiner*, 14 June 1818, 378–9.
95. WH to Francis Jeffrey, 12 May 1818; Beineke Library, Yale University (*Letters* 182). The dispatch postmark is 13 May; the receipt postmark 16 May. Hazlitt posted it at the Tothill Street post office, a few minutes' walk from his house.
96. WH to Archibald Constable, 28 July 1818; Tinker Collection, Gen MSS 310, Box 8, folder 364, Beineke Library, Yale University (*Letters* 184). The letter bears no postmark, no seal, and no address, suggesting it was delivered by hand.
97. Wu ii. 156.
98. Howe ix. 220.
99. For further information on the monetary system of the time, see St Clair, *The Godwins and the Shelleys*, 257–8.
100. Francis Jeffrey to WH, 3 May 1818; National Library of Scotland, MS 672 (Constable papers), 82r. The receipt postmark is dated 5 May.
101. Ibid. 81v.

Notes

Chapter 15

1. Howe ix. 179.
2. WH to Archibald Constable, n.d. [before 18 September 1818]; National Library of Scotland, MS 674, 74r (*Letters* 187). The MS text is a transcription in an unknown hand, and presumably a later copy—which makes it unlikely that, as Sikes claims, it was endorsed by Hazlitt (*Letters* 188). Sikes's text is from the *TLS* rather than the MS, of which he was apparently unaware; see P. P. Howe, 'Three Hazlitt Letters', *TLS* 21 March 1936, 244. Sikes's dating is '[September] 1818', but Jones advises 'Before 18 Sept 1818', which I have followed; see Jones, review of Sikes, *The Library* Series 6, 3 (1980), 356–62, esp. 359.
3. Alexander Henderson to Archibald Constable, 20 November 1818; National Library of Scotland, MS 674 (Constable papers), 150r.
4. In 1823, on a visit to London, William Maginn pumped Hazlitt's publisher, Colburn, for information on his colleagues, telling Blackwood: 'I have not time to give you particulars more minutely, but I will draw up a minute of everything he said, for I have picked up some strange information about Hazlitt, Patmore, B. Cornwall, C. Redding, &c.' (Margaret Oliphant, *Annals of a Publishing House: William Blackwood and his Sons, Their Magazine and Friends* (2 vols., Edinburgh, 1897), i. 396).
5. Alexander Henderson's list of books sent to him in Edinburgh from Paris and London, 1825–7, shows that Hazlitt sent him a complimentary copy of his last collection, *The Plain Speaker*; see National Library of Scotland, MS 155, 39v.
6. [John Wilson], 'Hazlitt Cross-Questioned', *Blackwood's Edinburgh Magazine* 3 (August 1818), 550–2, esp. 551. It is not easy to be sure where Wilson got every piece of information used in his article, but it is a safe conjecture that the items included here were provided by Henderson. The precise terms of this exchange are conjectural, based on Wilson's article.
7. Ibid. Again, the recent vintage of the information points to Henderson.
8. Wu viii. 116–17.
9. Ibid. 236.
10. Howe ix. 224. Air quality in Regency London was poorer than today, for a principal means of energy was wood-fires, which polluted the air. When, in his great sonnet 'Composed upon Westminster Bridge', Wordsworth described the city 'bright and glittering in the smokeless air' (l. 8), he did so pointedly: the air was smokeless because at 5.30am no one had yet lit their fires.
11. Wu vi. 163.
12. John Dix, *Lions: Living and Dead; or, Personal Recollections of the Great and Gifted* (London, 1852), 38.
13. Wu viii. 111–12.
14. Ibid. 24–5.
15. Ibid. 112. The passage about Millamant occurs in the second of the lectures; see ibid. v. 32–3.
16. Ibid. vi. 63.
17. See 'Translation from an Ancient Chaldee Manuscript', *Blackwood's Edinburgh Magazine* 2 (October 1817), 89–96, esp. 92. Strout attributes it principally to James Hogg, adding that it was rewritten by Lockhart, Wilson, and possibly others.
18. J. G. Lockhart, *The Life of Sir Walter Scott, Bart.* (Edinburgh, 1879), 779.
19. J. G. Lockhart, *Peter's Letters to his Kinsfolk*, ed. William Ruddick (Edinburgh, 1977), 38.
20. See Wu (2007) ii. 217.
21. Quoted Jones 290.

22. The testimony is that of De Quincey; see Robert Morrison, 'Richard Woodhouse's *Cause Book*: The Opium-Eater, the Magazine Wars, and the London Literary Scene in 1821', *Harvard Library Bulletin* 9.3 (Fall 1998), 7.

23. This would make better sense if, as Elsie Swann suggests, John Wilson met Hazlitt in the Lakes (presumably in 1803), though I cannot see on what evidence that is proposed; see Elsie Swann, *Christopher North < John Wilson >* (Edinburgh, 1934), 97. It is not a notion endorsed by Jones.

24. C. K. Sharpe to Robert Surtees, 1 October 1817; National Library of Scotland, MS 3700.

25. William Blackwood to P. G. Patmore, 20 April 1818; Champneys ii. 437. For a late Hazlittian dissection of the Blackwoodsmen, see 'Phrenology' (Wu (2007) ii. 211–17).

26. [John Wilson], 'Hazlitt Cross-Questioned', *Blackwood's Edinburgh Magazine* 3 (August 1818), 550–2, esp. 550.

27. Ibid.

28. Ibid. 550–1.

29. See, for instance, WH to Archibald Constable, n.d. [before 18 September 1818]; National Library of Scotland, MS 674, 74r, where he refers to the *Edinburgh Review*, saying: 'I sent a long article for the last, but you know I am expelled from it' (*Letters* 188).

30. Francis Jeffrey to WH, 20 September 1818; National Library of Scotland, MS 672, 83v–84r.

31. Z [J. G. Lockhart], 'Cockney School of Poetry No. IV', *Blackwood's Edinburgh Magazine* 3 (August 1818), 519–24, esp. 519.

32. Ibid. 524.

33. J. A. Hessey to John Taylor, 5 September 1818; Houghton Library, MS Keats 4.8.18.

34. WH to Archibald Constable, n.d. [before 18 September 1818]; National Library of Scotland, MS 674, 74r (*Letters* 187).

35. Wu (2007) ii. 388.

36. Edmund Blunden, *Keats's Publisher: A Memoir of John Taylor* (London, 1936), 55. It is a little unfair of Blunden to comment: 'Whoever had dealings with Hazlitt, sooner or later found him hard to please.'

37. Rollins i. 368.

38. *Keats Circle* i. 232.

39. Wu vi. 86. Haydon is a less reliable witness, but his testimony should be noted: 'Keats was a victim to personal abuse and want of nerve to bear it. . . . His ruin was owing to his want of decision of character and power of will, without which genius is a curse' (*Haydon Table Talk* ii. 71).

40. Francis Jeffrey to WH, 20 September 1818; National Library of Scotland, MS 672, 83r.

41. WH to William Blackwood, 18 September 1818; National Library of Scotland, MS 7200, 144r (Jones (1966) 277, *Letters* 189–90). The letter is incorrectly dated by Sikes to 19 September for, as Jones notes, it was written the day before. See Stanley Jones, review of Sikes, *The Library* Series 6, 3 (1980) 356–62, esp. 359. This error indicates that Sikes's copy-text is, in fact, Jones (1966) rather than the MS. The MS appears to be in the hand of Constable rather than that of his clerk.

42. William Blackwood to WH, 21 September 1818; Jones (1966) 277.

43. WH to James Balfour, 25 September 1818; Jones (1966) 277 (*Letters* 191). Balfour was also Constable's agent.

44. *The Times*, 21 September 1818, p. 2 col. 5.

Notes

45. William Blackwood to John Murray, 22 September 1818; Samuel Smiles, *Memoir and Correspondence of the Late John Murray* (2 vols., London, 1891), i. 482.

46. William Blackwood to John Murray, 25 September 1818; Smiles, *Memoir and Correspondence of the Late John Murray*, i. 482.

47. William Blackwood to John Murray, 2 October 1818; Smiles, *Memoir and Correspondence of the Late John Murray*, i. 485.

48. On 27 October he told Patmore that 'I have no doubt but that Constable is to pay the whole' of Hazlitt's expenses; see Champneys ii. 440. The date of this letter is misread by Champneys as 27 August, as Jones records (Jones 301 n 85). It is not likely that Constable was underwriting Hazlitt's legal battle.

49. Smiles, *Memoir and Correspondence of the Late John Murray*, i. 486.

50. [Macvey Napier], *Hypocrisy Unveiled and Calumny Detected: in a Review of Blackwood's Magazine* (3rd edn, Edinburgh, 1818), 6, 14.

51. See Philip Flynn, 'Blackwood's *Maga*, Lockhart's *Peter's Letters*, and the Politics of Publishing', *Studies in Romanticism* 45 (Spring 2006), 117–31, esp. 119.

52. Gordon i. 292.

53. It appeared also in *The Edinburgh Advertiser*, 27 October 1818, and was reported in the *Morning Chronicle* two days later. There is no chance that Hazlitt could have missed it.

54. Champneys i. 488.

55. Ibid. 489.

56. William Blackwood to John Murray, 30 October 1818; Murray papers.

57. J. A. Hessey to John Taylor, 23 October 1818; Houghton Library, MS Keats 4.8.19. His willingness to do this may owe something to the fact that, as Hessey reported, another bookseller, Fairbairn, 'has ordered 25 Lectures & 15 Shaksp: with many other things' (*Keats Circle* i. 53). Hazlitt's books were still, apparently, in demand.

58. Hazlitt's second meeting with Hessey took place on 24 October; on that day, as Keats told the George Keatses, 'I walked with Hazlitt as far as Covent Garden: he was going to play Rackets' (Rollins i. 402).

59. *Romantic Bards and British Reviewers*, ed. John O. Hayden (London, 1971), 325. Although it appeared in the *Quarterly* for April 1818, the issue itself was not published until 26 September. It is worth noting that a severe review from Croker succeeded in bringing a premature end to the career of Anna Laetitia Barbauld in 1813; see my *Romantic Women Poets: An Anthology* (Oxford, 1997), pp. xxii–xxiii, 8–9.

60. *Haydon Table Talk* ii 287. These were Keats's words to Haydon, but it is very likely he said something of the sort to Hazlitt as well.

61. For recent perspectives on Hazlitt's influence on this aspect of Keats's thought, see Uttara Natarajan, *Hazlitt and the Reach of Sense* (Oxford, 1998), 108–10, and Andrew Motion, *Keats* (London, 1997), 227–8.

62. See Stanley Jones, 'Hazlitt and the Game of Fives', *Charles Lamb Bulletin* NS 72 (October 1990), 284–5.

63. See Procter (1830) 479.

64. Bewick i. 137.

65. Howe xvii. 318.

66. Bewick i. 137–8.

67. Patmore iii. 130.

68. John Payne Collier, MS autobiography, f. 112 (Folger Shakespeare Library).

69. WH to Leigh Hunt, 21 April 1821; *Letters* 205.

70. William Blackwood to John Murray, 30 November 1818; Murray papers.

71. William Blackwood to John Murray, 27 October 1818; Champneys ii. 439–40. The date of this letter is misread by Champneys as 27 August, as Jones records (Jones 301 n 85).

72. William Blackwood to John Murray, 27 October 1818; Champneys ii. 440–1.

73. William Blackwood to John Murray, 16 December 1818; Smiles, *Memoir and Correspondence of the Late John Murray*, i. 493.

74. John Murray to William Blackwood, 9 January 1819; Smiles, *Memoir and Correspondence of the Late John Murray*, i. 493.

75. See Flynn, 'Blackwood's *Maga*, Lockhart's *Peter's Letters*, and the Politics of Publishing', 117 n 1.

76. Z., 'On the Cockney School of Prose Writers No.I', *New Monthly Magazine* 10 (October 1818), 198–202, esp. 198, 200, 201.

77. Z., 'On the Cockney School of Prose. No.II', *New Monthly Magazine* 10 (November 1818), 299–304, esp. 304.

78. William Godwin to Archibald Constable, 9 November 1818; National Library of Scotland, MS 327 (letters to Archibald Constable), 307r.

79. WH to Archibald Constable, n.d.; *Letters* 179. Sikes locates this item at the National Library of Scotland but as neither Jones nor I managed to find it Sikes's remains the sole available text. Sikes dates it 'January or February 1818', but the context makes clear it was written *c.*November or December 1818, prior to the beginning of the lectures on the comic writers.

80. *The Examiner*, 8 November 1818, 713.

81. 'He raised a tumult by abusing Gifford, which a few hissed at and many applauded' (Morley i. 225).

82. A member of the audience wrote to describe how Hazlitt 'made (as he not infrequently does) an unfortunate and irrelevant political allusion; which was instantly followed by rounds of applause from some, and hissing from other parts of the audience; by which hubbub the course of the lecture was suspended for some minutes' (A Friend to Order, 'To the Editor of the Times', *The Times*, 12 November 1818, p. 3 col. 5).

83. Bewick i. 145.

84. Morley i. 225.

85. Ibid. 226.

86. John Keats to George and Georgiana Keats, 14 February 1819; Rollins ii. 59.

87. John Keats to George and Georgiana Keats, 2 January 1819; Rollins ii. 24. For the dating of the visit to York Street see Rollins ii. 24 n 2.

88. Bewick i. 146–7.

89. His diary shows that he attended the first, second, fifth, and sixth lectures on the comic writers.

90. Howe xviii. 314; Wu (2007) i. 272.

91. For further details see Wu *Library*.

92. Others include Wordsworth's 'Recluse', Davy's epic poem about Moses, Southey's history of Levellers, and any number of works by Coleridge. What survives of Hazlitt's *History* is to be found at Howe ii. 123–48. Hazlitt was undoubtedly thinking of himself when, in 'On the Want of Money', he wrote: 'There is a set of poor devils, who live upon a printed *prospectus* of a work that never will be written, for which they solicit your name and half-a-crown' (Howe xvii. 182).

93. When he met him in 1805 Haydon encountered 'a little white-headed lion-faced man in an old flannel dressing-gown tied round his waist with a piece of rope' (Haydon, *Life* i. 28).
94. Howe xvi. 209.
95. Wu viii. 85.
96. Ibid. v. 152.
97. See Wu (2007) ii. 184.
98. Shaver 169–70.
99. Howe xx. 226.
100. Ibid.
101. Ibid. 227.
102. Ibid.
103. Ibid. 226.

Chapter 16

1. Howe xvii. 229.
2. Francis Place to Thomas Hodgskin, 8 September 1819; BL Add. MS 35153, 69r.
3. See F. W. Hackwood, *William Hone: His Life and Times* (London, 1912), 212.
4. The contract is in the Goodyear Collection at SUNY at Buffalo.
5. Hackwood, *William Hone: His Life and Times*, 212.
6. Wu iv. 219.
7. Ibid. 5. This passage has been described, aptly, by Charles Mahoney, as Hazlitt's 'systematic programme-statement'; see *Romantics and Renegades: The Poetics of Political Reaction* (Houndmills, 2003), 30.
8. As quoted in Ben Wilson, *The Laughter of Triumph* (London, 2005), 277.
9. WH to P. G. Patmore, [3 February 1819]; Howe vi. 385 (*Letters* 193). Sikes's text is from Howe rather than the MS, which is not now to be found. Jones apparently saw the MS and reports a postmark of 4 February and date of composition of 3 February; see his review of Sikes, *The Library* Series 6, 3 (1980), 356–62, esp. 359.
10. *Quarterly Review* 19 (July 1818), 424–34, esp. 434. This was the issue for July 1818, much delayed. Hazlitt borrowed it from Whitmore and Fenn's circulating library as soon as it was published (WH to Whitmore and Fenn, 2–7 February 1819; *Letters* 195. Sikes dates this note 'February 1819' but I follow Jones's more precise dating; see his review of Sikes, *The Library* Series 6, 3 (1980), 356–62, esp. 359). Though Hazlitt could not know it, the review was by Eaton Stannard Barrett whose comedy, *My Wife! What Wife?*, Hazlitt praised as 'very amusing' in 1815 (Wu iii. 67). Barrett was in no mood to reciprocate.
11. Wu v. 343.
12. Ibid.
13. Ibid. 343–4.
14. Ibid. 375.
15. Robert Southey to Tom Southey, 12 November 1808; *Selections from the Letters of Robert Southey*, ed. John Wood Warter (4 vols., London, 1856), ii. 107–8.
16. Including Robert Stodart's, 81 Strand.
17. Godwin's diary records receipt of a presentation copy on 11 March.
18. This copy is now in the Bodleian Library, Oxford.
19. Leigh Hunt to Mary Shelley, 9 March 1819; *Hunt Correspondence* i. 128.

20. *The Examiner*, 14 March 1819, 171–3, esp. 171. For more on reception of the *Letter*, public and private, see Wu v, pp. xxiv–vi.
21. Rollins ii. 76. By the time the *Letter to Gifford* appeared, as David Bromwich observes, 'Hazlitt seemed to Keats almost an embodiment of the modern idea of genius' (Bromwich 365).
22. This copy appeared in the Maggs catalogue no. 443 for 1923.
23. Wu vii. 204.
24. Graham Wallas, *The Life of Francis Place 1771–1854* (4th edn, London, 1925), 134.
25. Leslie G. Mitchell, *Lord Melbourne: 1779–1848* (Oxford, 1997), 80.
26. Lady Caroline's motives in assisting her brother-in-law were political in more senses than one: she was spiking the guns of one of Byron's closest friends. When consoling Hobhouse for having lost the election, Byron referred to her involvement in his own inimitable style: 'If I had guessed at your *opponent*—I would have made one among you Certes—and have f——d Caroline Lamb out of her "two hundred votes" although at the expence of a testicle— I think I could have neutralized her zeal with a little management—but alas! who could have thought of that Cuckoldy family's *standing* for a *member*—I suppose it is the first time that George Lamb ever *stood* for any thing' (Marchand vi. 107). For more on her involvement in this, see Paul Douglass, *Lady Caroline Lamb: A Biography* (New York, 2004), 215–16, and *The Whole Disgraceful Truth: Selected Letters of Lady Caroline Lamb*, ed. Paul Douglass (New York, 2006), 171–3.
27. *The Examiner*, 14 February 1819, 104.
28. Wu iv. 12–13.
29. Ibid. viii. 175.
30. Francis Place to John Cam Hobhouse, Friday 20 August 1819; BL Add. MS 36457, f. 340.
31. Ibid.
32. Wu viii. 351.
33. Ibid. ii. 307.
34. McGann v. 682–3.
35. Ibid. 683.
36. *Haydon Table Talk* ii. 368.
37. BL Add. MS 56540. I thank Peter Cochran for bringing this diary entry to my attention. John Murray's letter informing Byron that the note would not after all be published is to be found in *The Letters of John Murray to Lord Byron*, ed. Andrew Nicholson (Liverpool, 2007), 267. Byron was not pleased.
38. Mary Russell Mitford's *Literary Pocket-Book* for 1819, entry for 17 April 1819; BL C.60 b.7.
39. *Four Generations* i. 121.
40. George Ticknor, *Life, Letters, and Journals of George Ticknor* (2 vols., London, 1876), i. 293.
41. Ibid. 293–4. The witticism about Emperor Alexander occurs in an essay of 1815; see Howe xix. 139.
42. This point is conjectural, but Hazlitt was proud of his father, and would not have missed a chance of telling Ticknor about him.
43. This is William Henry Curran, son of the recently deceased John Philpot Curran, who during 1819 became involved with the Hunt and Hazlitt circle perhaps thanks to an introduction from Hazlitt.
44. Ticknor, *Life, Letters, and Journals of George Ticknor*, 294.

45. This is confirmed by Hunt's remark that 'I see a good deal of Lamb, Hazlitt, Coulson, the Novellos &c., but as much at their own houses as at mine' (Leigh Hunt to Mary Shelley, 25–7 July 1819; *Shelley Circle* vi. 847).
46. WH to Francis Jeffrey, 2 May 1820; Beineke Library, Yale University (*Letters* 200). Sikes does not report the dispatch postmark, 3 May, and receipt postmark of 6 May.
47. Procter (1877) 177.
48. Ibid. 178.
49. Ibid.
50. *Hazlitts* 176.
51. *Memoirs* i, p. xi.
52. Ibid. The Reynells were decayed gentry from Devonshire who traced their lineage back to the reign of Richard I. Carew Henry's father had been the first member of the family to go into trade. John Hunt was apprenticed to him and, when he began to publish, used Reynell as his printer—which explains why manuscripts of the most important poets of the day passed through Carew Henry's hands, including those of Byron, Shelley, and Keats.
53. Rollins ii. 59; Morley i. 230; Godwin's diary.
54. William Godwin to John Taylor, 14 June 1819; *Shelley Circle* vi. 834.
55. A year later Taylor wrote to an American bookseller offering 1,000 copies of *Lectures on the English Poets*, 'for we have overprinted that Work'; John Taylor to Michael Drury, 26 January 1820; *Keats Circle* i. 101.
56. William Godwin to John Taylor, 14 June 1819; *Shelley Circle* vi. 834.
57. Archibald Constable to WH, 25 June 1819; National Library of Scotland, MS 790, f. 548. The letter is quoted by Stanley Jones, 'Hazlitt in Edinburgh: An Evening with Mr. Ritchie of *The Scotsman*', *Etudes Anglaises* 17 (1964), 9–20, 113–27, 16 n 17.
58. WH to Francis Jeffrey, 25 September 1819; Beineke Library, Yale University (*Letters* 198). Sikes does not report the dispatch postmark of 27 September or receipt postmark of 30 September. The letter is postmarked Andover; that is, it was dispatched from Winterslow Hut on the Andover coach.
59. Jones says that Stodart's 'radical sympathies proved so inimical to his business affairs, that he became bankrupt the following year' (Jones 306).
60. WH to B. W. Procter, n.d.; MS in a private collection (Gates 653, *Letters* 177). Gates edited from the MS, Sikes from a copy owned by Keynes. Gates dates the dinner to '?1818', Sikes to '[April 1817]'; neither is satisfactory. Even if Sikes's dating were correct, his letter appears in the wrong place in his edition—it should be number 66 or 68 (not number 71). However, Farren's first appearance in London did not occur until 10 September 1818, so the letter must post-date that. Furthermore, the presence of Washington Irving indicates a date of 1819 at the earliest, given that he was invited to the dinner as a literary personality, and became known only in that year for his *Sketch-Book of Geoffrey Crayon*, which Hazlitt was to commend in *The Spirit of the Age* (Wu vii. 234). If the earliest year in which the dinner could have occurred is 1819, the most likely time for it, when all participants were in London, is the summer of that year.
61. Wu vii. 235. Meeting him in 1822, Francis Jeffrey drew a similar conclusion; he was 'agreeable, I think, *tête à tête*...very gentle and amiable' (Francis Jeffrey to Mrs Colden, 6 May 1822; *The Life of Lord Jeffrey*, ed. Lord Cockburn (2 vols., Edinburgh, 1852), ii. 206).
62. Howe xviii. 356.
63. Procter (1877) 173.

64. Ibid. The volumes in question were Dodsley's *Select Old Plays* (12 vols., 1744).
65. Wu viii. 211.
66. Procter (1877) 167.
67. Howe xvii. 67.
68. Ibid. 68.
69. Wu v. 227–8.
70. *Quarterly Review* 22 (July 1819), 158–63, esp. 162; *The Anti-Jacobin Review* 57 (December 1819), 312–24, esp. 312, 319, 322; *Edinburgh Monthly Review* 3 (March 1820), 297–309, esp. 309.
71. Months later, Southey stuck to the view that 'the meeting was unlawful, and in *terrorem populi* is to me perfectly clear.' See *The Life and Correspondence of the Late Robert Southey*, ed. Charles Cuthbert Southey (6 vols., London, 1849–50), iv. 360.
72. See Howe xx. 142. Scholars suggest Hazlitt may have had a hand in post-Peterloo journals such as *The White Hat*; see Wu (2007) ii. 499–501.
73. Howe xvii. 177.
74. Ibid. 183.
75. WH to B. R. Haydon, n.d.; Houghton Library, fMS Eng 1331 (11) vol. ix, 156v (*Letters* 196). Sikes dates the note to '[September, 1819]'. However, the note is glued into Haydon's diary, its position indicating that it was received by 13 August 1819, its text suggesting Hazlitt expected Haydon to drop by (at York Street) 'tomorrow morning before twelve'. Haydon is mistaken in supposing Hazlitt's note was originally sent *c.*October 1818—a claim made many years after the event; see Haydon, *Life* i. 411.
76. Pope ii. 495.
77. Leigh Hunt to WH, 22 September 1819; SUNY at Buffalo, Goodyear Collection (Gates 102).
78. *Memoirs* i. 253–4.
79. WH to Francis Jeffrey, 25 September 1819; Beineke Library, Yale University (*Letters* 198). Sikes does not report the dispatch postmark of 27 September 1819 (Andover) and the receipt postmark of 30 September. We do not know for sure that the money was to pay off a debt to Mrs Hine, but the possibility is a likely one.
80. Leigh Hunt to WH, 22 September 1819; SUNY at Buffalo, Goodyear Collection (Gates 102).
81. Howe xvii. 176.
82. WH to Leigh Hunt, 21 April 1821; *Letters* 205.
83. Haydon, *Life* i. 411.
84. Pope iii. 132–3. See also Stanley Jones, 'Haydon and Northcote on Hazlitt: A Fabrication', *Review of English Studies* 24 (1973), 165–78, esp. 176.
85. Patmore confirms they were 'the only things to which I ever knew him attach any value' (Patmore iii. 105).
86. Haydon, *Life* i. 411.
87. Howe xvii. 177.
88. WH to Leigh Hunt, 21 April 1821; *Letters* 205.
89. Howe, *Life* 294.
90. See Jeremy Bentham to Francis Place, 6 November 1819: 'When you were with me, neither of us could think of No. 19. Have you communicated with Carr? If not, do so, as soon as may be: were it only to stop me from being bothered with his Attorney on Tuesday when Koe is to be here' (*The Correspondence of Jeremy Bentham, Volume 9: January 1817 to June 1820*, ed. Stephen Conway (Oxford, 1989), 366).

91. See Jeremy Bentham to Richard Rush, 14 August 1821; *The Correspondence of Jeremy Bentham, Volume 10: July 1820 to January 1821* ed. Stephen Conway (Oxford, 1994), 383. It is not known whether the staircase survives, or where in America it was sent.
92. Wu vii. 78.
93. WH to Leigh Hunt, 21 April 1821; *Letters* 205.
94. *Correspondence of Jeremy Bentham, Volume 9*, 94.
95. Toward the end of his life, Hazlitt became increasingly bemused by the nature of friendship. His most undeceived account of it is to be found in 'Friends', published the day after his death in *The Atlas* (Wu (2007) ii. 402–7).
96. Howe xx. 343.
97. John Keats to Fanny Brawne, 13 October 1819; Rollins ii. 223.
98. John Keats to Charles Brown, 22 September 1819; Rollins ii. 177.
99. Ibid.
100. This exchange is largely inferred.
101. *Memoirs* i. 256.
102. John Keats to George and Georgiana Keats, 12 November 1819; Rollins ii. 228, 230.
103. Wu ii. 171.
104. John Keats to George and Georgiana Keats, 12 November 1819; Rollins ii. 230.
105. 'Surrey Institution', *The Examiner*, 7 November 1819, 714.
106. See Wu v. 267–8.
107. *Memoirs* i. 257.
108. See Bodleian Library, MS. Dep. b.215/6.
109. The audience on this occasion included Mary (John Hazlitt's wife), Godwin and his son William, and Talfourd. Mary Hazlitt was helpful to the lecturer as he prepared for the sixth in the series (*Four Generations* i. 121; W. C. Hazlitt believed this story to relate to the lectures on the English poets, but that cannot be, as Hazlitt did no more than glance at Sidney in the lecture on Thomson and Cowper). She was one of the unsung heroines of her day. Her husband being alcoholic, she generated a modest income by looking after insane gentlewomen, possibly at one of the local madhouses—one of whom may have been Mary Lamb (see Henry Crabb Robinson, Diary 11, 38r entry for Wednesday 26 January 1825; Dr Williams's Library—not in Morley).
110. Wu v. 339.
111. Wu v. 340. I follow the example of Stanley Jones, who also directs us to this passage (Jones 306).

Chapter 17
1. Howe ix. 219.
2. Pope ii. 315. The date of the meeting is provided by Scott in a letter to Baldwin of 18 January 1820: 'I have not spoken to [Hazlitt] for several years until Sunday last' (quoted O'Leary 118).
3. WH to B. R. Haydon, 11 August 1820; Houghton Library, fMS Eng 1331 (11) vol. ix f. 273 (*Letters* 201). The year was added to the letter by Haydon.
4. *Memoirs* i. 260.
5. Ibid. 269.
6. *Four Generations* i. 124.
7. In the MS of 'On the Fear of Death'; Wu vi. 342.

8. Howe xviii. 368.
9. See for instance the sentence beginning 'Cloud rolls over cloud' (Wu viii. 186). It has not previously been argued that this essay was composed at Winterslow.
10. *London Magazine* 1 (February 1820), 185–91, esp. 187, 188.
11. *Edinburgh Review* 34 (November 1820), 438–49, esp. 439.
12. Pope ii. 265.
13. Haydon, *Life* i. 403. There is some question about whether Haydon really did remember this or whether he made it up (as he did so much else). It is the only indication we have of Hazlitt's presence that evening.
14. Howe xvi. 209.
15. *The Reminiscences of Alexander Dyce*, ed. Richard J. Schrader (Ohio State University Press, 1972), 197.
16. Wu iii. 207–8.
17. Farington xvi. 5523.
18. Ibid.
19. 'Mr Haydon's Picture', *The Examiner*, 7 May 1820, 297–300.
20. For the English reception of Géricault's painting, see Christine Riding, 'The Raft of the Medusa in Britain: Audience and Context', *Constable to Delacroix: British Art and the French Romantics*, ed. Patrick Noon (London, 2003), 66–73. It is possible that it influenced the discarded first stanza of Keats's 'Ode on Melancholy'.
21. WH to Francis Jeffrey, 2 May 1820; Beineke Library, Yale University (*Letters* 199). The dispatch postmark is dated 3 May, the receipt postmark 6 May.
22. B. R. Haydon to WH, 22 May 1820; Beineke Library, Osborn Files Folder 6893. As well as being dated by its author, the letter is postmarked 22 May.
23. WH to B. R. Haydon, 11 August 1820; Houghton Library, fMS Eng 1331 (11) vol. ix f. 273 (*Letters* 201). Hazlitt dates the letter '11 August', Haydon having added the year.
24. Howe xvi. 181.
25. Ibid. 191.
26. Sir Thomas Lawrence to Joseph Farington, endorsed by Farington 'recd. Octr. 21/1820'; LAW/3/221, Royal Academy archives.
27. Wu vii. 236.
28. Ibid. iii 171.
29. *Macready's Reminiscences*, ed. Sir Frederick Pollock (London, 1876), 162.
30. *The Examiner*, 4 June 1820, 362–3.
31. James Sheridan Knowles to Leigh Hunt, n.d.; BL Add. MS 38524, 165v. The letter must have been written on or soon after 4 June 1820, when Hunt's review was published.
32. Howe xviii. 347.
33. F. Holland Day to W. C. Hazlitt, 9 August 1896; BL Add. MS 38907, f. 60. Day gives a different reading in his subsequent letter of 2 September: 'To Wm Hazlitt Esqr with the Authors sincere respects'; see 63r. The book was apparently sold at William Godwin's sale, which suggests that Hazlitt lent it to him at some point.
34. *The Hazlitts* 175. In this Hazlitt agreed with Lamb, who thought it 'The finest thing in the volume'; see *Lamb as Critic*, ed. Roy Park (London, 1980), 243.
35. *Memoirs* i. 261.
36. Wu vi. 342.

37. WH to Robert Baldwin, n.d.; Berg Collection, NYPL (Baker 404 n, *Letters* 202). Baker and Sikes date this letter 'September, 1820'. This cannot be correct because, as Jones points out, it refers to the proofs of 'On the Conversation of Authors', published in the *London Magazine* in September. A more likely dating would be 'some time between July and August 1820'; see Jones's review of Sikes, *The Library* Series 6, 3 (1980), 356–62, esp. 359. The MS of the letter, now in the Berg Collection, NYPL, gives little clue as to its exact date, although someone has endorsed it '1821' in pencil.

38. *Memoirs* i. 260.

39. Ibid. 263.

40. I cannot accept Wardle's assertion that the news 'could hardly have caused him deep grief' (Wardle 267).

41. Margaret Hazlitt to WH, 28 July 1820; *Hazlitts* 450. For William Hazlitt Sr's connection with the *Monthly Repository,* see my article, 'William Hazlitt (1737–1820) and the *Monthly Repository:* A Bibliographical Study', *Charles Lamb Bulletin* NS 136 (October 2006), 133–43.

42. Wu iv. 224–5.

43. *The Examiner,* 6 August 1820, 512.

44. WH to Rowland Hunter, 5 October 1823; MS in the possession of the author. This letter is hitherto unpublished and unrecorded.

45. See Bryant Lillywhite, *London Signs* (London, 1972).

46. Wu vi. 172.

47. Patmore iii. 78.

48. Ibid.

49. The exact date of their meeting is not known, but W. C. Hazlitt notes: 'I find his autograph on the title of a copy of the *Abridgment of Tucker,* 1807' (*Four Generations* i. 174).

50. *Four Generations* i. 173.

51. Ibid.

52. Wu vi. 178. 'Martin' in Wu's text should read 'Mounsey'.

53. Patmore ii. 316.

54. Ibid. iii. 81.

55. Ibid. 80.

56. William Hazlitt Jr to W. C. Hazlitt, [?1866]; BL Add. MS 38899, 83r. W. C. Hazlitt worked that recollection into a more elaborate story at *Memoirs* i. 300.

57. The occasion of these meetings is indicated by F. W. Hackwood, *William Hone: His Life and Times* (London, 1912), p.212.

58. Patmore iii. 84–5.

59. Wu vi. 6.

60. WH to Robert Baldwin, n.d.; Berg Collection, NYPL (Baker 404 n, *Letters* 202).

61. The rate-book for 1821, now at Holborn Public Library, shows that Walker paid £56 in rent.

62. See for instance Hazlitt's letter to Patmore postmarked 21 April 1822; *Letters* 255.

63. Procter (1877) 181.

64. Wu vii. 15.

65. Ibid.

66. Howe xvi. 45.

67. Stendhal, *On Love,* tr. Vyvyan Holland (London, 1928), 41 n.

68. Procter (1877) 181–2.

69. Wu vii. 8.
70. Ibid. 12.
71. The phrase occurs in the MS of *Liber Amoris* at SUNY at Buffalo. It is written in Hazlitt's hand and deleted in pencil.
72. Wu vi. 78.
73. Wu vi. 20–1. The suggestion that this passage was added in Winterslow was first made by Jones 316.
74. Wu vii. 12–13.
75. Ibid. 13.
76. Wu vi. 68. It is typical of his candour that he thought nothing of publishing these exclamations in the midst of 'The Indian Jugglers'. His enemies did not hesitate to use them against him; in the *Quarterly Review* J. Matthews cited them as a 'confession of the true scope of [Hazlitt's] own abilities' (*Quarterly Review* 26 (October 1821), 103–8, esp. 108).
77. John Scott, 'The Mohock Magazine', *The London Magazine* 2 (December 1820), 666–85, esp. 670.
78. J. G. Lockhart to Jonathan Christie, January 1821; quoted O'Leary 149.
79. O'Leary 149.
80. WH to John Scott, n.d.; Liverpool Central Library, Hornby Collection (*Letters* 203). Sikes dates it '[January] 1821', indicating that the year of composition is part of the text. It is not. Unhelpfully, the letter when edited by W. C. Hazlitt was dated 12 April 1820 (*Four Generations* i. 140). The MS gives no indication of when the letter was written; however, there is a dispatch postmark which, though smudged, is legible as 12 January 1821. It was posted at Crediton.
81. For years, Thomas Campbell claimed that Hazlitt egged Scott on, knowing he was in danger (see, for instance, Cyrus Redding, *Literary Reminiscences and Memoirs of Thomas Campbell* (London, 1860), 145). That was false to both men and not corroborated by any of the participants, nor is it regarded seriously by scholars; for instance, see Baker 406 n and Jones 317. John Scott was irascible enough without needing encouragement. Campbell hated Hazlitt for reasons of his own; see Wu (2007) ii. 332–3.
82. Wu (2007) i. 342.
83. Sir Walter Scott to J. G. Lockhart, 4 March 1821; *The Letters of Sir Walter Scott*, ed. H. J. C. Grierson (12 vols., London, 1932–79), vi. 374.
84. Robert Southey to Henry Herbert Southey, 5 March 1821; Curry ii. 225–6.
85. Lord Byron to John Murray, 21 April 1821; Marchand viii. 99.
86. *Lord Byron: The Complete Miscellaneous Prose*, ed. Andrew Nicholson (Oxford, 1991), 171. 'Poor Scott!', Horace Smith wrote to Shelley, then in Pisa, 'what a melancholy termination & how perfectly unnecessary' (Horace Smith to Percy Bysshe Shelley, 28 March 1821; Bodleian Library, Abinger Collection, Dep. c. 516 (Batch II)). For reactions by Wordsworth and Haydon see *The Letters of William and Dorothy Wordsworth III. The Later Years Part I 1821–1828*, ed. Ernest de Selincourt, rev. Alan G. Hill (Oxford, 1978), 43–4, and Pope ii. 313.
87. Morley i. 262.
88. *Haydon Table Talk* ii. 287.
89. Sir Walter Scott to B. R. Haydon, October 1822; *Letters of Sir Walter Scott* vii. 253.
90. For more on Lamb's response to Scott's death, see 'John Scott's Death and Lamb's "Imperfect Sympathies"', *Charles Lamb Bulletin* NS 114 (April 2001), 38–50.

91. Morley i. 262.
92. Robert Baldwin to WH, 5 March 1821; *Hazlitts* 465.
93. [Thomas Noon Talfourd], 'Hazlitt's Table Talk', *London Magazine* 3 (May 1821), 545–50, esp. 545.
94. For a summary of the critical reception, see Wu vi, pp. xi–xiii.
95. Leigh Hunt to WH, 20 April 1821; *Memoirs* i. 305. The original of this letter is not now to be found.
96. Wu vi. 130–1.
97. Ibid. 131.
98. Leigh Hunt to WH, 20 April 1821; *Memoirs* i. 305.
99. Ibid. 307.
100. WH to Leigh Hunt, 21 April 1821; *Letters* 204.
101. Ibid. 206.
102. Ibid.
103. Leigh Hunt to WH, shortly after 21 April 1821; *Memoirs* i. 310.
104. Ibid. 311.
105. Leigh Hunt to Mary and Percy Bysshe Shelley, 11 July 1821; *Hunt Correspondence* i. 166.
106. WH to Leigh Hunt, 21 April 1821; *Letters* 206.

Chapter 18

1. WH to Thomas Noon Talfourd, 1 December 1821; Wordsworth Library, WL MS Foot 3 [1998.71.3] (*Letters* 212). Sikes's text is taken from Howe, at the auction of whose library it was purchased by Michael Foot. Sikes does not record the postmark, slightly smudged, of 3 December.
2. John M'Creery to John Cam Hobhouse, 4 August 1821; BL Add. MS 36459, 80v.
3. 'He has failed upwards of £100 in my debt'; ibid. 78r.
4. He was not gazetted, but Hazlitt reported 'this failure of Warren's' in December; see WH to Thomas Noon Talfourd, 1 December 1821; Wordsworth Library, WL MS Foot 3 [1998.71.3] (*Letters* 211).
5. Robert Stodart to William Hone, 26 December 1821; University College library manuscript room, Ogden 73 (3 vols.), vol. i, f. 26. This note has not previously been cited in biographies of Hazlitt.
6. Stodart seems soon after to have sailed for Australia on a convict ship with his pregnant wife. See William Hone to Henry Brougham, 24 December 1821; BL Add MS 36459, 189r–v.
7. WH to Taylor and Hessey, 22 June 1821; Beineke Library, Yale University (*Letters* 208). The paper is watermarked 1818. Sikes does not record the dispatch postmark of 23 June.
8. *The Examiner*, 25 February 1821, 114.
9. Howe xix. 264.
10. News of Napoleon's death was known in Britain on 4 July 1821; see J. Landfear Lucas, 'News of Napoleon's Death', *Notes and Queries* ser. 12, 7 (1920), 409.
11. Thomas Pittman to WH, 16 July 1821; SUNY at Buffalo. The letter was posted in Canterbury and the dispatch postmark is the same as the date of composition. See Arthur Freeman and Janet Ing Freeman, ' "The Resort of the Illustrious Obscure": Hazlitt, Rackets, and the Coronation', *The Book Collector* 44 (1995), 27–36; see also Howe, *Life* 296–8.
12. 'Death of Napoleon Bonaparte', *The Examiner*, 8 July 1821, 417.

13. Lord Byron to Thomas Moore, 2 August 1821; Marchand viii. 166.
14. Thomas Noon Talfourd to Mary Russell Mitford, 10 July 1821; Reading Central Library, Talfourd letters: R/TU/TAL, vol. 2, item 9.
15. The printer was John M'Creery. This publication does not appear in Keynes, and the only known copy is at the Pforzheimer Library, NYPL. I thank Charles Carter, Librarian of the Pforzheimer, for letting me examine it.
16. Morley i. 265.
17. Wu ix. 45.
18. James Augustus Hessey to John Taylor, 5 October 1821; as quoted in Edmund Blunden, *Keats's Publisher: A Memoir of John Taylor* (London, 1936), 137.
19. Ibid.
20. Ibid.
21. Ibid. 138.
22. Wu ix. 47.
23. It was also, of course, a justification for the intense passion he felt for Sarah Walker, echoes of which are to be found throughout the essay: 'The heroical is the fanaticism of common life: it is the contempt of danger, of pain, of death, in the pursuit of a favourite idea. . . . A man in a passion, or who is worked up to a certain pitch of enthusiasm, minds nothing else' (Wu ix. 52).
24. W. C. Hazlitt describes him as 'the reputed natural son, by one of his numerous mistresses, of that famous military chieftain, the Duke of York, who supplied him with the means of starting in business' (*Four Generations* i. 168). Colburn's mysterious past assisted his business, which went from strength to strength during the 1810s. In 1818 he would become the publisher of Evelya's diary, and in 1825 he issued the first ever text of pepys's diary, edited by Lord Braybrooke.
25. Ibid. 168–9.
26. Francis Jeffrey to WH, 23 October 1821; Beineke Library, Osborn collection folder 8033. The dispatch postmark is dated 24 October 1821.
27. *John Clare by Himself*, ed. Eric Robinson and David Powell (Manchester, 1996), 142.
28. Wu vii. 41.
29. Ibid.
30. 'The Fight'; Morgan Library, MA 190, f. 11. Words enclosed in square brackets are deleted in the MS. See also Wu vii. 36, 250.
31. I take this to be the implication of Sarah Walker's letter to Hazlitt of 17 January 1822, in which she concludes: 'I hope Sir your little Son is quite well.' See Le Gallienne, facsimile opposite p. 209.
32. Pope iii. 132. This claim should be read in the light of Jones's comments, 'Haydon and Northcote on Hazlitt: A Fabrication', *Review of English Studies* 24 (1973), 165–78.
33. Bonner 196.
34. See Bennett i. 375.
35. Black's attempt failed because the proofs of domicile were not adequate. The connection between Black's unfortunate experience and that of Hazlitt is explored by Jones 89–90.
36. Wu ix. 67.
37. Pierce Egan, *Boxiana* (3 vols., London, 1812–24), i. 440.
38. See Wu ix. 67.
39. Ibid. 68.

40. For the purposes of the essay he was about to write, it was useful to pretend he was a stranger to the Fancy, as many readers were in that position, and it was a good way of drawing them in: 'Reader! have you ever seen a fight? If not, you have a pleasure to come' (ibid. 67).

41. According to W. C. Hazlitt, the idea of the essay was Patmore's, and Hazlitt then 'spoke to about it, and Colburn seemed to entertain the notion; so he determined to make a day, or rather two, of it' (*Memoirs* ii. 74).

42. In the MS of 'The Fight'; see Wilcox 22.

43. At this time, Parkes was articled to Amory and Coles of Throgmorton Street (to the immediate north of the Bank of England) and resident at 16 Mount Pleasant, not far from Southampton Buildings. He was also a good friend of William Hone. In 1822 he became a solicitor in Birmingham and two years later married Joseph Priestley's eldest daughter. Shortly after he became associated with the Bentham circle, particularly Francis Place. In 1852 he was in touch with William Hazlitt Jr, whom he asked for an introduction to a Mr Ellice (see Parkes Papers, UCL Manuscript Room).

44. Wu ix. 65–6.

45. Ibid. 67.

46. Ibid. 69.

47. Ibid.

48. Ibid. 70. Patmore, who was also there, recognized Hazlitt's achievement: 'Hazlitt could perceive and describe "at sight" the characteristics of anything, without any previous study or knowledge whatever, but by a species of intellectual intuition' (Patmore iii. 46). See also Tom Paulin, *The Day-Star of Liberty: William Hazlitt's Radical Style* (London, 1998), 82.

49. David Bromwich observes: 'the under-plot of "The Fight" is disclosed more plainly here than in any comparable stretch of the published version. Hazlitt's motive for going to see the boxers was by a single stroke, through his absorption in some violent spectacle, to throw off the load of tormenting jealousies which for months had kept him a haunted man' (Bromwich 437 n 10).

50. I take this to be the implication of the proposal to 'try the 100£ a year whenever the 3 apartments [are vacant]'—although these words are deleted in the MS. See WH to P. G. Patmore, 20–1 June 1822; SUNY at Buffalo (Le Gallienne 228, *Letters* 276).

51. WH to P. G. Patmore, *c*.8 or 9 June 1822; SUNY at Buffalo (Le Gallienne 224, *Letters* 270). Sikes dates the letter 18 June, probably following Le Gallienne. However, the dispatch postmark reads 10 June (the information given by Jones in his review of Sikes is erroneous, and corrected in his later article: see Stanley Jones, review of Sikes, *The Library* Series 6, 3 (1980), 356–62, esp. 360; Jones, 'Some Notes on the Letters of William Hazlitt', *The Library* Series 6, 5 (1983), 269–75, esp. 270).

52. Ibid.

53. Wu ii. 304 n.

54. Cyrus Redding, *Literary Reminiscences and Memoirs of Thomas Campbell* (2 vols., London, 1860), i. 297.

55. Cyrus Redding, 'The Life and Reminiscences of Thomas Campbell', *New Monthly Magazine* 79 (1847), 241–8, esp. 245.

56. See Cyrus Redding, *Fifty Years' Recollections, Literary and Personal* (3 vols., London, 1858), ii. 269. Hazlitt's essay, he later wrote, was 'a very vulgar thing' (*Past Celebrities Whom I Have Known* (2 vols., London, 1866), i.83). Hazlitt's only letter about the proofs was sent to Colburn; WH to Henry Colburn, 19 January 1822; *Four Generations* i. 193–4 (*Letters* 213).

Hazlitt dates the letter 'Saturday evening'. The reference to his 'departure for Scotland next week' makes it almost certain that the evening in question was that of 19 January. Sikes's text is from *Four Generations*; the present whereabouts of the MS is not known.

Colburn was not consistent in his attitude towards Hazlitt. On one hand he was almost certainly the reason why the *New Monthly* accepted his work; at the same time he had shares in the *Literary Gazette* (edited by William Jerdan) and the *John Bull*, which attacked Hazlitt viciously. And in 1823 he was unwise enough to tell William Maginn that Hazlitt 'is a fool, John Hunt a rogue, L. Hunt a puppy, Patmore a *bad young man* (his very words)' (see William Maginn to William Blackwood, 30 July 1823; Margaret Oliphant, *Annals of a Publishing House: William Blackwood and his Sons, Their Magazine and Friends* (2 vols., Edinburgh, 1897), i. 400).

57. Grace and Margaret Hazlitt to Sarah Stoddart Hazlitt, 22 March 1822; SUNY at Buffalo (published James A. Houck, 'Hazlitt's Divorce: A Family Letter', *English Language Notes* 18 (1980–1), 33–5).

58. WH to P. G. Patmore, *c.*19–25 February 1822; *Letters* 245. The MS is not now to be found. Though not dated by Hazlitt, the letter is conjecturally dated by Sikes to the 'middle of March 1822'. It was written 'three weeks, next Monday' after Hazlitt's arrival in Scotland. He landed in Edinburgh on 4 February; the third Monday after that was 25 February. Therefore this letter must have been written at some point during the preceding weeks, between Tuesday 19 February and Monday 25 February. It should therefore come after number 98 in Sikes's edition; see Stanley Jones, review of Sikes, *The Library* Series 6, 3 (1980), 356–62, esp. 359.

59. These exchanges are taken from WH to P. G. Patmore, 5 March 1822; *New Letters* 17.

60. WH to P. G. Patmore, *c.*19–25 February 1822; *Letters* 245–6.

61. Wu vii. 57. This is from one of the letters to James Sheridan Knowles, none of which has ever been known in any form but that published in *Liber Amoris*, leading me to suspect that they existed only as copy for the book. That is to say, the concept of the epistle was, in Part III of the volume, fictional. That being so, none of these letters have any place in Sikes.

62. On 19 December 1821 according to McGann and Weller.

63. This notebook survives today at SUNY at Buffalo in the Goodyear Collection.

64. Wu vii. 35.

65. Wu (2007) i. 377. It is possible, on grounds of content, to isolate parts of the published text attributable to Hazlitt; see Wu (2007) i. 369–73 and my 'Talking Pimples: Hazlitt and Byron in Love', *Romanticism* 10 (2004), 158–90.

66. WH to P. G. Patmore, 30 March 1822; SUNY at Buffalo (*Letters* 248). In the published text this was altered to read: 'Have you read Sardanapalus? How like the little Greek slave, Myrrha, is to *her*!' (Wu vii 28). Jones reports that 'although written in Edinburgh on 30 March the letter was dispatched from Renton Inn' (Stanley Jones, 'Some Notes on the Letters of William Hazlitt', *The Library* Series 6, 5 (1983) 269–75, p.270).

67. WH to Sarah Walker, 11–19 February 1822; SUNY at Buffalo (*Letters* 214). The equivalent passage in *Liber Amoris* is to be found at Wu vii. 20. Sikes dates the letter to 'February 1822'; the more specific dating is given by Stanley Jones, review of Sikes, *The Library* Series 6, 3 (1980), 356–62, esp. 359.

68. WH to P. G. Patmore, *c.*19–25 February 1822; *Letters* 245.

69. WH to Henry Colburn, 3 March 1822; Howe ix. 261, Baker 412, *Letters* 238. The original is not now to be found: Sikes and Baker draw their texts from Howe.

70. See Jones, 'Hazlitt's Missing Essay "On Individuality" ', *Review of English Studies* 28 (1977), 421–30, esp. 423.
71. As Jones observes, the winds in Edinburgh were strong enough to blow down the railings round the monument on Calton Hill and break the windows of St John's and St Giles's; see Jones, 'William Hazlitt at Renton House', *College Courant* 16.31 (1963), 15–20, esp. 17.
72. WH to Sarah Walker, 5 March 1822; *John Bull* 22 June 1823, p. 198 col. 1 (partial text at Le Gallienne 205). *John Bull* reports that the letter was postmarked Dunbar, 9 March 1822; a date of composition of 5 March might be proposed, when violent weather conditions were reported in Edinburgh. (Jones also favours this date; see Jones 322 n 14.) (Stanley Jones reprinted the *John Bull* text in his article, 'Hazlitt and *John Bull*: A Neglected Letter', *Review of English Studies* 17 (1966), 163–70, as did Sikes at *Letters* 241–4.) Although my copy-text is *John Bull* I do not preserve its italics, small caps, and other incidentals, as they are interpolations by a hand other than Hazlitt's.
73. Wu viii. 20.
74. Ibid. 20–1.
75. Sarah Walker to WH, 17 January 1822; Le Gallienne 209, where it is reproduced in facsimile on the opposite page. Sarah Walker to WH, 26 February 1822; *New Letters* 16.
76. WH to P. G. Patmore, 5 March 1822; *New Letters* 16.
77. *Memoirs* ii. 11. This passage does not occur among the fragments of this essay now preserved at the John Rylands library, Manchester.
78. WH to P. G. Patmore, 5 March 1822; *New Letters* 17.
79. WH to Sarah Walker, 5 March 1822; *John Bull* 22 June 1823, p. 198 col. 1 (*Letters* 242).
80. See the Manchester (Ireland) volume, 12r; Manchester Central Library.
81. WH to Henry Colburn, 3 March 1822; Howe xi. 261, Baker 412, *Letters* 238. The MS is not now to be found; Sikes and Baker use Howe as copy-text.

Chapter 19

1. Howe ix. 206.
2. WH to Taylor and Hessey, 10 April 1822; P. P. Howe, 'New Hazlitt Letters', *London Mercury* 7 (March 1923), 494–8, esp. 497 (*Letters* 252). WH to Taylor and Hessey, 16 April 1822; Morgan Library, MA number unassigned (*Letters* 253).
3. The news conveyed by Patmore can only be conjectured, as this is one of the few letters that has not survived.
4. WH to P. G. Patmore, 30 March 1822; SUNY at Buffalo (*Letters* 247).
5. Ibid. 247–8. Sikes's text is incomplete. The last sentence in the quotation is heavily deleted, but Patmore deciphered it.
6. WH to P. G. Patmore, *c.*7 April 1822; SUNY at Buffalo (*Letters* 249). The letter is not dated; however, it bears a dispatch postmark of 7 April 1822 at Edinburgh and an arrival postmark of 10 April in London.
7. Ibid. 251.
8. Ibid. The sentence beginning 'All she wants' to 'felt & all' is heavily deleted in the MS, but the reading re-entered in pencil by an unknown hand.
9. The quotation is from *Othello* IV. i. 70–1: 'To lip a wanton in a secure couch, | And to suppose her chaste!' See Jon Cook's useful analysis, *Hazlitt in Love* (London, 2007), 112–13.
10. WH to P. G. Patmore, *c.*21 April 1822; SUNY at Buffalo (*Letters* 254). The MS is undated, but the dispatch postmark is dated 21 April and the receipt postmark 25 April.

11. Ibid. 255.
12. Wu vii. 197.
13. Ibid.
14. Howe xvii. 95.
15. This speech is based on Jeffrey's letter to Charles Wilkes of 27 January 1822; see *Life of Lord Jeffrey*, ed. Lord Cockburn (2 vols., Edinburgh, 1852), ii. 197–8. Whether or not Jeffrey actually said this to Hazlitt, they are opinions he certainly held at this time.
16. Wu vii. 198.
17. Ibid. 124.
18. Patmore iii. 22.
19. For more on this, see Wu (2007) ii. 90–1.
20. *Haydon Table Talk* ii. 376.
21. WH to P. G. Patmore, 30 March 1822; SUNY at Buffalo (*Letters* 248).
22. See Stanley Jones, 'Hazlitt in Edinburgh: An Evening with Mr. Ritchie of *The Scotsman*', *Etudes Anglaises* 17 (1964), 9–20, 113–27, esp. 15–17.
23. Hazlitt's article on the Exhibition of Living Artists at Waterloo Place appeared in *The Scotsman* on 20 April 1822 (Howe xviii. 167).
24. Thomas Hodgskin to Francis Place, 19 May 1819; BL Add MS 35153, 61v.
25. As long before as 1817 Francis Place had informed him that 'Mr Bentham has the highest opinion of you and a strong desire to have you for his friend' (Francis Place to Thomas Hodgskin, 30 May 1817; BL Add. MS 35153, 6v).
26. Thomas Hodgskin to Francis Place, 4 November 1819; BL Add. MS 35153, 99v.
27. Thomas Hodgskin to Francis Place, 15 April 1822; BL Add. MS 35153, 208r.
28. 'On Dreams' and 'On Dr Spurzheim's Theory', composed at Renton Inn, published in *The Plain Speaker*.
29. George Combe, *A System of Phrenology* (2nd edn, Edinburgh, 1825), 223.
30. Stanley Jones, 'Hazlitt in Edinburgh: An Evening with Mr. Ritchie of *The Scotsman*', *Etudes Anglaises* 17 (1964), 9–20, 113–27, esp. 114.
31. Ibid. 113.
32. Wu ix. 171. The figures mentioned by Hazlitt were first identified by Jones, 'Hazlitt in Edinburgh: An Evening with Mr. Ritchie of *The Scotsman*', *Etudes Anglaises* 17 (1964), 9–20, 113–27, esp. 127.
33. Howe ix. 214.
34. Wu vi. 211.
35. In conversation with his wife; see Bonner 248.
36. These are enumerated in 'Hazlitt's "Sexual Harassment"', *Essays in Criticism* 50 (July 2000), 199–214, esp. 207–8.
37. WH to P. G. Patmore, *c.*21 April 1822; SUNY at Buffalo (*Letters* 255).
38. Grace and Margaret Hazlitt to Sarah Stoddart Hazlitt, 22 March 1822; SUNY at Buffalo (published James A. Houck, 'Hazlitt's Divorce: A Family Letter', *English Language Notes* 18 (1980–1), 33–5).
39. It is now at the British Library; see BL Add. MS 62943, ff. 23–4. I thank a number of friends and colleagues for assisting me in my analysis of this document: Nicholas Powell, David Graham, and Joshua Getzler.
40. For more on *The Correspondent* and Hazlitt's putative involvement in it, see Wu (2007) ii. 495–6.

Notes

41. Bonner 196.
42. Jones proposes that the suggestion that Walker was 'one eyed from disease!', a detail given by Hazlitt in the version of the tale he gave Haydon (see Pope ii. 374), was part of 'a perverse impulse to exaggerate his degradation' (Jones 333).
43. See the 'Summons of Divorce' transcribed by Sarah into her journal; Bonner 190–1.
44. Bonner 197.
45. The exchange is abstracted from Sarah's journal entry for 3 May 1822; Bonner 197.
46. This was reported in London by *The Examiner*, 9 April 1820, 234.
47. The gatehouse was preserved, and now forms part of the University of Glasgow in Kelvingrove.
48. From the *Glasgow Sentinel* 8 May 1822, as quoted by Stanley Jones, 'Hazlitt as Lecturer: Three Unnoticed Contemporary Accounts', *Etudes Anglaises* 15 (1962), 15–24, esp. 19.
49. Wu vii. 54.
50. Ibid. 40.
51. Ibid.
52. Ibid. 54.
53. Ibid. 56.
54. Ibid. 57.
55. Ibid. 58.
56. Ibid.
57. Ibid. 64.
58. WH to P. G. Patmore, 29 or 30 May 1822; BL RP 6712 (part xxi) (*Letters* 260). There are two postmarks on this letter: the dispatch postmark was stamped at Scarborough on 30 May; the arrival postmark 1 June. Sikes was not aware of the MS and takes *Liber Amoris* as copy-text, dating the letter '30 or 31 May 1822'; I follow the dating proposed by Jones, review of Sikes, *The Library* Series 6, 3 (1980), 356–62, esp. 359.
59. WH to P. G. Patmore, 30 May 1822; SUNY at Buffalo (*Letters* 263, Le Gallienne 216–17). The letter is not dated, but bears a dispatch postmark of 31 May (Edinburgh) and arrival postmark in London of 3 June (not recorded by either Sikes or Le Gallienne).
60. Howe ix. 219.
61. WH to P. G. Patmore, 30 May 1822; SUNY at Buffalo (*Letters* 263–4, Le Gallienne 217–18).
62. Ibid. (*Letters* 265, Le Gallienne 219).
63. WH to P. G. Patmore, *c.*19 June 1822; SUNY at Buffalo (*Letters* 257, Le Gallienne 220). Though undated, the MS is ascribed to 'May 1822' by Sikes. I follow the dating preferred by Jones in his review of Sikes, *The Library* Series 6, 3 (1980), 356–62, esp. 359. The letter should therefore be placed after number 116 in Sikes. The MS is reproduced in facsimile in Le Gallienne facing p. 236.
64. Wu vi. 291.
65. 'Hazlitt's Table-Talk', *Blackwood's Edinburgh Magazine* 12 (August 1822), 157–66, esp. 157.
66. Ibid. 163.
67. WH to P. G. Patmore, 27 June 1822; SUNY at Buffalo (*Letters* 279). The letter is not dated, and Sikes notes 'PM: 28 June 1822'. As Jones observes, it was written on 27 June (see his review of Sikes, *The Library* Series 6, 3 (1980) 356–62, esp. 360). The dispatch postmark (Edinburgh) is dated 28 June, the arrival postmark (London), 1 July.
68. WH to P. G. Patmore, 3–5 July 1822; SUNY at Buffalo (*Letters* 284). The letter was posted from Edinburgh on 4 July and arrived in London on 7 July.

69. WH to P. G. Patmore, 8 July 1822; SUNY at Buffalo (*Letters* 286).
70. This conversation is based on the entry for Saturday 13 July at Bonner 242.
71. WH to P. G. Patmore, [16–17 July 1822]; BL RP 6712 (xxi) Box 165 (*Letters* 289). The MS of this letter was formerly in the possession of W. C. Hazlitt and then in that of Lord Crewe. It came into the hands of a dealer and was put on the market in 1997, while I was editing *Liber Amoris*. I was not allowed to consult it and the purchase price of £20,000 was beyond my means. The dealer's catalogue contains the photograph of a single recto of the MS which is superior in quality to the photostat lodged with the British Library prior to export. See *Roy Davids Ltd* (London, 1997), 58. The MS text is different from the much-revised version in *Liber Amoris* (and Sikes, whose text derives from *Liber Amoris*), and to the best of my knowledge remains unpublished. Hazlitt simply dates the letter 'Tuesday', indicating 16 July as the date of composition. The postscript was added the following day.
72. WH to P. G. Patmore, [16–17 July 1822]; BL RP 6712 (xxi) Box 165 (*Letters* 289).
73. WH to P. G. Patmore, 27 June 1822; SUNY at Buffalo (*Letters* 278).
74. WH to P. G. Patmore, [16–17 July 1822]; BL RP 6712 (xxi) Box 165. Not included in Sikes's text (see *Letters* 289–90).
75. Bonner 246–8.
76. Wu vii. 68.
77. Ibid. 68–9.
78. Pope ii. 375–6. Many years later, Procter recalled that 'at the time of the furor caused by the heroine of the Liber Amoris he was—mad' (B. W. Procter to W. B. Donne, 21 September 1866; Osborn file 12317, Beineke Library, Yale University).
79. Pope ii. 382.
80. Procter (1877) 180.
81. Wu vii. 70.
82. WH to Francis Jeffrey, *c.*21–2 August 1822; Beineke Library, Yale University (*Letters* 291). The letter is undated, but the dispatch postmark reads '22 AU 1822'. It arrived in Edinburgh two days later. Instead of 'oddnesses', which is the correct reading, Sikes reads 'offenses'.

Chapter 20

1. Howe xx. 341.
2. As quoted by Alexander Ireland, *List of the Writings of William Hazlitt and Leigh Hunt* (London, 1868), 76.
3. Howe xvii. 356. 'On Footmen' was composed probably in April 1823, even though not published until September 1830.
4. Jenner would die of a stroke in January 1823. Hazlitt's brother John painted his portrait in 1809, and may have had something to do with the subscription; see Wu *Library* 52.
5. Part II was transcribed and prepared for the press (though chaotically) by Patmore, as W. C. Hazlitt explained: 'What he did was foolish and ineffectual enough; he copied out Hazlitt's MS., which he seems to have destroyed, and in preparing his transcript for the press marked passages and expressions for omission or modification, and made such a jumble of the work pure and simple and the letters addressed to him, and scraps of which we do not trace the source, that the biographer and editor have ever since been puzzled or misled' (Le Gallienne pp. xxxiv–xxxv).

6. This was certainly the opinion of Charles Ollier—who, however, is an unsympathetic witness. See W. M. Parker, 'Charles Ollier to William Blackwood', *Times Literary Supplement*, 7 June 1947, 288.

7. He was released on 3 June 1822, and was fortunate in missing the treadmill introduced on 25 June, on which all prisoners, male and female, were set to work.

8. *Monthly Literary Register* 4 (1 August 1822), 52–60, esp. 60; quoted in Wu vi, p. xiv.

9. Howe xi. 318.

10. Le Gallienne p. xxxv.

11. Lord Byron to Douglas Kinnaird, 26 October 1819; Marchand vi. 232.

12. Biographers suggest Shelley kept the sail hoisted in the midst of the storm. See, for instance, Newman Ivey White, *Shelley* (2 vols., London, 1947), ii. 377; Richard Holmes, *Shelley: The Pursuit* (London, 1974), 729, and Ann Wroe, *Being Shelley* (London, 2007), 387.

13. Leigh Hunt to John Hunt, 26 October 1822; Luther A. Brewer, *My Leigh Hunt Library, the Holograph Letters* (Iowa City, 1938), 155.

14. *His Very Self and Voice: Collected Conversations of Byron*, ed. Ernest J. Lovell, Jr (New York, 1954), 451.

15. Leigh Hunt, *Lord Byron and Some of his Contemporaries* (2 vols., London, 1828), i. 108–9.

16. Howe ix. 217.

17. Leigh Hunt to John Hunt, 26 December 1822; Gates 126.

18. WH to Francis Jeffrey, 2 October 1822; Beineke Library, Yale University (*Letters* 322). The underlining is Hazlitt's. Sikes does not record the dispatch postmark, 4 October, or the arrival postmark of 6 October. Nor does he record the place of posting—Whitchurch. It is not clear to me which of the various places of that name the letter was posted from, nor why Hazlitt was there.

19. Ibid.

20. Henry Crabb Robinson, Diary 10, 62v for Saturday 6 December 1823; Dr Williams's Library. Not in Morley.

21. Howe xvi. 223.

22. *John Bull*, 24 August 1823, 269. For more on this and its relation to a newly attributed Hazlitt item, see Wu (2007) ii. 1–2.

23. WH to unidentified creditors, n.d., in which Hazlitt declares his intention to 'pay off my arrears with the interest & the sum of fifty pounds' (MS in the possession of the author, hitherto unpublished). The letter is undated. However, its reference to 'a new volume of Essays from the London Magazine' could refer to *Table Talk*, volume 2, which was published 15 June 1822. It may be that this letter is related to that also addressed to unidentified creditors edited by Robinson (see *New Letters* 20).

24. It is now in the Keynes collection at Cambridge; a photograph of the inscription is at Keynes 16.

25. WH to Taylor and Hessey, 1–11 February 1823; P. P. Howe, 'New Hazlitt Letters', *London Mercury* 7 (March 1923), 494–8, esp. 498 (*Letters* 326). The whereabouts of the MS is not known. Sikes takes his text from Howe, dating it to '[February 1823]', but the contents indicate it pre-dates Hazlitt's arrest. That being the case, it is incorrectly positioned in Sikes, and ought to precede number 130.

26. In a letter from John Wilson to William Blackwood written in late September or early October 1823, it is reported that Taylor and Hessey no longer pay advances to contributors to the *London Magazine*: 'The rule is absolute owing to Hazlitts having cheated them out of

£3 10–. This is a secret.' See David Groves, ' "Disgusted with all the Cockneys": De Quincey, the *London Magazine*, and *Blackwood's Magazine*', *Notes and Queries* 47 (September 2000), 326–7.

27. See *Robson's London Commercial Directory, Street Guide, and Carriers' List for 1822* (4th edn, London, 1822), 311.

28. Although the address from which Hazlitt wrote to Talfourd has long been known, the connection with Walbancke and Whittle is made here for the first time.

29. WH to Thomas Noon Talfourd, 12 February 1823; Bodleian Library MS Autogr. d.5, 53r (*Letters* 325). Sikes notes the address incorrectly. Hazlitt had trouble remembering Talfourd's address, perhaps as a result of anxiety, and wrote: '26 or 27 Henrietta Street'. The sheet is a small quarto folded in half, for transmission by hand.

30. William Makepeace Thackeray, *Vanity Fair* (London, 1963), chapter 53.

31. Jones 278–9 n 5.

32. WH to unidentified creditors, shortly after 12 February; *New Letters* 20. Robinson is admirably cautious about his dating of the letter; without having seen the MS, it is hard to be sure, but the contents suggest that it post-dates the arrest of 1823.

33. *Hazlitts* 472. My search through the records of the various compters of the City of London (now at the Guildhall Record Office) failed to reveal any mention of Hazlitt either in 1823 or 1830. Nor does his name appear in the book containing actions in the Sheriff's Court.

34. He had seen it as early as May 1821 (see Howe xviii. 145).

35. *Haydon Table Talk* ii. 76.

36. For an example, see Pope ii. 455, entry for 26 January 1824.

37. Ibid. 423.

38. Ibid. 418. On 19 June Northcote told Farington he had neither seen the painting, nor 'does he admit him into his house' (Farington xvi. 5523).

39. David Blayney Brown in *Benjamin Robert Haydon 1786–1846* (Grasmere, 1996), 14.

40. See Hazlitt's journal of 4–16 March 1823, in Bonner 266–77. The text is reprinted with minor emendations in *Letters* 379–89. I have preferred to cite Bonner, as corrected by Jones (see Stanley Jones, 'Hazlitt's Journal of 1823: Some Notes and Emendations', *The Library* 26 (1971), 325–36). Various identifications have been offered for F, the most plausible of which is Jones's, who proposes Albany Fonblanque (1793–1872), 'philosophic radical' and journalist, who became political editor of *The Examiner* in 1826. The earliest evidence of Fonblanque's acquaintance with Hazlitt is his review of *Liber Amoris* in *The Examiner*, 11 May 1823.

41. Bonner 276.

42. Ibid. 275.

43. Ibid. 275.

44. Ibid. 277.

45. Ibid. 272; for this reading, see Stanley Jones, 'Hazlitt's Journal of 1823: Some Notes and Emendations', *The Library* 26 (1971), 325–36, esp. 331.

46. Howe xvii. 105.

47. As Jones notes, this appointment (dating from July 1820) was said by *The Scotsman* to be the most remarkable 'since Caligula made his horse a consul' (Jones 290)—Wilson lacking any qualification for it.

48. 'On the Scotch Character—By a Flunky', *Blackwood's Edinburgh Magazine* 13 (March 1823), 365–7, esp. 365. Strout attributes it to Wilson.

49. WH to Thomas Cadell, 19 April 1823; Folger Shakespeare Library (*New Letters* 21, Gates 655–6, *Letters* 327). Sikes dates the MS to 17 April but, as Robinson notes, it 'is clearly dated 19 April'. The letter is to be found at page 119 of a grangerized copy of the *Life of Kean* (Art Vol b8).

50. Thomas Cadell to William Blackwood, 19 April 1823; *Four Generations* i. 143. W. C. Hazlitt transcribes the date of Cadell's letter as 'Saturday . . . April 18, 1823'. That cannot be right, for Saturday was the 19th, rather than the 18th, of April. Cadell received Hazlitt's letter shortly before 3pm on Saturday 19 April, and wrote immediately to Blackwood, mistakenly writing the wrong date on it.

51. William Blackwood to Thomas Cadell, *c*.21 April 1823; quoted Theodore Besterman, 'Hazlitt and Maga', *Times Literary Supplement*, 22 August 1935, 525. In private, Blackwood feared a repetition of the earlier prosecution, as is clear from his correspondence with William Maginn, who offered his services as a spy, digging up dirt to throw at Hazlitt in the event of a court case. See William Maginn to William Blackwood, 30 April 1823, quoted Alan Lang Strout, 'William Maginn as Gossip', *Notes and Queries* 2 (June 1955), 263–5, esp. 263. A toned-down version of the letter appears in Margaret Oliphant, *Annals of a Publishing House: William Blackwood and his Sons, Their Magazine and Friends* (2 vols., Edinburgh, 1897), i. 389.

52. *The Examiner*, 1 June 1823, 361.

53. *The New European Magazine* 2 (June 1823), 518–21, esp. 521.

54. *The Literary Register* 17 May 1823, 305.

55. *Literary Gazette* 31 May 1823, 339.

56. *Blackwood's Edinburgh Magazine* 13 (June 1823), 640–6, esp. 645. The review has been doubtfully attributed to Lockhart.

57. WH to Sarah Walker, 5 March 1822; *John Bull*, 22 June 1823, p. 198 col. 1 (*Letters* 242). I have chosen to disregard incidentals—italics, small caps, and the like—which are probably editorial. *John Bull* remains the only copy-text.

58. Hazlitt later believed the culprit to have been J. W. Croker, Secretary to the Admiralty (and target of his first political commentary). Croker would have denied it; two years earlier, he protested to Murray that 'some persons have had the impudence & the falsehood to insinuate that I was, in some way or other, a supporter of the John Bull newspaper, of which I am as innocent as Mr Bennett or Mr Brougham can be' (J. W. Croker to John Murray, 17 May 1821; John Murray Archive). Few of Croker's political opponents would have found this persuasive, and in suspecting him Hazlitt followed the lead of Brougham, who described Croker as 'a prime favorite' of the King, one who 'repays his favour by squibs, & attacks of all kinds on both men & women out of power' (Henry Brougham to Leigh Hunt, 'Thursday' [21 March 1816]; BL Add. MS 38108, 163v. The quotation comes from a passage deleted by Brougham.).

59. Patmore ii. 350.

60. Wu (2007) ii. 13. Additional evidence that Hazlitt was meditating further attacks on Blackwood is given by the letter from him to Henry Leigh Hunt of summer/autumn 1823, published for the first time by Jones (see Jones 341 and n 74). The present whereabouts of this MS is not known.

61. Jones speculates that the letter was stolen by a lodger and sold to Hook (Jones 338–9).

62. *Blackwood's Edinburgh Magazine* 14 (October 1823), 484–503, esp. 488.

63. Chorley i. 126.

64. *De Quincey* x. 267. This is a compliment, but it reflects the rather poor opinion De Quincey entertained of Hazlitt otherwise, which probably owed much to resentment of Hazlitt's accusation of plagiarism. W. C. Hazlitt quotes further comment on *Liber Amoris* by De Quincey (*Memoirs* ii. 67), for which see *De Quincey* xv. 276.

65. None of which helped sales. Before the print run was exhausted, Hunt was compelled to reduce the price from 7*s*.6*d*. to 7*s*. See M. L. Poston, 'Hazlitt's "Liber Amoris" ', *Times Literary Supplement*, 14 August 1943, 396.

66. This is a subtlety which eludes feminists who have renewed the moral attack.

67. Wu viii. 113.

68. Joseph Parkes to William Hone, n.d. but endorsed 1823; BL Add. MS 40120, 205v.

69. Morley i. 296.

70. William Wordsworth to Julius Charles Hare, 28 May 1838; *The Letters of William and Dorothy Wordsworth: The Later Years iii: 1835-9*, ed. Ernest De Selincourt, rev. Alan G. Hill (Oxford, 1982), 595.

71. Tom Paulin, *The Day-Star of Liberty* (London, 1998), 45.

72. This is analysed in my 'Hazlitt's "Sexual Harassment" ', *Essays in Criticism* 50 (July 2000), 199–214.

73. See Hazlitt's portrait of Irving (Wu vii. 110).

74. Howe xviii. 173.

75. The sum is that cited by Haydon when telling Mary Russell Mitford about the commission in September 1823; see *Haydon Table Talk* ii. 79. For this, he may also have served the purpose of a 'white bonnet' during the auction; see Wu (2007) i. 444-5.

76. One book review for the *Literary Examiner* has come to light recently; see Wu (2007) i. 477-87.

77. Howe xx. 114.

78. Ibid.

79. Ibid. 122.

80. Ibid. 120.

81. The evidence appears in a letter from E. H. Barker to Henry Crabb Robinson of 15 June 1828: 'Hazlitt has then, it seems, flung his *dirt* at you. Basil Montagu *cut* him on account of the attack, which Hazlitt made on him in the notice of Irving the Scotch preacher, in Lord Byron's review. Montagu had been particularly kind to him, & was much annoyed at the double crime of ungrateful & contemptuous treatment experienced from Hazlitt. He hath a rare faculty of losing friendships, & in old age he will, like George Stevens, die of misanthropy' (Dr Williams's Library).

82. Howe ix. 172, 173, 212, 213.

83. Ibid. 201, 204, 215.

84. Ibid. 222.

85. *Hazlitts* 176.

86. *Literary Gazette*, 12 July 1823, 437.

87. *Literary Gazette*, 31 May 1823, 340.

88. Wu viii. 113.

89. *Literary Register*, 19 July 1823, 41.

90. Keynes describes it as 'a very scarce book at the present time' (Keynes 73), and I find less than 100 copies on WorldCat.

91. Wu (2007) i. 446.

92. Patmore iii. 72.

93. Wu (2007) i. 447.

94. Ibid. 474.

95. See ibid. 493–4. Beckford was extremely well read, and his copies of *Lectures on the English Poets* and *The Spirit of the Age* contain appreciative annotations. Of Hazlitt's essay on Lord Eldon, Beckford commented: 'His glaring faults & sneaking virtues were never displayed in truer colours—every line tells—every touch sparkles'; see Beckford shelfmarks 255 and 256, Beineke Library.

96. Interestingly, the connoisseur declares himself to be the author of the catalogue raisonne (Wu (2007) i. 500), which indicates that Hazlitt had been told that its author was someone fitting his description—though it is not clear who.

97. Ibid. 497.

98. Ibid. 499–500.

99. Ibid. 496.

100. WH to William Bewick, *c*.25 August 1823; Durham County Library, Darlington Branch (Jones (1977) 338). Not in Sikes. The dispatch postmark is dated 25 August, the receipt postmark (Edinburgh) 27 August. The advice given here echoes that given to Talfourd in December 1821: 'My dear Talfourd, if you have a girl that loves you and that you have regard for, lose no time in marrying, and think yourself happy, whatever else may happen' (*Letters* 212).

101. Bennett i. 373.

102. Morley i. 387.

103. Bennett i. 375.

104. *Haydon Table Talk* ii. 79.

105. Howe xx. 135.

106. Patmore iii. 107.

107. Ibid. 108.

108. This led to a misunderstanding by which Haydon believed himself to have been cheated by Hazlitt. For that story see Jones, 'Haydon and Northcote on Hazlitt: A Fabrication', *Review of English Studies* 24 (1973), 165–78.

109. WH to Rowland Hunter, 5 October 1823; MS in the possession of the author. Not hitherto published. The letter bears no address panel or postmark.

110. William Hazlitt, 'To the Editor of the London Magazine', *London Magazine* 8 (1823), 459–60. This article appears at *Letters* 329.

111. Ibid. 460.

112. Thomas De Quincey, 'To the Editor of the London Magazine', *London Magazine* 8 (1823), 570.

113. See *De Quincey* xv. 272–80. Procter too was 'struck ... by De Quincy's attacks on Hazlitt'; see B. W. Procter, *Charles Lamb: A Memoir* (London, 1869), 160. Elsewhere, he records Hazlitt as having said of De Quincey that he wrote well only 'whilst the opium was trickling from his mouth' (quoted Wardle 78 n).

114. See *Quarterly Review* 28 (1823), 493–536, p. 524. Later editions substitute 'sounder' for 'saner', which was Southey's preferred reading. The article, a review by Southey of Grégoire's *Histoire de la Théophilanthropie*, condemns the French Revolution while refuting accusations of apostasy—an acutely defensive piece.

115. *London Magazine* 8 (October 1823), 405.

116. See *The Examiner* (1823), 643–4, 660–1, 675.
117. Henry Crabb Robinson, *Reminiscences*, Vol. iv 1834–43, f. 475; Dr Williams's Library.
118. Charles Lamb to Sarah Stoddart, [?10 November 1823]; Lucas ii. 406.
119. Wu viii. 122.
120. He was certainly making visits to them by 25 January 1824, when he coincided with Henry Crabb Robinson.
121. The Lambs were looked after by Becky, the daughter of Mrs Tomlinson, who had been Hazlitt's housekeeper in York Street. She was both 'servant and tyrant' to the Lambs, just as her mother had been to the Hazlitts; see E. V. Lucas, *The Life of Charles Lamb* (2 vols., London, 1905), ii. 209.

Chapter 21

1. Howe xx. 345.
2. Bewick i. 163.
3. Ibid.
4. Jones explores these in greater detail in his invaluable booklet, 'The Second Mrs. Hazlitt—A Problem in Literary Biography' (University of Swansea, 1981), 12.
5. Pope ii. 441.
6. This is confirmed by the letter Hazlitt sent to Taylor and Hessey from Melrose, returning the proofs, postmarked 16 April 1824, now at the Wordsworth Library, Grasmere (*Letters* 333–4).
7. Howe xvii. 321.
8. James Sheridan Knowles to WH, 28 November 1823; Gates 657.
9. Bewick i. 167.
10. Ibid. 172–3. In an article for the *Morning Chronicle*, Hazlitt went further, defending Scott against those who criticized his novels because of his politics; see Wu (2007) i. 440–44.
11. Bewick i. 197.
12. Ibid.
13. Wu vii. 139.
14. Howe xvi. 270.
15. Clare 157–8.
16. Ibid. 157.
17. *Life of John Sterling*, as quoted in Richard Holmes, *Coleridge: Darker Reflections* (London, 1998), 543–4. It must be said that Carlyle's description is corroborated by the life mask taken in 1825; see Morton D. Paley, *Portraits of Coleridge* (Oxford, 1999), 81.
18. Clare 141.
19. John Clare to Thomas Hood, 28 May 1840, quoted Clare 308 n 197.
20. Howe x. 7.
21. Adapted from Hazlitt's remark in 'Thoughts on Taste', Howe xvii. 60.
22. This surmise is based not only on what we know of Hazlitt's love of the collection, but on his observations on the dress of those who visited; see Howe xx. 335–6.
23. Hazlitt had been projecting such a venture for years (he mentioned it in a letter as long before as December 1821). See WH to Thomas Noon Talfourd, 1 December 1821; Wordsworth Library, WL MS Foot 3 [1998.71.3] (*Letters* 212). Sikes's text is taken from Howe, at the auction of whose library it was purchased by Michael Foot. Sikes does not record the postmark, slightly smudged, of 3 December.

24. All of whom were issued with British passports; see Public Record Office passport records FO 610/01. On none of his visits to the Continent does Hazlitt appear to have applied for a passport, evidence of his distrust of government bureaucracy.
25. She visited Godwin on 30 June.
26. Mary Shelley to Leigh Hunt, 29 July 1824; Bennett i. 441–2.
27. As William St Clair points out, 'His handwriting deteriorated overnight into the uncontrolled scrawl of a very old man' (*The Godwins and the Shelleys* (London, 1989), 466).
28. The idea was apparently Sir James Mackintosh's; see *Four Generations* i. 157–8.
29. Howe xvi 408.
30. Ibid. 265.
31. Ibid.
32. Ibid. 266, 267.
33. Ibid. 270.
34. Ibid. 274.
35. Mary Shelley to Marianne Hunt, 10 October 1824; Bennett i. 452–3.
36. Before leaving for France, Sarah Stoddart Hazlitt also dined at the Godwins', on 22 October 1824.
37. Charles Lamb to Bernard Barton, *c.*17 August 1824; Lucas ii. 437. The letter was dated from its postmark.
38. John Hunt to Leigh Hunt, 31 August 1824; BL Add. MS 38108, 329r.
39. Edmund Blunden, *Keats's Publisher: A Memoir of John Taylor* (London, 1936), 163.
40. Sarah Stoddart to William Hazlitt Jr, 25 September 1824; Bonner 260.
41. The timing and sequence of events is confirmed by a letter from Richard Reynell to W. C. Hazlitt at BL Add. MS 38899, 248r–v. See also Bennett i. 378. Patmore, Procter and William Jr also worked on it at various times; see *Memoirs* i, p. xxviii, ii. 197.
42. *Memoirs* ii. 197. Copyright lasted for life or 28 years after publication, whichever was the longer. See also William St Clair, *The Reading Nation in the Romantic Period* (Cambridge, 2004), 224, 606.
43. Thomas Noon Talfourd to Mary Russell Mitford, 25 February 1840, item 74 Reading Central Library, Talfourd letters: R/TU/TAL.
44. This story is recounted in greater detail by Payson G. Gates, 'Hazlitt's *Select British Poets*: An American Publication', *Keats–Shelley Journal* 35 (1986), 168–82, and Geoffrey Bindman, 'Hazlitt against the Law: The Suppression of *Select British Poets*', *Charles Lamb Bulletin* NS 125 (January 2004), 10–16. Jeffrey C. Robinson analyses its aesthetics in *Unfettering Poetry: The Fancy in British Romanticism* (New York, 2006), chapters 8 and 9. Further information on Tegg is given by James J. and Patience P. Barnes, 'Reassessing the Reputation of Thomas Tegg, London Publisher, 1776–1846', *Book History* 3 (2000), 45–60, presented in digested form in their *New DNB* entry.
45. Howe x. 90.
46. Ibid. 91.
47. Ibid. 95.
48. Ibid.
49. Sarah Stoddart to William Hazlitt Jr, 25 September 1824; Bonner 260.
50. Howe x. 107.
51. Ibid. 106.
52. Ibid. 118. This point is reprised in *Characteristics* cccxxii (Howe ix. 213).

53. Ibid.
54. Ibid. xvii 209 n.
55. WH to Jean-Antoine Galignani,? November–December 1824; Pforzheimer Library, NYPL (*New Letters* 24). Not in Sikes. Robinson's rationale for dating is sound; there is no date and no watermark on the MS. The note is written in a very rough hand, but is certainly Hazlitt's.
56. Howe x. 246.
57. Ibid. 246–7.
58. Ibid. 247.
59. Stendhal, *The Life of Henry Brulard*, tr. John Sturrock (New York, 2002), 99.
60. See Robert Vigneron, 'Stendhal et Hazlitt', *Modern Philology* 35 (1938), 375–414, esp. 399, 404–7.
61. Hobhouse, journals ed. Peter Cochran; see http://www.hobby-o.com/milan.php.
62. Michael Foot, *Debts of Honour* (London, 1980), 37.
63. Howe x. 250.
64. *Haydon Table Talk* ii. 87.
65. See Henry Leigh Hunt to WH, 4 November 1824; SUNY at Buffalo: 'My father would like much to publish your volume himself, & would endeavour to comply with the condition. He will thank you to say what sum (in all) you expect for the copyright; & he will then write to you finally on the subject.' The arrival postmark in Paris is dated 7 November.
66. WH to Jean-Antoine Galignani, December 1824; Pforzheimer Library, NYPL (*New Letters* 25). Not in Sikes. As Robinson indicates, the MS is dated 'Dec^r.', but with no indication of year.
67. WH to Jean-Antoine Galignani, 28 December 1824; Pforzheimer Library, NYPL (*New Letters* 26). Not in Sikes. The MS is dated by Hazlitt.
68. Wu viii. 119.
69. Ibid. vii. 87.
70. Ibid. 124, 133.
71. Ibid. 141.
72. Ibid. 212.
73. Ibid. 214.
74. Ibid. 216.
75. Ibid. 161, 169.
76. Ibid. 103.
77. Ibid. 165.
78. Ibid. 198.
79. Ibid. 205.
80. Ibid. 220.
81. Ibid. 181.
82. Howe x. 177.
83. Ibid. 182.
84. Ibid.
85. Ibid. 184.
86. There is no record of his being granted a passport; see FO 612/1-71.
87. Howe x. 186.
88. Ibid. 191.

89. Ibid. 196.
90. Ibid. 195.
91. Ibid. 216.

Chapter 22

1. Howe xvii. 344.
2. Leigh Hunt to Elizabeth Kent, 12 February 1825; Gates 163.
3. Stillinger 1.
4. Morley i. 387.
5. Charles Brown to Joseph Severn, 6 June 1823; *New Letters From Charles Brown to Joseph Severn*, ed. Grant F. Scott and Sue Brown (Romantic Circles, University of Maryland). I am grateful to Grant Scott for bringing this quotation to my attention, and for supplying me with his edited text.
6. Charles Brown to John Hunt, 2 April 1825; BL Add. MS 38109, 8v (Stillinger 216).
7. John Hunt to Leigh Hunt, 6 June 1824; BL Add. MS 38108, 323r.
8. Howe xvi. 240.
9. An honourable exception to this is Geoffrey Carnall, who describes it as 'one of the more favourable assessments' of Landor's masterpiece in his *New DNB* article. Grayling is wrong to say that it was a 'bad review' (Grayling 318).
10. Howe xvi. 244.
11. See John Forster, *Walter Savage Landor. A Biography* (2 vols., London, 1869), ii. 201, and Super 177.
12. This is what Landor told Henry Crabb Robinson in 1831; see Morley i.391.
13. Wilson Landor, quoted by John Forster, *Walter Savage Landor. A Biography* (2 vols., London, 1869), ii. 203–4.
14. Super 177.
15. *Landor as Critic*, ed. Charles L. Proudfit (London, 1979), 111.
16. Super 544 n 4.
17. This direct speech is based on Forster, *Walter Savage Landor. A Biography*, ii. 208. It is inaccurate in some respects: Sarah Stoddart Hazlitt was not involved in the discovery so far as we know.
18. Ibid. 201; Super 177.
19. John Taylor to James Augustus Hessey, 19 April 1825; as quoted in Edmund Blunden, *Keats's Publisher: A Life of John Taylor* (London, 1936), 164.
20. So far as I can find, the note in praise of Hazlitt did not make it into the second edition, despite Blunden's observation that it appeared 'on cancel-pages' (ibid. 165). Landor does point out, in a note to one of the dialogues, that Bentham's 'merits and defects...are accurately and perspicuously laid down by M. Hazlitt in *The Spirits of the Age*' (*sic*); see *Imaginary Conversations* (2nd edn, 2 vols., London, 1826), ii. 373.
21. 'My Books', *The Literary Examiner* I (5 July 1823), 3–4. The manuscript of this essay is at BL Add. MS 38108, ff. 262–99; there are some interesting variants on the quoted text at 270r.
22. Morpurgo 372.
23. *Memoirs* ii. 304. Leigh Hunt was going to incorporate this paper into *Lord Byron and some of his Contemporaries* (1828), but resisted the temptation.

24. Edmund Blunden, *Leigh Hunt: A Biography* (London, 1930), 369.
25. Ibid. 371.
26. Howe x. 239.
27. [Leigh Hunt], 'The Wishing-Cap. No. I.', *Tait's Edinburgh Magazine* 2 (January 1833), 435–42, esp. 441. Some items from Hunt's collection are now at the Keats–Shelley Memorial House in Rome.
28. It is sometimes stated, erroneously, that Hunt introduced Hazlitt to Landor. Hazlitt was quite clear about this: 'he does not mention [in *Lord Byron and his Contemporaries*] that it was I who introduced him to Landor at Florence, which would have given me great satisfaction, though in the same passage there is sedulous mention of two other friends of his, as personally agreeable to him' (Howe xx. 161).
29. Leigh Hunt, *Lord Byron and Some of his Contemporaries* (2 vols., London, 1828), ii. 380–1.
30. Medwin (1839) 278–9.
31. Howe xvii. 266.
32. Super 179.
33. Howe x. 217.
34. Ibid. 220.
35. Ibid. 222–3.
36. Charles Brown to Joseph Severn, 23 February 1825; *New Letters From Charles Brown to Joseph Severn*, ed. Grant F. Scott and Sue Brown (Romantic Circles, University of Maryland). This text supercedes that at Stillinger 212–14, and is supplied by Grant Scott.
37. Morley i. 387.
38. WH to Jean-Antoine Galignani, 11 March 1825; Pforzheimer Library, NYPL (*New Letters* 27). The year does not appear on the letter, but it can only have been written in 1825. The paper is watermarked 1820.
39. This must be the implication of Robinson's observation that 'They are of no value' (Morley i. 387).
40. Howe x. 228.
41. Ibid. 230.
42. Ibid. 231.
43. Ibid. 231. There was, for a time, some question in my mind as to whether Rosa's was the house in which he lodged, as he says in *Notes of a Journey* that it 'is at present let out in lodgings' (ibid.); however, he wrote from number 33 to Landor on 22 March 1825 (*Letters* 337).
44. For information about 33 via Gregoriana I thank Josephine Greywoode of the Keats–Shelley Memorial House and Professor Dr Julian Kliemann of Bibliotheca Herziana.
45. Howe x. 233–4. The rusticity of this part of Rome is confirmed by Piranesi's 1748 map of the city; see Hein-Th. Schulze Altcappenberg and Ulf Sölter, *Giovanni Battista Piranesi: Vedute di Roma* (Berlin, 2007), 26–7.
46. Howe x. 234.
47. Ibid. 235.
48. Ibid.
49. Ibid.
50. Ibid. 237.
51. Ibid.
52. Ibid. 239.

53. Ibid.
54. Ibid. 237.
55. Ibid. 238.
56. Ibid. 240.
57. Ibid. 241.
58. WH to Charles Brown, 22 March 1825; Dreer Collection, Historical Society of Pennsylvania (*Letters* 336–7). This is one of Sikes's least correctly rendered texts. Firstly, the addressee was not Landor, as he supposes. Secondly, the letter is not dated by Hazlitt, although Sikes reads 'Rome, 28 March [1825]' (*Letters* 336). Brown did endorse the letter 'William Hazlitt/28 March 1825'—the day he received it. The endorsement is 'unmistakeably in the handwriting of Brown', as Jack Stillinger told Stanley Jones in a letter of 25 September 1980. (I thank Professor Stillinger for permission to quote from this letter. See also Stillinger 214.) The paper on which the letter was written bears a watermark identical to that on which Hazlitt wrote a note to Galignani on 11 March 1825, now at the Pforzheimer (*New Letters* 27).
59. WH to W. S. Landor, 9 April 1825; V&A, London, 48.E.2, f. 15 (*Letters* 338–9). The MS is endorsed 'Hazlett' in Landor's hand, and postmarked 'Rome' on the address panel.
60. Morley i. 317. As publication does not appear to have taken place until 11 January, that read by Robinson and his interlocutor (Horace Smith) may have been a proof copy.
61. Hobhouse, diary entry for 4 May 1825. I am grateful to Peter Cochran for this quotation.
62. Charles Brown to Leigh Hunt, 14 September 1829; Stillinger 285.
63. Charles Lamb to Bernard Barton, 10 February 1825; Lucas ii. 460.
64. William Godwin to Henry Colburn, 22 November 1824; V&A, Forster 48.E.4, f. 127. Godwin's views may be influenced by the fact that he was writing to its publisher.
65. Howe xvii. 135.
66. Charles Brown to Joseph Severn, 18 June 1826; *New Letters From Charles Brown to Joseph Severn*, ed. Scott and Brown.
67. Charles Brown to Joseph Severn, 27 June 1826; *New Letters From Charles Brown to Joseph Severn*, ed. Scott and Brown.
68. Howe xvii. 143.
69. This explains why Severn later told Henry Crabb Robinson that Hazlitt had 'ill-treated' him (Morley i. 378).
70. Admittedly, he mentions neither Keats nor Shelley when he alludes to the fact that 'the tombs in the English burying-ground were destroyed and defaced not long ago' (Howe x. 233), but he is sure to have visited the graves of these two poets he had once known.
71. *Haydon Table Talk* ii. 98.
72. Ibid. 99.
73. Howe x. 267.
74. Ibid. 278.
75. Ibid. 279.
76. Ibid. 283.
77. Wu ix. 129–30.
78. Ibid. viii. 116.
79. The Didot–Galignani editions were sources for Hazlitt's article on Scott; see Jones, 'Bad English in the Scotch Novels', *The Library* Series 6, 3 (1981), 202–16, esp. 214 n 35.
80. Wu viii. 316.

81. Ibid.
82. Written by Medwin in his *Life of Shelley* and quoted by Ernest J. Lovell Jr., *Captain Medwin: Friend of Byron and Shelley* (London, 1962), 196.
83. Wu vii. 49. It is worth noting that the MS of the original letter does not contain the passage referring to Vevey and Rousseau, though there is no reason to doubt the veracity of Hazlitt's claim in the text ultimately published in *Liber Amoris*—which, incidentally, his wife can be expected to have read.
84. Howe x. 292.
85. Ibid. 294.
86. Wu viii. 195.
87. *Edinburgh Review* 42 (April 1825), 254–60, esp. 254.
88. This is a rare poem from Hazlitt, and (contrary to Grayling) not the only one of his composition; see Wu (2007) i. 22.
89. Howe xx. 392. Another version of the poem is edited by Robinson 29–30.
90. Howe x. 299.
91. Ibid.
92. Ibid.
93. Ibid.
94. Ibid. 300–1.
95. Ibid. 302.
96. Ibid.
97. Charles Lamb to Henry Crabb Robinson, 29 March 1825; Lucas ii. 465.
98. Charles Lamb to William Ayrton, 3 October 1825; Lucas iii. 27.
99. *Haydon Table Talk* ii. 98.
100. Ibid. 99. The words 'well-behaved', which do not appear in the printed text, do appear in the original MS, according to Stanley Jones.
101. See Benjamin Robert Haydon to the Revd. J. Johns, 13 December 1838 (private collection), in which he mentions Hazlitt's 'very bad behaviour to me which I am willing to attribute to the malice of his second wife, because I did not sanction her, and would not suffer Mary to visit her' (although the original of this letter is preserved in a private collection, a copy may be found at BL Add. MS 74782A). Haydon's diary contains a number of fabrications about Hazlitt, as Jones has proved; see Stanley Jones, 'Haydon and Northcote on Hazlitt: A Fabrication', *Review of English Studies* 24 (1973), 165–78. Haydon's increasing volatility is indicated by the fact that in February 1829 he alienated even the indulgent Mary Russell Mitford, who protested to their mutual friend Thomas Noon Talfourd: 'Is it not very insulting? And is not the insult very uncalled for? What offence I have given him I really do not know. . . . I cannot tell you now how much this attack from an old friend has vexed me.' See Mary Russell Mitford to Thomas Noon Talfourd, n.d. (postmarked 8 March 1829); Bodleian Library, Montagu d. 38, 16r–v.
102. Leigh Hunt to WH, 20 June 1826; Houghton Library, Lowell collection (Gates 182). The reference must be to a visit made by Hunt to Down Street in late 1825.

Chapter 23

1. Howe xvii. 332.
2. William Godwin to Henry Colburn, 9 May 1826; V&A, Forster 48.E.3, 133v.
3. Wu viii. 185–6.

4. Godwin MS, *65M-10; Houghton Library, Harvard University. The 'Note on Hazlit', so-called in Godwin's diary, is a four-page MS entirely in Godwin's hand. To the best of my knowledge, it remains unpublished.
5. At least in the *London* Hazlitt referred to Godwin as 'the well-known author of —— and ——'; see *London Magazine* 1 (June 1820), 646–54, esp. 647. In the *London Magazine* text Godwin is also said to be wound up 'like an eight-day clock'.
6. Howe ix. 177.
7. Ibid.
8. Howe xi. 318.
9. Godwin noted in his diary: 'Call on Colburn & Northcote; adv. Ollier & Hazlit'.
10. For a full and accurate account of the publication of *Table Talk* (Paris, 1825), see *New Letters* 22–6.
11. Wu viii. 155.
12. *The Atlas* 28 May 1826, 26–7; *Monthly Review* 2 (June 1826), 113–22, esp. 122; *The Star Chamber* 1 (17 May 1826), 105. His reviewers had their way: the volume was still on sale in 1840, when it was advertised on Templeman's lists as a bargain, reduced from 24 shillings to 11 shillings. The obvious antidote is Tom Paulin's perceptive commentary on the volume in chapter 12 of his *The Day-Star of Liberty: William Hazlitt's Radical Style* (London, 1998), and the introduction to *William Hazlitt, The Plain Speaker: The Key Essays*, ed. Duncan Wu (Oxford, 1998).
13. Wu (2007) ii. 31.
14. *La Belle Assemblee* 4 (1826), 82; *Monthly Review* 2 (1826), 431–8, esp. 438; *The Atlas* 28 May 1826, 26.
15. Howe xiii, p. ix.
16. Ibid. p. x.
17. Although, as John Sutherland points out, the terms of the trust deed by which this was determined were unusually generous; see Sutherland, *The Life of Walter Scott* (Oxford, 1995), 295–7.
18. Shortly before he and Isabella left London, Leigh Hunt invited them to dinner, asking: 'Is there any hope that I might be permitted some day or other to try & bring you & Coleridge together again?' The answer was 'no'. See Leigh Hunt to WH, 20 June [1826]; Lowell Collection, Houghton Library, Harvard University (Gates 183). The MS bears no postmark and was probably transmitted by messenger.
19. Pope iii. 210.
20. WH to P. G. Patmore, 7 August 1826; BL RP 6003 (*Letters* 344). Sikes takes his text from Howe rather than the MS (see Howe xiii. 354), and as a result makes no reference either to the date marked on the letter by Hazlitt, 'August 7, Monday', or the postmark: '12 NOON/AUG 8/1826'.
21. WH to Jean-Antoine Galignani, 14 July 1826; Pforzheimer Library, NYPL (*New Letters* 32–3). Not in Sikes. The MS is not franked, indicating it was probably transmitted by hand. The year of composition is not written on the MS, and Robinson confesses it may date from 1828; 1826 seems more likely.
22. Stanley Jones, 'Two Hazlitt Quotations', *Notes and Queries* 23 (1976), 455–7, esp. 456.
23. Wu ix. 132.
24. Ibid. 138.

25. Ibid. 139.
26. WH to P. G. Patmore, 7 August 1826; BL RP 6003 (*Letters* 344).
27. Howe xvii. 175.
28. 'Boswell Redivivus—No. I', *New Monthly Magazine* 17 (1826), 113–18, esp. 113.
29. Hazlitt stole his title from a letter which appeared in the *Edinburgh Magazine* in 1819, to which he had been a contributor. See S.D., 'Boswell Redivivus, A Dream', *Edinburgh Magazine* 4 (October 1819), 304–10. This was not the first time someone had thought to preserve Northcote's table talk, the painter James Ward having done so between 1812 and 1821. The MS of his conversations is now at the Royal Academy and was published in part in 1901.
30. 'Boswell Redivivus—No. I', 113 n.
31. Veritas, 'Hazlitt and Northcote', *The Athenaeum*, 4 May 1833, 279–80.
32. 'Boswell Redivivus—No. I', 116.
33. 'Boswell Redivivus—No. II', *New Monthly Magazine* 17 (1826), 217–21, esp. 217.
34. 'Boswell Redivivus—No. III', *New Monthly Magazine* 17 (1826), 334–40, esp. 337.
35. 'Boswell Redivivus—No. VI', *New Monthly Magazine* 19 (1827), 277–80, esp. 277.
36. 'Boswell Redivivus—No. I', 114.
37. Ibid. 115.
38. Thomas Campbell to Leigh Hunt, 11 August 1826; *The Correspondence of Leigh Hunt*, ed. Thornton Leigh Hunt (2 vols., London, 1852), i. 251–2.
39. WH to Thomas Allsop, *c*.8 September 1826; Osborn files 7076, Beineke Library, Yale University (*New Letters* 34–5). Not in Sikes. Robinson is correct to record the postmark as 11 September 1826; the dealer Percy Dobell erroneously dates the letter to February 1826 in a letter retained at the British Library (see BL RP 72 (2)), and was responsible for the dating reported to Jones; see Jones, 'Some New Hazlitt Letters', *Notes and Queries* 24 (1977), 336–42.
40. *Memoirs* ii. 107 n. I follow the dating ascribed to this detail by Stanley Jones, 'The Dating of a Hazlitt Essay: Bibliography and Biography', *Etudes Anglaises* 33 (1980), 188–98, esp. 193. Erroneously, Grayling does not have William Hazlitt Jr going to Paris until 'the summer of 1827' (Grayling 332).
41. Howe xvii. 91.
42. Sir Walter Scott to John Gibson, 1826; *The Letters of Sir Walter Scott*, ed. H. J. C. Grierson (12 vols., London, 1936), x. 115.
43. Howe xi. 276.
44. Ibid. xvi. 401.
45. *Lamb and Hazlitt* 57.
46. *Racine et Shakspeare*, ed. Pierre Martino (Paris, 1970), 39. *Racine et Shakespeare* made a bigger splash in London than Stendhal's previous books: reading it in December 1826, Henry Crabb Robinson declared himself 'interested in the turn literature is taking in France' (Morley i. 343).
47. Quoted in Stendhal's 'Puff-Article' on *The Red and the Black*, Stendhal, *Mélanges de Littérature*, ed. Henri Martineau (3 vols., Paris, 1933), ii. 336.
48. G. Huntly Gordon to W. C. Hazlitt, 4 August 1866; BL Add. MS 38899, 82r.
49. G. Huntly Gordon to William Hazlitt Jr, 15 February 1866; BL Add. MS 38899, 16r. As Stanley Jones points out, William Jr referred W. C. Hazlitt to Gordon as an informant; see

Jones, 'The Dating of a Hazlitt Essay: Bibliography and Biography', *Etudes Anglaises* 33 (1980), 188–98, esp. 195–6.

50. G. Huntly Gordon to William Hazlitt Jr, 15 February 1866; BL Add. MS 38899, 17v.
51. Ibid.
52. G. Huntly Gordon to W. C. Hazlitt, 4 August 1866; BL Add. MS 38899, 82v.
53. Ibid.
54. Howe xx. 347.
55. Ibid. It is not certain that the reference is to Sabine, but the conjecture seems likely.
56. Ibid. xi. 276.
57. WH to Jean-Antoine Galignani; Pforzheimer Library, NYPL (*New Letters* 34). Not in Sikes. The MS is undated, and there is no date on the watermark. Robinson assigns it to '?July 1826–October 1827'; however, it is possible to be more specific. The note is likely to have been written at around the time of Lafayette's soiree, *c.*26 March 1827.
58. Howe xvi. 321. Cooper made no specific comment on Hazlitt, but of this evening told a correspondent: 'You often find yourself thrown by accident, in Paris, into a circle of some six or eight names you have often heard of, but which attract no sort of observation here.' See *The Letters and Journals of James Fenimore Cooper*, ed. James Franklin Beard (6 vols., Cambridge, MA, 1960–8), i. 204.
59. Howe xvi. 320.
60. 'Boswell Redivivus—No. VI', 277.
61. See Sir James Northcote to Thomas Campbell, 16 March 1827; Bodleian Library, MS Eng. Misc. e. 143, 40v.
62. Sir James Northcote to Thomas Campbell, 7 March 1827; Bodleian Library, MS Eng. Misc. e. 143, 37r–38v.
63. Thomas Campbell to Sir James Northcote, 9 March 1827; Bodleian Library, MS Eng. Misc. e. 143, 39r–40r.
64. Sir James Northcote to Thomas Campbell, 16 March 1827; Bodleian Library, MS Eng. Misc. e. 143, 40v–41r.
65. *Memoirs* ii. 212.
66. Reprinted in *The Examiner*, 17 June 1827, 378.
67. Wu (2007) ii. 55.
68. David Lester Richardson, *Literary Chit-Chat with Miscellaneous Poems* (Calcutta, 1858), 93.
69. The location of the meeting is indicated by Haydon; Pope iii. 302.
70. Richardson, *Literary Chit-Chat with Miscellaneous Poems*, 92.
71. Ibid. 91. The direct speech is mine, based on details given by Richardson.
72. Pope iii. 302.
73. Jules Douady was the first to argue for Hazlitt's presence in the first issue of the journal. Howe evidently disagreed, but Hazlitt's authorship of the article on Wordsworth is confirmed by my own examination of the text; see Wu (2007) ii. 32–6.
74. Ibid. 37–8.
75. Ibid. 38.
76. Richardson, *Literary Chit-Chat with Miscellaneous Poems*, 93.
77. Ibid. 99.
78. Ibid. 100.

Notes

Chapter 24

1. Morley i. 387.
2. Rollins ii. 59.
3. *Memoirs* ii. 196.
4. Ibid.
5. *Four Generations* i. 185.
6. Howe xvii. 236.
7. Ibid. 276.
8. Ibid.
9. Ibid. 417. This variant is reported by W. C. Hazlitt; I do not find it in the MS of the essay now at SUNY at Buffalo.
10. I have accepted Stanley Jones's hypothesis concerning the tour, and followed his dating; see Jones, 'The Dating of a Hazlitt Essay: Bibliography and Biography', *Etudes Anglaises* 33 (1980), 188–98, esp. 193.
11. Bewick i. 113.
12. *Memoirs* ii. 107 n.
13. Wu ix. 153.
14. WH to W. Underwood, 3 May 1828; *New Letters* 39.
15. I take this to be the implication of the occasional sightings of her in Lamb's letters at this period; see for instance Lucas iii. 149.
16. *Memoirs* ii. 196. Jones surmises that, when Isabella replied, she was on her way back to England from Switzerland, having accompanied her sister there; see 'The Second Mrs. Hazlitt—A Problem in Literary Biography' (booklet, University of Swansea, 1981), 16–17.
17. We are given the merest hint of his reaction in *Characteristics* cccxi, which I take to be a reflection on Isabella (among others): 'With women, the great business of life is love; and they generally make a mistake in it. They consult neither the heart nor the head, but are led away by mere humour and fancy. If instead of a companion for life, they had to choose a partner in a country-dance or to trifle away an hour with, their mode of calculation would be right. They tie their true-lover's knots with idle, thoughtless haste, while the institutions of society render it indissoluble' (Howe ix. 211).
18. Reginald Colby, *Mayfair: A Town within London* (London, 1966), 115.
19. *Memoirs* ii. 232–3. W. C. Hazlitt indicates that the manuscript was taken to the offices of *The Atlas*; that cannot be the case because Hazlitt did not write for that paper in 1827. It is more likely that the manuscript was placed in the care of one of the other papers for which he wrote.
20. *Four Generations* i. 201.
21. G. Huntly Gordon to W. C. Hazlitt, 4 August 1866; BL Add. MS 38899, 82v.
22. G. Huntly Gordon to William Hazlitt Jr 21 July 1866; BL Add. MS 38899, 58v.
23. I am grateful to Alan Crookham, Archivist at the National Gallery, for giving me access to period illustrations of Trafalgar Square. Hazlitt did not live to see the National Gallery complete, which did not open until 1838 (though he was acquainted with its corinthian columns, which came from the recently demolished Carlton House).
24. Henry Crabb Robinson to Dorothy Wordsworth, 7 December 1827; HCR papers, Dr Williams's Library. In the same letter Robinson noted that 'The solitude is much too great for him.'
25. Wu (2007) ii. 58–9.

26. John Sutherland admits that 'Scott's account is uncompromisingly Tory'; see *The Life of Walter Scott* (Oxford, 1995), 316.
27. Howe xvii. 255.
28. Ibid.
29. Ibid. 257.
30. His grandson reported that on his bill at Winterslow Hut for August 1821 'the items *tea* and *rice* are conspicuous' (*Memoirs* ii. 307).
31. Ibid. 216.
32. WH to Charles Cowden Clarke, 7 December 1827; *Letters* 349–50. Though reported to be at SUNY at Buffalo, this MS is not at present to be found.
33. Ibid.; *Letters* 349.
34. Ibid.; *Letters* 349.
35. WH to Jean-Antoine and Guillaume Galignani, 25 December 1827; Pforzheimer Library, NYPL (*New Letters* 36–7). Not in Sikes. Galignani's response was drafted on the MS of Hazlitt's proposal; a deleted comment reveals that the publishers regarded their reprinting of Scott's *Life* as a 'bad speculation' (*New Letters* 37). The paper is watermarked 'W. Brookman 1826'.
36. 'Mr Hazlitt's Napoleon', *The Athenaeum*, 2 January 1828, 8. See also WH to Charles Cowden Clarke, [January 1828]; *New Letters* 662 (*Letters* 356). Sikes's text is from *Four Generations* i. 191.
37. See Howe xix. 288–91.
38. WH to Henry Leigh Hunt, 16 January 1828; SUNY at Buffalo (*Letters* 354). The letter is addressed to 'H. L. Hunt, Esq.' and was presumably delivered by hand.
39. Pope iii. 302.
40. WH to James Augustus St John, 14 February 1828; not in Sikes. This letter is published in full, for the first time, by Charles E. Robinson, 'Two New Hazlitt Letters to His Editors', *Nineteenth-Century Prose* 36/1 (2009), 167–76, esp. 170. It was known to Jones from a description of the MS in an auction catalogue, see Jones (1977) 340.
41. Grayling dates publication to 'January 1828' (Grayling 335), but there is no evidence that the *Life* was available until the following month. The price of thirty shillings would not hold for long. In August 1828, Sir John Soane purchased the first two volumes of the *Life* for £17s 0d, from Priestley and Weale, 5 High Street, Bloomsbury. His copy survives today, with the receipt, at Sir John Soane's Museum, London.
42. *Literary Gazette*, 8 November 1828, 709. Charles Lamb to Charles Cowden Clarke, 25 February 1828, Lucas iii. 151–2.
43. See Robert E. Robinson, *William Hazlitt's Life of Napoleon Buonaparte: Its Sources and Characteristics* (Paris and Geneva, 1959), 27–35.
44. WH to Charles Cowden Clarke, 7 December 1827; *Letters* 348.
45. Howe xiii, p. ix.
46. Morley i. 356.
47. Anna Dorothea Benson Skepper Montagu to Jane Welsh Carlyle, 27 February 1828; as quoted in *The Collected Letters of Thomas and Jane Welsh Carlyle*, ed. Charles Richard Sanders (Durham, NC, 1970), iv. 364 n 2. Sanders does not indicate the location of the MS.
48. As the manuscript reveals; see Morgan Library, MA 2445, 2446. The MSS consist of doctored engravings and text in Northcote's hand. Hazlitt has emended and revised parts of it.

The title pages of the two volumes indicate 1825 as the date of composition, although the Morgan catalogue gives 1823–8.

49. Northcote's will gave 'to Mr William Hazlitt the Author the Sum of One Hundred Pounds'; see BL Add. MS 42524, 21r. It is dated 28 December 1829.

50. Patmore iii. 5.

51. Quoted from the text at *London Weekly Review*, 29 March 1828, 202.

52. Howe xviii. 377.

53. Wu (2007) ii. 86–7.

54. This is discussed by Nicholas Roe in *Fiery Heart: The First Life of Leigh Hunt* (London, 2005), 355.

55. 'The "Living Dog" and the "Dead Lion"', *The Times* 10 January 1828, p. 3 col. 3. Part of the MS of the poem, containing four stanzas, is at the Pforzheimer, NYPL (B.ana 0489).

56. *Quarterly Review* 37 (1828), 402–26, esp. 403.

57. Howe xi. 159.

58. Wu (2007) ii. 91.

59. See Leigh Hunt, 'Remarks Suggested by the Perusal of Mr Hazlitt's "Plain Speaker: Opinions on Books, Men, and Things"', *The Companion*, 12 March 1828, 113–28; 19 March 1828, 129–36.

60. Wu (2007) ii. 81.

61. WH to Isabella Jane Towers, 21 November 1827; *Letters* 347. Sikes records the MS as being at Stanford University.

62. WH to Charles Cowden Clarke, [January–February 1828]; Pforzheimer Library, NYPL, WH0016 (*Letters* 359). Sikes's text is from *Lamb and Hazlitt* 144. I follow Jones's proposed redating; see his review of Sikes, *The Library* Series 6, 3 (1980), 356–62, esp. 360. I am grateful to Charles Carter, Librarian at the Pforzheimer, for bringing this MS to my attention.

63. WH to Marianne Hunt or a servant in Leigh Hunt's employ, 2 March 1829; Jones (1977) 341 (*Letters* 361). Sikes is confused about whom the recipient can have been, indicating both Leigh Hunt and Henry Leigh Hunt. I have preferred Jones's ascription.

64. See Luther A. Brewer, *My Leigh Hunt Library: The Holograph Letters* (Iowa City, 1938), 175.

65. R. S. Rintoul to William Blackwood, 7 July 1828; National Library of Scotland, MS 4023.

66. At some point Charles Cowden Clarke was appointed to the 'Fine Arts' column.

67. [Robert Bell], 'William Hazlitt', *The Atlas*, 17 October 1830, 681–2, esp. 682.

68. See Wu (2007) i, pp. lv–lvii; ii. 142.

69. For a complete listing of Hazlitt's contributions to *The Atlas*, see Wu (2007) ii. 530–3.

70. WH to David Constable, 10 January 1828; *New Letters* 38 (*Letters* 352–3). Sikes erroneously claims the MS to be at the National Library of Scotland, but in fact takes his text from Howe, *Life* 360–1. The MS is at Delaware University Library. Glover may have possessed the MS in the early 1900s.

71. In the end, this must be conjecture, as hard evidence is not at present to be found. This is one point on which nearly all biographers disagree. Maclean says that Hazlitt did not go (Maclean 548). Baker (463) follows Howe (365) in thinking the review of Charles Kean in *The Examiner* on 15 June indicates Hazlitt's presence in Paris. However, Robinson points out that the review is probably based on information provided by someone else and that Hazlitt was 'writing from London at the end of May or in the first two weeks of June' (*New Letters* 41 n 2). Jones says that Hazlitt 'may have gone to Paris…in the summer of 1828'

(Jones 378)—and, in the end, I have taken this as license for my own conjecture. Grayling cites 'On Travelling Abroad' as evidence that Hazlitt was in Paris during the course of May (337); he is almost certainly wrong. I see no reason to doubt Robinson's dismissal of that essay as evidence for Hazlitt's presence in Paris at that time, though it does not rule out his presence there during July or August.

72. See Wu (2007) ii. 155–60. This may have been one of the 'details nouveaux' discovered by Jules Douady relating to 'un voyage en France que fit Hazlitt pendant l'été de 1828'; see Douady to W. C. Hazlitt, 20 February 1906; BL Add. MS 38911, 69v. Disappointingly, Douady does not elucidate those details in his *Vie de William Hazlitt* (Paris, 1907).

73. See *New Letters* 41 n 2.

74. It was reported in the *Morning Chronicle* on 6 August and *The Examiner* on 10 August.

75. David Lester Richardson, *Literary Chit-Chat with Miscellaneous Poems* (Calcutta, 1858), 94.

76. Ibid. By 'portrait of Gervartius', Richardson means Van Dyck's portrait of Cornelius van der Geest, and the landscape of Rubens was probably the famous autumn landscape with a view of Het Steen; both paintings are still to be seen in the National Gallery, London.

77. Ibid.

78. The quotation is the first line of a poem believed in Hazlitt's day to have been written by Sir Edward Dyer; see Wu vi. 4.

79. Howe xvii. 343.

80. See WH to the Salisbury Postmaster, 6 October 1828; Historical Society of Pennsylvania, Gratz Collection, Case 10, Box 30 (*Letters* 360). The letter bears no postmark.

81. WH to Charles Cowden Clarke or Henry Leigh Hunt, 28 October 1828; *New Letters* 42. Not in Sikes.

82. *Remains* i, p. lxiii.

83. See Jones 378 n 8.

84. Wu (2007) ii. 225–6.

85. Ibid. 219.

86. See Howe xx. 236, Wu ix. 187, Howe xx. 230, Wu (2007) ii. 226.

87. See Richard D. Altick, *The Cowden Clarkes* (Oxford, 1948), 63.

88. Frederick William Hackwood, *William Hone: His Life and Times* (London, 1912), 288.

Chapter 25

1. *The Complete Works of Montaigne*, tr. Donald M. Frame (London, 1967), 60.

2. *Memoirs* ii. 233. This was not the best residence for someone in uncertain health. John Payne Collier, who lived there in 1824, recalled that 'even my health was suffering from over application and want of good air in Bouverie Street' (MS autobiography, f. 127; Folger Shakespeare Library, M.a.230).

3. See Bodleian Library, Dep. b. 229/2.

4. James Ward found him working on it in March 1822; see Ward, 'Gossip for Artists', Royal Academy archive, WA/7, 85r.

5. *Remains* i, pp. lxv–lxvi. Despite carrying Northcote's name on its title page, *The Life of Titian* was as much Hazlitt's work as the *Conversations of Northcote*. The publishers' contract, signed by Hazlitt 'on behalf of James Northcote Esqre' declares that Hazlitt will 'make over a regular Assignment of the Copyright of the said Work to the said Henry Colburn

and Richard Bentley' (BL Add. MS 466611, f. 102). In May 1830, Colburn and Bentley paid Hazlitt £200 for 'Copyright of "Life of Titian" ' (BL Add. MS 46560, f. 57). Colburn and Bentley's records show that it went on sale in October at 28s. in boards (BL Add. MS 46667, f. 223). A total of 449 copies of the volume were remaindered in 1832 at 16s. (BL Add. MS 46674, ff. 16, 50).

6. He was there on 28 September 1829, when Godwin dropped by, and is mentioned in the twentieth of the conversations, which dates from August 1829 (see Howe xi. 305). He claims credit for work on the translation at *Remains* i, p. lxvi.

7. Howe xx. 245–6.

8. 'I was pleased to hear that you had been so good as to make some inquiries after me,' Hazlitt replied on 13 July, adding he would be pleased to write for him 'any thing that lies in my power'. See WH to Macvey Napier, 13 July 1829; BL Add. MS 34614, f. 121 (*Letters* 365). Sikes does not say that the dispatch postmark is dated 13 July and the Edinburgh postmark 15 July. Napier contacted Hazlitt through Owen Rees, of Longman. Rees's brother, Abraham, had tutored Hazlitt at Hackney, and was an old friend of Hazlitt's father.

9. WH to Macvey Napier, 21 July 1829; BL Add. MS 34614, f. 127 (*Letters* 366). Sikes does not report the arrival postmark of 23 July.

10. WH to Macvey Napier, [*c.*24 August 1829]; BL Add. MS 36414, f. 174 (*Letters* 367). Sikes's text is flawed: Hazlitt did not date the letter. However, Napier endorsed it on receipt: '26th August 1829'. It was probably, therefore, composed *c.*24 August or shortly earlier. It bears no postmark, suggesting that it was sent to Edinburgh with one of Hazlitt's articles.

11. See Charles Lamb to Walter Wilson, 15 November 1829; Lucas iii. 233.

12. Walter Wilson to William Hone, 23 September 1829; BL Add. MS 40120 (ff. 254–497), 330r.

13. William Hone to Thomas Hurst, 22 November 1829; F. W. Hackwood, *William Hone: His Life and Times* (London, 1912), 293.

14. *Memoirs* ii. 233.

15. *Hazlitts* 147.

16. Howe xx. 283–4.

17. These reviews have only recently been attributed to him; see Wu (2007) ii. 298–9. Hazlitt even sought to influence her choice of roles, advising her on one occasion to try comedy (Wu (2007) ii. 339).

18. Wu ix. 192–3.

19. Clarke 62.

20. John Mitford, notebooks; BL Add. MS 32566, 171v. Grayling's suggestion that the phrasing suggests a prostitute is plausible, but does not rule out the possibility that it refers to an actress.

21. Patmore ii. 301–2.

22. WH to Charles Kemble, 5 October 1829; Gates 663.

23. See Thomas Noon Talfourd to Mary Russell Mitford, 5 November 1829; John Rylands Library, English MSS 667, letter 37.

24. Mary Cowden Clarke, *My Long Life: An Autobiographic Sketch* (London, 1896), 84.

25. This is the implication of Lamb's letter to Walter Wilson of 15 November 1829 that reports Hazlitt's intention to review Wilson's life of Defoe (Lucas iii. 233). They had last met when Lamb came into town in July; see Lucas iii. 224.

26. Not in Howe. See Wu (2007) ii. 423.

27. Alexander Ireland, *William Hazlitt, Essayist and Critic: Selections from his Writings* (London, 1889), p. xlv. The precise date of publication is difficult to pin down. The implication of the advertisement that appeared in *The Examiner* on 26 September 1830, 622, is that it was published during the preceding week—that is, the week beginning Monday 20 September (see Maclean 604–5 n 352). The price for all four volumes was £2 10s 0d. It did not sell.

28. Wu ix. 193.

29. Wu (2007) ii. 314.

30. See *Survey of London Volume 33: The Parish of St Anne Soho* (London, 1966), 156.

31. W. C. Hazlitt confirms that 1830, the year of Hazlitt's death, 'marked nearly the close of the retention by Soho of its old character. Ever since the last quarter of the seventeenth century it had been a favourite resort of the nobility and gentry, before the West End was extended further toward Piccadilly and the Parks' (*Four Generations* i. 201).

32. *Memoirs* ii. 235.

33. Thomas Noon Talfourd to Mary Russell Mitford, 18 February 1830; Reading Central Library, Talfourd letters: R/TU/TAL, vol. ii, Item 54.

34. *Memoirs* ii. 235.

35. I do not find Hazlitt's name anywhere in the compter records at the Guildhall Record Office, nor in the book containing actions in the Sheriff's Court for 1830.

36. Wu (2007) ii. 354–5.

37. WH to Macvey Napier, 19 March 1830; BL Add. MS 34614, f. 308 (*Letters* 372). Sikes does not report that the letter was sent from London on 20 March and received in Edinburgh on 22 March.

38. This has only recently been attributed to Hazlitt; see Wu (2007) ii. 359 ff.

39. Howe xvi. 394.

40. Ibid. 402.

41. Ibid. 403.

42. Ibid. 395–6.

43. According to his diary, Godwin read the *Atlas* piece on 4 April 1830 (the day of its publication) and that in the *Edinburgh Review* on 20 August 1830 (published 17 May 1830).

44. See 'The Public', 'Friends', and 'Watch-Words'; Wu (2007) ii. 385–9, 402–7, 408–12.

45. There was some urgency attached to the latter, which Colburn and Bentley wanted to issue in April. The contract for the *Life of Titian* is at BL Add. MS 46611, f. 102.

46. See W. C. Hazlitt, *The Hazlitts: Part the Second* (Edinburgh, 1912), 1: 'Hazlitt appears to have cherished to the last a hope of leaving him sufficient to make any occupation unnecessary; but the best that can be pleaded for such a visionary notion is that he did not anticipate so early an abrupt a close of the scene, or the financial collapse of the firm which had engaged to pay him a handsome amount for the *Life of Napoleon*.'

47. Bewick ii. 122.

48. Howe xi. 367.

49. Bartholomew Dunsterville to James Northcote, 29 March 1830; Bodleian Library, MS. Eng. misc. e. 143, 69v.

50. James Northcote to Bartholomew Dunsterville, 5 April 1830; Bodleian Library, MS. Eng. misc. e. 143, 70v.

51. Wu (2007) ii. 373.

52. Ibid. 374.

53. Wu iii. 55.

54. Lucas iii. 281.

55. Richard Rosdew to James Northcote, 19 May 1830; Bodleian Library, MS. Eng. misc. e. 143, 74r.

56. *Haydon Table Talk* ii. 404.

57. James Northcote to Richard Rosdew, 21 July 1830; Bodleian Library, MS. Eng. misc. e. 143, 74v–75r.

58. Howe xi. 316.

59. WH to James Northcote, 29 July 1830; Bodleian Library, MS. Eng. misc. e. 143 (*Letters* 374). Sikes's copy-text is at Cornell University Library; I have corrected his text against that in Northcote's letter-book.

60. Allan Cunningham, *The Lives of the Most Eminent British Painters and Sculptors* (6 vols., London, 1829–33), vi. 108.

61. Ibid. 115–16.

62. *The Reminiscences of Alexander Dyce*, ed. Richard J. Schrader (Ohio, 1972), 239.

63. Wu ix. 194–5.

64. 'The Sick-Chamber' has sometimes been claimed as Hazlitt's last essay, but the error in dating is explained at Wu ix. 254.

65. Wu ix. 199.

66. Howe xix. 334 n.

67. Wu ix. 203–4.

68. *Four Generations* i. 197.

69. *Remains* i, p. lxvi.

70. Clarke 63.

71. Bentley and Colburn's records show that the volume sold for 10*s.* 6*d.* in boards (see BL Add. MS 46667, f. 174, dated 25 August 1830). Reviews were uninspiring and uninspired. As they all post-dated Hazlitt's death, they took the form of extended notices of his life. The least unfavourable was that in *The Examiner*, which described the volume as 'a very pleasant and a very suggestive publication' before embarking on an extended defence of Utilitarians who, it is claimed, 'do not treat the toys of life as the great machinery for human happiness' (*The Examiner* no. 1182 (26 September 1830), 615). The *Monthly Review* described Hazlitt as 'an ultra-radical' who 'was so fond of giving a political colour and tendency to every thing he touched, that he fell into the hands of a party who had no means of assisting his reputation' (*Monthly Review* 3rd Ser. 35 (October 1830), 275). The *Edinburgh Literary Journal* said that Hazlitt had no 'definite object in life' and 'an irascible and ungovernable temper' (*Edinburgh Literary Journal* no. 100 (9 October 1830), 221). In *The Athenaeum*, John Hamilton Reynolds attributed to him 'acerbities, hasty asperities, abrupt assertions, angry and bitter lamentations, which cloud nearly all his writings' (*The Athenaeum* (2 October 1830), 611). This was, as Hazlitt would have observed, 'the malice of a friend'. Despite these unhelpful reviews, the *Conversations* enjoyed a healthy sale.

72. WH to Basil Montagu, early September 1830; Cambridge University Library, Add. MS 8533/5 (*Letters* 376). The published text of this letter is incorrect; it actually reads: 'The second vol. of the Titian is at p.304, & will be done this week.' Sikes erroneously places the word 'I' before 'will', which suggests that Hazlitt was doing the proof-reading. In fact, Hazlitt studiously omits that word, indicating that someone else was doing it—as one would expect. The transcription error is perpetuated by Baker, who is dependent on Sikes (Baker 468).

Sikes dates the letter to 'early September', but it is possible to be more specific. Hazlitt helpfully dates the letter 'Monday morning', so that if it really dates from early September the most likely moment for its composition would be the morning of 6 September. It is most unlikely that it was written the following week, 13 September.

73. Both are now in the present author's possession.
74. Procter (1830) 478. It may be significant that a faint or high-pitched voice is a symptom of cholera in its advanced stages.
75. WH to Basil Montagu, 6 September 1830; Cambridge University Library, Add. MS 8533/5 (*Letters* 376).
76. *The Journal of William Charles Macready 1832–1851*, ed. J. C. Trewin (London, 1967), 22.
77. WH to Francis Jeffrey, September 1830; Thomas Carlyle, *Reminiscences*, ed. J. A. Froude (2 vols., London, 1881), ii. 38 (*Letters* 378). Sikes records that the addressee was 'the Editor of the *Edinburgh Review*' (Macvey Napier) before recording in a note that 'It was intended for Francis Jeffrey'. The addressee was Jeffrey.
78. This is clear from Bulwer's tribute to Hazlitt; see *Remains* i, pp. lxxxii–iii.
79. Ibid. p. lxxxiii.
80. WH to Longman and Co., 6 September 1830; Howe xvii. 429 (*Letters* 377).
81. Carlyle, *Reminiscences*, ii. 39.
82. Charles Lamb to Basil Montagu, 'Monday'; Beineke Library, Charles Lamb collection, Gen MSS 254 Box 1, Folder 5. Although the letter is dated only 'Monday', the most likely date is the last Monday of Hazlitt's life—13 September.
83. J. A. Hessey to John Clare, 15 September 1830; BL Egerton MS 2248, 263v.
84. *Memoirs* ii. 238.
85. Morley i. 424; Maclean 607. Jones (380) responds by saying that Robinson was incapable of invention, but Maclean's point is that his comments reflect a misreading (or deliberate distortion) of an article about Hazlitt's last days by Robinson's acquaintances—which is correct. Without alluding either to Maclean or Jones, Grayling reports Robinson as evidence that 'Hazlitt's incorrigible heart was again in pawn' (Grayling 339).
86. B. W. Procter to P. G. Patmore, 27 October 1830; Beineke Library, Osborn file 12324.
87. Ibid.
88. *Memoirs* ii 238.
89. Ibid.
90. Arnold Bennett, *The Evening Standard Years* (London, 1974), 414.
91. Maclean 608 n 357; Grayling 341.
92. *Memoirs* ii. 237.
93. Ibid. 238.
94. Jones 381.
95. Howe xx. 123.
96. This note is now to be found in the Goodyear Collection, SUNY at Buffalo. It is the source for the text quoted at *Memoirs* ii. 238.

Epilogue

1. S. T. Coleridge, *Notebooks*, ed. Kathleen Coburn and Anthony Harding (5 vols., Princeton, NJ, 1957–2002), v. 6467.
2. Attribution to Hazlitt is recent; see Wu (2007) ii. 402–12.

3. See B. W. Procter to P. G. Patmore, 13 October 1830 and 27 October 1830; Beineke Library, Osborn file 12324. The precise sum owed Mrs Stapleton was disputed, but on 27 October it was agreed that the outstanding amount was £8. 18s. 8d.

4. See Allan Cunningham, *The Lives of the Most Eminent British Painters and Sculptors* (6 vols., London, 1829–33), vi. 129.

5. Morley i. 397.

6. *The Edinburgh Literary Journal* no. 109, 11 December 1830, 353–4, esp. 353.

7. James Northcote to John J. Ruskin, 13 October 1830; John Ruskin, *Praeterita*, ed. A. O. J. Cockshut (Keele, 1994), 169.

8. *Memoirs* ii. 198.

9. *The Tatler* no. 14, Monday 20 September 1830, 53.

10. *Blackwood's Edinburgh Magazine* 28 (November 1830), 862, under 'Deaths'.

11. It was the last item in the paper; *The Times*, Monday 20 September 1830, p. 4 col. 5. This notice was reprinted in the *Evening Mail* later that day.

12. John Clare to James Hessey, 'after 15 September 1830'; Storey 517. The dating is Storey's. However, the reference to Hazlitt's obituaries suggests a more plausible date of 'after 20 September 1830'. According to Storey, the letter lacks a readable postmark.

13. See Charles Lamb to Thomas Noon Talfourd, [October 1830]; Houghton Library, *44M-409. Not in Lucas.

14. *The Collected Letters of Thomas and Jane Welsh Carlyle*, ed. Charles Richard Sanders (Durham, NC, 1970), iii. 234.

15. Morley i. 386.

16. Ibid. 387.

17. 'Horne knew Keats and Wells intimately, I believe'—Thomas Wade to R. M. Milnes, 27 January 1845; see *Keats Circle* ii. 115. See also Paul F. Matthiesen, 'Gosse's Candid "Snapshots"', *Victorian Studies* 8 (1965), 329–54, esp. 353.

18. R. H. Horne, 'Charles Wells', *The Academy*, Saturday 19 April 1879, 349–50, esp. 349. Not in Houck. A copy of the MS of this essay is to be found in the British Library, RP 794, 1r.

19. See B. W. Procter to P. G. Patmore, 29 October 1830; Beineke Library, Osborn file 12324.

20. Horne, 'Charles Wells', 349.

21. In later years Patmore was insistent that he was the only one of Hazlitt's friends to attend the funeral; see for instance Joanna Richardson, 'P. G. Patmore on Lamb and Hazlitt', *TLS*, 19 June 1953, 397.

22. Grayling questions the attribution to Wells, claiming Sarah Stoddart wrote the epitaph (Grayling 344); this can only be because he is unaware of Horne's article for *The Academy*; see note 18 above. Wells's authorship is attested also by W. C. Hazlitt (*Four Generations* i. 160).

23. See *The Examiner*, 26 September 1830, 615–16.

24. Ibid. 615.

25. 'The Fate of Genius', *The Atlas*, 26 September 1830, 634. This item is not recorded by Houck in his *Reference Guide*; it must have been by Bell.

26. This is a recent attribution; see Wu (2007) ii. 413–14.

27. *The Literary Examiner*, 1 November 1823, 286.

28. Wu (2007) ii. 416.

29. He was recalled as such by W. C. Hazlitt, *Four Generations* i. 160. Wells's son Charles was to become the subject of the song, 'The Man who Broke the Bank at Monte Carlo'.

30. Wu vii. 203. For Brougham's assistance, see Henry Brougham, first Baron Broughton and Vaux, to John, first Baron Romilly, 17 October 1853; BL Add. MS 38898, 42v–43r.
31. *Remains* i, pp. cix–x.
32. Ibid. pp. lxii–iii.
33. See Metropolitan Archive, London; PROB 12/246, p. 150.
34. These details were first disclosed by Jones 337 n 59.
35. Feminists today take a similar view; see my 'Hazlitt's "Sexual Harassment"', *Essays in Criticism* 50 (July 2000), 199–214.
36. *Four Generations* i. 203. This story is reminiscent of Hazlitt's amusement at hearing that the former inhabitant of 19 York Street was said to be a Mr Milford.
37. *Remains* i, p. lxxxiii.
38. John Forster, *The Life of Charles Dickens*, Book 6, section 6 (2 vols., London, 1950), ii. 76.
39. *The Letters of Robert Louis Stevenson*, ed. Bradford A. Booth and Ernest Mehew (5 vols. thus far, New Haven, 1994–), iii. 260.
40. Ibid. v. 217.
41. See for instance Horst Schroeder, 'An Unacknowledged Quotation in "Pen, Pencil and Poison"', *Notes and Queries* NS 43 (March 1996), 51–2.
42. Edward Thomas, *A Literary Pilgrim in England* (London, 1917), 129.
43. See Wu (2007) i, pp. liii–iv.
44. Jules Douady to WCH, 16 August 1905; BL Add. MS 388911.
45. Namely: 'My First Acquaintance with Poets', 'On the Pleasure of Painting', 'On the Conversation of Authors', 'On the Ignorance of the Learned', 'The Indian Jugglers', 'On Familiar Style', 'On Going a Journey', 'Character of Cobbett', 'The Fight', 'Merry England', 'On a Sun-Dial', 'A Farewell to Essay-Writing', 'Conversations as Good as Real' (one of the conversations with Northcote) and a selection from *Characteristics*.
46. Somerset Maugham, *The Summing Up* (London, 1976), 33.
47. [Virginia Woolf], 'William Hazlitt', *TLS*, 18 September 1930, 721–2, esp. 721. This essay was later revised for inclusion in *The Common Reader: Second Series* (London, 1932).
48. Wu viii. 113–14.

INDEX

Index

Index

Index

Index

Index

Index

Index

modernity of 238

money worries 186, 213, 220, 247, 252, 257–8, 332–3, 388, 391
  arrested for debt 333–4, 421
  bankruptcy of Hunt and Clarke 412
  borrows from Jeffrey 247, 276, 302
  cheated by accountant 421
  on death bed 429
  debt 181, 213, 247, 275–6, 302, 333–4, 404, 412
  dependence on Stoddart 221
  hides from bailiffs 276, 412
  pressure to repay creditors 421, 427
  reduced book sales 276–7

obituaries of 433, 436

painting career 63, 64, 77–8, 136
  commissioned to copy pictures from Louvre 79
  copying paintings in Louvre 80–1, 82, 83
  decline in abilities 137
  paints Coleridge 88, 89
  paints father's portrait 78
  paints Lamb 104
  recovers paintings sold to Haydon 343–4
  sells paintings to Haydon 277
  at Winterslow 125–6, 132

in Paris 409
  copying paintings in Louvre 80–1, 82, 83
  at ease in French society 392–4
  with Isabella 356–60
  joined by son 391
  meets Cosway 82–3
  meets Stendhal 359–60, 392–3
  researches biography of Napoleon 387–8
  sees Bonaparte 82

philosophy 12–13
  attacks on Utilitarians 193–4
  disinterestedness 13, 18, 63, 210
  gusto 210
  lectures on 138–9, 140–2

political commentary 156
  attack on monarchy 241

  attacks Liverpool administration 199–200
  attacks political turncoats 202–3
  attacks Southey 205–6, 207
  first political sketch 150–1
  Hone's trials 227, 233
  introduces into drama criticism 177
  introduces into literary criticism 176
  Political Essays 265–6
  in *The Yellow Dwarf* 233

politics:
  antipathy to hereditary monarchy 7
  belief in revolution 170
  childhood politicization 49
  Coleridge and Wordsworth 19
  criticism of George IV's coronation 299
  devastated by Napoleon's defeat 179–80
  entry into radical circles 64–7
  hatred of tyranny 266
  July Revolution 427–8
  reaction to Mackintosh's lectures 74
  republican 14, 64
  supports Napoleon 105, 159–60, 163, 174, 175, 405
  sympathy with France 6

posthumous reputation of 438–41

poverty 137, 140, 142, 143, 277, 389

prostitutes 59–60, 236, 300, 326

psychology 238

religion 15
  loses faith 60–1
  praise of dissenting ministers 34, 288–9

in Scotland 309–12
  divorce proceedings 318–19, 323–5, 367
  Edinburgh 309–10, 313
  Glasgow 319–20
  honeymoon 349–50
  lectures 320
  meets Jeffrey 314–16
  visits Ritchie 316–18

solitude 410, 421–2

sport:
  amateur boxer 304
  fives player 258–9

Index

Index

Index

Index

Index

Index

Index

Index

Index

Index